EDITOR'S LETTER

The term 'mixologist' has so far served to distinguish career cocktail bartenders from the likes of Doris, who pulls pints and ruins G&Ts at the local boozer two nights a week. But just as consumers were getting used to the term, bartenders have started calling themselves 'bar chefs'.

Now, when 'bar chef' is used to describe someone whose kitchen skills (like mine) run to using a juice extractor or muddling fresh herbs and fruits, I find this a bit poncy. With the honourable exception of sushi chefs, I and the Oxford English Dictionary are on the same side. A chef is someone who cooks - i.e., someone who both mixes and heats food.

However, there are some bartenders who spend almost as much time reducing over a hot stove as Gordon Ramsay. They make their own syrups, bitters and liqueurs, creating their own unique flavours. These are truly bar chefs - and one of the best-known of this new breed is Julien Gualdoni from London's Trailer Happiness.

A typical example of how Julien straddles the roles of bartender and chef is his excellent Solid Manhattan. More amuse-bouche than cocktail, this is served on a spoon. It consists of three parts: 1/ a whisky and bitters jelly base, served at room temperature 2/ a vermouth foam served on top of the jelly at –7°C, 3/ several small drops of maraschino concentrate placed on the foam.

Cheers

Simon Difford

simon@diffordsguide.com

PREPARATION OF THE JELLY:

1. Put 4 sheets of gelatine in a bowl with cold water for 10 minutes.
2. Heat 1 glass of Monkey Shoulder whisky to 20ºC in a saucepan.
3. Add the gelatine mixture, remove from heat and whisk for 30 seconds.
4. Pour the mixture into a plastic mould.
5. Cover with cling film and place in the fridge.

PREPARATION OF THE FOAM:

1. Put 2 sheets of gelatine in a bowl with cold water for 10 minutes.
2. Pour 2 glasses of sweet vermouth and 1.5 glasses of dry vermouth into a saucepan. Add the peel of 2 lemons and 2 spoons of crystallised sugar.
3. Heat the mixture to 20°C.
4. Add the gelatine mixture to the saucepan, remove from heat and whisk for 10 minutes.
5. Pour into cream whipping siphon.
6. Allow to cool for 20 minutes.
7. Charge siphon with nitrous oxide, shake briefly and place in the freezer.

PREPARATION OF THE MARASCHINO CONCENTRATE:

1. Pour a whole jar of maraschino cherries (including syrup) into a saucepan.
2. Heat and simmer but do not boil.
3. Reduce until half of the contents have evaporated.
4. Leave to cool for one hour.
5. Blend in food processor for two minutes.

ISBN: 0-9546174-7-9 **ISSN:** 1749-0855

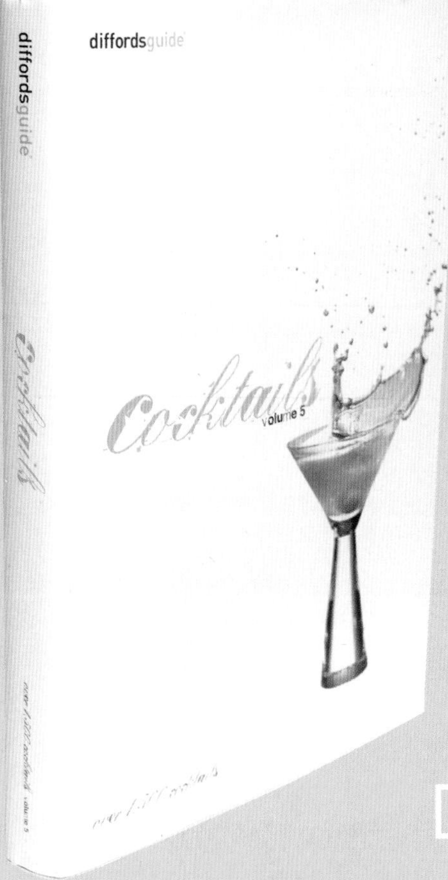

DIFFORDSGUIDE TO COCKTAILS

As I hope you'll see from this guide, we are passionate about bars, booze and cocktails. And our diffordsguide publications are aimed at people like us, be they professional bartenders, folk who like to make drinks at home or anyone who enjoys drinking in great bars.

The issue numbers on our covers are simpler than they might appear. We publish one book annually: 'diffordsguide to Cocktails'. In between editions we produce four quarterly softbacks, like the one you're reading. So, for example, we publish diffordsguide #5.1, #5.2, #5.3 and #5.4 in softback format over the year. Then we publish cocktails from all four mini-guides in one big, beefy, indexed hardback: 'diffordsguide to Cocktails vol.6'.

We used to publish a softback quarterly called 'diffordsguide to City Drinking' with reviews of the best bars in cities around the world. You'll find these now incorporated into the title you're reading. We figured it was better to produce one thick guide combining bars and cocktails than two separate, thinner titles - especially as many of you were buying both.

diffordsguide to Cocktails Hardback vol.5

ISBN: 0-9546174-2-8
Publication: UK October 2004 / USA October 2005
Cover price: UK £24.97, USA $34.97
An A-Z of over 1,500 colour illustrated cocktail recipes plus colourful illustrated pages on different fruits and their preparation.

diffordsguide to Cocktails Softback #5.1

ISSN: 1749-0855
Publication: November 2005
Cover price: UK £6.97, EU €9.97, USA $7.97, Canada $9.97
Featured bar, featured bartender, new stuff, bartender's kit and readers' cocktails - plus over 500 colour illustrated cocktail recipes from A-C with 92 new and 52 updated recipes besides those listed in vol.5.

diffordsguide to Cocktails Softback #5.2

ISBN: 0-9546174-6-0
ISSN: 1749-0855
Publication: February 2006
Cover price: UK £6.97, EU €9.97, USA $7.97, Canada $9.97
Wayne Collins demonstrates molecular gastronomy, Match bars London explored, the Tiki revival, bartender's kit and readers' cocktails - plus over 500 colour illustrated cocktail recipes from D-K including over 160 new recipes.

diffordsguide to Cocktails Softback #5.3

ISBN: 0-9546174-7-9
ISSN: 1749-0855
Publication: June 2006
Cover price: A guide to bars and drinking in Amsterdam, Atlanta, Cracow, London, Mexico City, New York, Prague and Singapore. Plus over 500 colour illustrated cocktail recipes from L-Q including over 170 new recipes.

diffordsguide to Cocktails Softback #5.4

ISBN: 0-9546174-8-7
ISSN: 1749-0855
Publication: August 2006
Cover price: 500 colour illustrated cocktail recipes from R-Z - almost 100 of them new - plus guides to drinking in the following cities: Auckland, Edinburgh, Hong Kong, London, Melbourne, New York, San Francisco and Stockholm.

diffordsguide to Cocktails Hardback vol.6

Publication: September 2006
Cover price: UK £24.97, USA $34.97
An A-Z of over 2,000 colour illustrated cocktail recipes including all those featured in #5.1, #5.2, #5.3 and #5.4 softback editions of diffordsguide to Cocktails and indexed by ingredients.

WHERE TO BUY diffordsguide

WWW.DIFFORDSGUIDE.COM

For subscriptions, individual Issues and back copies

UK WIDE RETAILERS

Books etc
Tel: +44 (0)20 7379 7313,
www.bordersstores.co.uk

Borders Books & Music
Tel: +44 (0)20 7379 7313,
www.bordersstores.co.uk

Harvey Nichols Department Stores
+44 (0)20 7235 5000,
www.harveynichols.com

Waterstone's
+44 (0)20 8742 3800,
www.amazon.co.uk

US WIDE RETAILERS

B-Dalton
Tel: 1 800 THE BOOK,
www.barnesandnoble.com

Barnes & Noble Superstores
Tel: 1 800 THE BOOK,
www.barnesandnoble.com

Books A Million
Tel: 1 800 201 3550,
www.booksamillion.com

Borders Books & Music
Tel: 1 888 81 BOOKS,
www.bordersstores.com

Tower Records
Tel: 1 800 ASK-TOWER
www.towerrecords.com

LONDON RETAILERS

The Conran Shop
81 Fulham Road, SW3 6RD
Tel: +44 (0)20 7589 7401, **www.**conran.com

The Conran Shop
55 Marylebone High Street,
W1U 5HS
Tel: +44 (0)20 7723 2223, **www.**conran.com

Daunt Books
83 Marylebone High Street,
W1U 4QW
Tel: +44 (0)20 7224 2295, **www.**dauntbooks.co.uk

Foyles
113-119 Charing Cross Road, WC2H 0EB
Tel: +44 (0)20 7437 5660, **www.**foyles.co.uk

Heal's Tottenham Court Road
196 Tottenham Court Road,
W1T 7LQ
Tel: +44 (0)20 7636 1666, **www.**heals.co.uk

Selfridges & Co.
400 Oxford Street, W1C 1JS
Tel:+44 (0)870 837 7377, **www.**selfridges.com

Stanfords Covent Garden
12-14 Long Acre, WC2E 9LP
Tel: +44 (0)20 7836 1321, **www.**stanfords.co.uk

Purves & Purves
222 Tottenham Court Road,
W1T 7QE
Tel: +44 (0)20 7580 8223, **www.**purves.co.uk

Vinopolis shop
1 Bank End, SE1 9BU
Tel: +44 (0)20 7940 8311, **www.**vinopolis.co.uk

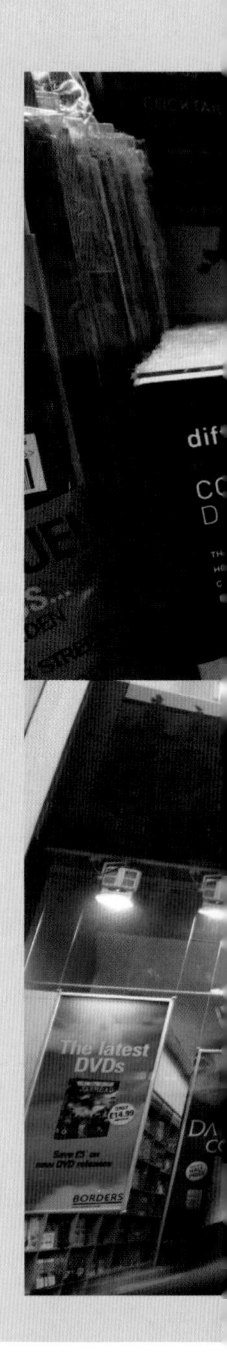

OTHER UK RETAILERS

Harris Interiors Gallery
33 Church Road, Lower Parkstone, Poole, BH14 8UF
Tel: +44 (0)1202 744 081,
www.harris-interiors.co.uk

Villeneuves Wines
49 A Broughton Street, Edinburgh, EH1 3RJ
Tel: +44 (0)131 558 8441,
www.villeneuvewines.com

Cornelius Wines
18-20 Easter Road, Edinburgh, EH7 5RG
Tel: +44 (0)131 652 2405

Please look for our quarterly guides on magazine racks as well as the book shelves of book retailers' cookery or travel departments. We are proud to produce publications which are hard to pigeonhole.

ONLINE E-TAILERS

www.b-opie.com
www.amazon.com
www.amazon.co.uk
www.drinkon.com
www.shaker-uk.com
www.thedrinkshop.com
www.urbanbar.com

Pringle
of Scotland
By Appointment To
Her Majesty The Queen
Manufacturers of
Knitted Garments
Pringle of Scotland Ltd
By Appointment To
Her Majesty Queen Elizabeth
The Queen Mother
Manufacturers of Knitted Garments
Pringle of Scotland Ltd
1815 Pringle of Scotland
2005_ Nineteen decades_
stockists 0800 360 200 pringlescotland.com

CONTENTS

Don't blame us:

- This guide is intended for adults of legal drinking age.
- Please enjoy alcohol and cocktails in a responsible manner.
- Consumption of alcohol in excess can be harmful to your health.
- The high sugar levels in some cocktails may mask their alcohol content.
- Please do not consume cocktails and drive or operate machinery.
- Great care should be exercised when combining flames and alcohol.
- Consumption of raw and unpasteurised eggs may be harmful to health.
- Please follow the alcohol content guidelines included in this guide where a shot is equal to 25ml or 1 US fluid ounce (29.6ml) at most. A 25ml measure of spirit at 40% alc./vol. is equal to 1 unit of alcohol. Most men can drink up to three to four units of alcohol a day and most women can drink up to two to three units of alcohol a day with out significant risks to their health.
- Women who are trying to conceive or who are pregnant should avoid getting drunk and are advised to consume no more than one to two units of alcohol once or twice a week.

diffordsguide are: CEO Ricky Agnew, **Publisher & Editor** Simon Difford, **Art Director** Dan Malpass, **Photography** Rob Lawson
Published by Sauce Guides Limited, Milngavie Business Centre, 17 Station Road, Milngavie, G62 8PG. **www.diffordsguide.com**

ISBN: 0-9546174-7-9 **ISSN:** 1749-0855

BRAND NEW

In the last issue I promised to evaluate some of the best known brands of vodka. Well, I've decided to extend this to an in-depth exploration of vodka, its history and its production with information and tasting notes on every single brand I've come across in the last decade. So you're going to have to wait for the full story till #6.1 is published this October. In the meantime, here's my view on the new vodkas and other stuff that has passed across my desk lately.

BARSOL QUEBRANTA PISCO

Peruvian Pisco
40% alc./vol. (80°proof)
www.barsolpisco.com
Producer: Bodega San, Isidro, Peru.
UK agent: N/A
US agent: Master Merchant LLC

This premium Peruvian pisco is made exclusively from Quebranta, a non-aromatic grape which produces a dryer style of pisco. Barsol is produced in one of the oldest alembic stills in South America, dating from the late 1800s. Like all Peruvian pisco, it is distilled to bottling strength rather than reduced with water after distillation.

Taste: A slightly smoky pear and hay nose leads to a green, grapy, grassy palate with fishy (herring) notes and hints of oats. A full flavoured pisco but without the harshness so often attributed to the spirit.

ABSOLUT RUBY RED

●●●●○

Absolut's eighth and latest flavour was unveiled in March this year. The Swedes took thirteen years to launch their first four flavoured variants but have been banging out a new one every year since 2003:

1986 -**Absolut Peppar** (chilli pepper)
1988 - **Absolut Citron** (lemon)
1992 - **Absolut Kurant** (blackcurrant)
1999 - **Absolut Mandrin** (orange)
2003 - **Absolut Vanilia** (vanilla)
2004 - **Absolut Raspberri** (raspberry)
2005 - **Absolut Apeach** (peach)
2006 - **Absolut Ruby Red** (grapefruit)

Indeed, some believe these annual launches are now central to the brand's continued growth. Significant volume is achieved just stocking shelves and warehouses across America.

This new grapefruit-flavoured vodka comes in the iconic Absolut bottle and, as always with Absolut flavours, the glass has been frosted. The Ruby Red bottle is distinguished by what look like a couple of balloons rising from its base – oddly, like the typography, these are more orange than red, let alone ruby. As a dyslexic, I also rather miss the creative spelling demonstrated on previous launches.

Like all the vodkas in the growing Absolut range, this is distilled and bottled in the small southern Swedish town of Åhus using winter wheat without any added sugar.

Taste: A perfumed, peachy grapefruit nose leads to a pleasingly bitter grapefruit palate with a subtle cracked black pepper, spirity bite.

CAPE NORTH

●●●●○

European Vodka
40% alc./vol. (80°proof)
www.capenorth.se
Producer: Gabriel Boudier, France, for Cape North Vodka Company AB, Drottningholm, Sweden
UK agent: Emporia Brands Ltd
US agent: Soon to be appointed

Cape North is the latest European vodka to hit the UK and US in a slick frosted bottle for a slice of the lucrative premium vodka market. The bottle suggests it is a Viking incursion, thanks to a prominent Swedish flag and the boast "made from Swedish spring water".

Gabriel Boudier, a family owned company based in Dijon, France, and famous for producing fruit liqueurs, take neutral spirit made from French winter wheat and redistill it in small copper pot stills. The resulting distillate is filtered through diatomaceous soil using a Kieselguhr filter. Finally, it is reduced to bottling strength with water shipped from one of Sweden's most famous springs.
Taste: A nose of raspberry and sucrose leads to a clean, very smooth, almost oily palate that suggests the addition of glycerine. Subtle orange zest and malty notes add interest. The extreme (possibly glycerine induced) smoothness of this vodka means it's bound to be a crowd pleaser.

THE GLENROTHES SELECT RESERVE

●●●●●

Speyside Single Malt Scotch Whisky
43% alc./vol. (86°proof) UK
40% alc./vol. (80°proof) US
www.theglenrothes.com
Producer: Glen Rothes Distillery (joint venture: The Edrington Group & Berry Bros & Rudd), Burnside Street, Rothes, Abbots Langley, Aberdeenshire, AB38 7AA, Scotland.
UK agent: Cutty Sark International
US agent: Skyy Spirits Inc.

The Glenrothes is distilled at Glen Rothes, beside the burn of Rothes which flows from the Mannoch Hills into the River Spey at Rothes-on-Spey. The distillery was founded in 1878 and the first spirit flowed from the stills on 28th December 1879, the night of the Tay Bridge Disaster when 75 people died after the new railway bridge over the River Tay collapsed in a storm.

The stills at Glen Rothes are exact replicas of the 1879 originals and have a very large boiling ball. This encourages reflux and helps to produce the light fruity, estery spirit for which the distillery is famous.

The Glenrothes is distilled from Scottish barley malted in traditional Saladin boxes using water from two local springs - the Ardcanny and Lady's Well - although it is reduced to bottling strength with purified municipal water. It is mainly aged in American and Spanish oak casks which have been seasoned with Oloroso sherry. Second-hand bourbon casks are used but to a lesser degree.

Although Glen Rothes distils a massive five million litres of spirit a year little more than 2% of this is bottled as a single malt. The bulk becomes a top dressing in blends such as Cutty Sark and The Famous Grouse.

Previously, the spirit that has been bottled as The Glenrothes single malt has only been available in very limited vintage releases and a few rare single cask bottlings. This new bottling, Select Reserve, is a vatting (blend) of casks from different, unspecified years. This means the blender can maintain a consistent style year on year.

The unusually shaped bottle is based on those used in the company's sample room: the 'handwritten' notes on the label continue the theme.

Taste: Linseed oil, Christmas fruit cake and vanilla are all evident on the nose, with the fruit and vanilla joined on the palate by a hint of spice. Glenrothes is fairly sweet with a creamy mouthfeel, making it wonderfully quaffable. A refreshing burst of citrus comes through in the long finish.

HANGAR ONE MANDARIN BLOSSOM

●●●●●

American Vodka
40% alc./vol.
www.hangarone.com
Producer: St George Spirits, Alameda, California, USA
UK agent: Not appointed
US agent: St George Spirits

This is one of four flavoured, super-premium vodkas from Hangar One. This boutique distillery takes its name from its location – the old Alameda Naval Air Station near San Francisco.

Hangar One is a joint enterprise from two Californian artisan distillers, Ansley Coale and Jörg Rupf. Previously, Coale was famed for his Germain-Robin brandy while Rupf was noted for his Aqua Perfecta eaux de vie, distilled from raspberries, pears, cherries and other fruits.

Rupf's expertise is used to distil eau de vie from fresh California fruit, using small Holstein pot stills. This, along with a distilled orange-flower infusion, is blended with spirit made from wheat grown on the Great Plains of the American Midwest. The team do not redistill this third-party spirit, reportedly believing that this would achieve nothing since the spirit is already highly rectified.

Like the rest of the Hangar One range, this is bottled without the addition of sugar. The chaps believe in using fresh fruit and don't like harsh filtration techniques so it's not unusual to find small residual solids, or "floaters" as they put it, in their vodka. I believe this adds to the charm of a truly artisanal product.
Taste: A perfumed, floral mandarin nose leads to an equally mandarin rich palate with a creamy mouthfeel. An intense, wonderfully natural honey and tangerine flavour comes through with orange flower water and a pleasant bitterness.

SONOMA SYRUP CO. INFUSED SIMPLE SYRUPS

●●●●●

American Sugar Syrups
0% alc./vol.
www.sonomasyrup.com
Producer: Sonoma Syrup Company, PO Box 819, Sonoma, California, CA 95476, USA
UK agent: Marblehead Brand Development
US agent: Sonoma Syrup Company

I first sampled these wonderful syrups at the Nightclub and Bar Show in Las Vegas last year. They are the creation of Karin Campion, a residential architect and keen amateur chef, who, in the summer of 2002 began marketing Meyer Lemon syrup, a flavoured syrup she originally created at home to sweeten cold black tea. The Williams-Sonoma chain took up her products and today they are among the retailer's top forty lines.

Karin works with a food technologist, Mark Caporale, who helps translate her home creations into quantities suitable for production at Wine Country Kitchens in Napa. The syrups are flavoured with fresh ingredients rather than essences and, although made without preservatives such as benzoate, are shelf-stable for one year. They should be stored in the same way as honey, without refrigeration which may cause clouding and separation.

The star of the range is the pomegranate syrup, which is made from real pomegranate juice and subtly brings classic cocktails to life. Try it against a cheap, cherry based grenadine and taste the difference.

While all the flavours are good, I'm also particularly keen on Lavender which works wonderfully with tequila and lime in a Margarita. New flavours are constantly being added as Karin experiments in her kitchen.

No.0 'Classic Simple Syrup' made with cane sugar and a hint of vanilla.
No.1 'Meyer Lemon Infused' with fresh California Meyer lemon juice and zest.
No.2 'Mint Infused' with natural spearmint leaves.
No.3 'Lavender Infused' with Matanzas Creek Sonoma grown lavender flowers.
No.4 'Vanilla Bean Infused' with Madagascar vanilla bean seeds.
No.5 'Cinnamon Infused' with Chinese and Vietnamese cassia cinnamon.
No.6 'Tangerine Infused' with fresh California tangerine juice.
No.7 'Peppermint Infused' with fresh peppermint leaves. Produced seasonally with limited supply.
No.8 'Pomegranate Syrup' 'natural grenadine' with Californian pomegranate juice.
No.9 'Lime Infused' with fresh Persian and Key lime juices.
No.10 'White Ginger Infused' with Hawaiian white ginger.

LEBLON

Brazilian Cachaça
40% alc./vol.
www.leblonspirit.com
Producer: Brazil & France by Leblon, 526 W 26th Street, New York City, NY 10001, USA
US agent: Leblon
UK agent: N/A

Leblon was launched in September 2005 by a former executive at LVMH, Steve Luttman, and ten partners. They raised $2 million to launch their spirit which takes its name from Leblon Beach in Rio de Janeiro.

This cachaça is distilled from fresh cane juice in Minas Gerais, Brazil, using an alembic copper still. It is then shipped to St. Sauvant, southern France, where it is briefly aged in cognac casks before bottling.
Taste: A nose hinting of unsalted butter and creamy, tinned sweetcorn leads to a very clean and refined palate which nonetheless retains that distinctive cachaça character. There is a long, slightly bitter, grassy/strawy finish.

THE MACALLAN AMBER

●●●◐○

Scottish Liqueur
25% alc./vol.
www.themacallan.com
Producer: The Macallan Distillery, Easter Elchies, Craigellachie, Banffshire, Scotland.
UK agent: N/A
US agent: Remy Amerique

A malt whisky liqueur from the makers of The Macallan. It is based on Macallan Scotch single malt whisky flavoured with sucrose, glucose, maple syrup and pecan. The aubergine-shaped bottle is modern and classy with screen-printed branding and a wooden stopper.

Taste: A nose of vanilla, whisky, maple syrup and soy sauce leads to a nutty, whisky palate with hints of maple syrup and vanilla. While sweet, Amber is not as syrupy as some liqueurs.

ORONOCO FAZENDA RESERVA

Brazilian Rum
40% alc./vol.
Producer: Fazenda Soledade, Rio de Janeiro, Brazil
UK agent: N/A
US agent: Southern Wine & Spirits

Launched in New York, Los Angeles and San Francisco at the tail end of 2005, this is Diageo's new rum offering. It is made by brothers Vicente and Roberto Bastos Ribiero, who are renowned cachaça makers.

Oronoco is distilled from Brazilian sugar cane grown on the lush mountain slopes of Novo Friburgo in the highlands of Rio de Janeiro state. The cane is harvested by hand and crushed within 24 hours of cutting, then the juice is fermented and distilled three times in copper stills. The resulting distillate is aged in Brazilian wood casks and blended with a little aged Venezuelan rum. Oronoco is packaged towards the premium end of the market in a very distinctive bottle with a label styled like cellar tasting notes and a thick, embossed leather girdle.
Taste: An almost colourless spirit with a nose of vanilla hot chocolate powder (right down to the powdered milk) leads to a vanilla-led palate with hints of milky chocolate and espresso coffee plus a spirity bite. It is hard to believe that the vanillaed, sweet palate is due solely to aging.

PAMA

American Pomegranate Liqueur
17% alc./vol.
www.pamaliqueur.com
Producer: Pama Spirits Co. (Heaven Hill Distilleries Inc.), Bardstown, KY 4004
UK agent: N/A
US agent: Wingard Imports Ltd (Heaven Hill Distillors Inc.)

The tall, elegant bottle proclaims this "the world's first true pomegranate liqueur". It goes on to claim that it "captures the complex, sweet yet tart taste and seductive colour of all-natural California pomegranates".

I'd beg to differ.

Pama is made with Californian pomegranate juice, sugar, vodka and a hint of tequila. The clear bottle features a stylized silver pomegranate tree with silver lettering that stands out against the deep crimson colour of the liqueur.
Taste: A nose reminiscent of a child's medicine leads to a palate like fortified, syrupy cranberry juice. The liqueur is clean and well balanced and the tequila hint adds bite and interest. However, it still seems somehow one dimensional and I can't help thinking it should be consumed on small, plastic spoons while holding your nose.

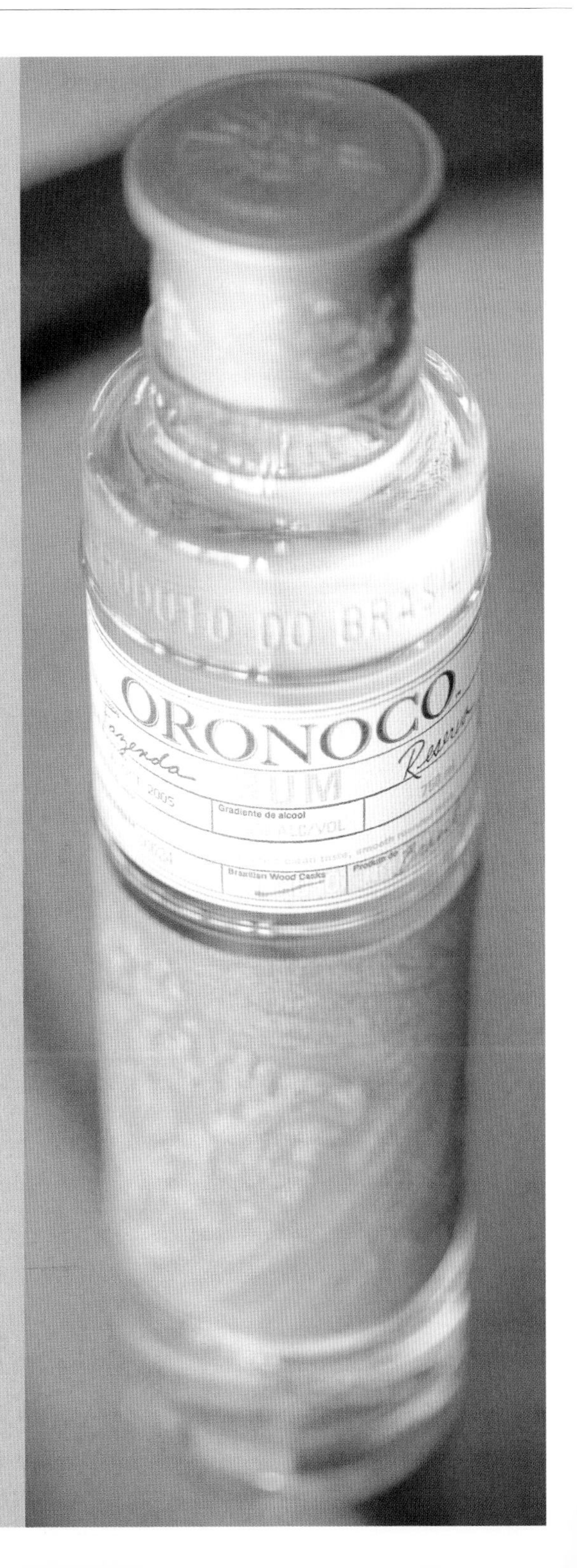

LA MAUNY RHUMS
MARTINIQUE AGRICOLE RUMS

www.rhumdemartinique.com
Producer: Bellonnie Bourdillon Distillerie, Rivière Pilote, 97211, Martinique, French West Indies.
UK agent: Emporia Brands Ltd
US agent: To be appointed

La Mauny was established in 1749 and bears the name of Ferdinand Poulain, Count de Mauny, who came to Martinique at the beginning of the 18th century and created a plantation in southern Martinique, the driest and sunniest part of the island. When the Bellonnie brothers took over the estate in 1920 they established this distillery. The brand is now the best selling rum on the island.

Martinique has its very own appellation: Martinique agricole rum (rhum agricole). In keeping with this La Mauny is made from sugar cane juice, not molasses, and the rums are distilled once only, using a twelve metre high column still.

For many years now La Mauny has been matured in casks previously used to age cognac. This makes it drier in style than most other Martinique rums, which are generally aged in casks with a bourbon heritage.

LA MAUNY 1979 VINTAGE

●●●●●

Martinique Rum
43% alc./vol.

This vintage rum is distilled from cane harvested in 1979 and aged for 10 years. It is one of the few La Mauny rums still available that has been aged in former bourbon casks. The decanter-style bottle is distinctive and luxurious.

Taste: A toffee, bitter chocolate nose leads to a slightly bitter, dry palate with smoky notes of over-ripe banana, golden syrup, spicy oak, fruit cake and espresso coffee. The finish is woody, spicy oak with hints of fruit cake.

LA MAUNY SUGAR CANE SYRUP

●●●●◐

0% alc./vol.

This is genuine sugar cane syrup. Sugar cane is squeezed to extract its rich juice, which is then filtered and bottled.

Taste: A golden syrup, strawy nose leads to a delicate, subtle moscavado sugar palate with hints of fudge. This is not as sweet as the home-made sugar syrup prescribed in this guide, so pour generously.

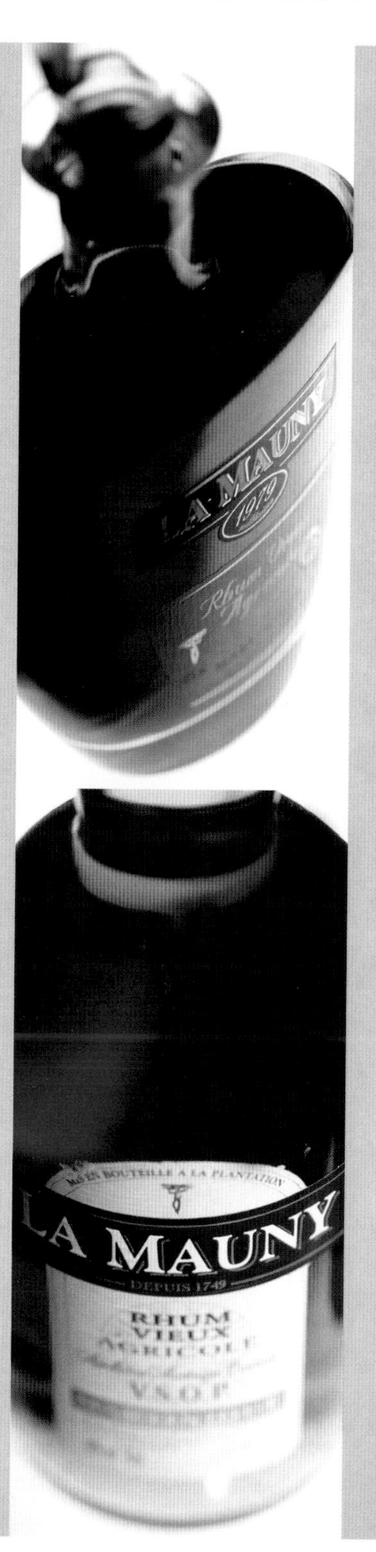

LA MAUNY RHUM BLANC

●●●●◐

Martinique Rum
50% alc./vol.

Sugar cane juice is allowed to slowly ferment over 24 hours, then distilled to around 70% alc./vol. in a column still. The rum is slowly reduced to bottling strength by the addition of demineralised water over a period of six to eight months.

Taste: A floral, pine fresh nose leads to a dry, fresh, clean palate with good cane character and subtle hints of grass, pear, cinnamon and delicate spice. This is a superb rum for making T-Punch, or any drink that relies on the unique character of Martinique agricole rum.

LA MAUNY ELEVÉ SOUS BOIS

●●●●○

Martinique Rum
40% alc./vol.

This rum is blended from rum aged in 18,000 litre oak tanks for eighteen months. Caramel is added to help achieve the dark golden colour. Elevé Sous Bois literally translates as 'Raised under wood'.

Taste: A nose of caramel and chocolate leads to a slightly sweet, toffee led palate. Subtle spicy notes of ginger, cinnamon and cracked black pepper add complexity.

LA MAUNY VSOP

●●●●◐

Martinique Rum
40% alc./vol.

'Dark' or 'aged' appellation rums from Martinique must be stored in casks for at least three years. This VSOP, a term with no official meaning in Martinique, is a blend of rums aged for between four and six years. No caramel is added: the rum's dark hue comes from the casks in which it is aged.

Taste: Coffee and woody notes on the nose lead to a dry woody palate with hints of hazelnut, milky toffee and an almost honeysuckle, pepperminty freshness. The long finish offers hints of nuts, oak and more milky toffee.

LA MAUNY 1995 VINTAGE

●●●●●

Martinique Rum
42% alc./vol.

This vintage rum is distilled from cane harvested in 1995 and aged for six-and-a-half years in casks previously used to mature cognac.

Taste: A eucalyptus, oaky, cigar box nose - almost like oil paint, in fact - leads to a wonderfully smooth, balanced palate. There is a slight sweetness with hints of vanilla, golden syrup and over-ripe banana, plus spicy notes of cinnamon and curry. This is by far my favourite La Mauny, made more approachable by its subtle sweetness.

STARBUCKS CREAM LIQUEUR

●●●●○

American Liqueur
15% alc./vol.
www.starbucksliqueurs.com
Producer: Fielding & Jones Ltd, Cincinnati, Frankfort, Kentucky (Fortune Brands and Starbucks Coffee Co.)
UK agent: N/A
US agent: Jim Beam Brands Co (Fortune Brands)

There's already one on virtually every street corner but this ubiquitous brand is heading for your drinks cabinet now. Launched in October 2005, this new cream liqueur follows the already established Starbucks Coffee Liqueur. Both are produced by a joint venture between Jim Beam Brands, a unit of Fortune Brands, and the Starbucks Coffee Company. Like other cream liqueurs, Starbucks should be stored in the refrigerator once opened.

Taste: Not too sweet, with a very creamy mouthfeel. On the palate comes well balanced coffee and cream with a slight alcohol bite and subtle hints of toffee. This is great in place of milk or cream in coffee.

10 CANE

●●●●●

Trinidadian Rum
40% alc./vol.
www.10cane.com
Producer: Angostura Ltd & Moet Hennessy Ltd, Laventille, Port of Spain, Trinidad, West Indies.
UK agent: Moet Hennessy UK Ltd
US agent: Schieffelin & Co.

Moet-Hennessy launched this new rum in the USA last May. It was a bold move as this is the first light white rum with super-premium positioning. Previously, top shelf, high ticket rums have been aged, sipping rums, but 10 Cane is intended to be mixed.

10 Cane is made using 75% of the cane juice extracted from the first pressing of hand cut Trinidadian sugar cane and is so named because it requires ten canes to distil enough rum to fill one 75cl bottle. It is double distilled in a French made alembic pot still at a purpose built distillery on Angostura property in Trinidad. (This is jointly operated by Moet Hennessy and Angostura.)

10 Cane is aged in first fill French oak casks with a cognac heritage for just six months, giving the rum a hint of oak and a slight yellow hue. The stylish, rectangular bottle is shaped a little like an old medicine bottle and features a howling monkey, a Trinidadian sign for the unexpected. It is finished with an orange flash, resembling a seal.

The only sad aspect of this brand's launch is the news that the marketeers at Moet Hennessy have decided not to try and re-educate the American people in the art of the Natural Daiquiri, but to rename the classic, straight-up Daiquiri a 'Sugar Shake Martini'.

Taste: Hints of fresh pear on the nose also come through on the palate, which is rich in sugar cane character with dominant vanilla and white pepper notes plus subtler hints of espresso and ripe banana. This rum is distinctly agricole in character but more subtly so than you would expect in Martinique. One to mix, not sip, but with real character.

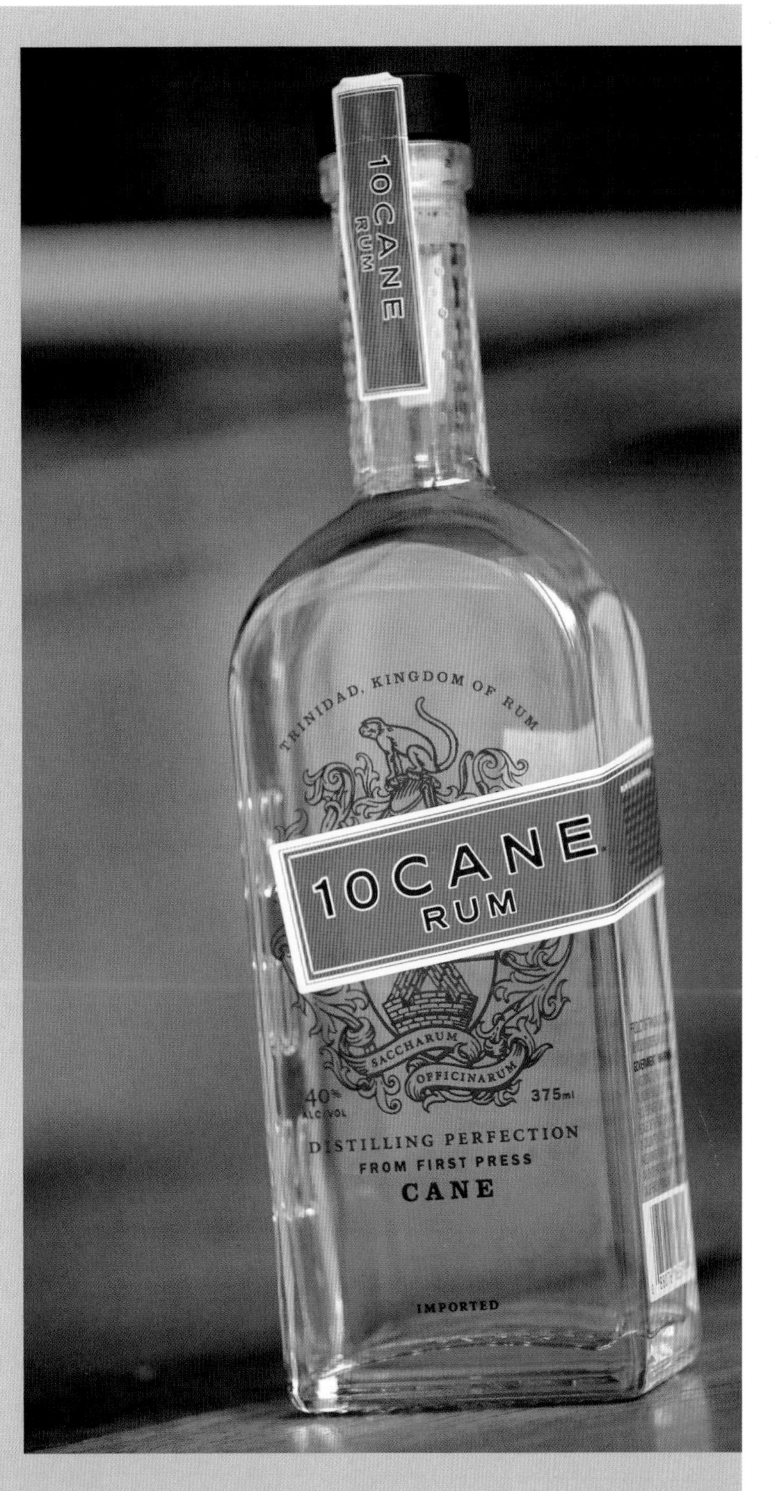

OLMECA TEZÓN

Highland Mexican Tequilas
Producer: Olmeca Distillery (Pernod-Ricard), Arandas, Jalisco, Mexico. NOM: 1111
UK agent: Marblehead Brand Development
US agent: Pernod Ricard USA

Pronounced 'Tes-zon', this range of 100% agave tequila is named after 'tezontle', the volcanic stone from which tahonas – the giant stone wheels that crush agave – are made.

Launched in the US in August last year and in March in the UK, this super-premium comes from Pernod-Ricard's Olmeca distillery. Many brands claim super-premium positioning but Tezón justifies it not only with the quality of the spirit but also with incredibly slick packaging.

The hand-blown and hand-finished bottle has metal plates on each side embossed with four symbols that represent Tezón's production process: an agave plant, fire (symbolising the slow roasting), a tahona stone and the 'spirit' of Tezón. Each bottle has a leather information tag attached to its neck and is finished with a black resin stopper. I have to say that unwrapping the bottle from its neatly folded tissue paper is more like unwrapping a Mont Blanc pen than a bottle of tequila.

Inside the fancy packaging lies a 100% blue agave tequila from Arandas, in the highlands of Jalisco. Only estate grown agave are used to make Tezón and the harvested piñas are traditionally slow-roasted for three days in steam-heated, 50 tonne Mampostería brick ovens. Unusually, the cooked piñas are crushed using a traditional millstone made from tezontle stone and the pulp and juice are then fermented together using a cultured yeast originally isolated from agave.

Olmeca use water drawn from a 211 metre artesian well on the estate, which is ideal for fermentation as it has a low PH and good mineral content. (Like most brands, they dilute to bottling strength with demineralised water.)

Tezón is double distilled in small batches using a 750 litre copper pot still. The agave fibres are added to the still with the fermented juice on first distillation.

TEZÓN BLANCO

40% alc./vol. (80°proof)
100% blue agave super-premium unaged tequila.

Taste: A subdued salty nose leads to a clean palate with a white pepper and salt spiciness plus subtle hints of fig, grapefruit, orange zest, espresso coffee, herbs and grass. The mouthfeel is creamy vanilla and the long finish is very clean with lasting pepper spice. Decent agave character is present throughout.

TEZÓN REPOSADO

●●●●◐

40% alc./vol. (80°proof)

100% blue agave super-premium tequila aged 8-10 months in seasoned white oak casks (ex bourbon).

Taste: A nose of stewed tea, bay leaves and caramel leads to a palate dominated by agave, chilli pepper and cracked black pepper. Subtle creamy vanilla/butterscotch notes refine the palate and there is long, sweet, smoky, burnt rubber finish.

TEZÓN AÑEJO

●●●●●

40% alc./vol. (80°proof)

100% blue agave super-premium tequila aged 18-20 months in seasoned oak casks (ex bourbon).

Taste: A nose of minty wet cement and breakfast tea leads to a beautifully balanced, agave rich palate. Hints of cracked black pepper, butterscotch, vanilla and subtle oak accompany faint charcoal and piny notes, and lead into a long, pleasing finish.

NO. 209 GIN

●●●●●

American Gin
46% alc./vol.
www.209gin.com
Producer: Distillery No. 209, Pier 50 Shed B, Mailbox 9, Terry A. Francois Blvd., San Francisco, CA 94158, USA
UK agent: N/A
US agent: Southern Wine & Spirits

The story of No. 209 Gin starts in 1870 when William Scheffler bought a patent for a pot still in New York. He travelled west and set up a distillery at Krug winery in St. Helena, Napa Valley, California. In 1880 he purchased a neighbouring winery called Edge Hill, which he registered in 1882.

As the 209th such distillery to register with the Federal Government, Scheffler was granted licence number 209 and his spirits received various awards, including a medal at the 1889 Grand Exposition in Paris.

Over a century later (in 2000), Leslie Rudd, the entrepreneur behind Standard Beverage Corp. and Dean & Deluca Foods, purchased the Edge Hill winery. While exploring his new acquisition Leslie came across an old hay barn with a faded emblem that read 'Registered Distillery 209'. So began his quest to resurrect the old 209 Distillery.

Sadly the old barn fell foul of modern distillery building regulations so a new site was found at Pier 50 in San Francisco. A custom-made copper pot still was acquired and an expert team assembled to formulate and distil the new gin. They sought to create a distinctive flavour and so chose bergamot orange peel from Southern Italy along with more usual gin botanicals such as Guatemalan cardamom, Chinese cassia bark, European coriander and the obligatory juniper berries. The botanicals are steeped in grain neutral alcohol overnight prior to traditional 'one shot' distillation.

No. 209 Gin is packaged in a smart bottle which resembles old Dutch jenever bottles. It was officially launched on 1st August last year. And Scheffler's 1889 French medal? It came up for auction in September 2004 and today is back at Distillery No. 209.

Taste: A fresh nose of lavender and juniper leads to a slightly sweet, clean, juniper-led palate with orange and lemon zest, plus hints of orris, rosewater, lavender and pine. The sweetness despite the high alcohol strength suggests the addition of sugar.

CITY DRINKING

The following pages feature our choice of the best hotels, restaurants and bars in nine frequently visited cities. Our aim is to continually review and improve on these selections and share these discoveries through the pages of this quarterly magazine.

I've personally visited and reviewed all of the following bars but also greatly rely on the local knowledge of a network of friends who represent drinks brands in their respective home cities around the world. These brands also support this title and without their help and patronage its publication would not be possible.

While I believe we can dispassionately feature premium liquor brands I do not believe the same can be said about the hotels, restaurants and bars we recommend. Hence, we DO NOT accept payment from such establishments or run advertising of any type from them.

We all have likes and dislikes which shape our opinions. The following are my own but I'm also keen to hear what are your favourite hotels, restaurants and bars.

Cheers
Simon Difford
simon@diffordsguide.com

Sleeping

Tasked with selecting the best hostelries a city has to offer, I've inevitably tended toward four and five star hotels; but not necessarily so as I personally favour small and boutique over large and corporate. Whether modern and minimalist or traditional, rooms should be reasonably sized but above all clean, comfortable and homely.

Many hotel inspectors grade hotels on such things as having a night porter and 24-hour room service. While these luxuries are welcome I'm more worried about whether the hotel has a great bar that's open late, a knowledgeable and friendly concierge, serves breakfast till late and offers an even later check-out without additional charge. In sunny climes a pool and terrace are always appreciated. As for the perfect hotel room, that should have the following:

- **Mini bar** (after all this title is first and foremost about drink).
- **Safe** large enough to take a lap-top.
- **Wardrobe space** with plenty of hangers with proper hooks.
- **Tea & coffee** making facilities.
- **A separate bath** (for girlfriend) and powerful hot shower (for me).
- **A full length and well lit make-up mirror** (also for my girlfriend).
- **Air conditioning** - and windows that can be opened.
- **Dressing gowns** to aid the feeling of being at home.
- **Iron and ironing board.**
- **Free wi-fi internet access** and a desk with plenty of power sockets.
- **Hi-fi** to plug iPod into.
- **Quality, and spotlessly clean towels and linen.**
- **Duvets** rather than heavy old blankets on a large comfortable bed.
- **Drapes or blinds** that stop the sun waking me up a couple of hours after I've left the last bar.

Eating

Obviously we're looking for restaurants that serve great food in pleasant surroundings but while designer décor can help make the restaurant experience, clean and simple with character can often be as good or better. A great restaurant should offer the following:

- **A bar** at which to sit and wait for late comers.
- **Attentive service,** but not overly so.
- **An aperitif drinks list.**
- **Great bread** or other nibbles.
- **An interesting and varied wine list.**
- **Friendly wait staff** with honest recommendations.
- **Choice of fish & vegetarian dishes** for the non-carnivorous.
- **Comfortable chairs and tables** well spaced apart.
- **Any music should be background.**
- **Clean toilets** with hand towels (plus mirrors for the girls).
- **Atmospheric lighting** but sufficient to read the menu and see what you're eating.
- **Unpretentious menu** that conveys what's on offer without the use of a culinary dictionary.
- **Choice of dessert wines** and digestive spirits and liqueurs.
- **Time to relax** without being rushed away for the next sitting.

Drinking

We're not just looking for upscale cocktail lounge bars - a characterful pub or dive bar could be as good or better. However, we are after great drinks, be they wine, beer, spirits or cocktails. A truly great bar would have a superb range of all of these, but certainly a lounge should have great cocktails, a pub great beer and a wine bar great wines.

Décor needn't be designer chic and I've noticed the best looking bars improve as they wear over the decades. Conversely bad bars need a refit every two or three years.

Atmosphere is difficult to pin down but bars either have it or they don't. Really great bars manage to achieve this with relatively few people.

The distinction between a restaurant, bar or club can be blurred, but for the record anywhere where the music takes precedence over the drinks is a club, and anywhere where you have to order food in order to sit down is a restaurant.

The following contribute to a great bar.

Grades

After much discussion and visiting establishments (some several times) I've awarded each a grade out of five according its range of drinks, service, décor, and ambience. These grades reflect my own tastes and yours may be very different - please let me know. (simon@diffordsguide.com)

Disgusting **Spectacular**

Recommendations

The following symbols appear at the foot of bar reviews where I consider the establishment reliably good at the following.

 **Cocktails**

 **Food**

 **Wine**

 **Beer**

 **Spirits**

 **Music**

- **Friendly welcome on the door** even if from bouncer turning you away.
- **Plenty of bar counter space** and comfortable bar stools with backs and foot rests.
- **Hooks under the bar counter** for handbags and jackets.
- **A good and varied beer selection** served in suitable cold glassware.
- **An interesting and varied wine list** with tasting notes and plenty of wines by the glass.
- **A reasonable choice of premium liquor brands** across all categories - not just vodka.
- **A list of well-made classic cocktails** with some contemporary twists, made using fresh ingredients and not sour mix.
- **A cocktail list -** I'm sick of hearing "we can make any cocktail you ask for" – really?
- **Shapely clean glassware.**
- **Complementary iced water** offered with drinks.
- **Finger food, nibbles and fries.**
- **Good espresso coffee** (preferably Illy).
- **If music's played it should suit the mood and be at an appropriate volume.**
- **Comfy chairs and tables.**
- **Friendly, efficient table service.**
- **Atmospheric lighting.**
- **Good ventilation,** particularly where smoking is allowed.
- **Friendly and varied clientele** but not too crowded.
- **Clean toilets** with hand towels but without challenging gender signs - I don't want an initiative test before I can pee. And I don't want to have to tip a toilet attendant for the privilege either.

AMSTERDAM

Time zone: Central European Time (GMT +1)
Airport: Amsterdam Schiphol (AMS)
Currency: Euros (€)

Holland's largest city was founded on and continues to thrive from its waterways and proximity to the North Sea. A staggering 165 canals – more even than Venice – criss-cross the city and I recommend a canal tour if you are visiting for the first time.

Amsterdam is flat and compact, so easy to explore on foot – but do as the locals do and cycle. There are twice as many cycles as people in the city and the streets are lined with bike lanes, making pedaling a real pleasure. Hire a bike for the duration of your stay and use it day and evening. Amsterdamers don't take cabs.

Amsterdam is a tolerant city, especially where vices are concerned, and thanks to this broad-minded attitude many tourists arrive in search of 'a smoke' and some extra-marital sex. But there is so much more to Amsterdam than hash bars and a red light district. Since the 17th century it has been one of Europe's most important trading cities and it has a rich history and culture.

Amsterdam Hotels

Amsterdam boasts some of the highest hotel occupancy rates of any European city. Even though 2004 saw a surge in luxury rooms you should still book well ahead, especially if you're after a room in the centre of town over a weekend. Even if you book ahead, many central places insist on a three night minimum stay.

Intercontinental Amstel Amsterdam

1 Professor Tulpplein, Amsterdam, 1018 GX, The Netherlands
Tel: +31 (0)20 622 6060,
www.amsterdam.intercontinental.com
Group: Intercontinental

This spectacular grand hotel opened in 1867 on the bank of the Amstel River and maintains its classical luxury. The original 111 rooms were converted in 1992 to create 55 rooms and 24 larger suites, all with mod cons such as air-conditioning, satellite TV, compact disc player and high speed internet access. The marble bathrooms are fitted with bathtub and separate shower. Facilities include indoor swimming pool, sauna, jacuzzi, steam room and gym.

The College Hotel

1 Roelof Hartstraat, Amsterdam, 1071 VE, The Netherlands
Tel: +31 (0)20 5711 511,
www.thecollegehotel.com
Group: The Stein Group

Built in 1894, the building that houses the aptly named College Hotel used to be a school. Not much has changed and nearly half the staff are catering students. Thankfully, it shares the same owner as the Dylan and the trainees are supervised to the extent that their keen service is often well above what you'd expect of a 'normal' hotel.

The interior is far from collegiate with seven earthy tones used throughout to create a modern but homely hotel. Rooms vary in size but tend to the bijou. All forty rooms boast luxurious bathrooms with heated tiles, mirrors and rain-like showers. Wifi internet is available at a price.

The Dylan Hotel

384 Keizersgracht, Amsterdam, 1016 GB, The Netherlands
Tel: +31 (0)20 530 2010,
www.dylanamsterdam.com
Group: The Stein Group

Better known to some as Blakes Hotel, the name under which it was designed in partnership with style guru Anouska Hempel, the woman behind Blakes in London, The Dylan is now part of the Stein Group. This ultra-stylish five star affair centres on an old workhouse built in 1772 and retains Anouska's harmonious 'ying yang' design, although it is currently being refurbished.

All forty rooms and suites are spacious and beautifully styled, have views either over the canal or over the rear courtyard, and feature spacious bathrooms, most with separate bath and shower.

Such style comes at a price, as does wifi internet access at nearly €30 per 24 hours, but the central location, stunning restaurant, beautiful design and friendly, efficient staff make it a worthwhile investment.

The Grand Amsterdam

197 Oudezijds Voorburgwal, Amsterdam, 1012 EX, The Netherlands
Tel: +31 (0)20 555 3111,
www.thegrand.nl
Group: Sofitel Demeure

The grand building which houses this grand hotel was a convent in the 15th century, a Royal Inn in the 16th century and subsequently the headquarters of the Dutch Admiralty. Its 182 generous rooms and suites are classically furnished and most have views over canals or courtyard. In-room amenities include air-con and broadband internet, while the hotel boasts a cosy lounge bar and a spa with pool and Turkish bath.

Lloyd Hotel

34 Oostelijke Handelskade, Amsterdam, 1019 BN, The Netherlands
Tel: +31 (0)20 561 3636,
www.lloydhotel.com
Group: Independent

Set in a century-old former prison in the regenerated Eastern Docklands area, Lloyd's 116 rooms vary tremendously according to designer and type. The cheapest 'Type A rooms' can be way out, are tiny and have shared baths. 'Type B' are larger and more traditional, with private baths, while 'Type C' are comparatively conservative and spacious. For the truly flush 'Type D rooms' boast essentials such as a bed that sleeps eight and a concert piano. You pays your money and you takes your choice. Mine would be another hotel.

Lute Suites

54-58 Amsteldijk Zuid, Amsterdam, 1184 VD, The Netherlands.
Tel: +31 (0)20 4722 462,
www.lutesuites.com

Famous Dutch designer Marcel Wanders oversaw the conversion of a row of 18th century cottages overlooking the Amstel River into seven stunningly contemporary, self contained luxury suites. Details include zinc bathrooms, egg-shaped baths, antique furniture, glass walls and ornate chandeliers.

Hotel Pulitzer

315-331 Prinsengracht, Amsterdam, 1016 GZ, The Netherlands
Tel: +31 (0)20 5235 235,
www.luxurycollection.com/pulitzer
Group: Starwood Hotels & Resorts

Hotel Pulitzer occupies twenty-five 17th and 18th century canal houses near the old city centre. The 230 rooms have canal views and original features such as wooden beams. Wifi internet is available in public areas and executive rooms.

Amsterdam Eating

The Dutch are not renowned for their culinary prowess and perhaps their most famous contribution to world cuisine is putting mayonnaise on their French fries (patates frites) instead of ketchup. To quote Vincent Vega in Pulp Fiction, "I seen 'em do it. And I don't mean a little bit on the side of the plate, they fuckin' drown 'em in it."

Less shocking staples of the Dutch diet include ham, cheese (particularly Edam and Gouda), deep fried meatballs (bitterballen), spicy rissoles (frikadellen) and seafood (particularly shrimps, herring and plaice).

But leave the packed lunch at home. Amsterdam has a rich restaurant scene with the best of world cuisine well represented. Much of Indonesia was a Dutch colony so this is the best place in Europe to sample Indonesian food. Japanese and Thai food are also very popular.

Blauw aan de Wal

99 Oudezÿds Achterburgwal, Centrum, Amsterdam, 1012 DD, The Netherlands
Tel: +31 (0)20 330 2257
Cuisine: Mediterranean

One of the hippest and probably the best Mediterranean restaurant in Amsterdam, Blauw aan de Wal is hidden away down a narrow street in the middle of the red light district.

Cinema Paradiso

184-186 Westerstraat, Jordaan, Amsterdam, 1015 MR, The Netherlands
Tel: +31 (0)20 623 7344, www.cinemaparadiso.info
Cuisine: Italian

Known as a hip place to see and be seen, Cinema Paradiso's food lies on the simple side of Italian cuisine. If you want to eat pizza and pasta with the style set you'll have to bowl up early (from 6pm) as they don't take bookings. They are closed on Mondays.

The College Hotel Restaurant

1 Roelof Hartstraat, Amsterdam, 1071 VE, The Netherlands
Tel: +31 (0)20 571 1511, www.thecollegehotel.com
Cuisine: Modern Dutch

In the former gymnasium of a former school, Chef Schilo van Coevorden and his (part-student) team serve up a contemporary take on the golden age of Dutch cuisine. Yes, there really was such a period, and this restaurant stands testament to it.

The Dylan Restaurant

The Dylan Hotel, 384 Keizersgracht, Amsterdam, 1016 GB, The Netherlands
Tel: +31 (0)20 530 2010, www.dylanamsterdam.com
Cuisine: International

The name may have changed but Blakes' great food, service and setting remain. Built in 1772, the hotel was once a workhouse. En route from the lobby to the restaurant you pass through the long gallery where the poor once lined up to receive bread baked in the ovens that still line the walls of the dining room. The eclectic menu combines influences from Japan, Thailand, Italy and France. The wine list is also suitably broad.

D'Vijff Vlieghen

294-302 Spuistraat, Centrum, Amsterdam, 1012 VX, The Netherlands
Tel: +31 (0)20 530 4060, www.fiveflies.nl
Cuisine: Modern Dutch

d'Vijff Vlieghen is located in a series of candlelit dining rooms spread across five 17th century buildings. It is named after Jan Janszoon Vijff Vlijghen, an art and antique dealer who opened a public house here in 1939. Each chair has a small copper plate engraved with the name of a famous guest. Organically grown local produce and an extensive wine list add to the appeal.

Fifteen

9 Pakhuis Amsterdam Jollemanhof, Amsterdam, 1019 GW, The Netherlands
Tel: +31 (0)900 343 8336, www.fifteen.nl
Cuisine: International

Jamie Oliver is not only influencing the standards of British school dinners but creating a stir in Amsterdam with this Dutch outpost of his school-cum-restaurant concept. This place is hipper than the naked celebrity himself and even boasts a comfortable lounge area.

Café Noa

84 Leidsegracht, Amsterdam, 1016 CR, The Netherlands
Tel: +31 (0)20 626 0802
Cuisine: Chinese (dim sum and noodles)

The acronymic name of this restaurant and bar stands for 'Noodles of Amsterdam'. With its white polished plaster walls, glass divide and open kitchen at the back, the décor is reminiscent of New York although the food is distinctly oriental. DJs ensure Noa has more of a clubby feel at weekends when you'll need to turn up early as there are no reservations.

Tempo Doeloe

75 Utrechtsestraat, Amsterdam, 1017 VJ, The Netherlands
Tel: +31 (0)20 625 6718, www.tempodoeloerestaurant.nl
Cuisine: Indonesian

The name is Indonesian for "the old days" and a traditional, homely place this is too. So much so that you have to ring the door bell to be let in. The décor is not impressive but the authentic Indonesian food is. An informative menu and staff will ensure your order is not beyond your own hot and spicy tolerances.

Visaandeschelde Rivierenbuurt

4 Scheldeplein, Rivierenbuurt, Amsterdam, 1078 GR, The Netherlands
Tel: +31 (0)20 675 1583, www.visaandeschelde.nl
Cuisine: International seafood

This small, contemporary, sixty seat restaurant is located across the street from the Rai convention centre and is noted for its seafood, with lobsters from its tank a speciality. The cuisine is truly international with influences from Japan, France and the Mediterranean. A terrace provides twenty further covers in summer.

Yamazato

Ground Floor, Hotel Okura, 333 Ferdinand Bolstraat, Amsterdam, 1072 LH, The Netherlands
Tel: +31 (0)20 678 8351, www.okura.nl
Cuisine: Japanese

The formal and business-like Okura Hotel boasts two restaurants with the coveted Michelin star. Widely regarded as Amsterdam's best Japanese restaurant, Yamazoto offers a bewildering choice of authentic Japanese cuisine, a Zen interior, a Japanese garden and a sushi bar.

Amsterdam Liquor Stores

De Bierkoning

125 Paleisstraat, Amsterdam, 1012 RK, The Netherlands
Tel: +31 (0)20 625 2336, www.bierkoning.nl

Head here for hundreds of different Belgian, German, English and Dutch beers, plus glasses, mugs and books on home brewing.

Cadenhead's

19 Huidenstraat, Amsterdam, 1016 ER, The Netherlands
Tel: +31 (0)20 330 6287, www.cadenhead.nl

The Amsterdam branch of the noted whiskey retailer.

Hart's Wijnhandel

27 Vijzelgracht, Amsterdam, 1017 HN, The Netherlands
Tel: +31 (0)20 623 8350

Listen to classical music as you peruse the large selection of jenevers and French and Italian wines at this peaceful shop.

De Gekraakte Ketel

3 Raamsteeg, Amsterdam, 31012VZ, The Netherlands
Tel: +31 (0)20 624 0745, www.crackedkettle.com

The Cracked Kettle beer shop and liquor store specialises in Dutch, Belgian and German beers, particularly those from smaller breweries.

Slijterij Wijnhandel Le Cellier

116 Spuistraat, Amsterdam, 1012 VA, The Netherlands
Tel: +31 (0)20 638 6573

This large store sells jenevers, liqueurs, a large selection of New World wines and over 75 types of beer.

Bols & Amsterdam

Bols is one of few brands in the world to boast a 430 year history. So justly proud is Bols of its Amsterdam roots and heritage that every bottle of liqueur has 'Bols Amsterdam 1575' boldly printed on its label.

Lucas Bols and his family founded their company in what was then the outskirts of Amsterdam, building a simple wooden shack to store ingredients and operating their copper pot still in the open air.

Amsterdam was rapidly becoming a major international port with Dutch seafaring merchants returning home from Asia, Africa and the Caribbean bearing exotic spices. The Bols family used these newly available spices to flavour their growing range of liqueurs and spirits.

By 1612, Amsterdam had grown to such an extent that Bols' little shed ('t Lootsje') was situated within the city walls. The stone building the family built to replace their wooden storage sheds can still be seen on Amsterdam's Rozengracht (Rose Canal).

Until 1816 the Bols distilleries remained in the hands of the family and successful recipes were passed from father to son. However, that year the direct family line terminated and the company was sold under the strict condition that the name would always be associated with it. Ever since the company has been named Erven Lucas Bols (The Heirs of Lucas Bols). The Latin words "Semper Idem" inscribed in the coat of arms mean "always the same", which to the distiller means "Always the same end product of the same high quality".

Many of the liqueurs still made by Bols today were originally created by Lucas Bols, although they now combine modern methods and technology with 430 years of experience. While Bols is proud of its heritage, it is constantly evolving new products to cater for new tastes and the needs of modern day bartenders. The shapely new award-winning Bols bottle is the only bottle designed by bartenders for bartenders.

Bols are perfect partners for our coverage of Amsterdam and its bars, hotels and restaurants due to their local knowledge of the city. Bols also sponsor www.specialnite.com, a website which features independently selected and reviewed venues and we recommend you use this as well as our guide.

Amsterdam Drinking

Compared to other major European cities, Amsterdam is something of a village. The population is well short of a million, so even with tourists included there are not enough cool young things with money to warrant more than a handful of truly upscale lounges. But Amsterdam has a great drinks history and heritage.

In the 17th century, during the Dutch Golden Age, Amsterdam was the centre of the European liquor industry, producing liqueurs and jenever (or genever), a juniper-flavoured spirit that was the forerunner to the now more familiar 'London dry gin'.

Jenever is made by blending two very different spirits together. The first, 'moutwijn' (malt-wine), is a kind of unaged whiskey made by double or triple pot-distilling a mixture of rye, malted barley and wheat. It is this that gives jenever its distinctive flavour. The second constituent is neutral alcohol, which is redistilled with a recipe of botanical flavourings, typically juniper, coriander, caraway and aniseed. This process is very similar to the way London gin is distilled and the result is essentially a gin. The two spirits are blended together and the amount of malt wine used determines the style of the jenever produced.

There are three basic styles of jenever - 'jonge' ('young'), the lightest style, with least malt wine, 'oude'('old'), which is not aged but is a traditional style and must include some malt wine, and 'korenwijn' ('corn wine'), which Bols spell 'corenwyn', which is cask aged and must contain at least 51% malt wine.

The Dutch drink jenever neat from small, ice-cold, tulip-shaped glasses. A 'Kopstoot' (pronounced 'Cop-Stout') literally translates as 'a blow for your head' and involves drinking a shot of ice-cold jenever followed by a glass of beer. Bols remain the biggest Dutch producer of both liqueurs and jenevers.

The Dutch along with their immediate neighbours, the Belgians, brew some great beers besides the familiar Heineken, Grolsch, Oranjeboom and Amstel. The Netherlands is home to the only Trappist brewery outside of Belgium, De Schaapskooi, at Tilburg in Brabant. Also look out for beers brewed by Alfa Brewery (noted for its Pils) and Gulpener. Amsterdam boasts a number of excellent bars that specialise in micro-brewed Dutch and Belgian beers (see Cafe Gollem, Cafe In De Wildeman and De Zotte). Also be sure to pay a visit to the excellent Brouwerij 't IJ brewery and bar housed in a windmill.

The traditional tasting houses (proeflokaalen) are literally outlet shops for a distiller or wine and spirits importer and unique to Amsterdam (see Proeflokaal De Drie Fleschjes, Proeflokaal and Proeflokaal Wynand Fockink).The Dutch answer to the local pub is the 'brown cafe', typically dimly lit and smoke filled with dark wooden panelling and furnishings. In summer seasonal beach bars lie in suburbs such as Bloemendaal aan Zee and Zandvoort - many Amsterdam bar operators run these huge temporary bars with some moving operations there for the summer.

Also unique to Amsterdam are its smoking coffee shops, or 'hash bars' where cannabis is openly sold and smoked. Perversely, while it's perfectly legal for such establishments to sell cannabis, it remains illegal for them to buy it. To quote Vincent Vega again, "Yeah, it's legal, but it ain't a hundred percent legal. I mean you can't walk into a restaurant, roll a joint, and start puffin' away. You're only supposed to smoke in your home or certain designated places." You'll find these coffee shops all over town, identifiable due to their names that normally include words like 'space', 'high' and 'happy'.

Amsterdam's bars typically open at 11am and close at 1am. Some around Leidseplein and Rembrandtplein remain open till 4am weekdays and 5am at weekends. This is also the area to head if you're interested in live bands and nightclubs but be aware that dress codes may apply. The minimum drinking age in The Netherlands is eighteen.

THE AMSTEL HOTEL BAR

1 Professor Tulpplein, Amsterdam, 1018 GX, The Netherlands

Tel: +31 (0)20 622 6060, www.amsterdam.intercontinental.com
Hours: Mon-Sun 11am-1am

Type: Hotel bar
Alfresco: Riverside terrace
Entry: Via hotel lobby
Highlights: Terrace & cocktails
Atmosphere: Starchy yet relaxed
Clientele: International hotel crowd
Dress code: Not too casual
Price guide: €€€
Bar snacks: Full menu

This classy, intimate, old-school bar is hidden in the depths of an equally classy old hotel. A long terrace gives onto the Amstel River and drinkers spill from the terrace on to the boats moored to it.

Inside the wooden panelled room, the nautical theme continues. A brass ship's clock, barometer and display case of nautical knots hang behind the granite topped bar. Blue leather bucket chairs line the tartan carpet and polished wooden tables are set for dinner (the extensive food menu and silver service befit such a hotel). Settle at the bar or out on the terrace and enjoy some very well made cocktails.

I hear a refurbishment is scheduled. Let's hope it includes a lighting change and an evolution in the music policy – because the location and drinks need no further amends.

ARC BAR

44 Reguliersdwarsstraat, Amsterdam, 1017 BM, The Netherlands

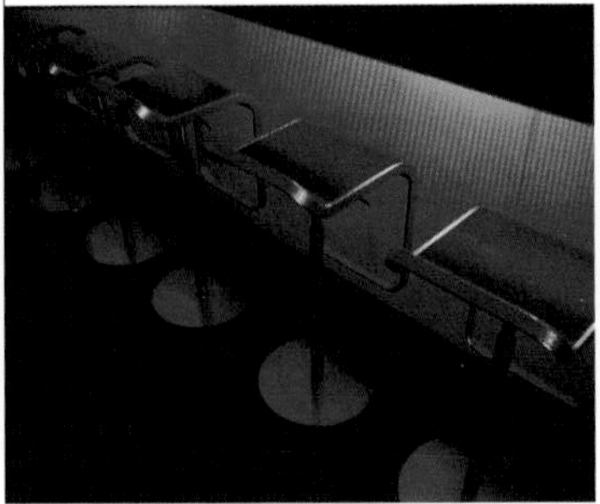

Tel: +31 (0)20 689 7070, www.bararc.com
Hours: Sun-Thu 4pm-1am, Fri-Sat 4pm-3am (happy hour 5-7pm)

Type: Gay restaurant bar
Alfresco: Street side terrace
Entry: Open door
Highlights: People watching
Atmosphere: Relaxed
Clientele: Gay blokes plus few straight
Dress code: Flamboyant designer casual
Price guide: €€€
Bar snacks: Full menu

This more than slightly gay restaurant and bar fronts Amsterdam's equally gay Reguliersdwarsstraat, its decked terrace producing an effect akin to the verandah of a camp beach hut.

The interior is clubby lounge with low slung seats and tables, and a decidedly eighties club look is heightened by design features including blue neon-lit stair rails. While the interior could be described as clean and modern, the same cannot be said of the garden this place backs onto: the large windows overlook a stagnant pond.

Unless you want to strut with the boys at the main bar, I'd head to the back left corner where a smaller cocktail bar lies. Here are served some surprisingly good cocktails, particularly when Ara Carvallo is manning the shaker.

BUBBLES & WINES

37 Nes, Amsterdam, 1012 KC, The Netherlands

Tel: +31 (0)20 422 3318, www.bubblesandwines.com
Hours: Mon-Sat 3:30pm-midnight

Type: Wine bar
Alfresco: No
Entry: Open door
Highlights: Wines by the glass, food
Atmosphere: Easy going
Clientele: Local office escapees & tourists
Dress code: Casual but not scruffy
Price guide: €€€
Bar snacks: Tapas-style bites

We stumbled upon this little place close to Dam Square by accident. I say stumbled, although we were riding past on pushbikes as normal when bar crawling in Amsterdam. Behind its narrow frontage lies a long, slender room outfitted in eighties retro brown and black, complete with velvet and bronzed mirrors.

As the name would suggest, the bar specialises in champagne and wine - fifty by the glass and 180 by the bottle. High-tech nitrogen wine savers (Enomatic System) ensure opened bottles stay fresh and tasting flights are enthusiastically served with the punch line "have a good flight" following notes on each of the wines poured.

Bubbles & Wines is owned by a young couple: Robert pours the wines while his wife prepares tapas-style gourmet bites in the kitchen. I particularly recommend the Bee Stings (truffle cheese, parmigiano and black pepper) but whatever you eat be sure to follow Robert's wine matching suggestion.

PROEFLOKAAL DE DRIE FLESCHJES

●●●○○

18 Gravenstraat, Amsterdam, 1012 NM, The Netherlands

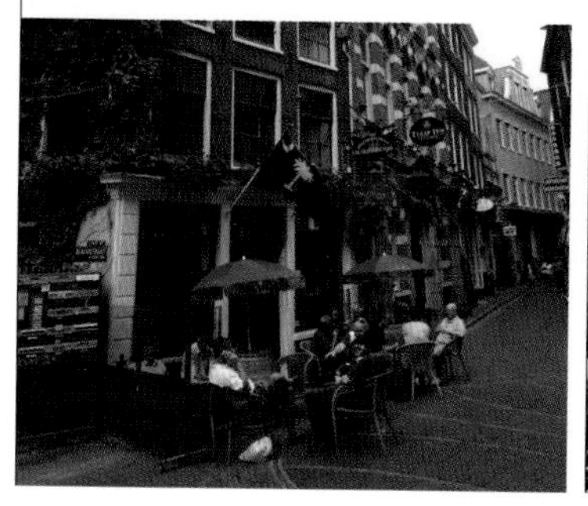

Tel: +31 (0)20 624 8443, www.driefleschjes.nl
Hours: Mon-Sat 2pm-8:30pm, Sun 3pm-7pm

Type: Old Dutch tasting house
Alfresco: Tables on street
Entry: Open door
Highlights: Heritage
Atmosphere: Restful
Clientele: Locals & tourists
Dress code: Anything goes
Price guide: €€
Bar snacks: Meatballs, cheese and sausages

Amsterdam used to be the centre of Europe's liqueur making and as London's old breweries commonly had a 'brewery tap' pub so these distilleries had their tasting house. This one, the name of which means 'The Three Little Bottles', opened in 1650 and was attached to the Bootz distillery. Although the distillery building still stands next door, it is now the Tulip Inn.

The distillery may have gone but the interior of this bar survives, like a working museum to the distillers' and liqueur makers' craft. Fittingly, both it and the Bootz brand name are now owned by Bols. A wall of old wooden vats faces the long wooden bar with old crock flasks and jenever bottles adding to the museum-like feel. The wide wooden floor is dusted with the traditional sand.

Tip van Bootz, Bols and Gravenbitter products line the shelves. Be sure to sample one of the five brands of Dutch jenever and almost forgotten Dutch liqueurs, such as Half-om-Half and Bitterkoekjeslikeur, which are still served in this tiny temple to Dutch distilling.

BROUWERIJ 'T IJ

●●●○○

7 Funenkade, Amsterdam, 1018 AL, The Netherlands

Tel: +31 (0)20 320 1786, www.brouwerijhetij.nl
Hours: Wed-Sun 3pm-8pm

Type: Brewery pub
Alfresco: Large terrace
Entry: All welcome
Highlights: Beer
Atmosphere: Surreal at times
Clientele: Cross section of locals & tourists
Dress code: Very casual
Price guide: €€
Bar snacks: Cheese and hardboiled eggs

Brouwerij 't Ij means 'brewery at Ij' - the lake behind the windmill which houses this brewery. In Dutch the name sounds like 'egg', hence the brewery's logo of an emu standing over an egg. Dutch humour may not translate well but beer aficionados will love this small, speciality brewery and I have to profess a liking for its well hopped and flavoursome Columbus amber ale.

The bar is slightly bizarre and scuzzy, but in an endearing way. Dusty empty beer bottles line narrow shelves that run around the walls of the room, the back half of which has white tiles and soap holders apparently marking where shower cubicles once stood. Long, well worn, wooden tables house an unusual bunch of locals, tourists and beer heads. On clement days drink alfresco on the large terrace in the shadow of the windmill's blades.

COLLEGE HOTEL BAR

●●●●○

1 Roelof Hartstraat, Amsterdam, 1071 VE, The Netherlands

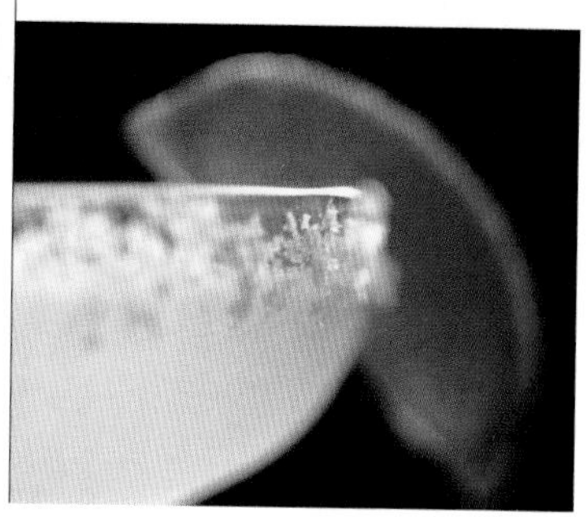

Tel: +31 (0)20 571 1511, www.thecollegehotel.com
Hours: Mon-Sun 11am-midnight

Type: Hotel/restaurant bar
Alfresco: Courtyard seating
Entry: Dedicated entrance or via lobby
Highlights: Décor & service
Atmosphere: Chilled
Clientele: Dinners & hotel guests
Dress code: Open collar smart
Price guide: €€€
Bar snacks: Full restaurant menu

A bar run by college kids sounds like a student union nightmare but the bar at this particular College is a plush, upmarket affair. The aptly named hotel is a working school with an annual intake of students learning as they serve its guests. With a little help from their supervisors these keen, eager to learn staff provide surprisingly good, attentive service.

The dimly lit room is wonderfully loungy and relaxed with an onyx lit bar, high stools surrounding tall round tables and plenty of comfy chairs and sofas.

As well as hotel residents, this bar attracts a more mature pre-dinner crowd of locals. The feel is decidedly upscale, something reflected in the large number of champagnes served by the glass.

The staff are keen to tackle any cocktail you may request and invent their own highly creative cocktails – sometimes a little too ambitious. All the same, a very classy bar.

CAFÉ DE STILL

●●●●○

326A Spuistraat, Amsterdam, 1012 VX, The Netherlands

Tel: +31 (0)20 427 6809, www.destill.nl
Hours: Mon-Wed 4pm-1am, Thu noon-1am, Fri-Sat noon-3am, Sun noon-1am

Type: Whiskey bar
Alfresco: Café style pavement seating
Entry: Open door
Highlights: Whisky selection
Atmosphere: Convivial
Clientele: Malt heads & tourists
Dress code: Casual
Price guide: €€€
Bar snacks: Olives, nuts, cheese & sausages

Café De Still lies practically opposite the rather better known Harry's Bar. It may be diminutive in its proportions but it carries a huge range of Scotch whiskies: over 350 different drams, tightly packed two deep on the narrow back bar shelves. Bottle lockers for regulars line the wall opposite the bar, each labelled with the name of its owner, many members of the drinks industry.

The small, cosy narrow room is dimly lit with mustard coloured walls, polished red wood furnishings and jazz quietly playing in the background. A brass water tap at the end of the bar caters for those needing to water down cask strength drams. (Café de Still also offers two beers on draught.)

Check the price when requesting a dram, as some are very rare and collectable, and priced accordingly. Credit cards are not accepted.

CAFE GOLLEM

●●●●○

4 Raamsteeg (btwn Spuistraat & Singel), Amsterdam, The Netherlands

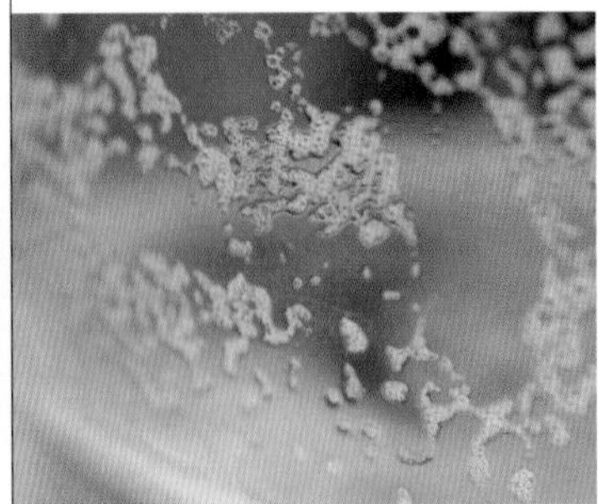

Tel: +31 (0)6 5241 7024, www.cafegollem.nl
Hours: Mon-Fri 4pm-1am, Sat-Sun 2pm-2am

Type: Traditional pub (brown café)
Alfresco: No
Entry: Subject to space
Highlights: Beers
Atmosphere: Very chilled
Clientele: Beer enthusiasts
Dress code: Very casual
Price guide: €€
Bar snacks: Only nuts etc

When Café Gollem opened in 1974 it was the first bar in Amsterdam to offer a large range of specialist Belgian and other foreign beers - owner Gerard Nooter imported many in the boot of his car. The current owner, Rick Hermans, offers over 200 different kinds of bottled beers, 95% of which are Belgian. He stocks the exclusive Westvleteren, and offers ten beers on tap, of which six change frequently.

The tiny, dimly lit, dark wood interior is quaint and rustic. Candles rest in wax-coated crock bottles and beer mats adorn the ceiling. There is a raised area beyond the bar with a balcony which often acts as a makeshift stage for stand-up comedians.

Chalkboards list the vast range of beers available. You'll not find many Budweiser drinkers here but the place gets packed with all manner of locals and tourists.

HARRY'S BAR

●●●●○

285 Spuistraat, Amsterdam, 1012 VR, The Netherlands

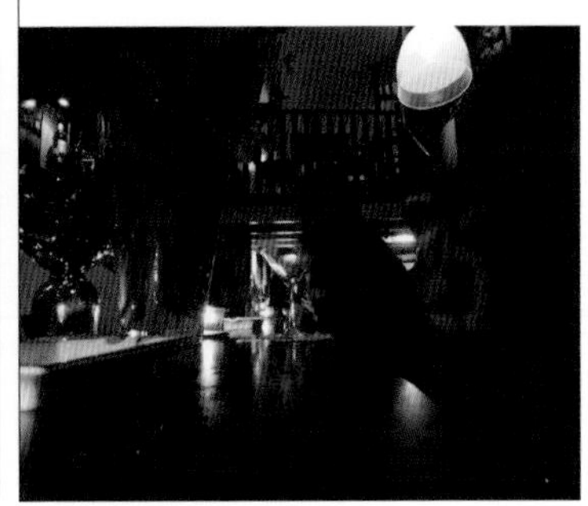

Tel: +31 (0)20 624 4384, www.harrysbar.nl
Hours: Sun-Thu 5pm-1am, Fri-Sat 5pm-3am

Type: Cocktail bar
Alfresco: Café style pavement seating
Entry: Open door
Highlights: Cocktails
Atmosphere: Buzzing
Clientele: Tourists & expats
Dress code: Casual
Price guide: €€€
Bar snacks: Nibbles

It appears that just about every city in the world boasts a Harry's Bar, paying deference to a lesser or greater degree to Harry MacElhone's Parisian original.

This Dutch outpost has no connection or resemblance to the Parisian version but does offer a better range of spirits. And if you make it clear to your white-clad bartender that you're not just another tourist after sweet, fluffy cocktails, you'll be served cocktails made to a standard close to those in Paris. Sadly, few locals come here and the tourists who do tend to be young with little understanding of what separates a good drink from a bad one.

Even taking into account the upstairs cigar lounge which overlooks the bar, the interior is small, buzzy and atmospheric. In summer the best spot is out front where you can enjoy the Martinis and people watch.

JIMMY WOO

18 Korte Leidsedwarsstraat, Amsterdam, 1017 RC, The Netherlands

Tel: +31 (0)20 626 3150, www.jimmywoo.nl
Hours: Thu-Sat 11pm-4am

Type: Club/ lounge bar
Alfresco: No
Entry: Guest list or a challenge
Highlights: Getting in
Atmosphere: Clubby
Clientele: Cool crowd & wannabees
Dress code: Designer casual
Price guide: €€€€
Bar snacks: Eat before you go

This lounge bar and club has a reputation for being the hardest in town to get into, unless you turn up unfashionably early (it opens at 11pm). Jimmy Woo lies down a narrow side street and has a typically unpromising entrance.

In keeping with the name, Eastern design influences prevail with pink glowing wall panels in the style of Japanese room dividers. Upstairs is a combination of lounge bar and club, while downstairs is out-and-out club.

After all the stress of getting your name on the guest list, you'll find many of the groups of girls are more Z than A-list. However, you'll have to really be someone or to have forked out to score one of the reserved tables.

Apart from the ubiquitous premium vodkas, other spirits are limited. Cocktails are reasonably well made, especially considering the clubby environment.

THE MANSION

2 Hobbemastraat (@ Vossiusstraat), Amsterdam, 1071 ZA, The Netherlands

Tel: +31 (0)20 616 6664, www.the-mansion.nl
Hours: Sun-Thu 6pm-1am, Fri-Sat 6pm-3am (basement Fri-Sat 10pm-3am)

Type: Lounge/restaurant bar, club
Alfresco: No
Entry: Guest list, reservations advised
Highlights: Cocktails, décor, food
Atmosphere: Cool club
Clientele: Cool 30-somethings
Dress code: Designer casual
Price guide: €€€€
Bar snacks: Restaurant upstairs

The multi-layered Mansion, which opened in December 2004, is one of several establishments in Amsterdam that combine restaurant, lounge and club. You enter the building at lounge level, via a series of connecting lounges with a mirrored back bar in each. Swanky decor includes crystal chandeliers, low black leather stools, black leather regency chairs and cherubs on both the Sistine ceiling and the carpet below. The other lounges are more clubby in feel with glamorous types surrounding mirror-topped high tables.

The various bars at Mansion stock a serious range of premium spirits which are used to great effect in a classically led cocktail list by some of the best bartenders in Amsterdam. There's also a choice of seven wines by the glass from the international list.

Descend the steep spiralling staircase for a dance in the small but cosy basement club or head upstairs for Asian inspired cuisine.

NL LOUNGE

169 Nieuwezijds Voorburgwal, Amsterdam, 1012 RK, The Netherlands

Type: Lounge bar/club
Alfresco: No
Entry: Cover charge
Highlights: Atmosphere
Atmosphere: Party
Clientele: Up for it
Dress code: Designer casual
Price guide: €€€
Bar snacks: Thai snacks

Just round the corner from Amsterdam's famous Supperclub lies this equally well established and well respected lounge. NL is not named after the nation's car registration code, as many mistakenly believe. Its full title is the more mundane 'Nieuwezijds Lounge' after the road on which it lies.

Once past the picky bouncers and through the red velvet drapes, NL is dominated by its black and red colour scheme, opaque illuminated bar and small dance floor with glitterball. Beyond that is a more loungy area with low comfortable seating.

Cocktails are an important part of the offering here and are lovingly made, so can take a while to arrive. The Mojitos in particular are worth the wait.

Although now positively geriatric in club years NL still manages to draw a young, hip crowd.

The Odeon

THE ODEON

●●●●○

460 Singel (btwn Beulingstraat & Koningsplein on west side of canal), Amsterdam, 1000 AB, The Netherlands

Tel: +31 (0)20 521 8555, www.odeontheater.nl
Hours: Wed 6pm-1am, Thu 6pm-4am, Fri-Sat 6pm-5am, Sun 6pm-4am

Type: Lounge bar/brasserie/restaurant/club
Alfresco: No
Entry: Cover charge for club
Highlights: Décor, cocktails
Atmosphere: Bar - relaxed, club - happening
Clientele: 30-somethings
Dress code: Designer casual
Price guide: €€€
Bar snacks: Eat in café or restaurant

Another of Amsterdam's multi-layered, multi-use venues, this one sits in a beautifully restored building overlooking a tree-lined canal. Originally built in 1663 as a beer brewery and rebuilt in the 1930s as Amsterdam's first real concert hall, it was later converted into a cinema. The present incarnation opened in April 2005 and from the bottom up includes a brasserie, lounge bar, restaurant and club.

The café-cum-brasserie is open seven days a week and handy to remember for refreshment but the tiny bar lying off the splendid marble hallway above is of more interest. Original 17th century cherubs flit across the high ceiling in dramatic contrast to the modern fashion photography that covers the panelled walls. Here British bartender Marty Bilsborough mixes some great drinks.

The upstairs club with its VIP gallery in the huge, ornate old theatre must rank as the most stunning nightclub space in the world.

CIEL BLUE BAR

23rd Floor, Hotel Okura, 333 Ferdinand Bolstraat, Amsterdam, 1072 LH, The Netherlands

Tel: +31 (0)20 678 7111
Hours: Daily until 1 am

Type: Lounge/restaurant bar
Alfresco: No
Entry: Via lift from lobby
Highlights: Cocktails
Atmosphere: Tad starchy
Clientele: Business types
Dress code: Smart
Price guide: €€€
Bar snacks: Head for hotel restaurants

Bar-wise, a city is not a real city without a Harry's Bar and a bar atop a skyscraper. We've already covered Amsterdam's Harry's and at 75 metres up on the 23rd floor this ensures that Amsterdam makes the city count. The bar and adjoining Michelin starred restaurants are perched on the top floor of the Okura Hotel, Amsterdam's second tallest building after the Rembrandt Tower.

On a clear day this bar's 'Blue Sky' title is apt as it offers incomparable views of the low-rise city. (The vertiginous viewing platform has been closed since a lunatic hopped over the edge to the sudden thump of death below.)

With its floral carpet and corporate design ethos, this small bar is no looker. It's also a little disappointing on the beer front with only Heineken on draught. However, friendly bartenders wearing waistcoats and bow ties make up for these failings with their classically led cocktails.

PROEFLOKAAL WYNAND FOCKINK

●●●◐○

31 Pijlsteeg, Amsterdam, 1012 HH, The Netherlands

Tel: +31 (0)20 639 2695, www.wynand-fockink.nl
Hours: Mon-Sun 3pm-9pm

Type: Dutch tasting house
Alfresco: Sit in alley
Entry: Open door
Highlights: Liqueur range
Atmosphere: Convivial
Clientele: Locals & tourists
Dress code: Casual
Price guide: €€
Bar snacks: Not a place to eat

The wonderfully named Wynard Fockink established his liqueur distillery in the Pijlsteeg around 1679. Back then it was usual for Dutch distilleries to have an adjoining 'tasting house' where the products from the distillery could be sampled and purchased. Sadly the distillery closed in 1955 but the Wynard Fockink tasting house remains almost unchanged from its seventeenth century heyday.

The interior looks more like an ancient apothecary's shop than a pub with earthenware pots, lines of bottles and a sand covered wooden floor. A small serving hatch houses the beer fonts and in summer drinkers gather in the street outside.

Wynard Fockink's range of sixty odd liqueurs and brandy weins are all still served here in the traditional way. The glass is placed on the low wooden counter and filled to the brim. You bend over to take the first sip before lifting the glass to consume the rest of the liqueur. Try the sweet and sour 'Half & half' or the Pruimpje Prikin (prick in a prune), made from squashed plums.

RAIN

●●●◐○

44 Rembrandtplein, Amsterdam, 1017 CV, The Netherlands

Tel: +31 (0)20 262 7078, www.rain-amsterdam.nl
Hours: Sun-Thu 5pm-2am, Fri-Sat 5pm-4am

Type: Lounge / restaurant / club
Alfresco: No
Entry: Subject to management & capacity
Highlights: Pick-up potential
Atmosphere: Clubby
Clientele: Party crowd
Dress code: Smart casual
Price guide: €€€
Bar snacks: Restaurant upstairs

Of all Amsterdam's new breed of restaurant, lounge bar and club combos, Rain is the blingest. Owned by sons of big money (the founder of the Mexx clothing empire and a successful real estate investment fund respectively), Rain has the look of a club where rock stars would come to be snapped by waiting paparazzi. Sadly like many rock stars it lacks the sophistication which gives bling its depth.

The bright bar dominates the dimly lit, predominantly black interior and overlooks a grey slate dance floor edged by loungy seating with low tables. Black pillars on which to rest drinks dot the edge of the dance floor. Rain is much more 'club and dance' than 'lounge and drink', even with able bartenders such as Lydia Soetadi making the cocktails.

Friday and Saturday nights see the upstairs restaurant area morph into a further club area. The door policy here appears more relaxed than other similar venues in town.

THE SUPPERCLUB

●●●○○

21 Jonge Roelensteeg, Amsterdam, 1012 PL, The Netherlands

Tel: +31 (0)20 344 6400, www.supperclub.nl
Hours: Sun-Thu 7pm-1am, Fri-Sat 7pm-3am

Type: Restaurant / club
Alfresco: No
Entry: Reservation advised
Highlights: Spectacle
Atmosphere: Tad debauched
Clientele: Businessmen to funsters
Dress code: Suits to rubber
Price guide: €€€€
Bar snacks: Ground floor restaurant

While many of us may leave breakfast breadcrumbs in the sheets at weekends, dinner in bed is wildly decadent. At least, it was back when this place first opened, serving not only dinner in a bed, but in a bed full of strangers. How the world has moved on. Now many restaurants and even nightclubs in comparatively reserved cities such as New York change sheets in place of tablecloths.

Elongated bunkbeds run the length of the large, high ceilinged room. The walls are white, the sheets are white, so naturally you're required to take your shoes off at the door. After your dinner and sweet in a communal bed the fun really starts as the bedroom turns to nightclub.

Downstairs past the gay & straight toilets (choose carefully), with urinals visible through the porthole windows, is the separate basement bar and adjoining black padded S&M dungeon-like lounge, complete with handcuffs and chains hanging from the walls. In general the food is OK, the DJs great, the drinks awful and the experience not to be missed.

Rain

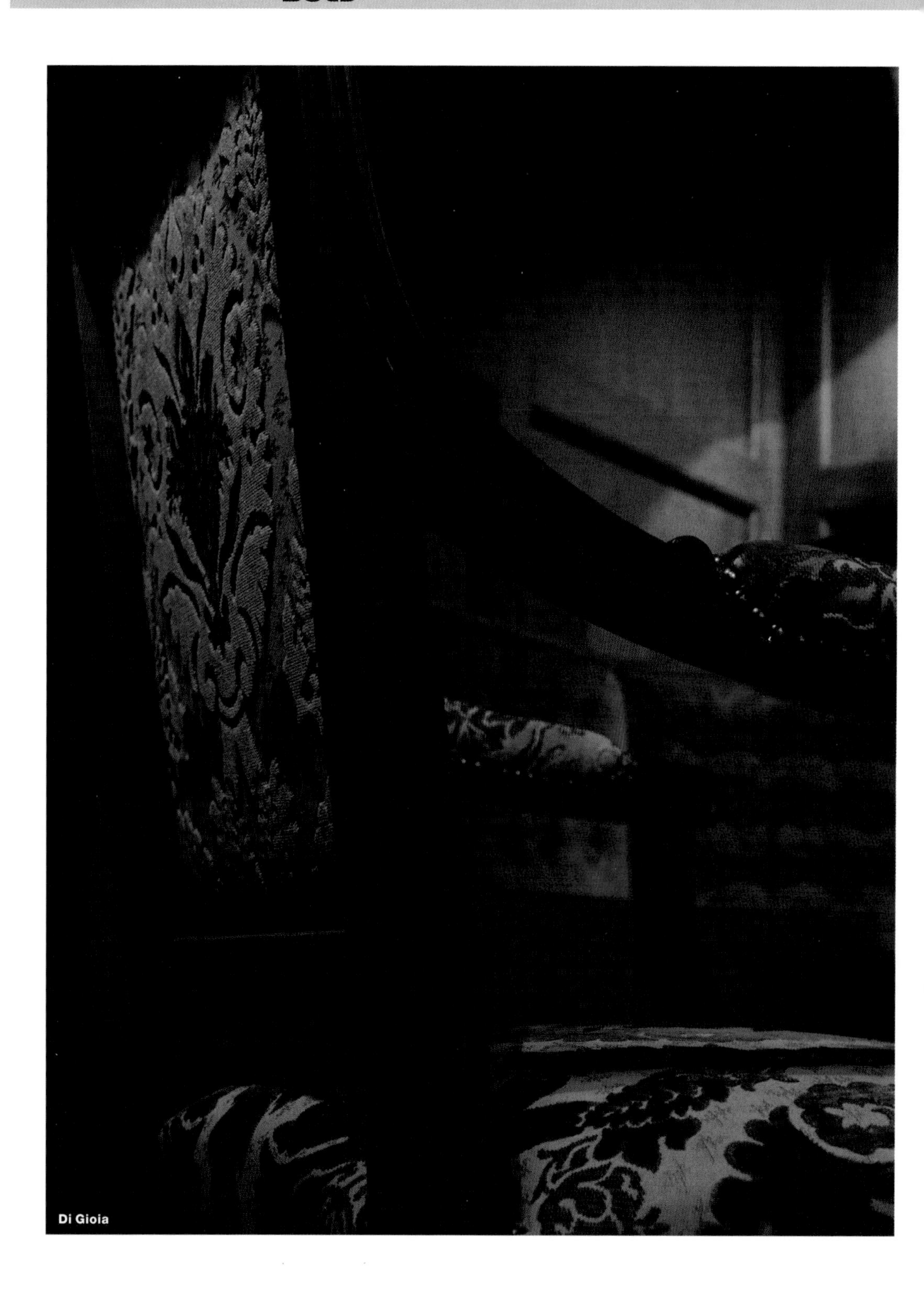

Di Gioia

DI GIOIA

45 Korte Leidese Dwarsstraat, Amsterdam, 1017 PW, The Netherlands

Tel: +31 20 626 6769, www.tao-group.nl
Hours: Sun-Thu 6pm-1am, Fri-Sat 6pm-3am

Type: Lounge bar
Alfresco: No
Entry: Open door
Highlights: Cocktails, decor
Atmosphere: Buzzy lounge
Clientele: 30-something cool set
Dress code: Designer casual
Price guide: €€€
Bar snacks: Not a place to eat

This lounge has changed its name but fairly little else. Formerly Suzy Wong, it is now named for mixologist extraordinaire Andrea di Gioia, who is a shareholder and in charge of the drinks.

The front section of the narrow, L-shaped bar retains its Parisian brothel feel with acres of red velvet, a mirrored ceiling and a pole dancing platform. The area behind is half gentleman's club, half Thai restaurant. There's a trophy cabinet and a hunting lodge ceiling, while bamboos flourish behind a glass wall. Efficient waitresses ply their way between the tables and the black leather, studded bar.

The cocktails here are of a good standard and enjoyed by a hip upscale crowd of local thirty-somethings. Di Gioia and its half-sibling, Jimmy Woo opposite, are oases of civilisation in what is Amsterdam's answer to the Haymarket.

CAFE IN DE WILDEMAN

3 Kolksteeg, Amsterdam, 1012 PT, The Netherlands

Tel: +31 (0)20 638 2348, www.indewildeman.nl
Hours: Mon-Thu noon-1am, Sat noon-2am

Type: Pub
Alfresco: Benches on lane
Entry: Open door
Highlights: Beer
Atmosphere: Relaxed but hectic some nights
Clientele: Tourists
Dress code: Casual
Price guide: €€
Food: Snack menu including Trappist cheese

This pub is housed in what was formerly a jenever and liqueur distillery's tasting house. The premises used to be dedicated to the production and sale of spirits and liqueurs but today this wonderfully old-school and unpretentious pub is all about the appreciation and enjoyment of beer.

Wildeman boasts a superb range of over 200 bottled and seventeen beers on draught. Most are Belgian and Dutch brews with Trappist beers a house speciality. However, there's also a good range of beers from around the world. Remember that 'triple' beers are lighter in style and 'double' tend to be rich and dark. If undecided, ask one of the knowledgeable staff for a recommendation.

Wildeman is tucked down a narrow pedestrian street and I can think of few better ways to spend an afternoon than sipping a Trappist beer on one of its outside wooden benches, eating Trappist cheese & pumpernickel and contemplating some meatballs.

DE ZOTTE

29 Raamstraaat, Amsterdam, 1016 XL, The Netherlands

Tel: +31 (0)20 626 8694
Hours: Mon-Thu 4pm-1am, Fri-Sat 2pm-3am

Type: Pub
Alfresco: No
Entry: Open door
Highlights: Beer, food
Atmosphere: Relaxed pub
Clientele: Locals
Dress code: Casual
Price guide: €€
Food: Chunky chips and more wholesome offerings

De Zotte is a wonderfully rustic traditional beer joint with a bare wooden floor and plywood panelled walls covered in tin beer signs. Mismatched old tables, chairs and bench seating house a mixed bunch of local students and tourists who've strayed from the beaten path or actively searched out this back street venue.

The real reason to come here is the beer. Belgian and Dutch brews dominate De Zotte's staggering list of well over 100 bottled and seven draught beers. The food is cheap and worth the quest with everything from chunky chips to more wholesome offerings such as escargot with calvados.

De Zotte literally means crazy and late on weekend evenings that pretty accurately sums up the atmosphere. To best appreciate the food and beer, visit during the day or early week.

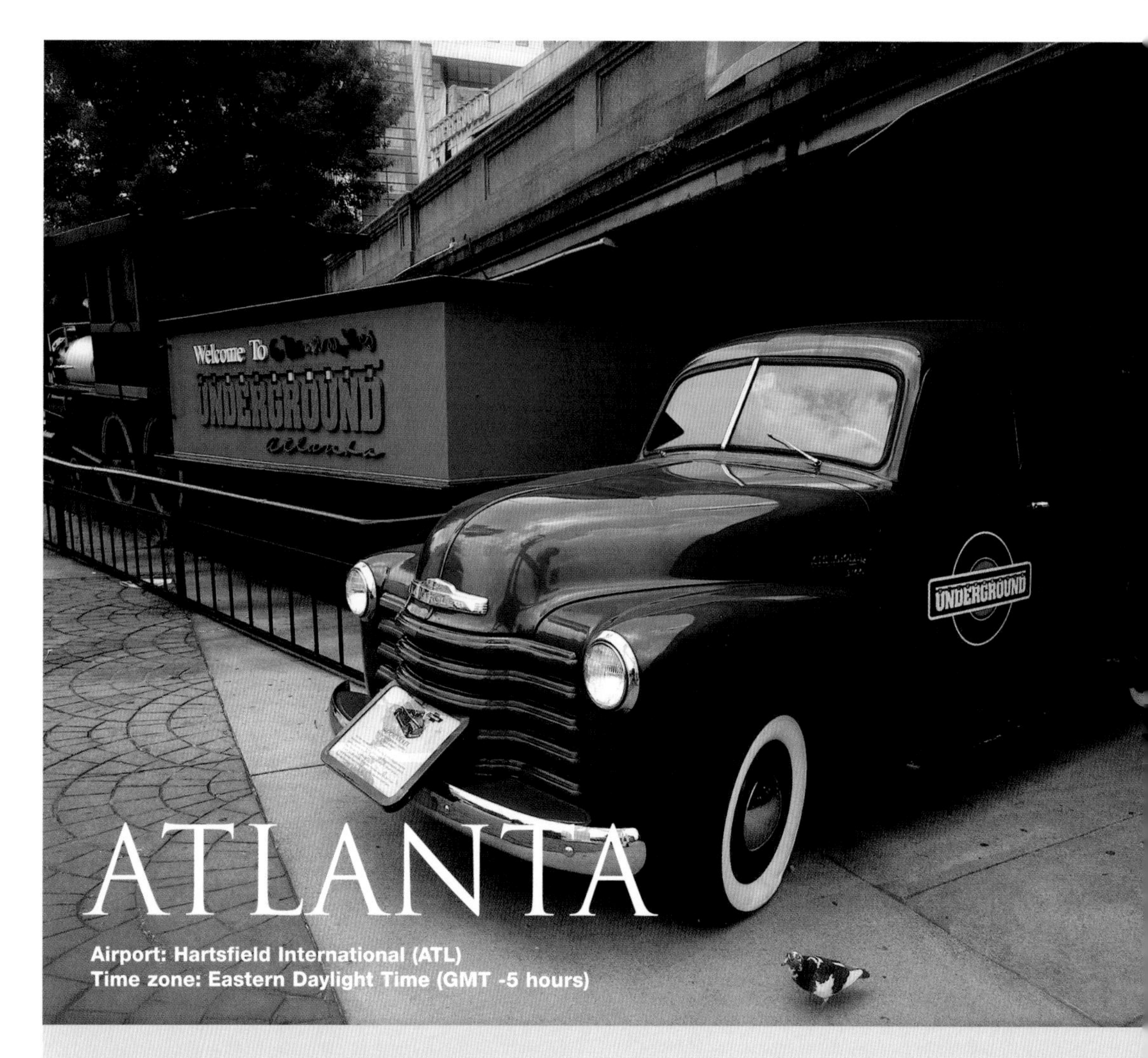

ATLANTA

Airport: Hartsfield International (ATL)
Time zone: Eastern Daylight Time (GMT -5 hours)

The capital of Georgia, birthplace of anti-segregationist leader Martin Luther King, site of the 1996 Olympic Games and home to CNN, Coca-Cola and Delta Airlines, Atlanta owes its growth from small town to metropolis to an accident of geography which made it a natural railroad hub. Today highways converge on the town and its airport is a hub for Delta and other airlines. This crossroads city attract much convention traffic.

Peachtree Street runs south to north from the downtown business and convention district, through trendy midtown to the upscale Buckhead shopping and business district. Confusingly this, the city's best known road, changes its name to Peachtree Road above midtown. Even more confusingly, since this is an area more noted for peanuts than peaches, this is one of dozens of streets with Peachtree in their title.

Atlanta Hotels

Unless travelling to Atlanta on business that necessitates your staying downtown, I'd recommend either choosing a midtown hotel or one of the many hotels in the Buckhead area. Small boutique hotels are yet to impact Atlanta, but of the many large corporate hotels in the city I favour the following.

Four Seasons Hotel

75 Fourteenth Street, Midtown, Atlanta, Georgia, GA 30309, USA
Tel: +1 404 881 9898,
www.fourseasons.com

This elegant hotel is not far away from the shops in Buckhill or the sights downtown. Originally built in 1991 as the Grand Hotel Atlanta, it was acquired by Four Seasons in 1998 and $65 million later offers 244 very plush rooms and suites with broadband internet access (subject to a daily charge). Its health club incorporates a 62ft/19m indoor pool with sun terrace and whirlpool bath plus steam and sauna rooms.

The Ritz-Carlton Buckhead Hotel

3434 Peachtree Road N.E. (@ Lenox Rd), Atlanta, Georgia, GA 30326, USA
Tel: +1 404 237 2700,
www.ritzcarlton.com

Set in the heart of the Buckhead financial and shopping district with two huge malls (Lenox Square and Phipps Plaza) lying on opposite corners, this hotel is a good bet for those seeking retail therapy. With its 553 rooms it's hardly boutique but with scale come amenities such as a heated indoor pool, sauna and steam baths, fitness centre and outdoor sundeck. Plush, classically appointed rooms include marble baths and dataport connection, at a cost. A second Ritz-Carton is situated downtown at the opposite end of the road - 181 Peachtree Street.

Atlanta Restaurants

Atlanta hardly has a reputation for culinary excellence but fine dining and a wide range of cuisines can be found all over this sprawling city. The Buckhead Life Restaurant Group has, since opening Pano's & Paul's in 1979, been very influential and now boasts a dozen of the best restaurants, as illustrated below.

A sales tax of 7% is added to all bills in Atlanta and, as with the rest of America, etiquette dictates that you should tip an additional fifteen to twenty percent.

Anis Bistro

2974 Grandview Avenue (Pharr Rd.), Buckhead, Atlanta, GA, USA 30305
Tel: +1 404 233 9889,
www.anisbistro.com
Cuisine: French bistro

This romantic little restaurant, in an old house on a residential street, serves traditional French bistro fare to Buckhead locals. The patio is my favourite spot.

Aria

490 E. Paces Ferry Road, (@ Maple Dr), Buckhead, Atlanta, Georgia, GA 30305, USA
Tel: +1 404 233 7673, www.aria-atl.com
Cuisine: Modern American

Gerry Klaskala opened this little place in a renovated house in Buckhead. Contemporary décor enhances the vibe, as do the slowly braised, roasted and stewed meats on which Klaskala has built his reputation.

Atlanta Fish Market

265 Pharr Road (btwn Peachtree St & Piedmont Rd), Buckhead, Atlanta, Georgia, GA 30305, USA
Tel: +1 404 262 3165,
www.buckheadrestaurants.com
Cuisine: Seafood

A thirty foot copper fish sculpture stands in front of the train station-styled building which houses this restaurant – it comes complete with veranda and rocking chairs. Inside the atmosphere is bustling bistro. The wide selection of seafood arrives wonderfully fresh and in a myriad of styles.

Bacchanalia

1198 Howell Mill Road (btwn 14th St & Huff Rd), Westside, Atlanta, GA 30318, USA
Tel: +1 404 365 0410 Ext.22,
www.starprovisions.com
Cuisine: Modern American

Seriously decadent fine cuisine served in a former meatpacking plant attracts serious foodies to chef-owners Anne Quatrano and Clifford Harrison's highly regarded restaurant.

Bone's

3130 Piedmont Road (Peachtree Rd), Buckhead, Atlanta, Georgia, GA 30305, USA
Tel: +1 404 237 2663,
www.bonesrestaurant.com
Cuisine: Steakhouse

As the name may suggest, Bones is hardly aimed at vegetarians. Expect business types enjoying juicy steaks accompanied by fine wines from the comprehensive list.

Buckhead Diner

3073 Piedmont Road, (E. Paces Ferry Rd.) Buckhead, Atlanta, Georgia, GA 30305, USA
Tel: +1 404 262 3336,
www.buckheadrestaurants.com
Cuisine: Modern American

Bigger and shinier than your everyday American stainless steel-fronted diner, this Buckhead restaurant takes the format upscale. It's always busy and passing celebrities often drop by.

Chops/Lobster Bar

Buckhead Plaza,
70 West Paces Ferry Road (@ Peachtree Rd), Buckhead, Atlanta, Georgia, GA 30305, USA
Tel: +1 404 262 2675,
www.buckheadrestaurants.com
Cuisine: Seafood & steakhouse

The dark wood dining room here serves some of the best steaks in America while the Lobster bar in the art deco styled basement serves superbly fresh fish to the less carnivorous.

Nan Thai Fine Dining

1350 Spring Street NW (@ 17th St), Midtown, Atlanta, Georgia, GA 30309, USA.
Tel: +1 404 870 9933,
www.nanfinedining.com
Cuisine: Thai

A simple but stunning dining room with exhibition kitchen, great service and regarded dishes by chef/co-owner Nan has made this one of Atlanta's most desirable restaurants.

Nikolai's Roof

Atlanta Hilton, 255 Courtland Street (btwn Baker & Harris Sts), Downtown Atlanta, Georgia, GA 30303, USA
Tel: +1 404 221 6362,
www.nikolaisroof.com
Cuisine: French & Russian

Floor to ceiling windows and a position high atop the Atlanta Hilton give diners spectacular views as they tuck into French and Continental cuisine with a heavy Russian accent. Caviar and ice-cold vodka are the preferred appetisers.

Pano's & Paul's

West Paces Ferry Shopping Centre, 1232 West Paces Ferry Road (Northside Pkwy), Buckhead, Atlanta, Georgia, GA 30327, USA
Tel: + 1 404 261 3662, www.buckheadrestaurants.com
Cuisine: Continental

The flagship of the Buckhead Life Restaurant Group, Pano's & Paul's has been at the head of fine dining in Atlanta for more than 25 years. Dover sole and venison are two of the favourites served in the warm, art deco styled interior. A very broad wine list offers plenty of choice from both old and new worlds.

Ritz-Carlton Buckhead Dining Room

Ritz-Carlton, 3434 Peachtree Road (@ Lenox Rd), Buckhead, Atlanta, Georgia, GA 30326, USA
Tel: +1 404 237 2700, www.ritzcarlton.com
Cuisine: French

Elegant fine dining set in a plush grand hotel. The need for jackets and the traditional setting can make the experience formal rather than atmospheric but the dishes are highly regarded.

Seeger's

111 West Paces Ferry Road NW (@ E. Andrews Dr), Buckhead Atlanta, Georgia, GA 30305, USA
Tel: +1 404 846 9779, www.seegers.com
Cuisine: Modern American

Renowned chef Guenter Seeger's constantly changing menu is a magnet for gastronauts who consider the stratospheric prices charged here superb value for money. Such a fine dining experience should be matched by fine wine and Seeger's offers more than 1,000 bins to choose from.

Atlanta Liquor Stores

Ansley Wine Merchants

1544 Piedmont Avenue, Atlanta, Georgia, GA 30324, USA
Tel: +1 404 876 6790

Ansley specializes in burgundies, but carries an impressive range of other wines from around the world plus beers and spirits. Friendly knowledgeable staff assist those in need of guidance.

Green's

2612 Buford Highway, Atlanta, Georgia, GA 30324, USA
Tel: +1 404 321 6232, www.greensbeverages.com

One of two well stocked branches in Atlanta, Green's offers a good range and friendly advice, which even runs to recommendations on which drinks books to buy.

Mac's Beer & Wine

21A Peachtree Place NW (@West Peachtree), Atlanta, Georgia, GA 30309, USA
Tel: +1 404 872 4897

A prominent, airy modern store with a growing reputation for its beer range.

Murphy's

997 Virginia Avenue Northeast, Virginia Highland, Atlanta, Georgia, GA 30306, USA
Tel: +1 404 872 0904, www.murphysvh.com

This well established restaurant also boasts a very slick wine bar and retail wine shop with weekly wine tastings and seminars.

Sherlock's Wine Merchant & The Cook's Warehouse

4062 Peachtree Road, Brookhaven, Atlanta, Georgia, GA 30319, USA
Tel: +1 404 949 9945, www.sherlocks.com

A combined wine merchant and retailer of cookware, kitchen appliances and kitchen gadgets.

Sherlock & Sanders Wine Cellar

3401 Northside Parkway, Atlanta, Georgia, GA 30327, USA
Tel: +1 404 233 1514, www.sherlocks.com

French wine specialist Jim Sanders established this noted wine merchants over 25 years ago.

ATLANTA DRINKING

While the bar scene in Atlanta is not as developed as in some other large US cities there's plenty to satisfy every taste, from dive bars to upscale lounges with plenty in between. There are also some good local brews such as Red Brick Ale, Peachtree Pale Ale, Sweet Georgia Brown, Sweetwater 420 and Terrapin Rye Pale Ale. Atlanta's nightlife is concentrated in five main areas.

Downtown is well past its 70s best with stray conference delegates helping to fill the clubs. In underground Atlanta these stay open till 4am.

Midtown is rapidly becoming the most upscale and stylish part of town with a wide variety of venues spread across a large area. This part of town hosts the annual Gay Pride Festival and its bars attract a mixed crowd year round. Atlantic Station, a huge new development at 17th Street, is the new locale to watch as bars and restaurants must surely move in to serve its new upscale residents.

Virginia Highland is a posh residential area with a decent splattering of quality neighbourhood pubs and bars, mostly along North Highland Avenue.

Little Five Points is a University area and bars here tend to be more wild and cutting edge with live music. Dress down or way out.

Buckhead is a financial and shopping district with its fair share of clubs and bars, many around the junction of Peachtree Road and East Paces Ferry Road. Two of note are Johnny's Hideaway (3771 Roswell Road), a nightclub attracting the over 40s (and in some cases 60s), and Tongue & Groove (3055 Peachtree Road), a cool nightclub attracting the local style set. On Friday and Saturday nights 20 & 30 somethings flock here for a good time.

Some bars stay open until 4am on Friday and Saturdays but Sunday and early week hours tend to be much shorter. In common with the rest of the US, legal drinking age is 21 years and it's usual to be asked for ID regardless of how old you look.

ATKINS PARK

794 North Highland Avenue NE, Virginia Highland, Atlanta, Georgia, GA 30306, USA

Tel: +1 404 876 7249, **www.**atkinspark.com
Hours: Mon-Sat 11am-4am, Sat 11am-3am, Sun 11am-midnight

Type: Neighbourhood bar
Alfresco: Side patio with fans
Entry: Open door
Highlights: Atmosphere, food
Atmosphere: Relaxed, friendly
Clientele: Virginia Highland locals
Dress code: Casual
Price guide: $$
Bar snacks: Full menu

Atkins Park began as a deli in 1922 and is Atlanta's oldest continuously licensed tavern. It's a traditional US neighbourhood bar and restaurant offering everything from kiddie meals to weekend brunches, late night drinking and late night feasting with food served until 2:30am.

Atkins Park's staff shirts profess "same as it ever was", and that's how it looks, agreeably worm around the edges, its dark wood and painted tin ceiling improving with age. The single roomed bar has diner style booths opposite a long wooden bar lined with brass name plates of its regulars. Neon bar signs and other drinking knick-knacks dot the room. There's a dining room next door and the bar snacks here are well above average, particularly the crab cakes. The atmosphere and music picks up when the restaurant closes at 11pm (midnight weekends).

Sixteen beers on draught plus twenty odd bottled beers, a good range of premium spirits and a friendly welcome from Nancy and the other bartenders make this neighbourhood bar worth journeying to.

FADÓ IRISH PUB

3035 Peachtree Road NE, Buckhead, Atlanta, Georgia, GA 30305, USA

Tel: +1 404 841 0066, **www.**fadoirishpub.com
Hours: Mon-Wed 11:30am-2am, Thu-Fri 11:30am-4am, Sat 10:30am-3am, Sun 10am-midnight

Type: Irish pub
Alfresco: Back yard
Entry: Open door
Highlights: The craik
Atmosphere: Relaxed to party
Clientele: Young Buckhead types
Dress code: Casual
Price guide: $$
Bar snacks: Boxty, fish 'n' chips in Guinness batter.

Just about every city in the world has a mock Irish pub: Guinness, toucan, Irish whiskey and all. Fadó is Atlanta's but, unlike most, is bordering on authentic with the Guinness being dispensed by Irishmen, salmon boxtys (stuffed Irish potato pancakes) on the menu and members of the local Gaelic football team among the regulars.

Fadó opened in 1996 and American readers may recognise the name, which incidentally means 'long ago' in Gaelic, as this Atlanta branch is the first of a chain of ten replicated in cities across the US.

The interior is divided into four areas around a central bar – a cottage pub with a fireplace, a Victorian pub with dark wood and stained glass, and so on. There's also an intimate back patio for those wanting to escape an atmosphere charged by televised soccer and Irish bands.

All in all this is a homely spot and a great place to sample a good traditional Irish breakfast washed down by a pint of the black stuff.

HALO LOUNGE

817 West Peachtree Street NW (entrance on 6th St), Midtown, Atlanta, GA 30308, USA

Tel: +1 404 962 7333, **www.**halolounge.com
Hours: Mon-Fri 4pm-3am, Sat 6pm-3am

Type: Lounge bar-styled club
Alfresco: No
Entry: Subject to management & capacity
Highlights: Great food & drinks
Atmosphere: Clubby but loungy
Clientele: Gay & straight mid-town style set
Dress code: Dressily casual
Price guide: $$$$
Bar snacks: Great nibbles & plates

The first thing to know about Halo is that the entrance is tucked around the corner on Sixth Street. Even so you could be forgiven for missing its discreet doorway.

The concrete bunker of a space lies under what was the grand 1920s Biltmore Hotel and was originally destined for the horses and carriages of the guests. Stairs that used to lead up to the hotel now finish at ceiling level and are something of a feature. The raw edges of bare concrete are softened by design features such as an underlit onyx bar and large blown-glass light fixtures. Halo is a hybrid of nightclub and chilled cocktail lounge, and attracts a stylish mixed gay & straight crowd. (Thursday nights are the gayest.)

A good spirits range including an impressive line-up of XO Cognacs reinforces upscale lounge aspirations while a short but innovative cocktail list, ten beers on draught, and a further 28 beers by the bottle and eleven wines by the glass mean there's something for every palate.

LOBBY LOUNGE

●●●○○

Ritz-Carlton Hotel, 3434 Peachtree Road N.E. (@ Lenox Rd), Buckhead, Atlanta, Georgia, GA 30326, USA

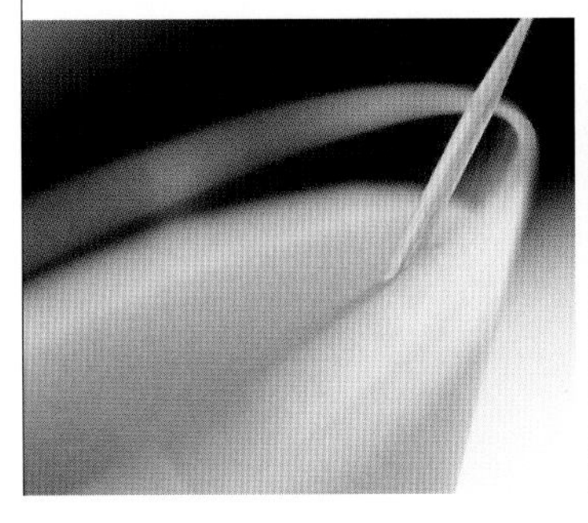

Tel: +1 404 237 2700, **www.**ritzcarlton.com
Hours: Daily till 1am

Type: Hotel lounge bar
Alfresco: No
Entry: Via hotel lobby
Highlights: Service
Atmosphere: Tad staid
Clientele: Business travellers & local hoi-polloi
Dress code: Nothing too casual
Price guide: $$$$
Bar snacks: Full menu

Atlanta boasts many large corporate hotels, each with their own lounge bar. However, this one at the Ritz-Carlton attracts an international lobby crowd mixed with local 'ladies who lunch', or at least 'chat over an afternoon coffee and cocktail'.

This lounge is a very civilized place. Plush, floral soft furnishings, carpet and drapes create a homely, if slightly stuffy feel. Windows look out onto the green belt that separates the hotel from the road network – not to mention the huge adjacent shopping malls that might help explain the attraction for those housewives.

The tab indexed bar menu has a respectable listing of spirits with a short explanation as to the production methods and history of each category. Cocktails centre on twists on the classic Martini and those after wine will find a choice of 27 by the glass.

If you are in Buckhead and seek impeccable service, a pianist and a plush lounge, then head here.

NEIGHBOR'S PUB

●●●○○

752C North Highland Avenue (@ St. Charles), Virginia Highland, Atlanta, Georgia, GA 30306, USA

Tel: +1 404 872 5440, **www.**neighborsatlanta.com
Hours: Mon-Sun 9am-late

Type: Neighbourhood pub
Alfresco: Large front patio
Entry: Open door
Highlights: Front patio
Atmosphere: Relaxed
Clientele: Locals
Dress code: Casual
Price guide: $$
Bar snacks: Full American menu

Lying in the posh suburb of Virginia Highlands, Neighbor's pub is just that, a neighbourly kind of place. However, posh it's not. The décor is basic and functional, with a bare wooden floor, khaki green walls and a black ceiling with exposed air-con ducting. Diner style booth seating lines the back wall and a fireplace occupies the middle of the room.

The most desirable spot is the huge front patio. Although it overlooks a car lot, on summer evenings this is the place to be. Powerful fans line the front roof to cool drinkers enjoying a choice of a dozen bottled beers or one of the 18 beers on draught, including the excellent local Sweetwater 420 IPA. The Jägermeister tap machine is worked hard to supply rounds of shots to chase the beer.

Free wifi, Monday karaoke, Braves games and other sports events are the draws inside this friendly neighbourhood bar.

PARK 75 LOUNGE

●●●◐○

Four Seasons Hotel, 75 Fourteenth Street, Midtown, Atlanta, Georgia, GA 30309, USA

Tel: +1 404 881 9898, **www.**fourseasons.com
Hours: Mon-Thu 4:30pm-midnight, Fri-Sat 4:30pm-1am

Type: Hotel lounge bar
Alfresco: Terrace
Entry: Via stairs from lobby
Highlights: Service
Atmosphere: Tad staid
Clientele: Hotel guests & locals
Dress code: Smart casual
Price guide: $$$$
Bar snacks: Kobe beef, Ahi tuna and barbecue pork etc

The lounge at this midtown Four Seasons lies a floor above the entrance lobby and is reached by ascending the sweeping stairway. It's a suitably plush affair, as you'd expect of such a grand hostelry: club chairs and sofas litter the warmly lit, classically appointed room. Smooth jazz schmoozes from a baby grand piano while a salmon pink marble topped bar sits altar-like at the end of the room. The sun ray mirror back bar is the focal point.

Such a cordial space attracts upscale locals as well as hotel guests who come here to enjoy cocktails and light fare, Saturday evenings frequently drawing a full house.

The friendly staff live up to Four Seasons' impeccable service standards and serve cocktails at your table from mini shakers. Cocktails are made with care but many employ the dreaded sour mix.

PRINCE OF WALES PUB

●●●○○

1144 Piedmont Avenue NE, (btwn 13th & 14th Sts), Midtown, Atlanta, Georgia, GA 30309, USA

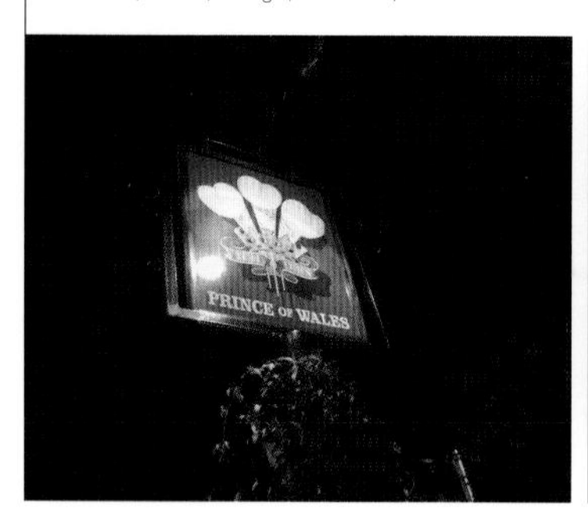

Tel: +1 404 237 1238
Hours: Mon-Wed 11:30am-1am, Thu-Fri 11:30am-2am, Sat 11:30am-3am, Sun 11:30am-midnight

Type: British-style pub
Alfresco: Large front patio
Entry: Open door
Highlights: Front patio
Atmosphere: Relaxed
Clientele: Locals of all ages
Dress code: Casual
Price guide: $$
Bar snacks: Fish 'n' chips, bangers & mash, pork chops etc.

The Prince of Wales is a British-style pub overlooking Piedmont Park's 14th Street entrance. It looks just like a traditional English countryside pub – only cleaner with American style service.

An old British red phone box sits at the front corner of the large brick-walled patio lined with wooden tables and edged with potted plants. Inside an island bar rests on the carpeted floor amid bare brick walls, wooden booths and red crushed velvet seating. A token photograph of John Lennon overlooks proceedings.

Pumps offering Guinness, Boddingtons, Harp, Fullers ES and Newcastle Brown Ale sit alongside the local Sweetwater IPA. The menu promises burgers, sandwiches, fish & chips, bangers & mash and shepherd's pie - therapy for homesick Brits.

In short, this is a well-run boozer. Don't expect a to-die-for wine list or fine cuisine. Do expect sports screens, trivia Tuesdays, cold beer and a warm welcome.

THE SUNDIAL LOUNGE

●●◐○○

Top Floor, Westin Peachtree Plaza Hotel, 210 Peachtree Street NW, Downtown, Atlanta, Georgia, GA 30303, USA

Tel: +1 404 659 1400, **www.**sundialrestaurant.com
Hours: Mon-Fri 4pm-midnight, Sat 2pm-midnight, Sun 2pm-11:30pm

Type: Cocktail lounge
Alfresco: No
Entry: Via express lift from 5th floor
Highlights: View
Atmosphere: Maybe back in the 70s
Clientele: Precious few
Dress code: Relaxed
Price guide: $$$
Bar snacks: Contemporary American

Take one of the twin glass-walled lifts that run from fifth floor of the Westin Hotel (the tallest hotel in the western hemisphere), offering views of Stone Mountain on the horizon as they speed up to the 72nd floor. This is the observatory level of what resembles a circular three tired wedding cake. The restaurant revolves below while the bar spins in the same direction above, offering 360-degree panoramic views of Atlanta and turning one full revolution every 35 minutes.

The neatly lined chairs and tables slowly revolve, as if you were on a carousel ride. On the way round you'll pass nameplates of towns in the distance, the bar and the grand piano on which live jazz is played on Wednesday and Thursday evenings. (The rest of the week the air is filled with cheesy background music.)

Constructed in the seventies, Sundial cries out for a refit. Its cocktails are stuck in a similar timewarp and should be avoided. Instead opt for one of the seventeen wines by the glass or a beer from the respectable list and enjoy the view from 723 feet.

TRADER VIC'S

●●●◐○

Hilton Towers Hotel, 255 Courtland Street NE (btwn Baker & Harris Sts), Downtown, Atlanta, Georgia, GA 30303, USA

Tel: +1 404 221 6339, **www.**tradervicsatlanta.com
Hours: Mon-Sat 5pm-midnight

Type: Tiki lounge
Alfresco: No
Entry: Via lift from hotel lobby
Highlights: Tiki drinks
Atmosphere: Relaxed
Clientele: Business types & tourists
Dress code: Smart casual
Price guide: $$$$
Bar snacks: Polynesian titbits and full meals

This outpost of the Trader Vic's chain lies in the basement, sorry "lower lobby", of the Hilton Hotel. Its kitsch tiki theme is in stark contrast to the bland, 22-floor modern hotel above.

Trader Vic's opened in the Hilton Atlanta in 1976, 39 years after Victor Jules Bergeron, or Trader Vic as he became known, first established his Polynesian themed restaurant in San Francisco. Fans of the genre will not be disappointed by this well run branch. This is classic Vic's with the mandatory South Pacific themed décor including glass floats, puffer fish and hand carved Tiki poles under bamboo rafters.

Vic's signature rum cocktails are also here, including his famous Mai Tai, all lovingly made to his original specifications and served in appropriately kitsch mugs, glasses or skeleton heads. They tend to the sweet, fruity side. So, should you not be in a tiki mood, there's a good range of spirits, particularly rum, and eight wines by the glass.

VICKERY'S BAR & GRILL

●●●●○

1106 Crescent Avenue NE (btwn 12th & 13th Sts), Midtown, Atlanta, Georgia, GA 30309, USA

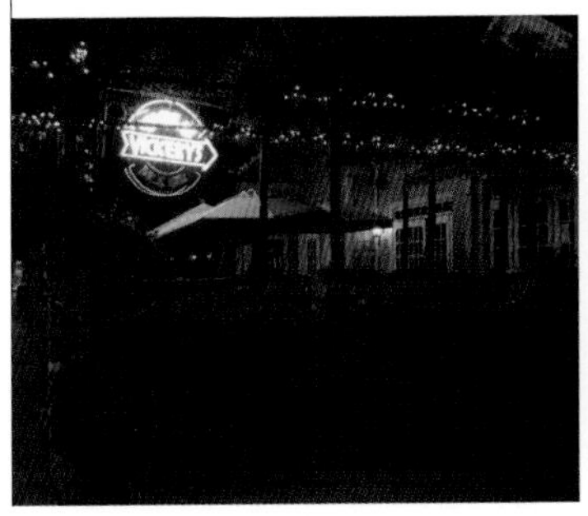

Tel: +1 404 881 1106, **www.**vickerys.com
Hours: Mon-Thu 11am-2am, Fri 11am-3am, Sat noon-3am, Sun 12:30pm-midnight

Type: Restaurant bar
Alfresco: Large front patio
Entry: Open door
Highlights: Atmosphere
Atmosphere: Warm, homely
Clientele: Locals, gay & straight
Dress code: Casual
Price guide: $$$
Bar snacks: Cajun/modern American full menu

Vickery's is named after Margaret Vickery, for whom this house was built and where until the late 1970s she lived and operated an antique and fabric shop. Rumor has it that Margaret Mitchell was a regular visitor and that a great deal of "Gone With The Wind" was written here. The neighbours must have had a shock in 1983 when three guys (Sam, Chip and Jerry) took over the house with a view to making it "a place to get a good stiff drink and a cheeseburger".

As it turns out, Vickery's neighbours are very lucky to have such a well-run, homely bar and restaurant on their doorstep. The warmly lit interior features intimate dining rooms running off a small bar with three Chesterfield-styled booths and red leather sofas on a bare wooden floor. The walls are two-thirds wood panelled and plantation blinds cover the windows. Out front is a large patio.

This is a hip place attracting a gay and straight clientele. There's a good range of premium spirits, three beers on draught (Pabst Blue Ribbon, Sam Adams and Sierra Nevada) and a good wine list.

VORTEX BAR AND GRILL

438 Moreland Avenue, Little Five Points, Atlanta, Georgia, 30307, USA

Tel: +1 404 688 1828, **www.**thevortexbarandgrill.com
Hours: Mon-Thu 11am-2am, Fri-Sat 11am-3am, Sun 11am-midnight

Type: Beer bar
Alfresco: Small area out front
Entry: Open door
Highlights: Beer & liquor selection
Atmosphere: Kitchen at a hell of a party
Clientele: Local Hell's Angels to accountants
Dress code: Whatever
Price guide: $$
Bar snacks: Legendary sirloin burgers & American menu

The Vortex bars are something of an institution in Atlanta, famous for their huge range of beers (80 bottled domestic beers, 90 bottled imported beers & 39 beers on draught), plus the burgers and liquor selection. Hank, Michael and Suzanne Benoit, three siblings from Los Angeles, opened the first Vortex Bar & Grill in 1992 at tiny midtown space. This was a huge success from day one. They opened their second place in Little Five Points on the site of a former vegetarian restaurant, on July 21st 1996, just three days before the opening ceremonies of the Olympic games.

The laughing skull entrance, heavy metal juke box and Hell's Angels bikes parked out front, coupled with a skeleton riding a BMW motorbike across the centre of the bar can give Vortex something of a hard ass feel. But don't be put off, everyone's welcome as long as they don't make a "jack-ass of themselves".

VORTEX BAR AND GRILL

878 Peachtree Street (@ 7th), Midtown, Atlanta, Georgia, GA 30309, USA

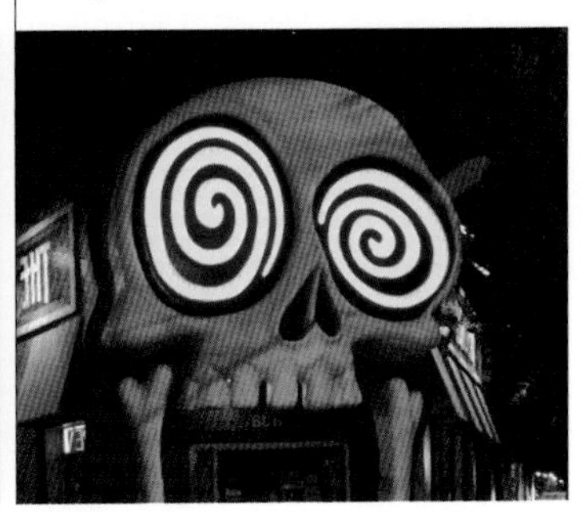

Tel: +1 404 875 1667, **www.**thevortexbarandgrill.com
Hours: Mon-Sat 11:30am-2am; Sun 11:30am-midnight

Type: Beer bar
Alfresco: No
Entry: Open door
Highlights: Beer & liquor selection
Atmosphere: Kitchen at a hell of a party
Clientele: Friendly local crowd
Dress code: Whatever
Price guide: $$
Bar snacks: Legendary burgers & American menu

The original tiny midtown Vortex relocated to this larger Peachtree Street address in 1997. Like the Little Five Points Vortex, the walls and ceiling are plastered with beer trays, neon signs, car licence plates and other clutter. However, as befits its midtown location, this Vortex is more approachable and an altogether classier affair than its Five Points sibling, attracting a friendly crowd of Midtown locals.

Both establishments share the same menu and extensive beer and spirits selection with banks of refrigerators lining the back bar. Expect 80 bottled domestic beers, 90 bottled imported beers, 39 beers on draught, 97 Scottish malts and nine wines by the glass, mostly from Housley's Century California winery.

The Vortex menu is a good read. Alongside the extensive list of beers are trenchant observations such as "Never snap your fingers or whistle at the Bartender, unless they happen to be a Cocker Spaniel," "If you can hear your tip hit the bar, chances are that you're being too cheap," and "Saint Patrick's Day and New Year's Eve. These are official Amateur Nights."

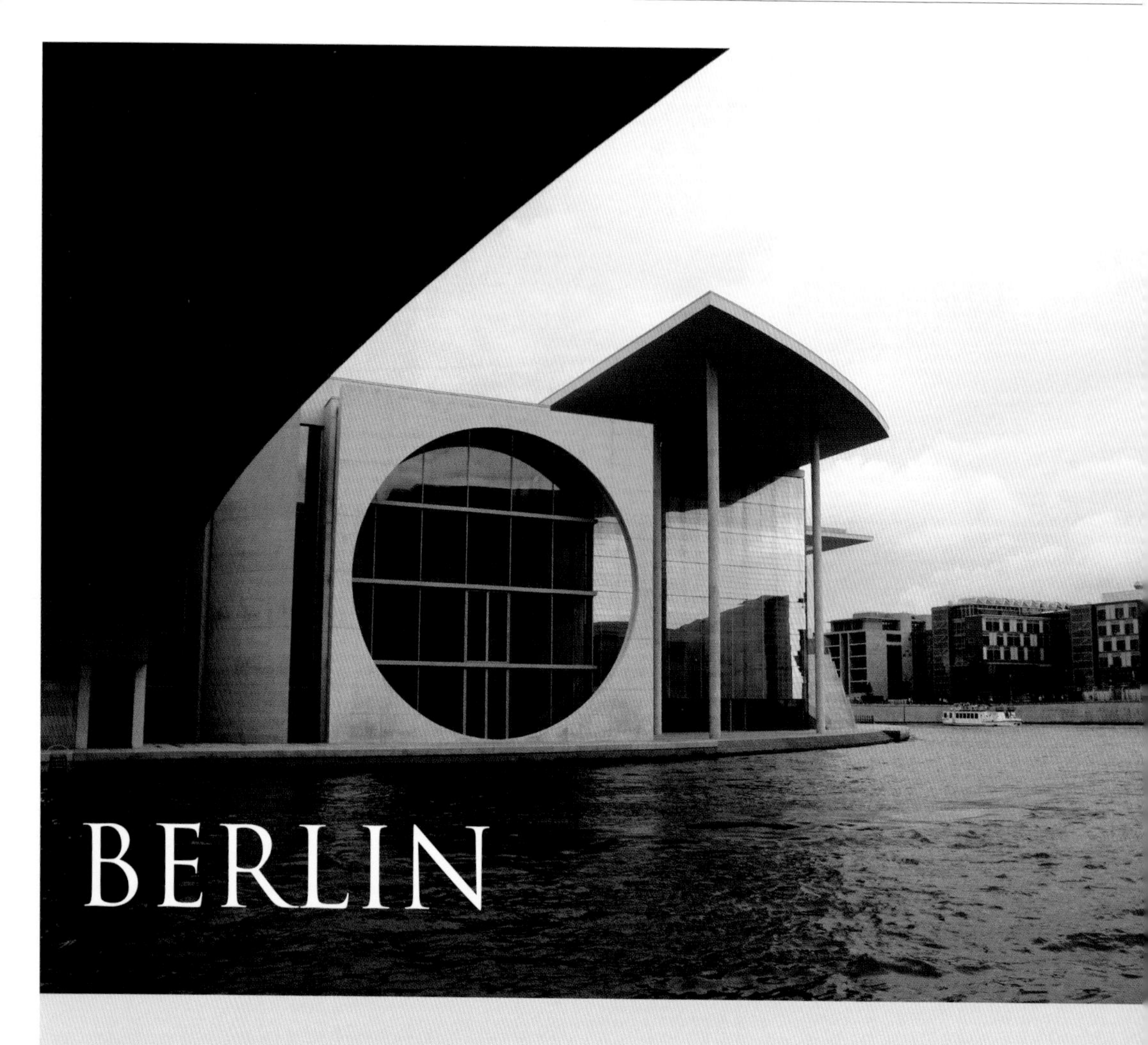

BERLIN

Airport: Tegel (TXL), Schonefeld (SXF)
Time zone: Central European Time (GMT +1)
Currency: Euro (€)

Berlin is famous as a city torn in two by war and reunited by peace, a portrayal which tends to mask the rich cultural and social scenes that preceded it. During the 'roaring twenties', Berlin was THE place where writers, filmmakers, artists and their patrons flocked. At the forefront of modern art, it boasted more theatres, film palaces and concert halls than practically any other European city and was rich in bars, restaurants and cafés. Since reunification, this old city has restored itself and is once again attracting leading artists and literary types.

The Berlin Wall was torn down in 1989 but the former East and West sides still show signs of the cultural, political and physical divide that existed for almost 30 years. There is plenty to see - from the graffiti-ed remnants of the wall and old watchtowers to the spectacular Norman Foster dome on the Reichstag.

Berlin Hotels

As you'd expect from one of Europe's greatest cities, Berlin is not short on luxury hotels – although many of its grand hotels were destroyed in 1945. The scene runs the gamut from futuristic, new build super-luxe to boutique conversions of historic buildings via pension-style apart-hotels.

Hotel Adlon Kempinski

77 Unter den Linden, Mitte, Berlin, 10117, Germany
Tel: +49 (0)30 2261 0, www.hotel-adlon.de
Group: Kempinski
Rooms: 394 (inc. 66 suites)

This modern, luxurious yet somewhat staid hotel occupies an unrivalled position opposite the Brandenburg Gate. All 328 rooms and 66 suites include air-con and marble bathrooms with separate bathtub and shower, while the basement spa boasts an 11 metre pool. If you require wifi you should specify this when booking.

Art Nouveau Hotel

59 Leibnizstrasse (btwn Mommsen & Sybel Strasse), Berlin, 10629, Germany
Tel: +49 (0)30 3277 440, www.hotelartnouveau.de
Group: Family owned
Rooms: 22 (inc. 3 suites)

Take the period lift to the fourth floor of this Art Nouveau building and discover a small, friendly, family run hotel. Rooms are clean, bright and spacious with original stucco ceilings and Mediterranean colour schemes but some of the bathrooms (actually shower rooms) are tiny. This pension-style hotel may lack luxury but the family home feel makes up for it. One of Berlin's best shopping streets (Kurfürstendamm) lies at the end of the road.

Bleibtreu Hotel

31 Bleibtreustrasse, Berlin, 10707, Germany
Tel: +49 (0)30 884 740, www.bleibtreu.com
Group: Privately owned
Rooms: 60

This contemporary hotel, just off the Kurfürstendamm shopping street, features a restaurant, an espresso bar, a deli and a flower shop, plus a 'wellness centre' which offers light therapy and a chi machine as well as more traditional steam baths. The boldly designed rooms feature cable TV, wifi, minibar and remote control lighting, plus fax, video connection and a cordless phone.

Brandenburger Hof

14 Eislebener Strasse, Berlin, 10789, Germany
Tel: +49 (0)30 214 050, www.brandenburger-hof.com
Group: Privately owned
Rooms: 82 (inc. 6 suites)

Elegant minimalism dominates this stylish converted mansion, just a short walk from the Kurfürstendamm shopping district. There's a Michelin-starred restaurant, a stunning winter garden with a glass-covered courtyard, plus a beauty and massage spa and oodles of modern art.

Dorint Sofitel Am Gendarmenmarkt

50-52 Charlottenstrasse, Berlin, 10117, Germany
Tel: +49 (0)30 203 750, www.sofitel.com
Group: Accor Hotels and Resorts
Rooms: 92 (inc. 22 suites)

Set on the Gendarmenmarkt (a famous square), this high-tech, futuristic boutique hotel is tailored for business and pleasure. There's a rooftop fitness centre, hammam, massage, sauna and solarium, plus the usual in-room wifi and self-service business centre. Service is as great as you'd expect.

Grand Hyatt

2 Marlene-Dietrich-Platz, Berlin, 10785, Germany
Tel: +49 (0)30 2553 1234, www.berlin.hyatt.com
Group: Hyatt
Rooms: 342 (inc. 16 suites)

This huge, modernist luxury hotel sits among the glass of Potsdamer Platz, the newbuild heart of the new Berlin, within easy reach of East Berlin's bars and clubs. The Feng Shui'd rooms are luxe and inventive, the interiors inspirational, the three restaurants stylish and the rooftop spa and indoor pool to die for. A fashionista favourite.

Lux II

9-13 Rosa-Luxemburg-Strasse, Mitte, Berlin, 10178, Germany
Tel: +49 (0)30 9362 800, www.lux11.com
Group: Chambers Group
Rooms: 72

This high-designed boutique hotel in the heart of Mitte combines hip elegance – an Aveda boutique, a designer clothing store, a lounge illuminated with video street scenes, and minimalist, geometric public spaces – with friendly, pension style mini-apartments at surprisingly reasonable prices.

Madison Potsdamer Platz

3 Potsdamer Strasse, Berlin, 10785, Germany
Tel: +49 (0)30 5900 500 00, www.madison-berlin.de
Group: Independent
Rooms: 166 suites

Sleekly stylish rather than spectacularly luxurious, the Madison is a calm space among the skyscrapers of Potsdamer Platz. The design is restrained and the individually designed suites have an apartment-like feel – long-stay is on offer. Facil, the bijou fifth-floor terrace restaurant with its retractable glass roof, is a real oasis.

Berlin Restaurants

In culinary cliché, Berlin offers little more than sausages, sauerkraut and dumplings. However, both the higher and lower ends of the food market have been enhanced by the fall of the Wall – don't miss a Berliner doner after a beer or three.

Traditional Berlin favourites, such as eisbein (fatty pork), sauerkraut (pickled cabbage) and matjes (pickled herring) are still available, as are the staples of potatoes, noodles, dumplings, meat and vegetables. But many German chefs are reinterpreting their inherited cuisine to create lighter, less fatty and more flavourful versions of the original classics.

The city contains over 12,000 restaurants, bars and cafes, serving cooking from almost every nation under the sun. Most haute cuisine outlets major in French cooking, although it's well worth surprising yourself with neue deutsche Küche, or German nouvelle cuisine: try Bamberger Reiter, if you can get a booking.

Should you wish, you could pass your entire stay without once tasting German cooking – but don't miss the traditional weekend breakfast, a vast brunch of cold meats, cheeses and fruit with orange juice and oodles of coffee. Most cafés serve breakfast until at least 4pm on Saturday and Sunday – perfect after a large night.

44

Swissôtel, 44 Augsburger Strasse, Wilmersdorf, Berlin, 10789, Germany
Tel: +49 (0)30 220 102 288,
www.swissotel.com
Cuisine: New French international

This surprisingly discreet, romantic place sits on the 5th floor of the vast and modern Swissôtel. Here chef Tim Raue produces imaginative, spectacular, French-styled cuisine. Try for the terrace above the Kurfürstendamm.

Alt Luxemburg

31 Windscheidstrasse, Charlottenburg, Berlin, 10627, Germany
Tel: +49 (0)30 323 8730,
www.altluxemburg.de
Cuisine: New French-Mediterranean

Karl Wannemacher's seriously good (frequently Michelin-starred) cuisine goes down a storm at this city standard near the Charlottenburg Castle. The environment is more conventional than glam but the food makes up for it.

Ana e Bruno

101 Sophie-Charlotte-Strasse, Charlottenburg, Berlin, 14059, Germany
Tel: +49 (0)30 325 7110, www.ana-e-bruno.de
Cuisine: New Italian

Elaborate, inventive Italian cooking comes courtesy of chef Bruno Pellegrini in a cosy, if hardly stunning, Charlottenburg eatery. You will need a reservation to try his inventive cuisine.

Bamberger Reiter

7 Regensburger Strasse, Schöneberg, Berlin, 10777, Germany
Tel: +49 (0)30 2196 6355, www.neuer-bamberger-reiter.de
Cuisine: Austrian and New German

An unappealing block surprises with Berlin's number one restaurant – a Tirolean-styled place where waitresses in dirndls serve 5-8 course menus of Michelin-starred cuisine. Book as far ahead as you can.

Borchardt

47 Französische Strasse, Mitte, Berlin, 10117, Germany
Tel: +49 (0)30 2038 7110
Cuisine: International

Established in 1853, this classy restaurant hasn't failed to move with the times. Actors, politicians, sports stars and models enjoy light, French-influenced cuisine amid its columned halls.

Die Quadriga

Brandenburger Hof, 14 Eislebener Strasse, Wilmersdorf, Berlin, 10789, Germany
Tel: +49 (0)30 2140 5650, www.brandenburger-hof.com
Cuisine: New French-Mediterranean

Two rooms of this elegant hotel house Die Quadriga and surround a striking Japanese garden. The menu is delicious and varied, the wine list all German and the service excellent. It is closed on Saturdays.

Lorenz Adlon

Hotel Adlon Kempinski, 77 Unter den Linden, Mitte, Berlin, 10117, Germany
Tel: +49 (0)30 22610, www.hotel-adlon.de
Cuisine: Classic French

Trad French cuisine stars in this traditional French-styled environment with views over the Brandenburg Gate. The wine list is voluminous, the service elegant, the cuisine haute and the experience luxe enough to justify the outlay.

Maxwell

22 Bergstrasse, Mitte, Berlin, 10115, Germany. Tel: +49 (0)30 280 7121, www.restaurant-maxwell.de
Cuisine: International

French, Asian, German and Italian cuisines meld to create a reasonably priced gourmet experience in this century-old brewery. The tall space is modern, the clientele funky and the staff amiable in the extreme.

Schwarzenraben

13 Neue Schönhauser Strasse, Mitte, Berlin, 10178, Germany
Tel: +49 (0)30 2839 1698, www.schwarzenraben.de
Cuisine: Italian

In a gorgeous, late nineteenth century conversion sits one of new Berlin's favourite restaurants. New East meets new Italian in this newish, narrow space.

VAU

54-55 Jägerstrasse, Mitte, Berlin, 10117, Germany
Tel: +49 (0)30 202 9730, www.vau-berlin.de
Cuisine: New French-Mediterranean

German TV chef Kolja Kleeberg has his way with incredible ingredients in this Mitte nouveau-classic. There's an elite wine list, wonderful service, some mercifully modern décor and the whole is well worth the credit card damage. Booking is essential.

Berlin Drinking

Berlin's bars have enjoyed legendary status ever since the 'roaring twenties' when swinging Berlin was Europe's party capital. The city is quickly regaining its reputation with a staggering variety of venues catering for the diversity of night owls. The scene encompasses everything from sophisticated cocktail lounges to dingy drinking dens and lasts till dawn or later. With no official closing time it's common for venues to stay open until the last guest leaves.

You'll find Berlin bars refreshingly unpretentious with few door or dress restrictions. For my money it is also the world's best city for classic cocktails. All kinds of bars feature voluminous cocktail lists filled with classic drinks, and all are reliably well made. Lurid modern concoctions are becoming fashionable but hopefully discernment will arrest this trend before too much damage is done.

Germans also take their beer very seriously and its quality can be traced back to the Beer Purity Law introduced by Duke Wilhelm IV in 1516. Traditionally pilsner lagers have been most popular but dark and wheat beers are beginning to catch up. Terms to look out for are 'Hell' (generally a lager, but technically any golden coloured, ordinary beer), 'Dunkel' (dark beer), 'Schwarzbier' (a very dark, generally sweetish style), 'weizenbier' (wheat beer), 'Bock' (strong beer brewed from barley) and 'Maibock' (a style of Bock brewed for May but often available in April or even late March). 'Berliner Weisse' is a Berlin speciality wheat beer. It is very sour and typically served in wine glasses mixed with fruit syrups ('mit Schuss').

The annual Berlin International Beer Festival at the beginning of August attracts around a million people to a mile long beer garden.

The climate around Berlin is too cold for grapes but you will find many wines from elsewhere in Germany. The German wine classification system is something of a nightmare. There are four main categories. First come the two most basic styles: 'Deutscher Tafelwein' (German table wine), the lowest classification, and 'Deutscher Landwein' (German country wine), which is equivalent to a French vin de pays. Then there are two categories of 'quality' wine, 'Qualitätswein bestimmter Anbaugebiete' (QbA) is the lower of the two, and sugar may be added during manufacture. 'Qualitätswein mit Prädikat' (QmP) are generally the best quality wines, and must be made from recognised grape varieties ripened to a specific level and grown in one district, to be stated on the label.

QmP wines are further divided according to the grapes' ripeness. 'Kabinett' refers to light wines made from fully ripened grapes, which are generally on the dry side. 'Spätlese' (late harvest) have a more intense flavour than Kabinett or QbA wines. 'Auslese' (select harvest) are made from extra ripe grapes, some with noble rot and are generally, although not always, sweet. 'Beerenauslese' (berries select harvest) are rich, sweet dessert wines made from hand-chosen, especially ripe grapes. 'Trockenbeerenauslese' (TBA) is the best German wine classification and refers to sweet, luscious honeyed wines made from the ripest of grapes. These tend to be sold in half bottles and are as rare as they are expensive. Outside these categories, there is also 'Eiswein' (icewine), made from grapes which are harvested while frozen, producing sweet yet sharp wines.

The majority of German wines have a degree of sweetness but dry ('trocken') and medium-dry ('halbtrocken') styles are increasingly popular. Also look out for sparkling wines ('Sekts'), which can be very good.

In Germany, schnaps (with one 'p') is a term for almost any hard liquor. Kornbranntwein is a clear, light, quality schnapps produced from corn and distilled in a pot still. The name literally means 'corn brandy' and is often shortened to korn. Korns may resemble rye whisky or be flavoured with herbs and spices. In northern Germany these spirits are a popular chaser to beer.

Whatever you drink and wherever you drink it, be sure you've brought your euros as many Berlin bars only take cash. German law restricts entry to bars to over 18 year olds.

BELLINI LOUNGE

42–43 Oranienburger Strasse (@ Auguststrasse), Mitte, East Berlin, 10117, Germany

Tel: +49 (0)30 9700 5618, **www.**bellinilounge.de
Hours: Mon-Thu 4pm-2am, Fri-Sat 4pm-5am

Type: Lounge bar
Alfresco: Pavement seating
Entry: Open door
Highlights: Cocktails
Atmosphere: Relaxed
Clientele: Laidback 30-somethings
Dress code: Stylishly casual
Price guide: €€€
Bar snacks: Not a place to snack

Some readers will recognise this address from its former incarnation as '808 Bar Lounge'. The name and the colour scheme of the main bar may have changed but the side lounge retains its long tropical fish tank and cosy banquette seating, and is still a great place to hide away on a romantic date.

The main bar is a meeting place for both gay and straight locals. Shaped like the stern of a ship, the room is dominated by a triangular island bar lined with stools. Black leather bucket chairs and small round cocktail tables, each with a flickering candle, sit against the walls. Outside, pavement tables front the café-style floor to ceiling windows.

The Bellini Lounge boasts an impressively comprehensive cocktail list with tens of classics listed beyond the eponymous Bellini. Those we sampled were very well made and service was attentive.

GREEN DOOR

50 Winterfeldstrasse, Schoeneberg, Berlin, 10781, Germany

Tel: +49 (0)30 215 2515, **www.**greendoor.de
Hours: Mon-Sun 6pm-3am

Type: Lounge bar
Alfresco: Pavement seating
Entry: Bouncer on busy nights
Highlights: Cocktails
Atmosphere: Relaxed, cool
Clientele: Mature style set
Dress code: Stylishly casual
Price guide: €€€
Bar snacks: Nibbles only (fried maize)

The man behind the Green Door is thespian Fritz Müller-Scherz, and the cocktail list here must approach the thickness of some of his scripts. His slogan "the power of positive drinking" sets the scene for this wonderful little lounge bar where beautifully crafted classic cocktails are stylishly delivered in a quaint setting that blends modernity with seventies design.

Beyond the eponymous green door is a long, narrow room lined in gingham and faux wood grain. An oak topped bar runs most of its length, facing a wavy wall broken by an illuminated drinks ledge. In the very back corner is the best table in the house (ring ahead and reserve).

The expertly made drinks take no prisoners but are tamed by accompanying small glasses of water. These are enjoyed by a stylish 30-something crowd. If you decide to join them be sure to bring cash as credit cards are not accepted.

GREENWICH

5 Gipsstrasse, Mitte, Berlin, 10119, Germany

Tel: +49 (0)30 2809 5566
Hours: Mon-Sat 7pm-2am (and later)

Type: Lounge bar
Alfresco: No
Entry: Subject to management & capacity
Highlights: Atmosphere
Atmosphere: Club VIP room
Clientele: Hip Mitte crowd
Dress code: Stylishly casual
Price guide: €€€
Bar snacks: Eat before you go

Greenwich can rightly claim to be Mitte's hippest bar. Only the glow of amber light escaping through the Venetian blinds betrays its modish anonymity.

The long room is split in two with high stools dotting the bar area at the front and loungy seating in the raised area at the back. The style is seventies with rolled brown leather-look walls. Huge aquariums line the space and watching the tropical fish slowly go about their evening is strangely relaxing. The atmosphere tends to the clubby side of lounge due to the sound system and the number of revellers crowded into the small space. Even for Mitte they are a very mixed bunch of hipsters.

Cocktails are acceptable but not up to the high quality of some I've enjoyed in Berlin.

DIE HAIFISCH BAR

25 Arndtstrasse (btwn Nostitz. & Friesen), Kreuzberg, West Berlin, 10965, Germany

Tel: +49 (0)30 691 1352
Hours: Mon-Sun 8pm-5am

Type: Lounge bar
Alfresco: No
Entry: Open door
Highlights: Cocktails, sushi
Atmosphere: Laidback
Clientele: Mature style set
Dress code: Designer casual
Price guide: €€
Bar snacks: Sushi

The name of this lounge translates as The Shark Bar and its apt logo of a shark with a chunk bitten from its underbelly is prominently featured on the illuminated signs outside. The space-age interior is white, almost clinical, but subtle art deco, Gaudiesque flourishes and touches such as disco balls and the Ken and Barbie dolls on the toilet signs help make Haifisch cosy rather than sterile.

A sushi counter lies at the back and the well-made sushi and sashimi is very reasonably priced. However, it's the cocktails, not the interior or the bar snacks, that make Haifisch one of my favourite bars in Berlin. They are best appreciated while sat at the L-shaped bar where you can witness the loving care that brings the impressive, classically led list to life and appreciate the incredibly friendly and attentive staff. You'll find yourself drinking with cool, laidback young professionals further mellowing to ambient techno tunes.

HARRY'S NEW-YORK BAR

Grand Hotel Esplanade, 15 Am Lützowufer, Tiergarten, West Berlin, 10785, Germany

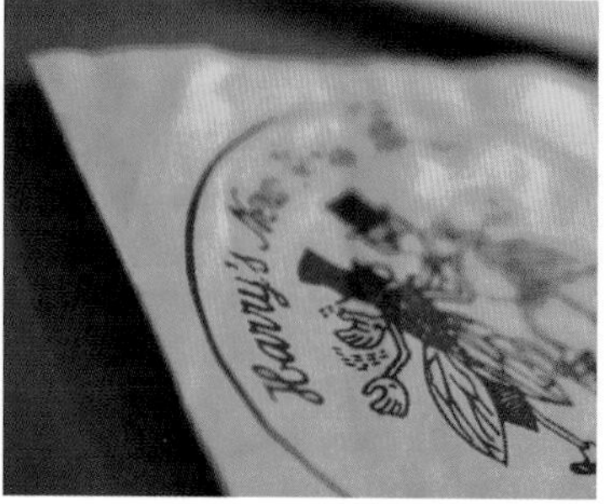

Tel: +49 (0)30 2547 8821
Hours: Mon-Sun 24 hours

Type: Hotel lounge bar
Alfresco: No
Entry: Via hotel lobby
Highlights: Cocktails
Atmosphere: Partly driven by live musicians
Clientele: International business set
Dress code: Suits to casual
Price guide: €€€€
Bar snacks: Not recommended for food

There appears to be at least one Harry's bar in every city, most attempting to emulate the famous Parisian watering hole. The Berlin version borrows much from the original, including the dancing flies logo and the American university pendants hanging behind the bar. Prints of all 43 US presidents recall the straw polls held in the Paris Harry's during presidential elections. However, this 1988 copy set off the dull lobby of a bland corporate hotel lacks the lived-in charm of the 1911 Parisian original. With its eighties smoked mirrors and walls covered in black film, I doubt charm will ever come with age.

All that said, discerning drinkers are well served with an impressive range of spirits and some of the best cocktails in Germany. The service is also impeccable.

Here you'll find the usual diverse international crowd that such a hotel attracts - lonely souls, romantic couples and boisterous business types lounging on the red vinyl high stools and low bucket chairs.

HUDSON BAR

10 Elssholtzstrasse, Schoeneberg, Berlin, 10781, Germany

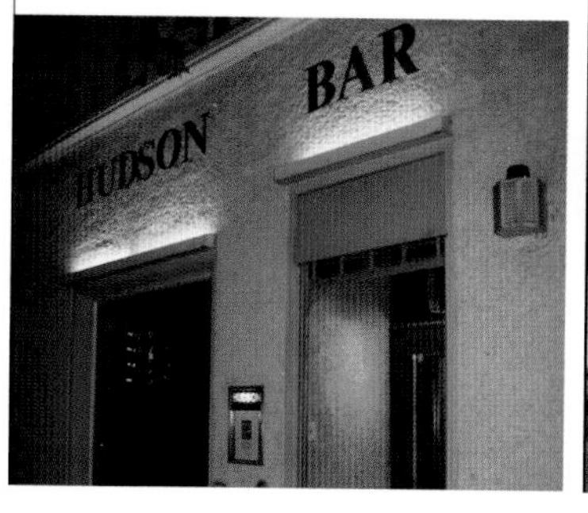

Tel: +49 (0)30 2199 7506, **www.**hudson-bar.de
Hours: Wed-Sat from 8pm

Type: Lounge bar
Alfresco: No
Entry: Buzz for entry
Highlights: Cocktails
Atmosphere: Laidback
Clientele: Unpretentious locals
Dress code: Casual
Price guide: €€€
Bar snacks: Not recommended for food

The Hudson Bar, which incidentally bears no relation to the New York hotel, is hidden away on an unlikely, residential back street. Once you've located it, you'll need to be buzzed in as if calling on one of the surrounding apartments.

I feel I should apologise to the friendly owners and staff, but I can only describe their interior as shockingly eighties without any redeeming features. Red neon lines the ceiling and pink neon reminds you of the bar's name, while a mix of cool jazz and scary Germanic music plays.

However, the impressive collection of spirits lining the walls and back bar is reason enough to visit. So too is the lengthy cocktail list that references all the classics to regarded cocktail books such as 'the 1928 Bon Vivant's Companion by Professor Jerry Thomas'. The owners and their laidback local clientele are unpretentious cocktail enthusiasts.

JULEP'S NEW YORK BAR

●●●●○

3 Giesebrechtstrasse, Charlottenburg, West Berlin, Germany

Tel: +49 (0)30 881 8823, **www.**juleps.de
Hours: Sun-Thu 5pm-1am, Fri-Sat 5pm-2am

Type: Lounge bar/restaurant
Alfresco: Decked terrace at front
Entry: Open door
Highlights: Atmosphere
Atmosphere: Warm & friendly
Clientele: Locals, American tourists & expats
Dress code: Casual
Price guide: €€€
Bar snacks: Full American food menu

Julep's lies on a tree-lined street in Charlottenburg, just doors away from Die Kurbel, Berlin's English-language cinema. It is New York by name and very American by nature – from the décor to the food, the drinks and even the customers' accents. Chalkboards listing specials hang on bare brick walls, while twirling ceiling fans, dark green banquettes and café-style chairs enhance the speakeasy look. The room is warmly lit and the long, dark wood bar is illuminated by antique desk lamps fixed above the back-bar mirrors. Light jazz helps to create a homely atmosphere.

All female staff serve American comfort food and mix the hundred-plus cocktails listed on the drinks menu. There are a number of Julep variations, and these should clearly be the drinks of choice. Sadly, the cocktails do not live up to the wonderful atmosphere, and beer seems more popular than mint drinks.

BAR AM LÜTZOWPLATZ

7 Lützowplatz, Tiergarten, West Berlin, Germany

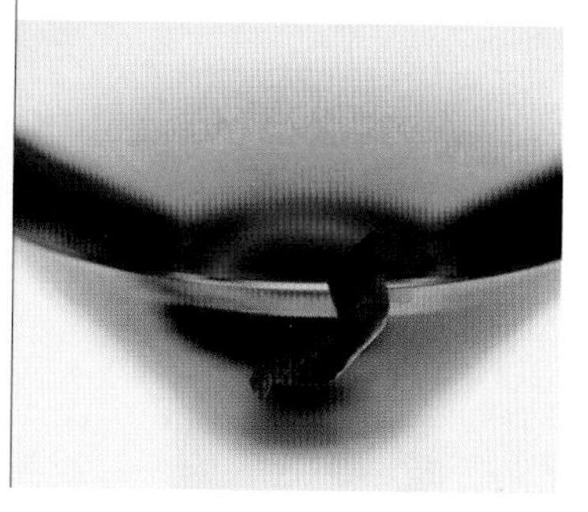

Tel: +49 (0)30 262 6807,
www.baramluetzowplatz.com
Hours: Mon-Sun 2pm-2am

Type: Lounge bar
Alfresco: Tables on street
Entry: Open door
Highlights: Cocktails
Atmosphere: Relaxed, laidback
Clientele: Local style set, tourists
Dress code: Stylishly casual
Price guide: €€€
Bar snacks: Wasabi coated peanuts (wasabi nüsse)

At sixteen metres long, Bar am Lützowplatz claims to have the longest bar counter in Berlin. The long, narrow room that houses it, with its curved mirrored ceiling and mustard coloured walls, feels rather like a windowless railway carriage. A bizarre, almost shrine-like image resembling Chairman Mao covers the end wall but the stools that line the light oak bar counter are inhabited by a good-looking crowd of moneyed young locals and tourists.

As you come to expect of bars in Berlin, Lützowplatz has a hugely impressive cocktail list, but also a good selection of champagnes and spirits. Also, as is typical in Berlin, cocktails are brilliantly made.

The only downside of Lützowplatz is that poor air-conditioning can make it feel like you are riding in the smoking carriage.

MOMMSEN-ECK

45 Mommsenstrasse (near Giesebrechtstrasse), Charlottenburg, Berlin, 10629, Germany

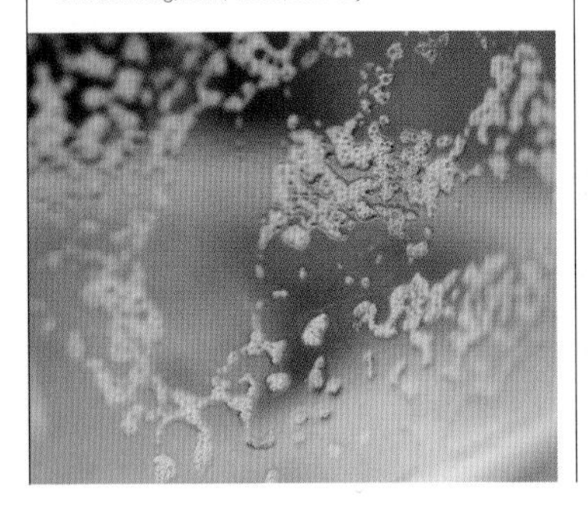

Tel: +49 (0)30 324 2580, **www.**mommsen-eck.de
Hours: Mon-Sun noon-2am

Type: Germanic gastro pub
Alfresco: Large front terrace
Entry: Open door
Highlights: Beer selection & breakfast
Atmosphere: Quiet, tad staid
Clientele: Locals, families out for dinner
Dress code: Smart casual
Price guide: €€
Bar snacks: Full traditional German menu

Mommsen-Eck is set in the residential back streets of Charlottenburg overlooking Hindemith square with its Bavarian fountain. The pub, as well as the street, are named in honour of a famous local resident, Theodor Mommsen (1817-1903), a lawyer and historian who received a Nobel Prize in 1902.

Mommsen-Eck has quite a history itself. It was established in 1905 and a portion of the original wall panelling has survived to this day. Over the years the place has been much extended and a large conservatory now dominates the frontage which opens out onto a terrace that meets the pavement.

Part restaurant, part pub, this is very much a locals' place, although a choice of 100 bottled beers from around the world and fourteen brews on draught rightly attracts visiting beer fanciers. Fashionable and stylish, it is not. However, your choice of beer will be served in the appropriate glass and the breakfasts are celebrated.

REINGOLD

11 Novalisstrasse, Mitte, Berlin, 10115, Germany

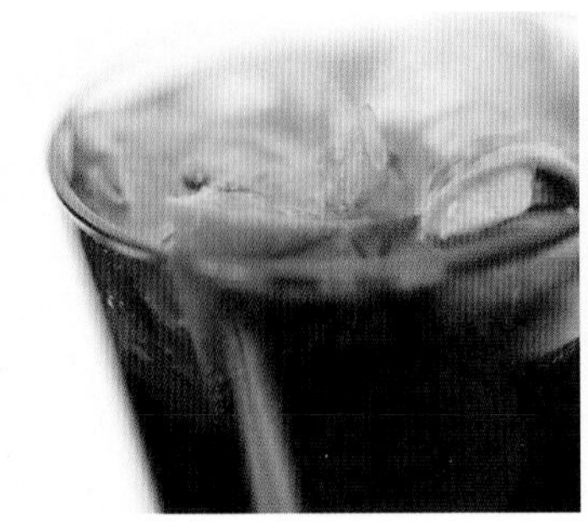

Tel: +49 (0)30 2838 7676, **www.**reingold.de
Hours: Mon-Sun 7pm-3am (& often till much later)

Type: Lounge bar
Alfresco: Large BBQ terrace
Entry: Open door
Highlights: Cocktails
Atmosphere: Chilled
Clientele: High-flying 30-somethings
Dress code: Cool casual
Price guide: €€€
Bar snacks: Ciabatta sandwiches, chips and olives

Reingold lies in the newly fashionable Mitte district and reflects how much this East Berlin area has changed since the Wall came down. Cabbies may be unfamiliar with this part of town and unhelpfully Reingold is hidden on an unlikely quiet side street.

The long, narrow, mustard and rust-coloured interior has a luxuriously decadent feel with images of the Côte d'Azur and capitalist old soaks enjoying the sun. The walnut bar stretches practically the length of the room and flickering candles illuminate the bucket chairs and tables.

Reingold has a monster cocktail list encompassing every classic you can think of and then some. All those I sampled were excellently made, and, if you arrive during "golden hour" (between 7-9pm), they are also reasonably priced at €6 each.

Reingold has atmosphere, décor and great drinks. Isn't capitalism a wonderful thing?

RIVA

142 Dircksenstrasse Bogen, Mitte, Berlin, 10178, Germany

Tel: +49 (0)30 2472 2688, **www.**riva-berlin.de
Hours: Mon-Sun 6pm-2am (or even later)

Type: Lounge bar
Alfresco: Rear patio
Entry: Subject to management & capacity
Highlights: Cocktails, atmosphere
Atmosphere: Laidback cool
Clientele: Young, hip, style set
Dress code: Stylishly casual
Price guide: €€€
Bar snacks: Maize, olives & Serrano ham

A single railway arch with net curtain covered windows at either end may not sound a very promising setting for a cool lounge bar, but once inside and under the psychedelic ceiling you'll be suitably impressed by Riva.

Named, rather inexplicably, after the 1970s Italian football star Luigi Riva, the tunnel-like, dimly-lit space is dominated by an oval island bar. Bar stools surround this with tables and banquettes on one side and standing room only on the other.

The extensive menu lists classic cocktails under dry, medium or sweet headings. When ordered, these are well made. The cool, hip crowd who come here also appreciate the Serrano ham which is finely sliced on a machine at the end of the bar and served with crisp breads and olives.

Riva also has a hidden gem in the form of its walled, decked garden. This is partly sheltered by the rear of the arch and is a remarkably secluded spot.

UNIVERSUM LOUNGE

153 Kurfürstendamm, Charlottenburg, West Berlin, Germany

Tel: +49 (0)30 8906 4995
Hours: Mon-Sun 6pm-3am

Type: Lounge bar
Alfresco: Large street-side patio
Entry: Open door
Highlights: Cocktails
Atmosphere: Laidback but cool
Clientele: Young style set
Dress code: Stylishly casual
Price guide: €€€
Bar snacks: No food

This designer lounge sits at the entrance to a 1920s Bauhaus Cinema. Although the street numbers don't make it obvious, it's easy to spot due to its large, street-side terrace shaded with white parasols and surrounded by bamboo.

Inside, the crescent-shaped lounge is quite literally space age. A lunar landscape covers one wall and golden stone fragments are stuck to the wallpaper. Cream leather banquette seating and stools surround the perimeter of the room and chainmail drapes cover the windows. This sleek, retro-futuristic '2001:a Space Odyssey ' interior is strangely warm and inviting.

On my two visits I encountered different bartenders both of whom served stunningly good cocktails from the bronze fronted bar.

VICTORIA BAR

102 Potsdamer Strasse (btwn Lützowstrasse & Pohlstrasse), Tiergarten, West Berlin, 10785, Germany

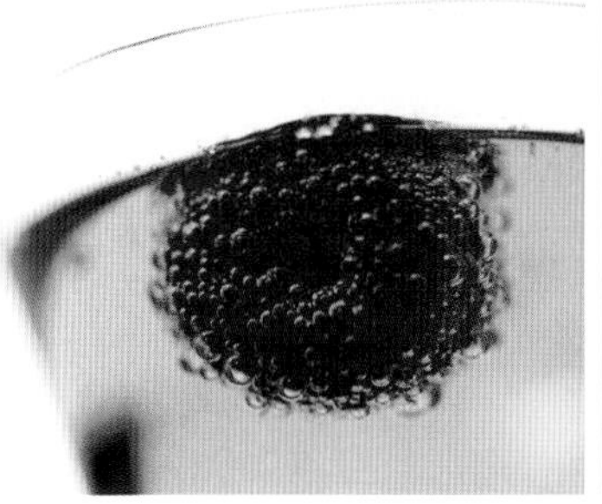

Tel: +49 (0)30 2575 9977, **www.**victoriabar.de
Hours: Mon-Thu 6:30pm-3am, Fri-Sat 6:30pm-4am

Type: Lounge bar
Alfresco: Pavement seating
Entry: Subject to management & capacity
Highlights: Cocktails
Atmosphere: Laidback but cool
Clientele: Mixed but mature locals
Dress code: Stylishly casual
Price guide: €€€€
Bar snacks: No food

Victoria lies on a street where you wouldn't expect to find such a cool, upmarket lounge bar. Perhaps this helps explain the diverse crowd of mature locals that flock here.

The long, narrow room exudes luxury and style. The dark planks of wood that vertically line the walls are interspersed with modern art and computer graphics. Twin lounge areas with booth seating lie at either end of the bar counter, which practically runs the length of the room and is fronted by a neat row of comfy, leather upholstered bar stools. The illuminated back bar is packed with premium spirits, shaded hanging lights emit a golden glow and the smoky atmosphere is filled with a mix of jazz, soul and reggae.

Mature bartenders in white shirts and Italian-style ties serve some spectacular cocktails from a choice of over 180, all listed by spirit base in an impressive red bound menu. The style continues with the small glass of soda water served to accompany each cocktail.

ZOULOU BAR

4 Hauptstrasse, Schöneberg, West Berlin, Germany

Tel: +49 (0)30 784 6894, **www.**zouloubar.de
Hours: Mon-Sun 7pm-6am

Type: Lounge bar
Alfresco: Few pavement tables
Entry: Open door
Highlights: Cocktails
Atmosphere: Very laidback
Clientele: Cool locals
Dress code: Casual
Price guide: €€
Bar snacks: Free maize nibbles

Behind a few pavement tables and an illuminated bamboo screen lies this small but very quaint cocktail bar. The unkind could label the 1950s styled interior scuzzy - the generous would say it oozed character. The two small rooms feature red banquette seating, nicotine coloured walls and framed sepia prints. An antique telephone and desk-lamps fixed to the ceiling add to the charm. Jazz plays in background, helping to create a wonderfully warm and relaxed atmosphere, even when there is just a couple of you and the bartender.

Cocktails here are expertly made and served with maize nibbles and accompanying water jug and glass. This is a proper bar, the kind of place you'd imagine Hemingway being drawn to. There's something wonderfully decadent about imbibing at Zoulou.

KRAKÓW (CRACOW)

Time zone: Central European Time (GMT +1 hours)
Airport: Kraków Balice (KRK)

Once the capital of Poland, Cracow (Kraków) lies in the southeast of the country on the banks of the Vistula (Wisla) River. It is a city of staggering architecture, vying with Venice in the competition for most beautiful city in Europe. Its people are incredibly hospitable, crime is low, the centre is compact and easy to navigate on foot, and it's cheap for visitors from the West. Is it any wonder that this UNESCO World Heritage Site is rapidly becoming one of Europe's 'must visit' tourist destinations?

Kraków is famed for its picturesque Main Market Square (Rynek Głowny), which was laid out in 1257 and encompasses the 16th-century Cloth Hall (Sukiennice). It is one of the largest and best-preserved medieval market squares in Europe. In the eastern corner lies the Church of St Mary (Kościół Mariacki) and from the taller of its two towers the famous bugle call (hejnał) is played on the hour, every hour. Legend has it that around 1241 a bugler was killed by an arrow whilst blowing the alarm to warn of a raid. For the past 700 or so years the melody has been sounded hourly from each of the tower's sides, the trumpeter stopping abruptly three-quarters of the way through to mark the moment when the arrow hit the original bugler.

The lanes of the Old Town (Stare Miasto) around the Main Market Square are ringed by the Planty, a tree lined park that marks where Cracow's city wall once stood. Wawel Castle, the seat of Polish kings from the 11th to the early 17th century, sits high on its own hill to the southern edge of town. A little further out is the Kazimierz district. For centuries, it was a centre of Jewish culture. Then the Nazis murdered most its residents, deporting those who survived to the Podgorze ghetto and thence to death in nearby Auschwitz (Oświęcim).

After World War II, Cracow and its people suffered under the Soviet-imposed regime. A lot has changed since the end of the Cold War, and Cracow and its people are now thriving under newfound freedom.

Kraków Hotels

The dramatic increase in Cracow's popularity as a tourist destination means that decent hotel rooms can be hard to come by. There are a few truly fantastic hotels in Cracow and, if you want a room in one, book early.

Amadeus Hotel

20 Ulica Mikolajska, Old Town, Kraków, 30-027, Poland
Tel: +48 (0)12 429 6070, www.hotel-amadeus.pl
Group: Independent

This small hotel on the edge of the Main Market Square has twenty bedrooms and two suites. All are air-conditioned with satellite TV, internet access and mini-bar. The hotel also boasts a gym and a sauna. All staff speak English and some Brits may be interested to hear that Prince Charles once stayed here.

Batory Hotel

19 Ulica Sołtyka, Kraków, 31-529, Poland
Tel: +48 (0)12 294 3030, www.hotelbatory.pl
Group: Independent

This pleasant, family-run hotel opened in 2000 and is named after the Polish King Stefan Batory. It is located in a former shoe factory just outside the Old Town and fifteen minutes walk from the Main Market Square. It is cosy, spotlessly clean and great value. All 29 rooms are furnished with simple pine furniture and have their own bathroom, television and internet access. The owners and staff are delightfully friendly.

Copernicus Hotel

16 Ulica Kanonicza, Old Town, Krakow, 31-002, Poland. Tel: +48 (0)12 424 3400, www.hotel.com.pl
Group: Likus Hotels & Resorts

State of the art technology and modern design sit sympathetically alongside medieval portals, beautiful frescoes, wooden beams and precious paintings in this stunning hotel close to Wawel Castle. The space is cleverly used, particularly the glass covered courtyard and the swimming pool squeezed into the basement.

Many of the 29 luxury rooms and suites feature original Renaissance painted sculptures, in addition to the more mundane air-conditioning, jacuzzi, satellite TV and mini-bar. The hotel's roof terrace offers views over Wawel Castle and the towers of the Old Town churches. President George W. Bush stayed here when he visited Cracow.

Grodek Hotel

4 Ulica Na Grodku, Old Town, Kraków, 31-028, Poland.Tel: +48 (0)12 431 9030, www.donimirski.com
Group: Domimirski

This recently opened hotel lies in a beautifully renovated townhouse, set in a charming cul-de-sac by the old Dominican Abbey in the heart of the Old Town.

Ostoya Palace Hotel

24 Ulica Piłsudskiego, Old Town, Kraków, 31-109, Poland
Tel: +48 (0)12 430 9000
Group: Independent

An elegant nineteenth century palace hosts this luxury hotel in the centre of the Old Town. All twenty four rooms feature air-conditioning, broadband internet, satellite TV, mini-bar, safe and bathroom.

Pod Róza Hotel

14 Ulica Floriańska, Old Town, Kraków, 31-021, Poland
Tel: +48 (0)12 424 3300, www.hotel.com.pl
Group: Likus Hotels & Resorts

The name means 'under the rose' and Pod Roza hotel lies in the centre of the Old Town, on Cracow's most fashionable shopping street, close to the Main Market Square. Its neo-classical facade conceals a luxurious modern hotel with 54 rooms. Previous guests include Chopin and Czar Alexander I.

Radisson SAS Hotel

17 Ul. Straszewskiego (@Zwierzyniecka), Old Town, Kraków, 31–101, Poland
Tel: +48 (0)12 618 8888, www.krakow.radissonsas.com
Group: Rezidor SAS Hospitality

This modern corporate hotel is superbly located in the Old Town, close to both the Market Square and Wawel Castle. Its 196 modern rooms all come with bath and shower, internet access, safe and air-conditioning. Besides this, the hotel features a gym, a sauna and underground parking.

Kraków Restaurants

Nearly 200 years of Austro-Hungarian occupation has left its mark on Cracovian cuisine and goulash and pepper casseroles are more prevalent here than in other parts of Poland. Other local specialties include wild duck (stewed with wild mushrooms and served with pearl barley), soups (borscht and zurek especially), apple pie and the local cheesecake, which is made with white curd cheese, eggs and raisins.

The area is also famous for sausages – particularly Lisiecka, from the village of Liszka outside Cracow. One of the most atmospheric places to try them is just over the bridge on Grzegórzecka. Late at night an old blue van parks up and the owner barbeques sausages over apple wood by the side of the road. For late night snacks in the Kazimierz district head to Plac Nowy, where traditional hot dishes are sold in the centre of the market place.

Amarone Restaurant

Hotel Pod Różą, 14 Ulica Floriańska, Kraków, 31-021, Poland
Tel: +48 (0)12 424 3381, www.hotel.com.pl
Cuisine: Italian

Amarone Restaurant lies in the glass covered courtyard of the Pod Różą Hotel and is widely regarded as Cracow's best Italian restaurant. The wine list offers a choice of over one hundred Italian bins stored in the hotel's medieval wine cellar.

Cyrano de Bergerac

26 Ulica Slawkowska, Krakow, 31-014, Poland
Tel: +48 (0)12 411 7288, www.cyranodebergerac.pl
Cuisine: French

Established in 1997, Cyrano de Bergerac serves fine French cuisine in two renovated cellars dating from the Middle Ages – during the summer, you can also eat in the courtyard above. By some way the best French restaurant in Cracow, Cyrano de Bergerac stands comparison with the world's finest. The French wine list is as extensive as you would expect.

A Dong

3 Ulica Brodzinskiego, Kazimierz, Krakow, 30-506, Poland
Tel: +48 (0)12 656 4872
Cuisine: Vietnamese/Chinese

Some way out of the centre lies probably the best oriental restaurant in Cracow. A Dong is famous for its Mongolian 'Seafood Boiler', where seafood is cooked at the table fondue-style.

Paese Restaurant

24 Ulica Poselka, Old Town, Krakow, 31-002, Poland. Tel: +48 (0)12 421 6273, www.paese.com.pl
Cuisine: Corsican/French

Named after the Corsican for land, Paese brings some Mediterranean warmth to Cracow. This is an extremely fashionable place to eat and a favourite of local politicians and celebrities. The reasonably priced wine list includes some interesting Corsican bins.

Pod Aniolami

35 Ulica Grodzka, Old Town, Krakow, 31-001, Poland. Tel: +48 (0)12 421 3999, www.podaniolami.pl Cuisine: Polish

Pod Aniołami serves renowned traditional Polish cuisine in Gothic cellars where blacksmiths once worked. An old anvil and other tools adorn the walls, making the place feel almost like a museum. The menu of Polish classics majors on specialities from the country's southern Tatra mountain region.

Renaissance Restaurant

Copernicus Hotel, 16 Ulica Kanonicza, Old Town, Krakow, 31-002, Poland
Tel: +48 (0)12 424 3421, www.hotel.com.pl
Cuisine: Traditional Polish

This restaurant overlooks the lobby atrium of the Copernicus Hotel and is set under a beautifully restored, finely painted wooden ceiling dating back to the 14th century. The menu includes traditional Polish dishes, many based on recipes from the old Polish court. The medieval wine cellar below holds more than 200 wines.

Wentzl Restaurant

Wentzl Hotel, 19 Rynek Glowny, Old Town, Krakow, 31-008, Poland
Tel: +48 (0)12 430 2664
Cuisine: Central European/French

First established in 1792 by John Wentzl, this restaurant is legendary. Nationalized after WWII, it operated under the name 'Pod Obrazem', meaning 'beneath the portrait', after the Baroque image of Mother Mary which adorns the front of the building. The signature dish here is 'Cracovian Maczanki', meat-stuffed pastry served with onion and caraway gravy..

Kraków Drinking

Cracow's Jagiellonian University is the oldest in Poland and in this city of less than a million inhabitants, over 100,000 are students. Come the weekend the local bars are packed. Truly upscale lounges have yet to evolve, and the best bars tend to offer simple drinks in wonderfully atmospheric environments.

The cafés and bars of the Main Market Square (Rynek Glowny) are the epicentre of tourist nightlife and sadly at weekends this area attracts hen and stag partying Brits in search of cheap beer and vodka. Thankfully, many of the best bars in the Old Town are hidden in medieval cellars, away from the tourists above. Follow the addresses given here, look for small signs hanging above innocent-looking doorways and, if all else fails, flag down a passing local.

The smaller market square in the Kazimierz district is where the trendy thirty-something locals head. The bars here tend to be quieter, more loungy and more convivial than the cellars of the Old Town.

Locals tend to drink Polish Zywiec beer chased with a startling array of Polish vodkas. 'Szarlotka', a long, mixed drink served with ice, is also popular and very tasty. Pronounced 'sha-lot-ka', this consists of Polish Zubrówka vodka mixed with apple juice and garnished with a lemon slice. The name literally translates as 'apple pie' and confusingly many Polish bars also sell a cake with exactly the same name. (Since the film 'Dances with Wolves' this drink has also earned the name 'Tatanka' after the Native American word for buffalo, in honour of the 'bison' vodka it contains.) Belvedere vodka served long over ice with pressed apple juice and garnished with a lemon slice is also a superbly refreshing drink. Alternatively, add honey to make a Cracow martini (see left).

The local headbanger's drink is 'Mad Dogs' (Wściekte Psy), a layered shot made with raspberry syrup, vodka and Tabasco. For a truly fiery experience make 'Very Mad Dogs', with Polish Pure Spirit at 79.9% alc./vol. instead of vodka.

Bar closing times vary between 1am and 4am but the Poles are wonderfully hospitable people and it's usual for bars to stay open till the last guest leaves. "Last orders" and "drink up please" are phrases you won't hear in Cracow.

The minimum legal drinking age in Poland is 18, and it is illegal to sell alcohol to someone who appears to be drunk. (Sadly this seems to apply mostly to young British males.) Many of the slicker bars and nightclubs also operate an over-21 policy.

The locals seem oblivious to the health risks of smoking and cellar bars tend to get cloudier as the night goes on.

CRACOW MARTINI

Glass: Martini
Garnish: Lemon zest twist

Method: STIR honey with vodka in base of shaker until honey dissolves. Add apple juice, SHAKE with ice and fine strain into chilled glass.

2 shot(s) **Belvedere vodka**
2 spoons **Runny honey**
2 shot(s) **Pressed apple juice**

Belvedere & Kraków

Vodka is Poland's national drink and the Polish word 'wódka' can be traced back to the 15th century. Allegedly, during the period of Soviet dominance, evidence of vodka's Polish origin was covered up.

Visitors to Cracow will soon discover that the city is Poland's spiritual home and vodka the local's drink of choice. Cracovians may start the night with a beer but subsequent rounds see them revert to type. The night always ends with farewell shots of vodka. Cracovians drink Polish vodka not just because they are patriotic but because of its unique style and quality.

Polish vodka is traditionally made using rye grain, and this is the most influential factor in its flavour. While it is common for small amounts of sugar or honey to be added to Western and Russian vodkas, Polish vodka is naturally sweet thanks to the sugars in the rye.

Belvedere Polish vodka is made from 100% Dańkowskie or 'Gold' Rye, a strain of rye grain that has been inter-crossed six times over a century and has only ever been successfully cultivated in Polish, Mazovian soil. After triple distillation in column stills, Belvedere is hand-finished in a traditional copper pot still, so can claim to be quadruple distilled.

Launched in 1996, Belvedere vodka is widely regarded as the world's first luxury vodka. The tall, slender, acid-etched bottle has a drawing of Poland's Presidential Palace screen-printed on to the back. Like the palace, its name appropriately translates as 'beautiful to see'.

Sadly for many of my Cracovian friends the premium nature of this vodka and the weakness of the zloty means Belvedere is only seen in the most upscale bars of Cracow. Thankfully, the bar at my favourite hotel in Cracow, Hotel Copernicus, not only stocks Belvedere but has a number of Martinis made with it on its cocktail list.

When in Cracow, stop by the small liquor store at number 8 Main Market Square and pick up a bottle of Belvedere. Store in your freezer and use in Martinis or sip neat from a shot glass. Be sure to savour the pleasing nose with its delicate vanilla hints and the wonderfully clean, silky smooth palate with its creamy mouthfeel and hints of vanilla, white chocolate and prickly black pepper.

40% alc./vol. (80°proof)
www.belvederevodka.com

ALCHEMIA

5 Ulica Estery, Plac Nowy, Kamimierz, Kraków, 31-056, Poland

Tel: +48 (0)12 421 2200, www.alchemia.com.pl
Hours: Mon-Sat noon-last guest leaves

Type: Lounge bar
Alfresco: Pavement tables
Entry: Open door
Highlights: Atmosphere
Atmosphere: Chilled
Clientele: Media, music & bohemian
Dress code: Casual
Price guide: ZZ
Bar snacks: Szarlotka cake

This wonderfully atmospheric bohemian place lies on the corner of Kasimierz Market Square. Light jazz by Charlie Parker and John Coltrane wafts through the four ground floor rooms, which have the look of an old couple's kitchen and parlour - particularly the small back room with its shrine-like dresser. The floors are a mix of wood, old bricks and tiles, while the place has a warm reddish glow thanks to the candles which are the only source of light. Early 20th century sepia photos line the walls.

Alchemia is one of the most fashionable bars of the moment. Local media and music types sit around its old wooden tables, drinking, smoking and discussing the merits of art. The vibe picks up later but the serious partying is restricted to the large cellar, often a venue for concerts and photography exhibitions. Beer, often flavoured with raspberry or ginger syrup, and shots of vodka are the most popular drinks but there's also half a dozen wines to choose from.

BOOGIE

9 Ulica Szpitalna (entrance on Ulica Tomasza), Kraków, 31-155, Poland

Tel: +48 (0)12 429 4306
Hours: Noon till 3am or last guest leaves

Type: Jazz lounge bar
Alfresco: No
Entry: Over 21s only
Highlights: Service, cocktails, jazz
Atmosphere: Rocking when bands play
Clientele: Local trendies & regular visitors
Dress code: Stylishly casual
Price guide: ZZZ
Bar snacks: Snack menu

Formerly known as Boogie Woogie, this jazz club cum lounge bar is a far cry from the 'pub in medieval cellar' Cracow stereotype. In a city like New York, Boogie would be just another bar, but here it personifies style.

The interior follows a two tone colour scheme and somehow, despite a white synthetic fur wall, a black vinyl ceiling and an ebony baby grand piano, manages to avoid complete tackiness. Huge black and white pictures of jazz performers such as Duke Ellington hang about the place. Low comfy black sofas and bucket chairs dot the floor and jazzsters surround the piano.

Smiley waitress serve adequately made cocktails at the table. There are only a few places in Cracow known for their cocktails, and this one attracts local trendy professionals and regular visitors from out of town.

ESZEWERIA

9 Ulica Józefa, Kazimierz, Kraków, 35-056, Poland

Tel: +48 (0)12 292 0458
Hours: Mon-Sun 11am-2am

Type: Café bar
Alfresco: Secluded rear garden
Entry: Open door
Highlights: Quaintness
Atmosphere: Wonderfully relaxed
Clientele: Couples, mosly locals
Dress code: Casual
Price guide: ZZ
Bar snacks: Pierogi and sernik (cheese cake)

The entrance to Eszeweria, with its shutters and potted plants, looks somehow enchanted, like an antique shop filled with incredible old relics waiting to be discovered.

By day Eszeweria operates as a café bar serving coffee, fresh pierogi and sernik (cheese cake). However, the magic of this intimate L-shaped bar is best appreciated at night when it's lit by old standard lamps, flickering candles and candelabras. Elderly wooden tables and chairs, rustic antiques and a bare brick floor combine with ambient, loungy jazz to create a quaint feel.

A doorway by the small bar area leads to a secluded garden with chairs and tables huddled under two huge parasols. Inside or out, this is a romantic spot for couples to spend an evening reminiscing over a drink or two.

ÓSMY DZIEŃ TYGODNIA

●●●◐○

4 Ulica Podbrzezie, Kazimierz, Kraków, Poland

Tel: +48 (0)12 8029285
Hours: Mon-Sun 4pm-2am or when the last guest leaves.

Type: Lounge bar
Alfresco: No
Entry: Open door
Highlights: Atmosphere
Atmosphere: Relaxed in a highbrow way
Clientele: Locals, artists & writers
Dress code: Casual
Price guide: ZZ
Bar snacks: Sandwiches, salads & cakes

The name literally translates as 'eighth day of the week' and, if there were such a day, it would definitely be a day of rest and contemplation, if you look at the regulars here. Behind the wooden shutters adorned with the bar's name lie three rooms connected by narrow doorways. All feature old tiled and wooden floors, exposed brickwork, mismatched old chairs and tables with candles in saucers.

Although atmospherically lit, Eighth Day is brighter than many other bars in the Kazimierz district, albeit with plenty of nooks and crannies to hide away in. A huge steel furnace in the far room makes this a particularly snug place in winter.

--Eighth Day is popular with artists, writers and poets, who gather round the little bar discussing how under-appreciated they are. Black and white photographs of them and examples of their work adorn the walls. Beatles tracks are popular here.

PAPARAZZI

●●●○○

9 Ulica Mikołajska, Old Town, Kraków, 31-027, Poland

Tel: +48 (0)12 429 4597, **www.**paparazzi.com.pl
Hours: Mon-Sun noon-2am & often much later

Type: Café bar
Alfresco: No
Entry: Over 21s only
Highlights: Atmosphere
Atmosphere: Relaxed daytime, party nighttimes
Clientele: Expats & moneyed locals
Dress code: Casual
Price guide: ZZZZ
Bar snacks: Light meal, toasts & baguettes (day)

Like its siblings in Warsaw, Zakopane and Wroclaw, this bar is adorned with old cameras and framed black and white photographs, celebrating the paparazzi and the celebrities they chase. It's a long narrow space with the bar counter and high stools at the front and a more loungy area beyond.

During the day English speaking business types meet over coffee and light snacks. However, as night falls Paparazzi morphs into a party zone for British and American expats.

Efficient, friendly staff dressed in black cope well, dispensing drinks quickly to the thirsty crowd. This is one of the few places in Cracow where orders for gin and tonics exceed those of Żywiec beer and vodka. It is also one of the city's few true cocktail bars, although the drinks do not excel in the international league.

PAUZA

●●●◐○

18 Ulica Florianska, Old Town, Kraków, Poland

Tel: +48 (0)12 422 4876, **www.**pauza.pl
Hours: Mon-Sun 4pm-2am or when last guest leaves

Type: Lounge bar
Alfresco: No
Entry: Flat door atop stairs
Highlights: Atmosphere
Atmosphere: Chilled, very cool
Clientele: Students and artists
Dress code: Cool casual
Price guide: ZZ
Bar snacks: Not a place to eat

Most of the other bars in Cracow's Old Town lie buried in medieval cellars, or firmly grounded at street level. Pauza is different.

Hidden in an archway off Ulica Florianska (a busy pedestrian street lined with bars and shops) is the wide wooden staircase that leads to Pauza's front door. It's like entering someone's apartment, which is what makes this place so cool. In fact, you actually are entering someone's apartment. A statement which not only challenges one's perceptions of Cracowian bars, but is currently challenging the city's licensing officials.

Literally translated, 'Pauza' means 'pause, take a break', and here you'll find students and artists chilling to beyond laidback. The three rooms are dimly lit with wooden parquet flooring strewn with low-slung sofas. The walls are plastered with 8-by-10 head shots of regulars and their relations – mostly pulling faces.

Being a converted apartment there is only one toilet, but you never know who you'll meet while waiting.

PIWNICA POD BARANAMI

27 Rynek Głowny, Old Town, Kraków, 31-010, Poland

Tel: +48 (0)12 421 2500,
www.piwnicapodbaranami.krakow.pl
Hours: Mon-Sun 7pm-till last guest leaves

Type: Cabaret pub
Alfresco: No
Entry: Via stone staircase
Highlights: Jazz
Atmosphere: Dependent on acts
Clientele: Tourists & locals
Dress code: Casual
Price guide: ZZ
Bar snacks: Not a place to eat

It's common in Poland for the word 'pod', meaning 'under', to appear in the name of a pub. In this case the full name translates as 'cellar under the rams'. In this case, the 'rams' are embedded in the name of the cinema above, but it's still logical enough compared to British pub names such as the Dog and Duck. The entrance lies off the Main Market Square behind the parasols of Trebeca Coffee.

Piwnica Pod Baranami is famous throughout Poland for the jazz and cabaret acts which appear on the small stage in the cavernous room next to the bar. The cabaret company that performs here was founded in 1956 by Piotr Skrzynecki, a celebrity of the day, and still does the Parisian thing every Saturday evening.

Each July sees the start of the pub's very own summer jazz festival (www.cracjazz.com).

Piwnica Pod Baranami is popular with locals and tourists. Sadly more are here for cheap beer than high culture.

ŚRÓDZIEMIE

8 Plac Wszystkich Świętych, Old Town, Kraków, Poland

Tel: +48 (0)12 429 6133
Hours: Mon-Fri noon-till last guest leaves, Sat-Sun 4pm-last guest leaves

Type: Themed pub
Alfresco: Small courtyard garden
Entry: Open door
Highlights: Watching a good match here
Atmosphere: Peaceful to party
Clientele: Students & tourists
Dress code: Casual
Price guide: ZZ
Bar snacks: Not a place to eat

This themed pub is a place of many purposes. The name means 'Middle Earth', with décor to match, but it's also a mecca for anyone who wants to watch English football league games.

From the street a long, tunnel-like entrance hallway leads to a small courtyard garden, whence steep stairs descend to the main chamber of Middle Earth. A naturally cavernous medieval stone and brick cellar has been transformed into a grotto, where Tolkien characters and a map of Middle Earth adorn the walls and ceiling.

The bar lies in an antechamber with tree roots growing through the ceiling and further Elvish types represented. Cocktails have names such as Arwena's Kiss (Malibu, pineapple juice, cream and grenadine), Tom Bombadil (blue curaćao, Galliano, orange juice) and Nazgul's Sting (tequila, lemon syrup and grenadine). The Polish favourite Mad Dog shots are also represented, in the form of Mad Ork shots.

Soccer matches permitting, weekday nights are quieter but come the weekend Śródziemie is packed with dancing students and tourists.

ŚWIĘTA KROWA

16 Ulica Floriańska, Old Town, Kraków, 31-021, Poland

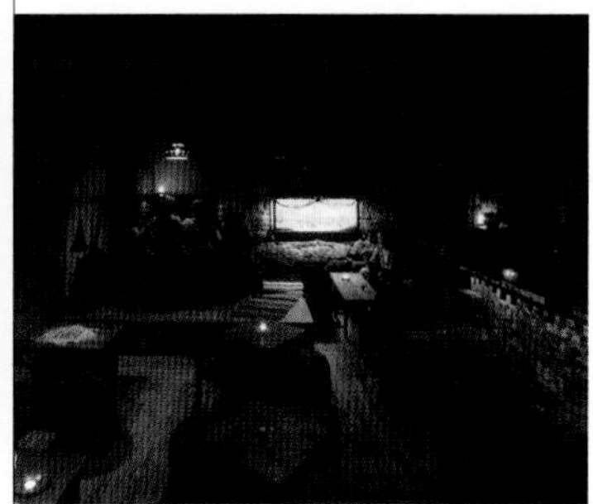

Tel: +48 (0)12 429 5951,
Hours: Mon-Sat noon-till late

Type: Lounge bar
Alfresco: No
Entry: If you can find it
Highlights: Cellar interior
Atmosphere: Chilled
Clientele: Students & locals
Dress code: Casual
Price guide: ZZ
Bar snacks: Not a place to eat

Cracow's Old Town has numerous bars in beautifully preserved medieval brick and stone cellars but this is by far my favourite. The name translates as 'Holy Cow' and you may well exclaim just that when you first descend into Święta Krowa. (To find the hidden entrance watch the street numbers and look for a painted swinging sign hanging below an illuminated Nike flash. Walk to the end of the entrance hallway under the sign and the stairs leading down to Święta Krowa are at the end on the right.) You will be greeted by burning incense, ambient jazz and lounge music.

The bar lies in one of two candle-lit chambers. Opposite is a chill-out lounge strewn with pouffe seating and low tables, which leads on to the bar's famous hanging garden. On cold winter nights order their hot drink made with Polish Krupnik honey liqueur and fresh ginger.

LONDON

Time zone: Greenwich Mean Time (GMT)
Airports: Heathrow (LHR), Gatwick (LGW), City (LCY), Stansted (STN)

London is Western Europe's biggest and, I believe, most vibrant city. And big it needs to be, as, even with its ancient, winding streets, there's one hell of a lot packed into its centre. I don't believe there's any city in the world that offers such a rich package of history, architecture, restaurants, theatres, galleries, museums, parks, shops and markets. Life is, however, not cheap. London is the world's second most expensive city – only Tokyo has a higher cost of living.

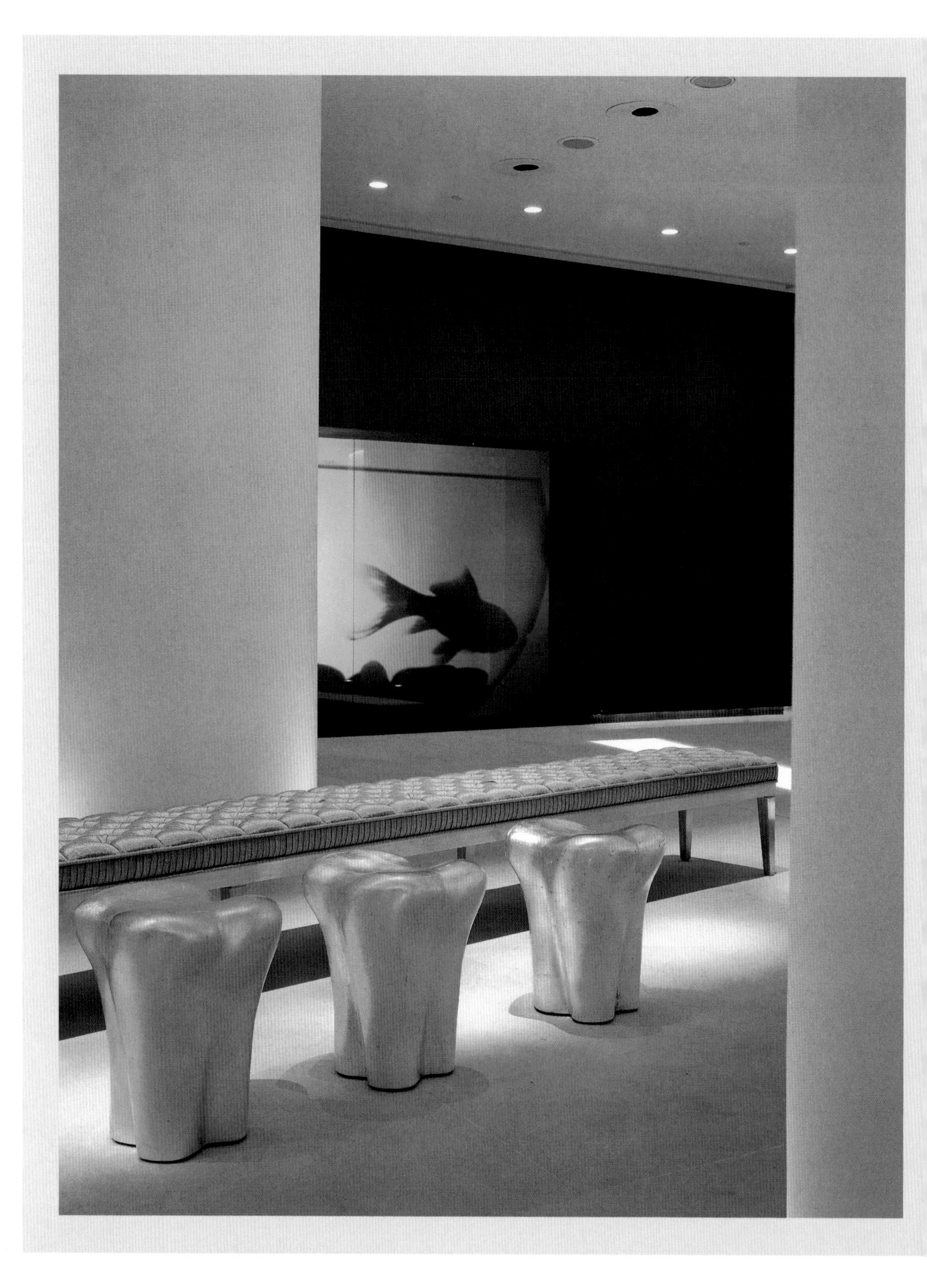

London Hotels

London is famed for its grand old hotels, such as the Ritz, the Savoy and Claridge's. The selection below features some of the more contemporary places to sleep, ranging from boutique hotels to West End glamour spots.

Charlotte Street Hotel

15-17 Charlotte Street, Bloomsbury, London, W1T 1RJ, England Tel: +44 (0)20 7806 2000, www.firmdale.com

Owned by the capital's boutique hotel pioneers, Tim and Kit Kemp, this luxury hotel takes its design cues from Virginia Woolf's Bloomsbury Set.

Great Eastern Hotel

Great Eastern Hotel

Liverpool Street, City of London, London, EC2M 7QN, England Tel: +44 (0)20 7618 5000, www.great-eastern-hotel.co.uk

Restaurant tycoon Sir Terence Conran has transformed this Victorian gothic station hotel into a hip, contemporary hangout on the edge of the Square Mile.

Malmaison Hotel

Charterhouse Square, Smithfield, London, EC1M 6AH, England Tel: +44 (0)20 7012 3700, www.malmaison.com

In leafy Charterhouse Square, between the City and Clerkenwell, is the London outpost of the Malmaison boutique hotel group. It offers affordable style, with great deals at weekends.

Metropolitan Hotel

Old Park Lane, London, W1K 1LB, England Tel: +44 (0)20 7447 1000, www.metropolitan.co.uk

This contemporary, very luxe hotel is known for its glamorous bar.

One Aldwych

One Aldwych

1 Aldwych, Aldwych, London, WC2B 4RH, England Tel: +44 (0)20 7300 1000, www.onealdwych.com

This modern, luxury hotel, poised between the City, West End and Theatreland, has a pool, a spa and lashings of contemporary art and design.

St Martins Lane Hotel

45 St. Martin's Lane, Covent Garden, London, WC2N 4HX, England Tel: +44 (0)20 7300 5500, www.morganshotelgroup.com

Ian Schrager created this hotel, which as you'd expect, features outré Philippe Starck interiors and fabulous bars.

Sanderson Hotel

50 Berners Street, Fitzrovia, London, W1T 3NG, England Tel: +44 (0)20 7300 1400, www.morganshotelgroup.com

Morgans' second London outpost is the home of Agua, an urban spa and fashionista destination.

The Soho Hotel

4 Richmond Mews, Soho, London, W1D 3DH, England Tel: +44 (0) 20 7559 3000, www.firmdale.com

Stylish, modern British boutique hotel from the Firmdale group. In the heart of Soho's film industry, it offers a screening room.

Sanderson Hotel

London Restaurants

London is a cosmopolitan city and its cuisine is shaped by influences from the many different cultures it encompasses. You can eat anything from Ethiopian to Danish, via Lebanese and Polish, but the following mixed bag tends towards the contemporary and upscale. Ring ahead to book and settle for an early table if nothing else is available.

The Capital Restaurant

The Capital Hotel, 22 Basil Street, Knightsbridge, London, SW3 1AT, England Tel: + 44 (0)20 7589 5171, www.capital-london.net/capital Cuisine: Modern French

This traditional hotel restaurant can feel a little stuffy but the cuisine is adventurous and excellent. Gents are requested to wear a jacket.

Cecconi's Restaurant

5a Burlington Gardens, Mayfair, London, W1S 3EP, England Tel: +44 (0)20 7434 1500 Cuisine: Modern Italian

Elegant food in a stylish, contemporary environment. If you haven't booked, try for one of the elevating tables at the bar.

Le Cercle

Phoenix House, 1 Wilbraham Place, Chelsea, London, SW1X 9AE, England Tel: +44 (0)20 7901 9999 Cuisine: Modern French

The team behind Club Gascon in Smithfield bring tapas-style French dishes to the Sloanes. Small portions allow you to sample more of the inspired flavour combinations.

The Cinnamon Club Restaurant

The Old Westminster Library, 30 Great Smith Street, Westminster, London, SW1P 3BU, England Tel: +44 (0)20 7222 2555, www.cinnamonclub.com Cuisine: Modern Indian

This high-end Indian restaurant in the heart of Westminster sometimes feels like an extension of the House of Commons bar. The small downstairs bar with its dodgy Bollywood screen back bar serves some very passable cocktails.

Deya Restaurant

34 Portman Square, Marylebone, London, W1H 7BY, England Tel: +44 (0)20 7224 0028, www.deya-restaurant.co.uk Cuisine: Modern Indian

Traditional Indian dishes are served with a contemporary twist in a modern environment in an elegant Grade II listed building. Deya is backed by film star Sir Michael Caine.

E&O Restaurant

14 Blenheim Crescent (corner Kensington Park Rd), Notting Hill, W11 1NN, England Tel: +44 (0)20 7229 5454, www.eando.co.uk Cuisine: Pan-Asian

The name is short for Eastern and Oriental, the cuisine which Will Ricker's restaurant serves to Notting Hill's in-crowd and a number of celebrities.

Eight Over Eight

392 King's Road, Chelsea, London, SW3 5UZ, England Tel: +44 (0)20 7349 9934, www.eightovereight.nu Cuisine: Pan-Asian

Will Ricker's Chelsea outpost serves Asian cuisine in minimalist surroundings to trendy young things and the odd celeb.

Gordon Ramsay at Royal Hospital Road

68 Royal Hospital Road, Chelsea, London, SW3 4HP, England Tel: +44 (0)20 7352 4441, www.gordonramsay.com Cuisine: Modern French

Celebrated chef Gordon Ramsay opened his first restaurant as owner in 1998 and it remains one of the very best in London, with three Michelin stars to prove it.

Gordon Ramsay at Claridge's

Claridge's Hotel, 55 Brook Street, Mayfair, London, W1A 2JQ, England Tel: +44 (0)20 7499 0099, www.gordonramsay.com Cuisine: French

Claridge's refurbished, art deco restaurant benefits from the Gordon Ramsay touch. Great food and service in refined surroundings.

Le Gavroche

43 Upper Brook Street, Mayfair, London, W1K 7QR, England Tel: +44 (0)20 7408 0881, www.le-gavroche.co.uk Cuisine: French

Le Gavroche was the first British restaurant to be awarded three Michelin stars. Michel Roux Junior, who now holds two stars, has built on his father's reputation for brilliant classic French cuisine in refined surroundings with service to match.

Valerian Noghin / Framescape

The Greenhouse Restaurant

27a Hays Mews, Mayfair, London, W1X 7RJ, England Tel: +44 (0)20 7499 3331
Cuisine: Modern eclectic

This contemporary, airy restaurant serves inventive and perfectly presented food. One of my favourites at the moment.

The Ivy

1-5 West Street, Covent Garden, London, WC2 9NE, England
Tel: + 44 (0)20 7836 4751,
www.caprice-holdings.co.uk
Cuisine: Eclectic

Still the number one restaurant in London for stars and rubberneckers, so getting a table is a challenge. The vast menu leads with Anglo-American comfort food.

J Sheekey

28-32 St Martin's Court, Covent Garden, London, WC2N 4AL, England
Tel: +44 (0)20 7240 2565,
www.caprice-holdings.co.uk
Cuisine: Seafood

This sister restaurant to the Ivy has a slightly clubby feel but is resolutely unpretentious. Seafood is simply served and perfectly done.

Levantine

26 London Street, Paddington, London, W2 1HH, England, Tel: +44 (0)20 7262 1111, www.levant.co.uk
Cuisine: Middle Eastern/Lebanese

The younger sibling of the established Levant in Wigmore Street offers plenty of spice in an Arabian Nights setting. Wonderful mezze dishes should be washed down with Lebanese wine.

Lindsay House

21 Romilly Street, Soho, London, W1D 5AF, England Tel: +44 (0)20 7439 0450,
www.lindsayhouse.co.uk
Cuisine: Modern European

Chef-patron Richard Corrigan serves fantastic, eclectic cuisine in this romantic townhouse in the heart of Soho.

Locanda Locatelli Restaurant

Churchill InterContinental Hotel, 8 Seymour Street, Marylebone, London W1H 7JZ, England Tel: +44 (0)20 7935 9088,
www.locandalocatelli.com
Cuisine: Modern Italian

My favourite of all London's Italian restaurants, headed by chef-patron Giorgio Locatelli, opens up a world beyond pasta. (Although the handmade pasta is also superb.)

Locanda Ottoemezzo

2-4 Thackeray Street, Kensington, London, W8 5ET, England
Tel: +44 (0)20 7937 2200.
Cuisine: Italian

This traditional, comfortable Italian restaurant, adorned with Fellini posters, sits just off High Street Kensington.

Maze

10-13 Grosvenor Square, Mayfair, London, W1K 6JP, England
Tel: +44 (0)20 7107 0000,
www.gordonramsay.com
Cuisine: Modern French fusion

The latest addition to Gordon Ramsay's empire, Maze offers a full à la carte menu, a market menu and a tapas-style grazing menu. Head chef Jason Atherton comes from Ramsay's Verre in Dubai.

Nobu Restaurant

The Metropolitan Hotel, 19 Old Park Lane (close to Hyde Park Corner), London, W1K 1LB, England
Tel: +44 (0)20 7447 4747,
www.noburestaurants.com
Cuisine: Japanese

Known for its celebrity clientele, this outpost of Nobu Matsuhisa's Nobu brand still serves the best Japanese food in London.

Pétrus

Berkeley Hotel, Wilton Place, Belgravia, London, SW1X 7RL, England
Tel: +44 (0)20 7235 1200,
www.gordonramsay.com
Cuisine: Modern French

Co-owned by Gordon Ramsay and his protegé Marcus Wareing, this no-smoking, Michelin-starred restaurant has a wine list as formidable as its name would suggest.

The Real Greek

14-15 Hoxton Market, Shoreditch, London, N1 6HG, England
Tel: +44 (0)20 7739 8212,
www.therealgreek.com
Cuisine: Greek

The first of chef Theodore Kyriakou's growing chain of Greek restaurants, this serves the best Hellenic food in London with a wine list to match. In a quiet location behind Hoxton Square, the attached Mezedopolio is a relaxing place for mezze and a glass of wine.

River Café

Thames Wharf, Rainville Road, Hammersmith, London, W6 9HA, England
Tel: +44 (0)20 7386 4200,
www.rivercafe.co.uk
Cuisine: Modern Italian

Since 1987 this converted 19th century warehouse on the banks of the Thames in residential Hammersmith has been famed for great food, simply produced from the best ingredients. Oh, and it also brought us Jamie Oliver.

The Square

6-10 Bruton Street (btwn Berkeley Sq & New Bond St), Mayfair, London, W1J 6PU, England
Tel: +44 (0)20 7495 7100,
www.squarerestaurant.com
Cuisine: Modern French

This serious restaurant lacks the theatre of some of its competitors but Philip Howard's modern interpretations of classic French dishes take centre stage. The predominantly suited audience appreciates them.

The Wolseley

160 Piccadilly, Piccadilly, London, W1J 9EB, England
Tel: +44 (0)20 7499 6996,
www.thewolseley.com
Cuisine: Modern European

Once the showroom for a long defunct luxury car named Wolseley, this Grade II listed building is now one of London's most glamorous restaurants with an array of A-list regulars. Some consider the food overrated but the space and atmosphere are beyond reproach.

Yauatcha

15 Broadwick Street, Soho, London, W1F 0DL, England
Tel: +44 (0)20 7494 8888
Cuisine: Chinese/dim sum

The latest innovation from Alan Yau, the visionary behind Wagamama and Hakkasan, sits under Ford's London head-quarters. The ground floor teahouse serves 100 different teas but those in the know flock to the basement for dim sum. Don't sit nattering before you order as a 90-minute timeslot may mean you miss out on pudding.

London Liquor Stores and Wine Shops

Berry Bros & Rudd
3 St James's Street, St James's, London, SW1A 1EG, England
Tel: +44 (0)20 7396 9669, www.bbr.com
This historic store stocks over 2500 bins from the great European wine regions, most of which are not displayed on shelves.

City Beverage Company
303 Old Street, Hoxton, London, EC1V 9LA, England
Tel: +44 (0)207 729 2111, www.citybeverage.co.uk
This local fine wine and spirits shop also has a great range of teas and coffees.

Corney & Barrow
194 Kensington Park Road, Notting Hill, London, W11 2ES, England
Tel: +44 (0)20 7221 5122
The parent wine merchant holds the UK agency for Pétrus and Domaine de la Romanée Conti inter alia and this little shop has remarkable depth of coverage.

Fortnum & Mason
181 Piccadilly, London, W1A 1ER, England
Tel: +44 (0)20 7734 8040, www.fortnumandmason.com
The classic department store has a range of over 1200 wines and some fine spirits – plus those celebrated teas.

Gerry's Wine and Spirits
74 Old Compton Street, Soho, London, W1V 5PA, England
Tel: +44 (0)20 7734 2053
This legendary Soho offie features a spectacular selection of spirits and liqueurs, with a focus on curios such as absinthe.

Handford
105 Old Brompton Road, South Kensington, London, SW7 3LE, England
Tel: +44 (0)20 7589 6113, www.handford.net
This wine merchant offers bins from around the world, most notably Southern France.

Harrods
87-135 Brompton Road, Knightsbridge, London, SW1X 7XL, England
Tel: +44 (0)20 7730 1234, www.harrods.com
The historic department store offers some fine wines and some extremely high-end spirits.

Harvey Nichols
109-125 Knightsbridge, Knightsbridge, London, SW1X 7RJ, England
Tel: +44 (0)20 7235 5000, www.harveynichols.com
The food hall of this hip department store has an interesting wine choice as well as some fine spirits and cigars.

Jeroboams
50-52 Elizabeth Street, Belgravia, London, SW1W 9PB, England
Tel: +44 (0)20 7730 8108, www.jeroboams.co.uk
This fine wine merchant also sells a good range of whiskies, Cognacs and eaux de vie. There are several other branches around the city.

Lea & Sandeman
170 Fulham Road, South Kensington, London, SW10 9PR, England
Tel: +44 (0)20 7244 0522, www.londonfinewine.co.uk
This wine merchant provides a good selection of bottles at reasonable prices with a focus on Italy and Burgundy.

Milroys
3 Greek Street, Soho, London, W1D 4NX, England
Tel: +44 (0)20 7437 2385, www.milroys.co.uk
The whiskey specialist features a great range of malts and a more than decent Bourbon offer too.

Selfridges
400 Oxford Street, London, W1A 1AB, England
Tel: +44 (0)20 7318 3730, www.selfridges.co.uk
The glorious food hall of this classic but hip department store conceals some equally tempting liquid goodies.

Soho Wine Supply
18 Percy Street, Soho, London, W1T 1DX, England
Tel: +44 (0)20 7636 8490, www.sohowine.co.uk
This bijou Soho store stocks interesting wines and some fine Champagnes.

Utobeer
Borough Market, Southwark Street, London, SE1 1TL, England
Tel: +44 (0)20 7394 8601, www.utobeer.co.uk
This Borough Market stall displays a vast range of bottled beers from around the world, alongside some unusual spirits and specialist liqueurs. The range changes regularly.

The Vintage House
42 Old Compton Street, Soho, London, W1D 4LR, England
Tel: +44 (0)20 7437 2592, www.sohowhisky.com
This Soho whisky specialist hosts an expansive selection of single malts plus casked whiskies.

Wimbledon Wine Cellar
1 Gladstone Road, Wimbledon, London, SW19 1QU, England
Tel: +44 (0)20 8540 9979, www.wimbledonwinecellar.com
This independent, local wine merchant offers a large range of fine wine.

London Drinking

London is currently leading the world's bar scene. Its top cocktail lounges see off New York's best, while its pubs compete with Dublin's. Add to that the fact that London is one of the world's biggest centres for imported wine and spirits and you can see why I'm very happy to call it home.

The following are my hundred favourite pubs, bars and clubs in the capital. I have chosen most for their drinks offering but a few are here for their ambience or historical interest.

A nationwide ban on smoking in all pubs, bars and clubs will come into force next year. At the moment many bars have designated areas for smoking and non-smoking: very few are entirely non-smoking. 24-hour licensing was introduced last year, amid much fanfare and political debate. However, this has not significantly affected the following bars, since licensing remains a local authority issue. Generally, most pubs shut at 11pm and most style bars close between 1 and 3am. With a very few exceptions only clubs are open after 3am and do not serve alcohol.

The legal minimum age for buying alcohol is 18. 16 and 17 year olds who are accompanied by a person aged over 18 are allowed to consume beer, wine or cider with a meal. In general, even if you are lucky enough to look under 21, you will only be asked for ID in pubs or bars which have a problem with under-age drinking.

OFFICIAL BEER
Budweiser
F.A. PREMIER LEAGUE
KING

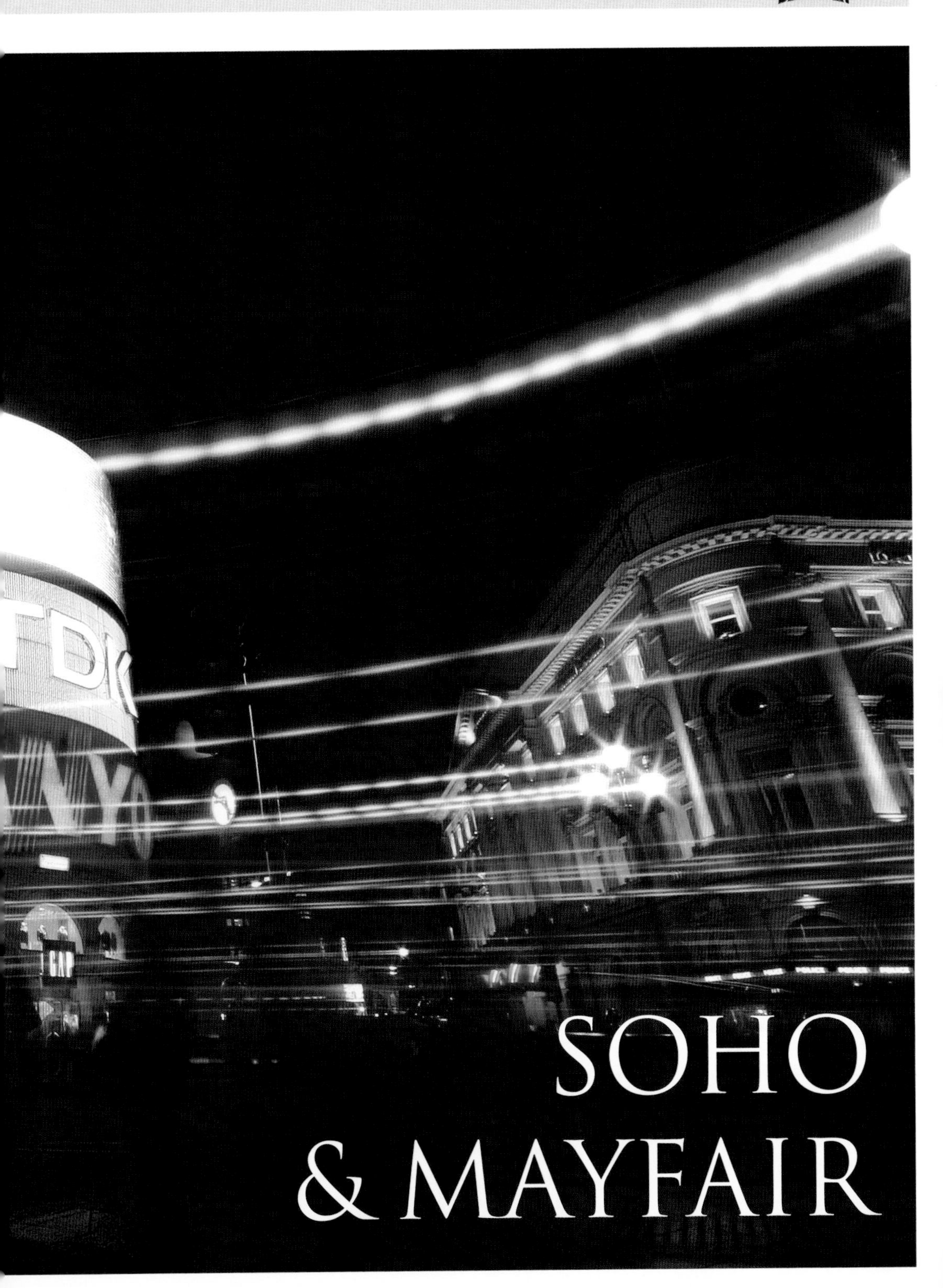

SOHO & MAYFAIR

AKBAR

●●●●○

The Red Fort, 77 Dean Street, Soho, London, W1D 3SH, England

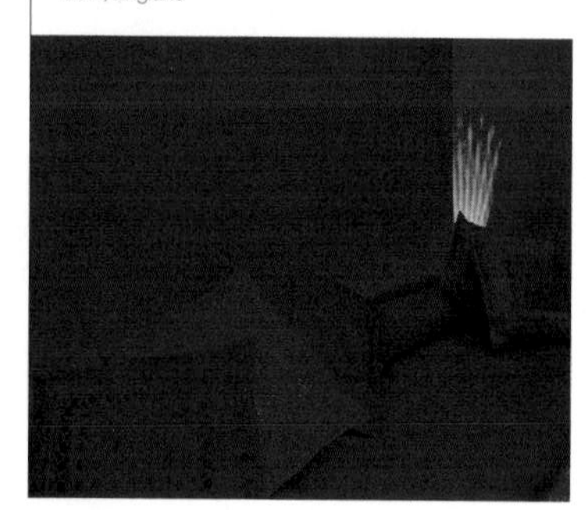

Tel: +44 (0)20 7437 2525, **www.**redfort.co.uk/akbar
Hours: Mon-Fri noon-1am, Sat 5.30pm-1am

Type: Lounge bar
Alfresco: No
Entry: Arrive early towards the weekend
Highlights: Cocktails, food
Atmosphere: Full-on/chilled
Clientele: Young trendy media types
Dress code: Smart/casual
Price guide: ££££
Food: Mughal court food (posh Indian)

Soho's famous Red Fort first opened in 1983 and became instantly renowned for its stylish design and a quality of food and service aeons beyond that of your average Tandoori. A serious fire in the kitchen closed the place down and it reopened in October 2001 after a complete refurbishment.

With this phoenix-like reincarnation came 'Akbar', the superb lounge bar in the basement, which takes its name from the greatest of the Mughal emperors. The small (70 capacity) room has simple but lush deÇcor and includes two intimate booths which are actually under Dean Street.

The tasty bar snacks should be washed down with one of the sublime cocktails which exploit typical Indian flavours such as date, jasmine, ginger, rosewater, mango and sweet spices.

Akbar's clientele is predominantly young and drawn from local media companies. The bijou space can get packed and the atmosphere DJ charged, but I prefer the place earlier in the week when it is quieter.

Akbar

ANNEX 3

6 Little Portland Street, Fitzrovia, London, W1W 7JE, England

Tel: +44 (0)20 7631 0700
Hours: Mon-Sat noon-midnight, Sun noon-8pm

Type: Lounge bar/restaurant
Alfresco: No
Entry: Best book ahead
Highlights: Punk interior
Atmosphere: Chilled
Clientele: Young trendy media types
Dress code: Designer casual
Price guide: ££££
Food: French bistro with an Asian twist

The latest offering from the three antique dealers behind Les Trois Garçons & Loungelover is no less restrained despite being their first foray out of funky Shoreditch. Annex's eclectic interior looks like it was designed by an ageing punk with a penchant for gilt, glitter and hard drugs. It's loud, bold and kitsch with snakeskin tables, 70s chandeliers, perspex Louis XV chairs, gold banquettes and a mosaic floor. The centrepiece is a rotating and illuminated fairground ride encased in a perspex box.

When this place first opened in November 05 the cocktail list was even more spectacular than the decor. Sadly by Christmas the whole bar team had walked out and the replacement cocktail list, while good, lacks that indefinable wow factor.

Annex is popular with young, trendy media types. In fact, it's so popular that I'd advise booking ahead. The food is better than many reviews suggest but is still style over substance.

ASTOR BAR AND GRILL

20 Glasshouse Street, Piccadilly, London, W1B 5DJ, England

Tel: +44 (0)20 7734 4888, **www.**astorbarandgrill.com
Hours: Mon-Sat 5pm-3am

Type: Lounge, restaurant bar
Alfresco: No
Entry: £10 cover after 10pm
Highlights: Amazing interior architecture
Atmosphere: Mellow
Clientele: After office crowd
Dress code: Smart with funky exceptions
Price guide: ££££
Food: Full menu available

This splendid art deco ballroom beneath the Regent Palace Hotel off Piccadilly dates back to 1919, the height of the ocean liner era. Its high coffered ceilings and network of columns, mouldings and friezes were concealed for years until 1994, when Oliver Peyton restored the room to its former glory and opened The Atlantic. Until its demise late in 2005 this was London's foremost lounge bar.

Thankfully, the splendid art deco space is protected by a Grade II listing and was not left empty for long. Astor opened in February 2006. The interior is little changed and the columns and panelling are as lavish as ever, but this bar-cum-club-cum-steakhouse is less than special. The food fails to live up to the surroundings, the cocktail list is disappointing compared to the Atlantic's heyday and the wine list is hardly good value.

An entrance charge (usually £10) may be payable after 10pm, so for a quick drink and a look at a splendid room, go early.

BHUTAN
MAGYAR POSTA
AIR MAIL
POSTA

Cocoon

THE AUDLEY

41 Mount Street (corner South Audley St), Mayfair, London, W1K 2RX, England

Tel: +44 (0)20 7499 1843
Hours: Mon-Sat 11am-11pm, Sun noon-10:30pm

Type: Traditional pub
Alfresco: Pavement tables
Entry: Open door
Highlights: Traditional cask ales & grub
Atmosphere: Relaxed
Clientele: Surprisingly varied
Dress code: Casual to smart suits
Price guide: £££
Food: Sandwiches to hearty meals

In the early 1880s the first Duke of Westminster set about rebuilding Mount Street and with this reconstruction came The Audley. Built in the neo-French Renaissance style, the red brick and pink terracotta frontage with its lush greenery is in harmony with the rest of the street.

Inside, this is a traditional grand old pub with a forest of dark carved wood offset by red leather banquettes and a floral carpet. The original chandeliers hang from the ornately moulded ceiling and the long bar counter traverses the two distinct sides of the Audley. Drinkers congregate on the left and diners on the right.

Four regular cask ales are supplemented by a changing guest beer while 17 wines by the glass feature on a brand-led list. Proper pub grub runs from gourmet sausages and mash, burgers, salads and sandwiches to roasts on Sundays.

COCOON

65 Regent Street (entrance on Air Street), London, W1B 4EA, England

Tel: +44 (0)20 7494 7600, **www.**cocoon-restaurants.com
Hours: Mon-Fri noon-3pm & 5:30pm-midnight, Sat 5:30pm-midnight, Sun 5:30pm-11pm

Type: Restaurant bar
Alfresco: No
Entry: Subject to management & capacity
Highlights: Food, cocktails, sake & shochu
Atmosphere: Relaxed
Clientele: Henrys & Henriettas
Dress code: Designer casual
Price guide: ££££
Food: Starters from Pan-Asian menu

This long, narrow venue with views over Regent Street was formerly the landmark l'Odeon restaurant. The original arched windows and claustrophobically low ceiling remain. However, the room now hosts a series of six spherical and interlocking dining areas, linked by a central walkway and divided by net drapes. The bar and lounge nestles in the middle of the row, and shares the rather garish space age decor of the whole.

According to Cocoon's blurb, the design was 'inspired by the lifecycle of the butterfly '. Yeah, right.

Whatever you may think of the high concept, the cocktails, whether classics or Cocoon's own Asian-influenced creations, are superb. The wine list features some interesting bins and there's an exceptional selection of shochu and sake.

Those with a weak bladder should be warned that the loos are in the basement and the trip involves a long walk and two sets of stairs. However, the incontinent and just plain lazy may like to note that there's also a solitary 'disabled' WC upstairs.

THE CUCKOO CLUB

●●●●○

Swallow Street, London, W1B 4EZ, England

Tel: +44 (0)20 7287 4300, **www.**thecuckooclub.com
Hours: Wed-Thu 7:30pm-3am, Fri-Sat 8pm-3:30am

Type: Members bar & club
Alfresco: No
Entry: Subject to management & capacity
Highlights: Cocktails (upstairs) & atmosphere
Atmosphere: Full-on party
Clientele: Style set
Dress code: Designer casual
Price guide: £££££
Food: Modern European food

The word 'club' usually suggests bad drinks, bad service and grotty spaces but a great party atmosphere. Thankfully there are a few clubs that manage to combine the standards of an upscale lounge with the buzz of a rave and the Cuckoo Club is a shining example.

The Cuckoo Club opened in November 2005 on the site of the former Stork Rooms and its 5,000 square feet is spread over two floors. This makes it feel more intimate than the 300 capacity might suggest.

The upstairs bar boasts an impressive array of spirits and, judging by my visit, some great cocktails. It starts off relatively sedately, picking up momentum and volume as the night turns to morning. Downstairs, the drinks offering is more basic but the atmosphere full-on from the start. Both floors feature flamboyant decor, theatrical drapes, gilded mirrors and ceilings where 350 LED lights pulsate in time with the music.

If you want to come and play here you'll need to blag your name on the list or, better, pass the A-list committee and splash out a few hundred quid on one of the coveted memberships.

CVO FIREVAULT

36 Great Titchfield Street, near Oxford Circus, London, W1W 8BQ, England

Tel: +44 (0)20 7636 2091, **www.**cvo.co.uk
Hours: Mon-Sat noon-11pm

Type: Lounge bar & restaurant
Alfresco: No
Entry: Ring first
Highlights: Food, decor
Atmosphere: Wonderfully ambient
Clientele: Media types
Dress code: Designer casual
Price guide: ££££
Food: Diverse snack & full menu

Five minutes walk from Oxford Circus, this is one of London's best hidden and most romantic bars. The unusual name is a reference to its owner, Caroline Van Outersterp, a fireplace designer who originally opened this as a basement showroom. She had the natty idea of combining her showroom with a restaurant and bar, something she's done brilliantly.

The ground level reception and cloakroom look like another of the area's many designer furniture shops. Descend the stairs and you'll find yourself in a clinical white space, divided by maze-like walls and net drapes. Fireplaces of all shapes and sizes are everywhere, set into the walls and even the tables. The combination of secluded spaces, comfy white leather sofas, ambient lighting and the warm glow of the flames is enchanting.

Such surroundings are the perfect setting for sipping cocktails and the list here features classics and twists on classics which when ordered are very well-made. The food is wonderfully diverse with classic French meeting Asian and North African dishes.

Highly recommended for romantic liaisons on cold winter's nights.

THE DOG & DUCK

18 Bateman Street (at Frith St), Soho, London, W1D 3AJ, England

Tel: +44 (0)20 7494 0697
Hours: Mon-Fri noon-11pm, Sat 6pm-11pm, Sun 7pm-10:30pm

Type: Traditional pub
Alfresco: No
Entry: Open door
Highlights: Decor and ale
Atmosphere: Relaxed
Clientele: Local office types, tourists
Dress code: Whatever
Price guide: £££
Food: Hot & cold traditional pub grub

The name Dog & Duck is so synonymous with traditional English pubs that it's practically generic. This particular Dog & Duck is deeply traditional, from the building's fabric to the food and drink.

The first pub here was built in 1734 on the site of the Duke of Monmouth's home. This was demolished in 1897 and replaced by the present building, which remains a glorious example of a late Victorian boozer. One of Soho's oldest and smallest pubs, its original, ornamental glazed tile and mirror interior is simply gorgeous. The Victorians were a practical lot and the tiles, like the pub's yellowish glazed brick façade, were designed to repel dirt.

Although several draught lagers and eleven wines by the glass cater for modern tastes, thankfully this tiny pub still offers four traditional cask draught ales - more than most pubs several times its size. The food menu is also disproportionately large, and packed with traditional pub fare such as sausage and mash, pies, sandwiches and even pickled eggs.

Cuckoo

43 South Molton

43 SOUTH MOLTON

43 South Molton Street, Mayfair, London, W1K 5RS, England

Tel: +44 (0)20 7647 4343, **www.**43southmolton.com
Hours: Mon-Sat noon-3pm & 6pm-2am

Type: Members' lounge bar/club
Alfresco: No
Entry: Members & guests only
Highlights: Cocktails
Atmosphere: Relaxed, loungy
Clientele: City boys & trust fund babes
Dress code: Designer casual
Price guide: ££££
Food: Tapas & Euro dishes

OK. So the name lacks a little imagination, but then this is one posh Mayfair address - and, given the eccentric country house theme of this members' club, what more appropriate moniker could there be? Molton Street is known for its designer boutiques and trust-funded babes who lunch. So it's hardly surprising that number 43 is attracting a suitably high net worth and fashionable young crowd, with City boys driving their Ferraris across town in pursuit of the aforementioned ladies of leisure.

43 uses all four floors of the site, formerly a restaurant called 'Knew'. The street level bistro looks more like a general store from an episode of Little Britain than an aristocratic pad. The first and second floors are cosier and kitted out in a shabby chic vein with mismatched comfy old armchairs and antique light fittings. Don't get too comfortable, however, for the action is generally in the basement below. Despite its grand title 'The Ballroom', this is actually an intimate club space.

Join the Mayfair set here and you'll benefit from sublime cocktails and great service from friendly staff.

FRENCH HOUSE

49 Dean Street, Soho, London, W1V 5HL, England

Tel: +44 (0)20 7437 2799
Hours: Mon-Fri 11am-11pm, Sun 11am-10:30pm

Type: Traditional pub
Alfresco: No
Entry: Subject to limited space
Highlights: All things French
Atmosphere: Crowded but friendly
Clientele: Conversationalists, all ages & walks
Dress code: Casual to suits
Price guide: ££
Food: Modern British restaurant above

When this tiny Soho boozer was built in 1937 it was named the York Minster. Just before the Second World War it was taken over by a Belgian, Victor Berlemont, who made it a haunt for singers and actors. During the war it became a meeting place for French exiles, including the future president Charles de Gaulle, which led to the nickname 'The House of the French', later shortened to the 'French House'.

Today this one room pub still attracts plenty of French folk and is reputedly the country's largest retail outlet for Ricard Pastis. Its walls display a unique collection of signed photographs of French entertainers and sportsmen. The first floor restaurant has something of a reputation, but surprisingly offers a modern British menu.

Its reputation and diminutive size means that most lunchtimes and early evenings the French House is so busy that entering one of its twin doors is a challenge, let alone getting to the bar. Winter afternoons are the best time to appreciate this hospitable little pub at its best.

YE GRAPES

16 Shepherd Market, Mayfair, London, W1J 7QQ, England

Tel: +44 (0)20 7499 1563
Hours: Mon-Sat 11am-11pm, Sun noon-10:30pm

Type: Traditional pub
Alfresco: Standing room outside
Entry: Open door
Highlights: Traditional cask ales
Atmosphere: Often very busy
Clientele: Office staff, locals, tourists
Dress code: Casual to suits
Price guide: £££
Food: Peanuts and crisps only

Ye Grapes lies in Shepherd Market, which is named after Edward Shepherd, the architect and developer who started building here in 1735, on the site of the May Fair, the annual fair which gave Mayfair its name. By 1882, when this pub was built, Shepherd Market was a well-known haunt for prostitutes.

Today the market is distinctly upscale but retains a quaint, village-like feel with narrow streets and tiny houses and shops. This very traditional, old Victorian pub with hanging baskets, green paintwork and glazed tiles fits right in.

As was common in pubs of the day, the interior was originally divided to accommodate different classes of drinker but today only high back snugs provide some anonymity. Cartoons, a deer head, a propeller and stuffed fish in cases dot the walls and abundant carved bunches of grapes recall the pub's name.

Traditional ales are a speciality here and the five pumps on the bar are often supplemented by a couple of firkins on the side.

ICEBAR & BELOW ZERO

29-33 Heddon Street, London, W1B 4BL, England

Tel: +44 (0)20 7478 8910,
www.belowzerolondon.com
Hours: Mon-Sun 12:30pm-11:30pm

Type: Lounge, restaurant & ice bar
Alfresco: No
Entry: Cover charge, book ahead
Highlights: The cold experience
Atmosphere: Chilled!
Clientele: The curious
Dress code: Smart casual
Price guide: ££££
Food: Sashimi to burgers (some dishes served on ice plates)

Below Zero and the Absolut Icebar sit adjoining each other and united by a common theme. Below Zero is a two storey lounge and restaurant which is pleasant enough and serves reasonable cocktails. But it's the Icebar, perhaps wrongly, that's of more interest. This is a miniature, artificially chilled version of the bar at the legendary Icehotel in Sweden.

The London version is basically a huge industrial freezer lined with ice blocks to resemble an igloo and maintained at -5°C. The stools, the tables, the bar counter and the spectacular ice carvings are made from ice imported from northern Sweden.

A forty minute slot in the Icebar costs £12 (£15 on Thursday, Friday and Saturday evenings) and the price includes your first Absolut cocktail, served in an outsize, hollow ice cube by a bartender wearing a ski suit. You are issued with a silver cape to keep you warm and gloves so you can hold your "glass". It's certainly worth doing once for the experience - as is spending a night at the Icehotel itself.

KABARET'S PROPHECY NIGHTCLUB

16-18 Beak Street, Soho, London, W1F 9RD, England

Tel: +44 (0)20 7439 2229,
www.kabaretsprophecy.com
Hours: Mon-Fri 4pm-3am, Sat 10pm-3am

Type: Lounge bar/members' club
Alfresco: No
Entry: Members & guest list
Highlights: Cocktails & vibe
Atmosphere: Full-on
Clientele: Style set (20-40)
Dress code: Designer casual
Price guide: £££££
Food: Very tasty international snacks & plates

This tiny basement club is a 70s schoolboy's dream. The bar front is made of Swarovski crystal, the walls are lined with LED pixels which produce an arcade style flicker and, naturally, the dancefloor is full of pretty young things. The frenzied design (and attractive clientele) continues in the toilets, where the walls are plastered with cartoon characters by Jamie Hewlett, the illustrator who created Tank Girl.

Unusually for a club, there is a very serious bar team - and a cocktail list to match. I can highly recommend both the bar snack menu and the cocktails, which are far above the standard for such places. Kabaret's Prophecy is open to members only from 10:30pm, but from 4-10pm Monday to Friday anyone can enjoy these delights.

With its flashing walls and pumping sound system, this is certainly no place to take your granny. However, it could be right for you.

THE LIVING ROOM W1

3-9 Heddon Street, London, W1B 4BE, England

Tel: 087 0166 2225, **www.**thelivingroomw1.co.uk
Hours: Mon-Sat 10am-1am, Sun 11am-midnight

Type: Lounge bar/restaurant
Alfresco: No
Entry: Subject to management & capacity
Highlights: Cocktails & vibe
Atmosphere: Relaxed party
Clientele: 20 & 30-somethings
Dress code: Designer casual
Price guide: £££
Food: Full modern British menu

Towns across the country are dotted with this successful brand of style bars cum restaurants, but this is the chain's flagship and accordingly distinguished by the W1 moniker. The setting is a former Post Office just off Regent Street, an address made famous on the cover of David Bowie's Ziggy Stardust album.

No living room is complete without the homely warmth of a flickering fire and the partition that divides the large ground floor incorporates three gas fires. On one side lies the lounge with its 17 metre bar, on the other an informal dining area with café style windows that can be thrown open in summer. A staircase leads up to a more formal first floor dining room with an open kitchen and galleried view of the bar below. A club is also set to open in the basement.

The modern British gastro grub attracts business types at lunchtime while evenings see their secretaries pile in for the well made cocktails. Although it trades until 1am, access after 11pm is by non-fee membership.

MAZE

10-13 Grosvenor Square, Mayfair, London, W1K 6JP, England

Tel: +44 (0)20 7107 0000, **www.**gordonramsay.com
Hours: Mon-Sun noon-1am

Type: Restaurant lounge bar
Alfresco: No
Entry: Subject to capacity
Highlights: Food, cocktails, wine
Atmosphere: Relaxed, informal
Clientele: Business types
Dress code: Smart casual
Price guide: ££££££
Food: Tiny tasting plates from 'Spring' menu

Grosvenor Square is the home of the US embassy and opposite its ugly concrete and steel security cordon sits yet another Gordon Ramsay restaurant. Unlike some of his others, however, this features a very serious bar. In fact, two bar stations jut out into the room. Covered by canopies of white tile and frosted glass, these illuminate the already clinical and brightly lit space with its white ceiling and polished white plaster walls.

Ramsay pulls a crowd and the banquette seating in the bar area fills up quickly, leading drinkers to congregate around the bars. This helps create a relaxed, informal atmosphere and the business types abandon their jackets and ties on entry in favour of open necked shirts.

The cocktail list is one of the most interesting in London and features many imaginative new creations and twists on the classics. All are brilliantly made and beautifully presented, while the skilled bartenders confidently handle requests for classics not on the list. Foodies are right to rave about executive chef Jason Atherton, but the chaps wielding the shakers are worthy of similar praise.

Maze

NOBU BERKELEY

15 Berkeley Street, Mayfair, London, W1J 8DY, England

Tel: +44 (0)20 7290 9222,
www.noburestaurants.com
Hours: Mon-Sat 6pm-2am

Type: Lounge bar/restaurant
Alfresco: No
Entry: Subject to management & capacity
Highlights: Food & cocktails
Atmosphere: Relaxed
Clientele: Wealthy, good looking
Dress code: Designer casual
Price guide: £££££
Food: Amazing sushi, sashimi, tempura

This ground floor bar and upstairs restaurant was the third Nobu to open in London and one has the feeling that even if they outnumbered McDonald's they'd all be busy. The draw is of course the faultlessly good sushi, sashimi, tempura and famed black cod in miso. The bar is pretty much guaranteed custom as trendy upscale restaurant patrons wait for a table or stop off for an after dinner drink. However, it has also become a destination in its own right.

The interior is so modern that it wouldn't seem out of place in Star Trek or Star Wars. The almost circular room is dominated by the bar, which is backed by whitened tree branches spouting out over black tiles.

Able bartenders construct tasty cocktails. There's a serious champagne list, ten sakes and eleven wines by the glass, while the choice of four beers includes Asahi Black and the wonderfully creamy and hoppy house beer, Nobu Special Reserve. Seats and tables tend to be reserved for VIPs.

CENTURY

61-63 Shaftesbury Avenue (btwn Wardour & Dean Sts), Soho, London, W1D 6LQ, England

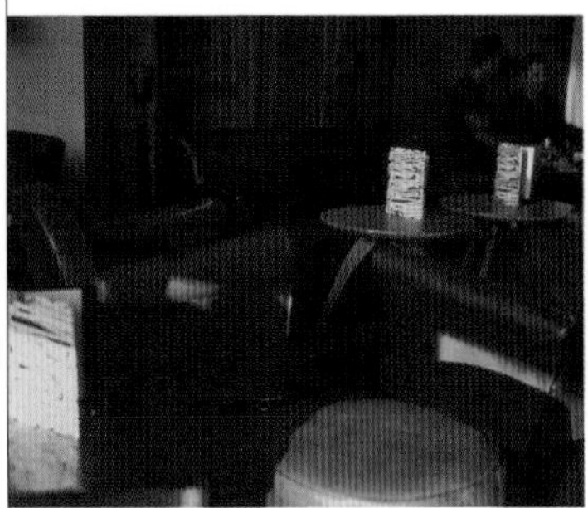

Tel: +44 (0)20 7534 3080, **www.**centuryclub.co.uk
Hours: Mon-Fri 8am-1am, Sat noon-2am

Type: Members lounge bar/restaurant
Alfresco: Roof terrace
Entry: Members & guests only
Highlights: Ambience, service & roof terrace
Atmosphere: Relaxed, home from home
Clientele: Soho media types
Dress code: Suits to designer jeans
Price guide: £££
Food: Platters to Shepherds' pie

I worried about including this bar in my London top 100 as it's the one I frequent the most. Happily it's a private members club and so a committee prevents it from getting too crowded with new drinkers - sorry.

Century opened in spring 2001 and its four floors boast three bars, a roof terrace and a restaurant (which offers good brasserie fare). The first floor bar, which is open from breakfast, is cosy with comfy chairs arranged round simple tables: modern art on the walls entertains the creative clientele which Century attracts. The second floor lounge bar opens from 4pm and tends to a living room feel, with warm lighting and a fireplace. The ambience is friendly and a comfy armchair here makes a relaxing spot to escape the bustle of Soho.

Membership costs £400 per year plus a £100 registration fee but it's worth every penny. However, please save your money and stay away - I want that armchair.

CIRCUS

Basement, 1 Upper James Street (corner Beak St), Soho, London, W1R 4BP, England

Tel: +44 (0)20 7534 4000
Hours: Mon-Wed noon-1.30am, Thu-Sat 12.30pm-3am

Type: Lounge bar
Alfresco: No
Entry: Possible charge for non-members after 11pm
Highlights: Cocktails, vibe
Atmosphere: Full-on / relaxed
Clientele: Soho-ites and local workers
Dress code: Chic is best
Price guide: £££
Food: Chips, spring rolls etc.

This split-level minimalist bar lies underneath the successful restaurant of the same name on the corner of Beak Street and Upper James Street. Black leather seating is scattered along the lengthy lower lounge which looks out onto an illuminated Japanese style garden of gravel and bamboo.

The well-stocked bar, complete with goldfish swimming in two giant bowls, knocks out classic cocktails as well as some interesting original concoctions. The food menu is short but every bit as good as that on offer in the restaurant above.

The clientele ranges from magazine styled local media darlings to the unstylish after office crowd. Circus enjoys a late licence but I'd advise arriving early as non-members have to pay an entry charge after 11pm.

CLARIDGE'S BAR

Claridges's Hotel, 55 Brook Street (corner Davies St.), Mayfair, London, W1A 2JQ, England

Tel: +44 (0)20 7629 8860, **www.**savoygroup.com
Hours: Mon-Sat midnight-1am, Sun 4pm-noon

Type: Hotel/lounge bar
Alfresco: No
Entry: Via hotel lobby or Davies St.
Highlights: Cocktails, service
Atmosphere: Quiet gentleman's club
Clientele: Mayfair set
Dress code: Gents requested to wear jackets
Price guide: ££££
Food: Caviar, sushi, salads, risotto etc

Tucked away under the staircase of Claridge's lobby is this quaint lounge bar, which acquired its warm Art Deco look in 1999 when the hotel embarked on its first major designer restoration since the 1930s. A Venetian chandelier drapes glass tendrils down in front of the white marble bar counter in this small but somehow stately room lined with comfy, red leather bar stools, chairs and banquettes. A similarly appointed, connecting room has a fireplace topped by a mirrored clock. Behind this lies the aptly named Snuggery, an intimate area which seats up to twenty.

Claridge's Bar boasts the best range of Louis Roederer Champagne in Britain with Vintage Cristal 1997 by the glass (£44). Service is impeccable. The skilled bartenders will make any classic you request as well as more contemporary creations from their own list.

Elderly regulars are joined by the young Mayfair set and diners from Gordon Ramsay's restaurant just across the lobby.

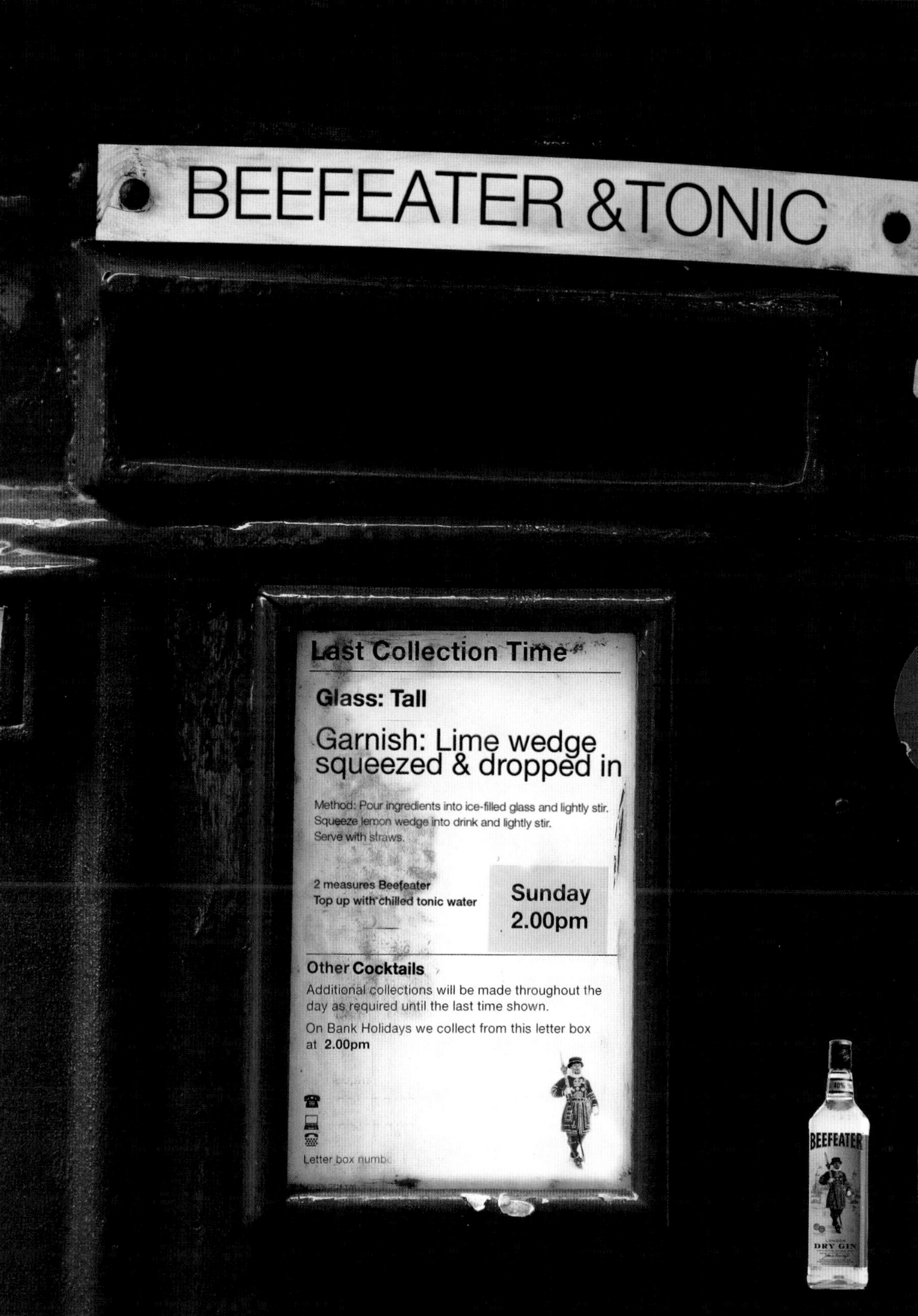

BEEFEATER &TONIC
Last Collection Time
Glass: Tall
Garnish: Lime wedge squeezed & dropped in
Method: Pour ingredients into ice-filled glass and lightly stir. Squeeze lemon wedge into drink and lightly stir. Serve with straws.
2 measures Beefeater
Top up with chilled tonic water
Sunday 2.00pm
Other Cocktails
Additional collections will be made throughout the day as required until the last time shown.
On Bank Holidays we collect from this letter box at 2.00pm
Letter box numb
BEEFEATER
LONDON
DRY GIN

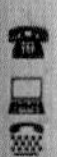

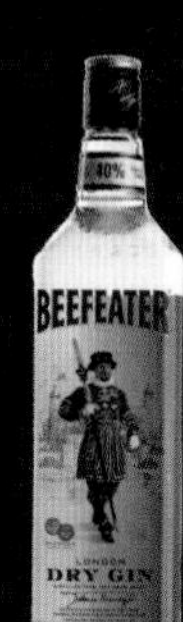

CRAZY BEAR BAR

●●●◐○

Basement, 26-28 Whitfield Street, Fitzrovia, London, W1T 2RG, England

Tel: +44 (0)20 7631 0088, **www.**crazybeargroup.co.uk
Hours: Mon-Fri 11am-11pm, Sat 6pm-11pm

Type: Lounge bar
Alfresco: No
Entry: Subject to management & capacity
Highlights: Interior design
Atmosphere: Relaxed
Clientele: Local office & diners
Dress code: Smart casual
Price guide: ££££
Food: Oriental

The restaurant on the ground floor of this Fitzrovia enclave looks so impressive that you may not want to descend the stairs to the bar. But with its leather floor and walls, art deco lamps, ostrich-skin chairs and padded booth tunnels, the basement delivers another visual treat.

The bar itself is sunken so, when seated at the bar, the bartenders are at your level. Behind them are five matching fireplaces salvaged from the Royal Automobile Club, which now warm their admirers with premium spirits rather than flames. Naturally, the toilets do not disappoint. The gents features an incredible mirrored floor.

The bar snacks and food served in the restaurant upstairs are Thai with pan-Asian elements. The cocktails can be disappointing so I'd recommend wine, Champagne, or a spirit and mixer. However, Crazy Bear is worth the journey for its interior alone.

FINO RESTAURANT

●●●●○

33 Charlotte Street (entrance on Rathbone Street), Fitzrovia, London, W1T 1RR, England

Tel: +44 (0)20 7813 8010, **www.**finorestaurant.com
Hours: Mon-Fri noon-3pm & 6pm-11pm, Sat 6pm-11pm

Type: Spanish tapas restaurant & bar
Alfresco: No
Entry: Around corner in Rathbone Street
Highlights: Cocktails, food, wine list
Atmosphere: Convivial - no music
Clientele: Local office crowd & traveing foodies
Dress code: Smart casual
Price guide: ££££
Food: Superb Spanish tapas

Put all your preconceptions of tapas bars aside and head down to this great little place in Fitzrovia. Don't, however, head down to the postal address, which bears no resemblance to the location of the front door. You need to enter from opposite the Rathbone Hotel, on Rathbone Street, around the corner from Charlotte Street.

The basement space feels slick, comfortable and convivial. Brightly coloured leather chairs and stools sit among the pale wood walls. The cocktail bar, tucked round to the right, is intimately proportioned. However, they prepare the most amazing cocktails - many of them topped with foaming heads created with nitrous oxide (laughing gas). My favourite is the Vanilla Daiquiri with Camomile Foam. The wine list is also inspired and, as the name would suggest, the establishment offers a great Sherry selection.

The food is modern tapas with a focus on fresh seafood. Order a few dishes to nibble or opt for one of their selections and eat at the kitchen bar.

FLORIDITA

●●●●○

Mezzo Basement, 100 Wardour Street, Soho, London, W1F 0TN, England

Tel: +44 (0)20 7314 4000, **www.**floriditalondon.com
Hours: Mon-Wed 5.30pm-2am, Thu-Sat 5.30pm-3am

Type: Cabaret bar
Alfresco: No
Entry: At a price after 8pm (£10)
Highlights: Cocktails & live entertainment
Atmosphere: Mellow
Clientele: After office crowd & tourists
Dress code: Smart
Price guide: £££££
Food: Cuban fusion

On this site in 1964 a little known group called the Rolling Stones played at the Marquee Club. Much later came Mezzo, part of Sir Terence Conran's huge gastro-empire. And Sir Terence still has a stake in this new venture, which is modelled on Havana's celebrated Floridita bar and housed in the basement of the Mezzo building.

From the ground floor tapas bar wide stairs descend to a huge bunker decorated in 80s shades of red, black and white. There's a 13 metre long bar and a stage, from which Latin American live music is played.

Even with live langosta (lobster) imported weekly from Cuba, the food here is hardly authentic, but having tried the food in Cuba that's surely a good thing. The cocktails are much better, with excellent classic Daiquiris and imaginative modern twists all made by a superb bar team.

GROUCHO CLUB

45 Dean Street (just North of Old Compton St), Soho, London, W1D 4QB, England

Tel: + 44 (0)20 7439 4685, **www.**thegrouchoclub.com
Hours: Mon-Sat 11am-3am, Sun 11am-midnight

Type: Private members club
Alfresco: No
Entry: Members & guests
Highlights: Vibe
Atmosphere: Mellow
Clientele: 25-50 arts, celebs and media
Dress code: Casual
Price guide: ££££
Food: Club sandwiches etc

The legendary Groucho Club was founded in 1985 by a group including Tony Mackintosh, the chocolate multimillionaire. The name derived from Groucho Marx's quip, "I don't care to belong to any club that would accept me as a member," and it was billed as a members-only hangout for non-clubby people. It quickly attracted many celebrity members, including actors and pop stars such as Mick Jagger.

Groucho was bought in 2001 by a group led by another chocolate heir (Joel Cadbury) and PR guru Matthew Freud, who gave the club a much needed spruce up. The Groucho's three bars, brasserie and more formal dining room still offer celebs and media types an exclusive and congenial haven in which to relax. Should they need overnight accommodation, the club has 19 well appointed bedrooms.

The Groucho offers great service, great cocktails and perhaps the best drinking companions of any London bar. The only problem is gaining membership: aspirants must be signed and seconded by accredited members then accepted by the membership committee, and, even if they pass these hurdles, may have to wait more than a year for membership.

HAKKASAN

8 Hanway Place, Fitzrovia, London, W1T 9HD, England

Tel: +44 (0)20 7927 7000, **www.**hakkasan.com
Hours: Mon-Wed noon-12.30am, Thu-Sat noon-2.30am, Sun noon-midnight

Entry: Dinner bookings take preference
Type: Lounge / restaurant bar
Alfresco: No
Highlights: Cocktails, spirits, food, vibe
Atmosphere: Full-on / relaxed
Clientele: Stylish business and Soho set
Dress code: Chic / smart
Price guide: ££££
Food: Modern Oriental

The hubbub of Oxford Street and the grime of Hanway Place do little to prepare the visitor for the elegance of Hakkasan, with its dramatic staircase leading down to a basement lobby bathed in a blue neon glow. The main room's architecture is among the most impressive of any London restaurant. Dark wood latticework screens divide the main space into restaurant, lounge and bar. These and the slate wall of the 16 metre bar are much copied by counterfeiters who always fail to achieve Hakkasan's wow factor.

Hakkasan is the vision of Alan Yau, who also brought us the Wagamama noodle bar chain. It buzzes with a business led clientele enhanced by some very beautiful women and successfully cool men. They are served dim sum to die for and some highly imaginative cocktails by waitresses who look like they have been squeezed into Chinese lanterns.

And the name? 'Hakka' is Chinese dialect and 'san' is the Japanese form of addressing someone.

HUSH

8 Lancashire Court (off Brook Street), Mayfair, London, W1S 1EY, England

Tel: +44 (0)20 7659 1500, **www.**hush.co.uk
Hours: Mon-Sat 11am-11pm

Type: Lounge/restaurant bar
Alfresco: Courtyard dining in summer
Entry: Subject to capacity
Highlights: The atmosphere
Atmosphere: The kitchen of a great party
Clientele: City types & Mayfair set
Dress code: Suits, glamour, designer jeans
Price guide: ££££
Food: Potato wedges to caviar

Hush is owned by Jamie Barber and Geoffrey Moore (son of Roger) and sits serenely in its Georgian townhouse in a cobbled courtyard off Mayfair's Brook Street. Clement weather sees diners from the popular ground floor brasserie spill out into the courtyard in continental style.

The lounge bar and a second, more upmarket restaurant known as 'Hush Up' lie at the top of a wood and perspex staircase. The Hush lounge is a cosy den of 70s softness, with velour banquettes and satin cushions. But the place to blag is the intimate wood-lined boudoir that seats ten and is filled with deep cushions.

Hush is close to Bond Street and next to the Versace store, so caters for ladies who lunch and suited young gentry who gather to enjoy an array of superbly conceived cocktails mixed by a very able bar crew. All in all, a very civilised experience which can also be great fun.

KEMIA BAR

●●●◐○

Momo, 25 Heddon Street (off Regent St.), Soho, London, W1B 4BH, England

Tel: +44 (0)20 7434 2011
Hours: Mon-Tue 7pm-1am, Wed 7pm-2am, Thu-Sat 7pm-3am

Type: Members bar/club
Alfresco: No
Entry: Mon-Wed: invited guests, Thu-Sat: members only
Highlights: Atmosphere
Atmosphere: Full-on party
Clientele: Elegant, classy, fun-loving models
Dress code: Expensive & stylish but casual
Price guide: ££££
Food: Mezze-style, served 7pm-11.30pm

At the end of a tiny cul-de-sac just off Regent Street, a doorway nestles alongside the fashionable Momo restaurant whence a narrow staircase leads down to a tiny basement club. Walking into Kemia Bar for the first time is like stepping into a bedouin tent which has been erected in a cave to find a visiting North African band and its entourage celebrating their first number one hit.

Authentically decorated in an Algerian/Moroccan vein, this low vaulted, incense burning den is lined with leather, organza and luxurious silk drapes. With its celebrated music policy the Kemia Bar is a gem for the sophisticated partygoer.

Drinks and food are in keeping with the theme, so mint is delivered by the truck load to supply cocktails such as the refreshing Momo Special or the Pepe. The ethos behind Momos, as Kemia Bar is better known, is fun and the place is full of sophisticated, beautiful, stylish people having lots of it.

KETTNERS CHAMPAGNE ROOMS

●●●◐○

29 Romilly Street, Soho, London, W1D 5HP, England

Tel: +44 (0)20 7734 6112, **www.**pizzaexpress.com/kettners
Hours: Mon-Sun 11am-1am

Type: Champagne bar
Alfresco: No
Entry: Subject to space and attire
Highlights: Champagne list
Atmosphere: Relaxed
Clientele: Sloane set, actors, tourists, locals
Dress code: Smart/chic
Price guide: £££££
Food: Pizzetine & ciabatta sandwiches

Kettners was opened in 1867 by Auguste Kettner, chef to Napoleon III, and it is said that both Oscar Wilde and Edward VII ate here. (It's also said that Wilde used to take rent boys to the upstairs rooms.) It underwent various incarnations until 1979, when it was purchased by Peter Boizot, founder of the Pizza Express chain.

This place looks nothing like a Pizza Express outlet (although the pizzas are very good). Consisting of a series of simply decorated yet grand rooms with comfy leather armchairs and wooden floors, it has the air of a gentlemen's club without the pretension.

Kettners is one of London's original champagne bars and remains one of few still offering 32 Grand Marques. A refined place to meet friends or lovers and chat while a bottle chills in the bucket.

THE KINGLY CLUB

●●●●○

4 Kingly Court, Soho, London, W1B 5PW, England

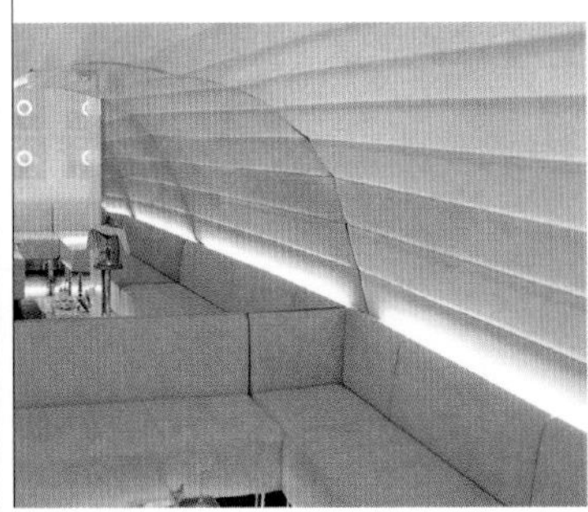

Tel: +44 (0)20 7287 9100, **www.**kinglyclub.co.uk
Hours: Mon-Sat 6pm-2am, Sun 6pm-12.30am

Type: Lounge bar, members club
Alfresco: No
Entry: Members & guest list
Highlights: Cocktails and vibe
Atmosphere: Relaxed
Clientele: Soho style set
Dress code: Anything but a tie
Price guide: ££££
Food: Sushi

This visually stunning bar sits in a subterranean tunnel that was once home to the legendary Pinstripe Club. During the 1960s it attracted famous revellers, allegedly including John Profumo and Christine Keeler, protagonists in the decade's greatest British sex scandal. However, the site was forgotten until the opening of The Kingly Club in August 2003.

The intimate space, with a capacity of only 125, is made to feel bigger thanks to mirrors, a white burnished, almost wet ice finish on the walls and some gorgeous fish tanks. Two intimate antechambers have cream leather booth seating.

This space age club can get claustrophobic but it always has atmosphere, beautiful people and great drinks.

Kentish Town
A400
Holloway
A503
Dry Martini
Method: Stir vermouth with ice and strain to discard excess, leaving the ice coated with vermouth. POUR Beefeater over vermouth coated ice, STIR and strain into a chilled glass.
Stop
Glass: Martini
Garnish: Olive or Lemon zest twist
3/4 measure Dry Vermouth
21/2 measures Beefeater
N
R
S
L
BEEFEATER
DRY GIN

Lotus Rooms

LAB

12 Old Compton Street (Charing Cross Rd end), Soho, London, W1V 5PG, England

Tel: +44 (0)20 7437 7820, **www.**lab-bar.com
Hours: Mon-Sat noon-midnight, Sun 3pm-10.30pm

Type: Lounge bar
Alfresco: No
Entry: Open to all subject to capacity
Highlights: Cocktails, atmosphere
Atmosphere: Party-like
Clientele: Young Soho set (20-35)
Dress code: Practically anything goes
Price guide: £££
Food: Food is not always available

Lab's name is a throwback to the long defunct London Academy of Bartenders, which was established by some of its founders, but this multi-award-winning venue remains a big name on the bar circuit.

The distinctive 70s retro decor sees rounded corners far outnumbering angles. The two long narrow, dimly lit bars (one on the ground floor, one in the basement) are either intimate or claustrophobic depending on your mood and the population density.

The beer and wine lists are also bijou, but if you drink anything other than a cocktail here you're missing out. The house cocktail style tends towards long fruity drinks rather than short strong ones. If the extensive list leaves you undecided, the bartenders will helpfully oblige with a recommendation.

Lab is busy pretty much nightly and even if there is no DJ expect loud music and a pumped up atmosphere. The bar attracts a friendly young crowd, mainly drawn from local offices.

LOTUS ROOMS

Bam-Bou, 1 Percy Street, Fitzrovia, London, W1P 0ET, England

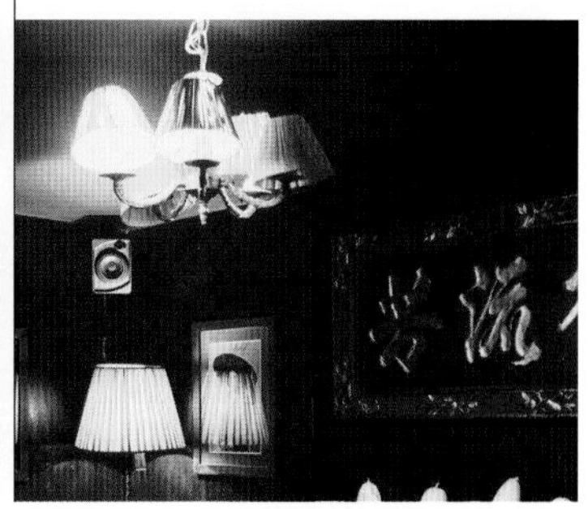

Tel: +44 (0)20 7323 9130, **www.**bam-bou.co.uk
Hours: Mon-Sat 6pm-1am

Type: Lounge bar / members bar
Alfresco: No
Entry: Members only (but try your luck)
Highlights: Atmosphere
Atmosphere: Mellow & relaxed
Clientele: Media types
Dress code: Designer, cool casual
Price guide: £££
Food: Prawn toast, spring rolls etc

This four-floored paean to French Vietnamese colonial style is quite seductive. The dark and lusty rooms, with cracked lacquered walls, are filled with opulent antiques and authentic furniture.

The ground and first floor restaurants serve Asian fare to diners. On the third floor, the bar is open to all and yet further up the winding staircase sits the tantalisingly titled Lotus Rooms. These are a series of small, interlocking rooms in an opium den vein, lined with comfy chairs and banquettes.

Appropriately themed around the Orient, many of the original cocktails are superb. The bar food continues the theme: dim sum are presented in steaming baskets. Chilled music, friendly armchair service and an open fire complete the karma-inducing experience.

Strictly speaking the Lotus Rooms are only open to members and their guests. However, my advice is to ring ahead. Unless there is a private booking you will probably be most welcome.

GARDEN
OF
EARTHLY
DELIGHTS
FAT CAP
JUSTICE

MATCH BAR

37-38 Margaret Street (nr Oxford Circus), London, W1G 0JF, England

Tel: +44 (0)20 7499 3443, **www.**matchbar.com
Hours: Mon-Sat 11am-midnight

Type: Lounge/restaurant bar
Alfresco: No
Entry: Subject to space rather than dress
Highlights: Cocktails
Atmosphere: Laid-back but bustling
Clientele: Business groups, friends, couples
Dress code: Anything goes - suits to jeans
Price guide: £££
Food: Cumberland sausage, tortillas, wraps, tapas, burgers etc.

Located just a stone's throw from Regent Street, Match consists of a small raised dining zone, a lengthy bar area which feels a little like a corridor and a cosy back room which is available for hire.

Like the other bars in the group, this place is primarily about good drinks, particularly cocktails. The list (as in the other two Match bars featured here) includes all the classics you'd hope for, as well as the many original cocktails created by Match bartenders over recent years. There is also a small but good selection of wines and beers.

The clientele is a mixture of the suited and the stylish and customers tend to get younger and more lively as the week draws to a close, when the atmosphere is usually DJ assisted. In this relatively small space, both the discerning, table-bound Martini drinker and the out & out party goer can be satisfied.

Milk & Honey

MILK & HONEY

●●●●●

61 Poland Street, Soho, London, W1F 7NU, England

Tel: 07000 655 469, **www.**mlkhny.com
Hours: Mon-Fri 7pm-3am, Sat 8pm-3am

Type: Members lounge club
Alfresco: No
Entry: Members only after 11pm (membership £250 p/a)
Highlights: Cocktails
Atmosphere: Relaxed/sombre
Clientele: Media & fashion kids
Dress code: Smart casual
Price guide: ££££
Food: Platters, oysters, caviar, venison etc.

Jonathan Downey, the man behind the Match bar chain, has teamed up with Sasha Petraske, owner of Milk & Honey in New York, to turn what was Papa Gaio into a larger copy of the famously secretive Manhattan club.

The austere exterior and lobby confer a satisfying feeling of entering a seedy den. Beyond are three dimly lit floors, all sharing the same 30s speakeasy decor. The two main bars are on the ground floor and basement with the smaller VIP 'Red Room' on the first floor.

The comfortably moody surroundings, secretive address and calm atmosphere, coupled with the best classic cocktails in London, make this a special place for seriously discerning drinkers. Members are requested to ring prior to visiting. Non-members can visit until 11pm provided a telephone reservation is made well in advance.

THE MET BAR

●●●● 

18-19 Old Park Lane, Mayfair, London, W1K 1LB, England

Tel: +44 (0)20 7447 4757, **www.**metropolitan.co.uk
Hours: Mon-Sat 10am-3am, Sun 10am-10.30pm

Type: Members' lounge bar
Alfresco: No
Entry: Strictly members & hotel guests
Highlights: Cocktails, music, atmosphere
Atmosphere: Chilled/late night party
Clientele: Celebs, hotel guests, music & media
Dress code: Gorgeously casual
Price guide: ££££
Food: Nibbles from Nobu

When The Met first opened at the end of last century it was consistently rammed with 'A' list celebs while hordes of paparazzi froze their nuts off outside. Unfortunately, most of the celebs moved on to the next place to be seen and some of the magic was lost. While lesser bars would have relaxed their door policy, The Met stuck strictly to its members and guests only rule. The strategy paid off for the celebs and that famous Met atmosphere have returned. On a good night it's like being at a friend's house party only with great DJs, bartenders and the odd TV personality.

With the exception of a new mural depicting people dancing, the decor has changed little. The original red, diner-style booths and tables are still crammed into a surprisingly small space. But The Met is about the music, the cocktails and the atmosphere, all of which can be fantastic. Unless you are a member, however, you'll need to book a room.

MEZZA

●●●  ○

100 Wardour Street, Soho, London, W1F 0TN, England

Tel: +44 (0)20 7314 4002, **www.**conran.com
Hours: Mon-Thu noon-2am, Fri-Sat midnight-3am

Type: Tapas bar
Alfresco: No
Entry: Subject to capacity
Highlights: Sherry, tapas & cocktails
Atmosphere: Loud, informal and fun
Clientele: After work & out of towners
Dress code: Casual to suits
Price guide: £££
Food: Spanish tapas

This bar, on the ground floor of Conran's old Mezzo building, has attracted much less press coverage than the larger Floridita restaurant below. But this slick Conran operation is certainly worthy of attention. The sherry list alone features more than twenty bins and the forty strong wine list is almost exclusively Spanish. The Hispanic theme continues throughout the menu, which features Spanish liqueurs, Spanish brandy and of course tasty tapas. The extensive cocktail list features classic drinks as well as contemporary interpretations, all prepared to a high standard.

Sit at the chef's counter, at the sweeping, pebble-fronted bar or at one of the many oak trimmed tables. The fortunate few score one of the four intimate booths. The decor is clean and modern and the atmosphere informal and fun. You'll find a mixed bunch of after workers alongside Conran fans from out of town.

MORTON'S

●●●●○

28 Berkeley Square, Mayfair, London, W1J 6EN, England

Tel: +44 (0)20 7499 0363, **www.**mortonsclub.com
Hours: Mon-Sat 8am-3am

Type: Members/lounge bar
Alfresco: No
Entry: Member and guests only
Highlights: Service
Atmosphere: Posy but relaxed
Clientele: Sloanes & mature trustafarians
Dress code: Smart/designer casual
Price guide: £££££
Food: Nibbles & platters

There has been a club called Morton's in a Georgian townhouse on Berkeley Square, Mayfair, for as long as I can remember but a change in ownership saw an altogether plusher space emerge in May 2004.

The new interior mixes original fixtures with contemporary decor. In the basement private dining room guests sit among the 2,300 bins that comprise the very impressive wine list. The ground floor bar features tan, stitched leather on both walls and banquettes, while handcrafted glass adorns the bar top. Backlit panels along one wall change hue to moderate the mood as the day progresses. A restaurant lies at the top of a sweeping staircase.

Five star service prevails throughout, while the Champagne and cocktail offerings live up to the standards set by the sommeliers. Morton's attracts a range of moneyed types who are happy to part with the £800 a year membership fee.

THE PLAYER LOUNGE BAR & KITCHEN

●●●●○

8 Broadwick Street, Soho, London, W1F 8HN, England

Tel: +44 (0)20 7494 9125, **www.**theplyr.com
Hours: Mon-Thu 5.30pm-1am, Fri 5.30pm-1am, Sat 6pm-3am

Type: Members lounge bar
Alfresco: No
Entry: Door charge may apply (members only after 11pm)
Highlights: Cocktails
Atmosphere: Club-like
Clientele: Young Soho set
Dress code: Designer jeans
Price guide: £££
Food: Spare ribs, crab fritters, cheese fondue

A simple doorway in the heart of Soho, the entrance to The Player would look complete if it had a sign saying 'model downstairs', a feel which is further enhanced by the lingerie in the window of Agent Provocateur next door. In fact, the basement houses a well stocked bar complete with black leather banquette seating and scarlet walls.

When The Player first opened in September 1998, it enjoyed immediate success, partly due to the presence of bar guru Dick Bradsell. However, he left, there were 'licensing difficulties' and eventually the Player closed. It was reopened by Jonathan Downey's Match group in October 2001, looking and feeling even better than it did before, with Dale DeGroff (New York's legendary bar meister) overseeing the excellent cocktails.

The Player attracts a young crowd partly drawn from nearby media and film companies.

THE RED LION

●●●◐○

1 Waverton Street (opp. Charles St.), Mayfair, London, W1J 5QN

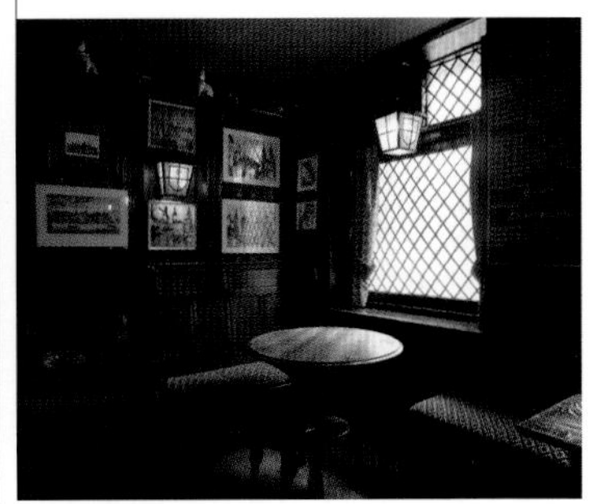

Tel: +44 (0)20 7499 1307
Hours: Mon-Fri 11:30-11pm, Sat 11:30pm-3pm & 6pm-11pm, Sun noon-3pm & 7pm-11pm

Type: Traditional pub
Alfresco: No
Entry: Open door
Highlights: Heritage & atmosphere
Atmosphere: Warm & convivial
Clientele: Well-heeled
Dress code: Not too casual - suits
Price guide: £££
Food: Fish & chips, pies, burgers etc.

With its quaint lattice windows and back street location, The Red Lion has the look and feel of a country pub. Originally it was. Back in the 18th century, it stood on an unmade road, close to the grounds of Chesterfield House, lordly seat of the Earls of Chesterfield. The house was demolished in 1937 and the old stable buildings that used to surround the pub were replaced with the grand houses we see today.

The interior has altered over the years as the clientele changed from stable lads to captains of industry. However, it retains an olde-worlde charm with open fires, a low ceiling, bare floorboards and dark panelled walls adorned with old prints and topped by shelves lined with Toby jugs, tea pots and other chinaware. Winged settles (high backed benches) add to its traditional appeal.

This little pub is busy enough at lunchtimes and early evening to justify as many as five traditional cask ales on draught. There's also a fair wine offering and reasonably priced pub grub.

REFUEL BAR

The Soho Hotel, 4 Richmond Mews, Richmond Buildings (off Dean St), Soho, London, W1D 3DH, England

Tel: +44 (0)20 7559 3000, **www.**sohohotel.com
Hours: Mon-Sat noon-3pm & 6pm-11pm, Sun noon-3pm & 6pm-10.30pm

Type: Lounge/hotel/restaurant bar
Alfresco: No
Entry: Subject to capacity
Highlights: Cocktails & champagne
Atmosphere: Relaxed
Clientele: Hotel guests and media office escapees
Dress code: Smart/casual
Price guide: £££££
Food: Platters serve 4 (e.g. Italian or Moroccan)

The Soho Hotel opened in summer 2004 at the end of a cul-de-sac off Dean Street and it's hard to believe that this slick boutique environment was constructed in the shell of a former multi-storey car park. The Refuel bar lies next to the hotel's restaurant, beyond the lobby and its impressive giant bronze cat.

The fairly bland room is dominated and brightened by a specially commissioned mural which illustrates the site's previous incarnation. Below it runs a long pewter bar lined with high stools, while low slung sofas and coffee tables occupy the narrow space between the bar and the restaurant.

Soho's most stylish media set appear to have settled in here, appreciating the efficient service offered by the friendly staff. A comprehensive champagne and wine list and an inspired range of excellent cocktails enhance the draw.

REX CINEMA & BAR

21 Rupert Street, Soho, London, W1V 7FE, England OR 13 Coventry Street, W1V 7FE

Tel: +44 (0)20 7287 0102, **www.**rexcinemaandbar.com
Hours: Tue-Sat 6pm-3am

Type: Lounge bar/nightclub/cinema
Alfresco: No
Entry: Members have priority
Highlights: Cocktails, films
Atmosphere: Chilled to full-on party
Clientele: Young social climbers
Dress code: Bling
Price guide: ££££
Food: Sushi, gourmet pizza, club sandwiches & desserts

A bouncer, a clipboard toting accomplice and a velvet rope protect the entrance to this subterranean art nouveau styled lounge. Deep velvets and crystal chandeliers contrast with raw exposed brickwork to create a feel rather similar to a film set.

Beyond the bar and a lobby-like space is a small but plushly appointed 75-seat cinema which screens current, classic and pre-release films (the Rex is named after a pre-war cinema group). Membership costs £250 per annum but provides free access to both bar and cinema.

The female-led bar team at Rex offer a great list of classically inspired cocktails which are brilliantly executed and delivered to your table. The atmosphere is more club-like towards the end of the week and at weekends, when DJs often play.

RIVOLI BAR

Ritz Hotel, 150 Piccadilly, London, W1J 9BR, England

Tel: +44 (0)20 7493 8181, **www.**theritzhotel.co.uk
Hours: 11:30am-11pm (1am for hotel residents)

Type: Hotel / lounge bar
Alfresco: No
Entry: Subject to dress
Highlights: Art Deco interior, cocktails
Atmosphere: Somewhat staid
Clientele: Trustafarians & crusty Mayfair money
Dress code: Gents must wear jacket & tie, no jeans
Price guide: £££££
Food: Posh sandwiches, sushi, omelette, salad Niçoise etc

When Cesar Ritz opened this graceful old hotel on 24th May 1906 it featured spectacular innovations such as a bathroom for each guestroom and double glazing. It was the first steel framed building of any significance in London and was praised for its French chateau style architecture and Louis XVI furnishings. Thanks to recent refurbishment it still oozes style and opulence, which continue in the Rivoli Bar just off the grand 'Long Gallery'.

Entering the Rivoli is like stepping into a bygone era. The interior is classic 1920s Art Deco. An onyx marble bar is surrounded by walls of polished camphor wood and illuminated Lalique glass panels. Etched glass windows peek onto Piccadilly. Four panels of verre églomisé (gilded and silvered mirror glass) reflect gilt leaf ceiling domes and polished bamboo.

This ornate room accommodates a mere 44 guests but it does so in some style. Champagne and well made cocktails are delivered by table service.

SANDERSON HOTEL BARS

●●●●○

Long Bar & Purple Bar, 50 Berners Street, Fitzrovia, London, W1P 3AD, England

Tel: +44 (0)20 7300 1400, **www.**sandersonhotel.com
Hours: Mon-Sat 11am-12.30am, Sun 11am-10.30pm

Type: Lounge/hotel bar
Alfresco: Courtyard
Entry: Hotel guests only in Purple bar
Highlights: Eye candy/pulling potential
Atmosphere: Chilled to party
Clientele: City boys, jet set, models
Dress code: To the hilt
Price guide: £££££
Food: Finger food - foie gras, smoked salmon

The jewel of Ian Schrager's Starck-designed Sanderson hotel, the Purple bar is like travelling celebrity class to Wonderland. It's snug and dimly lit, with miniature tables and chairs, decoratively cut mirror work and opulent deep purple furnishings in front of a solid stone bar. But you'll need to book a room as the Purple bar is designed for VVIPs and hotel residents only.

The Long Bar, Sanderson's slightly less exclusive second bar, is, well, long. The island bar sits in the centre of the white room, allowing the finance/fashion clientele, who ooze cash from every orifice, to check each other out from opposite sides.

Outside, a wooden decked courtyard with bamboo, candles, slate and running water is welcome relief. Grab yourself a seat and ask one of the waitresses who slink about in black dresses for the oversized cocktail list. Whatever you choose is likely to be eminently drinkable.

SHOCHU LOUNGE

Roka, 37 Charlotte Street, Fitzrovia, London, W1T 1RR, England

Tel: +44 (0)20 7580 6464
Hours: Mon-Sat 5.30pm-midnight, Sun 5.30pm-11pm

Type: Lounge bar
Alfresco: No
Entry: Subject to management & capacity
Highlights: Cocktails, spirits & food
Atmosphere: Chilled
Clientele: Mature office escapees
Dress code: Smart/casual
Price guide: £££
Food: Japanese farmhouse cuisine

Nestling below Roka, the West End sister restaurant to the stratospherically fashionable Zuma, this subterranean lounge takes its name from the traditional Japanese spirit. A kind of low-proof, flavoursome vodka, Shochu is very much the theme here and antique Japanese brewing and distilling vessels occupy a whole wall.

Various types of Shochu are available, either as a cocktail base or infused with flavours such as cherry blossom or green tea in one of the many glass jars that line the wall. Infusions are served in wonderful hand blown tumblers with a single huge ice cube chiselled from a large block of ice as you watch.

Beyond the natural timber island bar is a lounge area. I recommend the Japanese farmhouse nibbles from the kitchen above.

SKETCH

9 Conduit Street, Mayfair, London, W1S 2XG, England

Tel: +44 (0)8707 774 488, **www.**sketch.uk.com
Hours: Mon-Sat noon-2am

Type: Restaurant bar/supper club
Alfresco: No
Entry: Members and diners only
Highlights: Peeing in a pod
Atmosphere: Clinical to debauched
Clientele: Business types and the glamorous
Dress code: To the hilt
Price guide: ££££
Food: Finger food - foie gras, smoked salmon etc.

The interior of Sketch sets clinical 70s futurism against a grand backdrop. The high ceilings and detailing are original to the Georgian, Grade II listed building which houses this Michelin-starred restaurant, lounge and club.

Along with The Lecture Room, which is notoriously London's most expensive restaurant, Sketch also boasts a 150-seat brasserie-style restaurant with moving wallpaper called the Gallery, the East Bar and an affordable restaurant, Glade, in what was once the West Bar.

The East Bar is known as the capsule due to its ovoid design and is encircled by a double staircase which leads to the much talked about toilets, each housed in its own egg shaped white pod.

Sketch attracts a glamorous, well-heeled crowd, admitted because they have paid for annual membership or have previously reserved a table at one of the restaurants. Thanks to wonderfully polite staff the whole experience is far more approachable than it sounds - that's if your credit card is up to it.

SOHO HOUSE

40 Greek Street (corner Old Compton St), Soho, London, W1D 4EB, England

Tel: +44 (0)20 7851 1178, **www.**sohohouse.com
Hours: Mon-Sat noon-3am, Sun noon-10:30pm

Type: Members' club/restaurant/ lounge bar
Alfresco: Small roof deck
Entry: Members & guests only
Highlights: Exclusive retreat feel
Atmosphere: Relaxed, laid-back
Clientele: Folk from film, media & arts
Dress code: Stylish, designer casual
Price guide: ££££
Food: Plates to full meals

Soho House was founded in 1995 by Nick Jones, the husband of the TV newsreader Kirsty Young. It is a private members' club of some repute, popular with folk from the film and media industries - many of them celebrities.

There are two distinct sides to Soho House. One, accessed from an entrance at 21 Old Compton Street, houses a series of rooms and a loft terrace which can be hired by non-members for private functions or meetings. The other, quite separate, side is accessed from the members' entrance around the corner on Greek Street. This also consists of a series of rooms laid out over three floors with a first floor restaurant, second floor circle bar and a drawing room. My favourite area is the third floor Kitchen & Bar, an informal, open-plan restaurant and bar. A small roof deck offers views across the rooftops of Soho and is great for al fresco breakfasts, lunches or dinners.

Soho House is now rolling out globally - see New York for my take on Soho House New York.

TAMAN GANG

140a Park Lane (@ Oxford St), London, W1K 7AA, England

Tel: +44 (0)20 7518 3160, **www.**tamangang.com
Hours: Daily midday-1am

Type: Lounge/restaurant bar
Alfresco: No
Entry: Subject to management & capacity
Highlights: Cocktails & service
Atmosphere: Restrained
Clientele: Diners and a varied crowd
Dress code: Smart casual/designer
Price guide: ££££
Food: Pan-Asian

Owned by the founders of London's fashionable Chinawhite club, Taman gang takes its named from the Balinese for 'Park Lane'. Hidden in a basement under the Marriott Hotel near the corner of Park Lane and Oxford Street, its unassuming entrance belies the impressive space below.

The interior resembles a hidden chamber from Raiders Of The Lost Ark. Craftsmen were flown in from Bali to carve the limestone walls. The lighting is dim and the ceiling low, adding intimacy to the large room. The men's toilets feature erotic carvings and the women's have stalagmite and stalactite wash and dry units. These are something of a talking point among the glamorous folk Taman gang attracts.

This is primarily a restaurant but the small bar area is worth a visit in itself. Service is slick and both food and drinks are great. Cocktails are inventive, high quality and made with love.

TRADER VIC'S

Hilton Hotel (basement), 22 Park Lane, Mayfair, London, W1Y 4BE, England

Tel: +44 (0)20 7208 4113, **www.**tradervics.com
Hours: Mon-Thu 11.30am-3.30pm & 5pm-1am, Fri 11.30am-3.30pm & 5pm-3am, Sat 5pm-3am, Sun 5pm-10.30pm

Type: Lounge/cabaret/restaurant bar
Alfresco: No
Entry: Subject to management & capacity
Highlights: Cocktails
Atmosphere: Relaxed
Clientele: Suited older crowd
Dress code: Smart (but not strictly)
Price guide: £££££
Food: 'Tidbits' & 'bar bites' (try the Piri Piri Prawns)

In 1934, Victor Jules Bergeron, or Trader Vic as he became known, opened his first restaurant 'Hinky Dink's' in Oakland, San Francisco. Here he served Polynesian food with a mix of Chinese, French and American dishes cooked in Chinese wood-fired ovens. As well as his then exotic menu, Vic became famous for the rum based cocktails he created, particularly the Mai Tai.

He acquired the 'Trader' nickname due to offering free food and drinks to customers who brought him aged rums, which were then hard to obtain. After a trip to Tahiti in 1937 he changed the restaurant's name to Trader Vic's and the Tiki theme was born.

Vic died in 1984, but his brand lives on with branches around the world. I've visited a few and found this one to be by far the best. Here you'll find Vic's take on Polynesian food, great rum cocktails and South Pacific themed decor including shark's teeth, puffer fish and hand carved Tiki poles.

BEEFEATER & ELDERFLOWER

Glass: Tall
Garnish: Mint sprig
2 measures Beefeater
1 measure Elderflower cordial
Top up with chilled sparkling water
Method: Pour ingredients into ice-filled glass and lightly stir. Serve with straws.

VOLSTEAD

●●●●○

9 Swallow Street (btwn Regent Street & Piccadilly), Mayfair, London, W1R 7HD, England

Tel: +44 (0)20 7287 1919, **www.**volstead.com
Hours: Tue-Sat 7pm-3am

Type: Lounge bar / micro club
Alfresco: No
Entry: Arrive early towards the weekend
Highlights: Cocktails
Atmosphere: Chilled to mini party
Clientele: Mayfair in-crowd
Dress code: Designer lounge
Price guide: ££££
Food: Posh mini burgers, chips & caviar

Volstead is a 1920s inspired lounge-cum-club ironically named after Andrew Volstead, who created the act which launched Prohibition in the US. Although this is an intimately sized space – the capacity is only 150 - the owners, who also run Cocoon, have managed to squeeze in a small dancefloor complete with a decanter encrusted DJ booth. They have also managed to entice the flamboyant Mikey and Andreas away from Momo's Kemia Bar to draw Mayfair's moneyed and gorgeous set to their new place.

Banquettes line walls still clad with original strip mirrors from a previous incarnation as Sybilla's Club, an elite 1960s venue backed by the Beatle George Harrison and friends. The lighting is suitably dim and the DJ steers the mood from early evening cocktail jazz through lounge to out & out club as the atmosphere picks up.

The spirits offering is dominated by American whiskies and gin, as is the cocktail list, which features audacious contemporary creations rather than the predictable classics you might expect in a retro lounge. Alternatively wash the wagyu beef burgers down with vintage Veuve Clicquot, Dom Perignon or Krug, which are all available by the glass.

ZETA

●●●●○

35 Hertford Street (under Hilton Hotel), Mayfair, London, W1Y 7TG, England

Tel: +44 (0)20 7208 4067, **www.**zeta-bar.com
Hours: Mon-Tue 5pm-1am, Wed-Fri 5pm-3am, Sat 5pm-3am, Sun 8pm-1am

Type: Lounge bar
Alfresco: No
Entry: Members take precedence
Highlights: Atmosphere
Atmosphere: Party
Clientele: City crowd & the style set
Dress code: Casually couture
Price guide: ££££
Food: Oriental influence

Zeta is one of London's funkiest hotel bars, so you'll be surprised to hear that the name was inspired not by the sixth letter of the Greek alphabet, but by the brand name of a fire bell Robbie Bargh (the consultant behind this bar) spotted in another bar's toilets.

The interior has a subtly Oriental theme with delicate looking illuminated walls that appear to be made from brown packing paper. Apart from the odd out of place guest from the Hilton upstairs and businessmen celebrating winning or losing an award in another Park Lane hotel, Zeta is packed with city boys and model types enjoying sublime drinks from the impressive cocktail list.

Friday and Saturday nights here are huge. Subdued lighting, comfy chairs, attentive staff and DJs spinning chilled tunes combine to make this one of the hottest hotel bars in town.

Zeta

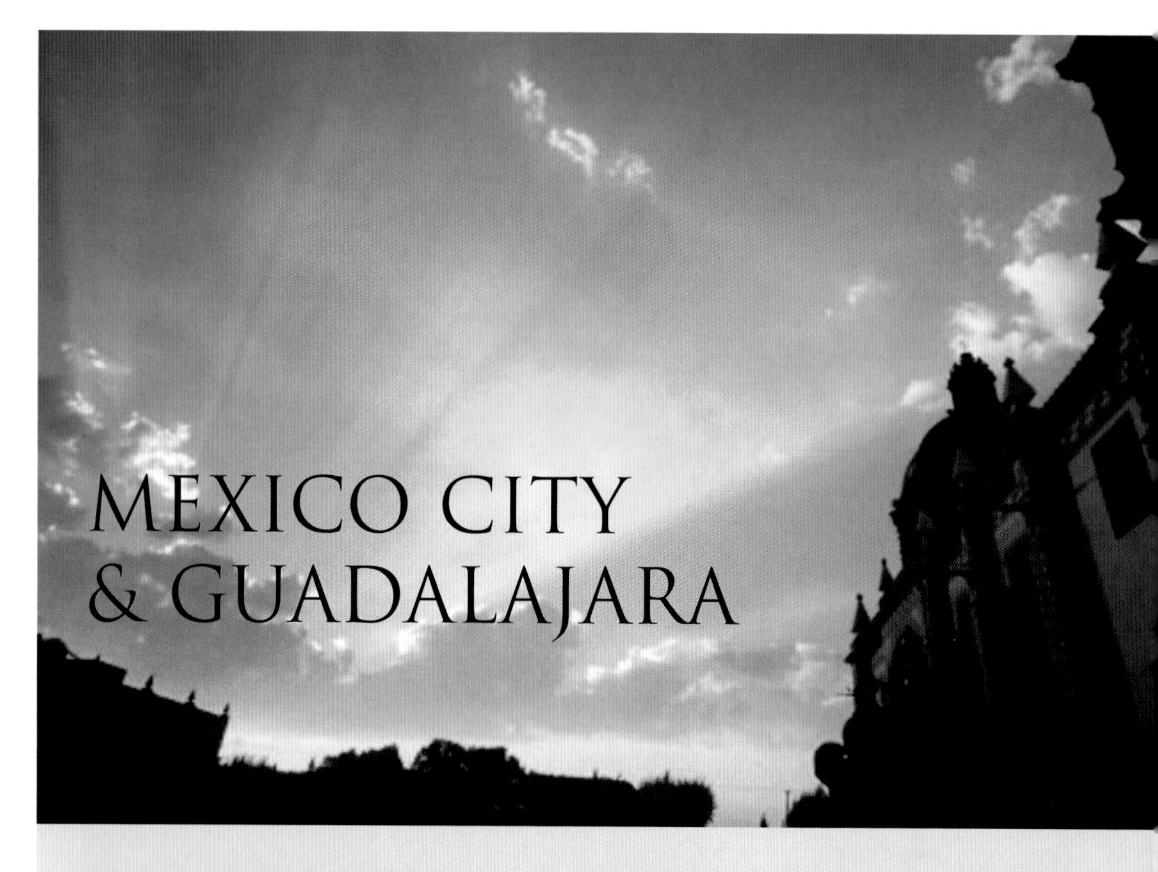

MEXICO CITY & GUADALAJARA

Airport (Mexico City): Benito Juárez International (MEX)
Airport (Guadalajara): Guadalajara Miguel Hidalgo (GDL)
Time zone: Central Time (GMT -6 hours)
Currency: Mexican Peso ($)

I've included Mexico's second city with our coverage of Mexico City as any discerning drinker staying in the capital should take the hour long flight or five hour drive to Guadalajara, the centre of the Tequila industry.

Mexico City is a sprawling city, and one of the world's largest. At 2,350m (7,350 feet) above sea level it is also the world's highest big city and some visitors suffer mild altitude sickness. Flanked by the Popocatepetl and Iztaccihuatl volcanoes, it lies in the base of a natural bowl, ringed by the Sierra Madre Mountains, which contributes to its extraordinarily high pollution. Armed street crime and kidnappings are rife, and I recommend exercising caution on public transport and traveling by telephone taxi after dark.

That said, Mexico City is also a vibrant city with a nightlife that only Latin America seems able to offer. The hub of the ancient Aztec Empire and the oldest capital of the New World,its aptly named Historic Centre (Centro Histórico) boasts relics and architecture from the Aztec and Colonial periods with Art Nouveau and Art Deco thrown in.

In the state of Jalisco, west central Mexico, and 1,552 metres (5,091 feet) above sea level, Guadalajara enjoys spring temperatures and abundant sunshine most of the year. This modern industrial city shares some of the crime problems of the capital but is more approachable with tree lined streets and majestic colonial buildings.

But for me the real reason to visit Guadalajara lies an hour's drive (35 miles/56 km) to the west on Hwy 15. Here you'll find the town of Tequila, surrounded by plantations of blue agave and home to a dozen distilleries. (Mexico's other major tequila region, Los Altos (the Highlands) is roughly the same distance away to the north-east of Guadalajara.) The villages around Guadalajara are a souvenir hunter's dream and the city is often said to be Mexico's retirement capital – so you'll meet plenty of American ex-pats.

Mexico Hotels

Mexico City is huge and sprawling but most of its decent hotels are clustered in the districts of Colonia Polanco, Zona Rosa and La Condesa. In this tough, crime-ridden city it's worth spending a little more to have a luxurious and secure base from which to explore.

There are few really stylish hotels in Guadalajara. Hotel Quinta Real stands head and shoulders above its nearest rivals such as Camino Real Hotel (www.caminoreal.com/guadalajara).

In both cities the better hotels have purified water and extended room service, and will be happy to arrange drivers to ferry you around – a luxury I'd strongly advise. The rainy season is June through September and, unless you're driven by discounted rack rates, these months are best avoided.

CONDESA df

102 Avenida Veracruz, Colonia Condesa, Mexico City, 06700, Mexico
Tel: +52 55 5241 2600,
www.condesadf.com
Group: Grupo Habita

Situated in the fashionable Condesa neighbourhood ('DF' stands for Distrito Federal), this is the sister to Habita, Mexico City's first boutique hotel. CONDESA df is arranged around a leafy triangular internal courtyard within a converted 1920s French Neoclassical apartment block. Its forty rooms and suites are decorated in subdued shades of cream, chocolate and turquoise with terrazzo tiling and walnut panelling, and mod-cons include air-con, iPods and wireless internet. The hotel has a cinema, a nightclub, a bar, a sushi bar (reviewed overleaf) and a swimming pool.

Four Seasons Hotel

500 Paseo de la Reforma, Colonia Juárez, Mexico City, 06600, Mexico
Tel: +52 55 5230 1818,
www.fourseasons.com/mexico
Group: Four Seasons Hotels and Resorts

This Mexico City outpost offers the classical opulence you'd expect from the luxury hotel brand across 200 rooms and 40 suites. Opened in 1994, the hotel resembles an eight-storey Mexican colonial mansion built around a landscaped, cloistered courtyard with a fountain. Even the 'moderate rooms' are elegantly appointed with wifi internet access and a marble bathroom with deep tub and separate shower. The luxury extends to a sun deck and outdoor elve acres of gardens and courtyards.

Habita Hotel

201 Avenida Presidente Masaryk, Colonia Polanco, Mexico City, 11560, Mexico
Tel: +52 55 5282 3100,
www.hotelhabita.com
Group: Grupo Habita

Mexico City's first boutique style hotel, Habita is housed in a functionalist 1950s apartment building wrapped in green frosted glass. It lies in the upscale Polanco neighbourhood on the city's most exclusive shopping street.

Its 32 rooms and four suites are minimalist in design but spacious, comfortable and well-equipped with broadband internet access, air-con and safes large enough to hold laptops. The seventh floor roof terrace is home to one of the city's most fashionable bars (reviewed overleaf) and the lower terrace houses a small pool, jacuzzi and gym.

Quinta Real Hotel

2727 Av. México, Fraccionamiento Monraz, Guadalajara, Jalisco, 44680, Mexico
Tel: +52 33 3669 0600,
www.quintareal.com
Group: Quinta Real Grand Class Hotels and Resorts

Quinta Real offers palatial luxury in a setting reminiscent of a colonial hacienda with antique-style furniture, original works of art, stucco ceilings, ivy-covered pink stone walls and cobbled walkways through lush gardens. The first of twelve such hotels across Mexico, it opened in 1986.

The fifty Master Suites and twenty-five Grand Class Suites all have marble bathrooms with a bathtub while the Presidential Suite offers a Jacuzzi, separate shower and terrace. Amenities include a regarded restaurant and outdoor swimming pool.

W Hotel

252 Campos Eliseos, Polanco, Mexico City, CP 11560, Mexico
Tel: +52 55 9138 1800,
www.whotels.com
Group: Starwood Hotels and Resorts

Situated in the trendy Polanco neighbourhood, this is the first W hotel in Latin America and its purpose-built 25-storey tower makes an impressive beginning. All 237 guest rooms feature cherry red décor, all-white beds and amenities such as hammock (in the bathroom), 29" interactive TV, CD & DVD player and minibar, plus more mundane essentials such as wifi internet. If you're feeling flush consider one of the Loft rooms or WOW Suites.

Mexico Restaurants

Forget your experiences at the local Tex-Mex - real Mexican food is amongst the world's most innovative, and stodgy dishes such as burritos, fajitas, taco shells and nachos are in fact of US origin. The indigenous mainstays of Mexican cuisine - such as chillis, tomatoes, potatoes, pumpkin, avocado, turkey, cocoa and vanilla - weren't even known to Europeans until well into the 15th century. Today's 'traditional' Mexican cuisine incorporates Hispanic and more general European influences. The most contemporary Mexican chefs also draw inspiration from Asia, while the cosmopolitan capital, like most big cities, offers a range of cuisines.

Mariachi music originated in the state of Jalisco and it is common for Mariachi bands dressed in black, silver-studded suits and large hats to roam Guadalajara's restaurants in search of patrons to serenade. They may cost more than your main course but their music is sure to help make the meal memorable. You'll also find Mariachi bands in Mexico City and Bar Jorongo in the Sheraton Maria Isabel Hotel attracts the biggest names.

Although hygiene standards are reasonably good you should avoid consuming tap water (unless purified by your hotel), salads, uncooked vegetables, unpeeled fruit and undercooked meat and fish.

Adonis

424 Calle Homero, Colonia Polanco, Mexico City, 11560, Mexico
Tel: +52 55 5531 6940
Cuisine: Lebanese

This Lebanese restaurant is renowned for its Middle Eastern and North African dishes. The décor and music will transport you to the east.

Asador La Vaca Argentina

25 Tomàs V. Gómez, col. Ladrón de Guervara, Guadalajara, Jalisco, México
Tel: +52 55 3615 2412
Cuisine: Argentinian

Practically opposite La Tequila (see under bars), this very popular restaurant is known for its steaks.

Los Almendros

164 Campos Elíseos, Colonia Polanco, Mexico City, Mexico
Phone: +52 55 5531 6646
Cuisine: Traditional Mexican

Close to the Habita Hotel, this is one of the best restaurants in Mexico City to experience real Mexican food. Expect hard-to-pronounce traditional dishes wonderfully spiced with habañero chillis and red onions.

La Casa de las Sirenas

32 Republica Guatemala, Centro Histórico, Mexico City, Mexico
Tel: +52 55 5704 3225
Cuisine: Mexican/Tex-Mex

Spread over four floors of a 16th-century mansion at the foot of the Templo Major ruins, this restaurant and bar has a spectacular setting. Its two bars offer over 250 varieties of tequila but the top floor restaurant with its terrace overlooking the cathedral makes it a must visit.

Cícero Centenario

195 Londres, Colonia Juárez, Mexico City, 06000 Mexico
Tel: +52 55 5518 4447
Cuisine: Modern Mexican

Tucked away in an 18th-century mansion, Cícero Centenario's interior is baroque (think Parisian brothel) and its food excellent. It's fashionable with the in crowd, as is the sister restaurant of the same name in Zona Rosa (+52 55 5525 6130).

Hacienda de los Morales

Col. Del Bosque, Polanco, Mexico City, 115110, Mexico
Tel: +52 55 5096 3054, www.haciendadelosmorales.com

This gourmet restaurant is one of a number of function rooms and bars located in a magnificent 16th century hacienda and its grounds. It's a tad formal but is noted for serving excellent traditional Mexican cuisine.

Ixchel

65 Medellín (@ Colima), Colonia Roma, Mexico City, Mexico
Tel: +52 55 5208 4055
Cuisine: Asian-Mediterranean fusion

Ixchel is fashionable with successful Mexican media types and is situated in a colonial-era mansion in the heart of Roma. Its terrace bar and blue velvet lounge are great places to enjoy a Margarita before or after dinner.

Kohinoor

999 Guillermo Gonzalez Camarena, Santa Fe, Mexico City, Mexico
Tel: +52 55 5292 1291
Cuisine: Indian

Mexicans have spice enough in their own cuisine so good Indian restaurants are relatively rare in Mexico City. However, if you need a curry fix then Kohinoor is the best in town. The decor is clean and bright and you can watch the chefs at work through the large glass window.

Les Moustaches

88 Río Sena, Cuauhtemoc, Mexico City, Mexico
Tel: +52 55 5533 3390, www.lesmoustaches.com.mx
Cuisine: French

Established in 1974, this regarded French restaurant is situated in a European style mansion near the US Embassy. Of its several rooms, the patio is the most attractive. Les Moustaches is particularly noted for its mussel soup and duck a l'orange.

El Sacromonte

1398 Pedro Moreno, Guadalajara, Jalisco, Mexico
Tel: +52 33 3825 5447
Cuisine: Traditional Mexican

This friendly little restaurant serves traditional Mexican dishes in a courtyard setting with a pianist playing over the natter of locals and ex-pats. You'll be one of the few tourists here but will be made to feel very welcome.

San Angel Inn

50 Calle Diego Rivera (@ Altavista), Colonia San Angel Inn, Mexico City, 01060, Mexico
Tel: +52 55 5616 1402, www.sanangelinn.com
Cuisine: International

Set in a 17th century hacienda on a cobbled street, this restaurant is a favourite with leading business folk. The food is good, and the Margaritas served in small silver carafes with accompanying mini ice-buckets are even better, and best enjoyed in the pretty courtyard. The wine list is also noteworthy.

Villa Maria

704 Homero, Colonia Polanco, Mexico City, Mexico
Tel: +52 55 5203 0306
Cuisine: Modern Mexican

This lively restaurant is famous for its creative Mexican menu and signature Tamarind Margarita. Set over two floors, downstairs is more casual with mariachi bands providing entertainment, while upstairs is more formal.

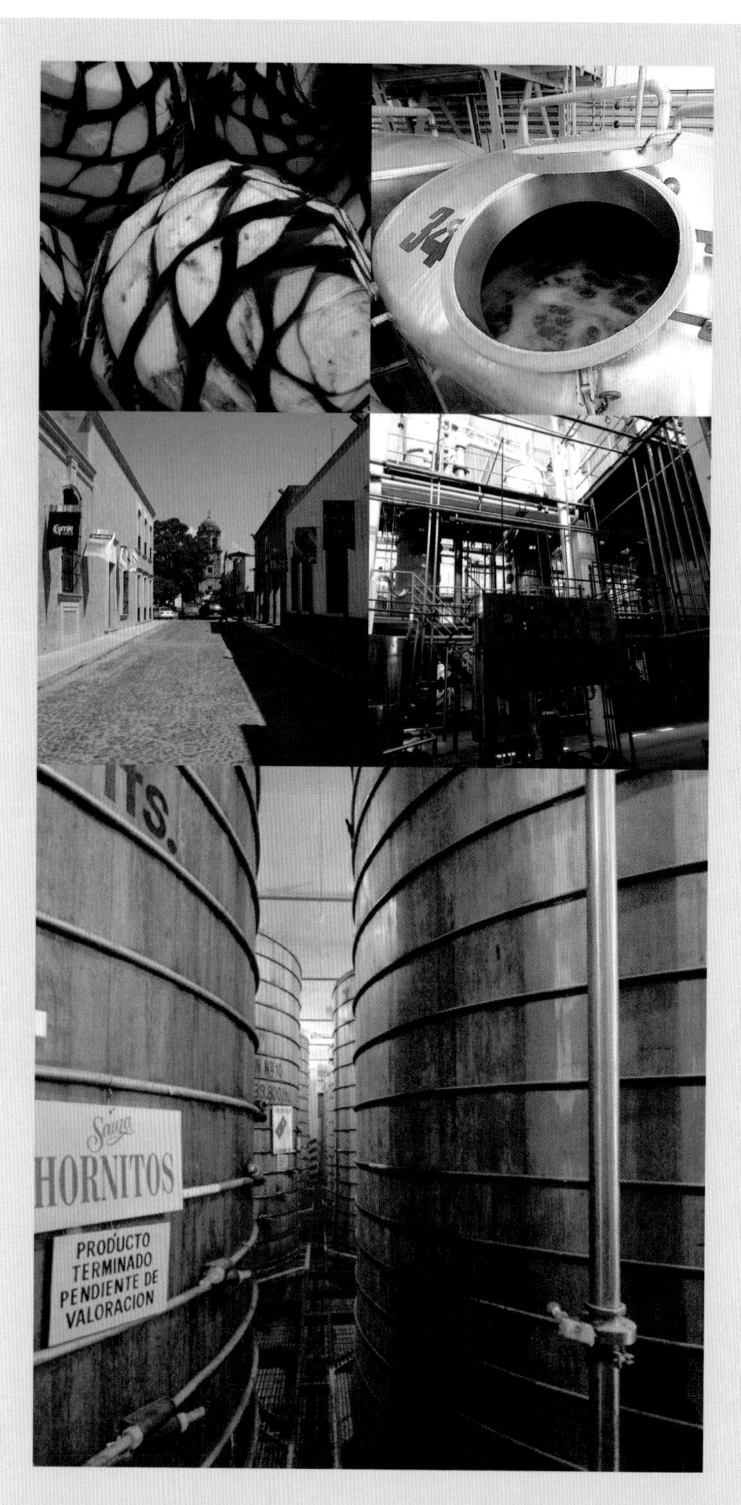

Sauza & Mexico

Sauza Tequila takes its name from Don Cenobio Sauza, the tequila pioneer who founded the brand in 1873, in the distillery where Sauza is still made today. He was the first distiller to label his agave spirit 'tequila' - after the town in which he lived and worked and the first producer to export the newly-named category to the US. Don Cenobio is also credited with technical innovations such as heating stills indirectly, using steam coils, rather than relying on the harsher direct heating favoured by other distillers.

Today, Sauza is Mexico's best selling tequila and the world's fastest growing spirit. The company stays true to Don Cenobio's history of innovation and leads the industry in its development of nursery cultivation of agave plants. By careful selection at the nursery stage, Sauza ensures that only the best agave plants – those with the highest sugar content – will make it to maturity, when their 'piñas' (cores), will be harvested to make Sauza tequila. Given the plants take between eight and fourteen years to reach full maturity, the investment protects the quality of future production.

Anyone who has visited a Mexican bar will understand why we decided to work with a tequila brand when visiting these cities - and Sauza, the original tequila, was the obvious choice. Whether you are in Mexico City, Guadalajara or elsewhere in Mexico you'll find Sauza tequila well represented on bar shelves. Unless you're a connoisseur, you'll probably also find the selection quite bewildering. On the following page are my own personal favourites from the Sauza range (visit www.sauzatequila.com to see the complete selection).

TEQUILA

Sauza Hornitos

100% agave
Age: Rested in large American oak vats for a minimum of two months.

This reposado tequila is made in small batches to produce its distinctive flavour. Unusually, the production process involves baking the agave, rather than steaming it, which gives this tequila a slightly smoky flavour. The name 'Hornitos' means 'little ovens'.
Taste: A floral, almost minty nose leads to an elegant and subtle palate with muscovado sweetness balanced by light, smoky, earthy, herby, grassy agave notes with hints of citrus.

Sauza Tres Generaciones Plata

100% agave
Age: Unaged

The name means 'three generations', after the three generations of the Sauza family who built the parent brand. Unusually, this tequila is distilled three times rather than two.
Taste: A floral, fruity nose leads to a subtle palate with delicate fruity notes. This is a good tequila in which to sample finely distilled agave unimpeded by the influence of oak ageing.

Sauza Tres Generaciones Reposado

100% agave
Age: Three to four months in new 200 litre charged American oak casks

The reposado version of the three-times distilled tequila above.
Taste: A fruity, ripe banana, melon and agave nose leads to a fruity agave palate with nicely integrated smoky, spicy oak. The finish yields more spicy oak.

Sauza Tres Generaciones Añejo

100% agave
Age: More than two years in once used 200 litre bourbon casks

All the agave in this 100% agave tequila is grown on Sauza's own estate.
Taste: A woody, vanilla-ed, slightly chocolate nose leads to a big palate of smoky, spicy oak balanced by fruity agave, chocolate and vanilla and followed by a lasting oaky, white pepper and spice finish.

Mexico Drinking

Nightlife in both Guadalajara and Mexico City is lively and varied and you are likely to have a good time. Mexico City's most popular nightlife districts are Polanco, San Angel, Coyoacan, Condesa and La Zona Rosa. Polanco is the most upscale and Condesa the newest hot spot. Plaza Garibaldi, on Eje Central (between Republica de Honduras and Republica de Peru) is lined with bars and restaurants, and mariachi bands play from 8pm onwards.

Mexico City's style bar scene changes phenomenally rapidly and bars seem to have an all too brief honeymoon period with the style set. Many fail within six months of opening and bars that have been open for a year are regarded as positively geriatric and probably due a refit. In a city where cabs are problematic I would advise ringing a venue before you set off across town. (Thanks to everyone who recommended bars for me to visit: if your favourite isn't listed, it could well be closed.)

Traditional cantinas remain male bastions and unaccompanied women will definitely draw attention. One of the oldest and most tourist friendly is La Nueva Opera (reviewed here) and a visit is a must.

In most Mexican bars the drink of choice is tequila or beer ('cerveza'). Light lagers ('cerveza rubia') such as Corona are the most popular style but there are a few tasty dark beers ('cerveza oscura') such as the widely distributed Negra Modelo.

Although Mexico is the Americas' oldest wine producing nation, Mexicans are not big wine drinkers and most of the grapes grown are used for brandy, which the Mexicans are very fond of.

The national spirit is, of course, Tequila. Be sure not to confuse it with mezcal, a quite different Mexican spirit which is also made from the core (piña) of the agave plant. Mezcal generally has a distinctively smoky flavour and often comes with a pickled 'worm' (actually a moth larva) in the bottle. Tequila never contains a 'worm'.

Tequila can only be made in specified regions of Mexico and is categorised according to the percentage of agave spirit it contains and the ageing period it undergoes. The cheapest tequilas are a blend of not less than 51% agave spirit with sugar cane spirit and are referred to as 'mixto' tequilas. The best tequilas are 100% agave with no sugar or other spirit added and are consequently more expensive.

The different styles of tequila are divided as follows, according to age and colour. 'Blanco' (also known as 'silver' or 'plata') is a clear tequila which has not been oak aged. 'Gold' tequila (also known as 'oro' or 'joven abocado') is produced in the same manner as blanco tequila, but with the addition of flavouring and usually caramel colouring, and frankly is best avoided. 'Reposado' means 'rested' and to be labelled as such the tequila must have been matured in oak tanks for a minimum of 60 days and a maximum of one year. 'Añejo' tequilas must be aged in oak barrels no larger than 450 litres for at least a year. Tequilas can be aged for as long as ten years, and connoisseurs compare the best 100% agave añejo tequilas to fine French cognac. They are prepared to pay similarly high prices.

In Mexico, tequila is traditionally served at room temperature in a two-ounce 'caballito' shot glass (the name means 'little horse') accompanied by a glass of sangrita and sometimes also lime juice. Sangrita is a spicy, non-alcoholic chaser, generally made with tomato, orange juice, lime juice, pomegranate juice, salt and hot chilli sauce. The recipe for sangrita varies wildly from one bar to the next and you'll quickly recognise a good one from pre-mixed bottled ones.

There are no licensing hours in Mexico and nightlife kicks off and ends late, although most bars and nightclubs close on Sundays. Bars typically close around 1am while clubs usually stay open till at least 3am. The legal drinking age in Mexico is 18.

Unless you are in a very upscale bar or hotel, it's advisable to ask for drinks 'sin hielo' (without ice) as this is likely to be made with the local tap water: you should also be aware of this danger when ordering cocktails.

In Mexico City you should avoid hailing cabs on the street, particularly the ubiquitous green and white Volkswagen Beetles. Have the hotel or restaurant call a radio cab for you. If you're planning a bar crawl, then ask your hotel to quote for a driver for the night: a luxury that comes at a surprisingly reasonable price.

Warnings aside, Mexicans are friendly people and know how to enjoy themselves. You'll have a great time.

AREA BAR AND TERRACE

●●●○○

Sixth Floor, Hotel Habita, 201 Avenida Presidente Masaryk, Colonia Polanco, Mexico City, Mexico

Tel: +52 55 5282 3100, **www.**hotelhabita.com
Hours: Mon-Sat 5pm-2:30am

Type: Hotel roof bar
Alfresco: Yes
Entry: Via lobby lift
Highlights: View
Atmosphere: Relaxed to party
Clientele: Models and media types
Dress code: Fashionably casual
Price guide: $$$$
Food: Snacks & meals available

Hotel roof terrace bars are currently in vogue around the globe and the one atop the designer Habita hotel is one of the most fashionable places to be in Mexico City after midnight. Edged on two sides by high white tiled walls, the other two sides are open to views over the rooftops of Polanco. The scarlet lights that mark skyscraper peaks add to the backdrop, as for that matter do the advertisements, music videos and Pink Panther cartoons projected onto the adjacent office building. With local model agencies well represented, there is also plenty to see in the bar itself. Other entertainment comes courtesy of the DJ and quality sound system.

Comfy white cubed armchairs mix with modern white plastic chairs on the wooden decked floor, while the main design feature is a 12 foot fireplace. Hibita's back bar is devoid of bottles and judging by our two visits, decent cocktails too. However, the beers are cold and the scene hot.

BAR MILAN

18-24 Milán, Zona Rosa, Mexico City, Mexico

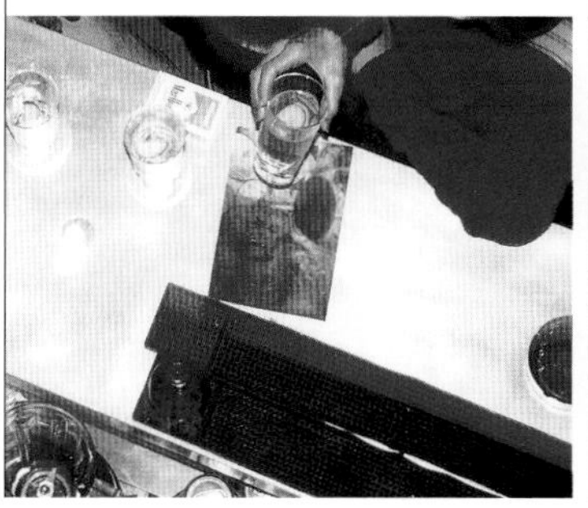

Tel: +52 55 5592 0031
Hours: Tue-Sat 6pm-3:30am, Sun 6pm-midnight

Type: Cantina-cum-club
Alfresco: No
Entry: Subject to management & capacity
Highlights: Atmosphere
Atmosphere: Rocking
Clientele: Young locals & tourists
Dress code: Casual
Price guide: $$$
Food: Tasty nibbles only

On the 1st of January 1993 three zeros were knocked off the Mexican currency: all of a sudden, a thousand pesos became just one. This may help to explain the popularity of Bar Milan, famous for operating its very own monetary system. Pass the bouncers on the door, follow the tunnel-like hallway through to the back and exchange your pesos for 'milagros' , the bar's own currency, whose name literally translates as 'miracles'. Work your way though the crowds of partying young locals to the bar and exchange your miracles for mojitos, the speciality here.

This is a hip place with a laidback party atmosphere, partly driven by the eclectic music which varies from rock to hip hop but is always loud. The décor is hip rather than designer with bare brick walls, a bizarre cactus-lined back bar and a spray-painted ceiling.

When leaving, remember to change what few miracles you have left back into pesos. They may not walk on water but they'll get you back to your hotel.

CAFEINA

73 Nuevo León, Condesa, Mexico City, Mexico

Tel: +52 55 5212 0090
Hours: Mon-Sun noon-2am

Type: Lounge bar
Alfresco: Narrow front terrace
Entry: Subject to management & capacity
Highlights: Cocktails, food, atmosphere
Atmosphere: DJ led
Clientele: Young, hip professionals
Dress code: Catwalk casual
Price guide: $$$$
Food: Extensive Italian menu

What makes some bars achingly fashionable while others just don't have it? Décor helps but celebrity patronage guarantees paparazzi and media attention which in turn drives style-conscious folk to vie behind the velvet ropes. Co-owned by Mexican actor Diego Luna, Cafeina really does have it.

Floor to ceiling sliding windows open onto a narrow terrace that runs the length of the frontage. The interior is decadent in feel. Black feather boas adorn one wall, and Persian rugs sit on a glossy white floor dotted with chaise longues and antique sofas juxtaposed with modern chrome wire chairs. A circular DJ booth takes centre stage and techno house blasts out, each beat shaking life into the otherwise slightly sterile candle-lit space.

The cocktail menu features Martinis listed under headings such as "Martini Classico" and "Popsicle Martini". The Italian menu is rather good and, like the chefs, the bartenders don't disappoint.

EL BAR

Four Seasons Hotel, 500 Paseo de la Reforma, Colonia Juárez, Mexico City, 06600, Mexico

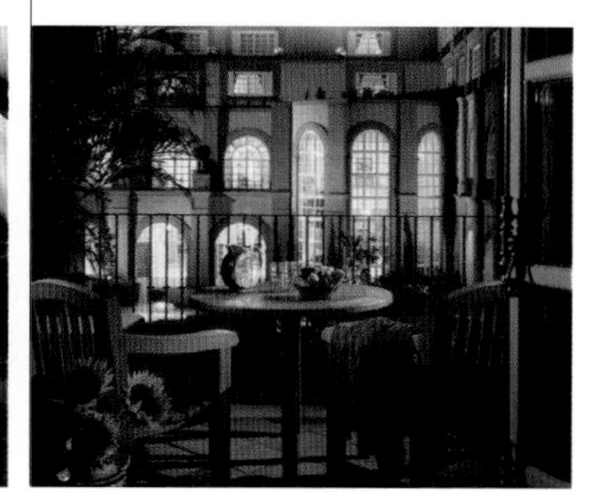

Tel: +52 55 5230 1818,
www.fourseasons.com/mexico
Hours: Mon-Fri 12:30pm-1am, Sat 1pm-1am, Sun 1pm-midnight

Type: Hotel lounge bar
Alfresco: Terrace
Entry: Via hotel lobby
Highlights: Tequila range, snacks
Atmosphere: Slightly staid
Clientele: Upmarket hotel guests & business types
Dress code: Nothing too casual
Price guide: $$$$
Food: Mexican hors d'oeuvres and appetisers

El Bar is a classically luxurious lounge in a classically luxurious hotel, which could, at first glance, be anywhere in the world: think polished wood, comfortable armchairs, high ceiling and book-lined walls. However, the contents of the cabinets on either side of the bar affirm that you are in Mexico, as this bar carries one of the largest ranges of 100% agave tequilas in the capital. (If the interior doesn't appeal, sit outside in the cloistered courtyard by the bubbling fountain.)

The service is excellent and, coupled with the range of tequila, makes this a great spot to conduct a comparative tasting. Classic cocktails are also competently made. During the week El Bar serves a daily changing lunch menu with Mexican hors d'oeuvres and appetizers during the evening.

A jazz trio grouped around the baby grand piano enlivens the otherwise staid atmosphere. This safe and luxurious bar suits the guests who choose to stay at this hotel.

LA NUEVA OPERA

10 Avenida Cinco de Mayo, Centro Histórico, Mexico City, Mexico

Tel: +52 55 5512 8959
Hours: Mon-Sat 1pm-midnight, Sun noon-6pm

Type: Traditional cantina
Alfresco: No
Entry: Open door
Highlights: History & décor
Atmosphere: Warm & friendly
Clientele: Locals of all walks
Dress code: Casual
Price guide: $$
Food: Not a place to eat

This downtown cantina is one of the oldest and most famous in Mexico. It dates back to around 1870 but little has changed since, oohhh, 1910, when the Mexican revolutionary hero Pancho Villa is said to have fired his revolver into the ceiling. You can still see the bullet hole – well, the black circle around it - roughly in the centre of the room, opposite the bar. Ask the bartender or one of the locals to point it out.

Stray away from beer or tequila here and you are likely to be disappointed. However, the grand old interior can't fail to impress. It's like walking into the saloon bar on a movie set, with ornate plaster ceilings, frosted windows, tiled floors, swirling carved wooden booth seating and long, dark wood bar counter.

The clientele ranges from old men who look as though they were here when Pancho got his gun out to trendy young couples stopping off between dinner and a club. Unlike your average Western saloon, however, the locals are a friendly bunch.

REXO

1 Saltillo (@ Vicente Suárez), Colonia Condesa, Mexico City, Mexico

Tel: +52 55 5553 5337
Hours: Mon-Sun 6pm-2am

Type: Lounge bar & restaurant
Alfresco: No
Entry: Subject to management & capacity
Highlights: Atmosphere
Atmosphere: Buzzy
Clientele: Diverse but hip
Dress code: Fashionably casual
Price guide: $$$
Food: Full menu

Exposed, black painted, industrial steel girders run across the ceilings of this clean and functional venue like old oak beams in a Tudor house. The space has been maximised in this small site by spreading the bar and restaurant across three floors, each connected by glass steps. The first two levels feature their own bar and sitting at the lower one is made more interesting by the glass back, which offers glimpses of passers-by. White walls are offset by black marble floors and white marble bar counters.

What the cocktails lack in finesse they make up for in potency, and they appear popular with a diverse bunch of regulars. Judging by my visits these include everything from the Condesa style set to courting couples and off-duty ambulancemen in uniform. Weekends are busier and more youthful.

SHELTY BAR

Nikko Hotel, 204 Avenida Campos Eliseos (facing Chapultepec Park), Colonia Polanco, Mexico City

Tel: + 52 55 5280 1111
Hours: Mon-Sat 4pm-1am, Sun 4pm-midnight

Type: Hotel lounge bar
Alfresco: No
Entry: Via lobby and lift or stairs
Highlights: Cocktails
Atmosphere: Lacking
Clientele: Business types
Dress code: No code but formal
Price guide: $$$$
Food: "Exquisite hors d'oeuvres"

I've seen Shelty described as similar to a British pub, but, as any Brit would tell you, that is way off the mark. Shelty is more like the lobby bar of a Scottish five star hotel. Red panelled walls and ceiling combine with a vibrant bottle green carpet, lurid cherry red armchairs, hunting prints, tartan and deer heads to create an effect every bit as tasteful as you'd expect from the second floor bar of a large, corporate hotel. Oh, and it lacks any atmosphere.

So why would you want to visit such a place? Great service and classic cocktails. If you're lucky, live piano music or sport on the television may help to liven things up. Alternatively, bring a posse and create your own vibe.

LA TEQUILA

●●●◐○

2916 Av. México, Guadalajara, Jalisco, Mexico

Tel: +52 33 3640 3110, **www.**latequila.com
Hours: Mon-Sat 6pm-1am

Type: Restaurant/lounge bar
Alfresco: No
Entry: Subject to management & capacity
Highlights: Food, tequila & cocktails
Atmosphere: Buzzy
Clientele: Locals & business types
Dress code: Nothing too casual
Price guide: $$$
Food: Great food, extensive Mexican menu

As the name would suggest, this restaurant and bar specialises in tequila. The ground floor restaurant serves decent traditional Mexican dishes and offers over 200 different types of tequila with which to wash them down. Antique photos of distilleries and plaques explaining tequila's history line the brick walls.

The upstairs bar also offers an extensive food menu and a good range of tequila but in a more informal, almost industrial setting with bare brick walls, exposed air-con ducting, high ceiling and back-lit bar with large sports screens. A huge bottle chandelier hangs over the slightly raised central dining area which is surrounded by underlit, glass-topped tables.

Food, service and cocktails are all good and this long established restaurant is popular with ex-pats and the business community. Pop in for a quick tequila and the pleasant atmosphere and plentiful supply of Japanese peanuts will lure you into staying all night.

LA TERRAZA

CONDESA df, 102 Avenida Veracruz, Colonia Condesa, Mexico City, 06700, Mexico

Tel: +52 55 5241 2600
Hours: Mon-Fri 6pm-11pm

Type: Hotel rooftop lounge
Alfresco: Yes
Entry: Via hotel lobby & lift
Highlights: Drinking alfresco
Atmosphere: Chilled
Clientele: Hip, fashionistas
Dress code: Designer casual
Price guide: $$$$
Food: Sushi

Like its sister hotel, Habita, CONDESA df is as much a fashionable night time entertainment destination as it is a traditional hotel. And La Terraza, its rooftop sushi bar, is one of the main attractions.

The V-shaped roof terrace looks down into the hotel's leafy central atrium and across the tree-lined avenues and park of Condesa. It is scattered with semicircular sofas, stools and patio heaters, with a sushi bar should you get peckish and a thermal bath should the mood take you. Like the rooftop bar of its Habita sibling, La Terraza is popular with local models and fashion types and access at weekends may be problematic if you're not a hotel resident.

A second bar lies downstairs, next to the restaurant. It is noted for its boudoir, a plush room with sofas, chocolate brown walls and thick carpets.

BAR TIKI

○○○○○

227 Querétaro, Colonia Roma, Mexico City, Mexico

Tel: +52 55 5584 2668, **www.**tiki.com.mx
Hours: Mon-Sat 6pm-late

Type: Tiki bar
Alfresco: No
Entry: Subject to management & capacity
Highlights: Cocktails
Atmosphere: TBC
Clientele: TBC
Dress code: TBC
Price guide: $$$$
Food: TBC

Those familiar with the London bar scene will be familiar with the names of Crispin Somerville and Jaspar Eyears, Englishmen who have foresaken Blighty to set up this Polynesian-themed bar in Mexico City.

Sadly, the slow progress of Mexican bureaucracy meant they had still not opened when I visited. However, those familiar with their previous operations will know to expect some pretty serious libations. Hence, I'm recommending it for cocktails without trying one. Email me and tell me if I got it wrong.

THE W LIVING ROOM

W Hotel, 252 Campos Eliseos Chapulaapec, Polanco, Mexico City, 11560, Mexico

Tel: +52 55 9138 1800, **www.**whotels.com
Hours: Sun-Wed 11pm-2am, Thu-Sat 11pm-4am

Type: Lobby lounge bar
Alfresco: Terrace
Entry: Via hotel lobby
Highlights: Cocktails
Atmosphere: Chilled
Clientele: Business types, leggy women & cool men
Dress code: Fashionably casual
Price guide: $$$$
Food: Mexican & Asian influenced seafood

Step through the front door of the W Hotel in Mexico City and you are greeted by the bar. How civilised! Turn left to check in at the glowing turquoise desk or dump your bags, turn right and lounge on the low slung, white leather cubed seating. The décor is ultra-modern. The sterile white walls, ceiling and floor are enlivened by scarlet lacquered cocktail tables and the red illuminated slots which dissect the walls. An opening in the floor reveals koi swimming in a pool which extends under the aptly named Red Lounge area. Stylish but rather uncomfortable-looking rectangular frame seats hang on chains from the ceiling.

This is one of the coolest W Hotel bars I've come across. It serves some of the best cocktails I've encountered in a W, with good renditions of classics plus contemporary offerings such as the Smoke Apple Cosmopolitan based on Ballantine's Scotch. If you're not in a cocktail mood then go for champagne, one of the four wines by the glass, or the ubiquitous Mexican beer.

photograph: linda duong

NEW YORK

Time zone: Eastern Standard Time (GMT -5 hours)
Airports: John F. Kennedy (JFK), La Guardia (LGA), Newark (EWR)

photograph: linda duong

This sprawling metropolis is one of the world's greatest and most cosmopolitan cities. Whether you most appreciate art, live music, culture, sport, shopping, eating or drinking, the Big Apple has it all on tap. And, thanks to its grid layout and numbered naming system, even the most befuddled imbiber will find it simple to navigate.

December through March can be frosty in the extreme, while in the summer the heat and humidity can be vicious. But, with the dollar weak against both the Euro and the pound, there has not been a better time for Europeans to visit the Empire State.

New York Hotels

Frank Sinatra called New York the city that never sleeps. He'd probably been looking at his hotel bills. Think small rooms, big prices and you won't go far wrong.

Chambers

15 West 56th Street (@ 5th Ave) New York City, NY 10019, USA Tel: +1 212 974 5656, www.chambershotel.com

Modern, high style hotel in the heart of Fifth Avenue's shopperama.

Dream Hotel

210 West 55th Street (btwn Broadway & 7th Ave), Manhattan, New York City, NY 10019, USA Tel: +1 212 247 2000, www.dreamny.com

It was a pretty way-out dream that inspired this modern hotel. All 228 rooms and suites are washed in blue light and feature wall mounted plasma TVs, preloaded iPods with Bose speakers, and broadband internet access.

Four Seasons Hotel

57 East 57th Street (btwn Park & Madison Aves), Midtown, New York, NY 10022, USA Tel: +1 212 758 5757, www.fourseasons.com

Trademark old school luxury in the heart of town.

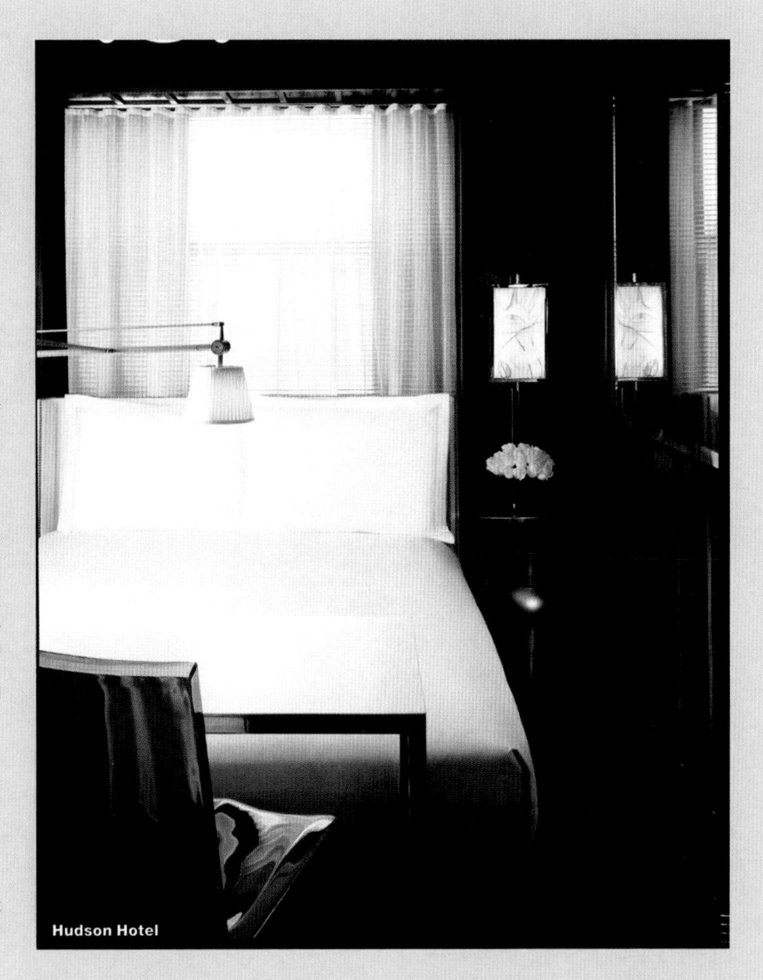

Hudson Hotel

Hotel Rivington

107 Rivington Street (@ Ludlow), Lower East Side, Manhattan, New York City, NY 10002, USA Tel: +1 212 475 2600, www.hotelonrivington.com

The Lower East Side is relatively low rise – that is, apart from this towering, glazed hotel. All the rooms and many of the showers in this very modern, very funky place offer great views of Manhattan.

Hudson Hotel

356 West 58th Street, New York City, NY 10019, USA Tel: +1 212 554 6000, www.morganshotelgroup.com

To really enjoy staying in this huge Starck designed Schrager created hotel you'll need to appreciate its lobby bars.

Mandarin Oriental Hotel

80 Columbus Circle (@ 60th St), New York, NY 10023, USA Tel: +1 212 805 8800, www.mandarinoriental.com

Highline, skyline luxe for the high-end consumer.

The Mercer Hotel

147 Mercer Street, New York City, NY 10012, USA Tel: +1 212 966 6060, www.mercerhotel.com

Fab, modern hotel. Go for a corner room if you can.

Morgans Hotel

237 Madison Avenue, New York City, NY 10016, USA Tel: +1 212 686 0300, www.morganshotelgroup.com

Ian Schrager's first hotel opened twenty years ago and still impresses.

Royalton Hotel

44 West 44th Street, New York City, NY 10036, USA Tel: +1 212 869 4400, www.morganshotelgroup.com

Schrager and Starck launched the concept of lobby socialising in this minimalist hotel, whose lobby runs the length of an entire block.

Soho Grand Hotel

310 West Broadway (@ Grand Street), New York City, NY 10013, USA Tel: +1 800 965 3000, www.sohogrand.com

Service can be disappointing and the rooms are small but this stylish hotel is located in the heart of Soho.

Public

New York Restaurants

New York's vibrant restaurant scene runs the gamut from expense account haute cuisine through to ethnic street food. The following recommendations are just a few of my personal favourites.

Aquavit

65 East 55th Street (btwn Park and Madison), New York City, NY 10022, USA
Tel: +1 212 307 7311,
www.aquavit.org
Cuisine: Scandinavian

Swedish chef Marcus Samuelsson presides over the country's finest Scandinavian restaurant, which moved to this new address last year.

Aureole

34 East 61st Street (btwn Madison & Park Aves), New York City, NY 10021, USA
Tel: +1 212 319 1660,
www.charliepalmer.com
Cuisine: Modern American

Leave room for pastry chef John Miele's spectacular desserts.

The Biltmore Room

290 Eighth Avenue (btwn 24th & 25th Sts), Chelsea, Manhattan, New York City, NY 10001, USA
Tel: +1 212 807 0111,
www.thebiltmoreroom.com
Cuisine: Modern international

Italian marble and brass fittings salvaged from the old Biltmore Hotel are married with crystal chandeliers in this fashionable lounge bar and restaurant. Superb food and attentive servers make for a rare combination of looks, style, cuisine and service.

Bouley Restaurant

120 West Broadway (@ Duane St), Tribeca, New York City, NY 10013, USA
Tel: +1 212 964 2525,
www.bouley.net
Cuisine: Modern French

Fantastic cuisine in this elegant setting, a reincarnation of one of the 90s' most celebrated restaurants.

Butter

415 Lafayette Street (btwn 4th St & Astor Pl), Noho, Manhattan, New York City, NY 10003, USA Tel: +1 212 253 2828,
www.butterrestaurant.com
Cuisine: Modern American

The curved cedar wood ceiling and large photographic mural of a birch forest give this restaurant a feel something like that of a Finnish sauna – although, with its moleskin booth seating, it's a sight more comfortable. The basement is more ski chalet but style does not completely overpower substance.

Public

Cru

24 Fifth Avenue (btwn 9th & 10th Sts), Greenwich Village, Manhattan, New York City, NY 10011, USA
Tel: +1 212 529 1700, www.cru-nyc.com
Cuisine: Modern Italian/Mediterranean

Cru is an oenophile's dream with 65,000 bottles of wine and a choice of 3,500 different bins. It also serves tasty modern Mediterranean cuisine with a six course tasting menu for $85. The dining room is easy on the eye with burnished wood and softly lit oil paintings.

Fiamma Osteria

206 Spring Street (btwn Sullivan St & 6th Ave), Soho, Manhattan, New York City, NY 10012, USA
Tel: +1 212 653 0100,
www.brguestrestaurants.com
Cuisine: Modern Italian

Part of the B.R. Guest estate and spread over three floors connected by a lift which overlooks the street, this large restaurant boasts a bold, eclectic interior. The Italian menu has plenty of modern twists while the excellent 500-strong wine list is bolstered by cocktails and 19 grappas accompanied by tasting notes. Expect efficient service by friendly staff.

Freeman's Restaurant

Freeman Alley (@ Rivington Street), Lower East Side, NY 10002, USA
Tel: +1 212 420 0012,
www.freemansrestaurant.com
Cuisine: Hunter's fayre

Lower East Side hipsters consume wild boar and whole roasted trout in a hunting lodge scene complete with moose and elk heads.

Chanterelle

2 Harrison Street (@ Hudson St), Tribeca, New York City, NY 10013, USA
Tel: +1 212 966 6960,
www.chanterellenyc.com
Cuisine: Modern French

Spectacular service, great presentation and fascinating combinations.

Daniel

60 East 65th Street (btw Park & Madison Aves), New York City, NY 10021, USA
Tel: +1 212 288 0033,
www.danielnyc.com

Named for its chef and owner, Daniel Boulud, who requests that gentlemen wear a jacket and tie.

Danube

30 Hudson Street (btwn Duane & Reade Sts), Tribeca, New York City, NY 10013, USA
Tel: +1 212 791 3771,www.thedanube.net
Cuisine: Austrian

Created by David Bouley, of Bouley, this refined restaurant serves Austrian cuisine lightened by Bouley's contemporary French-American touch.

Mas

39 Downing Street (btwn Bedford & Varick Sts), West Village, New York City, NY 10014, USA Tel: +1 212 255 1790
Cuisine: Modern American

Chef-owner Galen Zamarra serves adventurous modern American cuisine in an environment which mixes rustic and luxury.

Public

Gramercy Tavern

42 East 20th Street (btwn Broadway & Park Ave South), Flatiron, New York City, NY 10003, USA
Tel: +1 212 477 0777,
www.gramercytavern.com
Cuisine: Modern American

Fine dining in a warm, romantic tavern environment.

Kittichai

60 Thompson Hotel, 60 Thompson Street (btwn Broome & Spring Sts), Soho, Manhattan, New York City, NY 10012, USA
Tel: +1 212 219 2000,
www.kittichairestaurant.com
Cuisine: Modern Thai

Chef Ian Chalermkittichai serves brilliantly prepared contemporary Thai wonders to Soho hipsters who sit amidst the silk and orchids that surround the central pool of his restaurant on the ground floor of the fashionable Thompson Hotel.

March Restaurant

405 East 58th Street (btwn 1st Ave & Sutton Pl), New York City, NY 10022, USA
Tel: +1 212 754 6272,
www.marchrestaurant.com
Cuisine: Modern American

Share the dual tasting menu with your significant other.

Nobu

105 Hudson Street, Tribeca, New York City, NY 10013, USA Tel: +1 212 219 0500
Cuisine: Modern Japanese

Part-owned by Robert De Niro and famous for its Black Cod, this outpost of chef Matsuhisa's Nobu brand serves his trademark light and elegant dishes. Equally as good is the less grand, no reservations 'Next Door' Nobu.

Public Restaurant

210 Elizabeth Street (btwn Prince & Spring), Nolita, Manhattan, New York City, NY 10012, USA Tel: +1 221 343 7011,
www.public-nyc.com
Cuisine: Modern international

This former muffin factory retains an industrial feel but the warm modern décor, reclaimed fittings and individual smaller rooms make it cosy and snug. Well-travelled New Zealand chefs produce a well regarded eclectic menu.

Scalini Fedeli

165 Duane Street (btwn Greenwich & Hudson Sts), TriBeCa, New York City, NY 10013, USA Tel: +1 212 528 0400,
www.scalinifedeli.com
Cuisine: Modern Italian

The original home of Bouley now houses this elegant, antique-lined restaurant, which puts a supremely contemporary spin on Italian cuisine.

New York Drinking

New Yorkers are a fickle lot, always in search of the next 'in' place or area. The once so-hip Soho has been ousted by the warehouses of the Meatpacking District and Brooklyn is becoming more gentrified. Although it sometimes seems that bars and clubs can come and go in a New York minute, the best ones survive year after year, continually finding new discerning regulars.

2003's smoking ban prompted a growth in open air, rooftop venues where the addicted could once again enjoy their habit in the company of more health conscious friends. However, the most recent and exciting change in New York's bars is a move, at the top end of the scene, towards quality cocktails lovingly made with fresh juices. Sadly, quick drinks based on pre-packaged ingredients are still the norm in all but the very best venues.

Whatever you seek, be it pub, lounge or club, the diversity of New York's venues ensures your tastes will be catered for. That is, of course, assuming that you make it through the velvet rope - NYC has some of the world's hardest doors.

Most clubs close around 4am although some are open all night. It is illegal to serve alcohol after 4am (midnight on Sundays). The minimum drinking age is 21 and even greying 40-somethings may be asked for photo ID.

Fifty Seven Fifty Seven

APT

Dos Caminos

New York Liquor Stores

Astor Wines & Spirits
12 Astor Place (Broadway & Lafayette St), Manhattan, New York City, NY 10003, USA
Tel: +1 212 674 7500
www.astoruncorked.com

Best Cellars
1291 Lexington Avenue (@ 87th St), Manhattan, New York City, NY 10028, USA
Tel: +1 212 426 4200
www.bestcellars.com

Burgundy Wine Company
143 W. 26th St. (Seventh Ave), Manhattan, New York City, NY 10001, USA
Tel: +1 212 691 9092
www.burgundywinecompany.com

Crossroads Wines & Liquors
55 West 14th Street (@ Sixth Ave), Manhattan, New York City, NY 10011, USA
Tel: +1 212 924 3060

Elizabeth & Vine Inc.
253 Elizabeth Street, Manhattan, New York City, NY 10012, USA
Tel: +1 212 941 7943

Heights Chateau Wines & Liquors
123 Atlantic Avenue, Brooklyn, New York City, NY 11201, USA
Tel: +1 718 330 0963

Morrell & Company
1 Rockefeller Plaza (@ 49th St), Manhattan, New York City, NY 10020, USA
Tel: +1 212 688 9370
www.store.morrellwine.com

Park Avenue Liquor
292 Madison Avenue (btwn 40th & 41st Sts), Manhattan, New York City, NY 10017, USA
Tel: +1 212 685 2442
www.parkaveliquor.com

Seagrape Wines & Spirits
512 Hudson Street (@ West 10th St), West Village, Manhattan, New York City, NY 10014, USA Tel: +1 212 463 7688

Soho Wines & Spirits
461 West Broadway, Manhattan, New York City, NY 10012, USA
Tel: +1 212 777 4332,
www.sohowines.com

Spring Street Wine Shop
187 Spring Street, Soho, Manhattan, New York City, NY 10012, USA
Tel: +1 212 219 0521

Sherry-Lehmann Wine & Spirits
679 Madison Avenue (btwn 61st & 62nd Sts), Manhattan, New York City, NY 10021, USA Tel: +1 212 838 7500
www.sherry-lehmann.com

Vintage New York
482 Broome Street (Wooster St), Manhattan, New York City, NY 10013, USA
Tel: +1 212 226 9463
www.vintagenewyork.com

Vintage New York
2492 Broadway (@ 93rd St), Manhattan, New York City, NY 10025, USA
Tel: +1 212 721 9999
www.vintagenewyork.com

ANGEL'S SHARE

8 Stuyvesant Street (@ 9th St & Third Ave), East Village, New York City, NY 10003, USA

Tel: +1 212 777 5415
Hours: Daily 6pm-2:30am

Type: Lounge bar
Alfresco: No
Entry: Groups of 4 or fewer, subject to seating
Highlights: Cocktails & service
Atmosphere: Calm & refined
Clientele: Mixed bag of cocktail aficionados
Dress code: Smart casual
Price guide: $$$$
Bar snacks: Sashimi & dim sum to fried oysters

This is one of New York's most legendary bars but at first blush looks decidedly unpromising. Ascend the stairs to a very ordinary Japanese restaurant and you will find an unmarked door on your left, which looks more like the opening to the restaurant's broom cupboard than any stairway to heaven. Behind it lies Angel's Share, a cheaply appointed, Eastern-influenced lounge with booth banquettes, bare brickwork, subdued lighting and large, draped windows. A second, similarly appointed room lies beyond velvet curtains.

Angel's Share takes its name from the term given to alcohol lost through evaporation while ageing spirits. Above the bar a large oil painting depicts an oriental devil flanked by winged cherubs, one a little the worse for his angel's share.

Strictly enforced house rules dictate no standing, no shouting and no groups of more than four. Light jazz plays softly in the background. So what makes this place legendary? The relaxed atmosphere and perfectly made classic cocktails.

BAR NEXT DOOR

131 MacDougal Street (btwn 3rd & 4th Sts), Greenwich Village, Manhattan, New York City, NY 10012, USA

Tel: +1 212 529 5945, **www.**lalanternacaffe.com
Hours: Sun-Thu 6pm-2am, Fri-Sat 6pm-3am

Type: Wine bar/restaurant bar
Alfresco: Back patio
Entry: By stairs from street
Highlights: Wine selection/pizzas
Atmosphere: Cosy, romantic
Clientele: Local 30-somethings
Dress code: Casual
Price guide: $$$
Bar snacks: Panini, salads, pizza, cheese list

This atmospheric little bar lies in the basement of an old townhouse, adjoining and attached to a small trattoria called La Lanterna. Reached by a set of steep stone steps, it can be hard to spot, so look for 'La Lanterna' rather than 'Bar Next Door'.

Taller folk may need to mind their heads on the steps which lead down to the small, cosy room with a low ceiling, exposed brickwork and stone walls. An open fireplace and flickering candles add to the atmosphere in the otherwise dimly lit space. Simple wooden tables dot the room yet the best spot is at the small but well stocked bar, which carries a great range of grappa and whiskey. The Italian-led wine list has some excellent and well priced bins and 16 wines are available by the glass. The beer selection includes the likes of Leffe Braun, while the 'hot stuff' list of liqueur coffees is also popular with regulars. However, the real draw is the amazing pizzas from Lanterna next door.

THE BILTMORE ROOM

290 Eighth Avenue (btwn 24th & 25th Sts), Chelsea, Manhattan, New York City, NY 10001, USA

Tel: +1 212 807 0111, **www.**thebiltmoreroom.com
Hours: Mon-Sun 5pm-4am

Type: Restaurant/lounge bar
Alfresco: No
Entry: Subject to capacity
Highlights: Interior design
Atmosphere: Refined lounge
Clientele: Hipsters, business types and couples
Dress code: Nothing too casual
Price guide: $$$$
Bar snacks: Full restaurant menu

The old Biltmore Hotel near Grand Central Station provided much of the look of this atmospheric lounge bar and restaurant: many of its most striking features were salvaged from there. An impressive iron gate and bronze revolving door housing lead into a lounge where cosy black leather banquettes sit beneath a mahogany boxed ceiling and the long black granite bar is lined with mahogany cabinets. Brass-lined French doors lead through to the dining room with its elegant chandeliers and vaulted ceilings. Like the doors, the dumb waiter (now used as a cell-phone booth) came from the old hotel.

The cocktails are better than average and the wine list includes a choice of ten wines by the glass. But it is the splendid décor and food that attracts business types, wooing couples and the fashionably hip in droves. A late night menu is served Wednesday to Saturday till 2am.

BRANDY LIBRARY

25 North Moore Street (@ Varick St), Tribeca, Manhattan, New York City, NY 10013, USA

Tel: +1 212 226 5545, **www.**brandylibrary.com
Hours: Mon-Sun 4pm-4am

Type: Lounge bar
Alfresco: Small front terrace
Entry: No cover
Highlights: Cocktails, spirit selection, food
Atmosphere: Relaxed, sophisticated
Clientele: Switched on 30-somethings
Dress code: Smart casual/suits
Price guide: $$$$$
Bar snacks: "Figs & pigs", burgers, cheese plate etc.

The name hints at what to expect: wooden, floor to ceiling shelves lined with brandies from around the world. The selection is incredible, ranging from vintage Armagnacs and Cognacs to Yugoslavian slivovitz (plum brandy). Besides the brandies of the title, a full array of whiskies and rums also lines the shelves.

The 'librarians' tasked with climbing the sliding ladders and dispensing the bottles also mix great cocktails: 100 classic and contemporary drinks are listed. There are nine wines by the glass and a respectable beer selection. The substantial, leather bound catalogue is hardly a menu to fold and pocket, although you can purchase one for $125.

The service, décor and atmosphere are as special as the drinks selection. The Library has a warm amber glow and jazz plays softly. Comfy brown leather seats and long sofas separate the lounge area from the bar. This very classy joint caters to a discerning, fashionable crowd.

BROOKLYN SOCIAL

335 Smith Street (btwn Carroll & President Sts), Brooklyn, New York, NY 11231, USA

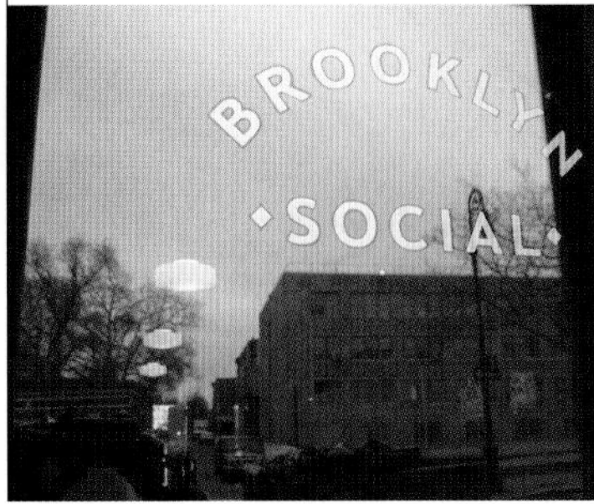

Tel: +1 718 858 7758
Hours: Mon-Thu 6pm-2am, Fri-Sat 6pm-4am, Sun 5pm-2am

Type: Lounge bar
Alfresco: Small back garden
Entry: No cover
Highlights: Cocktails and sandwiches
Atmosphere: Relaxed, laidback
Clientele: Hip locals
Dress code: Suitably casual
Price guide: $$$
Bar snacks: Hot ciabatta sandwiches

Things have changed in Brooklyn but the delightfully shabby décor of this former Sicilian social club remains untouched. Original art deco lamps hang over the curved oak bar and the half panelled walls are lined with sepia-tinted photographs of one-time club members and Brooklyn scenes. The small back room houses an old, well-worn pool table and leads through to a bijou back garden. Like the interior, the exterior is unspectacular but friendly: a small brass sign declares 'non-members welcome'.

Although the short 'speciality cocktails' list carries the odd classic it is far from vintage and includes some very well executed contemporary creations. Another, equally succinct 'hot pressed sandwiches' list offers a choice of three fillings in toasted ciabatta bread – all are very tasty.

The atmosphere is old school and laidback: a friendly bunch of 30-something locals relax to the jazz tunes playing on the jukebox.

DOUBLE SEVEN

418 West 14th Street (btwn Ninth & Tenth Aves), Meatpacking District, New York City, NY 10014, USA

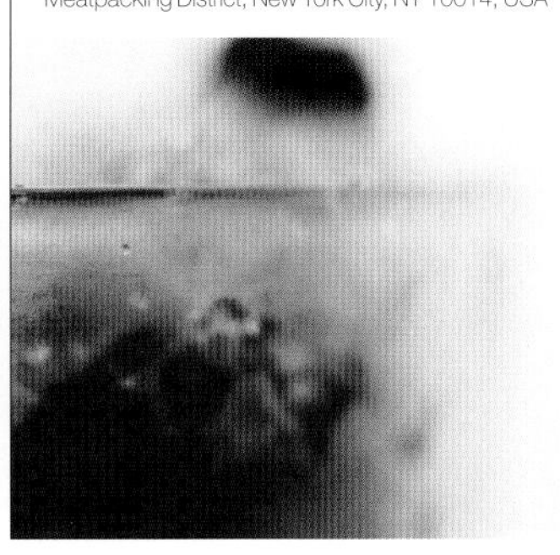

Tel: +1 212 981 9099
Hours: Mon-Fri 6pm-4am, Sat 8pm-4am

Type: Lounge bar
Alfresco: No
Entry: Subject to management & capacity
Highlights: Cocktails
Atmosphere: Chilled, friendly
Clientele: The fashionable & good looking
Dress code: Designer casual
Price guide: $$$$$
Bar snacks: Only Debauve & Gallais chocolates

Lying practically opposite Lotus nightclub and owned by the same operators, Double Seven is reached by passing heavy leather curtains and walking through an ovoid concrete tunnel. Beyond is a stylish lounge with black cork floors, a brown suede ceiling and crocodile-textured leather bar-top and banquettes. The wall opposite the bar is virtually an art installation: it is covered with 400 chunky, hand-blown amber glass tear drops. Metal mesh curtains screen the cosy, raised rear seating area.

Double Seven is rightly noted for its cocktails and the daily changing drinks menu is overseen by Sasha Petraske of Milk & Honey fame. Drinks are made with fresh juices and served with Debauve & Gallais chocolates flown in weekly from Paris.

Although occasionally overshadowed by the waitresses in their black, hourglass uniforms, the clientele is very fashion savvy. To avoid being disappointed by 'door discretion', arrive before 10pm at weekends.

DYLAN PRIME LOUNGE

62 Laight Street (corner of Greenwich St.), Tribeca, New York City, NY 10013, USA

Tel: +1 212 334 4783, **www.**dylanprime.com
Hours: Mon-Thu 6pm-11pm, Fri-Sat 6pm-midnight, Sun 5pm-10pm

Type: Lounge / restaurant bar
Alfresco: No
Entry: Subject to capacity
Highlights: Pie-Tinis
Atmosphere: Relaxed
Clientele: Locals, trendies, diners
Dress code: Smart casual – stylish
Price guide: $$$
Bar snacks: Full menu, great cheese fondue

This wonderfully atmospheric, candle-lit cocktail lounge is attached to the well-regarded Tribeca steak house of the same name. The décor is theatrical, with heavy drapes, shaded pendant lights and elaborate tapestry effects. The curved back bar resembles the stern of a Spanish galleon and is loaded with premium spirits.

The bar is well known in cocktail circles for it is here that Michael Waterhouse created the Key Lime Pie cocktail. This contemporary classic, now served in bars coast to coast, is one of several signature Pie-Tinis on the menu. In fact, Dylan Prime has even trademarked the term. While I wouldn't recommend a session on these dessert-style drinks, you should try at least one, perhaps the Lemon Meringue Pie. The quality of other cocktails is dependent on your server but the Manhattans are always great. Bar snacks are also noteworthy and I particularly recommend the cheese fondue.

The comfortable booths attract a mixed crowd of locals, after office types and travelling hipsters.

DOS CAMINOS

475 West Broadway (@ West Houston St), Soho, New York City, NY 10012, USA

Tel: +1 212 277 4300, **www.**brguestrestaurants.com
Hours: Mon-Thu noon-11pm, Fri-Sat noon-12:30am

Type: Mexican restaurant & bar
Alfresco: Yard with heaters
Entry: Not normally a problem
Highlights: Tequila range & guacamole
Atmosphere: Friendly & relaxed
Clientele: Soho set & office workers
Dress code: Casual
Price guide: $$$
Bar snacks: Mexican American fusion

Dos Caminos' functional stainless steel bar and fairly nondescript interior may not promise much but as soon as the friendly staff greet you at the door you know you're going to enjoy the place. And with well over 100 different brands and styles on offer, Tequila fanciers will love it.

Sip an añejo or choose one of the many blanco or reposado tequilas as the base for a mean Margarita. The Prickly Pear signature cocktail will bring joy to all lovers of frozen Margaritas, while if Tequila is not your thing you'll find a good range of Mexican beers. The spicy guacamole served with warm tortillas in large black tiki bowls is simply amazing.

The small side yard comes into its own in summer but even on chilly evenings gas heaters offer some warmth. There's a second Caminos at 373 Park Avenue South (@ 27th St). However, I prefer the Soho branch, which has more soul and is conveniently practically beneath the Pegu Club.

EAST SIDE COMPANY BAR

49 Essex Street (btwn Grand & Hester Sts), Lower East Side, Manhattan, New York City, NY 10002, USA

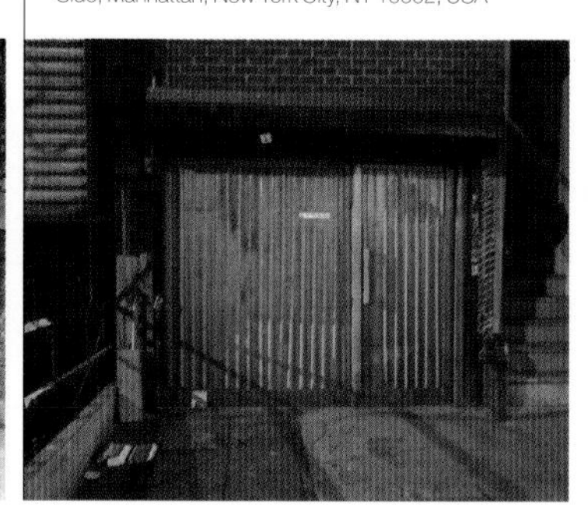

Tel: +1 212 614 7408
Hours: Mon-Sun 8pm-4am

Type: Lounge bar
Alfresco: No
Entry: Unwelcoming but go right in
Highlights: Cocktails
Atmosphere: Chilled, sophisticated
Clientele: Those in the know
Dress code: Smart casual
Price guide: $$$$
Bar snacks: Warm nuts served with drinks

Sasha Petraske of Milk & Honey fame and a group of partners opened this prohibition-style speakeasy in April 2005 and it attracts a discerning set of Lower East Side locals. While it is hardly a carbon copy, those familiar with Milk & Honey will see resemblances. Most obviously, it hardly shouts about its location. Only the small brass plaque on what look like wooden garage doors between Unique Hairstylists and The Pickle Guys confirms its existence.

Open the door and walk through the heavy curtain into a long, narrow, dimly lit room illuminated by flickering oil lamps. A long, zinc-topped bar sits under a pressed tin ceiling which curves down the walls to meet wooden panelling. Past the bar area is a lounge with a low ceiling, bare brick walls and secluded red booth seating, and a back room with stripy walls.

There is no cocktail list but classics are recommended and beautifully made. If the Martinis fail to tempt, there is Guinness on draught.

EMPLOYEES ONLY

●●●●○

510 Hudson Street (btwn Christopher & W 10th Sts), Tribeca, Manhattan, New York City, NY 10014, USA

Tel: +1 212 242 3021, **www.**employeesonlynyc.com
Hours: Mon-Sun 6pm-2am

Type: Restaurant/lounge bar
Alfresco: Small back garden
Entry: Subject to capacity – gets busy
Highlights: Cocktails
Atmosphere: Loud music but loungy
Clientele: 30-somethings out to party
Dress code: Cool casual
Price guide: $$$$
Bar snacks: Oysters, salads, Serbian charcuterie platter etc.

The fortune-teller sat in the window marks this bar out from other nearby venues: whether by tarot cards or palmistry you could know your future for only $15. Behind red velvet curtains lies an art deco lounge with a classic tin ceiling, carved wood panelling, marble floors, an onyx framed fireplace and a long, welcoming bar.

Past the bar and up a few steps is a small, sky-lit dining area. From here a sliding door leads to a small back yard with further seating for those hot summer evenings.

The five co-owners are all veterans of noted Manhattan bars and restaurants, which could help to explain Employees' popularity from opening. The bartenders are dressed in white jackets by Savoia and their cocktails live up to their reputation for mixology. There are seven wines by the glass and a beer selection that includes Pilsner Urquell and Anchor Steam.

Employees Only attracts a good looking crowd who dress to impress but it can get packed. There is only one toilet so you may want to stay off the beer.

LA ESQUINA (CORNER DELI)

●●●●○

106 Kenmare Street (@ Lafayette St), Manhattan, New York City, NY 10012, USA

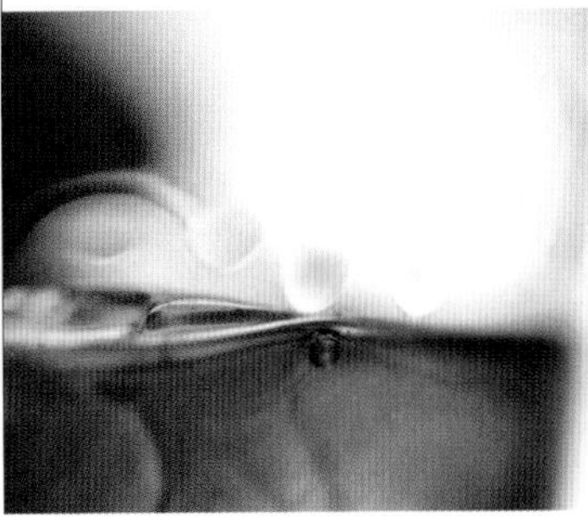

Tel: +1 646 613 7100
Hours: Mon-Sun 6pm-2am (Taqueria open noon-5am)

Type: Lounge bar/restaurant
Alfresco: No
Entry: Best to make a reservation
Highlights: Atmosphere
Atmosphere: Convivial, relaxed party
Clientele: Style set
Dress code: Designer casual
Price guide: $$$$
Bar snacks: Full modern Mexican menu

Even the name of this place is something of a secret. In true speakeasy style the entrance is marked 'employees only' and lies within a corner Taqueria. Doorman Dominic hovers, clipboard in hand, at the door which offers access to the basement and the lovely hostess. You reach the bar and restaurant by walking through the kitchen.

The room is divided by brick piers and wrought-iron railings. It is dimly lit with rustic, whitewashed brick walls and exposed service pipes run across the low ceiling.

The bar boasts more than eighty tequilas and the well made Margaritas are the drink of choice. Shots of tequila are served with sangrita in the Mexican vein.

La Esquina (its anagram is 'an equal sin') attracts a great crowd and the atmosphere is akin to the kitchen of a great house party. On the way out be sure to stop upstairs for a tasty chicken taco.

FIVE NINTH

●●●●○

5 Ninth Avenue (@ 13th St), Meatpacking District, New York City, NY 10014, USA

Tel: +1 212 929 9460, **www.**5ninth.com
Hours: Sun-Thu 6pm-midnight, Fri-Sat 6pm-4am

Type: Lounge/restaurant bar
Alfresco: Back yard
Entry: Subject to management & capacity
Highlights: Garden
Atmosphere: Warm
Clientele: Sophisticated West Village crowd
Dress code: Designer casual
Price guide: $$$$
Bar snacks: Fish cakes, imaginative sandwiches

Set in a mid-19th century townhouse, Five Ninth bar and restaurant has a wonderfully homely, almost romantic feel. You enter via the ground floor bar, which sets the scene for the rest of the building. Fireplaces, bare floorboards, exposed brickwork, wooden joists and dim lighting contribute to an interior that is rustic, yet cool and modern. Even the fridges behind the dark wood bar counter have been distressed.

Floor to ceiling glass doors set into the rear wall look out on an ivy-clad walled garden, which is ideal for summer drinking. An open tread staircase leads up to a restaurant lined with bookshelves, while the lounge on the top floor follows the same design cues.

The bar menu is a simple sheet of paper. Eleven nicely diverse wines are offered, all available by the glass. Half a dozen beers will please most palates, as will a similar number of well-made cocktails.

FLATIRON LOUNGE

●●●●◐

37 West 19th Street (btwn 5th & 6th Aves), Flatiron District, New York City, NY 10011, USA

Tel: +1 212 727 7741, **www.**flatironlounge.com
Hours: Sun-Wed 5pm-2am, Thu-Sat 5pm-4am

Type: Lounge bar
Alfresco: No
Entry: Line up behind the rope
Highlights: Art deco bar, flight of the day
Atmosphere: Decadent
Clientele: Hipsters
Dress code: Designer casual
Price guide: $$$$
Bar snacks: Not available

Both this lounge and its locale take their name from the landmark Flatiron Building, Manhattan's oldest surviving skyscraper, which dates back to 1902. The building's triangular shape resembles an iron – hence the name.

The Flatiron Lounge is a homage to the glory days of cocktails. An illuminated tunnel leads to an art deco-styled lounge, with mirrored tiles, red leather and pieces lifted from Manhattan's liquid history. There's a mirror from the Algonquin, where Dorothy Parker and her circle drank, while the 30-foot long mahogany bar is salvaged from The Ballroom, frequented by Sinatra and his pack. The whole is gently illuminated by Tiffany lamps.

Cocktails are king here and flights of taster size Martinis enable one to sample four different drinks in a single order – look out for the flight of the day. This is one of New York's most fashionable and talked about cocktail havens.

LITTLE BRANCH

●●●●○

22 Seventh Avenue South (btwn Clarkson & Leroy Sts), Greenwich Village, Manhattan, New York City, NY 10014, USA

Tel: +1 212 929 4360
Hours: Mon-Fri 7pm-3am, Sat 9pm-3am

Type: Lounge bar
Alfresco: No
Entry: Subject to capacity
Highlights: Cocktails
Atmosphere: Speakeasy
Clientele: Cocktail devotees
Dress code: Smart casual
Price guide: $$$$
Bar snacks: Snacks served with drinks

Sasha Petraske opened Milk & Honey in January 2000 in implausible premises on Manhattan's Lower East Side. It's best described as an upscale speakeasy for those who appreciate classic cocktails. Entrance is by referral and appointment only and this, coupled with its well disguised exterior, has given Milk & Honey urban myth status with many New Yorkers.

Both Sasha and Milk & Honey do very much exist, however. And in April 2005 Sasha opened this second lounge close to where he grew up in Greenwich Village. Although named 'Little Branch', it is twice the size of the original and, while fairly discreet, is open to all.

You enter the main area in the basement (there is a smaller, private hire space upstairs). Décor is similar to the original with a corrugated tin ceiling, pressed tin bar front and booth seating. Little Branch is far from plush but wonderfully cool and quirky. Cocktails are distinctly old school and, thanks to studious measuring of ingredients, consistently good.

MERC BAR

●●●●○

151 Mercer Street (btwn Houston & Prince), Soho, New York City, NY 10012, USA

Tel: +1 212 966 2727, **www.**mercbar.com
Hours: Sun-Mon 5pm-1:30am, Tue-Wed 5pm-2am, Thu 5pm-2:30am, Fri-Sat 5pm-3:30am

Type: Lounge/restaurant bar
Alfresco: Open fronted
Entry: Subject to capacity
Highlights: Atmosphere, decor
Atmosphere: Warm and friendly
Clientele: Soho locals
Dress code: Casual to designer
Price guide: $$$$
Bar snacks: Not available

The name of this wonderfully friendly bar does not refer to the German car manufacturer, but to the central Soho street on which it lies.

Entering the Merc is like walking into a mountain lodge, complete with trophy antlers. The walls are covered in old burlap, the ceiling displays its joists and the floor is of wide, timber boards. The mahogany bar counter has the regulation brass kick rail, while three large sepia photographs of Niagara Falls hang behind the bar.

All that dark wood coupled with flickering tealights help make this one of the warmest, most atmospheric bars I've visited. On summer evenings the front opens onto the street, creating a café feel.

The dozen or so long cocktail list changes by the season, although popular drinks such as the signature Vacation are permanent fixtures. However, it's not the mixology so much as the atmosphere and the friendly regulars that make this one of my longtime favourite New York bars.

MILK & HONEY

●●●●◐

134 Eldridge Street (just south of Delancey), Lower East Side, New York City, NY 10002, USA

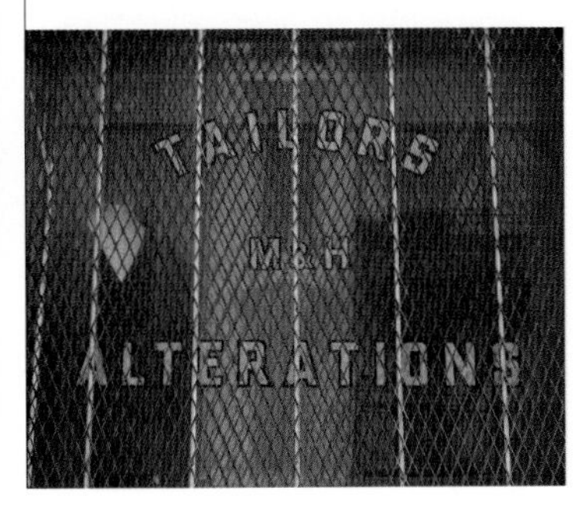

Tel: withheld
Hours: Daily 9pm-3:30am

Type: Lounge bar
Alfresco: No
Entry: Strictly members only
Highlights: Cocktails & atmosphere
Atmosphere: Chilled, relaxed
Clientele: Mature, refined, discerning
Dress code: Smart casual
Price guide: $$$$
Bar snacks: Warm nuts served with drinks

A grilled window marked 'Tailors M&H Alterations' helps give the façade of this legendary contemporary speakeasy the look of neglected commercial premises. A surveillance camera monitors the plain door, simply marked '134', and if you're a recognised member and have rung ahead to make a reservation, you'll be buzzed in.

Inside, beyond the black out curtains, is a single, candlelit room with simple décor and a pressed tin ceiling. There's a tiny bar with five fixed seats and leather lined circular booths run the length of the plainly painted brick wall. Here owner Sasha Petraske has perfected the classic cocktails from the Prohibition era. The drinks are simply amazing.

Those lucky enough to gain entry to this small and exclusive venue should note that you can only pay in cash and that the strictly enforced house rules include: "No name-dropping. No hooting, hollering, shouting or other loud behaviour. Gentlemen are required to remove their hats and may not introduce themselves to ladies."

MORRELL WINE BAR & CAFÉ

●●●●○

1 Rockefeller Plaza, 49th Street (btwn 5th & 6th Aves), Manhattan, New York City, NY 10020, USA

Tel: +1 212 262 7700, **www.**morrellwinebar.com
Hours: Mon-Sat 11:30-midnight, Sun noon-6pm

Type: Wine bar
Alfresco: Small sidewalk terrace
Entry: Subject to capacity
Highlights: Wine list & food
Atmosphere: Relaxed
Clientele: After work business crowd
Dress code: Suits/smart casual
Price guide: $$$$
Bar snacks: Tasty American-Italian plates and snacks

The Morrell family have owned what is one of New York's leading wine shops for over fifty years. This bright, airy wine bar with adjoining café is a relatively new foray for the family but has built a reputation in its own right over the last couple of years.

The heavy, metal ring-binder wine menu lists over 2,000 selections, divided into three sections: 'Market', 'Reserve' and 'By-the-Glass'. The 'Market' list offers some of the best made wines currently available on the market, the 'Reserve' contains over 100 rare wines, while the 'By-the-Glass' section boasts over 120 regularly changing wines complete with tasting notes and listed by grape variety with flights in mind.

Wine bottles of various sizes and origins are displayed around the modern, split-level, airy room with its wood block floor, plain light walls and curvy granite and stainless steel bar. A small terrace fronts the sidewalk where tables overlook the flags of Rockefeller Plaza.

Excellent American-Italian influenced food with wine pairings completes the offering which draws the after work business crowd.

PEGU CLUB

●●●●◐

77 West Houston Street (Btwn Laguardia Pl & Wooster St), New York City, NY 10012, USA

Tel: +1 212 473 7348, **www.**peguclub.com
Hours: Sun-Wed 5pm-2am, Thu-Sat 5pm-4am

Type: Lounge bar
Alfresco: No
Entry: Subject to management & capacity
Highlights: Cocktails
Atmosphere: Laidback lounge
Clientele: Discerning 30-somethings
Dress code: Designer casual
Price guide: $$$$
Bar snacks: Asian-inspired snack menu

Audrey Saunders, a leading light in New York's cocktail culture, has taken the inspiration and name for this bar from a club famous in the 1800s, the heyday of the British empire. The original Pegu Club in Rangoon, near the Gulf of Martaban in Burma, was the haunt of British colonial types and Kipling described it as "a funny little club always filled with lots of people either on their way up or on their way down".

This Pegu Club's entrance and cloakroom are at street level but the long, narrow lounge is perched above West Houston Street. Fittingly, the interior has an oriental influence and latticework covers the windows that run down one wall. Plush banquettes and comfy low chairs surround the tables which dot the room.

The original Pegu Club was famous for its eponymous, tart house cocktail and naturally this leads Audrey's list, which changes with the seasons and showcases creations by Audrey and her team. Infused spirits are a major component in their drinks, all of which are judiciously made and carefully measured.

PRAVDA

281 Lafayette Street (btwn Houston & Prince Sts), Soho, New York City, NY 10012, USA

Tel: +1 212 226 4944 , **www.**pravdany.com
Hours: Sun-Tue 5pm-1am, Wed-Thu 5pm-2am, Fri-Sat, 5pm-3am

Type: Lounge/restaurant bar
Alfresco: No
Entry: Subject to capacity - expect a line
Highlights: Service, atmosphere & drinks
Atmosphere: Chilled to party
Clientele: Friendly Soho locals, style set & tourists
Dress code: Designer casual
Price guide: $$$$
Bar snacks: Russian themed tapas style

This subterranean, Soviet themed bar and restaurant is owned by Keith McNally, the guru behind Balthazar, Pastis and Schiller's Liquor Bar. Of all his venues this is by far my favourite.

A narrow staircase leads down from the street to a room warmly lit by what look like Russian street lights. These illuminate nicotine-stained paintwork, faux-antique mirrors, a low vaulted ceiling, red banquettes and club armchairs. A discreet staircase leads up to a further small bar, which can be a good place to head if the main room gets too hectic. However, I prefer to stay in the basement, preferably at the curved, zinc topped bar where bottles of Pravda's own infused vodkas chill on ice.

The twenty or so cocktails on offer are speedily and superbly made by friendly bartenders. The Soviet theme continues in the excellent food menu which features blinis (potato pancakes) with smoked salmon.

PUCK FAIR

298 Lafayette Street (just south of Houston), Soho, New York City, NY 10012, USA

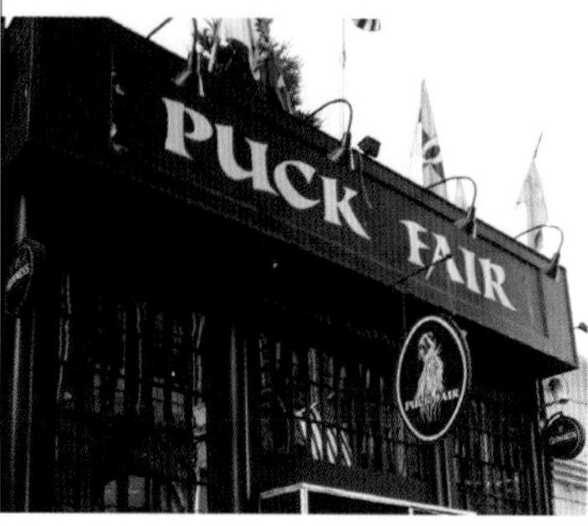

Tel: +1 212 431 1200, **www.**puckfairbarnyc.com
Hours: Daily 11am-4am

Type: Pub
Alfresco: No
Entry: Not normally a problem
Highlights: Beer selection
Atmosphere: Friendly local
Clientele: Local post-workers
Dress code: Casual
Price guide: $$$
Bar snacks: Five dollar fare and full meals

Located across the street from the landmark Puck Building in the heart of Soho, this distinctly Irish pub is named after the annual fair where a goat is paraded through the small town of Killorglin in County Kerry, Ireland, and crowned King Puck.

Puck Fair is one of the best beer bars in New York City. It looks the part with wooden floorboards, open rafters and bare brick walls. The long bar is divided into bite-sized portions by glazed pine panels, while further panels create a couple of secluded snugs. The rear balcony provides a vantage point from which to view lower Broadway's creative professionals letting their hair down after work.

Even the most demanding beer drinker should find something to suit their fancy here. The line of fourteen beer fonts includes two dedicated to Guinness along with others from Chimay Red to Anchor Porter. There is also a good range of bottled brews.

SOHO HOUSE NEW YORK

29-35 Ninth Avenue (@ 13th St), Meatpacking District, New York City, NY 10014, USA

Tel: +1 212 627 9800, **www.**sohohouseny.com
Hours: Sun-Thu 11am-3am, Fri-Sat 11am-4am

Type: Lounge bar
Alfresco: Roof top pool bar
Entry: Members & hotel residents only
Highlights: Roof top pool bar
Atmosphere: Chilled
Clientele: After work, style set, celebs
Dress code: Smart casual to catwalk
Price guide: $$$$
Bar snacks: Salads, sandwiches & full meals

When London's Nick Jones opened this boutique hotel and members club in 2003, it caused something of a stir. The rooftop pool quickly became the place to be seen parading your tan and designer swimwear.

The Circle bar lies on the top floor of the hotel, next to the restaurant, which is run by a former manager of London's Ivy. Its U-shaped, zinc topped bar juts out into a room furnished with 39 feet long, brown leather Chesterfield sofas on a herringbone parquet floor. The glass walls of the wine cellar house some appealing bins, although the quality of the drinks on the short cocktail list varies widely depending on your server. You'll still find the odd celeb drinking here, alongside the West Village professionals relaxing after work.

Sound appealing? Then book a hotel room. Or you could apply for membership, and, if the committee like the cut of your jib, pay the annual fee of $1,100 plus the $200 registration fee.

TEMPLE BAR

332 Lafayette Street (btwn Bleecker & Houston Sts), Soho, New York City, NY 10012, USA

Tel: +1 212 925 4242, **www.**templebarnyc.com
Hours: Mon-Thu 5pm-1am, Fri-Sat 5pm-2am

Type: Lounge bar
Alfresco: No
Entry: Subject to management & capacity
Highlights: Cocktails, refined warm interior
Atmosphere: Calm & friendly
Clientele: 30 something business/casual
Dress code: Designer casual/smart
Price guide: $$$$$
Bar snacks: Fresh oysters, prosciutto, guacamole, spare ribs etc.

The solid, polished cherry oak bar, wood panelled walls, plush seating and thick curtains give Temple Bar the look and feel of a classic five star hotel bar. Except the crusty old buffers you'd expect to find in such a venue have been replaced by professional, savvy thirty-somethings.

The bar menu features a selection of classic cocktails and aperitifs with something of an Italian bias. Besides contemporary favourites such as the Sakeini and Green Apple sit drinks such as the Bicicleta and the Venetian classic Sgroppino. An ample champagne and wine selection is followed by an impressive selection of 67 different vodkas listed by country of origin.

Temple Bar has stood the test of time. While it may no longer be über-trendy, those who prefer attentive service and well-made drinks in pleasant surroundings to chasing after the fashion pack are wise enough to continue frequenting this classy little bar.

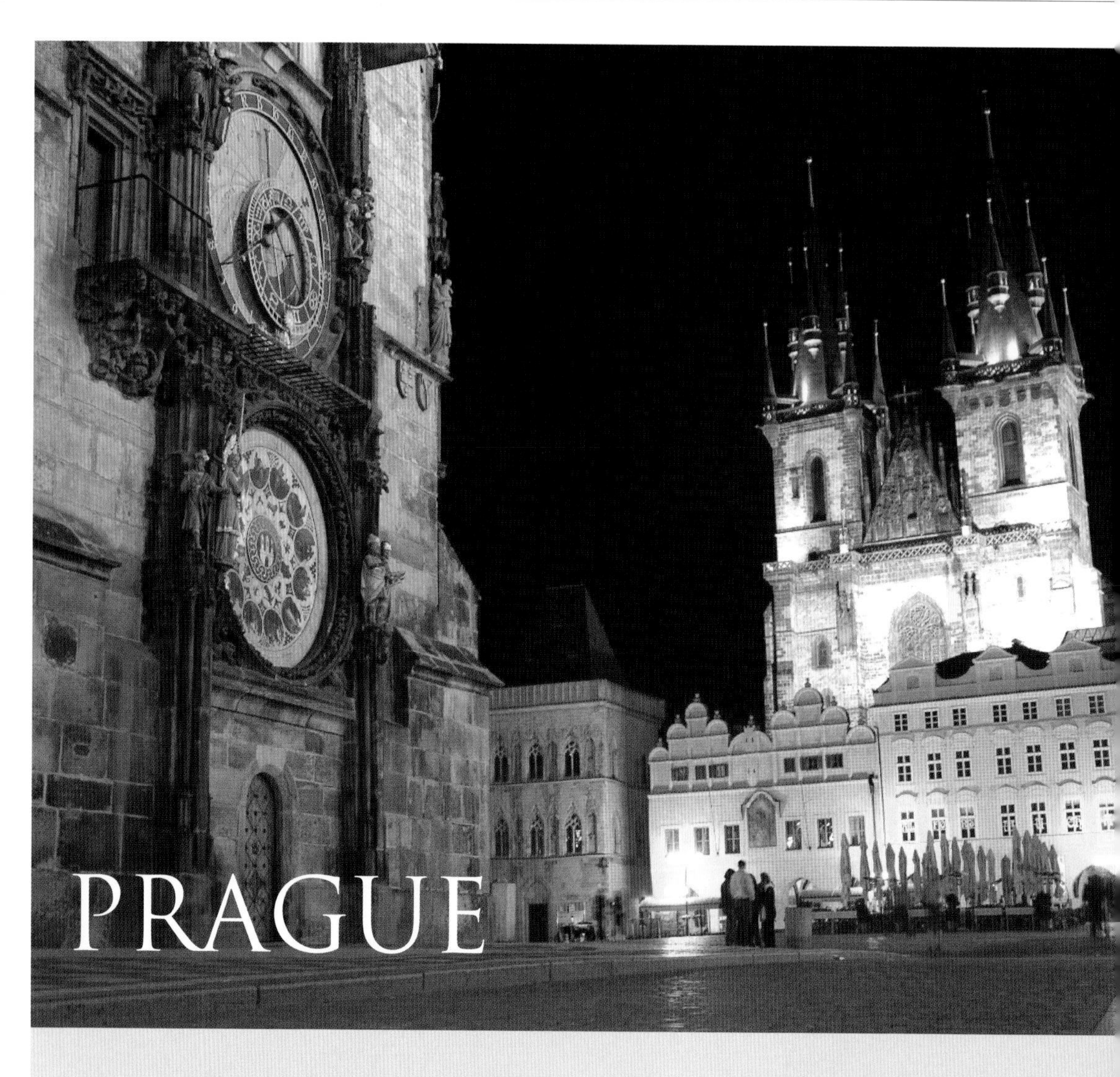

PRAGUE

Time zone: Central European Time (+1 GMT)
Airport: Prague Ruzyne (PRG)
Currency: Czech Koruna (K)

The capital of the Czech Republic, Prague (Praha) is one of central Europe's most beautiful cities. The Vltava river winds its way below the imposing castle which dominates the Old Town: cobbled lanes lined with ancient cottages alternate with Art Nouveau boulevards, fairytale turrets and scarlet rooves, and grand squares decked out in wedding cake pastels.

They don't call Prague the capital of Bohemia for nothing. In amid ten centuries worth of architecture and the trappings of the modern European capital, there are hundreds of galleries, plus concert halls, opera houses and theatres. And plenty of ancient pubs for those wannabe Kafkas to while away the long creative days.

Prague Hotels

The number of luxury hotels in Prague has grown enormously over the past few years. Many boutique hotels now challenge the luxury brands already established in the city - Four Seasons (www.fourseasons.com) and Radisson SAS (www.radisson.com) among them.

Alchymist Grand Hotel & Spa

19 Tržiště, Malá Strana, Prague 1, 118 00, Czech Republic
Tel: +420 257 286 011,
www.alchymisthotel.com
Group: Privately owned
Rooms: 9 (inc. 4 suites)

The Italian owners of this boutique hotel have restored and combined four late 15th century houses to create a seriously opulent space adorned with ancient art, ornate furniture and four poster beds. Besides the art, there's a small café bar, a health club with spa and indoor pool, a sushi bar and the usual broadband, safe and mini bar in rooms.

Aria Hotel

9 Tržiště, Prague 1, 118 00, Czech Republic
Tel: +420 225 334 111,
www.ariahotel.net
Group: Trziste a.s./ Aria hotel
Rooms: 52

One for the music lover, this hotel is dedicated to tunes: every single sound-proofed room is themed around an artist from Bach to Billie Holiday, and selections of their work are loaded into the room's computer. The baroque architecture is enlivened by bright skylights and a scarlet and pale yellow interior.

Hotel Carlo IV

13 Senovazne Namesti, Prague 1, 110 00, Czech Republic
Tel: +420 224 593 050,
www.boscolohotels.com
Group: Boscolo Hotels
Rooms: 152

This converted bank has been given a creative makeover, blending antique gold leaf and frescoes with slick, ultramodern glass and metal. The contemporary luxury extends to the bathrooms and the mosaic indoor pool, while broadband internet and aircon are standard.

Hotel Hoffmeister Wellness & Spa

7 Pod Bruskou, Mala Strana, Prague 1, 118 00, Czech Republic
Tel: +420 251 017 111,
www.hoffmeister.cz
Group: Small Luxury Hotels
Rooms: 38 (inc. 15 suites)

Created by Czech Martin Hoffmeister in honour of his father, Adolf, a diplomat, writer, artist and gourmet, this luxury hotel just below the castle maintains that family run feel. There's a gallery of Adolf's paintings and caricatures, plus a celebrated restaurant, wine cellar, bar and spa.

Hotel Josef

20 Rybná, Prague 1, 110 00, Czech Republic
Tel: +420 221 700 000,
www.hoteljosef.com
Group: Independent
Rooms: 110

Built into two houses around a quiet courtyard, this elegant, contemporary hotel was designed by Eva Jiricna, the celebrated Czech-born, London-based architect. The sculptural, stylish, hyper-modern interiors are enhanced by a small gym and the usual contemporary communication facilities.

Hotel Savoy

6 Keplerova, Prague 1, 118 00, Czech Republic
Tel: +420 224 302 430,
www.hotel-savoy.cz
Group: Vienna International Hotels and Resorts
Rooms: 61 (including 6 suites)

Like the Four Seasons, Hotel Savoy, to the west of Prague Castle, is a star-gazer's dream – rockers and actors flock to its Presidential Suite. The Art Nouveau building features spacious rooms kitted out in romantic décor, plus high speed internet, complimentary minibar and spa, a library, a beauty salon, a bar and a restaurant.

The Iron Gate Hotel

19 Michalská, Prague 1, 110 00, Czech Republic
Tel: +420 225 777 777
Group: Orchid Group
Rooms: 43 (all suites)

Set in a stunning, fourteenth century building in the core of the Old Town, all 43 of Iron Gate's boutique suites feature original antique furniture and many have original medieval frescoes and decorative wooden ceilings. Amenities include fully equipped kitchenettes, minibars, air-con, safes and internet access.

Pachtuv Palace

34 Karoliny Světlé, Staré Město, Prague 1, 110 00, Czech Republic
Tel: +420 234 705 111,
www.pachtuvpalace.com
Group: MaMaison Residences
Rooms: 50

This baroque palace on the riverfront just 50m from the Charles Bridge has been converted into an assortment of super-luxe, fully serviced apartments, available for periods from one night to several months. Amenities include laundry service, room service and fitness room, plus wifi in the lobby.

Residence Nosticova

1 Nosticova, Malá Strana, Prague 1, 118 00, Czech Republic
Tel: +420 257 312 513,
www.nosticova.com
Group: Privately owned
Rooms: 10

Sister to the Alchymist, this gorgeous converted palace houses ten self-contained, fully serviced apartments, all with kitchens plus lavish antiques and artwork. The only meal served is breakfast, but there is a wine bar downstairs and room service.

Riverside Hotel Prague

15 Janackovo Nabrezi, Prague 5, 150 00, Czech Republic
Tel: +420 225 994 611
Group: Orco Hotels Collection
Rooms: 45 (inc. 13 suites)

Set in a glorious Art Nouveau building on the left bank of the Vltava River, this early twentieth century hotel was remodelled in 2002. The rooms are elegant although less than huge, and breakfast, drinks and bar snacks are available on site.

Prague Restaurants

An inheritance of German and Hungarian cuisines, followed by forty years of domination by Soviet Russia, means that the Czech Republic is not known for its food. A typical Czech meal comprises roast pork, cabbage, sauce and sturdy dumplings to sop up the sauce. Think meat, gravy and carbohydrate and you won't be far wrong.

Traditional Czech dishes worth looking out for are cheese fried in breadcrumbs (smažený sýr), garlic soup (česneková polévka) and potato pancakes (bramborak). With over a hundred thousand registered hunters in the country, wild game can also be delicious – particularly boar, hare, duck, goose and venison.

As befits this cosmopolitan city, international cuisine is widely available, although in cheaper restaurants it too can tend to the stodgy. Steer clear of the tourist traps around the Charles Bridge, Wenceslas Square etc. – as you'd expect, these tend to price for their location rather than their food.

It is polite to tip 10-15% or, if a service charge (generally 10-12.5%) has already been added, to round up the total to the nearest K10.

Alcron

Radisson SAS Alcron Hotel, 40 Štepánská, Prague 1, 110 00, Czech Republic
Tel: +420 222 820 000,
www.radisson.com
Cuisine: Seafood

Regarded by many as serving the best seafood in Prague, the semicircular dining room features a beautifully restored Art Deco mural. After dinner head to the hotel's Be Bob Bar (reviewed overleaf) for Alcron cocktails.

Allegro

Four Seasons Hotel, 2A Veleslavínova, Prague 1, 110 00, Czech Republic
Tel: +420 221 427 000,
www.fourseasons.com
Cuisine: Italian/ Mediterranean

The riverside terrace and the dining room offering views of the river, Charles Bridge and the Castle combine with great cuisine and Four Seasons service to make this a favourite with business types. Regarded by some as the best restaurant in the Czech Republic, it can be a tad formal.

Bellevue

18 Smetanovo Nábrezí, Old Town, Prague 1, 110 00, Czech Republic
Tel: +420 222 221 438, www.pfd.cz
Cuisine: Czech

Prague Castle, the Charles Bridge and the Vltava river make a stunning backdrop to this regarded restaurant serving Czech and international dishes. A live pianist and summer terrace are added attractions.

Circle Line

12 Malostranské námestí, Prague 1, 110 00, Czech Republic
Tel: +420 257 530 023,
www.circleline.cz
Cuisine: French-influenced International

Fine, French-led cuisine is served in a relaxed and airy brasserie-style setting, whose luxury attracts suits aplenty from the nearby embassies.

David Restaurant

21 Tržiště, Malá Strana, Prague 1, 118 00, Czech Republic
Tel: +420 257 533 109,
www.restaurant-david.cz
Cuisine: Czech

This small, formal yet charming, family run restaurant lies on a cobbled street near the American Embassy. Regarded as one of the best Bohemian restaurants in Prague.

Don Giovanni

34 Karolíny Svetlé, Staré Město, Prague 1, 110 00, Czech Republic
Tel: +420 222 222 062,
www.dongiovanni.cz
Cuisine: Italian

Situated in the Old Town, only 50 metres from Charles Bridge, with views of the Vltava and the Castle, Don Giovanni is particularly noted for its risotto and seafood.

Francouzská A Plzeňská Restaurace
5 Náměstí Republiky, Prague 1, 110 00, Czech Republic
Tel: +420 222 002 770, www.frenchrest.obecnidum.cz
Cuisine: French/Czech International

Set in the wonderful, Art Nouveau Obecní dům on Staré Město, the French Restaurant blends styles from Baroque to Oriental with the Czech original to create a spectacular setting. The menu is as varied as the environment.

La Perle de Prague
80 Rašínovo Nábrezí, Prague 2, 120 00, Czech Republic
Tel: +420 221 984 160, www.laperle.cz
Cuisine: French

Sitting on top of the crazy, Frank Gehry-designed Dancing House is this high quality French restaurant, where the cooking is as striking as the views of the Prague skyline.

Le Café Colonial
6 Siroká, Prague 1, 110 00, Czech Republic
Tel: +420 224 818 322, www.lecafecolonial.cz
Cuisine: French

This Old Town café cum restaurant is a safe stop-off by night or day. The French-based menu has hints of Chinese and Indian flavourings, alongside grilled meats, pasta and the like.

Mlynec
9 Novotného Lávka, Prague 1, 110 00, Czech Republic
Tel: +420 221 082 208, www.praguefinedining.cz
Cuisine: International

High-end international cuisine is served in a casually cool environment complete with a terrace overlooking the Charles Bridge and the Castle. Not cheap.

Palác Kinskych
606/3 Tynská ulicka, Prague 1, 110 00, Czech Republic
Tel: +420 224 810 750, www.palac-kinskych.cz
Cuisine: Czech-International

In a barrel-vaulted cellar below the stunning Kinski Palace lies this formal yet friendly restaurant offering good Czech fusion cuisine and a more than decent wine list.

Pravda
17 Parízská, Prague 1, 110 00, Czech Republic
Tel: +420 222 326 203
Cuisine: International

A very stylish restaurant on Prague's most stylish street which attracts appropriately glammed-up customers. The broad-ranging menu is delivered by attentive servers.

Rybí trh
5 Týnský dvur, Prague 1, 110 00, Czech Republic
Tel: +420 296 767 447, www.rybitrh.cz
Cuisine: Seafood

Fish, fish and more fish adorn this Old Town restaurant: pick your favourite at the entrance and choose a sauce to go with it. There's everything from oysters to eels and shark.

U Maltézskych rytíru (The Maltese Knights)
Prokopská 10, Prague 1, 118 00, Czech Republic
Tel: +420 257 533 666
Cuisine: Czech

This intimate restaurant in a Gothic cellar takes its name from the medieval knights who once used the building above. It is family owned and the Czech cuisine is simple and good.

U Modré Kachnicky II (The Blue Duckling)
Michalská 16, Prague 1, 110 00, Czech Republic
Tel: +420 224 213 418, www.umodrekachnicky.cz
Cuisine: Czech-influenced haute cuisine

The second branch of this quirky, intimate, traditional little restaurant. Like its sibling it offers some gorgeous dishes – mainly Bohemian classics served with an haute cuisine twist.

V zátiátisí (Still-Life)
Liliová 1, Prague 1, 110 00, Czech Republic
Tel: +420 222 221 155, www.praguefinedining.cz
Cuisine: International

From the folks behind Bellevue, Circle Line and Mlýnec comes another elegant international restaurant – with decent vegetarian options – in an intimate riverfront space.

Prague Drinking

The biggest drink in Prague is beer (pivo) and the Czechs top the world's beer consumption league. Indeed, it is the Czechs we have to thank for inventing lager. In 1842 Josef Groll brewed the first bottom-fermented beer or 'Pilsner' in the town from which the style takes its name - 'Pilsen' in German,Plzeň in Czech.

80km (50 miles) southwest of Prague, Plzeň is still home to the brewery that developed Pilsner. And it still makes Plzeňský Prazdroj, the Czech beer whose name means 'original source', although we know it better in German, as Pilsner Urquell. The town is also home to the Gambrinus brewery and, while its beer is not as famous or exported, its domestic sales exceed Urquell's.

The country's biggest selling lager export, Budvar, is brewed in Budweis (České Budějovice), 150km (100 miles) south of Prague. As with Pilsner, it's the German name for this beer that the American brewers, Anheuser-Busch, 'adopted' in 1876. I'd like to comment on Budweiser's rights to the name but there's been enough litigation so I'll confine myself to commenting that, although the slightly sweet Budvar is not my favourite Czech beer, it's a sight tastier than Budweiser.

The other big name Czech lager is Staropramen (meaning 'ancient spring'). Prague Breweries, which is predominantly British owned, produce it at the Smíchov brewery.

Czech pubs, or beer halls (pivnice), are supplied by a single brewer (pivovar) so only one brand of beer is usually available, although each brewer makes different styles. Light beer (světlé) is the most common style on draught but strong dark beers (tmávé) and strong light beers resembling a German bock (kozel) are sometimes also available.

Unless otherwise specified, draught beer is served by the half-litre (pullítr), which is just under a pint. Smaller (male) 333ml measures are always available on request. Although Czech wine can be overly sweet, the best examples are surprisingly palatable. Most comes from South Moravia along the Austrian and Slovakian borders, with some from the small Bohemian vineyards on the banks of the river Labe.

The Czech national liquor is Becherovka, a bittersweet liqueur made in the Bohemian spa town of Karlovy-Vary, west of Prague. Becherovka is matured in oak and flavoured with cinnamon, cloves, nutmeg and herbs. It can be drunk neat over ice but is more commonly served with tonic water and a slice of lime or lemon in a mix known as a Beton.

When drinking in Prague, you are also likely to come across 'slivovice', a plum brandy originally from the border hills between Moravia and Slovakia. At 45% alc./vol. this is fiery stuff but appears bland when compared to the Czech Republic's most infamous spirit, absinth. This bitter, aniseed-flavoured drink is still illegal in the US and much of Europe. Czech absinth (spelt without the 'e') usually has a bluer tinge to its green colour and a more subtle aniseed flavour than French absinthe. Unlike French absinthes, Czech absinths do not usually turn cloudy when water is added.

Prague's bar scene has changed dramatically since 1995 when Bugsy's opened in the Old Town. Since then a host of similar 'American' cocktail bars have opened in the surrounding streets, the best of which are listed over the following pages. Bugsy's also led the trend for cocktail lists as bound books featuring a bewildering range of cocktails, rums and Scotch malt whiskies.

Beware of 'nightclubs'. In Prague this usually means a table-dancing club with a strip show. If you're looking to dance yourself, you want a 'disco' or 'dance club'.

The minimum drinking age in the Czech Republic is 18. It's common for bars to remain open until between 2am and 4am in the morning with clubs chucking out just in time for an early breakfast. Prague is hardly a style savvy city so don't stress over dress codes.

You should be aware that cheap flight after cheap flight lands hordes of hen and stag partying Brits on weekend breaks in search of cheap beer, vodka and debauchery. If you don't fancy sharing your evening's entertainment with them you may prefer to visit midweek.

ALCOHOL BAR

6 Dušní, Prague 1, Czech Republic

Tel: +420 241 430 762, **www.**alcoholbar.cz
Hours: Mon-Sun 7pm-2am

Type: Lounge bar/club
Alfresco: No
Entry: Open door
Highlights: Cocktails
Atmosphere: Rocking
Clientele: Locals, few tourists
Dress code: Casual
Price guide: KK
Bar snacks: Czech snacks available

Loud mainstream pop music rises from the basement and seeps out from Alcohol Bar's unattended street level vestibule. It may look and sound unpromising but this is one of Prague's best bars.

At the foot of the winding, open tread stairs lies a large, well-stocked cigar humidor and beyond that a long dark wood bar with a stepped back bar loaded with premium spirits. The cavernous cellar is vaulted and rich in nooks and alcoves. Artistic female nudity hangs about its red walls. The room, like the atmosphere, has a warm glow.

However, it's when one of the staff in their smart black shirts and ties hands you a tome of a menu listing some 230 cocktails, 200 Scotch malt whiskies, 75 rums and 20 different 100% agave tequilas that you realise this is no ordinary bar. And they don't just list loads of classic cocktails, they know how to make them.

Like the friendly bunch of (mainly) locals that huddle around its high tables, you're bound to develop a taste for Alcohol.

ALLEGRO BAR

Four Seasons Hotel, 2A Veleslavínova, Prague 1, 1098, Czech Republic

Tel: +420 221 427 000, **www.**fourseasons.com
Hours: Mon-Sun 11am-1am

Type: Hotel bar
Alfresco: No
Entry: Via hotel lobby
Highlights: Cocktails
Atmosphere: Subdued
Clientele: Business types & hotel guests
Dress code: Nothing too casual
Price guide: KKKK
Bar snacks: Tasty snack menu

There are many swanky hotels with blandly decorated, characterless bars and sadly Allegro, the bar at the luxurious Four Seasons Hotel, is fairly typical. With its wood panelled walls, circular cocktail tables, upholstered armchairs and baby grand piano it's not lacking in grandeur. It simply lacks character and atmosphere. In fact, it feels more like the boardroom of a crusty firm of accountants – with those we saw drinking here having about as much fun.

All that said, I've a feeling that those who choose to stay in Four Seasons hotels aren't seeking fun so much as luxury and great service. Here Allegro excels. Its friendly bartenders efficiently make and serve wonderful cocktails from a list that rather appropriately changes with the seasons. There are fifteen wines by the glass, two reds and two whites from Czech wineries, a good range of grappa and premium spirits, plus the mandatory local beers.

Allegro may be low on atmosphere, but it lacks nothing if all you desire is great drinks in a civilised environment.

BE BOP BAR

Radisson SAS Alcron Hotel, 40 Štěpánská, Prague 1, 110 00, Czech Republic

Tel: +420 221 821 111, **www.**renaissancehotels.com
Hours: Mon-Sun 10am-1am

Type: Lobby / lounge bar
Alfresco: No
Entry: Open door
Highlights: Cocktails & service
Atmosphere: Relaxed
Clientele: Hotel guests, business types
Dress code: Relaxed
Price guide: KKK
Bar snacks: Sandwiches and snacks to meals

The Radisson SAS sits on a street plagued by the stag and hen parties that spill out of neighbouring bars. However, within its portals lies something of an oasis, the Be Bop Bar. As soon as you enter the lobby area you'll be greeted by the civilised and relaxing sound of a three-piece jazz band (Mon-Sat 10pm till 1am) and an equally jazzy harlequin coloured carpet. The bar and lounge area lie to the right of the open plan lobby area (a shame as the bar's atmosphere would benefit from further separation). The décor is simple and modern with white walls, black leather banquette seating and a granite topped bar.

The cocktail menu is extensive with a page dedicated to Alcronies (I recommend the one by Charlie) and classics categorised according to spirit base. There's a good selection of Czech beers and four of the six wines by the glass are from local vineyards.

The bar is open for coffee during the day and also offers a broad food menu ranging from snacks, salads and sandwiches through to main courses and Czech specialities.

LA BODEGUITA DEL MEDIO

●●●●○

5 Kaprova, Prague 1, 110 00, Czech Republic

Tel: +420 224 813 922, **www.**bodeguita.cz
Hours: Mon-Sun 10am-2am

Type: Theme bar
Alfresco: No
Entry: Open door
Highlights: Mojitos
Atmosphere: Buzzing
Clientele: Locals
Dress code: Casual
Price guide: KK
Bar snacks: Full restaurant menu & dining room

La Bodeguita del Medio translates from Spanish as 'the pub in the middle of the street' and many readers will recognise this as the name of the bar in Havana, Cuba, that's famous for its Mojitos and past patrons including Nat King Cole and Ernest Hemingway.

This Prague copy opened sixty years after the original, in 2002. Like its inspiration, the walls are covered in signatures, framed photographs and mementoes from famous guests. The replication extends to the dark wooden bar, high round tables, tiled floor, Cuban music and buzzy Hispanic atmosphere. You could even believe you were in Cuba. That is until you try the Mojitos, which are stuffed with mint and, I'm pleased to say, considerably better than those served at the Havana Bodeguita.

Fittingly, a bust of Hemingway sits behind the bar overseeing the bartenders in white lab coats who keep the glasses of the predominantly local crowd charged.

BAZAAR MEDITERRANEE

●●●○○

40 Nerudova, Prague 1, 118 00, Czech Republic

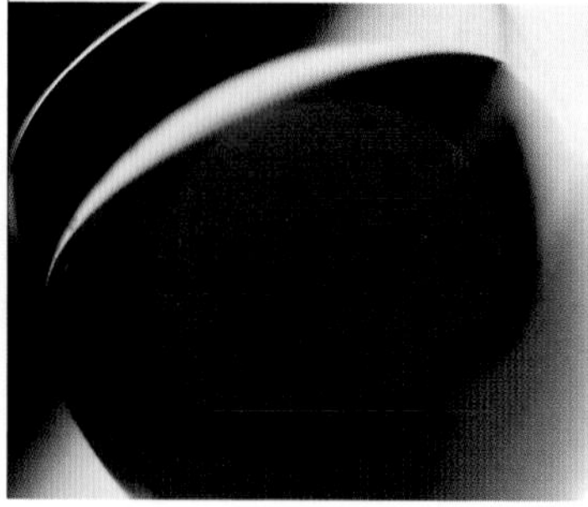

Telephone: +420 257 535 050, **www.**kampagroup.com
Hours: Mon-Sun noon-11pm

Type: Restaurant bar
Alfresco: Roof terrace
Entry: Via restaurant and stairs
Highlights: View
Atmosphere: Relaxed
Clientele: Tourists
Dress code: Casual
Price guide: KKK
Bar snacks: Full restaurant menu

The weather in Prague is hardly Mediterranean but on a sunny afternoon the roof terrace of this Mediterranean restaurant is the place to be. Bazaar Mediterranee is housed in a 17th century building on the hill below the castle and its roof terrace is reached by 69 numbered, winding steps. The ascent is rewarded with views over Prague's chimney tops, red tiled roofs and spires. The terrace is laid out as a garden complete with neatly trimmed box hedges, cushioned chairs surrounding small round tables and even a few sun loungers in their own sandy corner for those who'd rather be at the beach.

Sadly the cocktails are missable but with five wines by the glass plus local favourites such as Betons and cool Czech lager, this is a great place to take in the views after a visit to the castle.

BUGSY'S

●●●●◐

10 Pařížská, Staré Město, Prague 1, 110 00, Czech Republic

Tel: +420 224 810 287, **www.**bugsysbar.cz
Hours: Mon-Sun 7pm to 2am

Type: Lounge bar
Alfresco: No
Entry: Subject to management & capacity
Highlights: Cocktails, spirits selection
Atmosphere: Relaxed
Clientele: Business crowd, upmarket tourists
Dress code: Nothing too casual
Price guide: KKK
Bar snacks: Not a place to eat

When this cellar bar named after the American gangster Benjamin Siegel opened in 1995 it heralded a dramatic change in Prague's nightlife. Bugsy's brought cocktail culture to the city and trained many of the professionals who work in the bars that have followed in its wake.

Bugsy's bartenders wear white shirts with black bow ties and are expected to know how to make more than 400 cocktails according to the bar's exacting specifications. The spirits selection is also impressive and includes 150 Scotch malt whiskies and 75 of the world's rums. Bugsy's set the trend for Prague's best cocktail bars to use bound books as cocktail menus. (These are for sale as mementoes so please don't pocket them.) The bar underwent a major refurbishment in 2002 after the Vltava River burst its banks and flooded it. Sadly, little remains of the original interior and the new eighties look includes black furnishings and neon lights. It is only saved by Honza Jiříček's original illustrations.

Bugsy's lies just off the city's swankiest shopping street and attracts an upmarket business crowd, drawn by the great drinks.

U FLEKŮ

●●●◐○

11 Křemencova, Nove Mesto (New Town), Prague 1, 110 00, Czech Republic

Tel: +420 224 934 019, **www.**ufleku.cz/en
Hours: Mon-Sun 9am-11pm

Type: Traditional beer hall
Alfresco: Garden
Entry: Reservation for diners
Highlights: Beer and interior
Atmosphere: Dependent on room
Clientele: Tourists
Dress code: Casual
Price guide: KKK
Bar snacks: Traditional Czech cuisine

Prague's most famous beer hall (pivovar) is also a restaurant, working brewery and brewing museum. This huge sprawling place can 'feed and water' more than 1,200 guests (read: tourists) in its eight individually decorated rooms, halls and garden. The most famous and oldest of these is the Academy (Akademie). Others include the 200 seater Kabaret (Cabaret) hall where dancing revues vary from Czech polka through Baroque and Latin American. You may prefer the more intimate and sedate Kufr (Suitcase) hall.

The unusual name apparently dates from 1762 when entrepreneur Jakub Flekovskych and his wife purchased the pub and renamed it U Flekovskych, meaning 'At The Flekovskych'.

Much of the modern brewing equipment used today was installed in 1986 as part of a major refurbishment but many original pieces of brewing paraphernalia can be seen in the attached museum. This opened in 1999 to celebrate 500 years of brewing the house beer, 'Flekovský lezák', a strong dark beer which is only available on the premises and is reason enough to pay U Fleků a visit.

Museum and brewery tours Mon-Fri 10am-4pm (reservations required), Sat-Sun tours conditional on dining in the restaurant.

MONARCH

15 Na Perštyně, Old Town, Prague 1, 110 00, Czech Republic

Tel: +420 224 239 602, **www.**monarchvinnysklep.cz
Hours: Sun-Thu 3pm-10pm, Fri-Sat 3pm-11pm

Type: Wine bar
Alfresco: No
Entry: Open door
Highlights: Wine selection
Atmosphere: Relaxed
Clientele: Local wine lovers
Dress code: Casual
Price guide: KK
Bar snacks: Cheese, cold meats, fondue

This bright, airy wine bar is attached to a very serious wine shop. Both are owned by a wine importer and the selection of both new and old world bins is impressive with 20 by the glass and a good choice of vintages from the cellar below. Prices are also very reasonable and, if you particularly like a wine, you can buy a bottle or even a case to enjoy at home.

Aluminium industrial-styled lamps hang from the high ceiling and keep the large room perhaps a little too bright. Three large windows look out onto the street. The curvy, altar-like bar occupies one end of the room and the wine shop the other, with display cabinets full of bottles in between.

The cheese selection is as impressive as the wines and the helpful menu features animal images (cow, sheep and goat) to illustrate the origin of each cheese. Cold meats and cheese fondue are also served. Monarch is popular with local young professionals, so much so that you may have to wait for a table.

OCEAN DRIVE

7 V Kolkovně (Customs Street), Prague 1, 110 00, Czech Republic

Tel: +420 224 819 089, **www.**tretters.cz
Hours: Mon-Sun 4pm-2am

Type: Lounge bar
Alfresco: No
Entry: Open door
Highlights: Atmosphere
Atmosphere: Laid back
Clientele: Tourists
Dress code: Casual
Price guide: KKK
Bar snacks: Not a place to eat

Thoughts of Miami conjure up blue skies, palm trees and shimmering heat rising from a sandy beach where bikini clad babes stretch out in the sun and hunks play volleyball. Creating a Miami-themed bar in chilly Prague was ambitious to say the least, but that's what the owners of Tretter's have attempted to do at this second venue just a couple of doors down from their successful bar.

The somewhat contrived Ocean Drive look includes a two-tone, Art Deco-style interior with palm trees, tiled floor, red banquette seating, ceiling fans and palm trees. As you'd expect from a high-end Prague cocktail bar, the drinks list is a bound book, but the cocktails I sampled failed to live up to the standards of other neighbouring bars, including its sibling.

Ocean Drive lacks the atmosphere and the drinks offered by Tretter's and so is quieter. That may appeal to those seeking a more relaxed evening.

TRETTER'S BAR

3 V Kolkovně, Prague 1, 110 00, Czech Republic

Tel: +420 224 811 165, **www.**tretters.cz
Hours: Mon-Sun 7pm-3am

Type: Cocktail lounge bar
Alfresco: No
Entry: Open door
Highlights: Cocktails, atmosphere
Atmosphere: Buzzy, warm
Clientele: Media types to tourists
Dress code: Casual but stylish
Price guide: KKK
Bar snacks: Not a place to eat

Tretter's brilliantly matches the archetypal image of a cocktail bar. Its décor, bartenders, drinks and even customers all perfectly fit the bill.

The 1930s Parisian-style interior is dominated by a long, dark wood, tiled bar counter with large palms growing behind. Cosy alcoves line the burgundy walls which are covered with black and white framed photographs and a mural of girls in swimming costumes. Air-con ducting runs the length of the room, bolstered by whirling ceiling fans which struggle to cope with the heat and smoke generated by the cool crowd who gather here. Local fashion and film industry types sip cocktails alongside tourists and suited businessmen. The buzz, dim lighting and cool lounge tracks combine to create a great atmosphere.

Tretter's thick, diary-like book of drinks includes 150 classic cocktails plus fifty or so in-house creations. Classics are perfectly made and presented while Tiki-style drinks are garnished with an orchid. The accomplished bartenders also look the part, in their white, lab coat jackets and stripy ties. Tom Cruise wouldn't look out of place behind or at this bar.

ZANZIBAR

6 Lázeňská, Malá Strana, Prague 1, Czech Republic

Tel: +420 602 780 076
Hours: Mon-Sun 5pm-3am

Type: Mexican theme bar
Alfresco: No
Entry: Open door
Highlights: Cocktails & spirits
Atmosphere: Party
Clientele: Young tourists & few locals
Dress code: Casual
Price guide: KK
Bar snacks: More a place to imbibe

Think Zanzibar and you're transported to archipelago islands with golden sands and coral reefs. Meld such images with a vaulted room entered from a narrow lane in old Prague and the last thing you'd expect is this gaudy Mexican theme bar with its fire engine red bar counter, mustard coloured walls and scarlet floorboards. The need for sunglasses is about the only thing that connects this place to its namesake in the Indian Ocean.

Cocktail names stencilled on the walls and an impressive back bar selection with lines of Monin syrups and liqueurs induced me to order a round of drinks. What a pleasant surprise! ZanziBar may have tasteless décor but the cocktails are sublime. The serious spirits selection, including forty single malts, combines to show that looks can be deceiving.

ZanziBar attracts a youngish, friendly crowd of locals and tourists. The great Mojitos contribute to the party atmosphere.

SINGAPORE

Airport: Changi (SIN)
Time zone: Singapore Standard Time (GMT +8)
Currency: Singapore Dollar (S$)

On February 6th, 1819, Sir Stamford Raffles, an agent of the British East India Company, anchored off St John's Island and rowed into the Singapore River. At the mouth of the river he passed a rocky promontory topped with a monument inscribed in ancient script and was sure he'd discovered the lost city of Singapura. He raised the Union Jack and named the small island Singapore. Fort Fullerton, named after the first governor of the Straits settlement, was constructed on the hill a couple of years later.

Its strategic location, along the maritime route between India and China, meant that Singapore grew rapidly on the back of the spice and tea trade. By 1873, the land on which the fort stood was too valuable to remain under military use and it was demolished to make way for trade. Between 1919 and 1928, a grand building was erected to house the General Post Office, The Singapore Club and the Chamber of Commerce: it is now the Fullerton Hotel.

Today, independent Singapore is an ultra-modern city state of soaring skyscrapers and spotless, manicured streets, surrounded by fifty smaller islands. It is the world's busiest port and home to a mix of many different Asian peoples: in the bustling streets of Chinatown, Kampong Glam and Little India, religious monuments reside among colourful shophouses.

Singapore is also a shoppers' paradise with mall upon mall, all boasting designer brands and open late into the evening. However, such rapid commercial growth and safe, clean surroundings have come at the price of freedom of expression. Everything from public protest to chewing gum in the street to not flushing a public lavatory is punishable by law and the result is a somewhat sterile city of subservient people.

The tropical climate means that Singapore is either steaming hot, sunny and humid or humid and raining. Pack for sauna conditions and remember to bring an umbrella.

Singapore Hotels

Singapore has almost as many large luxury hotels as it does shopping malls and yet more are being constructed. Starwood's St Regis Hotel is perhaps the most notable.

When deciding what class of room to book, bear in mind that many Singapore hotels offer access to club lounges and other fringe benefits with suites.

Four Seasons Hotel

190 Orchard Boulevard, Singapore, 248646, Singapore
Tel: +65 6734 1110,
www.fourseasons.com/singapore
Group: Four Seasons Hotels and Resorts Rooms: 250

The Singapore outpost of the luxury brand offers elegant, modern rooms with Asian influences and local art. Floor to ceiling windows and walk-in closets come as standard, there's unlimited champagne at Sunday brunch, and, besides the pool and spa, there are air-conditioned tennis courts.

The Fullerton Hotel

1 Fullerton Square, Singapore, 049178, Singapore
Tel: +65 6733 8388,
www.fullertonhotel.com
Group: Sino Group of Hotels
Rooms: 400

Housed in the grandest building in Singapore with Doric columns and monumental porte cocheres, this truly impressive luxury hotel sits in the heart of the commercial district.

When booking it's worth digging deep to really indulge yourself. Heritage and Esplanade rooms are luxurious but suites come with access to the Straits Club and complementary breakfast, afternoon tea, evening cocktails and canapés. Many also boast private balconies or terraces looking over the Singapore River.

Whatever class of room your pocket allows, all have broadband internet access, mini-bar, bathroom with separate shower and an in-room safe that's not only large enough to hold a lap top, but also has a power point so it can recharge in safety.

Facilities include a 25-metre infinity pool and sun terrace, a gym, a spa and, should you require it, even a gorgeous 1962 vintage Rolls Royce. The Fullerton may be large and corporate, but it offers luxury surroundings, incredibly attentive service and a quiet, relaxed environment.

Raffles The Plaza

80 Bras Basah Road, Singapore, 189560, Singapore
Tel: +65 6339 7777,
www.singapore-plaza.raffles.com
Group: Raffles Hotels and Resorts
Rooms: 769

Named for Sir Stamford, founder of Singapore, this is the younger sibling of the celebrated, classic Raffles hotel across the road. All the rooms in this vast place are modern and very chic, particularly the bathrooms, while there are seventeen different bars and restaurants, plus private lounges for executive travellers and others.

Ritz-Carlton Millenia

7 Raffles Avenue, Singapore, 039799, Singapore
Tel: +65 6337 8888,
www.ritzcarlton.com
Group: The Ritz-Carlton Hotel Company
Rooms: 608

This 32-storey hotel features contemporary rooms decorated in eastern silks and Tibetan rugs, while amenities include a pool, a spa, a florist and a "romance concierge". Marble baths sit in front of large octagonal windows overlooking the marina or city: premiere suites provide access to the hotel's club lounge.

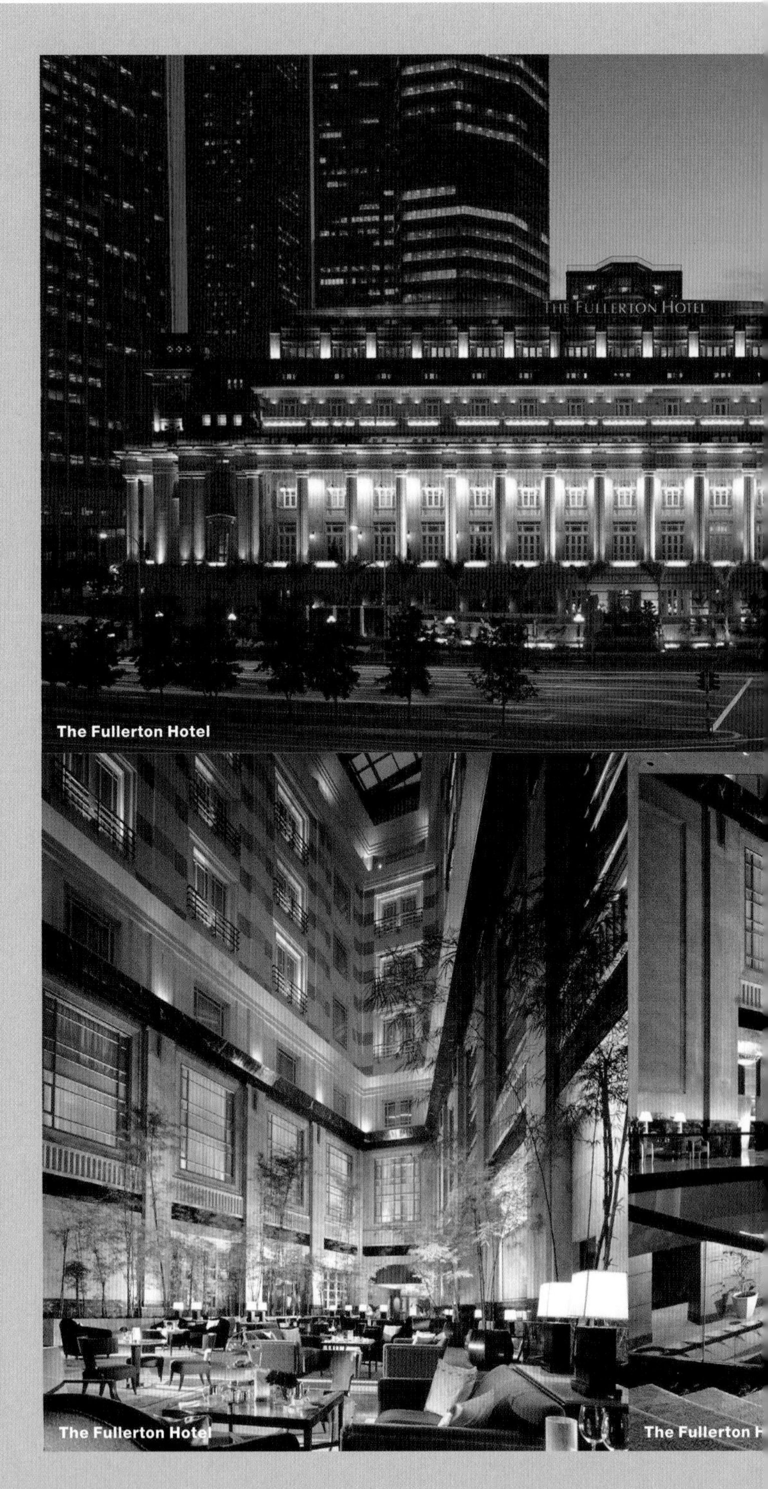

The Fullerton Hotel

The Fullerton Hotel

The Fullerton H

The Scarlet Hotel

33 Erskine Road, Chinatown, Singapore, 069333, Singapore
Tel: +65 6511 3333,
www.thescarlethotel.com
Group: Grace International
Rooms: 84

15 converted shophouses in Chinatown house this boutique hotel with a trio of restaurants and bars plus a sun terrace complete with open-air jacuzzi. I'd advise booking a 'Premium' or 'Executive' room as the lower end rooms are cramped, but suites here could add some colour into your relationship, quite literally. Service can sometimes be lacksadaisical and the long corridors claustrophobic but the Scarlet is reasonably priced, stylish and located in an area with some very atmospheric little bars.

The Sentosa Resort & Spa

2 Bukit Manis Road, Sentosa Island, 099891, Singapore Tel: +65 6275 0331,
www.thesentosa.com
Group: Beaufort
Rooms: 210 (inc. 43 suites) + 4 Garden Villas

Across a bridge from the City of Singapore lies the island of Sentosa where this resort sits on a cliff overlooking the South China Sea. There's 27 acres of woods, park and water gardens, a pool and some wonderful beaches, plus a golf course and the vast Spa Botanica next door.

Singapore Restaurants

As you'd expect from its location in the heart of Asia, Singapore has a rich and varied cuisine – all the way through from fine dining to simple "hawker centres" where arrays of stallholders offer flavoursome street food. Expect absolutely every Asian style of food, from Cantonese, Hainanese, Sichuan or Shanghainese, through Japanese, Indian, Malaysian, Indonesian and Thai. And, as befits a cosmopolitan city state with a large expat community, there is elegant European fine dining, too – most often business-friendly French cuisine.

Food comes colourfully to life during the city's many festivals – most notably the Chinese Mooncake Festival, which is celebrated in September. Mooncakes – sweet round pastries made from flour, oil and lotus seeds, available in many flavours – are served and lanterns are lit in a celebration of harvest.

Restaurants will add a 10% service charge, 5% GST and 1% government tax to the bill. This 16% is known as 'triple plus' and is mandatory. Tipping is not required on top.

Club Chinois

2-18 Orchard Parade Hotel, 1 Tanglin Road, Singapore, 247905, Singapore
Tel: +65 6834 0660, www.tunglok.com
Cuisine: Modern Chinese & dim sum

Pronounced 'Chin-Wha' in the French style, this club is known as the pioneer of modern Chinese food in Singapore and the interior is as contemporary as you'd expect. Signature dishes include five spiced foie gras, while the wine list is extensive and award winning.

Ember

Hotel 1929, 50 Keong Saik Road, Singapore, 089154, Singapore
Tel: +65 6347 1928, www.hotel1929.com
Cuisine: Modern European (with Asian twist)

In the new boutique Hotel 1929, in the heart of Chinatown, this small restaurant delivers modern European cuisine with Asian top notes. The design is original and glam, with tessellated mirrors and Japanese globe lamps. It is closed on Sunday and there is no lunch on Saturday.

Jade

Ground Floor, Fullerton Hotel, 1 Fullerton Square, Singapore, 049178, Singapore
Tel: +65 6877 8188, www.tunglok.com
Cuisine: Modern Chinese

Elegant, formal dining in a grand room of a grand hotel. The modern twists on classic Chinese cuisine plus the refined environment has attracted dignitaries including Bill Clinton.

Les Amis

2nd Floor, 16 Shaw Centre, 1 Scotts Road (entrance on Claymore Hill), Singapore, 228208, Singapore
Tel: +65 6733 2225, www.lesamis.com.sg
Cuisine: Modern French

This tiny, contemporary place is the flagship of the eponymous restaurant group. Expect modern French food produced with classic techniques from ingredients gathered the world over. The environment is elegantly minimalist.

Lingzhi Vegetarian Restaurant

5-1 Liat Tower, 541 Orchard Road, Singapore, 238881, Singapore
Tel: +65 6734 3788, www.tunglok.com
Cuisine: Vegetarian dim sum

Lingzhi is renowned for its monkey head mushroom dishes and the generally wide variety of fungi used in its cuisine. The vegetarian and vegan food here is so good that even steadfast carnivores won't notice they're not eating meat. There's a second branch at Far East Square, 7-10 Amoy Street.

My Humble House

2nd Floor, Esplanade Mall, 8 Raffles Avenue, Singapore, 039802, Singapore
Tel: +65 6423 1881, www.tunglok.com
Cuisine: Neo-classic Chinese

Set in the Esplanade, a striking modern arts complex, this fine dining restaurant is not in the slightest bit humble. The presentation of dishes is a work of art. The name derives from the traditional Cantonese phrase "Welcome to my humble abode", addressed to visiting guests.

Noble House

6-13 UIC Building, 5 Shenton Way, Singapore, 068808, Singapore Tel: +65 6227 0933, www.tunglok.com Cuisine: Classic Cantonese

This vast place in Singapore's thriving business district seats 520 and has six private dining rooms with the ever popular Karaoke TV. The traditional Cantonese cuisine attracts Singapore's financial movers and shakers, particularly at lunchtimes.

Oso Ristorante

27 Tanjong Pagar Road, Singapore, 088450, Singapore Tel: +65 6327 8378, www.oso.sg Cuisine: Italian

Chef Diego Chiarini serves elegant, simple Italian cuisine in a stylish environment with visible kitchen. The menu varies according to what is fresh and good that day but you can expect old favourites from tirami su to bresaola prepared with a lightness of touch.

Paddy Fields

The Copperdome, 368 Alexandra Road, Anchorport, Singapore, 159952, Singapore Tel: +65 6472 3822, www.tunglok.com Cuisine: Thai

Another outpost of the Tung Lok empire, this serves authentically spicy and flavourful Thai cuisine. Don't miss the clay pot jumbo prawns with glass noodles and the grilled shoulder of pork with garlic chilli dip.

Pierside Kitchen and Bar

One Fullerton, 1 Fullerton Road, Singapore, 049214, Singapore Tel: +65 6438 0400, www.piersidekitchen.com Cuisine: Seafood (with Japanese influence)

This minimalist, waterfront spot offers fabulous views over the harbour and – unusually for these parts – alfresco dining. The environment is stylish, the cuisine inventive and the clientele hip. Closed on Saturday lunch and Sundays.

Raffles Grill by Jacques & Laurent Pourcel

Raffles Hotel, 1 Beach Road, Singapore, 189673, Singapore Tel: +65 6337 1886, www.raffleshotel.com Cuisine: French

The flagship restaurant of this grand, landmark colonial hotel has been known as the island's number one, and celebrated, two-Michelin-star twin chefs Jacques and Laurent Pourcel keep the classic French cuisine top notch. There is no lunch on Saturday and the restaurant is closed Sunday.

Saint Pierre

Central Mall, 3 Magazine Road, Singapore, 059570, Singapore Tel: +65 6438 0887, www.saintpierre.com.sg Cuisine: Modern French

Buzzy, informal and modern, Saint Pierre combines a Belgian chef with Asian and European ingredients and new French cooking techniques to great effect. Reservations are recommended to enjoy some very fine food in a notably unstuffy environment.

San Marco

8th Floor, Fullerton Hotel, 1 Fullerton Square, Singapore, 049178, Singapore Tel: +65 6438 4404, www.fullertonhotel.com Cuisine: French-influenced Italian

This tiny Italian restaurant lies in the former lighthouse perched on top of the Fullerton Hotel, commanding spectacular views of the bay and the city skyline. Expect inventive, contemporary cuisine in a surprisingly funky environment. Closed on Saturday lunch and Sundays.

Tung Lok Restaurant

4-7/9 Liang Court Complex, 177 River Valley Road, Singapore, 179030, Singapore Tel: +65 6336 6022, www.tunglok.com Cuisine: Cantonese & dim sum

The flagship of the Tung Lok group – the finest restaurant group in Singapore – this has an almost stately ambience. The shark's fin dishes are celebrated and the broad wine list includes a range of champagnes. There are eight private dining rooms.

Tung Lok Seafood Gallery

2nd Floor East Coast Recreation Centre, Building B, 1000 East Coast Parkway, Singapore, 449876, Singapore Tel: +65 6246 0555, www.tunglok.com Cuisine: Seafood & sashimi

This is Singapore's foremost seafood restaurant, and its sheer scale – 450 capacity and ten private dining rooms – means the kind of fast turnover that ensures incredible freshness. Be sure to try the wasabi prawns and chilli crab.

The Fullerton Hotel

Singapore Bars

Bars in Singapore tend to be designed to appeal to the masses and few are noteworthy on the international scale. In general, drinks are disappointing and cocktails best avoided. Quiet, sophisticated lounges are scarce, but karaoke (KTV) bars are plentiful. Indeed, music is a theme in Singapore nightlife and live bands and DJs are commonplace.

Bottle service is popular in both bars and clubs: customers purchase a bottle of spirit and mixers which they share with friends at their table. If the bottle remains unfinished it is labelled and held by the bar for their next visit. This bottle culture appears to impact wine selections and even wine bars offer little choice by the glass.

For the same reason, carbonated mixers are served in jugs. When you order a G&T the bartender will pour the tonic into a jug so you can add it to your gin. By the time the twice poured tonic arrives in your drink, it's already on the warm and flat side.

Smoking is banned in all restaurants and bars that serve food eaten with utensils (which include chopsticks). Consequently most bars serve only finger food.

Getting around the bars by taxi is cheap, and, even better, air-conditioned. However, at peak times you're advised to book by phone rather than chance finding one on the street.

Singapore is not a late city, especially during the week when most bars close soon after midnight. Weekends see bars remain open till around 2am with clubs closing at 3am or later. Fridays and Saturdays also see the in vogue places packed despite the cover charges. There are plenty of clubs but only one of real note – Zouk on River Valley Road, which houses the internationally regarded Velvet Underground. Dress codes tend to be on the casual side of smart-casual and the minimum age for drinking alcohol is 18 years.

BAR OPIUME

1 Empress Place, Asian Civilisations Museum (next to IndoChine Waterfront), Singapore, 179555, Singapore

Tel: +65 6339 2876, **www.**indochine.com.sg
Hours: Sun-Thu 5pm-2am, Fri-Sat 5pm-3am

Type: Lounge bar
Alfresco: Large riverside patio
Entry: Open door
Highlights: Location
Atmosphere: Relaxed to party
Clientele: Office escapees, few tourists
Dress code: Office attire, fashion casual
Price guide: $$$
Food: Dim sum

Part of the huge IndoChine empire and positioned next to one of the company's large 'Waterfront' restaurants, Bar Opiume benefits from location, location, location. It sits on the bank of the Singapore River with a large patio and views of Boat Quay on the opposite bank.

The outside patio is covered in black leather box sofas and definitely the place to be. Inside, the bar is a little lacking in character. Despite the illuminated bar counter which changes colour, twin chandeliers and sports television screens are the most memorable design features. The look is club-like and later on that's what the place becomes.

The cocktail list is extensive and the signature Opium Martini with home infused lemongrass vodka can be great. However, we experienced some awful drinks so be warned.

BLU BAR

24th Floor Tower Wing, Shangri-La Hotel, 22 Orange Grove Road, Singapore, 258350, Singapore

Tel: +65 6213 4598, **www.**shangri-la.com
Hours: Sun-Thu 5pm-1am, Fri-Sat 5pm-2am

Type: Hotel bar
Alfresco: No
Entry: Via lift from lobby
Highlights: View
Atmosphere: Staid
Clientele: Business types & couples
Dress code: Smart casual
Price guide: $$$$
Food: Vegetable tempura, dumplings & other snacks

This bar, perched up on the 24th floor of the Shangri-La Hotel, is appropriately named. The frankly blue interior is swanky, modern and polished to the point of near sterility, with only art deco detailing to soften the harsh lines. The bar sits by the adjoining restaurant and an island bar counter in the shape of a running track dominates the room. Bar stools surround it and the high, glass topped round tables that dot the room. Arched windows rise from the floor to the double-height ceiling offering a spectacular view of the city below.

The lengthy wine list includes some 27 by the glass, among them Krug and Dom Perignon champagnes. Cocktails are also on offer but are far from special.

The Blu Bar is a hotel bar with a view but little more.

Brewerkz

BREEZE

●●●◐○

The Scarlet Hotel, 33 Erskine Road, Chinatown, Singapore, 069333, Singapore

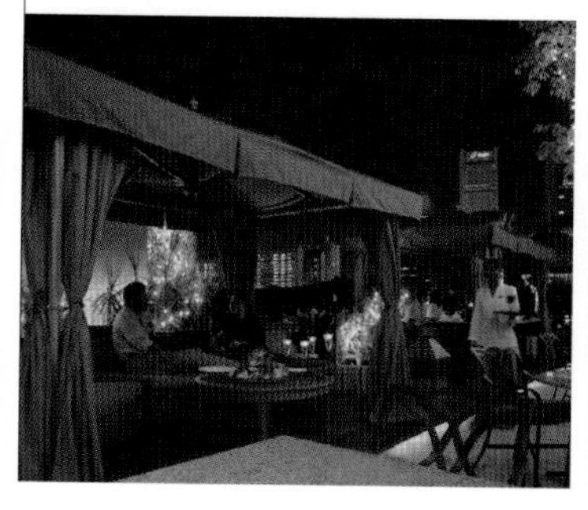

Tel: +65 6511 3333, **www.**thescarlethotel.com
Hours: Mon-Thu 7pm-midnight, Fri-Sat 7am-2am

Type: Hotel bar
Alfresco: Roof terrace
Entry: Via lift from lobby
Highlights: The breeze
Atmosphere: Chilled
Clientele: Hotel guests & couples
Dress code: Fashionably casual
Price guide: $$$$
Food: Crab Rangoon, calamari, salads etc

Breeze is an appropriate name for this bar. In steamy Singapore this open air, rooftop lounge offers an escape from the usual humidity or air-conditioning into good old fashioned air. You'll need to book at least three days ahead to reserve a table and there is a no standing policy.

Although on a hotel roof, Breeze is only on the fourth floor. But this is low-rise Chinatown so the view down a tree lined street and over the surrounding tiled roofs is pleasant enough. It's a romantic spot with tables under pagodas, day beds, subtle illumination and flickering night lights. There is no shelter, so if it rains guests are relocated to the Desire restaurant on the first floor.

A tapas menu with grills, seafood platters, salads and suchlike befits the Mediterranean styled décor. There is a choice of eight wines by the glass plus cocktails such as the Earl Grey Martini, which read well on the menu but can be disappointing when consumed.

BREWERKZ & WINE GARAGE

01-05/06 Riverside Point, 30 Merchant Road, Singapore, 058282, Singapore

Tel: +65 6438 7438, **www.**brewerkz.com
Hours: Mon-Thu noon-midnight, Fri-Sat noon-1am, Sun 11am-midnight

Type: Sports/beer bar
Alfresco: Seating overlooking river
Entry: Open door
Highlights: Beers
Atmosphere: Relaxed, party
Clientele: Sports & beer fans
Dress code: Office attire / casual
Price guide: $$$
Food: American-style

This very American sports bar is unlike most other such venues – it has great beer. In fact, Brewerkz offers the best beers I've sampled in a brew pub anywhere in the world.

The industrial interior features exposed steel girders, stainless steel brewing vessels and other brewing equipment. TV screens, pool tables and even a dartboard make sports fans feel at home. The open front with its outside seating offers views across the Singapore River to the hideously garish Clarke Quay "festival village" opposite.

Brew master Scott Robertson makes a dozen beers here and you can sample a flight of eight 2oz tasters for $12.50. Scott brews a style to suit all palates from his easy drinking Golden Ale through to the black Oatmeal Stout. The hoppy Xtra IPA at 7.2% abv is an amazingly tasty, balanced brew. Eleven interesting imported beers such as Canadian Maudite and Belgian Pauwel Kwak are also available. If wine is your thing, then head for the Wine Garage next door.

DIVINE SOCIETY

1F Parkview Square, 600 North Bridge Road, Singapore, 188778, Singapore

Tel: +65 6396 4466
Hours: Mon-Sat noon-11pm

Type: Wine bar
Alfresco: No
Entry: Members only
Highlights: Architecture
Atmosphere: Formal
Clientele: Business types
Dress code: Suits
Price guide: $$$$$
Food: Measly cheese plate

Parkview Square is the most impressive and expensive office building in Singapore. It is affectionately known by expats as the Gotham City building as its grandiose art deco architecture bears a striking resemblance to the edifice in the Batman movies. Parkview's lobby is spectacular. Italian frescoes cover the soaring ceiling, gold trimmed marble adorns the floors and walls, and there is not a column in sight.

With its twelve metre tall, 3000 bottle wine cellar, Divine Society suits this ostentatious lobby. Bottles are plucked from the tower by tutu clad, winged 'wine angels' suspended on wires. It's quite a spectacle – you can see right up their skirts!

Theoretically only members who've paid some S$3000 a year are admitted but the smartly attired are rarely challenged, especially on Saturdays when it's all but deserted. A second Martini bar sponsored by The Macallan lies opposite.

Despite the huge selection, a mere half dozen or so wines and one champagne are available by the glass. All in all, Divine Society fails to live up to its magnificent surroundings.

INTROBAR

●●●○○

Lobby Level 1, Swissotel Stamford, Singapore

Tel: +65 6431 3176
Hours: Sun-Thu 11am-1am, Fri-Sat 11am-3am

Type: Hotel bar
Alfresco: No
Entry: Open door
Highlights: Cocktails & service
Atmosphere: Relaxed but dull
Clientele: Business types
Dress code: Business attire
Price guide: $$$$
Food: Pizzas, chicken wings, calamari etc

Set on the ground floor of the Swissotel Stamford and Raffles Plaza complex, this rather bland bar lacks the view offered by the New Asia bar seventy floors above. Thankfully it also lacks the tack and terrible drinks we experienced there.

Introbar is a hotel lobby bar and looks the part - corporate, modern and bland. However, it is comfortable enough with plentiful banquette seating divided by mahogany panels.

Take a seat at the underlit onyx bar and order yourself a pizza and a cocktail. Neither will be spectacular but both will satisfy and the service you receive will be friendly and efficient.

Introbar may not be the most exciting or fashionable venue but it is a safe bet for drinks and service. If you must go up to New Asia for the view, try to gain access to the galleried mezzanine level where you can sit, sip and watch the hoi-polloi below.

LONG BAR

●●◐○○

Raffles Hotel, 1 Beach Road, Colonial District, Singapore, 189673, Singapore

Tel: +65 6431 6156, **www.**raffleshotel.com
Hours: Sun-Thu 11am-12:30am, Fri-Sat 11am-1:30am

Type: Lounge bar
Alfresco: Terrace
Entry: Tourists welcome
Highlights: Décor
Atmosphere: Better when band sparks up
Clientele: Tourists
Dress code: Casual (shorts commonplace)
Price guide: $$$$
Bar snacks: Beer battered fish & chips, spicy chicken wings

The Long Bar at the Raffles Hotel is one of the world's legendary bars, famous for being where, some time between 1911 and 1915, Ngiam Tong Boon created the Singapore Sling. The 1887 hotel with its neo-Renaissance architecture is a reminder of past British colonial splendour and the Long Bar's duplex interior looks the part with ceiling fans, cane furniture and plantation shutters. Bowls of complementary peanuts line the bar counter and it is customary to discard your shells onto the beautiful mosaic floor, which becomes a tad slippery as a result.

The original Long Bar was situated near the hotel's lobby on the ground floor. This is, in fact, a 1980s reproduction tucked away upstairs around the side of the hotel. Like the bar, the famous Sling has changed - for the worse. It is premixed and dispensed from plastic jugs filled from a tap in the corner of the bar. The other cocktails, including the famous Million Dollar Cocktail, are also lamentable.

If you are any kind of discerning drinker you will feel both compelled to visit this bar and bitterly disappointed by the reality. However, the tourists appear to love it, and its Slings.

MEZZA9 MARTINI BAR

●●●○○

Grand Hyatt Singapore, 10 Scotts Road, Singapore, 228211, Singapore

Tel: +65 6738 1234, **www.**singapore.grand.hyatt.com
Hours: Mon-Sun 10:30am-2am

Type: Lounge bar
Alfresco: No
Entry: Behind wine cellars
Highlights: Wine list & snacks
Atmosphere: Lacklustre
Clientele: Locals, few tourists
Dress code: Whatever
Price guide: $$$
Bar snacks: Cheese plate & other snacks

Ascend the wide, sweeping staircase from the lobby of the Grand Hyatt to Mezza9, a kind of upmarket food court with nine different food and drink venues. It's a nice concept but all the different counters and groups of seats can be a little daunting.

One of the nine venues is a Martini Bar and thankfully this is set apart from the chaos in its own space. There are two entrances, one on either side of the building, both partially hidden behind large, walk-in wine cellars with glass fronts. Once inside you'll find a long, dimly lit lounge with comfy chairs. The bar with its long polished wooden counter sits in its own conservatory which protrudes from the front of the hotel.

There's an extensive wine list (22 by the glass) and plenty of cocktails. While the wines may live up to their billing, all the cocktails we tried were disappointing.

This quiet, relaxed space provides a break from the crowds in nearby tourist haunts but remains a tad soulless and boring.

POST BAR

●●●◐○

The Fullerton Hotel, 1 Fullerton Square, Singapore, 049178, Singapore

Tel: +65 6877 8120, **www.**fullertonhotel.com
Hours: Mon-Fri noon-2am, Sat-Sun 2:30pm-2am

Type: Lobby lounge bar
Alfresco: No
Entry: Via hotel lobby
Highlights: Service, drinks
Atmosphere: Relaxed to party
Clientele: Hotel guests, expats
Dress code: Office attire, fashion casual (no shorts)
Price guide: $$$$
Bar snacks: Oysters to light meals

This bar sits off the main atrium of the impressive Fullerton Hotel in the heart of Singapore's financial district, so it's not surprising that, apart from the odd international traveller, most customers are expats from nearby offices.

It is housed in what was once the main transaction hall of the General Post Office and the original wall motifs, lofty ceiling and pillars remain. However, don't expect a museum piece. The Post Bar is a modern affair with a long island bar that's underlit and continually changes colour. The large, airy room features white walls, high chairs at round tables and groupings of low armchairs. As well as the main bar there's a dedicated Martini bar with a wide range of premium gin and vodka brands.

Cocktails can be very good here but regulars seem to favour Dom Perignon and oysters.

QUE PASA

●●●●○

7 Emerald Hill Road (off Orchard Road), Singapore, 229291, Singapore

Tel: +65 6235 6626, **www.**emeraldhillgroup.com
Hours: Sun-Thu 6pm-2am, Fri-Sat 6pm-3am

Type: Tapas / wine bar
Alfresco: Shaded & decked front terrace
Entry: Subject to capacity (no standing)
Highlights: Food, wine
Atmosphere: Relaxed to party
Clientele: Expats & tourists
Dress code: Office attire, fashion casual
Price guide: $$$
Bar snacks: Tapas, pizza & snacks

Que Pasa means 'what's happening?' in Spanish and it's an appropriate name for this rustic looking wine and tapas bar on Singapore's pretty party street, Emerald Hill.

Housed in a 1910 Straits Chinese shophouse, the ground floor resembles a grocery store with provisions on display. In the main room, wine bottles are stacked on floor to ceiling shelves, old wooden tables and benches house groups of drinkers and wine barrel lids are used as tabletops.

The wine cellar houses an extensive collection of premium bins and is reserved for privileged regulars. There is another, quieter bar on the second floor plus 'The Salon', a private lounge equipped with old leather Chesterfields, wing armchairs, glass display cabinets and a gentlemen's club feel. To gain access to this you'll need to order a 'premium' - i.e. expensive - bottle of wine.

A warm, relaxed, shabby chic atmosphere prevails, making this a pleasant place to share tapas and a bottle of wine from the extensive list. The selection by the glass is limited.

UNION BAR

81 Club Street, Chinatown, Singapore, Singapore

Tel: +65 6327 4990
Hours: Mon-Thu 5pm-1am, Fri-Sat 5pm-3am

Type: Lounge bar
Alfresco: Small front terrace
Entry: Open door
Highlights: Atmosphere
Atmosphere: Cosy
Clientele: Expats & tourists
Dress code: Casual
Price guide: $$$
Bar snacks: Oysters, pizza and light bites

Since about 70% of Singapore's population is Chinese, the concept of Chinatown may seem a little superfluous. It dates back to 1822 when Sir Stamford Raffles, founder of modern Singapore, attempted to reduce racial tensions by designating parts of the island as areas for specific races to settle. Today, Chinatown's low rise skyline contrasts with the modern skyscrapers around it and its small, cosy bars seem a million miles away from the bling emporia which are commonplace in other parts of the city. Of all Chinatown's atmospheric little hideaways, the Union is my favourite.

Drinkswise the offering is basic, without great wines, beers or cocktails. But the rustic rendered and bare brick walls, flickering night lights and low, comfy chairs create a simple appeal. Modern art adorns the walls and strangely makes this long, narrow space feel more New York than Singapore. Only I don't know a bar in New York that feels so homely.

BARTENDING BASICS

PLEASE READ THE FOLLOWING INSTRUCTIONS BEFORE ATTEMPTING TO FOLLOW THE RECIPES IN THIS GUIDE.

By definition any drink which is described as a cocktail contains more than one ingredient. So if you are going to make cocktails you have to know how to combine these various liquids. Firstly, as in cooking, there is a correct order in which to prepare things and with few exceptions that runs as follows:

1. Select glass and chill or pre-heat (if required).
2. Prepare garnish (if required).
3. Pour ingredients.
4. Add ice (if required - add last to minimise melt).
5. Combine ingredients.
6. Add garnish (if required).
7. Consume or serve to guest.

Essentially, there are four different ways to mix a cocktail: shake, stir, blend and build. (Building a drink means combining the ingredients in the glass in which the cocktail will be served.)

A fifth construction method, 'layering', isn't strictly mixing. The idea here is to float each ingredient on its predecessor without the ingredients merging at all. At the heart of every cocktail lies at least one of these five methods. So understanding these terms is fundamental.

SHAKE

When you see the phrase 'shake with ice and strain', you should place all the necessary ingredients with cubed ice in a cocktail shaker and shake briskly for about twenty seconds. Then you should strain the liquid into the glass, leaving the ice behind in the shaker.

Shaking not only mixes a drink. It also chills and dilutes it. The dilution is as important to the resulting cocktail as using the right proportions of each ingredient. If you use too little ice it will quickly melt in the shaker, producing an over-diluted cocktail - so always fill your shaker at least two-thirds full of fresh ice.

Losing your grip while shaking is likely to make a mess and could result in injury, so always hold the shaker with two hands and never shake fizzy ingredients.

Although shakers come in many shapes and sizes there are two basic types.

STANDARD SHAKER

A standard shaker consists of three parts and hence is sometimes referred to as a three-piece shaker. The three pieces are **1.** a flat-bottomed, conical base or 'can', **2.** a top with a built-in strainer and **3.** a cap.

I strongly recommend this style of shaker for amateurs due to its ease of use. Be sure to purchase a shaker with a capacity of at least one pint as this will allow the ice room to travel and so mix more effectively.

TO USE:

1. Combine all ingredients in the base of the shaker and fill two-thirds full with ice.
2. Place the top and cap firmly on the base.
3. Pick up the closed shaker with one hand on the top and the other gripping the bottom and shake vigorously. The cap should always be on the top when shaking and should point away from guests.
4. After shaking briskly for a count of around 20 seconds, lift off the cap, hold the shaker by its base with one finger securing the top and pour the drink through the built-in strainer.

BOSTON SHAKER

A Boston shaker comprises two flat-bottomed cones, one larger than the other. The large cone, or 'can', is made of stainless steel while the smaller cone can be either glass or stainless steel. I prefer glass as this allows both mixer and guest to see the drink being made.

Avoid Boston shakers that rely on a rubber ring to seal. I use Alessi Boston tins as I find these seal without a thump and open with the lightest tap. However good your Boston shaker, these devices demand an element of skill and practice is usually required for a new user to become proficient.

TO USE:

1. Combine ingredients in the glass or smaller of the two cans.

2. Fill the large can with ice and briskly upend over the smaller can (or glass), quickly enough to avoid spilling any ice. Lightly tap the top with the heel of your hand to create a seal between the two parts.

3. Lift shaker with one hand on the top and the other gripping the base and shake vigorously. The smaller can (or glass) should always be on the top when shaking and should point away from guests.

4. After shaking for around 20 seconds, hold the larger (base) can in one hand and break the seal between the two halves of the shaker by tapping the base can with the heel of your other hand at the point where it meets the upper can (or glass).

5. Before pouring place a strainer with a coiled rim (also known as a Hawthorne strainer) over the top of the can and strain the mixture into the glass, leaving the ice cubes behind.

STIR

If a cocktail recipe calls for you to 'stir with ice and strain', stir in a mixing glass using a bar spoon with a long, spiralling stem. If a lipped mixing glass is not available, one half of a Boston shaker, or the base of a standard shaker, will suffice.

Combine the ingredients in the mixing glass, adding the ice last. Slide the back of the spoon down the inside of the mixing glass and stir the drink. Then strain into a glass using a strainer (or the top of a standard shaker if you are using a standard shaker base in place of a mixing glass).

Some bartenders (and I'm one) prefer to use the flat end of a bar spoon to stir a drink. Simply place the flat end on top of the ice in the mixing glass and start to stir, working the spoon down the drink as you go.

FINE STRAIN

Most cocktails that are served 'straight up' without ice benefit from an additional finer strain, over and above the standard strain which keeps ice cubes out of the drink. This 'fine strain' removes small fragments of fruit and fine flecks of ice which can spoil the appearance of a drink. All you need to do is strain a cocktail through the strainer you would normally use while holding a fine sieve, like a tea strainer, between the shaker and the glass. Another popular term for this method is 'double strain'.

BLEND

When a cocktail recipe calls for you to 'blend with ice', place ingredients and ice into a blender and blend until a smooth, even consistency is achieved. Ideally you should use crushed ice, as this lessens wear on the blender's blades. Place liquid ingredients in the blender first, adding the ice last, as always. If you have a variable speed blender, always start slowly and build up speed.

LAYER

As the name would suggest, layered drinks include layers of different ingredients, often with contrasting colours. This effect is achieved by carefully pouring each ingredient into the glass so that it floats on its predecessor.

The success of this technique is dependent on the density (specific gravity) of the liquids used. As a rule of thumb, the less alcohol and the more sugar an ingredient contains, the heavier it is. The heaviest ingredients should be poured first and the lightest last. Syrups are non-alcoholic and contain a lot of sugar so are usually the heaviest ingredient. Liqueurs, which are high in sugar and lower in alcohol than spirits, are generally the next heaviest ingredient. The exception to this rule is cream and cream liqueurs, which can float.

One brand of a particular liqueur may be heavier or lighter than another. The relative temperatures of ingredients may also affect their ability to float or sink. Hence a degree of experimentation is inevitable when creating layered drinks. Layering can be achieved in one of two ways. The first involves pouring down the spiral handle of a bar spoon, keeping the flat, disc-shaped end of the spoon over the surface of the drink. Alternatively you can hold the bowl end of a bar spoon (or a soup spoon) in contact with the side of the glass and over the surface of the drink and pour over it.

The term 'float' refers to layering the final ingredient on top of a cocktail.

MUDDLE

Muddling means pummelling fruits, herbs and/or spices with a muddler (a blunt tool similar to a pestle) so as to crush them and release their flavour. (You can also use a rolling pin.) As when using a pestle and mortar, push down on the muddler with a twisting action.

Only attempt to muddle in the base of a shaker or a suitably sturdy glass. Never attempt to muddle hard, unripe fruits in a glass as the pressure required could break the glass. I've witnessed a bartender slash his hand open on a broken glass while muddling and can't over-emphasize how careful you should be.

FLAME

The term ignite, flame or flambé means that the drink should be set alight. Please exercise extreme care when setting fire to drinks. Be particularly careful not to knock over a lit drink and never attempt to carry a drink which is still alight. Before drinking, cover the glass so as to suffocate the flame and be aware that the rim of the glass may be hot.

ICE

A plentiful supply of fresh ice is essential to making good cocktails. When buying bagged ice avoid the hollow, tubular kind and the thin wafers. Instead look for large, solid cubes of ice. I have a Hoshizaki ice machine which produces large solid cubes, and thoroughly recommend it.

When filling ice cube trays, use bottled or filtered water to avoid the taste of chlorine often apparent in municipal water supplies. Your ice should be dry, almost sticky to the touch. Never use 'wet' ice that has started to thaw.

When serving a drink over ice, always fill the glass with ice, rather than just adding a few cubes. This makes the drink much colder, the ice lasts longer and so melting ice does not dilute the drink.

Never use ice in a cocktail shaker twice, even if it's to mix the same drink as last time. You should always throw away ice after straining the drink and use fresh ice to fill the glass if required.

Unless otherwise stated, all references to ice in this guide mean cubed ice. If crushed ice is required for a particular recipe, the recipe will state 'crushed ice'. This is available commercially. Alternatively you can crush cubed ice in an ice-crusher or simply bash a bag of it with a rolling pin.

If a glass is broken near your ice stocks, melt the ice with warm water, clean the container and re-stock with fresh ice. If this occurs in a busy bar and you are not immediately able to clean the ice well, mark it as being contaminated with a liberal coating of red grenadine syrup and draw ice from another station.

MEASURING

Balancing each ingredient within a cocktail is key to making a great drink. Therefore the accuracy with which ingredients are measured is critical to the finished cocktail.

In this guide I've expressed the measures of each ingredient in 'shots'. Ideally a shot is 25ml or one US fluid ounce (29.6ml), measured in a standard jigger. (You can also use a clean medicine measure or even a small shot glass.) Whatever measure you use should have straight sides to enable you to accurately judge fractions of a shot. Look out for measures which are graduated for quarter and half shots.

The measure 'spoon' refers to a bar spoon, which is slightly larger than a standard teaspoon.

Some bartenders attempt to measure shots by counting time and estimating the amount of liquid flowing through a bottle's spout. This is known as 'free-pouring' and can be terribly inaccurate. I strongly recommend the use of a physical measure.

GARNISHES

Garnishes are used to decorate cocktails and are often anchored to the rim of the glass. Strictly speaking, garnishes should be edible, so please forget about paper parasols. Anything from banana chunks, strawberries or redcurrants to coffee beans, confectionery, basil leaves and slices of fresh ginger can be used as a garnish. The correct garnish will often enhance the aroma and flavour as well as the look of a drink.

Fruit should be unblemished and washed prior to use. Olives, in particular, should be washed thoroughly to prevent oil from spoiling the appearance of a drink. Cut citrus fruits have a maximum shelf life of 24 hours when refrigerated. Cherries and olives should be stored refrigerated and left in their own juices.

Olives, cherries, pickled onions and fresh berries are sometimes served on cocktail sticks. A whole slice of citrus fruit served on a cocktail stick 'mast' is known as a 'sail': this is often accompanied by a cherry.

Celery sticks may be placed in drinks as stirring rods while cinnamon sticks are often placed in hot drinks and toddies.

To sprinkle chocolate on the surface of a drink you can either shave chocolate using a vegetable peeler or crumble a Cadbury's Flake bar. The instruction 'dust with chocolate' refers to a fine coating of cocoa powder on the surface of a drink. (When dusting with nutmeg it is always best to grate fresh nutmeg as the powdered kind lacks flavour.)

Citrus peels are often used as a garnish. Besides the variations listed under 'zest twist' overleaf, thin, narrow lengths of citrus peel may be tied in a 'knot'. A 'Horse's Neck' is the entire peel of either an orange, a lemon or a lime, cut in a continuous spiral and placed so as to overhang the rim of the glass.

Wedges of lemons and limes are often squeezed into drinks or fixed to the glass as a garnish. A wedge is an eighth segment of the fruit. Cut the 'knobs' from the top and bottom of the fruit, slice the fruit in half lengthwise, then cut each half into four equal wedges lengthwise.

Mint sprigs are often used to garnish cups and juleps.

ZEST TWIST

This term refers to flavouring a drink by releasing the aromatic oils from a strip of citrus zest. Using a knife or peeler, cut a half inch (12mm) wide length of zest from an unwaxed, cleaned fruit so as to leave just a little of the white pith. Hold it over the glass with the thumb and forefinger of each hand, coloured side down. Turn one end clockwise and the other anticlockwise so as to twist the peel and force some of its oils over the surface of the drink. Deposit any flavoursome oils left on the surface of the peel by wiping the coloured side around the rim of the glass. Finally, drop the peel onto the surface of the drink. (Some prefer to dispose of the spent twist.)

A flamed zest twist is a dramatic variation on this theme which involves burning the aromatic oils emitted from citrus fruit zest over the surface of a drink. Lemons and limes are sometimes treated in this way but oranges are most popular. Firm, thick-skinned navel oranges, like Washington Navels, are best.

You will need to cut as wide a strip of zest as you can, wider than you would for a standard twist. Hold the cut zest, peel side down, between the thumb and forefinger about four inches above the drink and gently warm it with a lighter flame. Then pinch the peel by its edges so that its oils squirt through the flame towards the surface of the drink - there should be a flash as the oils ignite. Finally, wipe the zest around the rim of the glass.

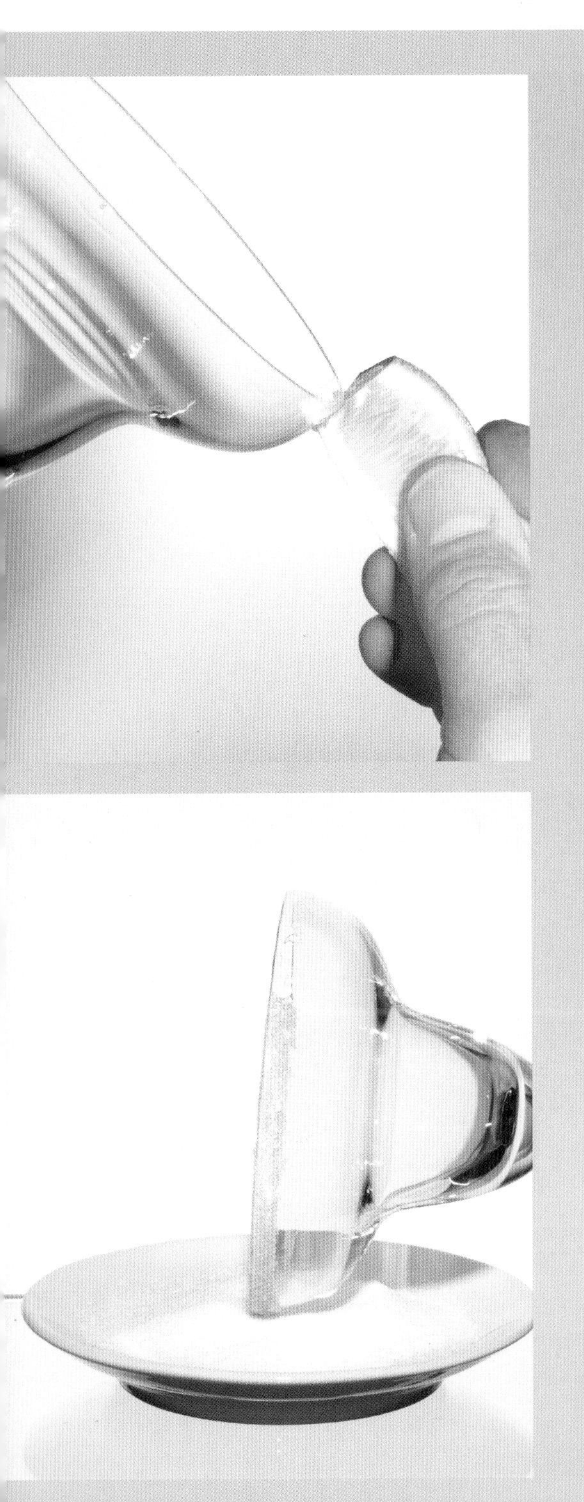

SALT/SUGAR RIM

Some recipes call for the rim of the glass to be coated with salt, sugar or other ingredients such as desiccated coconut or chocolate: you will need to moisten the rim first before the ingredient will hold. When using salt, whip a cut wedge of lime around the outside edge of the rim, then roll the outside edge through a saucer of salt. (Use sea salt rather than iodised salt as the flavour is less biting.) For sweet ingredients like sugar and chocolate, either use an orange slice as you would a lime wedge or moisten a sponge or paper towel with a suitable liqueur and run it around the outside edge of the glass.

Whatever you are using to rim the glass should cling to the outside edge only. Remember, garnishes are not a cocktail ingredient but an optional extra to be consumed by choice. They should not contaminate your cocktail. If some of your garnish should become stuck to the inside edge of the glass, remove it using a fresh fruit wedge or a paper towel.

It is good practice to salt or sugar only two-thirds of the rim of a glass. This allows the drinker the option of avoiding the salt or sugar. If you rim glasses some hours prior to use, the lime juice or liqueur will dry, leaving a crust of salt or sugar crystals around the rim. The glasses can then be placed in a refrigerator to chill ready for use.

A professional piece of equipment with the unfortunate title of a 'rimmer' has three sections, one with a sponge for water or lime juice, one containing sugar and another containing salt. Beware, as this encourages dipping the glass onto a moist sponge and then into the garnish, and so contaminating the inside of the glass.

#1

SPICY BEANS

Canadian readers will probably already be aware of these long, thin pickled beans. They are a popular alternative to celery in those parts as a garnish for 'Caesar' cocktails, a Canadian twist on the Bloody Mary. They originate with Blaze Denoon, who started picking beans in Vancouver in 1995. For more see www.blazesbeans.com.

The Bloody Caesar is credited to Walter Chell. When Marco's Italian restaurant opened at the Calgary Inn, Canada, in 1969, Walter was inspired by the flavour of Spaghetti Vongole (spaghetti with clams). So he used Clamato juice in place of tomato juice in his Bloody Mary style cocktail.

#2 FLOWERING JASMINE TEA ROSETTES

These hand-sewn tea flowers are produced in China near the borders of Laos and Vietnam. White, green and black tea leaves are picked early in the morning then shaped and hand-sewn with cotton thread around chrysanthemum flowers while still damp. The resulting balls are dried with fresh jasmine flowers which give the tea its delicate flavour and aroma. When they are infused in hot water, they open up into a chrysanthemum flower surrounded by tea leaf petals. While intended for brewing hot tea, they make an unusual and aromatic cocktail garnish.

#3 FLAMING ZEST BOAT

I'm indebted to the folk at Absinthe in San Francisco for this potentially dangerous garnish. Not only does it add to the theatrical style of Tiki drinks but my inner child finds floating fire boats irresistible.

Make your zest boat by chopping a lime or lemon in half lengthwise and scraping away the flesh from one half. Float your boat on top of the drink and carefully pour in its cargo of high-strength dark rum - for example Woods 100 or Pusser's Naval rum. Lastly, and very carefully please, ignite the rum.

This is almost certainly against the rules of the nanny state and definitely constitutes a fire hazard. All the same, dear readers, I trust you to be responsible and careful. To prevent the predictable trail of carnage I will add:

1/ Only use a fraction of a shot of rum or it will burn for ages.
2/ Be aware that the flame may be blue and so almost invisible.
3/ Don't even move the glass, let alone drink from it, until the flame is out.
4/ Don't blame me if your bar goes up in smoke.

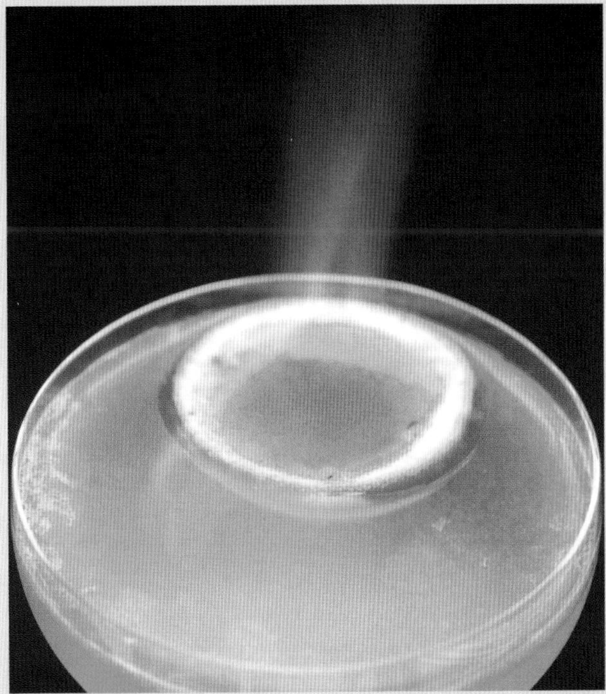

COCKTAILS L-Q

L.A. ICED TEA

Glass: Sling
Garnish: Split lime wedge
Method: SHAKE first seven ingredients with ice and strain into ice-filled glass. Top with soda.

1/2	shot(s)	Ketel One vodka
1/2	shot(s)	Plymouth gin
1/2	shot(s)	Light white rum
1/2	shot(s)	Cointreau / triple sec
1/2	shot(s)	Midori melon liqueur
1	shot(s)	Freshly squeezed lime juice
1/2	shot(s)	Sugar (gomme) syrup
Top up with		Soda water (club soda)

Comment: Long and lime green with subtle notes of melon and fresh lime.

LAGO COSMO

Glass: Martini
Garnish: Orange zest twist
Method: SHAKE all ingredients with ice and fine strain into chilled glass.

1 1/2	shot(s)	Cranberry flavoured vodka
3/4	shot(s)	Cointreau / triple sec
1 3/4	shot(s)	Freshly squeezed orange juice
1/4	shot(s)	Freshly squeezed lime juice
1/2	shot(s)	Sugar (gomme) syrup

Origin: Discovered in 2003 at Nectar @ Bellagio, Las Vegas, USA.
Comment: A Cosmo with cranberry vodka in place of citrus vodka and orange juice in place of cranberry juice.

LAVENDER & BLACK PEPPER MARTINI [NEW]

Glass: Martini
Method: Pour the syrup into an ice filled mixing glass. Add the vodka and black pepper. STIR and super-fine strain into chilled glass.

2 1/2	shot(s)	Ketel One vodka
1/4	shot(s)	Sonoma Lavender sugar syrup
2	twist	Freshly ground black pepper

Origin: Adapted from a recipe created in 2006 by Richard Gillam at The Kenilworth Hotel, Warwickshire, England.
Comment: Subtly sweetened and lavender flavoured vodka with a bump and grind of spicy pepper.

LANDSLIDE

Glass: Shot
Method: Refrigerate ingredients then LAYER in chilled glass by carefully pouring in the following order.

1/2	shot(s)	Luxardo Amaretto di Saschira liqueur
1/2	shot(s)	Bols crème de banane
1/2	shot(s)	Baileys Irish Cream liqueur

Comment: A sweet but pleasant combination of banana, almond and Irish cream liqueur.

LAVENDER MARTINI [NEW]

Glass: Martini
Garnish: Lemon zest twist
Method: STIR all ingredients with ice and strain into chilled glass.

2 1/2	shot(s)	Lavender infused Ketel One vodka
3/4	shot(s)	Parfait amour liqueur
1/4	shot(s)	Dry vermouth

Origin: Created in 2006 by yours truly.
Comment: Infusing lavender in vodka tends to make it bitter but the parfait amour adds sweetness as well as flavour and colour.

THE LAST WORD [NEW]

Glass: Martini
Garnish: Lime wedge on rim
Method: SHAKE all ingredients with ice and fine strain into chilled glass.

3/4	shot(s)	Plymouth gin
3/4	shot(s)	Green Chartreuse
3/4	shot(s)	Luxardo maraschino liqueur
3/4	shot(s)	Freshly squeezed lime juice
1/2	shot(s)	Chilled mineral water (omit if wet ice)

Origin: An old classic championed in 2005 by the team at Pegu Club, New York City, USA.
Comment: Chartreuse devotees will love this balanced, tangy drink. I'm one.

LAVENDER MARGARITA [NEW]

Glass: Coupette
Garnish: Lime wedge
Method: SHAKE all ingredients with ice and fine strain into chilled glass.

2	shot(s)	Sauza Hornitos tequila
1	shot(s)	Freshly squeezed lime juice
1/2	shot(s)	Sonoma lavender infused sugar syrup

Origin: Created in 2006 by yours truly.
Comment: Lavender lime and tequila combine harmoniously.

LAZARUS

Glass: Martini
Garnish: Float three coffee beans
Method: SHAKE all ingredients with ice and fine strain into chilled glass.

1	shot(s)	Ketel One vodka
1	shot(s)	Kahlúa coffee liqueur
1/2	shot(s)	Rémy Martin cognac
1	shot(s)	Espresso coffee (cold)

Origin: Created in 2000 by David Whitehead at Atrium, Leeds, England.
Comment: A flavoursome combination of spirit and coffee.

A B C D E F G H I J K L M N O P Q R S T U V W X Y Z

LCB MARTINI

Glass: Martini
Garnish: Lemon zest twist
Method: SHAKE all ingredients with ice and fine strain into chilled glass.

2	shot(s)	**Ketel One vodka**
3/4	shot(s)	**Sauvignon Blanc/unoaked Chardonnay wine**
2	shot(s)	**Freshly squeezed pink grapefruit juice**
1/4	shot(s)	**Sugar (gomme) syrup**

Origin: Created by yours truly in 2004 and named after Lisa Clare Ball, who loves both Sauvignon and pink grapefruit juice.
Comment: A sweet and sour, citrus fresh Martini.

LEAP YEAR MARTINI [NEW]

Glass: Martini
Garnish: Lemon peel twist
Method: SHAKE all ingredients with ice and fine strain into chilled glass.

2	shot(s)	**Plymouth gin**
1/2	shot(s)	**Grand Marnier liqueur**
1/2	shot(s)	**Sweet (rosso) vermouth**
1/4	shot(s)	**Freshly squeezed lemon juice**

Origin: Harry Craddock created this drink for the Leap Year celebrations at the Savoy Hotel, London, on 29th February 1928 and recorded it in his 1930 Savoy Cocktail Book.
Comment: This drink, which is on the dry side, needs to be served ice-cold.

LEAVE IT TO ME MARTINI [NEW]

Glass: Martini
Garnish: Lemon zest twist
Method: SHAKE all ingredients with ice and fine strain into chilled glass.

1 1/2	shot(s)	**Plymouth gin**
1/2	shot(s)	**Bols apricot brandy**
3/4	shot(s)	**Sweet (rosso) vermouth**
1/2	shot(s)	**Freshly squeezed lemon juice**
1/4	shot(s)	**Sonoma pomegranate (grenadine) syrup**

Origin: Adapted from a recipe in Harry Craddock's 1930 Savoy Cocktail Book.
Comment: Gin, apricot, vermouth and lemon create an old fashioned but well balanced drink.

THE LEGEND

Glass: Martini
Garnish: Blackberries on stick
Method: SHAKE all ingredients with ice and fine strain into chilled glass.

2	shot(s)	**Ketel One vodka**
1	shot(s)	**Freshly squeezed lime juice**
1/4	shot(s)	**Bols blackberry (crème de mûre) liqueur**
1/4	shot(s)	**Sugar (gomme) syrup**
4	dashes	**Fee Brothers orange bitters**

Origin: Created in the late 1990s by Dick Bradsell for Karen Hampsen at Legends, London, England.
Comment: The quality of orange bitters and blackberry liqueur used dramatically affect the flavour of this blush coloured cocktail.

LEMON BEAT

Glass: Rocks
Garnish: Lemon slice
Method: STIR honey with cachaça in the base of shaker to dissolve honey. Add other ingredients, **SHAKE** with ice and strain into ice-filled glass.

2	spoons	**Clear runny honey**
2	shot(s)	**Cachaça**
1	shot(s)	**Freshly squeezed lemon juice**

Comment: Simple but effective. Use quality cachaça and honey and you'll have a great drink.

LEMON BUTTER COOKIE

Glass: Old-fashioned
Garnish: Lemon zest twist
Method: SHAKE all ingredients with ice and strain into glass filled with crushed ice.

3/4	shot(s)	**Zubrówka bison vodka**
3/4	shot(s)	**Ketel One vodka**
3/4	shot(s)	**Krupnik honey liqueur**
2	shot(s)	**Pressed apple juice**
1/2	shot(s)	**Almond (orgeat) syrup**
1/8	shot(s)	**Freshly squeezed lemon juice**

Origin: Created in 2002 by Mark 'Q-Ball' Linnie and Martin Oliver at The Mixing Tin, Leeds, England.
Comment: An appropriate name for a most unusually flavoured drink modelled on the Polish Martini.

LEMON CHIFFON PIE

Glass: Coupette
Garnish: Grated lemon zest
Method: BLEND all ingredients with crushed ice and serve with straws.

1	shot(s)	**Light white rum**
1	shot(s)	**Bols white crème de cacao**
1	shot(s)	**Freshly squeezed lemon juice**
2	scoops	**Vanilla ice cream**

Comment: Creamy and tangy – like a lemon pie. Consume in place of dessert.

LEMON CURD MARTINI [NEW]

Glass: Martini
Garnish: Lemon wedge on rim
Method: SHAKE all ingredients with ice and fine strain into chilled glass.

3	spoons	**Lemon curd**
2	shot(s)	**Ketel One Citroen vodka**
1/2	shot(s)	**Freshly squeezed lemon juice**

Origin: Created by yours truly.
Comment: This almost creamy cocktail is named after and tastes like its primary ingredient. Martini purists may justifiably baulk at the absence of vermouth and the presence of fruit.

LEMON DROP

Glass: Shot
Garnish: Sugar coated slice of lemon
Method: **SHAKE** all ingredients with ice and fine strain into chilled glass.

1/2	shot(s)	**Ketel One vodka**
1/2	shot(s)	**Cointreau / triple sec**
1/2	shot(s)	**Freshly squeezed lemon juice**

Comment: Lemon and orange combine to make a fresh tasting citrus shot.

LEMON DROP MARTINI [NEW]

Glass: Martini
Garnish: Lemon zest twist
Method: **SHAKE** all ingredients with ice and fine strain into chilled glass.

2	shot(s)	**Ketel One Citroen vodka**
1	shot(s)	**Cointreau / triple sec**
3/4	shot(s)	**Freshly squeezed lemon juice**
1/2	shot(s)	**Sugar (gomme) syrup**

Comment: Sherbety lemon.

LEMON LIME & BITTERS

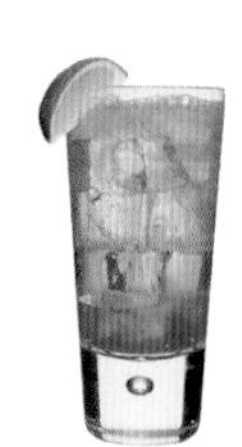

Glass: Collins
Garnish: Lime wedge
Method: Squeeze lime wedges and drop into glass. **ADD** Angostura bitters and fill glass with ice. **TOP** with lemonade, stir and serve with straws.

4	fresh	**Lime wedges**
5	dashes	**Angostura aromatic bitters**
Top up with		**7-Up**

AKA: LLB
Origin: Very popular in its homeland, Australia.
Comment: If you're unlucky enough to be the driver, this refreshing long drink is a good low alcohol option.

LEMON MARTINI [NEW]

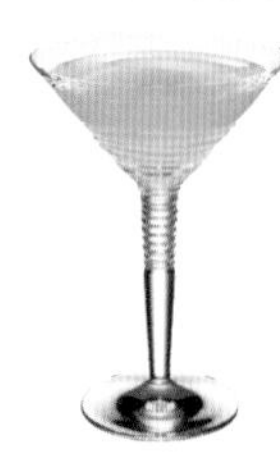

Glass: Martini
Garnish: Lemon zest twist
Method: **MUDDLE** lemongrass in base of shaker. Add other ingredients, **SHAKE** with ice and fine strain into chilled glass.

1	inch	**Lemongrass chopped**
2	shot(s)	**Ketel One vodka**
1/4	shot(s)	**Dry vermouth**
1	shot(s)	**Freshly squeezed lemon juice**
1/2	shot(s)	**Sugar (gomme) syrup**

Origin: Created in 2006 by yours truly.
Comment: A complex, delicately lemon Vodkatini.

LEMON MERINGUE MARTINI [UPDATED]

Glass: Martini
Garnish: Lemon zest twist
Method: **SHAKE** all ingredients with ice and fine strain into chilled glass.

2	shot(s)	**Ketel One Citroen vodka**
1	shot(s)	**Baileys Irish Cream liqueur**
1	shot(s)	**Freshly squeezed lemon juice**
1/4	shot(s)	**Sugar (gomme) syrup**

Origin: Adapted from a drink created in 2000 by Ben Reed, London, England.
Comment: Slightly creamy in consistency, this tangy lemon drink is indeed reminiscent of the eponymous dessert.

LEMON MERINGUE PIE'TINI

Glass: Martini
Garnish: Pie rim (wipe outside edge of rim with cream mix and dip into crunched up Graham Cracker or digestive biscuits)
Method: **SHAKE** first three ingredients with ice and fine strain into chilled and rimmed glass. **SHAKE** cream and Licor 43 without ice so as to mix and whip. **FLOAT** cream mix by pouring over back of a spoon.

1	shot(s)	**Luxardo Limoncello liqueur**
1	shot(s)	**Sugar (gomme) syrup**
1	shot(s)	**Freshly squeezed lemon juice**
2	shot(s)	**Double (heavy) cream**
1/2	shot(s)	**Cuarenta Y Tres (Licor 43) liqueur**

Origin: Created by Michael Waterhouse at Dylan Prime, New York City.
Comment: Rich and syrupy base sipped through a vanilla cream topping.

LEMON SORBET

Glass: Martini (saucer)
Garnish: Strips of lemon rind
Method: Heat water in pan and add sugar. Simmer and stir until sugar dissolves, add lemon juice and grated lemon rind and continue to simmer and stir for a few minutes. Take off the heat and allow to cool. Fine strain into a shallow container and stir in liqueur and orange bitters. Beat egg whites and fold into mix. Place in freezer and store for up to 3-4 days before use.

3/4	cup(s)	**Mineral water**
1	cup(s)	**Granulated white sugar**
1/2	cup(s)	**Freshly squeezed lemon juice**
5	rinds	**Fresh lemon (avoid the pith when grating)**
1/4	cup(s)	**Luxardo Limoncello liqueur**
2	spoons	**Fee Brothers orange bitters**
2	fresh	**Egg whites**

Variant: To make any other citrus flavour sorbet, simply substitute the juice and peel of another fruit such as grapefruit, lime or orange.
Comment: My favourite recipe for this dessert and occasional cocktail ingredient.

LEMONY [NEW]

Glass: Martini
Garnish: Maraschino cherry
Method: **SHAKE** all ingredients with ice and fine strain into chilled glass.

2	shot(s)	Plymouth gin
1/2	shot(s)	Yellow Chartreuse liqueur
1/2	shot(s)	Luxardo Limoncello liqueur
1/2	shot(s)	Freshly squeezed lemon juice
1/2	shot(s)	Chilled mineral water (omit if wet ice)

Comment: Lemon subtly dominates this complex, herbal drink.

LEMONGRAD

Glass: Collins
Garnish: Lemon wedge squeezed over drink
Method: **SHAKE** first three ingredients with ice and strain into ice-filled glass. **TOP** with tonic and lightly stir.

2	shot(s)	Ketel One Citroen vodka
1	shot(s)	Elderflower cordial
1/2	shot(s)	Freshly squeezed lemon juice
Top up with		Tonic water

Origin: Created in 2002 by Alex Kammerling, London, England.
Comment: A great summer afternoon drink. Fresh lemon with elderflower and quinine.

LEMONGRASS COSMO [NEW]

Glass: Martini
Garnish: Lemon zest twist
Method: **MUDDLE** lemongrass in base of shaker. **ADD** other ingredients, **SHAKE** with ice and fine strain into chilled glass.

1/4	stem	Fresh lemongrass (finely chopped)
1	shot(s)	Ketel One Citroen vodka
1	shot(s)	Cointreau / triple sec
1 1/2	shot(s)	Cranberry juice
1/2	shot(s)	Freshly squeezed lemon juice

Origin: Adapted from a drink discovered in 2005 at Opia, Hong Kong, China
Comment: Lemongrass adds complexity to this balanced Cosmo.

LENINADE

Glass: Martini
Garnish: Orange zest twist
Method: **SHAKE** all ingredients with ice and fine strain into chilled glass.

1 1/2	shot(s)	Ketel One Citroen vodka
1	shot(s)	Freshly squeezed lemon juice
1/4	shot(s)	Sugar (gomme) syrup
1/4	shot(s)	Cointreau / triple sec
3	dashes	Fee Brothers orange bitters

Origin: Created by Dick Bradsell at Fred's, London, England, in the late 80s.
Comment: Orange undertones add citrus depth to the lemon explosion.

LIFE (LOVE IN THE FUTURE ECSTASY)

Glass: Old-fashioned
Garnish: Mint leaf
Method: **MUDDLE** mint in base of shaker. Add next three ingredients, **SHAKE** with ice and fine strain into glass filled with crushed ice. **DRIZZLE** tea liqueur over drink.

7	leaves	Fresh mint
1 1/2	shot(s)	Ketel One vodka
1	shot(s)	Freshly squeezed lime juice
1/2	shot(s)	Sugar (gomme) syrup
1	shot(s)	Tea liqueur

Origin: Adapted from a drink created in 1999 by Nick Strangeway at Ché, London, England, for Martin Sexton (writer and artistic entrepreneur).
Comment: Refreshing tea and mint.

LIGHT BREEZE

Glass: Collins
Garnish: Lemon slice
Method: **POUR** all ingredients into ice-filled glass. **STIR** and serve with straws.

3	shot(s)	Cranberry juice
2	shot(s)	Freshly squeezed golden grapefruit juice
2	shot(s)	Pernod anis

Origin: Created in 2000 by yours truly at the Light Bar, London, England (hence the name).
Comment: A Seabreeze based on anis rather than vodka, with aniseed depth and sweetness.

LIGHTER BREEZE

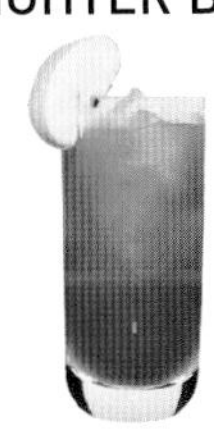

Glass: Collins
Garnish: Apple wedge on rim
Method: **POUR** all ingredients into ice-filled glass. **STIR** and serve with straws.

3	shot(s)	Pressed apple juice
2	shot(s)	Cranberry juice
1/2	shot(s)	Elderflower cordial
2	shot(s)	Pernod anis

Comment: Long, fragrant and refreshing.

LIMA SOUR [NEW]

Glass: Old-fashioned
Garnish: Lemon zest string
Method: **BLEND** all ingredients with one 12oz scoop of crushed ice. Serve with straws.

2	shot(s)	Pisco
1/2	shot(s)	Luxardo maraschino liqueur
3/4	shot(s)	Freshly squeezed golden grapefruit juice
3/4	shot(s)	Freshly squeezed lime juice
3/4	shot(s)	Sugar (gomme) syrup

Origin: Created before 1947 by Jerry Hooker.
Comment: A refreshing blend of pisco, maraschino and citrus.

LIME BLUSH (MOCKTAIL) [NEW]

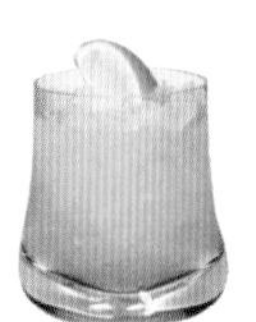

Glass: Old-fashioned
Garnish: Lime wedge
Method: **SHAKE** all ingredients with ice and strain into glass filled with crushed ice.

2	shot(s)	**Freshly squeezed lime juice**
1/2	shot(s)	**Roses lime cordial**
1/2	shot(s)	**Sonoma pomegranate (grenadine) syrup**
1/2	shot(s)	**Sugar (gomme) syrup**

Origin: Adapted from a drink discovered in 2005 at Blue Bar, Four Seasons Hotel, Hong Kong, China.
Comment: Refreshingly sweet and sour.

LIME BREEZE

Glass: Collins
Garnish: Lime wedge
Method: **SHAKE** all ingredients with ice and fine strain into ice-filled glass.

2	shot(s)	**Lime flavoured vodka**
3	shot(s)	**Cranberry juice**
1 1/2	shot(s)	**Freshly squeezed golden grapefruit juice**

Comment: A lime driven Sea Breeze.

LIME SOUR

Glass: Old-fashioned
Garnish: Lime wedge on rim
Method: **SHAKE** all ingredients with ice and strain into ice-filled glass.

2	shot(s)	**Lime flavoured vodka**
1 1/4	shot(s)	**Freshly squeezed lime juice**
1/4	shot(s)	**Sugar (gomme) syrup**
1/2	fresh	**Egg white**

Comment: Fresh egg white gives this drink a wonderfully frothy top and smoothes the alcohol and lime juice.

LIMEADE (MOCKTAIL) [NEW]

Glass: Collins
Garnish: Lime wedge
Method: **SHAKE** all ingredients with ice and fine strain into ice filled glass.

2	shot(s)	**Freshly squeezed lime juice**
1	shot(s)	**Sugar (gomme) syrup**
3	shot(s)	**Chilled mineral water**

Variant: Shake first two ingredients & top with sparkling water.
Comment: A superbly refreshing alternative to lemonade.

LIMELITE

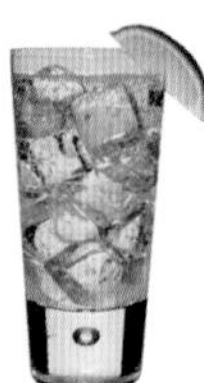

Glass: Collins
Garnish: Lime wedge
Method: **SHAKE** first four ingredients with ice and strain into ice-filled glass. **TOP** with 7-Up.

2	shot(s)	**Lime flavoured vodka**
1/2	shot(s)	**Cointreau / triple sec**
1/2	shot(s)	**Freshly squeezed lime juice**
1/4	shot(s)	**Sugar (gomme) syrup**
Top up with		**7-Up**

Comment: Long and citrussy.

LIMEOSA

Glass: Flute
Method: **SHAKE** first two ingredients with ice and fine strain into chilled glass. **TOP** with champagne and gently stir.

1	shot(s)	**Lime flavoured vodka**
2	shot(s)	**Freshly squeezed orange juice**
Top up with		**Piper-Heidsieck brut champagne**

Comment: Why settle for a plain old Buck's Fizz when you could add a shot of lime-flavoured vodka?

LIMERICK

Glass: Collins
Garnish: Lime wedge squeezed over drink
Method: **SHAKE** first three ingredients with ice and strain into ice-filled glass. **TOP** with soda water and lightly stir.

2	shot(s)	**Lime flavoured vodka**
1	shot(s)	**Freshly squeezed lime juice**
1/2	shot(s)	**Sugar (gomme) syrup**
Top up with		**Soda water (club soda)**

Origin: I created this twist on the classic Vodka Rickey in 2002.
Comment: A refreshing lime cooler.

LIMEY

Glass: Martini
Garnish: Lime zest twist
Method: **SHAKE** all ingredients with ice and fine strain into chilled glass.

2	shot(s)	**Lime flavoured vodka**
1/2	shot(s)	**Freshly squeezed lime juice**
1/2	shot(s)	**Sugar (gomme) syrup**
1/8	shot(s)	**Rose's lime cordial**
3	dashes	**Angostura aromatic bitters**
1/2	shot(s)	**Chilled mineral water (omit if wet ice)**

Origin: I created and named this drink after the British naval tradition of mixing lime juice with spirits in an attempt to prevent scurvy. This practice gained British sailors the nickname 'limeys'.
Comment: A rust coloured drink with a delicately sour flavour.

LIMEY COSMO

Glass: Martini
Garnish: Lime wedge on rim
Method: **SHAKE** all ingredients with ice and fine strain into chilled glass.

1½	shot(s)	Lime flavoured vodka
1	shot(s)	Cointreau / triple sec
1¼	shot(s)	Cranberry juice
¼	shot(s)	Freshly squeezed lime juice
½	shot(s)	Rose's lime cordial

Comment: If you like Cosmopolitans, you'll love this zesty alternative.

LIMNOLOGY

Glass: Martini
Garnish: Lime zest twist
Method: **STIR** all ingredients with ice and fine strain into chilled glass.

2	shot(s)	Lime flavoured vodka
1	shot(s)	Rose's lime cordial
¾	shot(s)	Chilled water

Origin: The name means the study of the physical phenomena of lakes and other fresh waters – appropriate for this fresh green drink.
Comment: A vodka Gimlet made with lime flavoured vodka.

LIMEY MULE

Glass: Collins
Garnish: Lime wedge
Method: **SHAKE** first three ingredients with ice and strain into ice-filled glass. **TOP** with ginger ale, lightly stir and serve with straws.

2	shot(s)	Lime flavoured vodka
1	shot(s)	Freshly squeezed lime juice
½	shot(s)	Sugar (gomme) syrup
Top up with		Ginger ale

Comment: Made with plain vodka this drink is a Moscow Mule. This variant uses lime flavoured vodka.

LIMONCELLO MARTINI [NEW]

Glass: Martini
Garnish: Lemon zest twist
Method: **SHAKE** all ingredients with ice and fine strain into chilled glass.

1½	shot(s)	Ketel One vodka
1½	shot(s)	Luxardo Limoncello liqueur
1	shot(s)	Freshly squeezed lemon juice

Origin: Adapted from a drink created in 2005 by Francesco at Mix, New York City, USA.
Comment: If you like the liqueur you'll love the cocktail.

LIMINAL SHOT

Glass: Shot
Method: Refrigerate ingredients then **LAYER** in chilled glass by carefully pouring in the following order.

½	shot(s)	Sonoma pomegranate (grenadine) syrup
½	shot(s)	Bols blue curaçao
¾	shot(s)	Lime flavoured vodka

Comment: The name means transitional, marginal, a boundary or a threshold. Appropriate since the layers border each other.

LIMOUSINE

Glass: Old-fashioned
Method: Place bar spoon in glass. **POUR** ingredients into glass and stir.

2	shot(s)	Lime flavoured vodka
1	shot(s)	Honey liqueur
4	shot(s)	Hot camomile tea

Origin: Created in 2002 by yours truly.
Comment: In winter this hot drink is a warming treat. In summer serve cold over ice.

LIMITED LIABILITY

Glass: Old-fashioned
Method: **SHAKE** all ingredients with ice and strain into ice-filled glass.

2	shot(s)	Lime flavoured vodka
¾	shot(s)	Freshly squeezed lime juice
1	shot(s)	Honey liqueur

Origin: Created in 2002 by yours truly.
Comment: A sour and flavoursome short - honey and lime work well together.

LINSTEAD

Glass: Martini
Garnish: Lemon zest twist
Method: **SHAKE** all ingredients with ice and fine strain into chilled glass.

2	shot(s)	The Famous Grouse Scotch whisky
2	shot(s)	Pressed pineapple juice
¼	shot(s)	Sugar (gomme) syrup
⅛	shot(s)	La Fée Parisian 68% absinthe

Comment: Absinthe and pineapple come through first, with Scotch last. A great medley of flavours.

LIQUORICE ALL SORT

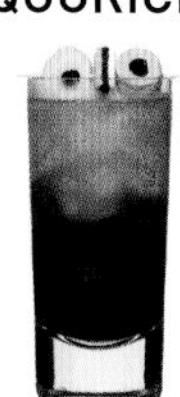

Glass: Collins
Garnish: Liquorice Allsort sweet
Method: **SHAKE** first four ingredients with ice and strain into ice-filled glass. **TOP** with lemonade.

1 shot(s) **Opal Nera black sambuca**
1 shot(s) **Bols crème de bananes**
1 shot(s) **Bols strawberry (fraise) liqueur**
1 shot(s) **Bols blue curaçao**
Top up with **7-Up / lemonade**

Origin: George Bassett (1818-1886), a manufacturer of liquorice sweets, did not invent the Liquorice Allsort that carries his name. That happened 15 years after George died when a salesman accidentally dropped a tray of sweets, they fell in a muddle and the famous sweet was born.
Comment: This aptly named, semi-sweet drink has a strong liquorice flavour with hints of fruit.

LIQUORICE MARTINI

Glass: Martini
Garnish: Piece of liquorice
Method: **STIR** all ingredients with ice and strain into chilled glass.

2 shot(s) **Plymouth gin**
1/4 shot(s) **Opal Nera black sambuca**
1/8 shot(s) **Sugar (gomme) syrup**

Origin: Created in 2003 by Jason Fendick, London, England.
Comment: Gin tinted violet, flavoured with liquorice and slightly sweetened.

LIQUORICE SHOT

Glass: Shot
Method: **SHAKE** all ingredients with ice and fine strain into chilled glass.

1/2 shot(s) **Ketel One vodka**
1/2 shot(s) **Luxardo white sambuca**
1/2 shot(s) **Crème de cassis**

Comment: For liquorice fans.

LIQUORICE WHISKY SOUR

Glass: Old-fashioned
Garnish: Cherry & lemon slice (sail)
Method: **SHAKE** all ingredients with ice and strain into ice-filled glass.

2 shot(s) **The Famous Grouse Scotch whisky**
1/2 shot(s) **Ricard pastis**
1 shot(s) **Freshly squeezed lemon juice**
1/2 shot(s) **Sugar (gomme) syrup**
1/2 fresh **Egg white**
3 dashes **Angostura aromatic bitters**

Origin: Created in 2006 by yours truly.
Comment: Pastis adds a pleasing hint of liquorice to the classic Whisky Sour.

LISA B'S DAIQUIRI

Glass: Martini
Garnish: Grapefruit zest twist
Method: **SHAKE** all ingredients with ice and fine strain into chilled glass.

2 1/2 shot(s) **Vanilla infused Havana Club rum**
1/2 shot(s) **Freshly squeezed lime juice**
1/2 shot(s) **Sonoma vanilla bean sugar syrup**
1 shot(s) **Freshly squeezed pink grapefruit juice**

Origin: Created in 2003 by yours truly for a gorgeous fan of both Daiquiris and pink grapefruit juice.
Comment: Reminiscent of a Hemingway Special, this flavoursome, vanilla laced Daiquiri has a wonderfully tangy bitter-sweet finish.

LITTLE ITALY [NEW]

Glass: Martini
Garnish: Orange zest twist
Method: **STIR** all ingredients with ice and fine strain into chilled glass.

2 shot(s) **Bourbon whiskey**
1 shot(s) **Sweet (rosso) vermouth**
1/2 shot(s) **Cynar liqueur**

Origin: Adapted from a drink discovered in 2006 at Pegu Club, New York City, USA.
Comment: A sweet, Manhattan-style drink, bittered with Cynar.

LIVINGSTONE [NEW]

Glass: Shot
Garnish: Lemon peel twist
Method: **SHAKE** all ingredients with ice and fine strain into chilled glass.

2 shot(s) **Plymouth gin**
1 shot(s) **Dry vermouth**
1/4 shot(s) **Sugar (gomme) syrup**

Variant: Use pomegranate syrup in place of sugar and you have a Red Livingstone, named after London's 'lefty' mayor, Ken.
Origin: This 1930s classic was named after Doctor Livingstone, the famous African missionary.
Comment: The classic gin and vermouth Martini made more approachable with a dash of sugar.

LOCH ALMOND

Glass: Collins
Garnish: Float amaretti biscuit
Method: **POUR** all ingredients into ice-filled glass, stir and serve with straws.

1 1/2 shot(s) **The Famous Grouse Scotch whisky**
1 1/2 shot(s) **Luxardo Amaretto di Saschira liqueur**
Top up with **Ginger ale**

Comment: If you haven't got to grips with Scotch but like amaretto, try this spicy almond combination.

LOLA

Glass: Martini
Garnish: Orange zest twist
Method: **SHAKE** all ingredients with ice and fine strain into chilled glass.

1½	shot(s)	Mount Gay Eclipse golden rum
½	shot(s)	Mandarine Napoléon Liqueur
½	shot(s)	Bols white crème de cacao
1	shot(s)	Freshly squeezed orange juice
½	shot(s)	Double (heavy) cream

Origin: Created in 1999 by Jamie Terrell, London, England.
Comment: Strong, creamy orange.

LOLITA MARGARITA [NEW]

Glass: Coupette
Garnish: Lime wedge on rim
Method: **STIR** honey with tequila in base of shaker to dissolve honey. Add other ingredients, **SHAKE** with ice and fine strain into chilled glass.

2	spoons	Runny honey
2	shot(s)	Sauza Hornitos tequila
1	shot(s)	Freshly squeezed lime juice
2	dashes	Angostura aromatic bitters

Origin: Named after the novel by Vladimir Nabokov which chronicles a middle-aged man's infatuation with a 12 year old girl. Nabokov invented the word 'nymphet' to describe her seductive qualities.
Comment: A fittingly seductive Margarita.

LONDON CALLING

Glass: Martini
Garnish: Orange zest twist
Method: **STIR** all ingredients with ice and strain into chilled glass.

2	shot(s)	Plymouth gin
1¼	shot(s)	Plymouth sloe gin liqueur
½	shot(s)	Sweet (rosso) vermouth
2	dashes	Fee Brothers orange bitters

Origin: Discovered in 2003 at Oxo Tower Bar & Brasserie, London, England.
Comment: A traditionally styled sweet Martini with a dry, fruity finish.

LONDON COCKTAIL [NEW]

Glass: Martini
Garnish: Orange zest twist
Method: **SHAKE** all ingredients with ice and fine strain into chilled glass.

2½	shot(s)	Plymouth gin
⅛	shot(s)	La Fée Parisian 68% absinthe
⅛	shot(s)	Sugar (gomme) syrup
2	dashes	Fee Brothers orange bitters
½	shot(s)	Chilled mineral water (omit if wet ice)

Origin: Adapted from a recipe in Harry Craddock's 1930 Savoy Cocktail Book.
Comment: Chilled, diluted and sweetened gin invigorated by a hint of absinthe.

LONDON FOG [NEW]

Glass: Old-fashioned
Garnish: Orange zest twist
Method: Fill glass with ice. Add ingredients in the following order and **STIR**. Add more ice to fill.

1	shot(s)	Plymouth gin
2	shot(s)	Chilled mineral water
1	shot(s)	Pernod anis

Comment: Dry liquorice and aniseed.

LONELY BULL

Glass: Old-fashioned
Garnish: Dust with freshly grated nutmeg
Method: **SHAKE** all ingredients with ice and strain into ice-filled glass.

1½	shot(s)	Sauza Hornitos tequila
1½	shot(s)	Kahlúa coffee liqueur
¾	shot(s)	Double (heavy) cream
¾	shot(s)	Milk

Comment: Like a creamy iced coffee – yum.

LONG BEACH ICED TEA [UPDATED]

Glass: Sling
Garnish: Lemon slice
Method: **SHAKE** all ingredients with ice and strain into ice-filled glass. Serve with straws.

½	shot(s)	Kahlúa coffee liqueur
½	shot(s)	Sauza Hornitos tequila
½	shot(s)	Light white rum
½	shot(s)	Plymouth gin
½	shot(s)	Ketel One vodka
1	shot(s)	Freshly squeezed lime juice
½	shot(s)	Sugar (gomme) syrup
2	shot(s)	Cranberry juice

Comment: One of the more grown-up 'Iced Tea' cocktails.

LONG FLIGHT OF STAIRS [NEW]

Glass: Collins
Garnish: Apple or pear slice
Method: **SHAKE** all ingredients with ice and strain into ice-filled glass. Serve with straws.

1	shot(s)	Pear flavoured vodka
1	shot(s)	Calvados or applejack brandy
1	shot(s)	Pear & cognac liqueur
2½	shot(s)	Pressed apple juice

Origin: Created in 2005 by yours truly as a homage to the G.E. Club's 'Stairs Martini'.
Comment: A seriously tasty, strong, long drink. The name is a reversal of the London rhyming slang 'apples and pears' (stairs).

LONG ISLAND ICED TEA

Glass: Sling
Garnish: Lemon slice
Method: **SHAKE** first seven ingredients with ice and strain into ice-filled glass. **TOP** with cola, stir and serve with straws.

1/2	shot(s)	Light white rum
1/2	shot(s)	Plymouth gin
1/2	shot(s)	Ketel One vodka
1/2	shot(s)	Sauza Hornitos tequila
1/2	shot(s)	Cointreau / triple sec
1	shot(s)	Freshly squeezed lime juice
1/2	shot(s)	Sugar (gomme) syrup
Top up with		Cola

Origin: This infamous drink reached the height of its popularity in the early 1980s. It looks like iced tea disguising its contents - hence the name.
Comment: A cooling combination of five different spirits with a hint of lime and a splash of cola.

LONG ISLAND SPICED TEA

Glass: Collins
Method: **SHAKE** first seven ingredients with ice and strain into ice-filled glass. **TOP** with cola, lightly stir and serve with straws.

1/2	shot(s)	Spiced rum
1/2	shot(s)	Ketel One vodka
1/2	shot(s)	Plymouth gin
1/2	shot(s)	Sauza Hornitos tequila
1/2	shot(s)	Cointreau / triple sec
1	shot(s)	Freshly squeezed lime juice
1/2	shot(s)	Sugar (gomme) syrup
Top up with		Cola

Comment: A contemporary spicy twist on an American classic.

LOTUS ESPRESSO [NEW]

Glass: Martini
Garnish: Float three coffee beans
Method: **SHAKE** all ingredients with ice and fine strain into chilled glass.

2	shot(s)	Ketel One vodka
1/2	shot(s)	Kahlúa coffee liqueur
1/2	shot(s)	Maple syrup
1	shot(s)	Espresso coffee (cold)

Origin: Adapted from a drink discovered in 2005 at Lotus Bar, Sydney, Australia.
Comment: Coffee to the fore but with complex, earthy bitter-sweet notes.

LOTUS MARTINI

Glass: Martini
Garnish: Mint leaf
Method: Lightly **MUDDLE** mint (just to bruise) in base of shaker. Add other ingredients, **SHAKE** with ice and fine strain into chilled glass.

7	fresh	Fresh mint leaves
2	shot(s)	Plymouth gin
1/4	shot(s)	Bols blue curaçao
1 1/2	shot(s)	Lychee syrup from tinned fruit
1/4	shot(s)	Sonoma pomegranate (grenadine) syrup

Origin: Created in 2001 by Martin Walander at Match Bar, London, England.
Comment: This violet coloured drink may have an unlikely list of ingredients, but – boy! - does it look and taste good.

LOUD SPEAKER MARTINI [NEW]

Glass: Martini
Garnish: Lemon peel twist
Method: **SHAKE** all ingredients with ice and fine strain into chilled glass.

1 1/2	shot(s)	Plymouth gin
1 1/2	shot(s)	Rémy Martin cognac
1/2	shot(s)	Sweet (rosso) vermouth
1/4	shot(s)	Freshly squeezed lemon juice
1/4	shot(s)	Sugar (gomme) syrup

Origin: Adapted from a recipe in the 1930 Savoy Cocktail Book by Harry Craddock. He says, "This it is that gives Radio Announcers their peculiar enunciation. Three of them will produce oscillation, and after five it is possible to reach the osculation stage."
Comment: I've added a dash of sugar to the original recipe which I found too dry.

LOUISIANA TRADE

Glass: Old-fashioned
Garnish: Lime wedge
Method: **SHAKE** all ingredients with ice and strain into glass filled with crushed ice.

2	shot(s)	Southern Comfort
1/2	shot(s)	Maple syrup
1	shot(s)	Freshly squeezed lime juice
1/4	shot(s)	Sugar (gomme) syrup

Origin: Created in 2001 by Mehdi Otmann at Zeta, London, England.
Comment: Peach and apricot with the freshness of lime and the dense sweetness of maple syrup.

HOW TO MAKE SUGAR SYRUP

To make your own sugar syrup, gradually pour TWO cups of granulated sugar into a saucepan containing ONE cup of hot water. Stir as you pour and carry on stirring and simmering until the sugar is dissolved. Do not let the water even come close to boiling and only simmer for as long as it takes to dissolve the sugar. Allow syrup to cool and pour into an empty bottle. Ideally, you should finely strain your syrup into the bottle to remove any undissolved crystals which could otherwise encourage crystallisation. If kept in a refrigerator this mixture will last for a couple of months.

LOVE JUNK

Glass: Old-fashioned
Garnish: Apple wedge
Method: **SHAKE** all ingredients with ice and strain into ice-filled glass.

2	shot(s)	Ketel One vodka
1/2	shot(s)	Midori melon liqueur
1/2	shot(s)	Peach schnapps liqueur
1 1/2	shot(s)	Pressed apple juice

Comment: A light, crisp, refreshing blend of peach, melon and apple juice, laced with vodka.

LOVED UP

Glass: Martini
Garnish: Berries on stick
Method: **SHAKE** all ingredients with ice and fine strain into chilled glass.

1 1/2	shot(s)	Sauza Hornitos tequila
1/2	shot(s)	Cointreau / triple sec
1/2	shot(s)	Chambord black raspberry liqueur
1/2	shot(s)	Freshly squeezed lime juice
1	shot(s)	Freshly squeezed orange juice
1/4	shot(s)	Sugar (gomme) syrup

Origin: Adapted from a cocktail discovered in 2002 at the Merc Bar, New York City, where the original name was listed as simply 'Love'.
Comment: Tequila predominates in this rusty coloured drink, which also features orange and berry fruit.

LUCKY LILY MARGARITA [NEW]

Glass: Coupette
Garnish: Pineapple wedge dusted with pepper on rim
Method: **STIR** honey with tequila in base of shaker to dissolve honey. **ADD** other ingredients, **SHAKE** with ice and fine strain into chilled glass.

2	spoons	Runny honey
2	shot(s)	Sauza Hornitos tequila
1	shot(s)	Pressed pineapple juice
3/4	shot(s)	Freshly squeezed lime juice
5	grinds	Black pepper

Origin: Adapted from a drink discovered in 2006 at All Star Lanes, London, England.
Comment: Spicy tequila and pineapple tingle with balance and flavour.

FOR MORE INFORMATION SEE OUR
INGREDIENTS APPENDIX ON PAGE 254

LUCKY LINDY

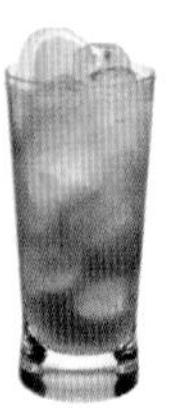

Glass: Collins
Garnish: Lemon wheel
Method: **STIR** honey with bourbon in base of shaker so as to dissolve honey. Add lemon juice, **SHAKE** with ice and strain into ice-filled glass. **TOP** with 7-Up, lightly stir and serve with straws.

3	spoon(s)	Runny honey
2	shot(s)	Bourbon whiskey
1/2	shot(s)	Freshly squeezed lemon juice
Top up with		7-Up

Origin: Adapted from a drink discovered in 2003 at The Grange Hall, New York City, USA.
Comment: A long refreshing drink that combines whisky, citrus and honey – a long chilled toddy without the spice.

LUSH

Glass: Flute
Garnish: Raspberry in glass
Method: **POUR** vodka and liqueur into chilled glass. **TOP** with champagne and lightly stir.

1	shot(s)	Ketel One vodka
1/2	shot(s)	Chambord black raspberry liqueur
Top up with		Piper-Heidsieck brut champagne

Origin: Created in 1999 by Spike Marchant at Alphabet, London, England.
Comment: It is, are you?

LUTKINS SPECIAL MARTINI [NEW]

Glass: Martini
Garnish: Orange zest twist
Method: **SHAKE** all ingredients with ice and fine strain into chilled glass.

1 1/2	shot(s)	Plymouth gin
1	shot(s)	Dry vermouth
1/2	shot(s)	Bols apricot brandy liqueur
3/4	shot(s)	Freshly squeezed orange juice

Origin: Adapted from a recipe in Harry Craddock's 1930 Savoy Cocktail Book.
Comment: I've tried many variations on the above formula and none are that special.

DRINKS ARE GRADED AS FOLLOWS:

● DISGUSTING ●◐ PRETTY AWFUL ●● BEST AVOIDED ●●◐ DISAPPOINTING ●●● ACCEPTABLE ●●●◐ GOOD ●●●● RECOMMENDED ●●●●◐ HIGHLY RECOMMENDED ●●●●● OUTSTANDING / EXCEPTIONAL

LUX DAIQUIRI

Glass: Martini (large)
Garnish: Maraschino cherry
Method: **BLEND** all ingredients with one 12oz scoop of crushed ice and serve in chilled glass.

3	shot(s)	**Light white rum**
3/4	shot(s)	**Freshly squeezed lime juice**
1/2	shot(s)	**Luxardo maraschino liqueur**
1/4	shot(s)	**Sugar (gomme) syrup**
1/4	shot(s)	**Maraschino syrup (from cherry jar)**

Origin: This was one of two cocktails with which I won a Havana Club Daiquiri competition in 2002. I named it after Girolamo Luxardo, creator of the now famous liqueur, 'Luxardo Maraschino'. My educated sub also informs me Lux is Latin for light.
Comment: A classic frozen Daiquiri heavily laced with maraschino cherry.

LUXURY COCKTAIL [UPDATED]

Glass: Martini
Method: **SHAKE** all ingredients with ice and fine strain into chilled glass.

2	shot(s)	**Plymouth gin**
3/4	shot(s)	**Pimm's No.1 Cup**
1/2	shot(s)	**Bols crème de bananes**
3/4	shot(s)	**Sweet (rosso) vermouth**
1/4	shot(s)	**Rose's lime cordial**
3	dashes	**Angostura aromatic bitters**

Comment: Sticky banana followed by a bitter, refined aftertaste.

LUXURY MOJITO

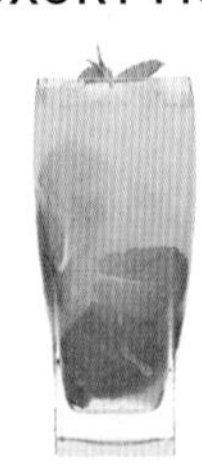

Glass: Collins
Garnish: Mint sprig
Method: **MUDDLE** mint in glass with sugar and lime juice. Fill glass with crushed ice, add rum and Angostura, then **TOP** with champagne and stir.

12	fresh	**Mint leaves**
1/4	shot(s)	**Sugar (gomme) syrup**
1	shot(s)	**Freshly squeezed lime juice**
2	shot(s)	**Appleton Estate V/X aged rum**
3	dashes	**Angostura aromatic bitters**
Top up with		**Piper-Heidsieck brut champagne**

Comment: A Mojito made with aged rum and topped with champagne instead of soda water: more complex than the original.

LYCHEE & BLACKCURRANT MARTINI

Glass: Martini
Garnish: Peeled lychee in glass
Method: **SHAKE** all ingredients with ice and fine strain into chilled glass.

2	shot(s)	**Plymouth gin**
1/2	shot(s)	**Soho lychee liqueur**
1/4	shot(s)	**Crème de cassis**
1/4	shot(s)	**Rose's lime cordial**
3/4	shot(s)	**Chilled mineral water (omit if wet ice)**

Origin: Created by yours truly in 2004.
Comment: Light, fragrant and laced with gin.

LYCHEE & ROSE PETAL MARTINI

Glass: Martini
Garnish: Float rose petal
Method: **STIR** all ingredients with ice and strain into chilled glass.

2	shot(s)	**Plymouth gin**
1	shot(s)	**Rose petal vodka liqueur**
1	shot(s)	**Lychee syrup from tinned fruit**
2	dashes	**Peychaud's aromatic bitters**

Origin: Created in 2002 by Dick Bradsell for Opium, London, England.
Comment: Light pink in colour and subtle in flavour.

LYCHEE & SAKE MARTINI

Glass: Martini
Garnish: Peeled lychee in glass
Method: **STIR** all ingredients with ice and strain into chilled glass.

1 1/2	shot(s)	**Plymouth gin**
2	shot(s)	**Sake**
3/4	shot(s)	**Soho lychee liqueur**

Origin: Created in 2004 by yours truly.
Comment: A soft, Martini styled drink with subtle hints of sake and lychee.

LYCHEE MAC

Glass: Old-fashioned
Garnish: Peeled lychee in drink
Method: **SHAKE** all ingredients with ice and strain into ice-filled glass.

2 1/4	shot(s)	**The Famous Grouse Scotch whisky**
1	shot(s)	**Soho lychee liqueur**
3/4	shot(s)	**Stone's green ginger wine**

Origin: Created by yours truly in 2004.
Comment: Peaty Scotch with sweet lychee and hot ginger.

LYCHEE MARTINI

Glass: Martini
Garnish: Whole lychee from tin
Method: **STIR** all ingredients with ice and fine strain into chilled glass.

2	shot(s)	**Ketel One vodka**
1/2	shot(s)	**Soho lychee liqueur**
1/2	shot(s)	**Dry vermouth**
1	shot(s)	**Lychee syrup from tinned fruit**

Origin: Thought to have been first made in 2001 at Clay, a Korean restaurant in New York City, USA.
Comment: If you like lychee you'll love this delicate Martini.

LYCHEE RICKEY [NEW]

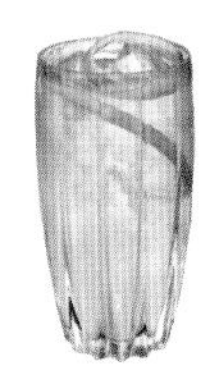

Glass: Collins (small 8oz)
Garnish: Immerse length of lime peel in drink.
Method: SHAKE first three ingredients with ice and strain into ice-filled glass. **TOP** with soda water.

2	shot(s)	**Plymouth gin**
1	shot(s)	**Soho lychee liqueur**
1/2	shot(s)	**Freshly squeezed lime juice**
Top up with		**Soda water (club soda)**

Origin: Adapted from a drink discovered in 2005 at Club 97, Hong Kong, China.
Comment: The lychee liqueur dominates this surprisingly dry Rickey.

LYNCHBURG LEMONADE

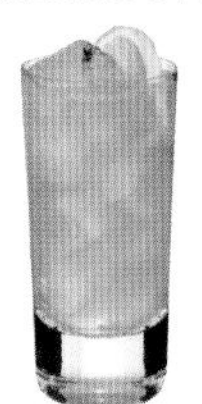

Glass: Collins
Garnish: Lemon slice
Method: SHAKE first three ingredients with ice and strain into ice-filled glass. **TOP** with 7-Up.

1 1/2	shot(s)	**Jack Daniel's Tennessee whiskey**
1	shot(s)	**Cointreau / triple sec**
1	shot(s)	**Freshly squeezed lemon juice**
Top up with		**7-Up**

Variant: With three dashes Angostura aromatic bitters.
Origin: Created for the Jack Daniel's distillery in - yep, you guessed it - Lynchburg, Tennessee.
Comment: Tangy, light and very easy to drink.

M.G.F.

Glass: Martini
Garnish: Orange zest twist
Method: SHAKE all ingredients with ice and fine strain into chilled glass.

1	shot(s)	**Orange flavoured vodka**
1	shot(s)	**Ketel One Citroen vodka**
1	shot(s)	**Pressed pink grapefruit juice**
1	shot(s)	**Freshly squeezed lemon juice**
1/2	shot(s)	**Sugar (gomme) syrup**

Origin: Discovered in 2003 at Claridge's Bar, London, England.
Comment: Short and sharp.

MAC ORANGE [UPDATED]

Glass: Old-fashioned
Garnish: Orange zest twist
Method: SHAKE all ingredients with ice and fine strain into chilled glass.

2	shot(s)	**The Famous Grouse Scotch whisky**
1	shot(s)	**Stone's ginger wine**
1	shot(s)	**Freshly squeezed orange juice**
1/4	shot(s)	**Sugar (gomme) syrup**
3	dashes	**Fee Brothers orange bitters**

Comment: A Whisky Mac with orange topping off the ginger.

MACKA [NEW]

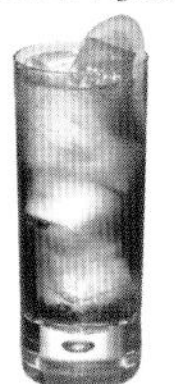

Glass: Collins
Garnish: Lemon slice
Method: SHAKE first four ingredients with ice and strain into ice-filled glass. **TOP** with soda.

2	shot(s)	**Plymouth gin**
1/2	shot(s)	**Dry vermouth**
1/2	shot(s)	**Sweet (rosso) vermouth**
1/2	shot(s)	**Crème de cassis**
Top up with		**Soda water (club soda)**

Comment: A long fruity drink for parched palates.

MAD MONK MILKSHAKE

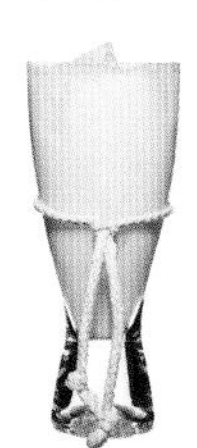

Glass: Collins
Garnish: Tie cord around glass
Method: SHAKE all ingredients with ice and strain into ice-filled glass.

2	shot(s)	**Frangelico hazelnut liqueur**
1	shot(s)	**Baileys Irish Cream liqueur**
1/4	shot(s)	**Kahlúa coffee liqueur**
1	shot(s)	**Double (heavy) cream**
2	shot(s)	**Milk**

Variant: Blend instead of shaking and serve frozen.
Comment: Long, creamy and slightly sweet with hazelnut and coffee.

MADRAS

Glass: Collins
Garnish: Orange slice
Method: SHAKE all ingredients with ice and strain into ice-filled glass.

2	shot(s)	**Ketel One vodka**
3	shot(s)	**Cranberry juice**
2	shot(s)	**Freshly squeezed orange juice**

Comment: A Seabreeze with orange juice in place of grapefruit juice, making it slightly sweeter.

MADROSKA

Glass: Collins
Garnish: Orange slice
Method: SHAKE all ingredients with ice and strain into ice-filled glass.

2	shot(s)	**Ketel One vodka**
2 1/2	shot(s)	**Pressed apple juice**
1 1/2	shot(s)	**Cranberry juice**
1	shot(s)	**Freshly squeezed orange juice**

Origin: Created in 1998 by Jamie Terrell, London, England.
Comment: A Madras with more than a hint of apple juice.

MAE WEST MARTINI

Glass: Martini
Garnish: Melon wedge on rim
Method: **SHAKE** all ingredients with ice and fine strain into chilled glass.

2	shot(s)	**Ketel One vodka**
1/2	shot(s)	**Luxardo Amaretto di Saschira liqueur**
1/4	shot(s)	**Midori melon liqueur**
1 1/2	shot(s)	**Cranberry juice**

Comment: A rosé coloured, semi-sweet concoction with a cherry-chocolate flavour.

VIC'S ORIGINAL 1944 MAI TAI

Glass: Mai Tai (16oz old-fashioned)
Garnish: Half spent lime shell, mint sprig, pineapple cube & cherry on stick
Method: "Cut lime in half; squeeze juice over shaved ice in a Mai Tai (double old-fashioned) glass; save one spent shell. Add remaining ingredients and enough shaved ice to fill glass. Hand shake. Decorate with spent lime shell, fresh mint, and a fruit stick."

1	fresh	**Lime**
2	shot(s)	**17 yo Wray & Nephew Jamaican rum**
1/2	shot(s)	**Dutch orange curaçao liqueur**
1/4	shot(s)	**Orgeat (almond) sugar syrup**
1/4	shot(s)	**Rock candy syrup**

Comment: In the words of the master, from his Bartender's Guide.

MAI TAI #2 (BEAUMONT-GANTT'S FORMULA)

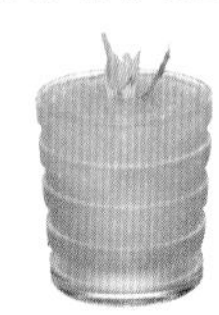

Glass: Old-fashioned
Garnish: Mint sprig
Method: Lightly muddle mint in base of shaker (just to bruise). Add other ingredients, **SHAKE** with ice and strain glass filled with crushed ice.

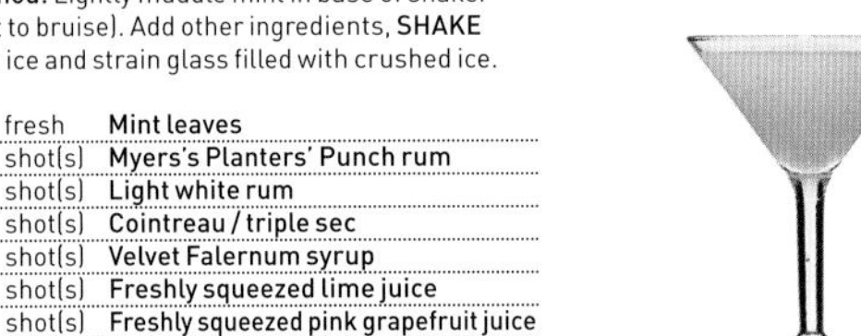

12	fresh	**Mint leaves**
1 1/2	shot(s)	**Myers's Planters' Punch rum**
1	shot(s)	**Light white rum**
3/4	shot(s)	**Cointreau / triple sec**
1/2	shot(s)	**Velvet Falernum syrup**
1	shot(s)	**Freshly squeezed lime juice**
1	shot(s)	**Freshly squeezed pink grapefruit juice**
2	dashes	**Angostura aromatic bitters**

Origin: It is claimed that Ernest Raymond Beaumont-Gantt first served this drink in 1933 at his Don The Beachcomber's bar in Hollywood, California. This is some ten years earlier than Bergeron's Mai Tai-Roa Aé moment in cocktail history.
Comment: Whichever of the two created the drink; it is Trader Vic that made it famous and it is his recipe that endures.

DRINKS ARE GRADED AS FOLLOWS:

● DISGUSTING ●◐ PRETTY AWFUL ●● BEST AVOIDED
●●◐ DISAPPOINTING ●●● ACCEPTABLE ●●●◐ GOOD
●●●● RECOMMENDED ●●●●◐ HIGHLY RECOMMENDED
●●●●● OUTSTANDING / EXCEPTIONAL

MAI TAI #3 (DIFFORD'S FORMULA)

Glass: Old-fashioned
Garnish: Mint sprig & lime wedge
Method: **SHAKE** all ingredients with ice and strain into glass filled with crushed ice.

2	shot(s)	**Aged rum**
1/2	shot(s)	**Cointreau / triple sec**
3/4	shot(s)	**Freshly squeezed lime juice**
1/2	shot(s)	**Orgeat (almond) syrup**
1/4	shot(s)	**Sugar (gomme) syrup**

Origin: My adaptation of Victor Bergeron's (Trader Vic's) 1944 classic.
Comment: I love Daiquiris and this is basically a classic Daiquiri with a few bells and whistles.

MAIDEN'S BLUSH [NEW]

Glass: Martini
Garnish: Lemon peel twist
Method: **SHAKE** all ingredients with ice and fine strain into chilled glass.

2	shot(s)	**Plymouth gin**
1/2	shot(s)	**Cointreau / triple sec**
1/2	shot(s)	**Sonoma pomegranate (grenadine) syrup**
1/4	shot(s)	**Freshly squeezed lemon juice**
1/2	shot(s)	**Chilled mineral water (omit if wet ice)**

Origin: Adapted from a recipe in Harry Craddock's 1930 Savoy Cocktail Book.
Comment: Pale pink, subtle and light.

MAIDEN'S PRAYER [UPDATED]

Glass: Martini
Garnish: Orange zest twist
Method: **SHAKE** all ingredients with ice and fine strain into chilled glass.

1 1/2	shot(s)	**Plymouth gin**
1	shot(s)	**Cointreau / triple sec**
1	shot(s)	**Freshly squeezed orange juice**
1/2	shot(s)	**Freshly squeezed lemon juice**

Origin: Adapted from a recipe in Harry Craddock's 1930 Savoy Cocktail Book.
Comment: Fresh, zesty orange with a pleasing twang of alcohol.

MAINBRACE

Glass: Martini
Garnish: Orange zest twist
Method: **SHAKE** all ingredients with ice and fine strain into chilled glass.

1 1/2	shot(s)	**Plymouth gin**
1 1/2	shot(s)	**Cointreau / triple sec**
1 1/2	shot(s)	**Freshly squeezed golden grapefruit juice**

Comment: Full-on grapefruit laced with gin and a hint of orange. Tart finish.

MAI TAI

In 1934, Victor Jules Bergeron, or Trader Vic as he became known, opened his first restaurant in Oakland, San Francisco. He served Polynesian food with a mix of Chinese, French and American dishes cooked in wood-fired ovens. But he is best known for the rum based cocktails he created.

One evening in 1944 he tested a new drink on two friends from Tahiti, Ham and Carrie Guild. After the first sip, Carrie exclaimed,"Mai Tai-Roa Aé", which in Tahitian means 'Out of this world - the best!'.

So Bergeron named his drink the Mai Tai. The original was based on 17 year old Jamaican J.Wray & Nephew rum which Vic in his own guide describes as being "surprisingly golden in colour, medium bodied, but with the rich pungent flavour particular to the Jamaican blends". Vic states he used "rock candy" syrup. This is an old term for the type of strong sugar syrup I prescribe in this guide. You could dangle a piece of string in it to encourage crystallisation and make rock candy.

When supplies of the Jamaican 17-year-old rum dwindled, Vic started using a combination of dark Jamaican rum and Martinique rum to achieve the desired flavour. Sheer demand in his chain of restaurants later necessitated the introduction of a Mai Tai pre-mix (still available from www.tradervics.com).

Others, particularly Ernest Raymond Beaumont-Gantt, then owner of a Hollywood bar called Don the Beachcomber's, have also laid claim to the creation of this drink. But as Vic says in his own Bartender's Guide, "Anybody who says I didn't create this drink is a dirty stinker."

MAJOR BAILEY #1 [NEW]

Glass: Sling
Garnish: Mint sprig
Method: Lightly **MUDDLE** (only bruise) mint with gin in base of shaker. Add other ingredients, **SHAKE** with ice and fine strain into glass half filled with crushed ice. **CHURN** (stir) drink with the ice using a barspoon. Top the glass to the brim with more crushed ice and churn again. Serve with straws.

12	fresh	**Mint leaves**
2	shot(s)	**Plymouth gin**
1/4	shot(s)	**Freshly squeezed lime juice**
1/4	shot(s)	**Freshly squeezed lemon juice**
1/2	shot(s)	**Sugar (gomme) syrup**

Origin: Adapted from a recipe in the 1947 Trader Vic's Bartender's Guide by Victor Bergeron.
Comment: As Victor says of this gin based Julep, "This is a hell of a drink."

MAJOR BAILEY #2 [NEW]

Glass: Sling
Garnish: Mint sprig
Method: **BLEND** all ingredients with one 12oz scoop of crushed ice and serve with straws.

2	shot(s)	**Light white rum**
1	shot(s)	**Cointreau / triple sec**
1	shot(s)	**Pressed pineapple juice**
1/2	shot(s)	**Freshly squeezed lemon juice**
1/4	shot(s)	**Sugar (gomme) syrup**

Origin: Adapted from a drink created by Victor Bergeron.
Comment: Made well, this is a long, fruity, brilliant frozen Daiquiri.

MAGIC BUS

Glass: Martini
Garnish: Lime wedge on rim
Method: **SHAKE** all ingredients with ice and fine strain into chilled glass.

1	shot(s)	**Sauza Hornitos tequila**
1	shot(s)	**Cointreau / triple sec**
1	shot(s)	**Cranberry juice**
1	shot(s)	**Freshly squeezed orange juice**

Comment: Orange and cranberry laced with tequila.

MALCOLM LOWRY [NEW]

Glass: Old-fashioned
Garnish: Lime wedge
Method: **SHAKE** all ingredients with ice and strain into ice-filled glass.

1	shot(s)	**Sauza Hornitos tequila**
1/2	shot(s)	**Wray & Nephew overproof white rum**
1/4	shot(s)	**Cointreau / triple sec**
1/2	shot(s)	**Freshly squeezed lime juice**
1/4	shot(s)	**Sugar (gomme) syrup**

Origin: Created by drinks author David Broom. Named after Malcolm Lowry's 1947 novel 'Under the Volcano' which explores a man's battle with alcoholism in Mexico.
Comment: A suitably 'hard' and flavoursome Daiquiri-like drink.

MAMBO

Glass: Collins
Garnish: Orange slice
Method: **SHAKE** all ingredients with ice and strain into ice-filled glass.

1	shot(s)	**Ketel One vodka**
1	shot(s)	**Cointreau / triple sec**
1	shot(s)	**Bols apricot brandy liqueur**
1/4	shot(s)	**Campari**
3	shot(s)	**Freshly squeezed orange juice**

Origin: Created by Nichole Colella.
Comment: A slightly bitter, tangy, orange, cooling drink.

MAN-BOUR-TINI

Glass: Martini
Garnish: Orange zest twist
Method: **SHAKE** all ingredients with ice and fine strain into chilled glass.

1	shot(s)	**Mandarine Napoléon liqueur**
3/4	shot(s)	**Bourbon whiskey**
1/2	shot(s)	**Freshly squeezed lime juice**
2	shot(s)	**Cranberry juice**
1/4	shot(s)	**Sugar (gomme) syrup**

Origin: Created in 1999 by yours truly.
Comment: A rounded, fruity, bourbon based drink with mandarin and lime sourness.

MANDARINE COLLINS

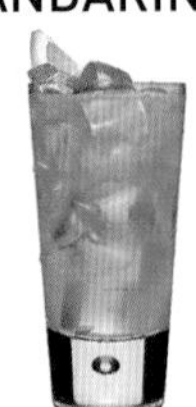

Glass: Collins
Garnish: Half orange slice
Method: **SHAKE** first three ingredients with ice and strain into ice-filled glass. **TOP** with soda.

1 1/2	shot(s)	**Plymouth gin**
1	shot(s)	**Mandarine Napoléon liqueur**
1	shot(s)	**Freshly squeezed lemon juice**
Top up with		**Soda water (club soda)**

Comment: A tangy, long refreshing drink with an intense mandarin flavour.

MANDARINE SIDECAR [NEW]

Glass: Martini
Garnish: Sugar rim (optional) & lemon zest twist
Method: **SHAKE** all ingredients with ice and fine strain into chilled glass.

1 1/2	shot(s)	**Rémy Martin cognac**
1	shot(s)	**Mandarine Napoléon liqueur**
1	shot(s)	**Freshly squeezed lemon juice**
3/4	shot(s)	**Chilled mineral water (omit if wet ice)**
1/8	shot(s)	**Sugar (gomme) syrup**

Comment: Wonderfully tart and strong in flavour.

MANDARINE SONGBIRD [NEW]

Glass: Collins
Garnish: Orange slice
Method: SHAKE first three ingredients with ice and fine strain into ice-filled glass. TOP with ginger beer.

2	shot(s)	Mandarine Napoléon liqueur
1/2	shot(s)	Freshly squeezed lemon juice
3/4	shot(s)	Freshly squeezed orange juice
Top up with		Ginger beer

Comment: Long, spicy orange.

MANDARINE SOUR

Glass: Old-fashioned
Garnish: Lemon slice
Method: SHAKE all ingredients with ice and strain into ice-filled glass.

2	shot(s)	Mandarine Napoléon liqueur
1	shot(s)	Freshly squeezed lemon juice
1/4	shot(s)	Sugar (gomme) syrup
1/2	fresh	Egg white

Comment: Sour, but with a strong mandarin sweetness.

MANDARINTINI [NEW]

Glass: Martini
Garnish: Orange slice on rim
Method: SHAKE all ingredients with ice and fine strain into chilled glass.

1 1/2	shot(s)	Orange flavoured vodka
1/2	shot(s)	Campari
1/2	shot(s)	Grand Marnier liqueur
1 1/2	shot(s)	Pressed apple juice

Origin: Adapted from a drink discovered in 2005 at Aqua Spirit, Hong Kong, China.
Comment: This bittersweet palate cleanser looks like pink grapefruit juice.

MANDARITO [UPDATED]

Glass: Collins
Garnish: Mint sprig
Method: Lightly MUDDLE mint (just to bruise) in base of glass. Add next four ingredients, half fill glass with crushed ice and CHURN (stir). Fill glass to brim with more crushed ice and CHURN some more. TOP with soda, stir and serve with straws.

12	fresh	Mint leaves
1 1/2	shot(s)	Mandarine Napoléon liqueur
1	shot(s)	Ketel One vodka
1	shot(s)	Freshly squeezed lime juice
1/8	shot(s)	Sugar (gomme) syrup
Top up with		Soda water (club soda)

Comment: A vodka Mojito with mandarin accents.

MANGO BATIDA

Glass: Collins
Garnish: Mango slice
Method: SHAKE all ingredients with ice and strain into ice-filled glass.

2 1/2	shot(s)	Cachaça
2	shot(s)	Sweetened mango purée
1	shot(s)	Freshly squeezed lemon juice

Origin: Formula by yours truly in 2004.
Comment: Depending on the sweetness of the mango purée, this drink may benefit from the addition of a dash of sugar syrup.

MANGO COLLINS

Glass: Collins
Garnish: Lemon slice
Method: SHAKE first three ingredients with ice and strain into ice-filled glass. TOP with soda, stir and serve with straws.

2	shot(s)	Plymouth gin
2	shot(s)	Sweetened mango purée
1 1/2	shot(s)	Freshly squeezed lemon juice
Top up with		Soda water (club soda)

Origin: Formula by yours truly in 2004.
Comment: Lemon juice and gin combine with mango in this refreshing tall drink.

MANGO DAIQUIRI

Glass: Martini
Garnish: Lime wedge on rim
Method: SHAKE all ingredients with ice and fine strain into chilled glass.

2	shot(s)	Light white rum
2	shot(s)	Sweetened mango purée
1/2	shot(s)	Freshly squeezed lime juice

Origin: Formula by yours truly in 2004.
Variant: Blended with 12oz scoop crushed ice and an additional half shot of sugar syrup.
Comment: Tropical yet potent and refreshing.

MANGO MARGARITA #1 (SERVED 'UP')

Glass: Coupette
Garnish: Lime wedge on rim
Method: SHAKE all ingredients with ice and fine strain into chilled glass.

2	shot(s)	Sauza Hornitos tequila
1	shot(s)	Sweetened mango purée
1	shot(s)	Cointreau / triple sec
1	shot(s)	Freshly squeezed lime juice

Origin: Formula by yours truly in 2004.
Comment: The character of the tequila is not overwhelmed by the fruit.

MANGO MARGARITA #2 (FROZEN) [NEW]

Glass: Coupette
Garnish: Mango slice on rim
Method: **BLEND** all ingredients with 12oz scoop crushed ice. Serve with straws.

2	shot(s)	**Sauza Hornitos tequila**
¾	shot(s)	**Sweetened mango purée**
1	shot(s)	**Cointreau / triple sec**
½	shot(s)	**Freshly squeezed lime juice**
¼	shot(s)	**Sugar (gomme) syrup**

Origin: Formula by yours truly in 2006.
Comment: Mango first and Margarita second.

MANGO MARTINI

Glass: Martini
Garnish: Mango slice on rim
Method: **SHAKE** all ingredients with ice and fine strain into chilled glass.

2½	shot(s)	**Ketel One Citroen vodka**
2	shot(s)	**Sweetened mango purée**

Origin: Formula by yours truly in 2004.
Comment: This drink doesn't work nearly so well with plain vodka – if citrus vodka is not available, try using gin.

MANGO PUNCH

Glass: Collins
Garnish: Mango slice (dried or fresh)
Method: **SHAKE** all ingredients with ice and fine strain into glass filled with crushed ice.

2	shot(s)	**Wray & Nephew overproof rum**
3	shot(s)	**Sweetened mango purée**
¾	shot(s)	**Freshly squeezed lime juice**
¾	shot(s)	**Sugar (gomme) syrup**

Origin: Created in 2004 by yours truly.
Comment: A distinctly tropical cocktail flavoured with mango.

MANGO RUM COOLER

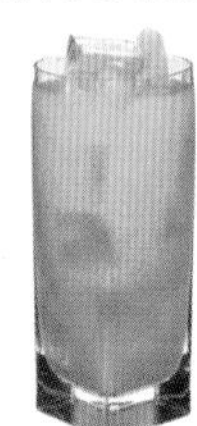

Glass: Collins
Garnish: Mango slice (dried or fresh)
Method: **SHAKE** all ingredients with ice and strain into ice-filled glass.

2½	shot(s)	**Light white rum**
1½	shot(s)	**Sweetened mango purée**
1	shot(s)	**Pressed apple juice**
1½	shot(s)	**Freshly squeezed lemon juice**

Origin: Created in 2004 by yours truly.
Comment: Long, fruity and cooling.

MANHATTAN DRY

Glass: Martini
Garnish: Twist of orange (discarded) & two maraschino cherries
Method: **STIR** all ingredients with ice and strain into chilled glass.

2½	shot(s)	**Bourbon whiskey**
1	shot(s)	**Dry vermouth**
3	dashes	**Angostura aromatic bitters**

Variant: Served over ice in an old-fashioned glass.
Comment: A bone dry Manhattan for those with dry palates.

MANHATTAN PERFECT

Glass: Martini
Garnish: Twist of orange (discarded) & two maraschino cherries
Method: **STIR** all ingredients with ice and strain into chilled glass.

2½	shot(s)	**Bourbon whiskey**
½	shot(s)	**Sweet (rosso) vermouth**
½	shot(s)	**Dry vermouth**
3	dashes	**Angostura aromatic bitters**

Variant: Served over ice in an old-fashioned glass.
Comment: The Manhattan version most popularly served – medium dry.

MANHATTAN SWEET

Glass: Martini
Garnish: Twist of orange (discarded) & two maraschino cherries
Method: **STIR** all ingredients with ice and strain into chilled glass.

2½	shot(s)	**Bourbon whiskey**
1	shot(s)	**Sweet (rosso) vermouth**
⅛	shot(s)	**Syrup from jar of maraschino cherries**
3	dashes	**Angostura aromatic bitters**

Variant: Served over ice in an old-fashioned glass.
Comment: I must confess to preferring my Manhattans served sweet, or perfect at a push. The Manhattan is complex, challenging and moreish. Best of all, it's available in a style to suit every palate.

MANHATTAN ISLAND

Glass: Martini
Garnish: Maraschino cherry
Method: **STIR** all ingredients with ice and fine strain into chilled glass.

2	shot(s)	**Rémy Martin cognac**
1	shot(s)	**Sweet (rosso) vermouth**
3	dashes	**Angostura aromatic bitters**
⅛	shot(s)	**Luxardo Maraschino liqueur**

Comment: A twist on the classic Harvard, or brandy based Manhattan.

MANHATTAN

Like so many cocktails, the origins of the Manhattan are lost in time. The drink started appearing in cocktail books around the 1880s and popular legend states that it was created on 18 November 1874 at the Manhattan Club in New York City for Lady Randolph Churchill, American mother of Winston. She was at a party to celebrate the successful gubernatorial campaign of Samuel Jones Tilden. (The celebrated Manhattan Club was opposite the site that is now the Empire State Building). Others claim it was invented in the 1860s by a man called Black who ran a saloon on Broadway.

The Manhattan was originally made with rye whiskey but it is now common to use bourbon. When Scotch is substituted it becomes a Rob Roy, with brandy (cognac) it is a Harvard and it is a Star Cocktail when made with applejack.

Some time in 2005 it became conventional in some bars to garnish a Manhattan with two cherries as a 9/11 tribute.

MARGARITA

Basically a Sidecar made with tequila in place of cognac, there are many people who claim to have invented the Margarita. The following are just a few of the more plausible stories: the last is most widely regarded as fact.

Pancho Morales, a bartender from Juarez, Mexico, was asked to make a 'Magnolia' but couldn't remember the ingredients, so threw something together. Although it was not what the customer ordered, she loved it. Her name was Margarita.

Carlos Herrera created the cocktail for a lady called Marjorie who drank no spirit but tequila. He added Cointreau and lime and the unique salt rim which caught people's attention at the bar.

Daniel (Danny) Negrete created the drink in 1936 for his girlfriend, called Margarita, when he was the manager of Garci Crespo Hotel in Puebla, Mexico.

Vernon Underwood was president of Young's Market Company, who in the 1930s had started distributing Cuervo tequila. He went to Johnny Durlesser, head bartender of the Tail O' The Cock in LA, and asked him to create something using his spirit. He named it after his wife Margaret and hispanicised her name to Margarita.

Sara Morales, an expert in Mexican folklore, claimed the Margarita was created in 1930 by Doña Bertha, owner of Bertha's Bar in Taxco, Mexico.

The drink could be named after Margarita Island, located in the Caribbean north of Venezuela, two-and-a-half hours from Miami. Margarita is also the Spanish equivalent of the girl's name 'Margaret', and the Spanish word for daisy.

In 1948 a socialite called Margaret Sames was hosting a party at her cliff-side house in Acapulco, Mexico. Among her guests was Nicky Hilton of the famous hotel family (and one of Liz Taylor's many ex-husbands). Looking for something to pep up the party, Margaret began to experiment at the bar and created the first Margarita. She thought nothing of it until, when flying home to San Antonio from Acapulco airport, she saw a bar advertising 'Margarita's Drink', a cocktail with exactly the same ingredients as her own.

MAPLE OLD-FASHIONED

Glass: Martini
Garnish: Orange zest twist
Method: **STIR** one shot of the bourbon with two ice cubes in a glass. Add maple syrup and Angostura and two more ice cubes. **STIR** some more and add another two ice cubes and the rest of the bourbon. **STIR** lots more so as to melt the ice, then add fresh ice to complete the drink. The melting and stirring in of ice cubes is essential to the dilution and taste of this drink.

2	shot(s)	**Bourbon whiskey**
1/2	shot(s)	**Maple syrup**
2	dashes	**Angostura aromatic bitters**

Origin: Discovered in 2004 at Indigo Yard, Edinburgh, Scotland.
Comment: Maple syrup replaces sugar in this reworking of the classic Old-fashioned.

MAPLE LEAF [NEW]

Glass: Old-fashioned
Garnish: Lemon zest twist
Method: **SHAKE** all ingredients with ice and strain into ice-filled glass.

2	shot(s)	**Bourbon whiskey**
1/2	shot(s)	**Freshly squeezed lemon juice**
1/4	shot(s)	**Maple syrup**

Comment: This trio combine wonderfully with maple to the fore.

MAPLE POMME [NEW]

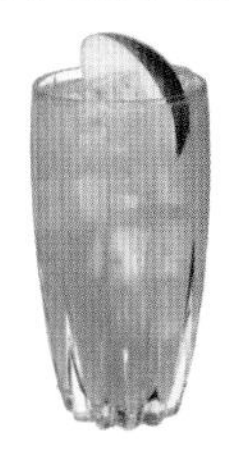

Glass: Collins
Garnish: Apple wedge
Method: **SHAKE** first four ingredients with ice and strain into ice-filled glass. **TOP** with ginger ale, lightly stir and serve with straws.

2	shot(s)	**The Famous Grouse Scotch whisky**
1/2	shot(s)	**Freshly squeezed lemon juice**
1	shot(s)	**Pressed apple juice**
1/2	shot(s)	**Maple syrup**
Top up with		**Ginger ale**

Origin: Adapted from a short drink created in 2005 by Tonin Kacaj at Maze, London, England.
Comment: Scotch based drink for warm weather.

MARACUJA BATIDA [NEW]

Glass: Collins
Garnish: Lemon slice
Method: Cut passion fruit in half and scoop out flesh into shaker. Add other ingredients, **SHAKE** with ice and fine strain into ice-filled glass.

2	fresh	**Passion fruit**
2	shot(s)	**Cachaça**
3/4	shot(s)	**Freshly squeezed lemon juice**
3/4	shot(s)	**Sugar (gomme) syrup**

Variant: Serve blended with crushed ice (add half a shot of passion fruit syrup to the above recipe).
Origin: The Batida is a traditional Brazilian drink and 'maracuja' means passion fruit in Portuguese.
Comment: Cachaça combines with passion fruit.

MARAMA RUM PUNCH [NEW]

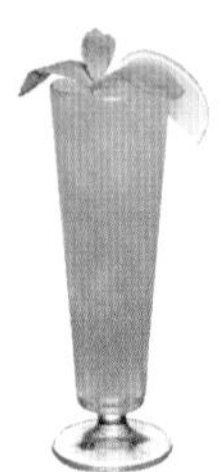

Glass: Sling
Garnish: Mint sprig & lime wedge
Method: Lightly **MUDDLE** mint (just to bruise). Add next five ingredients, **SHAKE** with ice and strain into ice-filled glass. **TOP** with 7-Up, lightly stir and serve with straws.

12	fresh	**Mint leaves**
1 1/2	shot(s)	**Wray & Nephew overproof rum**
1/2	shot(s)	**Cointreau / triple sec**
1/2	shot(s)	**Freshly squeezed lime juice**
1/2	shot(s)	**Almond (orgeat) syrup**
3	dashes	**Angostura aromatic bitters**
Top up with		**7-Up**

Comment: A tangy, well-balanced punch.

MARGARITA #1 (STRAIGHT-UP)

Glass: Coupette
Garnish: Salt rim & lime wedge
Method: **SHAKE** all ingredients with ice and fine strain into chilled glass.

2	shot(s)	**Sauza Hornitos tequila**
1	shot(s)	**Cointreau / triple sec**
1	shot(s)	**Freshly squeezed lime juice**

Variant: Margaritas made with premium tequilas are sometimes referred to as 'Deluxe' or 'Cadillac' Margaritas.
Tip: For the perfect salt rim, liquidise sea salt to make it finer, then run a lime wedge around the outside edge of the glass before dipping the rim in salt. Rimming only half the glass with salt gives the drinker the option of enjoying the cocktail with or without salt.
Comment: One of the great classics.

MARGARITA #2 (ON THE ROCKS)

Glass: Old-fashioned
Garnish: Salt rim & lime wedge
Method: **SHAKE** all ingredients with ice and strain into ice-filled glass.

2	shot(s)	**Sauza Hornitos tequila**
1	shot(s)	**Cointreau / triple sec**
1	shot(s)	**Freshly squeezed lime juice**

Comment: Tangy citrus, tequila and salt.

MARGARITA #3 (FROZEN) [UPDATED]

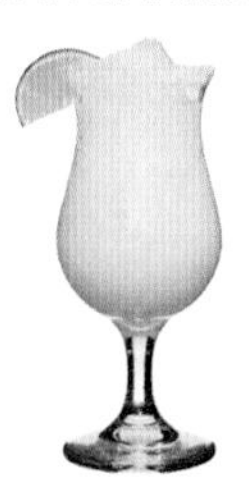

Glass: Martini
Garnish: Maraschino cherry
Method: **BLEND** all ingredients with 12oz scoop of crushed ice. Serve heaped in the glass and with straws.

1 1/2	shot(s)	**Sauza Hornitos tequila**
3/4	shot(s)	**Cointreau / triple sec**
3/4	shot(s)	**Freshly squeezed lime juice**
1/2	shot(s)	**Sugar (gomme) syrup**

Variant: With fruit and/or fruit liqueurs.
Comment: Citrus freshness with the subtle agave of tequila served frozen.

MARGARITA #4 (SALT FOAM FLOAT) [NEW]

Glass: Coupette
Garnish: Lime wedge on rim
Method: Combine first three ingredients, **POUR** into cream whipping siphon and **CHARGE** with nitrous oxide. Shake and place siphon in a refrigerator for one hour prior to making drink. **SHAKE** next three ingredients with ice and fine strain into chilled glass. **SQUIRT** salt foam over surface of drink from siphon.

4	spoons	**Sea salt**
1	pint	**Chilled mineral water**
2	fresh	**Egg whites**
2	shot(s)	**Sauza Hornitos tequila**
1	shot(s)	**Cointreau / triple sec**
1	shot(s)	**Freshly squeezed lime juice**

Comment: Classic Margarita with a salty foam topping.

MARGUERITE MARTINI [NEW]

Glass: Martini
Garnish: Orange zest twist
Method: **SHAKE** all ingredients with ice and fine strain into chilled glass.

2	shot(s)	**Plymouth gin**
½	shot(s)	**Dry vermouth**
1	dash	**Fee Brothers orange bitters**

Origin: Adapted from a recipe in Harry Craddock's 1930 Savoy Cocktail Book.
Comment: A slightly wet yet bone dry classic Martini with a hint of orange.

MARIA THERESA MARGARITA [NEW]

Glass: Martini
Garnish: Lime wedge on rim
Method: **STIR** honey with tequila in base of shaker to dissolve honey. **ADD** other ingredients, **SHAKE** with ice and fine strain into chilled glass.

2	spoons	**Runny honey**
2	shot(s)	**Sauza Hornitos tequila**
1	shot(s)	**Cranberry juice**
½	shot(s)	**Freshly squeezed lime juice**

Origin: Adapted from a Tiki drink created by Victor Bergeron (Trader Vic).
Comment: Originally sweetened with sugar syrup, this is better smoothed with honey.

MARMALADE MARTINI [NEW]

Glass: Martini
Garnish: Orange zest twist
Method: **SHAKE** all ingredients with ice and fine strain into chilled glass.

4	spoons	**Orange marmalade**
2	shot(s)	**Plymouth gin**
½	shot(s)	**Freshly squeezed lemon juice**

Origin: Adapted from a recipe in the 1930 Savoy Cocktail Book by Harry Craddock (the original recipe serves six people).
Comment: Harry wrote of his own drink, "By its bitter-sweet taste this cocktail is especially suited to be a luncheon aperitif."

MARMARITA [NEW]

Glass: Coupette
Garnish: Wipe Marmite (yeast extract) around rim
Method: **SHAKE** all ingredients with ice and fine strain into chilled glass.

2	shot(s)	**Sauza Hornitos tequila**
1	shot(s)	**Cointreau**
1	shot(s)	**Freshly squeezed lime juice**

Origin: Created in 2005 by Simon (Ginger) at Blanch House, Brighton, England.
Comment: A Margarita with a Marmite rim. After all, yeast extract is slightly salty.

MARNY COCKTAIL [NEW]

Glass: Martini
Garnish: Orange zest twist
Method: **SHAKE** all ingredients with ice and fine strain into chilled glass.

2	shot(s)	**Plymouth gin**
1	shot(s)	**Grand Marnier liqueur**
2	dashes	**Fee Brothers orange bitters (optional)**

Origin: Adapted from a recipe in Harry Craddock's 1930 Savoy Cocktail Book.
Comment: Spirit and liqueur in harmony.

MARQUEE [UPDATED]

Glass: Martini
Garnish: Raspberries on stick
Method: **SHAKE** all ingredients with ice and fine strain into chilled glass.

1½	shot(s)	**Bourbon whiskey**
1½	shot(s)	**Cranberry juice**
½	shot(s)	**Chambord black raspberry liqueur**
½	shot(s)	**Freshly squeezed lemon juice**
¼	shot(s)	**Sugar (gomme) syrup**

Origin: Created in 1998 by Giovanni Burdi at Match EC1, London, England.
Comment: Raspberry and bourbon combine perfectly in this short, slightly sweet, fruity drink.

MARTINEZ [UPDATED]

Glass: Martini
Garnish: Lemon zest twist
Method: **STIR** all ingredients with ice and strain into chilled glass.

1½	shot(s)	**Plymouth gin**
1½	shot(s)	**Sweet (rosso) vermouth**
¼	shot(s)	**Cointreau / triple sec**
2	dashes	**Fee Brothers orange bitters (optional)**

Variant: Use maraschino liqueur in place of orange liqueur.
Origin: Supposedly the forerunner of the modern Dry Martini, this was created in 1870 by 'Professor' Jerry Thomas using a sweet style of gin known as 'Old Tom'.
Comment: This medium dry Martini is somewhat more approachable than a Dry Martini.

THE MARTINI

The origin of the classic Martini is disputed and shrouded in mystery. Many books have been written on the subject, and it's a topic which can raise temperatures among drinks aficionados. Most agree that it was created some time around the turn of the last century.

When or wherever the Martini was actually invented, and however it acquired its name, for several decades the name was only applied to a drink containing gin and vermouth in varying proportions. Then came the Vodkatini which extended the meaning of the name. But even then, if a drink didn't contain gin and/or vodka and vermouth it simply wasn't a Martini. Purists hold to this definition today.

Language and the meaning of words are changing faster than ever, and today pretty much any drink served in a V-shaped glass is popularly termed a 'Martini' regardless of its contents. These contemporary, non-traditional Martinis are sometimes referred to as Neo-martinis or Alternatinis and the pages of this guide are filled with such drinks.

I believe a drink should at least be based on gin or vodka to properly be termed a Martini, and ideally should also include vermouth. However, you'll find plenty of drinks in my guides called 'Something' Martini containing all manner of fruits and liqueurs and not a single drop of vermouth – their only claim to the name is the V-shaped glass they are served in.

Even the name of the iconic glass has changed. The old guard of bartending still insist on referring to it as a 'Cocktail Glass'. To my understanding that's now a generic term for glasses designed to hold cocktails, a term which also encompasses the likes of Hurricanes, Slings and Coupettes. Today a V-shaped glass is commonly known as a Martini glass.

For those seeking traditional Martinis based on gin and/or vodka with vermouth and without muddled fruit and suchlike, here are a few classic variations.

Dickens Martini – without a twist.
Dirty Martini – with the brine from an olive jar.
Dry Martini (Traditional) – stirred with gin/vodka.
Dry Martini (Naked) – frozen gin/vodka poured into a frozen glass coated with vermouth.
Franklin Martini - named after Franklin Roosevelt and served with two olives.
Gibson Martini – with two onions instead of an olive or a twist.
Martinez – said to be the original Martini.
Vesper Martini – James Bond's Martini, with gin and vodka.
Vodkatini – very dry, vodka based Martini.
Wet Martini – heavy on the vermouth.

Please also see entries in this guide under: Dry Martini (Traditional), Dry Martini (Naked), Dirty Martini, Martinez, Medium Martini, Vesper Martini, Vodkatini and Wet Martini.

●●●◐○

MARTINI ROYALE

Glass: Martini
Garnish: Lemon zest twist
Method: **STIR** vodka and crème de cassis with ice and strain into chilled glass. **TOP** with chilled champagne.

$1\frac{1}{2}$	shot(s)	Ketel One vodka
$\frac{1}{2}$	shot(s)	Crème de cassis liqueur
Top up with		Piper-Heidsieck brut champagne

Origin: Created in 2001 by Dick Bradsell at Monte's, London, England.
Comment: The Kir Royale meets the vodkatini in this pink but powerful drink.

●●●●◐

MARTINI SPECIAL [NEW]

Glass: Martini
Garnish: Orange zest twist
Method: Fill glass with ice and pour absinthe and Angostura over ice. **TOP** with chilled mineral water and leave to stand. **SHAKE** gin, vermouth and orange water with ice. **DISCARD** contents of standing glass and fine strain shaken drink into washed glass.

$\frac{1}{4}$	shot(s)	La Fée Parisian 68% absinthe
4	dashes	Angostura aromatic bitters
2	shot(s)	Plymouth gin
$\frac{3}{4}$	shot(s)	Sweet (rosso) vermouth
$\frac{1}{8}$	shot(s)	Orange flower water

Origin: Adapted from a recipe in Harry Craddock's 1930 Savoy Cocktail Book.
Comment: Aromatic, very dry and very serious – yet it has a frothy head.

●●●●○

MARTINI THYME

Glass: Martini
Garnish: Thread three green olives onto thyme sprig
Method: **MUDDLE** thyme in base of shaker. **ADD** other ingredients, **SHAKE** with ice and fine strain into chilled glass.

2	sprigs	Lemon thyme (remove stalks)
1	shot(s)	Plymouth gin
$\frac{3}{4}$	shot(s)	Green Chartreuse
$\frac{1}{4}$	shot(s)	Sugar (gomme) syrup

Origin: A combination of two very similar drinks, that both originally called for thyme infused gin. The first I discovered at The Lobby Bar (One Aldwych, London) and the other came from Tony Conigliaro at Isola, London, England.
Comment: A wonderfully fresh herbal Martini with the distinctive taste of Chartreuse. You'll either love it or hate it.

DRINKS ARE GRADED AS FOLLOWS:

● DISGUSTING ●◐ PRETTY AWFUL ●● BEST AVOIDED
●●◐ DISAPPOINTING ●●● ACCEPTABLE ●●●◐ GOOD
●●●● RECOMMENDED ●●●●◐ HIGHLY RECOMMENDED
●●●●● OUTSTANDING / EXCEPTIONAL

●●●●●

MARY PICKFORD

Glass: Martini
Garnish: Maraschino cherry
Method: **SHAKE** all ingredients with ice and fine strain into chilled glass.

2	shot(s)	Light white rum
$1\frac{1}{2}$	shot(s)	Pressed pineapple juice
$\frac{1}{4}$	shot(s)	Sonoma pomegranate (grenadine) syrup
$\frac{1}{8}$	shot(s)	Luxardo maraschino liqueur

Origin: Created in the 1920s (during prohibition) by Fred Kaufman at the Hotel Nacîonal de Cuba, Havana for the silent movie star. She was in Cuba filming a movie with her husband Douglas Fairbanks and Charlie Chaplin.
Comment: When made correctly, this pale pink cocktail has a perfect balance between the fruit flavours and the spirit of the rum.

●●●●◐

MARY QUEEN OF SCOTS [NEW]

Glass: Martini
Garnish: Sugar rim & maraschino cherry
Method: **SHAKE** all ingredients with ice and fine strain into chilled glass.

$1\frac{1}{2}$	shot(s)	The Famous Grouse Scotch whisky
$\frac{3}{4}$	shot(s)	Drambuie liqueur
$\frac{3}{4}$	shot(s)	Green Chartreuse

Origin: Discovered in 2006 on Kyle Branch's Cocktail Hotel blog (www.cocktailhotel.blogspot.com). Mary Stuart, Mary Queen of Scots, was born on December 8th 1542 at Linlithgow Palace in West Lothian. On February 8th 1587, she was executed in the Great Hall of Fotheringhay.
Comment: Slightly sweet but herbal, serious and strong.

●●●●○

MARY ROSE

Glass: Martini
Garnish: Lime twist (discard) & rosemary sprig
Method: **MUDDLE** rosemary in base of shaker. **ADD** other ingredients, **SHAKE** with ice and fine strain into chilled glass.

1	sprig	Fresh rosemary
2	shot(s)	Plymouth gin
1	shot(s)	Green Chartreuse liqueur
$\frac{1}{2}$	shot(s)	Sugar (gomme) syrup
$\frac{1}{2}$	shot(s)	Chilled mineral water (omit if wet ice)

Origin: Created in 1999 by Philip Jeffrey at the Great Eastern Hotel, London, England. Named after King Henry VIII's warship, sunk during an engagement with the French fleet in 1545 and now on display in Portsmouth.
Comment: Herbal, herbal and herbal with a hint of spice.

MAURICE MARTINI [NEW]

Glass: Martini
Garnish: Orange zest twist
Method: **SHAKE** all ingredients with ice and fine strain into chilled glass.

1 1/2	shot(s)	**Plymouth gin**
3/4	shot(s)	**Dry vermouth**
3/4	shot(s)	**Sweet (rosso) vermouth**
1/4	shot(s)	**La Fée Parisian 68% absinthe**
3/4	shot(s)	**Freshly squeezed orange juice**

Origin: Adapted from a recipe in Harry Craddock's 1930 Savoy Cocktail Book.
Comment: A perfect Martini with an aromatic burst of absinthe and a hint of orange.

MAT THE RAT

Glass: Collins
Garnish: Lime wedge
Method: **SHAKE** first four ingredients with ice and strain into ice-filled glass. **TOP** with 7-Up, lightly stir and serve with straws.

2	shot(s)	**Spiced rum**
1/2	shot(s)	**Cointreau / triple sec**
1 1/2	shot(s)	**Freshly squeezed orange juice**
1/2	shot(s)	**Freshly squeezed lime juice**
Top up with		**7-Up**

Origin: A popular drink in UK branches of TGI Friday's, where it was created.
Comment: Whether or not Mat was a rat, we shall never know. However, the drink that's named after him is long and thirst-quenching.

MATADOR

Glass: Collins
Garnish: Pineapple wedge on rim
Method: **SHAKE** all ingredients with ice and strain into ice-filled glass.

2	shot(s)	**Sauza Hornitos tequila**
1	shot(s)	**Cointreau / triple sec**
1	shot(s)	**Freshly squeezed lime juice**
2	shot(s)	**Pressed pineapple juice**

Comment: A long Margarita with pineapple juice. The lime and tequila work wonders with the sweet pineapple.

MAURESQUE

Glass: Collins (10oz max)
Method: **POUR** pastis and almond syrup into glass. Serve iced water separately in a small jug (known in France as a 'broc') so the customer can dilute to their own taste (I recommend five shots). Lastly, add ice to fill glass.

1	shot(s)	**Ricard pastis**
1/2	shot(s)	**Almond (orgeat) syrup**
Top up with		**Chilled mineral water**

Origin: Pronounced 'Mor-Esk', this drink is very popular in the South of France.
Comment: Long, refreshing aniseed, liquorice and almond.

MAYAN

Glass: Old-fashioned
Garnish: Float 3 coffee beans
Method: **SHAKE** all ingredients with ice and strain into ice-filled glass.

1 1/2	shot(s)	**Sauza Hornitos tequila**
1/2	shot(s)	**Kahlúa coffee liqueur**
2 1/2	shot(s)	**Pressed pineapple juice**

Comment: Tequila, coffee and pineapple juice combine in this medium dry short drink.

MAYAN WHORE

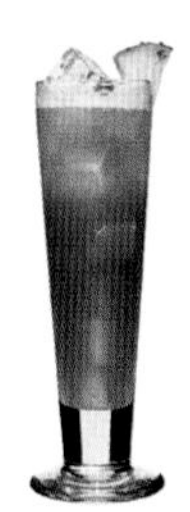

Glass: Sling
Garnish: Split pineapple wedge
Method: **SHAKE** first three ingredients with ice and strain into ice-filled glass. **TOP** with soda, **DO NOT STIR** and serve with straws.

2	shot(s)	**Sauza Hornitos tequila**
1 1/2	shot(s)	**Pressed pineapple juice**
3/4	shot(s)	**Kahlúa coffee liqueur**
Top up with		**Soda water (club soda)**

Comment: An implausible ménage à trois: coffee, tequila and pineapple, served long.

MAYFAIR COCKTAIL [NEW]

Glass: Martini
Garnish: Orange zest twist
Method: **MUDDLE** cloves in base of shaker. Add other ingredients, **SHAKE** with ice and fine strain into chilled glass.

2	dried	**Cloves**
2	shot(s)	**Plymouth gin**
1	shot(s)	**Bols apricot brandy**
1	shot(s)	**Freshly squeezed orange juice**
1/4	shot(s)	**Sugar (gomme) syrup**

Variant: With World's End Pimento Dram liqueur in place of sugar.
Origin: Adapted from a recipe in Harry Craddock's 1930 Savoy Cocktail Book.
Comment: The kind of spiced drink you'd usually expect to be served hot.

THE MAYFLOWER MARTINI

Glass: Martini
Garnish: Edible flower petal
Method: **SHAKE** all ingredients with ice and fine strain into chilled glass.

1 1/2	shot(s)	**Plymouth gin**
1/2	shot(s)	**Bols apricot brandy liqueur**
1	shot(s)	**Pressed apple juice**
1/4	shot(s)	**Elderflower cordial**
1/2	shot(s)	**Freshly squeezed lemon juice**

Origin: Created in 2002 by Wayne Collins for Maxxium UK.
Comment: Fragrant balance of English fruits and flowers.

MAXIM'S COFFEE (HOT) [NEW]

Glass: Toddy
Garnish: Float 3 coffee beans
Method: POUR all ingredients into warmed glass and STIR.

1	shot(s)	Rémy Martin cognac
1/2	shot(s)	Bénédictine D.O.M. liqueur
1/4	shot(s)	Galliano liqueur
Top up with		Hot filter coffee

Comment: An interesting herbal cognac laced coffee.

M.C. MARTINI [UPDATED]

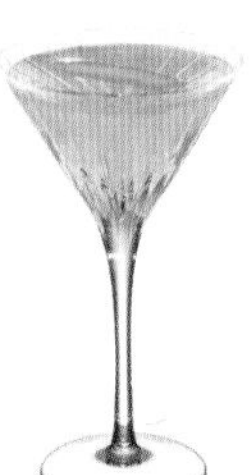

Glass: Martini
Garnish: Lime zest twist
Method: SHAKE all ingredients with ice and fine strain into chilled glass.

2	shot(s)	Plymouth gin
1	shot(s)	Sauvignon Blanc wine
1/2	shot(s)	Elderflower cordial

Origin: Created in 2003 by yours truly for Marie Claire magazine.
Comment: If you're an "independent, stylish and image-conscious woman who wants to get the best out of her life", then this drink was created for you. If you're not, drink this floral Martini and dream of meeting (or being) such a woman.

MEDICINAL SOLUTION [NEW]

Glass: Collins
Garnish: Lime wedge
Method: SHAKE first five ingredients with ice and strain into ice-filled glass. TOP with tonic water, lightly stir and serve with straws.

1 1/2	shot(s)	Oude jenever
1/2	shot(s)	Green Chartreuse liqueur
1/2	shot(s)	Freshly squeezed lime juice
1/4	shot(s)	Sugar (gomme) syrup
3	dashes	Angostura aromatic bitters
Top up with		Tonic water

Origin: Created in 2006 by yours truly.
Comment: Every ingredient, apart from the sugar, has at some time been consumed for its medicinal qualities. Even the sugar is still used to make bitter tasting medicine more palatable. Some might say that's just what I've done here.

MEDIUM MARTINI [NEW]

Glass: Martini
Garnish: Orange zest twist
Method: STIR all ingredients with ice and strain into chilled glass.

1 1/2	shot(s)	Plymouth gin
3/4	shot(s)	Dry vermouth
3/4	shot(s)	Sweet (rosso) vermouth

Origin: Adapted from a recipe in Harry Craddock's 1930 Savoy Cocktail Book.
Comment: A classic Martini served perfect and very wet. I prefer mine shaken which is the method Harry specifies in his guide.

MELON BALL

Glass: Shot
Method: SHAKE all ingredients with ice and fine strain into chilled glass.

1/2	shot(s)	Ketel One vodka
1/2	shot(s)	Midori melon liqueur
3/4	shot(s)	Freshly squeezed orange juice

Comment: A vivid green combination of vodka, melon and orange.

MELON COLLIE MARTINI

Glass: Martini
Garnish: Crumbled Cadbury's Flake bar
Method: SHAKE all ingredients with ice and fine strain into chilled glass.

1	shot(s)	Light white rum
1/2	shot(s)	Malibu coconut rum
3/4	shot(s)	Midori melon liqueur
1/4	shot(s)	Bols white crème de cacao
3/4	shot(s)	Double (heavy) cream
3/4	shot(s)	Milk

Origin: Created in 2003 by Simon King at MJU, Millennium Hotel, London, England.
Comment: Something of a holiday disco drink but tasty all the same.

MELON DAIQUIRI #1 (SERVED 'UP')

Glass: Martini
Garnish: Melon slice or melon balls
Method: Cut melon into 8 segments and deseed. Cut cubes of flesh from skin of one segment and MUDDLE in base of shaker. Add other ingredients, SHAKE with ice and fine strain into chilled glass.

1/8	fresh	Cantaloupe / Galia melon
2	shot(s)	Light white rum
1/2	shot(s)	Midori melon liqueur
1/2	shot(s)	Freshly squeezed lime juice
1/8	shot(s)	Sugar (gomme) syrup

Comment: A classic Daiquiri with the gentle touch of melon.

MELON DAIQUIRI #2 (SERVED FROZEN)

Glass: Martini (large 10oz)
Garnish: Melon slice or melon balls
Method: Cut melon into 8 segments and deseed. Cut cubes of flesh from skin of one segment and place in blender. Add other ingredients and BLEND with half scoop crushed ice. Serve with straws.

1/8	fresh	Cantaloupe / Galia melon
2	shot(s)	Light white rum
1/2	shot(s)	Midori melon liqueur
1/2	shot(s)	Freshly squeezed lime juice
1/4	shot(s)	Sugar (gomme) syrup

Comment: A cooling, fruity Daiquiri.

MELON MARGARITA #1 (SERVED 'UP')

Glass: Coupette
Garnish: Melon slice or melon balls
Method: Cut melon into 8 segments and deseed. Cut cubes of flesh from skin of one segment and **MUDDLE** in base of shaker. Add other ingredients, **SHAKE** with ice and fine strain into chilled glass.

1/8	fresh	Cantaloupe / Galia melon
2	shot(s)	Sauza Hornitos tequila
1	shot(s)	Midori melon liqueur
1	shot(s)	Freshly squeezed lime juice

Comment: Looks like stagnant pond water but tastes fantastic.

MELON MARGARITA #2 (SERVED FROZEN)

Glass: Coupette
Garnish: Melon slice or melon balls
Method: Cut melon into 8 segments and deseed. Cut cubes of flesh from skin of one segment and place in blender. Add other ingredients and **BLEND** with 6oz scoop crushed ice. Serve with straws.

1/8	fresh	Cantaloupe / Galia melon
2	shot(s)	Sauza Hornitos tequila
1	shot(s)	Midori melon liqueur
1/2	shot(s)	Freshly squeezed lime juice

Comment: Melon and tequila always combine well - here in a frozen Margarita.

MELON MARTINI #1

Glass: Martini
Garnish: Split lime wedge
Method: **SHAKE** all ingredients with ice and fine strain into chilled glass.

2 1/4	shot(s)	Ketel One vodka
1	shot(s)	Midori melon liqueur
1/2	shot(s)	Freshly squeezed lime juice
1/4	shot(s)	Sugar (gomme) syrup

Comment: Bright green, lime and melon with more than a hint of vodka. Do it properly - have a fresh one.

MELON MARTINI #2 (FRESH FRUIT)

Glass: Martini
Garnish: Melon wedge on rim
Method: Cut melon into 8 segments and deseed. Cut cubes of flesh from skinof one segment and **MUDDLE** in base of shaker. Add other ingredients, **SHAKE** with ice and fine strain into chilled glass.

1/8	fresh	Cantaloupe / Galia melon
2	shot(s)	Ketel One vodka
1/4	shot(s)	Sugar (gomme) syrup

Variant: Substitute Midori melon liqueur for sugar syrup.
Comment: Probably the most popular of all the fresh fruit martinis.

MELONCHOLY MARTINI

Glass: Martini
Garnish: Mint sprig
Method: **SHAKE** all ingredients with ice and fine strain into chilled glass.

1	shot(s)	Ketel One vodka
1	shot(s)	Midori melon liqueur
1/2	shot(s)	Cointreau / triple sec
1/2	shot(s)	Malibu coconut rum liqueur
1	shot(s)	Pressed pineapple juice
3/4	shot(s)	Double (heavy) cream
1/4	shot(s)	Freshly squeezed lime juice

Origin: Created in 2002 by Daniel O'Brien at Ocean Bar, Edinburgh, Scotland.
Comment: Sweet, but the flavours in this smooth, tangy, lime-green drink combine surprisingly well.

MELLOW MARTINI

Glass: Martini
Garnish: Fresh lychee on a stick
Method: **SHAKE** all ingredients with ice and fine strain into chilled glass.

1 1/2	shot(s)	Ketel One vodka
1/2	shot(s)	Soho lychee liqueur
1/2	shot(s)	Bols crème de bananes liqueur
1 1/2	shot(s)	Pressed pineapple juice

Comment: A fruity, tropical drink with a frothy head. Too fluffy to be a Martini.

MENEHUNE JUICE [NEW]

Glass: Old-fashioned
Garnish: Lime wedge, mint & Menehune
Method: **SHAKE** all ingredients with ice and strain into glass filled with crushed ice. Serve with straws.

2	shot(s)	Light white rum
1/2	shot(s)	Cointreau / triple sec
3/4	shot(s)	Freshly squeezed lime juice
1/4	shot(s)	Almond (orgeat) sugar syrup
1/4	shot(s)	Sugar (gomme) syrup

Origin: Adapted from a recipe in the 1947-72 Trader Vic's Bartender's Guide by Victor Bergeron.
Comment: Slightly sweet and strong. According to Vic, "One sip and you may see a Menehune."

MERRY WIDOW #1 [NEW]

Glass: Martini
Garnish: Lemon zest twist
Method: **STIR** all ingredients with ice and strain into chilled glass.

1 1/2	shot(s)	Plymouth gin
1 1/2	shot(s)	Dry vermouth
1/4	shot(s)	La Fée Parisian 68% absinthe
1/4	shot(s)	Bénédictine D.O.M. liqueur
3	dashes	Angostura aromatic bitters
1/2	shot(s)	Chilled water

Origin: Adapted from a recipe in Harry Craddock's 1930 Savoy Cocktail Book.
Comment: Aromatic, complex, strong and bitter.

MERRY WIDOW #2

Glass: Martini
Garnish: Orange zest twist
Method: **STIR** all ingredients with ice and strain into chilled glass.

1 1/4	shot(s)	**Ketel One vodka**
1 1/4	shot(s)	**Dubonnet Red**
1 1/4	shot(s)	**Dry vermouth**
1	dash	**Fee Brothers orange bitters**

Comment: Aromatic and complex - for toughened palates.

MERRY-GO-ROUND MARTINI [NEW]

Glass: Martini
Garnish: Olive & lemon zest twist
Method: **STIR** all ingredients with ice and fine strain into chilled glass.

2	shot(s)	**Plymouth gin**
1/2	shot(s)	**Dry vermouth**
1/2	shot(s)	**Sweet (rosso) vermouth**

Origin: Long lost classic variation on the Dry Martini.
Comment: Stir this 'perfect' Martini around and then get merry.

MESA FRESCA [NEW]

Glass: Collins
Garnish: Lime wheel
Method: **SHAKE** all ingredients with ice and strain into ice-filled glass.

2	shot(s)	**Sauza Hornitos tequila**
3	shot(s)	**Freshly squeezed pink grapefruit juice**
1	shot(s)	**Freshly squeeezed lime juice**
1/2	shot(s)	**Sugar (gomme) syrup**

Origin: Discovered in 2005 at Mesa Grill, New York City, USA.
Comment: Sweet and sour tequila and grapefruit.

MEXICAN [NEW]

Glass: Martini
Garnish: Pineapple wedge on rim
Method: **SHAKE** all ingredients with ice and fine strain into chilled glass.

2	shot(s)	**Sauza Hornitos tequila**
1 1/2	shot(s)	**Pressed pineapple juice**
1/4	shot(s)	**Sonoma pomegranate (grenadine) syrup**

Variant: Substitute sugar syrup for pomegranate syrup.
Comment: Fresh pineapple makes this drink.

MET MANHATTAN

Glass: Martini
Garnish: Orange zest twist
Method: **SHAKE** all ingredients with ice and fine strain into chilled glass.

2	shot(s)	**Bourbon whiskey**
1	shot(s)	**Grand Marnier liqueur**
1/2	shot(s)	**Bols butterscotch liqueur**
2	dashes	**Fee Brothers orange bitters**

Origin: The Met Bar, Metropolitan Hotel, London, England.
Comment: Smooth and rounded bourbon with a hint of orange toffee.

METROPOLITAN

Glass: Martini
Garnish: Flamed orange twist
Method: **SHAKE** all ingredients with ice and fine strain into chilled glass.

2	shot(s)	**Raspberry flavoured vodka**
1/2	shot(s)	**Cointreau / triple sec**
1	shot(s)	**Cranberry juice**
1/2	shot(s)	**Freshly squeezed lime juice**
1/4	shot(s)	**Rose's lime cordial**

Origin: Created in 1993 by Chuck Coggins at Marion's Continental Restaurant & Lounge, New York City. Marion's was originally opened in 1950 by fashion model Marion Nagy, who came to the States after seeking asylum while swimming for Hungary in the Paris Peace Games after WWII.
Comment: A Cosmo with more than a hint of blackcurrant.

MEXICAN 55 [NEW]

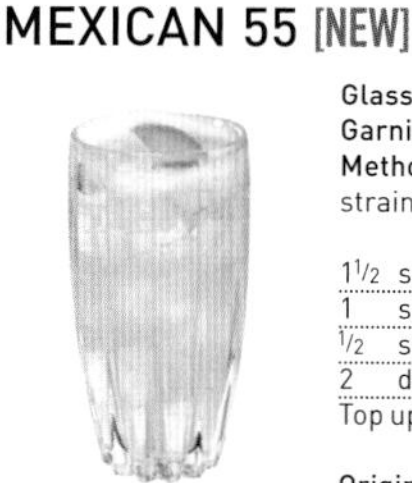

Glass: Collins
Garnish: Lime wedge
Method: **SHAKE** first four ingredients with ice and strain into ice-filled glass. **TOP** with champagne.

1 1/2	shot(s)	**Sauza Hornitos tequila**
1	shot(s)	**Freshly squeezed lemon juice**
1/2	shot(s)	**Sugar (gomme) syrup**
2	dashes	**Angostura aromatic bitters**
Top up with		**Piper-Heidsieck brut champagne**

Origin: An adaptation of the classic French '75 created in 1988 at La Perla, Paris, France. The name comes from Fidel Castro's statement that bullets, like wine, came in vintages and Mexican '55 was a good year (for bullets).
Comment: Suitably hard, yet surprisingly refreshing and sophisticated.

MEXICAN COFFEE (HOT) [NEW]

Glass: Toddy
Garnish: Three coffee beans
Method: Place bar spoon in glass. **POUR** tequila into glass, **TOP** with coffee and stir. **FLOAT** cream.

1	shot(s)	**Sauza Hornitos tequila**
1/4	shot(s)	**Sugar (gomme) syrup**
Top up with		**Hot filter coffee**
Float		**Double (heavy) cream**

Tip: Lightly whip or simply shake cream in container before pouring over the bowl of a spoon. It also helps if the cream is gently warmed.
Comment: Tequila's answer to the Irish Coffee.

MEXICAN MANHATTAN [NEW]

Glass: Martini
Garnish: Maraschino cherry
Method: STIR all ingredients with ice and strain into chilled glass.

2	shot(s)	Sauza Hornitos tequila
1	shot(s)	Red (rosso) vermouth
3	dashes	Angostura aromatic bitters

Comment: You've tried this with bourbon, now surprise yourself with an aged tequila.

MEXICAN MARTINI

Glass: Martini
Garnish: Pineapple leaf on rim
Method: SHAKE all ingredients with ice and fine strain into chilled glass.

2	shot(s)	Sauza Hornitos tequila
1/4	shot(s)	Crème de cassis
2	shot(s)	Pressed pineapple juice

Origin: Discovered in 2004 at Indigo Yard, Edinburgh, Scotland.
Comment: Tequila, pineapple and blackcurrant combine in this medium dry cocktail.

MEXICAN MELON BALL [NEW]

Glass: Collins
Garnish: Melon balls on stick
Method: Cut melon into 8 segments and deseed. Cut cubes of flesh from skin of one segment and MUDDLE in base of shaker. Add other ingredients, SHAKE with ice and fine strain into ice-filled glass.

1/8	fresh	Cantaloupe / Galia melon
2	shot(s)	Sauza Hornitos tequila
2	shot(s)	Freshly squeezed orange juice
1/4	shot(s)	Sugar (gomme) syrup

Origin: Adapted from a drink discovered at the Flying V Bar & Grill, Tucson, Arizona, USA.
Comment: Orange and melon laced with tequila.

MEXICAN MULE

Glass: Collins
Garnish: Lime wedge
Method: SHAKE first three ingredients with ice and strain into ice-filled glass. TOP with ginger beer, lightly stir and serve with straws.

1 1/2	shot(s)	Sauza Hornitos tequila
3/4	shot(s)	Freshly squeezed lime juice
1/4	shot(s)	Sugar (gomme) syrup
Top up with		Ginger beer

AKA: El Burro
Comment: A tequila based version of the Moscow Mule.

MEXICAN SURFER

Glass: Martini
Garnish: Lime wedge on rim
Method: SHAKE all ingredients with ice and fine strain into chilled glass.

2	shot(s)	Sauza Hornitos tequila
1 1/2	shot(s)	Pressed pineapple juice
1/2	shot(s)	Rose's lime cordial

Comment: Frothy topped, easy to make, and all too easy to drink.

MEXICAN TEA (HOT) [NEW]

Glass: Toddy
Garnish: Lime slice
Method: Place bar spoon in warmed glass. POUR all ingredients into glass and stir.

2	shot(s)	Sauza Hornitos tequila
1/2	shot(s)	Sugar (gomme) syrup
Top up with		Hot black breakfast tea

Comment: Tiffin will never be the same again.

MEXICO CITY

Glass: Coupette
Garnish: Lime wedge on rim
Method: SHAKE all ingredients with ice and fine strain into chilled glass.

1 1/2	shot(s)	Sauza Hornitos tequila
3/4	shot(s)	Grand Marnier liqueur
1/2	shot(s)	Freshly squeezed lime juice
1/2	shot(s)	Cranberry juice
1/4	shot(s)	Sugar (gomme) syrup

Origin: Adapted from a cocktail discovered in 2002 at the Merc Bar, New York City.
Comment: This pinky-red Margarita benefits from a hint of cranberry.

MEXICANO (HOT) [NEW]

Glass: Toddy
Garnish: Dust with nutmeg & cinnamon
Method: POUR tequila and liqueur into warmed glass and top with coffee. FLOAT cream over drink.

1	shot(s)	Sauza Hornitos tequila
1/2	shot(s)	Grand Marnier liqueur
Top up with		Hot filter coffee
Float		Double (heavy) cream

Tip: Lightly whip or simply shake cream in container before pouring over the bowl of a spoon. It also helps if the cream is gently warmed.
Comment: A spicy, flavour-packed hot coffee.

MIAMI BEACH [NEW]

Glass: Martini
Garnish: Pineapple wedge & cherry
Method: **SHAKE** all ingredients with ice and fine strain into chilled glass.

2	shot(s)	**Plymouth gin**
1½	shot(s)	**Pressed pineapple juice**
¼	shot(s)	**Sugar (gomme) syrup**

Comment: Fruity and well proportioned – like the babes on Miami Beach. Sorry.

MIAMI DAIQUIRI

Glass: Martini
Garnish: Mint leaf
Method: **SHAKE** all ingredients with ice and fine strain into chilled glass.

2	shot(s)	**Light white rum**
¼	shot(s)	**White crème de menthe**
½	shot(s)	**Freshly squeezed lime juice**
⅛	shot(s)	**Sugar (gomme) syrup**
¾	shot(s)	**Chilled mineral water (omit if wet ice)**

Origin: My adaptation of a classic.
Comment: The merest hint of mint in a refreshing Daiquiri with a dry finish.

MICHELADA [NEW]

Glass: Collins
Garnish: Lime wedge
Method: **STIR** first six ingredients in bottom of glass. Fill glass with ice and **TOP** with beer.

¾	shot(s)	**Freshly squeezed lime juice**
⅛	shot(s)	**Soy sauce**
3	drops	**Tabasco pepper sauce**
2	dashes	**Worcestershire sauce**
1	pinch	**Celery salt**
1	pinch	**Black pepper**
Top up with		**Beer**

Origin: A Mexican classic.
Comment: Made with lager this spicy drink is sometimes called a White Mary. It's best made with a dark, flavoursome beer.

MILANO [NEW]

Glass: Old-fashioned
Garnish: Orange slice
Method: **STIR** all ingredients with ice and strain into ice-filled glass.

1	shot(s)	**Ketel One vodka**
1	shot(s)	**Campari**
1	shot(s)	**Sweet (rosso) vermouth**

AKA: Negrosky
Comment: A Negroni with vodka in place of gin.

MILANO SOUR [NEW]

Glass: Old-fashioned
Garnish: Lemon slice & maraschino cherry (sail)
Method: **SHAKE** all ingredients with ice and fine strain into ice-filled glass.

1½	shot(s)	**Plymouth gin**
1	shot(s)	**Galliano liqueur**
1	shot(s)	**Freshly squeezed lemon juice**
½	fresh	**Egg white**

Origin: Created in 2006 by your truly.
Comment: Delicate anise and peppermint with citrus freshness.

MILHO VERDE BATIDA [NEW]

Glass: Collins
Garnish: Cinnamon dust
Method: **BLEND** all ingredients with 12oz scoop crushed ice. Serve with straws.

2½	shot(s)	**Cachaça**
70	grams	**Sweetcorn (canned)**
1½	shot(s)	**Sweetened condensed milk**

Origin: A classic Brazilian drink.
Comment: Quite possibly your first sweetcorn cocktail.

MILK & HONEY MARTINI

Glass: Martini
Garnish: Grate fresh nutmeg over drink
Method: **STIR** Scotch with honey in base of shaker to dissolve honey. Add other ingredients, **SHAKE** with ice and fine strain into chilled glass.

2	shot(s)	**The Famous Grouse Scotch whisky**
3	spoons	**Runny honey**
½	shot(s)	**Honey liqueur**
¾	shot(s)	**Double (heavy) cream**
¾	shot(s)	**Milk**

Origin: Created in 2002 by yours truly.
Comment: The rich flavour of Scotch is tamed by honey and cream.

MILK PUNCH [UPDATED]

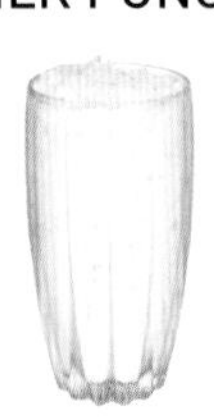

Glass: Collins
Garnish: Dust with freshly grated nutneg
Method: **SHAKE** all ingredients with ice and strain into glass filled with crushed ice.

1	shot(s)	**Rémy Martin cognac**
½	shot(s)	**Goslings Black Seal rum**
½	shot(s)	**Sonoma vanilla bean sugar syrup**
2	shot(s)	**Milk**
1	shot(s)	**Double (heavy) cream**

Comment: The cream, vanilla and sugar tame the cognac and rum.

MINT JULEP

This is the ultimate Deep South cocktail, famously served at the Kentucky Derby. The name derives from the Arabic word 'julab', meaning rosewater, and the first known written reference dates back to 1803. At that time it could be made with rum, brandy or whiskey, but by 1900 whiskey had become the preferred ingredient.

The Mint Julep reached Britain in 1837, thanks to the novelist Captain Frederick Marryat, who complained of being woken at 7am by a slave brandishing a Julep. He popularised it through his descriptions of American Fourth of July celebrations.

When making a Mint Julep it is important to only bruise the mint as crushing the leaves releases the bitter, inner juices. Also be sure to discard the stems, which are also bitter.

It is imperative that the drink is served ice cold. Cocktail etiquette dictates that the shaker containing the mint and other ingredients should be placed in a refrigerator with the serving glass for at least two hours prior to adding ice, shaking and serving.

Variations on the Mint Julep include substituting the bourbon for rye whiskey, rum, gin, brandy, calvados or applejack brandy. Another variation calls for half a shot of aged rum to be floated on top of the bourbon-based julep.

MOJITO

Between the wars, and especially during Prohibition, Cuba had a thriving international bar culture. In fact, when Prohibition was announced, numerous companies outfitted ferries for the overnight booze cruise to the island. At the heart of this bar culture were Cuba's bartenders, many of them trained at the Association Cantineros Cuba - the legendary Havana bar school.

A classic, long blend of rum, lime and mint, the Mojito was probably invented after Americans introduced the locals to the Mint Julep. Bodeguita del Medio is usually credited with the first Mojito and this is apparently where Hemingway went for his.

In January 2003 the Mojito had something of a boost when the newly released Bond film, Die Another Day, saw James visit Cuba and order a Mojito in preference to his more usual Vodka Martini.

MOJITO VARIATIONS

Apple Mojito
Apple Virgin Mojito
Bajan Mojito
Bajito
French Mojito
Ginger Mojito
Rude Mojito
Luxury Mojito
Milky Mojito
Mojito
Mojito de Casa
Momo Special
Orange Mojito
Pineapple Mojito
Strawberry & Balsamic Mojito

MILKY MOJITO

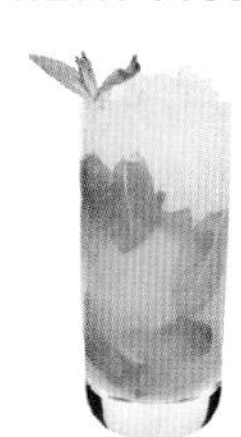

Glass: Collins
Garnish: Mint spring
Method: Lightly **MUDDLE** (just to bruise) mint in glass. Fill glass with crushed ice, add sugar, lime juice and anise. **TOP** with soda, stir and serve with straws.

12	fresh	Mint leaves
1	shot(s)	Freshly squeezed lime juice
3/4	shot(s)	Sugar (gomme) syrup
2	shot(s)	Pernod anis
Top up with		Soda water (club soda)

Comment: An anise laced alternative to a Mojito. The name refers to the opaque white colour of the drink after soda is added to the anis.

THE MILLION DOLLAR COCKTAIL

Glass: Martini
Garnish: Lemon zest twist (round like an egg yolk in the foam)
Method: **SHAKE** all ingredients with ice and fine strain into chilled glass.

2	shot(s)	Plymouth gin
1	shot(s)	Sweet (rosso) vermouth
1/2	shot(s)	Pressed pineapple juice
1/4	shot(s)	Sonoma pomegranate (grenadine) syrup
1/2	fresh	Egg white

Origin: This classic cocktail is thought to have been created around 1910 by Ngiam Tong Boon at The Long Bar, Raffles Hotel, Singapore. Boon is more famous for the Singapore Sling.
Comment: Serious, yet superbly smooth and a bit fluffy.

MILLION DOLLAR MARGARITA [NEW]

Glass: Old-fashioned
Garnish: Lime wedge
Method: **SHAKE** all ingredients with ice and strain into ice-filled glass.

1 1/2	shot(s)	Sauza Hornitos tequila
1 1/2	shot(s)	Grand Marnier (Cuvée du Centenaire)
1/2	shot(s)	Freshly squeezed lime juice

Origin: Discovered in 2006 at Maison 140 Hotel, Los Angeles, USA where I paid a mere $41.14 plus tip for the drink.
Comment: The proportions of this Margarita accentuate the liqueur.

MILLIONAIRE [NEW]

Glass: Martini
Garnish: Quarter orange slice on rim
Method: **SHAKE** all ingredients with ice and fine strain into chilled glass.

2	shot(s)	Bourbon whiskey
1/2	shot(s)	Cointreau/ triple sec
1/2	shot(s)	Freshly squeezed lemon juice
1/4	shot(s)	Sonoma pomegranate (grenadine) syrup
1/2	fresh	Egg white

Comment: Rust coloured tangy citrus smoothed and served straight-up.

MILLIONAIRE'S DAIQUIRI

Glass: Martini
Garnish: Star fruit
Method: **SHAKE** all ingredients with ice and fine strain into chilled glass.

1 3/4	shot(s)	Light white rum
3/4	shot(s)	Plymouth sloe gin
3/4	shot(s)	Bols apricot brandy liqueur
3/4	shot(s)	Freshly squeezed lime juice
1/4	shot(s)	Sonoma pomegranate (grenadine) syrup

Origin: This heralds from a classic cocktail known simply as the Millionaire. Originally sloe gin was the main base ingredient, but David Embury once wrote, "Since the sloe gin, which is a liqueur, predominates in this drink, I do not regard it as a true cocktail." Thus above is my modern adaptation.
Comment: The colour of this cocktail, due to sloe liqueur and grenadine, belies a surprisingly dry finish.

MILLY MARTINI

Glass: Martini
Garnish: Pineapple wedge on rim
Method: Lightly **MUDDLE** basil (just to bruise) in base of shaker. Add other ingredients, **SHAKE** with ice and fine strain into chilled glass.

5	fresh	Basil leaves
2	shot(s)	Plymouth gin
2	shot(s)	Pressed pineapple juice
1/2	shot(s)	Sugar (gomme) syrup
2	dashes	Fee Brothers orange bitters

Origin: Created in 2003 by Shelim Islam at the GE Club, London, England.
Comment: Gin and pineapple with a pleasing hint of basil.

MIMOSA

Glass: Flute
Garnish: Orange zest twist
Method: **POUR** ingredients into chilled glass and gently stir.

1/2	shot(s)	Grand Marnier liqueur
1 3/4	shot(s)	Freshly squeezed orange juice
Top up with		Piper-Heidsieck brut champagne

Variant: When made with mandarin juice this becomes a Puccini.
Origin: Created in 1925 at the Ritz Hotel in Paris and named after the tropical flowering shrub.
Comment: The British version of this drink was invented by a Mr. McGarry, barman at Buck's Club, in the early 20th century, using grenadine in place of orange liqueur. Naturally enough, he called it the Buck's Fizz.

DRINKS ARE GRADED AS FOLLOWS:

DISGUSTING · PRETTY AWFUL · BEST AVOIDED · DISAPPOINTING · ACCEPTABLE · GOOD · RECOMMENDED · HIGHLY RECOMMENDED · OUTSTANDING / EXCEPTIONAL

●●●●◐

MINT COCKTAIL [NEW]

Glass: Martini
Garnish: Mint leaf
Method: Lightly **MUDDLE** (just to bruise) mint in base of shaker. Add other ingredients, **SHAKE** with ice and fine strain into chilled glass.

12	fresh	**Mint leaves**
2	shot(s)	**Plymouth gin**
1	shot(s)	**Sauvignon Blanc wine**
1/4	shot(s)	**Bols white crème de menthe**
1/4	shot(s)	**Sugar (gomme) syrup**

Origin: Adapted from a recipe in Harry Craddock's 1930 Savoy Cocktail Book.
Comment: A great grassy, minty digestif with a good balance between acidity and sweetness.

●●●●○

MINT COLLINS [NEW]

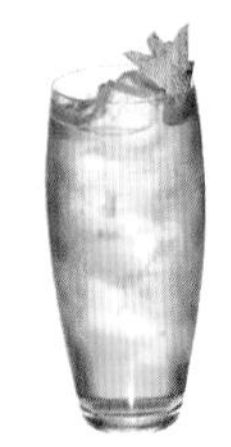

Glass: Collins
Garnish: Mint sprig
Method: Lightly **MUDDLE** (just to bruise) mint in base of shaker. Add next three ingredients, **SHAKE** with ice and fine strain into chilled glass. **TOP** with soda, lightly stir and serve with straws.

12	fresh	**Mint leaves**
2	shot(s)	**Plymouth gin**
1	shot(s)	**Freshly squeezed lemon juice**
1/2	shot(s)	**Sugar (gomme) syrup**
Top up with		**Soda water (club soda)**

Origin: Adapted from a recipe in the 1947-72 Trader Vic's Bartender's Guide by Victor Bergeron.
Comment: Exactly what the name promises.

●●●●●

MINT DAIQUIRI [NEW]

Glass: Martini
Garnish: Mint leaf
Method: Lightly **MUDDLE** (just to bruise) mint in base of shaker. Add other ingredients, **SHAKE** with ice and fine strain into chilled glass.

12	fresh	**Mint leaves**
2	shot(s)	**Light white rum**
1/2	shot(s)	**Freshly squeezed lime juice**
1/4	shot(s)	**Sugar (gomme) syrup**
1/2	shot(s)	**Chilled mineral water (omit if wet ice)**

Origin: Created in 2006 by yours truly.
Comment: A short, concentrated Mojito.

●●●◐○

MINT FIZZ

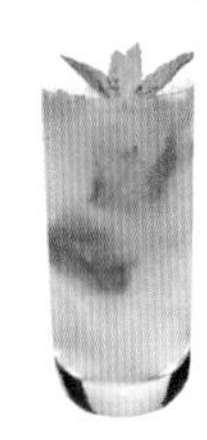

Glass: Collins
Garnish: Mint sprig
Method: Lightly **MUDDLE** mint (just to bruise) in base of shaker. Add other ingredients apart from soda, **SHAKE** with ice and fine strain into ice-filled glass. **TOP** with soda, lightly stir and serve with straws.

7	fresh	**Mint leaves**
2	shot(s)	**Plymouth gin**
1	shot(s)	**Freshly squeezed lime juice**
1/4	shot(s)	**White crème de menthe**
1/2	shot(s)	**Sugar (gomme) syrup**
Top up with		**Soda (from siphon)**

Comment: Long, refreshing citrus and mint fizz.

●●●●●

MINT JULEP

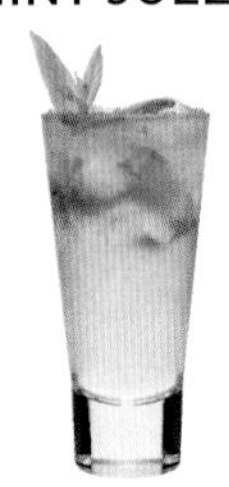

Glass: Collins
Garnish: Mint sprig and slice of lemon
Method: Lightly **MUDDLE** (only bruise) mint in base of shaker. Add other ingredients, **SHAKE** with ice and strain into glass half filled with crushed ice. **CHURN** (stir) the drink with the crushed ice using a bar spoon. Top up the glass with more crushed ice and **CHURN** again. Repeat this process until the drink fills the glass and serve with straws.

12	fresh	**Mint leaves**
2 1/2	shot(s)	**Bourbon whiskey**
3/4	shot(s)	**Sugar (gomme) syrup**
3	dashes	**Angostura aromatic bitters**

Comment: This superb drink is better if the shaker and its contents are placed in the refrigerator for several hours prior to mixing, allowing the mint flavours to infuse in the bourbon.

●●●●◐

MINT LIMEADE (MOCKTAIL) [NEW]

Glass: Collins
Garnish: Mint sprig
Method: Lightly **MUDDLE** (just to bruise) mint in base of shaker. Add next three ingredients, **SHAKE** with ice and fine strain into ice-filled glass. **TOP** with 7-Up, lightly stir and serve with straws.

12	fresh	**Mint leaves**
1 1/2	shot(s)	**Freshly squeezed lime juice**
1	shot(s)	**Pressed apple juice**
3/4	shot(s)	**Sugar (gomme) syrup**
Top up with		**7-Up**

Origin: Created in 2006 by yours truly.
Comment: Superbly refreshing - mint and lime served long.

●●●●◐

MINT MARTINI [NEW]

Glass: Martini
Garnish: Mint leaf
Method: Lightly **MUDDLE** (just to bruise) mint in base of shaker. Add next three ingredients, **SHAKE** with ice and fine strain into chilled glass. **TOP** with 7-Up, lightly stir and serve with straws.

12	fresh	**Mint leaves**
1 1/2	shot(s)	**Ketel One vodka**
1/2	shot(s)	**Dry vermouth**
1/4	shot(s)	**Bols green crème de menthe**
1 1/2	shot(s)	**Sauvignon Blanc wine**
1/4	shot(s)	**Sugar (gomme) syrup**

Origin: Created in 2005 by yours truly.
Comment: An after dinner palate cleanser.

DRINKS ARE GRADED AS FOLLOWS:

● DISGUSTING ●◐ PRETTY AWFUL ●● BEST AVOIDED
●●◐ DISAPPOINTING ●●● ACCEPTABLE ●●●◐ GOOD
●●●● RECOMMENDED ●●●●◐ HIGHLY RECOMMENDED
●●●●● OUTSTANDING / EXCEPTIONAL

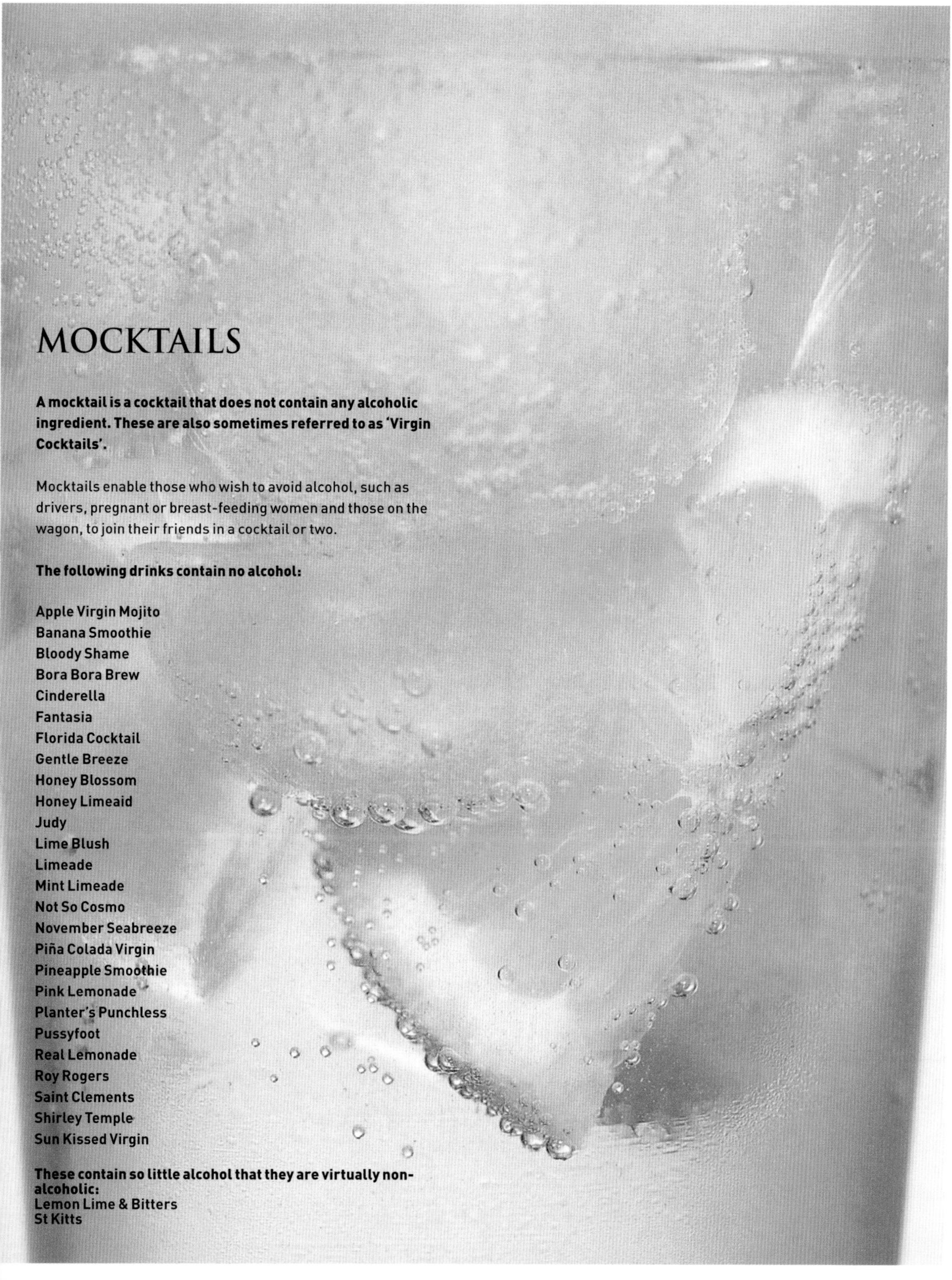

MOCKTAILS

A mocktail is a cocktail that does not contain any alcoholic ingredient. These are also sometimes referred to as 'Virgin Cocktails'.

Mocktails enable those who wish to avoid alcohol, such as drivers, pregnant or breast-feeding women and those on the wagon, to join their friends in a cocktail or two.

The following drinks contain no alcohol:

Apple Virgin Mojito
Banana Smoothie
Bloody Shame
Bora Bora Brew
Cinderella
Fantasia
Florida Cocktail
Gentle Breeze
Honey Blossom
Honey Limeaid
Judy
Lime Blush
Limeade
Mint Limeade
Not So Cosmo
November Seabreeze
Piña Colada Virgin
Pineapple Smoothie
Pink Lemonade
Planter's Punchless
Pussyfoot
Real Lemonade
Roy Rogers
Saint Clements
Shirley Temple
Sun Kissed Virgin

These contain so little alcohol that they are virtually non-alcoholic:
Lemon Lime & Bitters
St Kitts

MISS MARTINI

Glass: Martini
Garnish: Raspberries on stick
Method: **MUDDLE** raspberries in base of shaker. Add other ingredients, **SHAKE** with ice and fine strain into chilled glass.

7	fresh	Raspberries
2	shot(s)	Ketel One vodka
1/2	shot(s)	Chambord black raspberry liqueur
1/4	shot(s)	Double (heavy) cream
1/4	shot(s)	Milk
1/8	shot(s)	Sugar (gomme) syrup

Origin: Created in 1997 by Giovanni Burdi at Match EC1, London, England.
Comment: A pink, fruity and creamy concoction.

MISSIONARY'S DOWNFALL [NEW]

Glass: Collins
Garnish: Mint sprig
Method: Lightly **MUDDLE** mint (just to bruise) in base of shaker. Add other ingredients, **SHAKE** with ice and strain into glass filled with crushed ice.

12	fresh	Mint leaves
2	shot(s)	Light white rum
1/2	shot(s)	Peach schnapps liqueur
1 1/2	shot(s)	Freshly squeezed lime juice
1/2	shot(s)	Sugar (gomme) syrup
2	shot(s)	Freshly squeezed pineapple juice

Origin: Created in the 1930s by Don The Beachcomber at his restaurant in Hollywood, California, USA.
Comment: Superbly balanced and refreshing rum, lime, mint and a hint of peach.

MISSISSIPPI PUNCH [UPDATED]

Glass: Collins
Garnish: Lemon slice
Method: **SHAKE** all ingredients with ice and strain into glass filled with crushed ice.

1 1/2	shot(s)	Bourbon whiskey
3/4	shot(s)	Rémy Martin cognac
3/4	shot(s)	Freshly squeezed lemon juice
1	shot(s)	Sugar (gomme) syrup
2	shot(s)	Chilled water

Comment: Balanced and refreshing.

MISSISSIPPI SCHNAPPER

Glass: Martini
Garnish: Orange zest twist
Method: **SHAKE** all ingredients with ice and fine strain into chilled glass.

2	shot(s)	Jack Daniel's Tennessee whiskey
3/4	shot(s)	Peach schnapps liqueur
1/2	shot(s)	Cointreau / triple sec
1/4	shot(s)	Freshly squeezed lime juice
1/4	shot(s)	Sugar (gomme) syrup

Origin: Created in 1999 by Dan Cottle at Velvet, Manchester, England.
Comment: Orange predominates with peach sweetness balanced by whiskey and lime.

MISTER STU

Glass: Collins
Garnish: Pineapple wedge on rim
Method: **SHAKE** all ingredients with ice and strain into ice-filled glass. Serve with straws.

2	shot(s)	Sauza Hornitos tequila
1/2	shot(s)	Luxardo Amaretto di Saschira liqueur
1/2	shot(s)	Malibu coconut rum liqueur
1 1/2	shot(s)	Pressed pineapple juice
1 1/2	shot(s)	Freshly squeezed orange juice

Comment: There's a touch of the disco about this foamy drink, but it is still complex and interesting.

MITCH MARTINI

Glass: Martini
Garnish: Lemon zest twist
Method: **SHAKE** all ingredients with ice and fine strain into chilled glass.

2	shot(s)	Zubrowka bison vodka
2	shot(s)	Pressed apple juice
1/2	shot(s)	Freshly squeezed lemon juice
1/4	shot(s)	Passion fruit syrup

Origin: Created in 1997 by Giovanni Burdi at Match EC1, London, England.
Comment: One of London's most popular contemporary classics.

MOCHA MARTINI

Glass: Martini
Garnish: Dust with cocoa powder
Method: **SHAKE** first four ingredients with ice and fine strain into chilled glass. **FLOAT** cream in centre of drink.

1 1/2	shot(s)	Bourbon whiskey
1	shot(s)	Cold espresso coffee
1/2	shot(s)	Baileys Irish Cream liqueur
1/2	shot(s)	Bols brown crème de cacao
1/2	shot(s)	Double (heavy) cream

Comment: Made with great espresso, this drink is a superb, richly flavoured balance of sweet and bitter.

MODERNISTA [NEW]

Glass: Martini
Garnish: Lemon zest twist
Method: **SHAKE** all ingredients with ice and fine strain into chilled glass.

2	shot(s)	Plymouth gin
1/2	shot(s)	Goslings Black Seal rum
1/4	shot(s)	Pernod anis
1	shot(s)	Carlshamns Swedish Torr Flaggpunsch
1/4	shot(s)	Freshly squeezed lemon juice
1	dash	Fee Brothers orange bitters

Origin: Adapted from a drink created by Ted Haigh (AKA Dr. Cocktail) and derived from the 'Modern Cocktail'. See Ted's book, 'Vintage Spirits & Forgotten Cocktails'.
Comment: A massive flavour hit to awaken your taste buds.

MOJITO

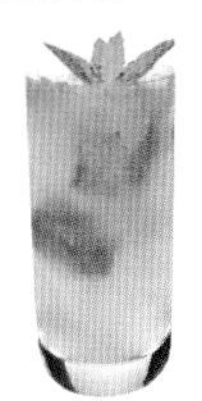

Glass: Collins
Garnish: Mint sprig
Method: Lightly **MUDDLE** mint (just to bruise) in base of glass. Add rum, lime juice and sugar. Half fill glass with crushed ice and **CHURN** (stir) with bar spoon. Fill glass with more crushed ice and **CHURN** some more. **TOP** with soda, stir and serve with straws.

12	fresh	**Mint leaves**
2	shot(s)	**Light white rum**
3/4	shot(s)	**Freshly squeezed lime juice**
1/4	shot(s)	**Sugar (gomme) syrup**
Top up with		**Soda water (club soda)**

Variant: Add a dash or two of Angostura aromatic bitters.
Comment: When well made, this Cuban cousin of the Mint Julep is one of the world's greatest and most refreshing cocktails.

MOJITO DE CASA [NEW]

Glass: Collins
Garnish: Mint sprig
Method: Lightly **MUDDLE** mint (just to bruise) in base of glass. Add tequila, lime juice and sugar. Half fill glass with crushed ice and **CHURN** (stir) with bar spoon. Fill glass with more crushed ice and **CHURN** some more. **TOP** with soda, stir and serve with straws.

12	fresh	**Mint leaves**
2	shot(s)	**Sauza Hornitos tequila**
3/4	shot(s)	**Freshly squeezed lime juice**
1/2	shot(s)	**Sugar (gomme) syrup**
Top up with		**Soda water (club soda)**

Origin: Created at Mercadito, New York City, USA.
Comment: A tequila based Mojito.

MOLOTOV COCKTAIL

Glass: Martini
Garnish: Lemon zest
Method: **SHAKE** all ingredients with ice and fine strain into chilled glass.

1 1/2	shot(s)	**Lime flavoured vodka**
1 1/4	shot(s)	**Parfait Amour liqueur**
1/2	shot(s)	**Freshly squeezed lemon juice**
1/2	shot(s)	**Opal Nera black sambuca**

Origin: I created this drink after a visit to the Rajamäki distillery in Finland. At the start of the Second World War the plant was used to produce Molotov cocktails, inflammatory bombs with which the Finns put hundreds of Soviet tanks out of action.
Comment: I selected the ingredients to represent the four liquids used in the wartime weapon. Vodka, which is clear, stands for alcohol, parfait amour shares the purple hue of paraffin, lemon juice represents gasoline and black sambuca replaces tar.

LA MOMIE

Glass: Shot
Method: **POUR** pastis into chilled glass and **TOP** with chilled water.

1/2	shot(s)	**Ricard pastis**
Top up with		**Chilled water**

Origin: Pronounced 'Mom-Ee', this shot is very popular in the South of France.
Comment: A bite-sized aniseed tipple.

MOMISETTE

Glass: Collins (10oz max)
Method: **POUR** pastis and almond syrup into glass. Serve with bottle of sparkling water so the customer can dilute to their own taste. (I recommend five shots.) Lastly, add ice to fill glass.

1	shot(s)	**Ricard pastis**
1/4	shot(s)	**Almond (orgeat) syrup**
Top up with		**Sparkling mineral water**

Origin: A traditional French drink, the name of which literally translates as 'tiny mummy'.
Comment: Complex balance of anis, almond and liquorice.

MOMO SPECIAL

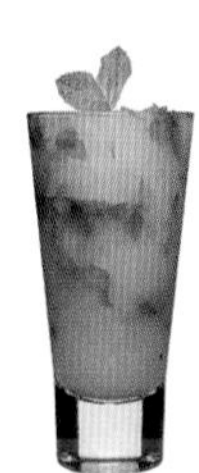

Glass: Collins
Garnish: Mint sprig
Method: Lightly **MUDDLE** mint (just to bruise) in base of shaker. Add next three ingredients, **SHAKE** with ice and strain into ice-filled glass. **TOP** with soda, lightly stir and serve with straws.

12	fresh	**Mint leaves**
2	shot(s)	**Ketel One vodka**
1/2	shot(s)	**Freshly squeezed lime juice**
1/2	shot(s)	**Sugar (gomme) syrup**
Top up with		**Soda water (club soda)**

Origin: Created in 1998 by Simon Mainoo at Momo, London, England.
Comment: Enrich the minty flavour by macerating the mint in the vodka some hours before making.

MONA LISA

Glass: Collins
Garnish: Orange slice
Method: **SHAKE** first three ingredients with ice and strain into ice-filled glass. **TOP** with tonic water.

1	shot(s)	**Green Chartreuse liqueur**
3	shot(s)	**Freshly squeezed orange juice**
2	dashes	**Angostura aromatic bitters**
Top up with		**Tonic water**

Comment: Chartreuse fans will appreciate this drink, which is also an approachable way for novices to acquire a taste for the green stuff.

MONARCH MARTINI

Glass: Martini
Garnish: Lemon zest twist
Method: Lightly **MUDDLE** mint (just to bruise) in base of shaker. Add other ingredients, **SHAKE** with ice and fine strain into chilled glass.

7	fresh	**Mint leaves**
1½	shot(s)	**Plymouth gin**
½	shot(s)	**Freshly squeezed lemon juice**
¾	shot(s)	**Elderflower cordial**
½	shot(s)	**Sugar (gomme) syrup**
½	shot(s)	**Chilled mineral water (omit if wet ice)**

Origin: Created in 2003 by Douglas Ankrah at Townhouse, London, England. Doug's original recipe omitted water and included a dash of peach bitters.
Comment: Wonderfully floral and minty – worthy of a right royal drinker.

MONKEY GLAND #1

Glass: Martini
Garnish: Orange zest twist
Method: **SHAKE** all ingredients with ice and fine strain into chilled glass.

2	shot(s)	**Plymouth gin**
¼	shot(s)	**La Fée Parisian 68% absinthe**
1½	shot(s)	**Freshly squeezed orange juice**
¼	shot(s)	**Sonoma pomegranate (grenadine) syrup**

Origin: Created in the 1920s by Harry MacElhone at his Harry's New York Bar in Paris. The Monkey Gland takes its name from the work of Dr Serge Voronoff, who attempted to delay the ageing process by transplanting monkey testicles.
Comment: Approach with caution. Due diligence reveals a dangerous base of gin and absinthe.

MONKEY GLAND #2

Glass: Old-fashioned
Garnish: Orange slice
Method: **SHAKE** all ingredients with ice and strain into ice-filled glass.

2	shot(s)	**Plymouth gin**
1¼	shot(s)	**Freshly squeezed orange juice**
½	shot(s)	**Bénédictine D.O.M. liqueur**
¼	shot(s)	**Sonoma pomegranate (grenadine) syrup**

Comment: A somewhat off-putting name for a very palatable cocktail.

MONKEY SHINE

Glass: Martini
Garnish: Cinnamon rim
Method: **SHAKE** all ingredients with ice and fine strain into chilled glass.

2	shot(s)	**Mount Gay Eclipse golden rum**
1	shot(s)	**Malibu coconut rum liqueur**
1	shot(s)	**Pressed pineapple juice**

Origin: An adaptation of a drink discovered in 2003 at the Bellagio Resort & Casino, Las Vegas.
Comment: The sweet, tropical fruitiness of this drink is set off by the spicy rim.

MONKEY WRENCH

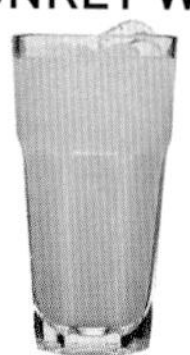

Glass: Collins
Method: **POUR** rum into ice-filled glass. Top with grapefruit juice, **STIR** and serve with straws.

2	shot(s)	**Mount Gay Eclipse golden rum**
Top up with		**Freshly squeezed pink grapefruit juice**

Comment: Simple but pleasant.

MONK'S CANDY BAR

Glass: Martini
Garnish: Sprinkle with nutmeg
Method: **SHAKE** all ingredients with ice and fine strain into chilled glass.

1	shot(s)	**Frangelico hazelnut liqueur**
½	shot(s)	**Bols butterscotch liqueur**
½	shot(s)	**Kahlúa coffee liqueur**
1	shot(s)	**Double (heavy) cream**
1	shot(s)	**Milk**

Comment: Creamy and sweet, with hazelnut, butterscotch and coffee.

MONK'S HABIT

Glass: Collins
Garnish: Orange slice
Method: **SHAKE** all ingredients with ice and strain into ice-filled glass.

1½	shot(s)	**Light white rum**
½	shot(s)	**Cointreau / triple sec**
1	shot(s)	**Frangelico hazelnut liqueur**
3	shot(s)	**Pressed pineapple juice**
¼	shot(s)	**Sonoma pomegranate (grenadine) syrup**

Comment: Fruit and nut laced with rum. Slightly sweet.

MONTE CARLO

Glass: Collins
Garnish: Maraschino cherry
Method: **POUR** first three ingredients into empty glass. **ADD** soda water to half fill glass. Fill glass with ice and then top up with more soda. (This avoids 'shocking' the anis with the ice.) Serve with straws.

1	shot(s)	**Pernod anis**
½	shot(s)	**Luxardo maraschino liqueur**
¾	shot(s)	**Freshly squeezed lime juice**
Top up with		**Soda water (club soda)**

Origin: An adaptation of a Martini style drink created in 2002 by Alex Turner, London, England.
Comment: A long, fragrant, almost floral summer cooler with lots of aniseed.

DRINKS ARE GRADED AS FOLLOWS:

● DISGUSTING ●◐ PRETTY AWFUL ●● BEST AVOIDED
●●◐ DISAPPOINTING ●●● ACCEPTABLE ●●●◐ GOOD
●●●● RECOMMENDED ●●●●◐ HIGHLY RECOMMENDED
●●●●● OUTSTANDING / EXCEPTIONAL

A B C D E F G H I J K L **M** N O P Q R S T U V W X Y Z

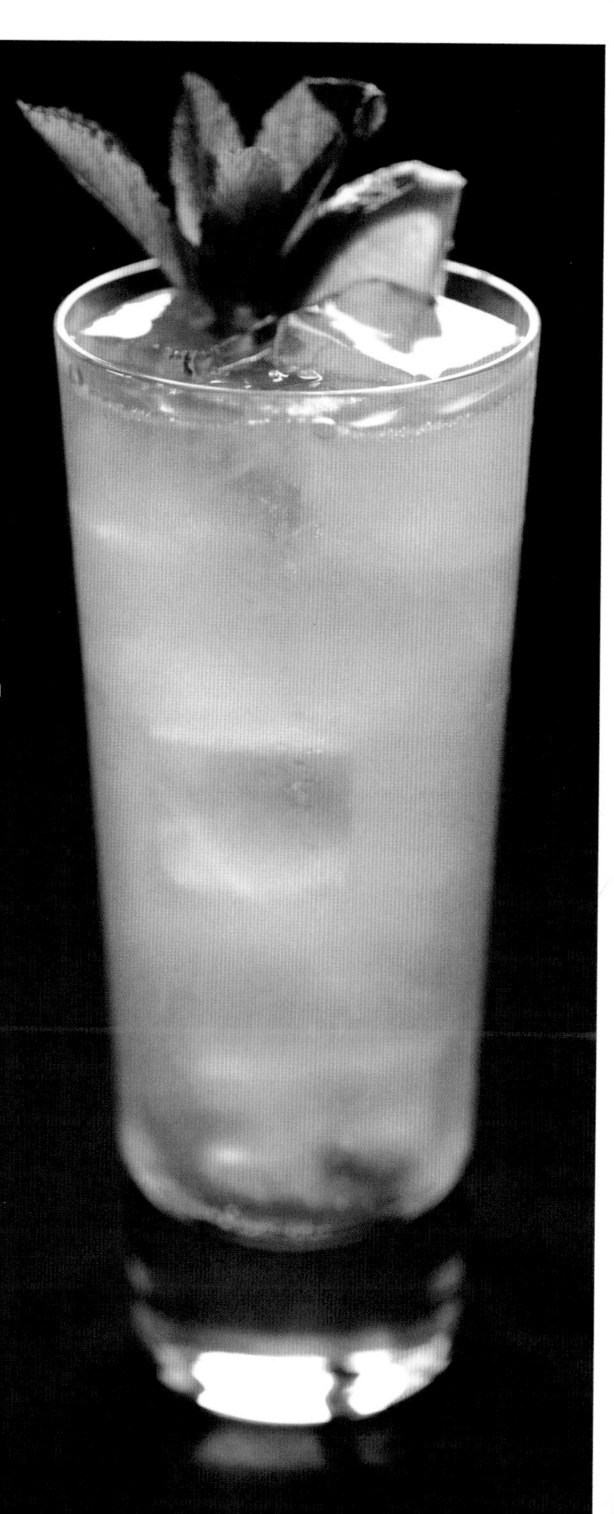

MOSCOW MULE

This classic combination was born in 1941. John G. Martin had acquired the rights to Smirnoff vodka for Heublein, a small Connecticut based liquor and food distributor. Jack Morgan, the owner of Hollywood's famous Cock'n'Bull Saloon, was trying to launch his own brand of ginger beer. The two men met at New York City's Chatham Bar and hit on the idea of mixing Martin's vodka with Morgan's ginger beer and adding a dash of lime to create a new cocktail, the Moscow Mule.

To help promote the drink, and hence their respective products, Morgan had the idea of marketing the Moscow Mule using specially engraved mugs. The five ounce mugs were embossed with a kicking mule and made at a copper factory a friend of his had recently inherited. The promotion helped turn Smirnoff into a major brand.

MONTE CARLO IMPERIAL [NEW]

Glass: Martini
Garnish: Mint leaf
Method: **SHAKE** first three ingredients with ice and fine strain into chilled glass. **TOP** with champagne.

$1^1/_2$	shot(s)	**Plymouth gin**
$^1/_2$	shot(s)	**Freshly squeezed lemon juice**
$^1/_2$	shot(s)	**Bols white crème de menthe**
Top up with		**Piper-Heidsieck brut champagne**

Origin: Adapted from a recipe in Harry Craddock's 1930 Savoy Cocktail Book.
Comment: A classic, minty digestif.

MONTEGO BAY [NEW]

Glass: Old-fashioned
Garnish: Lime wedge
Method: **SHAKE** all ingredients with ice and strain into ice-filled glass.

$1^1/_2$	shot(s)	**Martinique agricole rum (50% alc./vol.)**
$^1/_2$	shot(s)	**Freshly squeezed lime juice**
$^1/_2$	shot(s)	**Cointreau / triple sec**
$^1/_4$	shot(s)	**Sugar (gomme) syrup**
2	dashes	**Angostura aromatic bitters**

Origin: Adapted from a recipe in the 1947-72 Trader Vic's Bartender's Guide by Victor Bergeron.
Comment: The name suggests Jamaica but the recipe requires agricole rum. This pungent style of rum is not Jamaican.

MONZA

Glass: Collins
Garnish: Slice of apple
Method: Cut passion fruit in half and scoop flesh into shaker. Add other ingredients, **SHAKE** with ice and strain into ice-filled glass.

1	fresh	**Passion fruit**
2	shot(s)	**Ketel One vodka**
2	shot(s)	**Campari**
2	shot(s)	**Pressed apple juice**
$^1/_4$	shot(s)	**Sugar (gomme) syrup**

Origin: A classic cocktail promoted by Campari and named after the Italian Grand Prix circuit.
Comment: If you like Campari you'll love this.

MOONRAKER [NEW]

Glass: Martini
Garnish: Maraschino cherry
Method: **SHAKE** all ingredients with ice and fine strain into chilled glass.

$1^1/_2$	shot(s)	**Rémy Martin cognac**
$1^1/_2$	shot(s)	**Dubonnet red**
$^3/_4$	shot(s)	**Peach schnapps liqueur**
$^1/_4$	shot(s)	**Pernod anis**

Origin: Adapted from a recipe in the 1947-72 Trader Vic's Bartender's Guide by Victor Bergeron.
Comment: A diverse range of flavours come together surprisingly well.

MOON RIVER [NEW]

Glass: Martini
Garnish: Mint leaf
Method: **SHAKE** all ingredients with ice and fine strain into chilled glass.

$1^1/_2$	shot(s)	**Plymouth gin**
$^1/_2$	shot(s)	**Bols apricot brandy liqueur**
$^1/_2$	shot(s)	**Cointreau / triple sec**
$^1/_4$	shot(s)	**Galliano liqueur**
$^1/_2$	shot(s)	**Freshly squeezed lemon juice**
$^1/_2$	shot(s)	**Chilled mineral water (omit if wet ice)**

Origin: Adapted from a drink discovered in 2005 at Bar Opiume, Singapore.
Comment: There's a hint of aniseed in this fruity, sweet and sour drink.

MOONLIGHT MARTINI [NEW]

Glass: Martini
Garnish: Lemon zest twist
Method: **SHAKE** all ingredients with ice and fine strain into chilled glass.

$1^1/_2$	shot(s)	**Plymouth gin**
$^1/_4$	shot(s)	**Kirsch eau de vie**
1	shot(s)	**Sauvignon Blanc wine**
$1^1/_4$	shot(s)	**Freshly squeezed pink grapefruit juice**

Origin: Adapted from a recipe in Harry Craddock's 1930 Savoy Cocktail Book.
Comment: Craddock describes this as "a very dry cocktail". It is, but pleasantly so.

MOONSHINE MARTINI [NEW]

Glass: Martini
Garnish: Maraschino cherry
Method: **SHAKE** all ingredients with ice and fine strain into chilled glass.

$1^1/_2$	shot(s)	**Plymouth gin**
1	shot(s)	**Dry vermouth**
$^1/_2$	shot(s)	**Luxardo maraschino liqueur**
$^1/_8$	shot(s)	**La Fée Parisian 68% absinthe**

Origin: Adapted from a recipe in the 1930 Savoy Cocktail Book by Harry Craddock.
Comment: A wet Martini with balanced hints of maraschino and absinthe.

MORAVIAN COCKTAIL [NEW]

Glass: Old-fashioned
Garnish: Orange slice & cherry
Method: **SHAKE** all ingredients with ice and strain into ice-filled glass.

$^3/_4$	shot(s)	**Slivovitz plum brandy**
$^3/_4$	shot(s)	**Becherovka Czech liqueur**
$1^1/_2$	shot(s)	**Rosso (sweet) vermouth**

Origin: Discovered in 2005 at Be Bop Bar, Prague, Czech Republic.
Comment: The hardcore, Czech answer to the Italian Negroni.

MORNING GLORY

Glass: Old-fashioned
Garnish: Lemon zest twist
Method: **SHAKE** all ingredients with ice and strain into ice-filled glass.

1	shot(s)	**Rémy Martin cognac**
3/4	shot(s)	**Grand Marnier liqueur**
1/8	shot(s)	**La Fée Parisian 68% absinthe**
1/2	shot(s)	**Freshly squeezed lemon juice**
1/4	shot(s)	**Sugar (gomme) syrup**
2	dashes	**Angostura aromatic bitters**
1/2	shot(s)	**Chilled mineral water (omit if wet ice)**

Origin: My interpretation of a classic.
Comment: Sophisticated and complex – one for sipping.

MORNING GLORY FIZZ

Glass: Old-fashioned
Garnish: Lime wheel
Method: **SHAKE** first six ingredients with ice and strain into ice-filled glass. **TOP** with soda water from a siphon.

1	shot(s)	**The Famous Grouse Scotch whisky**
1/4	shot(s)	**La Fée Parisian 68% absinthe**
3/4	shot(s)	**Freshly squeezed lime juice**
3/4	shot(s)	**Freshly squeezed lemon juice**
1/4	shot(s)	**Sugar (gomme) syrup**
1/2	fresh	**Egg white**
Top up with		**Soda water from a siphon**

Comment: Considered a morning after pick-me-up but is great at any time.

MOSCOW LASSI

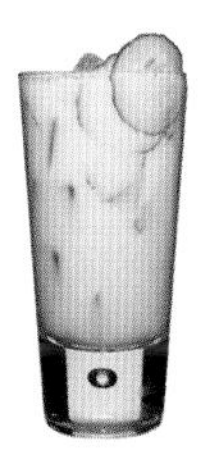

Glass: Collins
Garnish: Cucumber slices
Method: **MUDDLE** cucumber in base of shaker. Add other ingredients. **SHAKE** with ice and fine strain into ice-filled glass.

2	inches	**Chopped & peeled cucumber**
1	shot(s)	**Sweetened mango purée**
1 1/2	shot(s)	**Ketel One vodka**
2	shot(s)	**Pressed apple juice**
3	spoon(s)	**Natural yoghurt**
1/4	shot(s)	**Sugar (gomme) syrup**

Origin: Created in 2001 by Jamie Stephenson at Gaucho Grill, Manchester, England.
Comment: One to serve with your Indian takeaway.

MOSCOW MULE [UPDATED]

Glass: Collins (or copper mug)
Garnish: Lime wedge & mint sprig
Method: **SHAKE** first four ingredients with ice and strain into ice-filled glass. **TOP** with ginger beer and stir.

2	shot(s)	**Ketel One vodka**
1/2	shot(s)	**Freshly squeezed lime juice**
1/4	shot(s)	**Sugar (gomme) syrup**
3	dashes	**Angostura aromatic bitters**
Top up with		**Ginger beer**

Origin: My take on the drink created in 1941 by John G. Martin and Jack Morgan.
Comment: A long, vodka based drink with spice provided by ginger beer and Angostura.

MOTOX [NEW]

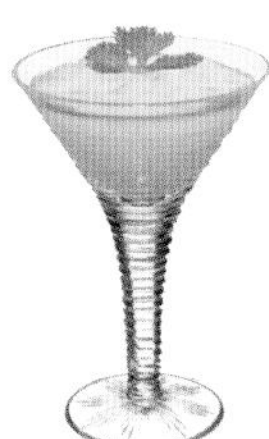

Glass: Martini
Garnish: Coriander leaf
Method: **MUDDLE** ginger and coriander in base of shaker. Add other ingredients, **SHAKE** with ice and fine strain into chilled glass.

1	slice	**Root ginger (thumbnail sized)**
10	fresh	**Coriander leaves**
1 1/2	shot(s)	**Ketel One Citroen vodka**
1/2	shot(s)	**Luxardo limoncello liqueur**
1	shot(s)	**Pressed pineapple juice**
1	shot(s)	**Pressed apple juice**

Origin: Adapted from a drink discovered in 2005 at Mo Bar, Landmark Mandarin Oriental Hotel, Hong Kong.
Comment: Each sip is fruity, lemon fresh and followed by a hot ginger hit.

MOUNTAIN [NEW]

Glass: Martini
Garnish: Maraschino cherry
Method: **SHAKE** all ingredients with ice and fine strain into chilled glass.

2	shot(s)	**Bourbon whiskey**
3/4	shot(s)	**Dry vermouth**
3/4	shot(s)	**Sweet (rosso) vermouth**
1/2	fresh	**Egg white**

Comment: A perfect Manhattan smoothed by egg white.

MOUNTAIN SIPPER

Glass: Old-fashioned
Garnish: Orange zest twist
Method: **SHAKE** all ingredients with ice and strain into ice-filled glass.

2	shot(s)	**Jack Daniel's Tennessee whiskey**
1	shot(s)	**Cointreau / triple sec**
1	shot(s)	**Cranberry juice**
1	shot(s)	**Freshly squeezed grapefruit juice**
1/8	shot(s)	**Sugar (gomme) syrup**

Comment: Fruity citrus flavours balance the richness of the whiskey.

MRS ROBINSON #1

Glass: Old-fashioned
Garnish: Three raspberries
Method: **MUDDLE** raspberries in base of shaker. Add next four ingredients, **SHAKE** with ice and strain into ice-filled glass. **TOP** with soda, lightly stir and serve with straws.

8	fresh	**Raspberries**
2	shot(s)	**Bourbon whiskey**
1	shot(s)	**Bols raspberry (framboise) liqueur**
1/4	shot(s)	**Freshly squeezed lemon juice**
1/4	shot(s)	**Sugar (gomme) syrup**
Top up with		**Soda water (club soda)**

Origin: Created in 2000 by Max Warner at Long Bar, Sanderson, London, England.
Comment: Rich raspberry fruit laced with bourbon.

MRS. ROBINSON #2 [NEW]

Glass: Martini
Garnish: Quarter orange slice on rim
Method: **SHAKE** all ingredients with ice and fine strain into chilled glass.

$2\frac{1}{2}$	shot(s)	**Ketel One vodka**
1	shot(s)	**Freshly squeezed orange juice**
$\frac{1}{2}$	shot(s)	**Galliano liqueur**

Origin: Discovered in 2006 on Kyle Branch's Cocktail Hotel blog. (www.cocktailhotel.blogspot.com).
Comment: A short Harvey Wallbanger.

MUDDY WATER

Glass: Old-fashioned
Garnish: Float 3 coffee beans
Method: **SHAKE** all ingredients with ice and strain into ice-filled glass.

1	shot(s)	**Ketel One vodka**
1	shot(s)	**Kahlúa coffee liqueur**
1	shot(s)	**Baileys Irish Cream liqueur**

Comment: Coffee and whiskey cream with added vodka.

MUDSLIDE

Glass: Hurricane
Garnish: Crumbled Cadbury's Flake bar
Method: **BLEND** all ingredients with two 12oz scoops of crushed ice and serve with straws.

$1\frac{1}{2}$	shot(s)	**Baileys Irish Cream liqueur**
$1\frac{1}{2}$	shot(s)	**Kahlúa coffee liqueur**
$1\frac{1}{2}$	shot(s)	**Ketel One vodka**
3	scoops	**Vanilla ice cream**

Comment: A simply scrumptious dessert drink with whiskey cream and coffee.

MULATA DAIQUIRI

Glass: Martini
Garnish: Lime wedge on rim
Method: **SHAKE** all ingredients with ice and fine strain into chilled glass.

2	shot(s)	**Appleton Estate V/X aged rum**
$\frac{1}{2}$	shot(s)	**Bols brown crème de cacao**
$\frac{1}{2}$	shot(s)	**Freshly squeezed lime juice**
$\frac{1}{4}$	shot(s)	**Sugar (gomme) syrup**

Comment: A classic Daiquiri with aged rum and a hint of chocolate.

MUCKY BOTTOM [NEW]

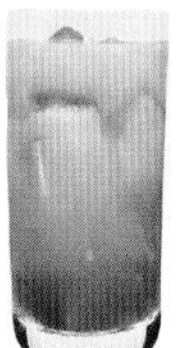

Glass: Collins
Method: **SHAKE** first three ingredients with ice and strain into ice-filled glass. **POUR** coffee liqueur around top of drink - this will fall to the base of the glass and create the mucky bottom.

2	shot(s)	**Malibu coconut rum liqueur**
1	shot(s)	**Pernod anis**
3	shot(s)	**Freshly squeezed grapefruit juice**
$\frac{3}{4}$	shot(s)	**Kahlúa coffee liqueur**

Origin: Created in 2003 by yours truly. (Formerly named Red Haze.)
Comment: Four very strong and distinctive flavours somehow tone each other down.

MUJER VERDE [NEW]

Glass: Martini
Garnish: Lime zest twist
Method: **SHAKE** all ingredients with ice and fine strain into chilled glass.

1	shot(s)	**Plymouth gin**
$\frac{1}{2}$	shot(s)	**Green Chartreuse liqueur**
$\frac{1}{2}$	shot(s)	**Yellow Chartreuse liqueur**
$\frac{1}{2}$	shot(s)	**Freshly squeezed lime juice**
$\frac{1}{4}$	shot(s)	**Sugar (gomme) syrup**
$\frac{3}{4}$	shot(s)	**Chilled mineral water (omit if wet ice)**

Origin: Discovered in 2006 at Absinthe, San Francisco, where 'D Mexican' resurrected this drink from his hometown of Guadalajara.
Comment: The name means 'Green Lady'... and she packs a Chartreuse punch.

MULE'S HIND LEG

Glass: Martini
Garnish: Apricot slice on rim
Method: **SHAKE** all ingredients with ice and fine strain into chilled glass.

1	shot(s)	**Plymouth gin**
1	shot(s)	**Bénédictine D.O.M. liqueur**
1	shot(s)	**Calvados or applejack brandy**
$\frac{1}{4}$	shot(s)	**Maple syrup**
$\frac{3}{4}$	shot(s)	**Bols apricot brandy liqueur**
$\frac{1}{2}$	shot(s)	**Chilled mineral water (omit if wet ice)**

Origin: My version of a classic 1920s recipe.
Comment: Apricot and maple syrup dominate this medium sweet drink.

HOW TO MAKE SUGAR SYRUP

To make your own sugar syrup, gradually pour TWO cups of granulated sugar into a saucepan containing ONE cup of hot water. Stir as you pour and carry on stirring and simmering until the sugar is dissolved. Do not let the water even come close to boiling and only simmer for as long as it takes to dissolve the sugar. Allow syrup to cool and pour into an empty bottle. Ideally, you should finely strain your syrup into the bottle to remove any undissolved crystals which could otherwise encourage crystallisation. If kept in a refrigerator this mixture will last for a couple of months.

MULLED WINE

Glass: Toddy
Garnish: Cinnamon stick
Method: **MUDDLE** cloves in base of mixing glass. Add rest of ingredients apart from boiling water, **STIR** and fine strain into warmed glass. **TOP** with boiling water and **STIR**.

5	whole	Dried cloves
1	pinch	Freshly grated nutmeg
1	pinch	Ground cinnamon
1½	shot(s)	Warre's Otima Tawny Port
1½	shot(s)	Red wine
¼	shot(s)	Grand Marnier liqueur
½	shot(s)	Freshly squeezed lemon juice
Top up with		Boiling water

Variant: Better if several servings are made and the ingredients warmed in a saucepan.
Comment: Warming, soothing and potent.

MYRTLE MARTINI

Glass: Martini
Garnish: Sugar rim
Method: **SHAKE** all ingredients with ice and fine strain into chilled glass.

2	shot(s)	Ketel One vodka
½	shot(s)	Crème de myrtille (bilberry) liqueur
2	shot(s)	Pressed apple juice
¼	shot(s)	Sugar (gomme) syrup
¼	shot(s)	Freshly squeezed lime juice

Origin: Created in 2003 at Cheyne Walk Brasserie & Salon, London, England.
Comment: A fruity concoction to remember should you find yourself with a bottle of crème de myrtille.

MYSTIQUE

Glass: Old-fashioned
Garnish: Orange zest twist
Method: **SHAKE** all ingredients with ice and strain into ice-filled glass.

½	shot(s)	The Famous Grouse Scotch whisky
¾	shot(s)	Drambuie liqueur
½	shot(s)	Peach schnapps liqueur
¼	shot(s)	Luxardo maraschino liqueur
3	dashes	Fee Brothers orange bitters

Origin: Created by Greg Pearson at Mystique, Manchester, England in 1999. Joint winner of the Manchester Food & Drink Festival cocktail competition.
Comment: Honeyed, peachy, orange Scotch.

MYSTIQUE MARTINI

Glass: Martini
Garnish: Raspberries on stick
Method: **STIR** all ingredients with ice and fine strain into chilled glass.

2	shot(s)	The Famous Grouse Scotch whisky
1	shot(s)	Tuaca Italian liqueur
¾	shot(s)	Chambord black raspberry liqueur

Origin: Created in 2002 by Tim Halilaj, Albania.
Comment: Rust coloured and fruit charged.

NACIONAL DAIQUIRI #1 [NEW]

Glass: Martini
Garnish: Maraschino cherry
Method: **SHAKE** all ingredients with ice and fine strain into chilled glass.

2	shot(s)	Light white rum
¾	shot(s)	Bols apricot brandy liqueur
½	shot(s)	Freshly squeezed lime juice
¾	shot(s)	Chilled mineral water (omit if wet ice)

Origin: An old classic named after the Hotel Nacional, Havana, Cuba, where it was created.
Comment: A sophisticated complex apricot Daiquiri.

NACIONAL DAIQUIRI #2 [NEW]

Glass: Martini
Garnish: Maraschino cherry
Method: **SHAKE** all ingredients with ice and fine strain into chilled glass.

2	shot(s)	Light white rum
½	shot(s)	Bols apricot brandy liqueur
1½	shot(s)	Pressed pineapple juice
½	shot(s)	Freshly squeezed lime juice

Comment: An apricot Daiquiri with extra interest courtesy of pineapple.

NANTUCKET

Glass: Collins
Garnish: Lime wedge
Method: **SHAKE** all ingredients with ice and strain into ice-filled glass.

2	shot(s)	Light white rum
3	shot(s)	Cranberry juice
2	shot(s)	Freshly squeezed golden grapefruit juice

Origin: Popularised by the Cheers bar chain, this is named after the beautiful island off Cape Cod.
Comment: Essentially a Seabreeze with rum in place of vodka.

NAPOLEON MARTINI [NEW]

Glass: Martini
Garnish: Lemon peel twist
Method: **SHAKE** all ingredients with ice and fine strain into chilled glass.

2	shot(s)	Plymouth gin
¼	shot(s)	Cointreau / triple sec
½	shot(s)	Dubonnet Red
¼	shot(s)	Fernet Branca
½	shot(s)	Chilled mineral water (omit if wet ice)

Origin: Adapted from a recipe in Harry Craddock's 1930 Savoy Cocktail Book.
Comment: A beautifully balanced, very approachable, rust coloured Martini.

NARANJA DAIQUIRI

Glass: Martini
Garnish: Orange slice on rim
Method: **SHAKE** all ingredients with ice and fine strain into chilled glass.

1 3/4	shot(s)	**Light white rum**
3/4	shot(s)	**Grand Marnier liqueur**
1	shot(s)	**Freshly squeezed orange juice**
1/2	shot(s)	**Freshly squeezed lime juice**
1/8	shot(s)	**Sugar (gomme) syrup**

Comment: The Latino version of an orange Daiquiri.

NATURAL DAIQUIRI

Glass: Martini
Garnish: Lime wedge
Method: **SHAKE** all ingredients with ice and fine strain into chilled glass.

2	shot(s)	**Light white rum (or aged rum)**
1/2	shot(s)	**Freshly squeezed lime juice**
1/4	shot(s)	**Sugar (gomme) syrup**
1/2	shot(s)	**Chilled mineral water (omit if wet ice)**

Variant: Flavoured syrups may be substituted for sugar syrup. Alternatively you can use flavoured rum (see Vanilla Daiquiri) or add fresh fruit and/or fruit juice and/or fruit liqueur (see Melon Daiquiri etc.).
Origin: Created in 1896 by Jennings Cox, an American engineer who was working at a mine near Santiago, Cuba.
Comment: A deliciously simple, clean, refreshing sour drink.

NAUTILUS [NEW]

Glass: Collins (or Nautilus seashell)
Garnish: Mint sprig
Method: **SHAKE** all ingredients with ice and strain into ice-filled glass. Serve with straws.

2	shot(s)	**Sauza Hornitos tequila**
2	shot(s)	**Cranberry juice**
1	shot(s)	**Freshly squeezed lime juice**
1/2	shot(s)	**Sugar (gomme) syrup**

Origin: Adapted from a drink created by Victor Bergeron (Trader Vic).
Comment: Basically a Margarita lengthened with cranberry juice.

NAVIGATOR [NEW]

Glass: Martini
Garnish: Lemon zest twist
Method: **SHAKE** all ingredients with ice and fine strain into chilled glass.

2	shot(s)	**Plymouth gin**
1	shot(s)	**Luxardo Limoncello liqueur**
1	shot(s)	**Freshly squeezed pink grapefruit juice**

Origin: Created in 2005 by Jamie Terrell, London, England.
Comment: This fruity, grapefruit-led drink is pleasantly bitter and sour.

NAVY GROG

Glass: Old-fashioned
Garnish: Lemon wedge
Method: **STIR** honey with rum in base of shaker to dissolve honey. Add next three ingredients, **SHAKE** with ice and strain into ice-filled glass.

3	spoons	**Runny honey**
1 1/2	shot(s)	**Pusser's Navy rum**
1/4	shot(s)	**Freshly squeezed lime juice**
2 1/2	shot(s)	**Chilled mineral water**
2	dashes	**Angostura aromatic bitters**

Variant: Also great served hot. Top with boiling water and garnish with a cinnamon stick.
Comment: An extremely drinkable, honeyed cocktail.

NEGRONI

Glass: Old-fashioned
Garnish: Orange zest twist
Method: **STIR** all ingredients with ice and strain into ice-filled glass.

1	shot(s)	**Plymouth gin**
1	shot(s)	**Campari**
1	shot(s)	**Sweet (rosso) vermouth**

Variant: Serve in a Collins glass topped with soda water (club soda).
Origin: This drink takes its name from Count Camillo Negroni. In the mid-1920s, while drinking at the Casoni Bar in Florence, Italy, he is said to have asked for an Americano 'with a bit more kick'.
Comment: Bitter and dry, but very tasty.

NEGUS (HOT)

Glass: Toddy
Garnish: Dust with freshly ground nutmeg
Method: Place bar spoon in warmed glass. **POUR** all ingredients into glass and **STIR**.

3	shot(s)	**Warre's Otima Tawny Port**
1	shot(s)	**Freshly squeezed lemon juice**
1/2	shot(s)	**Sugar (gomme) syrup**
Top up with		**Boiling water**

Variant: Bishop
Origin: Colonel Francis Negus was the MP for Ipswich from 1717 to 1732. He created this diluted version of the original Bishop.
Comment: A tangy, citrussy hot drink.

NEVADA DAIQUIRI

Glass: Martini
Garnish: Lime wedge on rim
Method: **SHAKE** all ingredients with ice and fine strain into chilled glass.

2	shot(s)	**Pusser's Navy rum**
1	shot(s)	**Freshly squeezed grapefruit juice**
1/2	shot(s)	**Freshly squeezed lime juice**
1/2	shot(s)	**Sugar (gomme) syrup**

Comment: A pungent Daiquiri with the intense flavour of Navy rum.

NEW ORLEANS MULE [NEW]

Glass: Collins
Garnish: Lime wedge
Method: **SHAKE** first four ingredients with ice and fine strain into ice-filled glass. **TOP** with ginger beer.

2	shot(s)	Bourbon whiskey
1	shot(s)	Kahlúa coffee liqueur
1	shot(s)	Pressed pineapple juice
1/2	shot(s)	Freshly squeezed lime juice
Top up with		Ginger beer

Comment: A spicy, full-flavoured taste of the South.

NEW ORLEANS PUNCH

Glass: Collins
Garnish: Lemon slice
Method: **SHAKE** all ingredients with ice and strain into glass filled with crushed ice. Serve with straws.

1 1/2	shot(s)	Bourbon whiskey
3/4	shot(s)	Appleton Estate V/X aged rum
1 1/2	shot(s)	Chambord black raspberry liqueur
3/4	shot(s)	Freshly squeezed lemon juice
3	shot(s)	Cold black camomile tea

Comment: Raspberry is the predominant flavour in this long drink.

NEW YEAR'S ABSOLUTION [NEW]

Glass: Old-fashioned
Garnish: Mint sprig
Method: **STIR** honey with absinthe in base of shaker until honey dissolves. Add apple juice, **SHAKE** with ice and strain into ice-filled glass. **TOP** with ginger ale and stir.

2	spoons	Runny honey
1	shot(s)	La Fée Parisian 68% absinthe
1	shot(s)	Pressed apple juice
Top up with		Ginger ale

Comment: The green fairy, tamed with honey and spiced with ginger.

NEW YORKER

Glass: Martini
Garnish: Orange zest twist
Method: **SHAKE** all ingredients with ice and fine strain into chilled glass.

2	shot(s)	Bourbon whiskey
1	shot(s)	Claret (red wine)
1/2	shot(s)	Freshly squeezed lemon juice
1/2	shot(s)	Sugar (gomme) syrup

Comment: Sweet 'n' sour whiskey and wine.

NEW PORT CODEBREAKER

Glass: Collins
Method: **SHAKE** all ingredients with ice and strain into ice-filled glass.

1	shot(s)	Sauza Hornitos tequila
1	shot(s)	Pusser's Navy rum
1/2	shot(s)	Warninks advocaat
1/2	shot(s)	Coco López cream of coconut
4	shot(s)	Freshly squeezed orange juice

Origin: Adapted from a cocktail discovered in 1999 at Porter's Bar, Covent Garden, London.
Comment: This straw yellow drink is a most unusual mix of ingredients.

NIAGARA FALLS

Glass: Flute
Garnish: Physalis
Method: **SHAKE** first four ingredients with ice and strain into chilled glass. **TOP** with ginger ale, stir and serve with straws.

1	shot(s)	Ketel One vodka
1	shot(s)	Grand Marnier liqueur
1/2	shot(s)	Freshly squeezed lemon juice
1/4	shot(s)	Sugar (gomme) syrup
Top up with		Ginger ale

Comment: Ginger ale and orange complement each other, fortified by vodka.

NICE PEAR-TINI

Glass: Martini
Garnish: Pear slice on rim
Method: **SHAKE** all ingredients with ice and fine strain into chilled glass.

1	shot(s)	Rémy Martin cognac
1/2	shot(s)	Pear & cognac liqueur
1/2	shot(s)	Poire William eau de vie
2	shot(s)	Freshly extracted pear juice
1/4	shot(s)	Sugar (gomme) syrup

Origin: Created in 2002 by yours truly.
Comment: Spirited, rich and fruity.

NICKY FINN [NEW]

Glass: Martini
Garnish: Lemon zest twist
Method: **SHAKE** all ingredients with ice and fine strain into chilled glass.

1	shot(s)	Rémy Martin cognac
1	shot(s)	Cointreau / triple sec
1	shot(s)	Freshly squeezed lemon juice
1/4	shot(s)	Pernod anis

Origin: Adapted from a recipe in 'Cocktail: The Drinks Bible for the 21st Century' by Paul Harrington and Laura Moorhead.
Comment: Basically a Sidecar spiked with an aniseedy dash of Pernod.

A B C D E F G H I J K L M N O P Q R S T U V W X Y Z

NICKY'S FIZZ [NEW]

Glass: Collins
Garnish: Orange slice
Method: **SHAKE** first two ingredients with ice and strain into ice-filled glass. **TOP** with soda, lightly stir and serve with straws.

2 shot(s) **Plymouth gin**
2 shot(s) **Freshly squeezed grapefruit juice**
Top up with **Soda water (from siphon)**

Comment: A dry, refreshing, long drink.

NIGHT & DAY [NEW]

Glass: Flute
Garnish: Orange zest twist
Method: **POUR** ingredients into chilled glass.

½ shot(s) **Campari**
½ shot(s) **Grand Marnier liqueur**
Top up with **Piper-Heidsieck brut champagne**

Comment: Dry, aromatic, orange champagne.

NIGHTMARE MARTINI

Glass: Martini
Garnish: Maraschino cherry
Method: **SHAKE** all ingredients with ice and fine strain into chilled glass.

1 shot(s) **Plymouth gin**
1 shot(s) **Dubonnet Red**
½ shot(s) **Bols cherry brandy liqueur**
2 shot(s) **Freshly squeezed orange juice**

Comment: Pleasant enough, with hints of cherry. Hardly a nightmare.

NINE-20-SEVEN

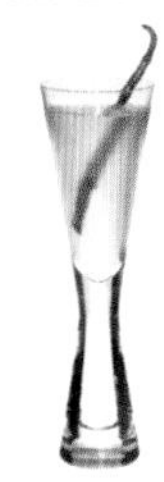

Glass: Flute
Method: **POUR** ingredients into chilled glass and lightly stir.

¼ shot(s) **Vanilla flavoured vodka**
¼ shot(s) **Cuarenta Y Tres (Licor 43)**
Top up with **Piper-Heidsieck brut champagne**

Origin: Created in 2002 by Damian Caldwell at Home Bar, London, England. Damian was lost for a name until a customer asked the time.
Comment: Champagne with a hint of vanilla.

FOR MORE INFORMATION SEE OUR
INGREDIENTS APPENDIX ON PAGE 254

NOBLE EUROPE

Glass: Old-fashioned
Garnish: Orange slice in glass
Method: **SHAKE** all ingredients with ice and strain into glass filled with crushed ice.

1½ shot(s) **Tokaji Hungarian wine**
1 shot(s) **Ketel One vodka**
1 shot(s) **Freshly squeezed orange juice**
1 dash **Vanilla essence**

Origin: Created in 2002 by Dan Spink at Browns, St Martin's Lane, London, England.
Variant: Also great served 'up' in a Martini glass.
Comment: A delicious cocktail that harnesses the rich, sweet flavours of Tokaji and delivers them very approachably.

NOME

Glass: Martini
Garnish: Mint leaf
Method: **STIR** all ingredients with ice and strain into chilled glass.

1½ shot(s) **Plymouth gin**
1 shot(s) **Yellow Chartreuse**
1½ shot(s) **Tio Pepe Fino sherry**

AKA: Alaska Martini
Origin: A classic cocktail whose origin is unknown.
Comment: This dyslexic gnome is dry and interesting.

NOON [NEW]

Glass: Martini
Garnish: Orange zest twist
Method: **SHAKE** all ingredients with ice and strain into chilled glass.

1½ shot(s) **Plymouth gin**
¾ shot(s) **Dry vermouth**
¾ shot(s) **Sweet (rosso) vermouth**
¾ shot(s) **Freshly squeezed orange juice**
2 dashes **Angostura aromatic bitters**
½ fresh **Egg white**

Comment: This classic cocktail is smooth and aromatic.

NORTHERN LIGHTS

Glass: Martini
Garnish: Star anise
Method: **SHAKE** all ingredients with ice and fine strain into chilled glass.

1½ shot(s) **Zubrówka bison vodka**
¾ shot(s) **Apple schnapps liqueur**
1 shot(s) **Pressed apple juice**
½ shot(s) **Freshly squeezed lime juice**
½ shot(s) **Pernod anis**
½ shot(s) **Sugar (gomme) syrup**

Origin: Created in 2003 by Stewart Hudson at MJU Bar, Millennium Hotel, London, England.
Comment: Wonderfully refreshing: apple and anis served up on a grassy vodka base.

A B C D E F G H I J K L M **N** O P Q R S T U V W X Y Z

NORTH POLE MARTINI [NEW]

Glass: Martini
Method: **SHAKE** first four ingredients with ice and fine strain into chilled glass. **FLOAT** cream over drink.

2	shot(s)	**Plymouth gin**
1	shot(s)	**Luxardo maraschino liqueur**
1/2	shot(s)	**Freshly squeezed lemon juice**
1/2	fresh	**Egg white**
Float		**Double (heavy) cream**

Origin: Adapted from a recipe in the 1947-72 Trader Vic's Bartender's Guide by Victor Bergeron.
Comment: An Aviation smoothed by egg white and cream.

NOT SO COSMO (MOCKTAIL)

Glass: Martini
Garnish: Orange zest twist
Method: **SHAKE** all ingredients with ice and fine strain into chilled glass.

1	shot(s)	**Freshly squeezed orange juice**
1	shot(s)	**Cranberry juice**
1	shot(s)	**Freshly squeezed lime juice**
1	shot(s)	**Freshly squeezed lemon juice**

Origin: Discovered in 2003 at Claridge's Bar, London, England.
Comment: This non-alcoholic cocktail may look like a Cosmo but it doesn't taste like one.

NOVEMBER SEABREEZE (MOCKTAIL)

Glass: Collins
Garnish: Lime wedge
Method: **SHAKE** first three ingredients with ice and strain into ice-filled glass. **TOP** with soda, gently stir and serve with straws.

2	shot(s)	**Cranberry juice**
2	shot(s)	**Pressed apple juice**
1	shot(s)	**Freshly squeezed lime juice**
Top up with		**Soda water (club soda)**

Comment: A superbly refreshing fruity drink, whatever the time of year.

NO. 10 LEMONADE [NEW]

Glass: Collins
Garnish: Lemon slice
Method: **MUDDLE** blueberries in base of shaker. Add next three ingredients, **SHAKE** with ice and fine strain into ice filled glass. **TOP** with soda, lightly stir and serve with straws.

12	fresh	**Blueberries**
2	shot(s)	**Light white rum**
1 1/2	shot(s)	**Freshly squeezed lemon juice**
3/4	shot(s)	**Sugar (gomme) syrup**
Top up with		**Soda water (club soda)**

Origin: Adapted from a drink discovered in 2006 at Double Seven, New York City, USA.
Comment: Basically a long blueberry Daiquiri.

NUTCRACKER SWEET [NEW]

Glass: Martini
Garnish: Dust with cocoa powder
Method: **SHAKE** all ingredients with ice and fine strain into chilled glass.

2	shot(s)	**Ketel One vodka**
1	shot(s)	**Bols white crème de cacao**
3/4	shot(s)	**Luxardo Amaretto di Saschira liqueur**

Comment: After dinner, fortified almond and chocolate.

NUTS & BERRIES

Glass: Martini
Garnish: Float raspberry and almond flake
Method: **STIR** all ingredients with ice and strain into chilled glass.

1	shot(s)	**Raspberry flavoured vodka**
1	shot(s)	**Almond flavoured vodka**
1/4	shot(s)	**Frangelico hazelnut liqueur**
1/4	shot(s)	**Chambord black raspberry liqueur**
1	shot(s)	**7-Up**

Origin: Created in 2004 by yours truly.
Comment: The inclusion of a carbonate (7-Up) may annoy some classical bartenders but it adds flavour, sweetness and dilution.

NUTTY BERRY'TINI

Glass: Martini
Garnish: Float mint leaf
Method: **SHAKE** all ingredients with ice and fine strain into chilled glass.

2	shot(s)	**Cranberry flavoured vodka**
1/2	shot(s)	**Bols cherry brandy liqueur**
1/2	shot(s)	**Frangelico hazelnut liqueur**
1/4	shot(s)	**Luxardo maraschino liqueur**
1	shot(s)	**Cranberry juice**
1/2	shot(s)	**Freshly squeezed lime juice**

Origin: Created by yours truly in 2003.
Comment: Cranberry vodka and juice, sweetened with cherry liqueur, dried with lime juice and flavoured with hazelnut.

NUTTY NASHVILLE

Glass: Martini
Garnish: Lemon zest twist
Method: **STIR** honey with bourbon in base of shaker to dissolve honey. Add other ingredients, **SHAKE** with ice and fine strain into chilled glass.

2	spoon(s)	**Runny honey**
2	shot(s)	**Bourbon whiskey**
1	shot(s)	**Frangelico hazelnut liqueur**
1	shot(s)	**Krupnik honey liqueur**

Origin: Created in 2001 by Jason Fendick at Rockwell, Trafalgar Hotel, London, England.
Comment: Bourbon and hazelnut smoothed and rounded by honey.

NUTTY RUSSIAN

Glass: Old-fashioned
Method: SHAKE all ingredients with ice and strain into ice-filled glass.

1½	shot(s)	**Ketel One vodka**
¾	shot(s)	**Frangelico hazelnut liqueur**
¾	shot(s)	**Kahlúa coffee liqueur**

Comment: A Black Russian with hazelnut liqueur.

NUTTY SUMMER

Glass: Martini
Garnish: Drop three dashes of Angostura aromatic bitters onto surface of drink and stir around with a cocktail stick - essential to both the look and flavour.
Method: SHAKE all ingredients with ice and fine strain into chilled glass.

1½	shot(s)	**Warninks advocaat**
¾	shot(s)	**Luxardo Amaretto di Saschira liqueur**
¾	shot(s)	**Malibu coconut rum liqueur**
¾	shot(s)	**Pressed pineapple juice**
½	shot(s)	**Double (heavy) cream**

Origin: Created in 2001 by Daniel Spink at Hush Up, London, England.
Comment: This subtle, dessert style cocktail is packed with flavour. A superb after dinner tipple for summer.

OATMEAL COOKIE

Glass: Shot
Method: SHAKE all ingredients with ice and fine strain into chilled glass.

½	shot(s)	**Bols butterscotch liqueur**
¼	shot(s)	**Goldschläger cinnamon schnapps**
¾	shot(s)	**Baileys Irish Cream liqueur**

Comment: A well balanced, creamy shot with hints of butterscotch and cinnamon.

OÁZA [NEW]

Glass: Old-fashioned
Garnish: Lime wedge
Method: SHAKE all ingredients with ice and strain into ice-filled glass.

2	shot(s)	**Becherovka**
¾	shot(s)	**Freshly squeezed lime juice**
¼	shot(s)	**Sugar (gomme) syrup**

Origin: A popular drink in the Czech Republic where Becherovka, a herbal liquor, is the national drink.
Comment: Herbal and bittersweet. Not for everyone.

ODDBALL MANHATTAN DRY [NEW]

Glass: Martini
Garnish: Two maraschino cherries
Method: STIR all ingredients with ice and strain into chilled glass.

2½	shot(s)	**Bourbon whiskey**
1	shot(s)	**Dry vermouth**
½	shot(s)	**Yellow Chartreuse liqueur**
3	dashes	**Angostura aromatic bitters**

Comment: Not as oddball as it sounds, the Chartreuse combines harmoniously.

O'HENRY [NEW]

Glass: Collins
Garnish: Lemon slice
Method: SHAKE first two ingredients with ice and strain into ice-filled glass. **TOP** with ginger ale, lightly stir and serve with straws.

2	shot(s)	**Bourbon whiskey**
1	shot(s)	**Bénédictine D.O.M. liqueur**
Top up with		**Ginger ale**

Origin: Discovered in 2006 at Brandy Library, New York City, USA.
Comment: Herbal whiskey and ginger.

OH GOSH!

Glass: Martini
Garnish: Lemon zest twist
Method: SHAKE all ingredients with ice and fine strain into chilled glass.

1½	shot(s)	**Light white rum**
1	shot(s)	**Cointreau / triple sec**
½	shot(s)	**Freshly squeezed lime juice**
¼	shot(s)	**Sugar (gomme) syrup**
½	shot(s)	**Chilled mineral water (omit if wet ice)**

Origin: Created by Tony Conigliaro in 2001 at Isola, London, England. A customer requested a Daiquiri with a difference – when this was served he took one sip and exclaimed "Oh gosh!".
Comment: A very subtle orange twist on the classic Daiquiri.

OIL SLICK

Glass: Shot
Method: Refrigerate ingredients then **LAYER** in chilled glass by carefully pouring in the following order.

¾	shot(s)	**Opal Nera black sambuca**
¾	shot(s)	**Baileys Irish Cream liqueur**

Comment: Whiskey cream and liquorice.

OLD FASHIONED #1 (CLASSIC VERSION)

Glass: Old-fashioned
Garnish: Orange (or lemon) twist
Method: **STIR** one shot of bourbon with two ice cubes in a glass. **ADD** sugar syrup and Angostura and two more ice cubes. **STIR** some more and add another two ice cubes and the rest of the bourbon. **STIR** lots more and add more ice.

2½	shot(s)	**Bourbon whiskey**
½	shot(s)	**Sugar (gomme) syrup**
3	dashes	**Angostura aromatic bitters**

Origin: Said to have been created between 1900 and 1907, at the Pendennis Club, Louisville, Kentucky, USA.
Comment: The melting and stirring in of ice cubes is essential to the dilution and taste of this classic.

OLD FASHIONED #2 (US VERSION)

Glass: Old-fashioned
Garnish: Orange zest twist & maraschino cherry
Method: **MUDDLE** orange and cherries in base of shaker. Add other ingredients, **SHAKE** with ice and fine strain into ice-filled glass.

2	whole	**Maraschino cherries**
1	fresh	**Orange slice (cut into eight segments)**
2	shot(s)	**Bourbon whiskey**
⅛	shot(s)	**Maraschino syrup (from the cherry jar)**
2	dashes	**Angostura aromatic bitters**

Comment: This drink is often mixed in the glass in which it is to be served. Shaking better incorporates the flavours produced by muddling and fine straining removes the orange peel and cherry skin.

OLD FASHIONED CADDY [NEW]

Glass: Old-fashioned
Garnish: Orange slice & cherry (sail)
Method: **SHAKE** all ingredients with ice and strain into ice-filled glass.

2	shot(s)	**The Famous Grouse Scotch whisky**
½	shot(s)	**Bols cherry liqueur**
½	shot(s)	**Sweet (rosso) vermouth**
2	dashes	**Angostura aromatic bitters**

Origin: Created in 2005 by Wayne Collins, London, England.
Comment: Rich, red and packed with flavour.

OLD PAL [UPDATED]

Glass: Old-fashioned
Garnish: Orange slice
Method: **STIR** all ingredients with ice and strain into ice-filled glass.

1¼	shot(s)	**Bourbon whiskey**
1¼	shot(s)	**Dry vermouth**
1¼	shot(s)	**Campari**

Comment: Dry and bitter.

OLE

Glass: Martini
Garnish: Orange wheel on rim
Method: **SHAKE** all ingredients with ice and fine strain into chilled glass.

2	shot(s)	**Rémy Martin cognac**
¾	shot(s)	**Cuarenta Y Tres (Licor 43) liqueur**
1½	shot(s)	**Freshly squeezed orange juice**

Comment: Vanilla, orange and brandy combine well.

OLYMPIC [NEW]

Glass: Martini
Garnish: Orange zest twist
Method: **SHAKE** all ingredients with ice and fine strain into chilled glass.

1¼	shot(s)	**Rémy Martin cognac**
1¼	shot(s)	**Grand Marnier liqueur**
1¼	shot(s)	**Freshly squeezed orange juice**

Origin: Adapted from a recipe in Harry Craddock's 1930 Savoy Cocktail Book.
Comment: The perfect balance of cognac and orange juice. One to celebrate the 2012 Games perhaps.

ONION RING MARTINI

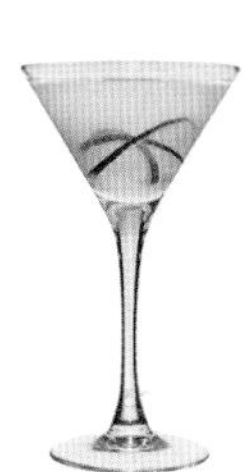

Glass: Martini
Garnish: Onion ring
Method: **MUDDLE** onion in base of shaker. Add other ingredients, **SHAKE** with ice and fine strain into chilled glass.

2	ring(s)	**Fresh red onion**
1	shot(s)	**Sake**
2	shot(s)	**Plymouth gin**
3	dashes	**Fee Brothers orange bitters**
⅛	shot(s)	**Sugar (gomme) syrup**

Origin: Reputed to have been created at the Bamboo Bar, Bangkok, Thailand.
Comment: Certainly one of the most obscure Martini variations – drinkable, but leaves you with onion breath.

OPAL [UPDATED]

Glass: Martini
Garnish: Orange zest twist
Method: **SHAKE** all ingredients with ice and fine strain into chilled glass.

2	shot(s)	**Plymouth gin**
½	shot(s)	**Cointreau / triple sec**
1¼	shot(s)	**Freshly squeezed orange juice**
¼	shot(s)	**Sugar (gomme) syrup**
⅛	shot(s)	**Orange flower water (optional)**

Origin: Adapted from the 1920s recipe.
Comment: Fresh, fragrant flavours of orange zest and gin.

OPAL CAFÉ

Glass: Shot
Method: SHAKE first two ingredients with ice and fine strain into chilled glass. **FLOAT** thin layer of cream over drink.

1/2	shot(s)	Opal Nera black sambuca
1/2	shot(s)	Cold espresso coffee
Float		Double (heavy) cream

Comment: A great liquorice and coffee drink to sip or shoot.

ORANGE BLOOM MARTINI [NEW]

Glass: Martini
Garnish: Maraschino cherry
Method: SHAKE all ingredients with ice and fine strain into chilled glass.

2	shot(s)	Plymouth gin
1	shot(s)	Cointreau / triple sec
1	shot(s)	Sweet (rosso) vermouth

Origin: Adapted from a recipe in the 1930s edition of the Savoy Cocktail Book by Harry Craddock.
Comment: Strong, fruity zesty orange laced with gin.

OPENING SHOT

Glass: Shot
Method: SHAKE all ingredients with ice and fine strain into chilled glass.

1	shot(s)	Bourbon whiskey
1/2	shot(s)	Sweet (rosso) vermouth
1/8	shot(s)	Sonoma pomegranate (grenadine) syrup

Variant: Double the quantities and strain into a Martini glass and you have the 1920s classic I based this drink on.
Comment: Basically a miserly Sweet Manhattan.

ORANGE BLOSSOM

Glass: Old-fashioned
Garnish: Orange zest twist
Method: SHAKE all ingredients with ice and strain into ice-filled glass.

1 1/2	shot(s)	Plymouth gin
1/2	shot(s)	Cointreau / triple sec
1 1/2	shot(s)	Freshly squeezed orange juice
1/2	shot(s)	Freshly squeezed lime juice
1/8	shot(s)	Sonoma pomegranate (grenadine) syrup

Variant: Served long in a Collins glass this becomes a Harvester.
Comment: Gin sweetened with liqueur and grenadine, and soured with lime.

OPERA

Glass: Martini
Garnish: Orange zest twist
Method: SHAKE all ingredients with ice and fine strain into chilled glass.

2	shot(s)	Plymouth gin
2	shot(s)	Dubonnet Red
1/4	shot(s)	Luxardo maraschino liqueur
3	dashes	Fee Brothers orange bitters

Origin: Adapted from the classic 1920s cocktail.
Comment: Dubonnet smoothes the gin while maraschino adds floral notes.

ORANGE BRÛLÉE [NEW]

Glass: Martini
Garnish: Dust with cocoa powder
Method: SHAKE first three ingredients with ice and fine strain into chilled glass. **FLOAT** thin layer of cream over drink and turn glass to spread evenly.

1 1/2	shot(s)	Luxardo Amaretto di Saschira liqueur
1 1/2	shot(s)	Grand Marnier liqueur
3/4	shot(s)	Rémy Martin cognac
1/4	shot(s)	Double (heavy) cream

Origin: Created in 2005 by Xavier Laigle at Bar Le Forum, Paris, France.
Comment: A great looking, beautifully balanced after-dinner drink.

ORANG-A-TANG [UPDATED]

Glass: Sling
Garnish: Orange slice on rim
Method: SHAKE first five ingredients with ice and strain into ice-filled glass. **FLOAT** layer of rum over drink.

1 1/2	shot(s)	Ketel One vodka
3/4	shot(s)	Cointreau / triple sec
2	shot(s)	Freshly squeezed orange juice
1/2	shot(s)	Freshly squeezed lime juice
1/4	shot(s)	Sonoma pomegranate (grenadine) syrup
1/2	shot(s)	Wood's 100 old navy rum

Comment: Orange predominates in this long, tangy, tropical cooler.

ORANGE CUSTARD MARTINI

Glass: Martini
Garnish: Orange zest twist
Method: SHAKE all ingredients with ice and fine strain into chilled glass.

2	shot(s)	Warninks advocaat
1	shot(s)	Tuaca Italian liqueur
1/2	shot(s)	Grand Marnier liqueur
1/4	shot(s)	Vanilla syrup

Origin: I created this drink in 2002 after rediscovering advocaat on a trip to Amsterdam.
Comment: A smooth, creamy orangey dessert cocktail.

ORANGE DAIQUIRI #1 [NEW]

Glass: Old-fashioned
Garnish: Orange zest twist
Method: SHAKE all ingredients with ice and fine strain into ice-filled glass.

2	shot(s)	Aged rum
3/4	shot(s)	Freshly squeezed orange juice
1/2	shot(s)	Freshly squeezed lime juice
1/4	shot(s)	Sugar (gomme) syrup

AKA: Bolo
Origin: My take on a popular drink.
Comment: Far more serious than it looks. Sweet and sour in harmony.

ORANGE DAIQUIRI #2

Glass: Martini
Garnish: Orange zest twist
Method: SHAKE all ingredients with ice and fine strain into chilled glass.

2	shot(s)	Clément Créole Shrubb liqueur
1/2	shot(s)	Freshly squeezed lime juice
3/4	shot(s)	Chilled mineral water (omit if wet ice)

Variant: Derby Daiquiri
Origin: I conceived this drink in 1998, after visiting the company which was then importing Créole Shrubb. I took a bottle to London's Met Bar and Ben Reed made me my first Orange Daiquiri.
Comment: Créole Shrubb is an unusual liqueur made by infusing orange peel in casks of mature Martinique rum.

ORANGE MARTINI [NEW]

Glass: Martini
Garnish: Orange zest twist
Method: SHAKE all ingredients with ice and fine strain into chilled glass.

2	shot(s)	Plymouth gin
1	shot(s)	Freshly squeezed orange juice
1/2	shot(s)	Sweet (rosso) vermouth
1/4	shot(s)	Sugar (gomme) syrup
3	dashes	Fee Brothers orange bitters

Origin: Adapted from the Orange Cocktail and Orange Martini Cocktail in the 1930s edition of the Savoy Cocktail Book by Harry Craddock.
Comment: A sophisticated, complex balance of orange and gin.

ORANGE MOJITO

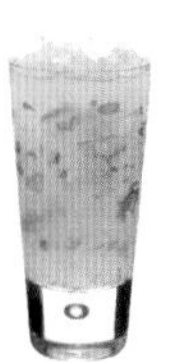

Glass: Collins
Garnish: Mint sprig
Method: Lightly **MUDDLE** mint (just to bruise) in base of glass. Add other ingredients and half fill glass with crushed ice. **CHURN** (stir) with bar spoon. Fill with more crushed ice and churn some more. **TOP** with soda, stir and serve with straws.

8	fresh	Mint leaves
1 1/2	shot(s)	Orange flavoured vodka
1/2	shot(s)	Mandarine Napoléon liqueur
1/2	shot(s)	Light white rum
1	shot(s)	Freshly squeezed lime juice
1/2	shot(s)	Sugar (gomme) syrup
Top up with		Soda water (club soda)

Origin: Created in 2001 by Jamie MacDonald while working in Sydney, Australia.
Comment: Mint and orange combine to make a wonderfully fresh drink.

ORANJINIHA

Glass: Collins
Garnish: Orange slice in glass
Method: SHAKE all ingredients with ice and strain into glass filled with crushed ice.

2	shot(s)	Orange flavoured vodka
3	shot(s)	Freshly squeezed orange juice
1	shot(s)	Freshly squeezed lemon juice
1	shot(s)	Sugar (gomme) syrup

Origin: Created in 2002 by Alex Kammerling, London, England.
Comment: A tall, richly flavoured orange drink.

ORCHARD BREEZE

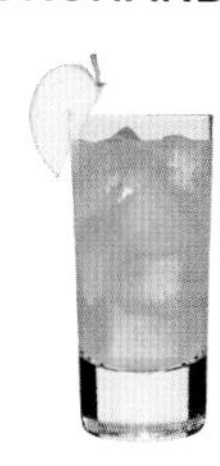

Glass: Collins
Garnish: Apple slice on rim
Method: SHAKE all ingredients with ice and strain into ice-filled glass.

2	shot(s)	Ketel One vodka
2 1/2	shot(s)	Pressed apple juice
1 1/2	shot(s)	Sauvignon Blanc wine
3/4	shot(s)	Elderflower cordial
1/4	shot(s)	Freshly squeezed lime juice

Origin: Created in 2002 by Wayne Collins for Maxxium UK.
Comment: A refreshing, summery combination of white wine, apple, lime and elderflower laced with vodka.

HOW TO MAKE SUGAR SYRUP

To make your own sugar syrup, gradually pour TWO cups of granulated sugar into a saucepan containing ONE cup of hot water. Stir as you pour and carry on stirring and simmering until the sugar is dissolved. Do not let the water even come close to boiling and only simmer for as long as it takes to dissolve the sugar. Allow syrup to cool and pour into an empty bottle. Ideally, you should finely strain your syrup into the bottle to remove any undissolved crystals which could otherwise encourage crystallisation. If kept in a refrigerator this mixture will last for a couple of months.

ORIENTAL GRAPE MARTINI

Glass: Martini
Garnish: Grapes on stick
Method: **MUDDLE** grapes in base of shaker. Add other ingredients, **SHAKE** with ice and fine strain into chilled glass.

12	fresh	**Seedless white grapes**
1½	shot(s)	**Ketel One vodka**
1½	shot(s)	**Sake**
¼	shot(s)	**Sugar (gomme) syrup**

Variants: Double Grape Martini, Grape Martini, Grapple.
Origin: Created by yours truly in 2004.
Comment: Sake adds some oriental intrigue to what would otherwise be a plain old Grape Martini.

ORIENTAL TART

Glass: Martini
Garnish: Peeled lychee in drink
Method: **SHAKE** all ingredients with ice and fine strain into chilled glass.

1½	shot(s)	**Plymouth gin**
1	shot(s)	**Soho lychee liqueur**
2	shot(s)	**Freshly squeezed golden grapefruit juice**

Origin: Created in 2004 by yours truly.
Comment: A sour, tart, fruity Martini with more than a hint of lychee.

OSMO [NEW]

Glass: Martini
Garnish: Orange zest twist
Method: **SHAKE** all ingredients with ice and fine strain into chilled glass.

2	shot(s)	**Sake**
½	shot(s)	**Cointreau / triple sec**
¼	shot(s)	**Freshly squeezed lime juice**
1½	shot(s)	**Cranberry juice**
⅛	shot(s)	**Sugar (gomme) syrup**

Origin: Adapted from a drink discovered in 2005 at Mo Bar, Landmark Mandarin Oriental Hotel, Hong Kong, China.
Comment: A sake based Cosmopolitan.

OUZI

Glass: Shot
Method: **SHAKE** all ingredients with ice and fine strain into chilled glass.

¾	shot(s)	**Ketel One vodka**
½	shot(s)	**Ouzo**
¼	shot(s)	**Sugar (gomme) syrup**
¼	shot(s)	**Freshly squeezed lemon juice**

Comment: A lemon and liquorice shooter.

PAGO PAGO [NEW]

Glass: Martini
Garnish: Lime wedge on rim
Method: **SHAKE** all ingredients with ice and fine strain into chilled glass.

2	shot(s)	**Mount Gay golden rum**
¼	shot(s)	**Green Chartreuse liqueur**
½	shot(s)	**Bols white crème de cacao**
½	shot(s)	**Freshly squeezed lime juice**
⅛	shot(s)	**Sugar (gomme) syrup**
½	shot(s)	**Chilled mineral water (omit if wet ice)**

Comment: A Daiquiri with a liqueur twist.

PAINKILLER

Glass: Collins
Garnish: Pineapple wedge & cherry
Method: **SHAKE** all ingredients with ice and strain into ice-filled glass.

2	shot(s)	**Pusser's Navy rum**
2	shot(s)	**Pressed pineapple juice**
1	shot(s)	**Freshly squeezed orange juice**
1	shot(s)	**Coco López cream of coconut**

Origin: From the Soggy Dollar Bar on the island of Jost Van Dyke in the British Virgin Islands. The bar's name is logical, as most of the clientele are sailors and there is no dock. Hence they have to swim ashore, often paying for drinks with wet dollars.
Comment: Full-flavoured and fruity.

PAISLEY MARTINI

Glass: Martini
Garnish: Lemon zest twist
Method: **STIR** all ingredients with ice and strain into chilled glass.

2½	shot(s)	**Plymouth gin**
½	shot(s)	**Dry vermouth**
¼	shot(s)	**The Famous Grouse Scotch whisky**

Comment: A dry Martini for those with a penchant for Scotch.

PALOMA [NEW]

Glass: Collins
Garnish: Lime wedge & salt rim
Method: **SHAKE** first four ingredients with ice and strain into ice-filled glass. **TOP** with soda, lightly stir and serve with straws.

2	shot(s)	**Sauza Hornitos tequila**
3	shot(s)	**Freshly squeezed pink grapefruit juice**
½	shot(s)	**Freshly squeezed lime juice**
¼	shot(s)	**Agave syrup (from health food shop)**
Top up with		**Soda water (club soda)**

Origin: The name is Spanish for 'dove' and the cocktail is well-known in Mexico.
Comment: A long, fruity, Margarita.

PALE RIDER

Glass: Collins
Garnish: Lime wedge
Method: SHAKE all ingredients with ice and strain into ice-filled glass.

2	shot(s)	Raspberry flavoured vodka
1/2	shot(s)	Peach schnapps liqueur
2	shot(s)	Cranberry juice
1	shot(s)	Pressed pineapple juice
1	shot(s)	Freshly squeezed lime juice
1/2	shot(s)	Sugar (gomme) syrup

Origin: Created in 1997 by Wayne Collins at Navajo Joe, London, England.
Comment: Sweet and fruity.

PALL MALL MARTINI [NEW]

Glass: Martini
Garnish: Orange zest twist
Method: SHAKE all ingredients with ice and fine strain into chilled glass.

1	shot(s)	Plymouth gin
1	shot(s)	Dry vermouth
1	shot(s)	Sweet (rosso) vermouth
1/4	shot(s)	Bols white crème de cacao
1	dashes	Fee Brothers orange bitters

Comment: A classic Martini served 'perfect' with the tiniest hint of chocolate.

PALOOKAVILLE

Glass: Collins
Garnish: Lemon wedge
Method: SHAKE all ingredients with ice and strain into ice-filled glass.

2	shot(s)	Zubrowka bison vodka
3/4	shot(s)	Apple schnapps liqueur
2	shot(s)	Pressed apple juice
3/4	shot(s)	Freshly squeezed lemon juice
3/4	shot(s)	Elderflower cordial

Origin: Adapted from a cocktail Chris Edwardes created for Norman Cook, AKA Fatboy Slim, at Blanch House, Brighton, England and named after Cook's 2004 album, which is named in turn after a place mentioned by Marlon Brando in On The Waterfront.
Comment: The Polish combo of zubrówka and apple benefits from a distinctly English touch of elderflower.

PALERMO

Glass: Martini
Garnish: Vanilla pod
Method: SHAKE all ingredients with ice and fine strain into chilled glass.

1 1/2	shot(s)	Vanilla infused light white rum
1	shot(s)	Sauvignon Blanc wine
1 1/4	shot(s)	Pressed pineapple juice
1/4	shot(s)	Sugar (gomme) syrup

Origin: Adapted from a cocktail discovered in 2001 at Hotel du Vin, Bristol, England.
Comment: This smooth cocktail beautifully combines vanilla rum with tart wine and the sweetness of the pineapple juice.

PALM BEACH [NEW]

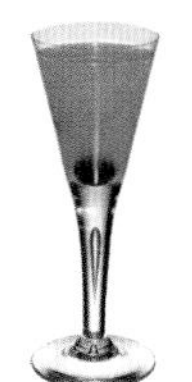

Glass: Martini
Garnish: Maraschino cherry
Method: SHAKE all ingredients with ice and fine strain into chilled glass.

2 1/2	shot(s)	Plymouth gin
1/2	shot(s)	Sweet (rosso) vermouth
1	shot(s)	Freshly squeezed pink grapefruit juice

Origin: A classic from the 1940s.
Comment: Dry, aromatic and packs one hell of a punch.

PALM SPRINGS

Glass: Collins
Garnish: Apple slice & mint sprig
Method: SHAKE all ingredients with ice and strain into glass filled with crushed ice.

4	fresh	Mint leaves
1	shot(s)	Passoã passion fruit liqueur
1	shot(s)	Mount Gay Eclipse golden rum
1/4	shot(s)	Freshly squeezed lime juice
1	shot(s)	Pressed apple juice
2	shot(s)	Cranberry juice

Comment: Sweet and aromatic.

PALMA VIOLET MARTINI

Glass: Martini
Garnish: Parma Violet sweets
Method: SHAKE all ingredients with ice and fine strain into chilled glass.

1 1/2	shot(s)	Ketel One vodka
1/4	shot(s)	Peach schnapps liqueur
1/2	shot(s)	Freshly squeezed lemon juice
1	shot(s)	Benoit Serres violet liqueur
1/4	shot(s)	Sugar (gomme) syrup
1	dash	Fee Brothers orange bitters
1/2	shot(s)	Chilled mineral water (omit if wet ice)

Origin: Created in 2001 by Jamie Terrell at LAB, London, England.
Comment: A subtly floral drink with a delicate colour.

PANCHO VILLA [NEW]

Glass: Martini (saucer)
Garnish: Pineapple wedge on rim
Method: SHAKE all ingredients with ice and fine strain into chilled glass.

1	shot(s)	Light white rum
1	shot(s)	Plymouth gin
1	shot(s)	Bols apricot brandy liqueur
1/4	shot(s)	Bols cherry brandy liqueur
1/4	shot(s)	Pressed pineapple juice
1/2	shot(s)	Chilled mineral water (omit if wet ice)

Origin: Adapted from a recipe in the 1947-72 Trader Vic's Bartender's Guide by Victor Bergeron.
Comment: To quote Victor Bergeron, "This'll tuck you away neatly - and pick you up and throw you right on the floor".

PAPPY HONEYSUCKLE

Glass: Martini
Garnish: Physalis fruit
Method: **STIR** honey with whiskey in base of shaker to dissolve honey. Add other ingredients, **SHAKE** with ice and fine strain into chilled glass.

1½	shot(s)	Black Bush Irish whiskey
2	spoons	Runny honey
1¼	shot(s)	Sauvignon Blanc wine
1½	shot(s)	Pressed apple juice
¼	shot(s)	Passion fruit syrup
¼	shot(s)	Freshly squeezed lemon juice

Origin: Created in 2002 by Shelim Islam at the GE Club, London, England.
Comment: Fresh and fruity with honeyed sweetness.

PARADISE #1 [NEW]

Glass: Martini
Garnish: Orange zest twist
Method: **SHAKE** all ingredients with ice and fine strain into chilled glass.

2	shot(s)	Plymouth gin
1	shot(s)	Apricot brandy liqueur
1	shot(s)	Freshly squeezed orange juice
¼	shot(s)	Freshly squeezed lemon juice

Origin: Proportioned according to a recipe in the 1930 edition of the Savoy Cocktail Book by Harry Craddock.
Comment: Orange predominates in this strong complex cocktail.

PARADISE #2

Glass: Martini
Garnish: Orange zest twist
Method: **SHAKE** all ingredients with ice and fine strain into chilled glass.

2	shot(s)	Plymouth gin
¾	shot(s)	Bols apricot brandy liqueur
1¾	shot(s)	Freshly squeezed orange juice
3	dashes	Fee Brothers orange bitters (optional)

Origin: This 1920s recipe has recently been revitalised by Dale DeGroff.
Comment: When well made, this wonderfully fruity cocktail beautifully harnesses and balances its ingredients.

PARADISE #3 [NEW]

Glass: Martini
Garnish: Orange zest twist
Method: Cut passion fruit in half and scoop flesh into shaker. Add other ingredients, **SHAKE** with ice and fine strain into chilled glass.

1	fresh	Passion fruit
2	shot(s)	Plymouth gin
¾	shot(s)	Bols apricot brandy liqueur
¾	shot(s)	Freshly squeezed orange juice

Comment: Thick, almost syrupy. Rich and fruity.

PARIS SOUR [NEW]

Glass: Old-fashioned
Garnish: Lemon zest twist
Method: **SHAKE** all ingredients with ice and strain into ice-filled glass.

2	shot(s)	Bourbon whiskey
1¼	shot(s)	Dubonnet Red
¼	shot(s)	Sugar (gomme) syrup
½	shot(s)	Freshly squeezed lemon juice
½	fresh	Egg white

Origin: Created in 2005 by Mark at Match Bar, London, England.
Comment: A wonderfully accommodating whiskey sour – it's easy to make and a pleasure to drink.

PARISIAN MARTINI [NEW]

Glass: Martini
Garnish: Lemon peel twist
Method: **SHAKE** all ingredients with ice and fine strain into chilled glass.

1¼	shot(s)	Plymouth gin
1¼	shot(s)	Crème de cassis
1¼	shot(s)	Dry vermouth

Origin: A drink created in the 1920s to promote crème de cassis. This recipe is adapted from one in Harry Craddock's Savoy Cocktail Book.
Comment: Full-on rich cassis is barely tempered by gin and dry vermouth.

PARISIAN SPRING PUNCH

Glass: Collins
Garnish: Lemon zest knot
Method: **SHAKE** first four ingredients with ice and strain into ice-filled glass. **TOP** with champagne and serve with straws.

1	shot(s)	Calvados or applejack brandy
½	shot(s)	Dry vermouth
¼	shot(s)	Freshly squeezed lemon juice
¼	shot(s)	Sugar (gomme) syrup
Top up with		Piper-Heidsieck brut champagne

Comment: Dry apple and champagne – like upmarket cider.

PARK AVENUE [NEW]

Glass: Martini
Garnish: Maraschino cherry
Method: **SHAKE** all ingredients with ice and fine strain into chilled glass.

2	shot(s)	Plymouth gin
½	shot(s)	Grand Marnier liqueur
½	shot(s)	Sweet (rosso) vermouth
1	shot(s)	Pressed pineapple juice

Origin: A classic from the 1940s.
Comment: Very fruity and well-balanced rather than dry or sweet.

PARK LANE

Glass: Martini
Garnish: Orange zest twist
Method: SHAKE all ingredients with ice and strain into chilled glass.

2	shot(s)	Plymouth gin
3/4	shot(s)	Bols apricot brandy liqueur
3/4	shot(s)	Freshly squeezed orange juice
1/8	shot(s)	Sonoma pomegranate (grenadine) syrup
1/2	fresh	Egg white

Comment: This smooth, frothy concoction hides a mean kick.

PARLAY PUNCH [NEW]

Glass: Collins
Garnish: Lime wedge
Method: SHAKE all ingredients with ice and strain into ice-filled glass.

1 1/2	shot(s)	Bourbon whiskey
1	shot(s)	Southern Comfort
1	shot(s)	Pressed pineapple juice
1	shot(s)	Cranberry juice
1/2	shot(s)	Freshly squeezed orange juice
1/2	shot(s)	Freshly squeezed lime juice

Origin: Adapted from a recipe discovered at Vortex Bar, Atlanta, USA.
Comment: Too many of these tangy punches and you'll be parlaying till dawn.

PARMA NEGRONI [NEW]

Glass: Collins
Garnish: Orange slice
Method: SHAKE first five ingredients with ice and strain into ice-filled glass. TOP with tonic water, lightly stir and serve with straws.

1	shot(s)	Plymouth gin
1	shot(s)	Campari
1	shot(s)	Freshly squeezed pink grapefruit juice
2	dashes	Angostura aromatic bitters
1/2	shot(s)	Sugar (gomme) syrup
Top up with		Tonic water

Origin: Discovered in 2005 at Club 97, Hong Kong, China.
Comment: Negroni drinkers will love this fruity adaptation.

PASS-ON-THAT

Glass: Collins
Garnish: Crown with passion fruit half
Method: Cut passion fruit in half and scoop flesh into shaker. Add other ingredients, SHAKE with ice and fine strain into ice-filled glass.

1	fresh	Passion fruit
1	shot(s)	Ketel One vodka
1	shot(s)	Passoã passion fruit liqueur
3	shot(s)	Cranberry juice

Comment: Full-on passion fruit and berries.

PASSBOUR COOLER

Glass: Collins
Garnish: Orange slice in glass
Method: SHAKE all ingredients with ice and strain into ice-filled glass.

1 1/2	shot(s)	Bourbon whiskey
3/4	shot(s)	Passoã passion fruit liqueur
3/4	shot(s)	Bols cherry brandy liqueur
3	shot(s)	Cranberry juice

Comment: Cherry and bourbon with passion fruit.

PASSION FRUIT CAIPIRINHA

Glass: Old-fashioned
Method: MUDDLE lime wedges in the base of sturdy glass (being careful not to break the glass). Cut the passion fruit in half and scoop out the flesh into the glass. POUR cachaça and sugar syrup into glass, add crushed ice and CHURN (stir) with barspoon. Serve with straws.

1	fresh	Passion fruit
3/4	fresh	Lime cut into wedges
2	shot(s)	Cachaça
3/4	shot(s)	Sugar (gomme) syrup

Comment: A tasty fruit Caipirinha. You may end up sipping this from the glass as the passion fruit pips tend to clog straws.

PASSION FRUIT COLLINS

Glass: Collins
Garnish: Lemon slice
Method: Cut passion fruit in half and scoop out flesh into shaker. Add next three ingredients, SHAKE with ice and fine strain into ice-filled glass. TOP with soda, stir and serve with straws.

2	fresh	Passion fruit
2	shot(s)	Plymouth gin
1 1/2	shot(s)	Freshly squeezed lemon juice
1/2	shot(s)	Passion fruit syrup
Top up with		Soda water (club soda)

Origin: Formula by yours truly in 2004.
Comment: This fruity adaptation of the classic Collins may be a tad sharp for some: if so, add a dash more sugar.

PASSION FRUIT DAIQUIRI

Glass: Martini
Garnish: Lime wedge on rim
Method: Cut passion fruit in half and scoop out flesh into shaker. Add other ingredients, SHAKE with ice and fine strain into chilled glass.

2	fresh	Passion fruit
2	shot(s)	Light white rum
1/2	shot(s)	Freshly squeezed lime juice
1/2	shot(s)	Sugar (gomme) syrup

Origin: Formula by yours truly in 2004.
Comment: The rum character comes through in this fruity cocktail.

PIMM'S CUP

This quintessential English summer tipple is usually accredited to James Pimm, who in 1823-4 began trading as a shellfish-monger in London's Lombard Street. He later moved to nearby number 3 Poultry, also in the City of London, where he established Pimm's Oyster Warehouse. It is here, in 1840, that he is said to have first served this drink.

Others dispute this, maintaining that James Pimm only unwittingly lent his name to the drink. They say the true credit lies with his successor, Samuel Morey, who is recorded as having taken out a retail liquor licence in 1860. This would appear to be when the oyster bar first offered its customers spirits. Many establishments of the day mixed house spirits to serve with liqueurs and juices as 'cups', in reference to the tankards in which they were sold. Naturally the 'cup' made at Pimm's Oyster Bar was named after the establishment which retained the goodwill of its founder.

Pimm's restaurant became very popular and changed hands a couple more times. Eventually Horatio David Davies, a wine merchant and owner of cafes in London bought the business. He became Sir Horatio, a Member of Parliament and between 1897-1898, Lord Mayor of London. He formed Pimm's into a private company in 1906, which was controlled by family trusts for another 57 years after his death.

The precise date that the drink Pimm's was first sold outside restaurants and bars controlled by the Pimm's company is unknown. However, it is certain that the original product, No.1, was based on gin and flavoured with numerous botanicals including quinine. A second Pimm's product based on Scotch (Pimm's No.2 Cup) was launched and a third (Pimm's No.3 Cup) was based on brandy. Pimm's became popular in Britain in the 1920s and took off internationally after the Second World War. Other versions were then introduced: Pimm's No.4 based on rum, Pimm's No.6 on vodka and Pimm's No.7 on rye whiskey.

PASSION FRUIT MARGARITA

Glass: Coupette
Garnish: Salt & lime wedge rim
Method: Cut passion fruit in half and scoop out flesh into shaker. Add other ingredients, **SHAKE** with ice and fine strain into chilled glass.

1 fresh **Passion fruit**
2 shot(s) **Sauza Hornitos tequila**
1 shot(s) **Cointreau / triple sec**
1 shot(s) **Freshly squeezed lime juice**
1/4 shot(s) **Passion fruit syrup**

Origin: Formula by yours truly in 2004.
Comment: The flavour of tequila is very evident in this fruity adaptation.

PASSION FRUIT MARTINI #1

Glass: Martini
Garnish: Physalis (cape gooseberry)
Method: Cut passion fruit in half and scoop out flesh into shaker. Add other ingredients, **SHAKE** with ice and fine strain into chilled glass.

1 fresh **Passion fruit**
2 shot(s) **Ketel One vodka**
1/2 shot(s) **Sugar (gomme) syrup**

Origin: Formula by yours truly in 2004.
Comment: A simple but tasty cocktail that wonderfully harnesses the flavour of passion fruit.

PASSION FRUIT MARTINI #2

Glass: Martini
Garnish: Physalis (Cape gooseberry)
Method: Cut passion fruit in half and scoop out flesh into shaker. Add other ingredients, **SHAKE** with ice and fine strain into chilled glass.

2 fresh **Passion fruit**
2 shot(s) **Ketel One vodka**
1/2 shot(s) **Passion fruit syrup**

Origin: Formula by yours truly in 2004.
Comment: Not for Martini purists, but a fruity, easy drinking concoction for everyone else.

PASSION FRUIT MARTINI #3

Glass: Martini
Garnish: Float passion fruit half
Method: Cut passion fruit in half and scoop out flesh into shaker. Add other ingredients, **SHAKE** with ice and fine strain into chilled glass.

2 fresh **Passion fruit**
2 shot(s) **Plymouth gin**
1/2 shot(s) **Cointreau / triple sec**
1/4 shot(s) **Freshly squeezed lemon juice**
1/2 shot(s) **Passion fruit syrup**
1/2 fresh **Egg white**

Origin: Formula by yours truly in 2004.
Comment: Full-on passion fruit with gin and citrus hints.

PASSION KILLER

Glass: Shot
Method: Refrigerate ingredients then **LAYER** in chilled glass by carefully pouring in the following order.

1/2 shot(s) **Midori melon liqueur**
1/2 shot(s) **Passoã passion fruit liqueur**
1/2 shot(s) **Sauza Hornitos tequila**

Comment: Tropical fruit and tequila.

PASSION PUNCH [NEW]

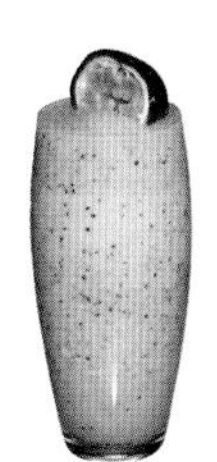

Glass: Collins (or individual scorpion bowl)
Garnish: Half passion fruit
Method: Cut passion fruit in half and scoop flesh into blender. Add other ingredients and **BLEND** with 12oz scoop crushed ice. Serve with straws.

1 fresh **Passion fruit**
2 shot(s) **Plymouth gin**
1/4 shot(s) **Rémy Martin cognac**
3/4 shot(s) **Freshly squeezed lime juice**
3/4 shot(s) **Sugar (gomme) syrup**
2 dashes **Angostura aromatic bitters**

Origin: Adapted from a recipe in the 1947-72 Trader Vic's Bartender's Guide by Victor Bergeron.
Comment: To quote the Trader, "A robust libation with the opulence of 'down under'."

PASSIONATE RUM PUNCH

Glass: Collins
Garnish: Passion fruit quarter
Method: Cut passion fruit in half and scoop out flesh into shaker. Add other ingredients, **SHAKE** with ice and fine strain into glass filled with crushed ice.

3 fresh **Passion fruit**
2 1/4 shot(s) **Wray & Nephew overproof rum**
3/4 shot(s) **Freshly squeezed lime juice**
1 shot(s) **Sugar (gomme) syrup**
1/2 shot(s) **Passion fruit syrup**

Origin: Formula by yours truly in 2004.
Comment: Rum and fruit combine brilliantly in this tropical punch style drink.

PASSOVER

Glass: Collins
Garnish: Orange slice
Method: **SHAKE** all ingredients with ice and strain into ice-filled glass.

2 shot(s) **Ketel One vodka**
1 shot(s) **Passoã passion fruit liqueur**
3 shot(s) **Freshly squeezed pink grapefruit juice**

Comment: Tropical and sweet.

PIÑA COLADA

Three Puerto Rican bartenders contest the ownership of this drink. Ramón Marrero Pérez claims to have first made it at the Caribe Hilton hotel's Beachcomber Bar in San Juan on 15th August 1954 using the then newly available Coco López cream of coconut. Ricardo Garcia, who also worked at the Caribe, says that it was he who invented the drink. But Ramón Portas Mingot says he created it in 1963 at the Barrachina Bar in Old San Juan.

It is commonly accepted that the Piña Colada was created and heavily promoted at the Caribe Hilton Hotel and the hotel credits Ramón Marrero Pérez with the invention. Opening in 1949 at a prime beachfront location, the Caribe was the first luxury hotel in San Juan and became a popular destination for the rich and famous who helped spread the popularity of the drink.

The name 'Piña Colada' literally means 'strained pineapple', a reference to the freshly pressed and strained pineapple juice used in the drink's preparation. Another essential ingredient, 'cream of coconut', is a canned, non-alcoholic, thick, syrup-like blend of coconut juice, sugar, emulsifier, cellulose, thickeners, citric acid and salt. The original brand, Coco López, was created in the early 1950s by Don Ramón López-Irizarry after receiving a development grant from the Puerto Rican government. Cream of coconut had previously been made but López-Irizarry mechanised the labour intensive process. The brand was launched in 1954 and is directly linked to the creation of the Piña Colada at the Caribe.

PAVLOVA SHOT

Glass: Shot
Method: Refrigerate ingredients then **LAYER** in chilled glass by carefully pouring in the following order.

3/4	shot(s)	**Chambord black raspberry liqueur**
3/4	shot(s)	**Ketel One vodka**

Comment: Pleasant, sweet shot.

PEACH DAIQUIRI

Glass: Martini
Garnish: Peach wedge on rim
Method: SHAKE all ingredients with ice and fine strain into chilled glass.

2	shot(s)	**Light white rum**
1	shot(s)	**Peach schnapps liqueur**
1/2	shot(s)	**Freshly squeezed lime juice**
1/2	shot(s)	**Chilled mineral water (omit if wet ice)**

Origin: My take on the Cuban Daiquiri de Melocoton.
Comment: A classic Daiquiri with a hint of peach liqueur.

PEACH MELBA MARTINI

Glass: Martini
Garnish: Float flaked almonds
Method: SHAKE all ingredients with ice and fine strain into chilled glass.

1 1/2	shot(s)	**Vanilla flavoured vodka**
3/4	shot(s)	**Peach schnapps liqueur**
3/4	shot(s)	**Chambord black raspberry liqueur**
1	shot(s)	**Double (heavy) cream**
1	shot(s)	**Milk**

Origin: Melba is a name given to various dishes dedicated to Dame Nellie Melba, the 19th century Australian opera singer. Peach Melba was created in 1892 by the world famous chef Georges-Auguste Escoffier, who was the business partner of César Ritz.
Comment: Not quite Peach Melba dessert, but rich and tasty all the same.

PEANUT BUTTER & JELLY SHOT

Glass: Shot
Method: SHAKE all ingredients with ice and fine strain into chilled glass.

1/2	shot(s)	**Chambord black raspberry liqueur**
1/2	shot(s)	**Frangelico hazelnut liqueur**
1/2	shot(s)	**Baileys Irish Cream liqueur**

Comment: Does indeed taste a little like peanut butter and jelly (jam in the UK).

PEAR & CARDAMOM SIDECAR

Glass: Martini
Garnish: Pear slice on rim
Method: MUDDLE cardamom in base of shaker. Add other ingredients, **SHAKE** with ice and fine strain into chilled glass.

2	pods	**Green cardamom**
1	shot(s)	**Rémy Martin cognac**
3/4	shot(s)	**Cointreau / triple sec**
3/4	shot(s)	**Pear & cognac liqueur**
3/4	shot(s)	**Freshly squeezed lemon juice**
1/8	shot(s)	**Sugar (gomme) syrup**
1/2	shot(s)	**Chilled mineral water (omit if wet ice)**

Origin: Adapted from a drink created in 2002 by Jason Scott at Oloroso, Edinburgh, Scotland.
Comment: A wonderful meld of aromatic ingredients.

PEAR & ELDERFLOWER MARTINI

Glass: Martini
Garnish: Pear slice on rim
Method: SHAKE all ingredients with ice and fine strain into chilled glass.

2	shot(s)	**Ketel One vodka**
2	shot(s)	**Freshly extracted pear juice**
1/2	shot(s)	**Elderflower cordial**

Origin: Created in 2001 by Angelo Vieira at St. Martins, London, England.
Comment: Pear and elderflower are a match made in St Martins Lane.

PEAR & VANILLA RICKEY

Glass: Collins
Garnish: Lime wedge
Method: SHAKE first three ingredients with ice and strain into ice-filled glass. **TOP** with 7-Up, lightly stir and serve with straws.

1	shot(s)	**Vanilla flavoured vodka**
1	shot(s)	**Pear & cognac liqueur**
1	shot(s)	**Freshly squeezed lime juice**
Top up with		**7-Up**

Comment: Vanilla and pear create a creamy mouthful cut by lime juice.

PEAR DROP

Glass: Shot
Method: SHAKE all ingredients with ice and fine strain into chilled glass.

1/2	shot(s)	**Ketel One Citroen vodka**
1/2	shot(s)	**Soho lychee liqueur**
1/2	shot(s)	**Pear & cognac liqueur**

Comment: Sweet, sticky and strong.

PEAR DROP MARTINI

Glass: Martini
Garnish: Pear drop sweet in drink
Method: **SHAKE** all ingredients with ice and fine strain into chilled glass.

1¼	shot(s)	**Pear & cognac liqueur**
1	shot(s)	**Luxardo Limoncello liqueur**
1	shot(s)	**Poire William eau de vie**
1	shot(s)	**Freshly extracted pear juice**

Origin: Created in 2002 by yours truly.
Comment: Not as sticky as the sweet it takes its name from but full-on tangy pear.

PEAR SHAPED #1 (DELUXE VERSION)

Glass: Martini
Garnish: Pear slice on rim
Method: Cut passion fruit in half and scoop out flesh into base of shaker. Add other ingredients, **SHAKE** with ice and fine strain into chilled glass.

1	fresh	**Passion fruit**
1½	shot(s)	**The Famous Grouse Scotch whisky**
1	shot(s)	**Pear & cognac liqueur**
1	shot(s)	**Freshly extracted pear juice**
1	shot(s)	**Pressed apple juice**
¼	shot(s)	**Freshly squeezed lime juice**

Comment: Wonderful balance of flavours but pear predominates with a dry yet floral finish.

PEAR SHAPED #2 (POPULAR VERSION)

Glass: Collins
Glass: Pear wedge on rim
Method: **SHAKE** all ingredients with ice and strain into ice-filled glass.

2	shot(s)	**The Famous Grouse Scotch whisky**
1	shot(s)	**Pear & cognac liqueur**
3	shot(s)	**Pressed apple juice**
½	shot(s)	**Freshly squeezed lime juice**
¼	shot(s)	**Sonoma vanilla bean sugar syrup**

Origin: Adapted from a drink created in 2003 by Jamie Terrell at Dick's Bar, Atlantic, London, England.
Comment: Scotch, pear and apple combine wonderfully in this medium-sweet long drink.

PEDRO COLLINS

Glass: Collins
Garnish: Orange slice & cherry on stick (sail)
Method: **SHAKE** first three ingredients with ice and strain into ice-filled glass. **TOP** with soda, lightly stir and serve with straws.

2	shot(s)	**Light white rum**
1	shot(s)	**Freshly squeezed lime juice**
½	shot(s)	**Sugar (gomme) syrup**
Top up with		**Soda water (club soda)**

Comment: This rum based Tom Collins is basically a long Daiquiri with soda.

PEGGY MARTINI [NEW]

Glass: Martini
Garnish: Orange zest twist
Method: **SHAKE** all ingredients with ice and fine strain into chilled glass.

2	shot(s)	**Plymouth gin**
1	shot(s)	**Dry vermouth**
¼	shot(s)	**La Fée Parisian 68% absinthe**
¼	shot(s)	**Dubonnet Red**
½	shot(s)	**Chilled mineral water (omit if wet ice)**

Origin: Adapted from a recipe in the 1930s edition of the Savoy Cocktail Book by Harry Craddock.
Comment: Very dry and aromatic. Sadly this will appeal to few palates.

PEGU CLUB [NEW]

Glass: Martini
Garnish: Lime wedge on rim
Method: **SHAKE** all ingredients with ice and fine strain into chilled glass.

2	shot(s)	**Plymouth gin**
1	shot(s)	**Cointreau / triple sec**
½	shot(s)	**Freshly squeezed lime juice**
¼	shot(s)	**Sugar (gomme) syrup**
1	dash	**Angostura aromatic bitters**
1	dash	**Fee Brothers orange bitters**
½	shot(s)	**Chilled mineral water (omit if wet ice)**

Origin: Created in the 1920s at the Pegu Club, an expat gentlemen's club in British colonial Rangoon, Burma.
The recipe was first published in Harry MacElhone's 1927 'Barflies and Cocktails'. In his seminal 1930 Savoy Cocktail Book, Harry Craddock notes of this drink, "The favourite cocktail of the Pegu Club, Burma, and one that has travelled, and is asked for, round the world."
Comment: I've added a dash of sugar to the original recipe to reduce the tartness of this gin based Margarita-like concoction.

PENDENNIS COCKTAIL [NEW]

Glass: Martini
Garnish: Maraschino cherry
Method: **SHAKE** all ingredients with ice and fine strain into chilled glass.

2	shot(s)	**Plymouth gin**
1	shot(s)	**Bols apricot brandy liqueur**
½	shot(s)	**Freshly squeezed lime juice**
1	dash	**Peychauds aromatic bitters**
¾	shot(s)	**Chilled mineral water (omit if wet ice)**

Origin: This classic is named after the Pendennis Club in Louisville, Kentucky, which is popularly supposed to be the birthplace of the Old-fashioned.
Comment: Tangy, subtle, sweet and sour.

A B C D E F G H I J K L M N N P Q R S T U V W X Y Z

PISCO PUNCH

The creation of the Pisco Punch is usually credited to Professor Jerry Burns of San Francisco's Bank Exchange. However, its origin could lie in the late 1800s, when the drink was served aboard steamships stopping in Chile en route to San Francisco. The following story of the Pisco Punch and the Bank Exchange comes from the 1973 edition of the California Historical Quarterly and Robert O'Brien's book, 'This Was San Francisco'.

The Bank Exchange was a ballroom that opened in 1854 and survived the earthquake and fire of 1906. Its popularity never waned and only Prohibition brought about its demise. Much of the Bank Exchange's notoriety was due to the Pisco Punch, so much so that the establishment gained the nickname 'Pisco John's' after one of its original owners.

The recipe was handed down from owner to owner in absolute secrecy. Duncan Nichol, the Scottish immigrant who owned the bar from the late 1870s until it closed, inherited it from the previous owners, Orrin Dorman and John Torrence, and is thought to have carried it to his grave.

PEPPER & VANILLA'TINI

Glass: Martini
Garnish: Strip yellow pepper
Method: **SHAKE** all ingredients with ice and fine strain into chilled glass.

1	shot(s)	Vanilla-infused Ketel One vodka
3/4	shot(s)	Pepper vodka
1	shot(s)	Cuarenta Y Tres (Licor 43) liqueur
3/4	shot(s)	Tuaca liqueur
1	shot(s)	Freshly extracted yellow bell pepper juice

Origin: Created in 2002 by yours truly.
Comment: Vanilla and pepper seem to complement each other in a sweet and sour kind of way.

PEPPERED MARY

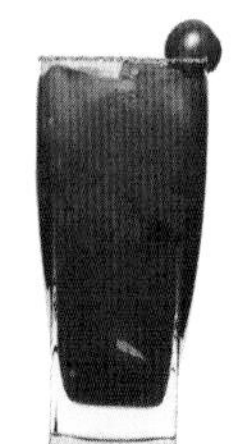

Glass: Collins
Garnish: Peppered rim & cherry tomato
Method: **SHAKE** all ingredients with ice and fine strain into chilled glass.

2	shot(s)	Pepper vodka
2	shot(s)	Freshly extracted yellow bell pepper juice
2	shot(s)	Pressed tomato juice
1/2	shot(s)	Freshly squeezed lemon juice
7	drops	Tabasco hot pepper sauce
1	spoon	Lea & Perrins Worcestershire sauce

Origin: Created in 2003 by yours truly.
Comment: Hot and sweet pepper spice this Bloody Mary.

PERFECT ALIBI

Glass: Collins
Garnish: Mint leaf & lime squeeze
Method: **MUDDLE** ginger in base of shaker. Add other ingredients, **SHAKE** with ice and fine strain into ice-filled glass.

2	fresh	Thumb-nail sized slices root ginger
1/2	shot(s)	Sugar (gomme) syrup
1 1/2	shot(s)	Krupnik honey liqueur
1/2	shot(s)	Bärenjäger honey liqueur
3	shot(s)	Cold black jasmine tea (fairly weak)

Origin: Created in 2001 by Douglas Ankrah for Akbar, London, England.
Comment: A very unusual and pleasant mix of flavours.

PERFECT JOHN

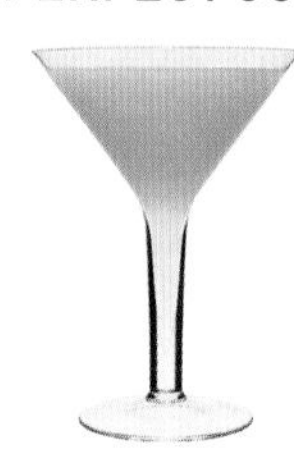

Glass: Martini
Garnish: Orange zest twist
Method: **SHAKE** all ingredients with ice and fine strain into chilled glass.

1	shot(s)	Ketel One vodka
3/4	shot(s)	Cointreau / triple sec
1 1/2	shot(s)	Freshly squeezed orange juice
1/4	shot(s)	Galliano liqueur

Comment: A straight-up Harvey Wallbanger with Cointreau.

PERFECT MARTINI [NEW]

Glass: Martini
Garnish: Orange zest twist
Method: **SHAKE** all ingredients with ice and fine strain into chilled glass.

1 1/4	shot(s)	Plymouth gin
1 1/4	shot(s)	Dry vermouth
1 1/4	shot(s)	Sweet (rosso) vermouth
1	dash	Fee Brothers orange bitters (optional)

Variant: Merry-Go-Round Martini
Origin: Adapted from a recipe in the 1930 edition of the Savoy Cocktail Book by Harry Craddock.
Comment: The high proportion of vermouth makes this Martini almost sherry-like.

PERIODISTA DAIQUIRI [NEW]

Glass: Martini
Garnish: Lime wedge
Method: **SHAKE** all ingredients with ice and fine strain into chilled glass.

1 1/2	shot(s)	Light white rum
1/2	shot(s)	Freshly squeezed lime juice
1/2	shot(s)	Grand Marnier liqueur
1/2	shot(s)	Apricot brandy liqueur
1/2	shot(s)	Chilled mineral water (omit if wet ice)

Comment: Basically an orange and apricot Daiquiri.

PERNOD & BLACK MARTINI

Glass: Martini
Garnish: Blackberries
Method: **MUDDLE** blackberries in base of shaker. Add other ingredients, **SHAKE** with ice and fine strain into chilled glass.

7	fresh	Blackberries
1/2	shot(s)	Pernod anis
1 1/2	shot(s)	Ketel One vodka
1/2	shot(s)	Bols blackberry (crème de mûre) liqueur
1	shot(s)	Freshly squeezed lime juice
1/8	shot(s)	Sonoma vanilla bean sugar syrup
3/4	shot(s)	Chilled mineral water (omit if wet ice)

Origin: Created in 2003 by yours truly.
Comment: Pernod enhances the rich, tart flavours of blackberry.

PERROQUET

Glass: Collins (10oz / 290ml max)
Method: **POUR** pastis and mint syrup into glass. Serve iced water separately in a small jug (known in France as a 'broc') so the customer can dilute to their own taste (I recommend five shots). Lastly, add ice to fill glass.

1	shot(s)	Ricard pastis
1/4	shot(s)	Green mint (menthe) syrup
Top up with		Chilled mineral water

Origin: Very popular throughout France, this drink is named after the parrot due to the bird's brightly coloured plumage.
Comment: The traditional French café drink with a hint of sweet mint.

PERRY-TINI

Glass: Martini
Garnish: Pear slice on rim
Method: **SHAKE** first three ingredients with ice and fine strain into chilled glass. **TOP** with champagne.

1 shot(s) **Poire William eau de vie**
1 shot(s) **Pear & cognac liqueur**
2 shot(s) **Freshly extracted pear juice**
Top up with **Piper-Heidsieck brut champagne**

Origin: Created in 2002 by yours truly.
Comment: Pear with a hint of sparkle.

PETER PAN MARTINI [NEW]

Glass: Martini
Garnish: Orange zest twist
Method: **SHAKE** all ingredients with ice and fine strain into chilled glass.

2 shot(s) **Plymouth gin**
1 shot(s) **Dry vermouth**
1 shot(s) **Freshly squeezed orange juice**
3 dashes **Fee Brother's peach bitters**

Origin: Adapted from a recipe in the 1930 edition of the Savoy Cocktail Book by Harry Craddock.
Comment: Orange predominates in this complex cocktail.

PETTO MARTINI [NEW]

Glass: Martini
Garnish: Orange zest twist
Method: **SHAKE** all ingredients with ice and fine strain into chilled glass.

2 shot(s) **Plymouth gin**
1 shot(s) **Dry vermouth**
1 shot(s) **Sweet (rosso) vermouth**
¼ shot(s) **Freshly squeezed orange juice**
⅛ shot(s) **Luxardo maraschino liqueur**

Origin: Adapted from a recipe in the 1930 edition of the Savoy Cocktail Book by Harry Craddock.
Comment: A wonderfully aromatic classic Martini served 'perfect' with a hint of orange juice and maraschino.

PHARMACEUTICAL STIMULANT

Glass: Old-fashioned
Garnish: Float three coffee beans
Method: **SHAKE** all ingredients with ice and strain into ice-filled glass.

2 shot(s) **Ketel One vodka**
½ shot(s) **Kahlúa coffee liqueur**
2 shot(s) **Espresso coffee (cold)**
¼ shot(s) **Sugar (gomme) syrup**

Origin: Created in 1998 by Dick Bradsell at The Pharmacy, London, England.
Comment: A real wake-up call and the drink that led to many an Espresso Martini.

PICCA

Glass: Martini
Garnish: Maraschino cherry
Method: **SHAKE** all ingredients with ice and fine strain into chilled glass.

1½ shot(s) **The Famous Grouse Scotch whisky**
1 shot(s) **Galliano liqueur**
1 shot(s) **Sweet (rosso) vermouth**
¾ shot(s) **Chilled mineral water (omit if wet ice)**

Comment: Bittersweet whisky.

PICCADILLY MARTINI [NEW]

Glass: Martini
Garnish: Lemon zest twist
Method: **SHAKE** all ingredients with ice and fine strain into chilled glass.

2 shot(s) **Plymouth gin**
1 shot(s) **Dry vermouth**
⅛ shot(s) **La Fée Parisian 68% absinthe**
⅛ shot(s) **Sonoma pomegranate (grenadine) syrup**

Origin: Adapted from a recipe in Harry Craddock's 1930 Savoy Cocktail Book.
Comment: A classic Martini tempered by a hint of pomegranate and absinthe.

PICHUNCHO MARTINI

Glass: Martini
Garnish: Orange zest twist
Method: **SHAKE** all ingredients with ice and fine strain into a chilled glass.

2¼ shot(s) **Pisco**
1½ shot(s) **Sweet (rosso) vermouth**
¼ shot(s) **Sugar (gomme) syrup**

Origin: Based on a traditional Chilean drink: pisco and vermouth served on the rocks.
Comment: This drink craves the best pisco and the best sweet vermouth. Find those and measure carefully and it's sublime.

PIERRE COLLINS

Glass: Collins
Garnish: Orange slice & cherry on stick (sail)
Method: **SHAKE** first three ingredients with ice and strain into ice-filled glass. **TOP** with soda, lightly stir and serve with straws.

2 shot(s) **Rémy Martin cognac**
1 shot(s) **Freshly squeezed lemon juice**
½ shot(s) **Sugar (gomme) syrup**
Top up with **Soda water (club soda)**

Comment: A Tom Collins made with cognac. The cognac's character shines through.

PILGRIM COCKTAIL

Glass: Martini
Garnish: Dust with grated nutmeg
Method: **SHAKE** all ingredients with ice and fine strain into chilled glass.

1½	shot(s)	Mount Gay Eclipse golden rum
½	shot(s)	Grand Marnier liqueur
1	shot(s)	Freshly squeezed orange juice
¾	shot(s)	Freshly squeezed lime juice
¼	shot(s)	World's End Pimento Dram liqueur
3	dashes	Angostura aromatic bitters

Variant: Can also be served hot by simmering ingredients gently in a saucepan.
Comment: Whether you serve this hot or cold, it's a delicately spiced drink to warm the cockles.

PIMM'S COCKTAIL

Glass: Martini
Garnish: Lemon & orange zest twist
Method: **SHAKE** first four ingredients with ice and strain into chilled glass. **TOP** with champagne.

2	shot(s)	Pimm's No.1 Cup
½	shot(s)	Plymouth gin
¼	shot(s)	Freshly squeezed lemon juice
¼	shot(s)	Sugar (gomme) syrup
Top up with		Piper-Heidsieck brut champagne

Comment: Luxuriate in this quintessentially English tipple.

PIMM'S CUP (OR CLASSIC) [UPDATED]

Glass: Collins
Garnish: Mint sprig
Method: **POUR** Pimm's into glass half filled with ice. Add fruit and fill glass with more ice. **TOP** with 7-Up (or ginger ale), lightly stir and serve with straws.

2	shot(s)	Pimm's No. 1 Cup
1	slice	Lemon
1	slice	Orange
2	slices	Cucumber
1	sliced	Strawberry
Top up with		7-Up (or ginger ale)

Origin: Usually credited to James Pimm in 1840 but more likely to have been first made by Samuel Morey in the 1860s.
Comment: You've not properly experienced an English summer until you've drunk one of these whilst sheltering from the rain.

PIMM'S ROYAL

Glass: Flute
Garnish: Berries on stick with cucumber peel
Method: **POUR** Pimm's into chilled glass and **TOP** with champagne.

1	shot(s)	Pimm's No.1 Cup
Top up with		Piper-Heidsieck brut champagne

Comment: Dry, subtle and refreshing.

PIÑA MARTINI [NEW]

Glass: Martini
Garnish: Pineapple wedge on rim
Method: **SHAKE** all ingredients with ice and fine strain into chilled glass.

2	shot(s)	Ketel One vodka
1¾	shot(s)	Pressed pineapple juice
¼	shot(s)	Freshly squeezed lime juice
⅛	shot(s)	Sugar (gomme) syrup

Origin: Created in 2005 by yours truly.
Comment: Rich pineapple but not too sweet.

PIÑA COLADA

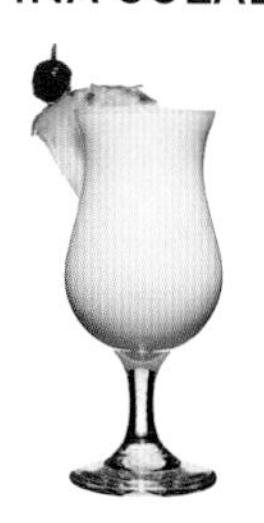

Glass: Hurricane (or hollowed out pineapple)
Garnish: Pineapple wedge & cherry
Method: **BLEND** all ingredients with one 12oz scoop crushed ice and serve with straws.

2	shot(s)	Mount Gay golden rum
3	shot(s)	Pressed pineapple juice
2	shot(s)	Coco López cream of coconut
½	shot(s)	Double (heavy) cream

Variant: Made with dark rums.
Comment: A wonderful creamy, fruity concoction that's not half as sticky as the world would have you believe. Too much ice will detract from the creaminess and kill the drink.

PIÑA COLADA VIRGIN (MOCKTAIL)

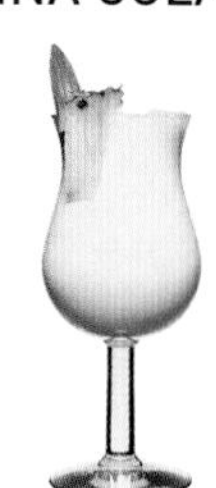

Glass: Hurricane
Garnish: Pineapple wedge & cherry on rim
Method: **BLEND** all ingredients with 18oz of crushed ice and serve with straws.

6	shot(s)	Pressed pineapple juice
¾	shot(s)	Double (heavy) cream
¾	shot(s)	Milk
2	shot(s)	Coco López cream of coconut

AKA: Snow White
Comment: A Piña Colada with its guts ripped out.

PINEAPPLE & CARDAMOM DAIQUIRI

Glass: Martini
Garnish: Pineapple wedge on rim
Method: **MUDDLE** cardamom in base of shaker. Add other ingredients, **SHAKE** with ice and fine strain into chilled glass.

4	pods	Green cardamom
2	shot(s)	Light white rum
1¾	shot(s)	Pressed pineapple juice
¼	shot(s)	Freshly squeezed lime juice
¼	shot(s)	Sugar (gomme) syrup

Origin: Adapted from Henry Besant's Pineapple & Cardamom Martini.
Comment: One of the tastiest Daiquiris I've tried.

PINEAPPLE & CARDAMOM MARTINI

Glass: Martini
Garnish: Pineapple wedge on rim
Method: **MUDDLE** cardamom in base of shaker. Add other ingredients, **SHAKE** with ice and fine strain into chilled glass.

4	pods	**Green cardamom**
2	shot(s)	**Ketel One vodka**
2	shot(s)	**Pressed pineapple juice**
1/4	shot(s)	**Sugar (gomme) syrup**

Origin: Created in 2002 by Henry Besant at Lonsdale House, London, England.
Comment: This is about as good as it gets: a spectacular pairing of fruit and spice.

PINEAPPLE & GINGER MARTINI

Glass: Martini
Garnish: Pineapple wedge on rim
Method: **MUDDLE** ginger in base of shaker. Add other ingredients, **SHAKE** with ice and fine strain into chilled glass.

2	slices	**Fresh root ginger (thumbnail sized)**
2	shot(s)	**Ketel One vodka**
2	shot(s)	**Pressed pineapple juice**
1/8	shot(s)	**Sugar (gomme) syrup**

Comment: Smooth, rich pineapple flavour with hints of vodka and ginger.

PINEAPPLE & SAGE MARGARITA [NEW]

Glass: Coupette
Garnish: Pineapple wedge on rim
Method: Lightly **MUDDLE** sage in base of shaker. Add other ingredients, **SHAKE** with ice and fine strain into chilled glass.

5	fresh	**Sage leaves**
2	shot(s)	**Sauza Hornitos tequila**
1	shot(s)	**Pressed pineapple juice**
1/2	shot(s)	**Freshly squeezed lime juice**
1/4	shot(s)	**Agave syrup (from health food store)**

Origin: Adapted from a drink created in 2005 at Green & Red Bar, London, England.
Comment: Herbal tequila and sweet pineapple in harmony.

PINEAPPLE BLOSSOM

Glass: Martini
Garnish: Pineapple wedge on rim
Method: **SHAKE** all ingredients with ice and fine strain into chilled glass.

2	shot(s)	**The Famous Grouse Scotch whisky**
1	shot(s)	**Pressed pineapple juice**
1/2	shot(s)	**Freshly squeezed lemon juice**
1/2	shot(s)	**Sugar (gomme) syrup**

Origin: My interpretation of a classic.
Comment: Richly flavoured but drier than you might expect.

PINEAPPLE DAIQUIRI #1 (ON-THE-ROCKS) [NEW]

Glass: Old-fashioned
Garnish: Pineapple wedge & cherry
Method: **SHAKE** all ingredients with ice and fine strain into ice-filled glass.

2	shot(s)	**Light white rum**
1	shot(s)	**Pressed pineapple juice**
1/2	shot(s)	**Freshly squeezed lime juice**
1/4	shot(s)	**Sugar (gomme) syrup**

Origin: Formula by yours truly.
Comment: Rum and pineapple are just meant to go together.

PINEAPPLE DAIQUIRI #2 (FROZEN) [NEW]

Glass: Martini (Large)
Garnish: Pineapple wedge & cherry
Method: **BLEND** all ingredients with two 12oz scoops crushed ice and serve with straws.

2	shot(s)	**Light white rum**
1 1/2	shot(s)	**Pressed pineapple juice**
1/2	shot(s)	**Freshly squeezed lime juice**
3/4	shot(s)	**Sugar (gomme) syrup**

Origin: Formula by yours truly.
Comment: Fluffy but very tasty.

PINEAPPLE FIZZ

Glass: Collins
Garnish: Lime wedge & cherry
Method: **SHAKE** first four ingredients with ice and strain into ice-filled glass. **TOP** with soda, lightly stir and serve with straws.

2	shot(s)	**Mount Gay Eclipse golden rum**
1 1/2	shot(s)	**Pressed pineapple juice**
1	shot(s)	**Freshly squeezed lime juice**
1/2	shot(s)	**Sugar (gomme) syrup**
Top up with		**Soda water (club soda)**

Comment: A Pineapple Daiquiri lengthened with soda. Surprisingly tasty and refreshing.

PINEAPPLE MARGARITA

Glass: Coupette
Garnish: Pineapple wedge on rim
Method: **SHAKE** all ingredients with ice and fine strain into chilled glass.

2	shot(s)	**Sauza Hornitos tequila**
3/4	shot(s)	**Cointreau / triple sec**
1 1/2	shot(s)	**Pressed pineapple juice**

Variant: Add half a shot of pineapple syrup, blend with 12oz scoop of crushed ice and serve frozen.
Comment: A Tequila Margarita with a pineapple fruit kick.

PINEAPPLE MOJITO

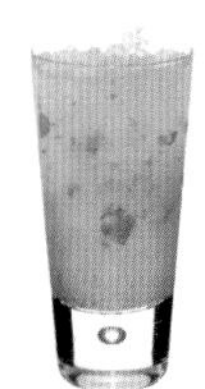

Glass: Collins
Method: Lightly **MUDDLE** mint (just to bruise) in glass. **POUR** other ingredients into glass and half fill with crushed ice. **CHURN** (stir) with barspoon. Fill glass with more crushed ice, churn and serve with straws.

12	fresh	Mint leaves
2	shot(s)	Light white rum
3/4	shot(s)	Cuarenta Y Tres (Licor 43) liqueur
2	shot(s)	Pressed pineapple juice
1	shot(s)	Freshly squeezed lime juice

Origin: Discovered in 2003 at Apartment 195, London, England.
Comment: A fruity, vanilla-ed twist on the classic Mojito.

PINEAPPLE SMOOTHIE (MOCKTAIL) [NEW]

Glass: Collins
Garnish: Pineapple wedge
Method: **BLEND** all ingredients with 12oz scoop crushed ice. Serve with straws.

2 tblspoon		Natural yoghurt
2 tblspoon		Runny honey
4	shot(s)	Pressed pineapple juice

Comment: Fluffy in every sense of the word.

PINI [NEW]

Glass: Martini
Garnish: Maraschino cherry
Method: **SHAKE** all ingredients with ice and fine strain into chilled glass.

2	shot(s)	Pisco
1/2	shot(s)	Rémy Martin cognac
1/4	shot(s)	Bols white crème de cacao
1/4	shot(s)	Sugar (gomme) syrup
1/2	shot(s)	Chilled mineral water (omit if wet ice)

Comment: Use a great pisco and you'll have a wonderfully complex drink.

PINK CLOUD [NEW]

Glass: Martini
Method: **SHAKE** all ingredients with ice and fine strain into chilled glass.

1	shot(s)	Luxardo Amaretto di Saschira liqueur
1	shot(s)	Sonoma pomegranate (grenadine) syrup
1	shot(s)	Bols white crème de cacao
3/4	shot(s)	Evaporated milk (sweetened)

Origin: Adapted from a recipe in the 1947-72 Trader Vic's Bartender's Guide by Victor Bergeron.
Comment: To make this sweet after dinner drink I've used amaretto and pomegranate syrup in place of crème de noyaux. This almond flavoured liqueur made from apricot and peach stones is not currently available in the UK. US readers should use 2 shots of crème de noyaux in place of the first two ingredients.

PINK DAIQUIRI [NEW]

Glass: Martini
Garnish: Lime wedge on rim
Method: **SHAKE** all ingredients with ice and fine strain into chilled glass.

2	shot(s)	Light white rum
1/2	shot(s)	Freshly squeezed lime juice
1/2	shot(s)	Sonoma pomegranate (grenadine) syrup
1/4	shot(s)	Luxardo maraschino liqueur
3	dashes	Angostura aromatic bitters
1/2	shot(s)	Chilled mineral water (omit if wet ice)

AKA: Daiquiri No.5
Origin: A classic from the 1930s.
Comment: The quality of pomegranate syrup will make or break this delicate Daiquiri.

PINK FLAMINGO

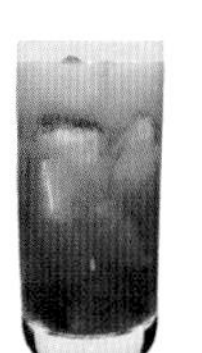

Glass: Collins
Garnish: Apple wheel
Method: **SHAKE** all ingredients with ice and fine strain into chilled glass.

2	shot(s)	Orange flavoured vodka
1	shot(s)	Sour apple liqueur
1/2	shot(s)	Freshly squeezed lime juice
1	shot(s)	Cranberry juice

Origin: Created in 2002 by Wayne Collins for Maxxium UK.
Comment: Soapy and citrus flavoured – but in a nice way.

PINK GIN #1 (TRADITIONAL) [UPDATED]

Glass: Martini
Garnish: Lemon zest twist
Method: **RINSE** chilled glass with Angostura bitters. **POUR** gin and water into rinsed glass and **STIR**.

2	dashes	Angostura aromatic bitters
2	shot(s)	Plymouth gin (from freezer)
2	shot(s)	Chilled mineral water

Origin: Gin was a favourite of the Royal Navy – along with rum, which was served as a daily ration right up until the 70s. It was often mixed with healthy ingredients to make them more palatable. Pink gin was originally used against stomach upsets, as Angostura aromatic bitters were considered medicinal.
Comment: A traditionally made Pink Gin without ice.

PINK GIN #2 (MODERN)

Glass: Martini
Garnish: Lemon zest twist
Method: **STIR** all ingredients with ice and strain into chilled glass.

2	shot(s)	Plymouth gin
2	shot(s)	Chilled mineral water
1	dash	Angostura aromatic bitters

Comment: Normally I'd advocate liberal use of Angostura bitters but this refined and subtle drink benefits from frugality.

PINK GIN & TONIC

Glass: Collins
Garnish: Lime slice
Method: **POUR** gin and Angostura bitters into ice-filled glass, **TOP** with tonic, lightly stir and serve with straws.

2	shot(s)	**Plymouth gin**
4	dashes	**Angostura aromatic bitters**
Top up with		**Tonic water**

Comment: Basically a G&T with an extra pep of flavour from Angostura, this has a wider appeal than the original Pink Gin.

PINK GRAPEFRUIT MARGARITA [NEW]

Glass: Coupette
Garnish: Lime wedge on rim
Method: **SHAKE** all ingredients with ice and fine strain into chilled glass.

2	shot(s)	**Sauza Hornitos tequila**
1	shot(s)	**Freshly squeezed pink grapefruit juice**
1/2	shot(s)	**Freshly squeezed lime juice**
1/4	shot(s)	**Sugar (gomme) syrup**

Comment: Delivers exactly what the name promises.

PINK HOUND

Glass: Martini
Garnish: Lemon zest twist
Method: **SHAKE** all ingredients with ice and fine strain into chilled glass.

2	shot(s)	**Plymouth gin**
1 3/4	shot(s)	**Freshly squeezed pink grapefruit juice**
1/4	shot(s)	**Sugar (gomme) syrup**

Comment: A flavoursome balance of sweet and sour.

PINK LADY [UPDATED]

Glass: Martini
Garnish: Lemon zest twist
Method: **SHAKE** all ingredients with ice and fine strain into chilled glass.

2	shot(s)	**Plymouth gin**
1/2	shot(s)	**Freshly squeezed lemon juice**
1/2	shot(s)	**Sonoma pomegranate (grenadine) syrup**
1/2	fresh	**Egg white (optional)**

Variant: With the addition of half a shot apple brandy.
Origin: A classic cocktail named after a successful 1912 stage play.
Comment: Despite the colour, this is sharp and alcoholic.

PINK LEMONADE (MOCKTAIL)

Glass: Collins
Garnish: Lemon slice
Method: **SHAKE** first three ingredients with ice and strain into ice-filled glass. **TOP** with soda and serve with straws.

2	shot(s)	**Freshly squeezed lemon juice**
1/2	shot(s)	**Sonoma pomegranate (grenadine) syrup**
1/4	shot(s)	**Sugar (gomme) syrup**
Top up with		**Soda water (club soda)**

Origin: Discovered in 2004 in New York City.
Comment: A tall, pink, tangy, alcohol free cocktail.

PINK PALACE [NEW]

Glass: Martini
Garnish: Lemon twist
Method: **SHAKE** all ingredients with ice and fine strain into chilled glass.

2	shot(s)	**Plymouth gin**
1/2	shot(s)	**Grand Marnier**
1/2	shot(s)	**Freshly squeezed lemon juice**
1/4	shot(s)	**Sonoma pomegranate (grenadine) syrup**

Origin: The signature drink at The Polo Lounge, Beverly Hills Hotel, Los Angeles, USA. The hotel, which is lovingly termed the 'Pink Palace', inspired The Eagles' Hotel California and graces the album cover.
Comment: A great drink but rarely done justice at the Polo Lounge.

PINK SIN MARTINI

Glass: Martini
Garnish: Dust with cinnamon powder
Method: **SHAKE** all ingredients with ice and fine strain into chilled glass.

1 1/2	shot(s)	**Ketel One vodka**
1	shot(s)	**Bols white crème de cacao**
3/4	shot(s)	**Goldschläger cinnamon schnapps liqueur**
1	shot(s)	**Cranberry juice**

Comment: This looks a little like a Cosmo but delivers sweet cinnamon and chocolate.

PINK TUTU

Glass: Old-fashioned
Garnish: Orange slice
Method: **SHAKE** all ingredients with ice and strain into ice-filled glass.

1	shot(s)	**Peach schnapps liqueur**
1/2	shot(s)	**Ketel One vodka**
1/2	shot(s)	**Campari**
2	shot(s)	**Freshly squeezed grapefruit juice**
1/4	shot(s)	**Sugar (gomme) syrup**

Origin: Created in 1999 by Dominique of Café Rouge, Leeds, England.
Comment: A cocktail that's both bitter and sweet.

PINKY PINCHER [NEW]

Glass: Old-fashioned
Garnish: Mint sprig, orange & lemon slice
Method: **SHAKE** all ingredients with ice and strain into ice-filled glass.

2	shot(s)	**Bourbon whiskey**
1	shot(s)	**Freshly squeezed orange juice**
1	shot(s)	**Freshly squeezed lemon juice**
$\frac{1}{4}$	shot(s)	**Orgeat (almond) sugar syrup**
$\frac{1}{4}$	shot(s)	**Sugar (gomme) syrup**

Origin: Adapted from a drink created by Victor Bergeron (Trader Vic).
Comment: Fruity, sweetened bourbon.

PINO PEPE [NEW]

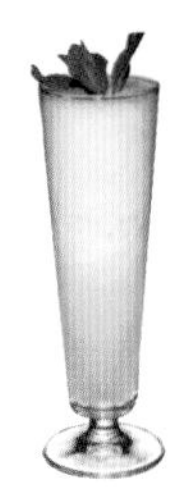

Glass: Sling (or pineapple shell)
Garnish: Mint sprig
Method: **BLEND** all ingredients with 12oz scoop crushed ice. Pour into glass (or pineapple shell) and serve with straws. If using a pineapple shell, serve with ice cubes.

1	shot(s)	**Light white rum**
1	shot(s)	**Ketel One vodka**
$\frac{1}{2}$	shot(s)	**Cointreau /triple sec**
2	shot(s)	**Pressed pineapple juice**
$\frac{1}{2}$	shot(s)	**Freshly squeezed lime juice**
$\frac{1}{4}$	shot(s)	**Freshly squeezed lemon juice**
$\frac{1}{2}$	shot(s)	**Sugar (gomme) syrup**

Origin: Adapted from a recipe in the 1947-72 Trader Vic's Bartender's Guide by Victor Bergeron.
Comment: To quote Trader Vic, "Lethal but smooth – pineapple at its best".

PIRATE DAIQUIRI

Glass: Martini
Garnish: Lime wedge on rim
Method: **SHAKE** all ingredients with ice and fine strain into chilled glass.

$\frac{3}{4}$	shot(s)	**Wray & Nephew overproof rum**
$\frac{3}{4}$	shot(s)	**Pusser's Navy rum**
$\frac{1}{2}$	shot(s)	**Goldschläger cinnamon schnapps liqueur**
$\frac{1}{2}$	shot(s)	**Freshly squeezed lime juice**
$\frac{1}{4}$	shot(s)	**Sonoma pomegranate (grenadine) syrup**
$\frac{3}{4}$	shot(s)	**Chilled mineral water (omit if wet ice)**

Origin: Created in 2004 by yours truly.
Comment: Why the name? Well, the rums are hard and nautical, the lime protects against scurvy, the liqueur contains gold and the syrup is red as blood.

DRINKS ARE GRADED AS FOLLOWS:

● DISGUSTING ●◐ PRETTY AWFUL ●● BEST AVOIDED
●●◐ DISAPPOINTING ●●● ACCEPTABLE ●●●◐ GOOD
●●●● RECOMMENDED ●●●●◐ HIGHLY RECOMMENDED
●●●●● OUTSTANDING / EXCEPTIONAL

PISCO COLLINS

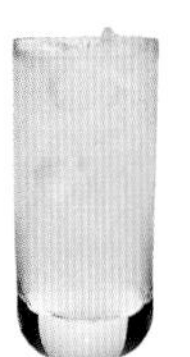

Glass: Collins
Garnish: Orange slice & cherry on stick (sail)
Method: **SHAKE** first three ingredients with ice and strain into ice-filled glass. **TOP** with soda, lightly stir and serve with straws.

2	shot(s)	**Pisco**
1	shot(s)	**Freshly squeezed lime juice**
$\frac{1}{2}$	shot(s)	**Sugar (gomme) syrup**
Top up with		**Soda water (club soda)**

Comment: The most aromatic and flavoursome of the Collins family.

PISCO PUNCH #1 (DIFFORD'S FORMULA)

Glass: Collins
Garnish: Pineapple wedge on rim
Method: **MUDDLE** cloves in base of shaker. Add other ingredients except for champagne, **SHAKE** with ice and strain into ice-filled glass. **TOP** with champagne.

4	dried	**Cloves**
$2\frac{1}{4}$	shot(s)	**Pisco**
$1\frac{3}{4}$	shot(s)	**Pressed pineapple juice**
$\frac{1}{4}$	shot(s)	**Freshly squeezed orange juice**
$\frac{1}{2}$	shot(s)	**Freshly squeezed lemon juice**
$\frac{1}{2}$	shot(s)	**Sugar (gomme) syrup**
Top up with		**Piper-Heidsieck brut champagne**

Origin: Created in 2003 by yours truly.
Variant: This recipe is improved by using the marinade prescribed in Alfredo Micheli's Pisco Punch in place of sugar syrup. If using the marinade drop one of the marinated pineapple wedges and cloves into the drink as the garnish.
Comment: A tangy, balanced combination of rich flavours. The quality of pisco used is crucial to the success of a Pisco Punch.

PISCO PUNCH #2 (ALFREDO MICHELI'S FORMULA)

Glass: Goblet
Garnish: Pineapple wedge on rim
Method: **MUDDLE** orange and pineapple in base of shaker. Add pisco and pineapple marinade, **SHAKE** with ice and fine strain into ice-filled glass. **TOP** with no more than 2 shots of soda water.

2	fresh	**Orange slices**
3		**Marinaded pineapple wedges**
2	shot(s)	**Pisco**
$\frac{3}{4}$	shot(s)	**Pineapple marinade**
Top up with		**Soda water (club soda)**

Recipe for marinade: Core and remove the rind from one ripe pineapple. Cut the pineapple into rings and then into wedges and place in a deep container. Add 30 cloves and one litre of sugar syrup and marinate for 24 hours.
Origin: Alfredo Micheli (who went by the nickname Mike) was employed at the Bank Exchange and spied on Duncan Nichol to learn how to make this legendary drink. After he believed he'd learnt the secret he left to start serving at a newly opened competitor to the Bank Exchange, Paoli's on Montgomery Street.
Comment: This subtly flavoured drink is justifiably legendary.

PUNCH

Long before the Martini, the V-shaped glass and the cocktail shaker, the drink of choice at society gatherings was punch and the punch bowl was the centre of activity at every party. Punch had existed in India for centuries before colonialists brought it back to Europe some time in the latter half of the 1600s. The name derives from the Hindi word for five, 'panch', and refers to the five key ingredients: alcohol, citrus, sugar, water and spices.

In India, it was made with arrack (the Arabic word for liquor and a local spirit distilled from palm sap or sugar cane). Back in Britain it was common for punches to be spiced with nutmeg or tea.

The classic proportions of a punch follow a mnemonic, 'one of sour, two of sweet, three of strong and four of weak.' It refers to lime juice, sugar, rum and water: the fifth element, spice, was added to taste. To fill a Collins glass I translate it as follows - all shaken with ice, strained and served over crushed ice.

1 sour =	3/4 shot(s)	**Freshly squeezed lemon or lime juice**
2 sweet =	1 1/2 shot(s)	**Sugar (gomme) syrup (sweet)**
3 strong =	2 1/4 shot(s)	**Spirit (preferably overproof)**
4 weak =	3 shot(s)	**Chilled mineral water (or fruit juice)**
5 spice =	3 dashes	**Angostura aromatic bitters**

The basic punch principle of balancing sweet and sour with spirit and dilution remains key to making a good cocktail to this day. Indeed, the essential punch ingredients - spirit, citrus, sugar and water - lie at the centre of most modern day cocktails including the Daiquiri, Sour, Margarita, Caipirinha and Sidecar. Today's hip bartenders are now also reintroducing the fifth punch ingredient by muddling or macerating herbs and spices in their cocktails.

Two traditional punches remain on today's cocktail lists, the 'Rum Punch' and the 'Hot Whisky Punch', now better known as the 'Hot Toddy'. Also bear in mind that the Gin Punch probably led to the creation of the Collins.

PISCO PUNCH #3 (LANES' FORMULA) [UPDATED]

Glass: Collins
Garnish: Pineapple wedge on rim
Method: **SHAKE** first four ingredients with ice and strain into glass filled with crushed ice. **TOP** with soda, lightly stir and serve with straws.

2½	shot(s)	**Pisco**
½	shot(s)	**Freshly squeezed lemon juice**
1	shot(s)	**Pressed pineapple juice**
½	shot(s)	**Sugar (gomme) syrup**
Top up with		**Soda water (club soda)**

Origin: This recipe is said to herald from John Lanes, manager of the famous Bank Exchange when it closed in 1919.
Comment: Pisco's character comes through the fruit in this long, refreshing classic.

PISCO PUNCH #4 (PROSSER'S FORMULA)

Glass: Martini
Garnish: Grapes on rim
Method: **MUDDLE** grapes in base of shaker. Add other ingredients, **SHAKE** with ice and fine strain into chilled glass.

20	fresh	**Seedless white grapes**
2½	shot(s)	**Pisco**
1	shot(s)	**Pressed pineapple juice**
⅛	shot(s)	**La Fée Parisian 68% absinthe**

Origin: Jack Koeppler, the bartender at the Buena Vista Café in San Francisco who's also famous for being the first bartender in America to serve Irish Coffee, was given this recipe by the son of its creator, a fellow San Franciscan by the name of Mr Prosser. I've adapted this recipe from his, which originally comprised: 2 shots white grape juice, 2 shots pisco, 1 spoon pineapple juice and 1 spoon absinthe.
Comment: An aromatic take on the Pisco Punch.

PISCO NARANJA

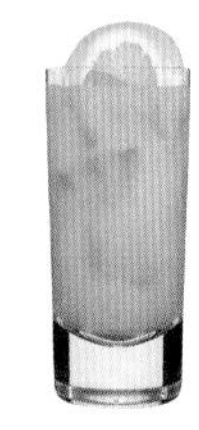

Glass: Collins
Garnish: Orange slice
Method: **SHAKE** all ingredients with ice and strain into ice-filled glass.

2	shot(s)	**Pisco**
3	shot(s)	**Freshly squeezed orange juice**
1	shot(s)	**Grand Marnier liqueur**

Origin: I based this recipe on the traditional Chilean combination of pisco and orange juice.
Comment: Aromatic brandy and orange juice pepped up and sweetened with a slug of orange liqueur.

FOR MORE INFORMATION SEE OUR
INGREDIENTS APPENDIX ON PAGE 254

PISCO SOUR (TRADITIONAL RECIPE) [NEW]

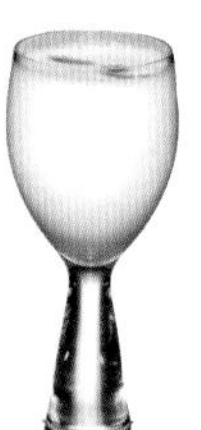

Glass: Goblet
Garnish: Three drops of Angostura bitters
Method: **BLEND** all ingredients with 12oz scoop crushed ice and serve with straws.

2	shot(s)	**Pisco**
1	shot(s)	**Freshly squeezed lime juice**
1	shot(s)	**Sugar (gomme) syrup**
½	fresh	**Egg white**

Variant: Dust with cinnamon powder.
Origin: Believed to have first been created in the 1920s, the Pisco Sour has since become the national drink of both Chile and Peru.
Comment: One of the few really brilliant blended drinks.

PISCO SOUR (DIFFORD'S VERSION)

Glass: Old-fashioned
Garnish: Three drops of Angostura bitters
Method: **SHAKE** all ingredients with ice and fine strain into chilled glass.

2½	shot(s)	**Pisco**
1	shot(s)	**Freshly squeezed lime juice**
½	shot(s)	**Sugar (gomme) syrup**
½	fresh	**Egg white**

Origin: My adaptation of the Chilean and Peruvian classic.
Comment: Traditionally this drink is blended with crushed ice, but I prefer it served straight-up. Be sure to drink it quickly while it's cold.

PISCOLA

Glass: Collins
Garnish: Lime wedge
Method: **POUR** pisco and bitters into ice-filled glass. **TOP** with cola, **STIR** and serve with straws.

2½	shot(s)	**Pisco**
3	dashes	**Angostura aromatic bitters**
Top up with		**Cola**

Origin: A popular long drink in its native Chile.
Comment: A 'brandy' and cola with a hint of angostura. Try it and see why the Chileans enjoy it.

PLANTATION PUNCH [NEW]

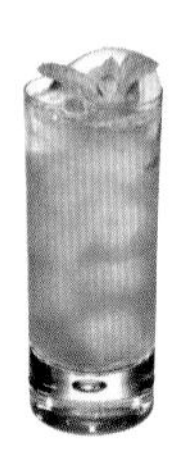

Glass: Collins
Garnish: Orange slice & mint sprig
Method: **SHAKE** first five ingredients with ice and strain into ice-filled glass. **TOP** with soda.

1½	shot(s)	**Southern Comfort**
1	shot(s)	**Light white rum**
¾	shot(s)	**Freshly squeezed lemon juice**
¼	shot(s)	**Sugar (gomme) syrup**
2	dashes	**Angostura aromatic bitters**
Top up with		**Soda water (club soda)**

Comment: Southern Comfort drives this tropical punch.

PLANTER'S PUNCH

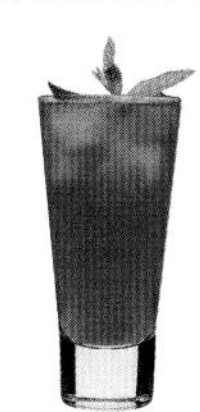

Glass: Collins
Garnish: Orange slice & mint sprig
Method: **SHAKE** all ingredients with ice and strain into ice-filled glass.

1½	shot(s)	**Myers's Planters' Punch rum**
1	shot(s)	**Freshly squeezed lime juice**
½	shot(s)	**Sugar (gomme) syrup**
2	shot(s)	**Chilled mineral water**
3	dashes	**Angostura aromatic bitters**

Origin: Invented in the late 19th century by the founder of Myers's rum, Fred L. Myers. The recipe on the back of each bottle is known as the 'Old Plantation formula' and uses the classic rum punch proportions of 1 sour (lime), 2 sweet (sugar), 3 strong (rum) and 4 weak (water). Rather than this or the American formula (1 sweet, 2 sour, 3 weak and 4 strong), I've followed David A. Embury's recommendation of 1 sweet, 2 sour, 3 strong and 4 weak.
Comment: A twangy punch which harnesses the rich flavours of Myers's rum.

PLANTER'S PUNCHLESS (MOCKTAIL) [NEW]

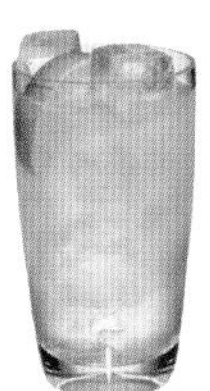

Glass: Collins
Garnish: Lime wedge
Method: **SHAKE** first three ingredients with ice and strain into ice-filled glass. **TOP** with 7-Up, lightly stir and serve with straws.

2	shot(s)	**Pressed apple juice**
¾	shot(s)	**Freshly squeezed lime juice**
¼	shot(s)	**Sonoma pomegranate (grenadine) syrup**
Top up with		**7-Up**

Comment: A pleasant, if uninspiring, driver's option.

PLANTEUR [NEW]

Glass: Collins
Garnish: Orange slice
Method: **SHAKE** all ingredients with ice and strain into ice-filled glass.

2	shot(s)	**Martinique blanc agricole rum (50% alc./vol.)**
3½	shot(s)	**Freshly squeezed orange juice**
¼	shot(s)	**Sonoma pomegranate (grenadine) syrup**

Comment: Handle with extreme care.

PLATINUM BLONDE [NEW]

Glass: Martini
Garnish: Freshly grated nutmeg
Method: **SHAKE** all ingredients with ice and fine strain into chilled glass.

1½	shot(s)	**Aged rum**
1½	shot(s)	**Grand Marnier liqueur**
½	shot(s)	**Double (heavy) cream**
½	shot(s)	**Milk**

Comment: An after dinner sipper.

PLAYA DEL MAR [UPDATED]

Glass: Martini
Garnish: Pineapple wedge on rim
Method: **SHAKE** all ingredients with ice and fine strain into chilled glass.

1	shot(s)	**Sauza Hornitos tequila**
½	shot(s)	**Cointreau / triple sec**
1	shot(s)	**Cranberry juice**
¾	shot(s)	**Pressed pineapple juice**
½	shot(s)	**Freshly squeezed lime juice**
¼	shot(s)	**Sugar (gomme) syrup**

Origin: This cocktail was created in 1997 by Wayne Collins at Navajo Joe, London, England. The name translates as 'Beach of the Sea'.
Comment: A fruity complex taste with a hint of tequila.

PLAYMATE MARTINI

Glass: Martini
Garnish: Orange zest twist
Method: **SHAKE** all ingredients with ice and fine strain into chilled glass.

1	shot(s)	**Rémy Martin cognac**
1	shot(s)	**Grand Marnier liqueur**
1	shot(s)	**Bols apricot brandy liqueur**
1	shot(s)	**Freshly squeezed orange juice**
½	fresh	**Egg white**
3	dashes	**Angostura aromatic bitters**

Comment: Smooth and easy drinking.

PLUM COCKTAIL

Glass: Martini
Garnish: Plum quarter on rim
Method: Cut plum into quarters, remove stone and peel. **MUDDLE** plum in base of shaker. Add other ingredients, **SHAKE** with ice and fine strain into chilled glass.

1	fresh	**Plum (stoned and peeled)**
2	shot(s)	**Zuta Osa Slivovitz plum brandy**
¼	shot(s)	**Dry vermouth**
¼	shot(s)	**Sugar (gomme) syrup**

Origin: Formula by yours truly in 2004.
Comment: The slivovitz adds woody, brandied notes to the plum.

PLUM DAIQUIRI

Glass: Martini
Garnish: Lime wedge on rim
Method: Cut plum into quarters, remove stone and peel. **MUDDLE** plum pieces in base of shaker. Add other ingredients, **SHAKE** with ice and fine strain into chilled glass.

1	fresh	**Plum (stoned and peeled)**
2	shot(s)	**Light white rum**
½	shot(s)	**Freshly squeezed lime juice**
½	shot(s)	**Sugar (gomme) syrup**

Origin: Formula by yours truly in 2004.
Comment: Depending on the ripeness of the plums, you may need to adjust the quantity of sugar.

A B C D E F G H I J K L M N O P Q R S T U V W X Y Z

PLUM MARTINI

Glass: Martini
Garnish: Plum quarter on rim (unpeeled)
Method: Cut plum into quarters, remove stone and peel. **MUDDLE** plum pieces in base of shaker. Add other ingredients, **SHAKE** with ice and fine strain into chilled glass.

1	fresh	Plum (stoned and peeled)
2	shot(s)	Ketel One vodka
3/4	shot(s)	Dry vermouth
1/2	shot(s)	Sugar (gomme) syrup

Origin: Formula by yours truly in 2004.
Variant: Substitute vanilla sugar syrup for plain sugar syrup.
Comment: Fortified plum juice in a Martini glass.

PLUM PUDDING MARTINI

Glass: Martini
Garnish: Grate fresh nutmeg over drink
Method: Cut plum into quarters, remove stone and peel. **MUDDLE** plum pieces in base of shaker. Add other ingredients, **SHAKE** with ice and fine strain into chilled glass.

1	fresh	Plum (stoned, peeled & chopped)
1	shot(s)	Raspberry flavoured vodka
1	shot(s)	Vanilla flavoured vodka
1/2	shot(s)	Luxardo Amaretto di Saschira liqueur
1/8	shot(s)	Goldschläger cinnamon liqueur

Origin: Created in 2004 by yours truly.
Comment: Spicy and fruity.

PLUM SOUR [NEW]

Glass: Old-fashioned
Garnish: Orange zest twist
Method: **MUDDLE** plum in base of shaker. Add other ingredients, **SHAKE** with ice and fine strain into ice-filled glass.

1	fresh	Plum (stoned and chopped)
2	shot(s)	Ketel One vodka
1	shot(s)	Freshly squeezed lemon juice
1/2	shot(s)	Sugar (gomme) syrup
1/2	fresh	Egg white

Comment: Soft, ripe plums are key to this fruity sour.

POET'S DREAM

Glass: Martini
Garnish: Squeezed lemon zest twist
Method: **STIR** all ingredients with ice and strain into chilled glass.

1	shot(s)	Plymouth gin
1	shot(s)	Bénédictine D.O.M. liqueur
1	shot(s)	Dry vermouth
3/4	shot(s)	Chilled mineral water (omit if wet ice)

Origin: Adapted from a recipe in the 1949 edition of Esquire's Handbook for Hosts.
Comment: Subtle, honeyed and herbal.

POGO STICK [NEW]

Glass: Martini (large)
Garnish: Mint sprig
Method: **BLEND** all ingredients with 12oz scoop crushed ice. Serve with straws.

2	shot(s)	Plymouth gin
1/2	shot(s)	Pressed pineapple juice
1/2	shot(s)	Freshly squeezed pink grapefruit juice
1/2	shot(s)	Freshly squeezed lime juice
1/2	shot(s)	Sugar (gomme) syrup

Origin: Adapted from a recipe in the 1947-72 Trader Vic's Bartender's Guide by Victor Bergeron.
Comment: To quote Trader Vic, "A refreshing blend of gin with pineapple and grapefruit juice... a real romper".

POINSETTIA [UPDATED]

Glass: Flute
Garnish: Quarter slice of orange on rim
Method: **POUR** first two ingredients into chilled glass. **TOP** with champagne.

1/2	shot(s)	Cointreau / triple sec
1	shot(s)	Cranberry juice
Top up with		Piper-Heidsieck brut champagne

Comment: Fruity champagne.

POLISH MARTINI [UPDATED]

Glass: Martini
Garnish: Lemon zest twist
Method: **SHAKE** all ingredients with ice and fine strain into chilled glass.

1	shot(s)	Ketel One vodka
1	shot(s)	Zubrówka bison vodka
3/4	shot(s)	Krupnik honey liqueur
1 1/2	shot(s)	Pressed apple juice

Origin: Created by Dick Bradsell, for his (Polish) father-in-law, Victor Sarge.
Comment: A round, smooth and very tasty alternatini.

POLLY'S SPECIAL

Glass: Martini
Garnish: Grapefruit wedge on rim
Method: **SHAKE** all ingredients with ice and fine strain into chilled glass.

1 3/4	shot(s)	The Famous Grouse Scotch whisky
1	shot(s)	Freshly squeezed grapefruit juice
1	shot(s)	Grand Marnier liqueur
1/4	shot(s)	Sugar (gomme) syrup

Origin: I adapted this recipe from a 1947 edition of Trader Vic's Bartender's Guide.
Comment: Sweet, sour, flavoursome and balanced – for grown-ups who like the taste of alcohol.

●●●◐○

POMEGRANATE BELLINI [NEW]

Glass: Flute
Method: Cut pomegranate in half and juice using a citrus juicer. **SHAKE** first three ingredients with ice and fine strain into chilled glass. **TOP** with sparkling wine.

1	shot(s)	**Freshly squeezed pomegranate juice**
1/2	shot(s)	**Cuarenta Y Tres (Licor 43) liqueur**
1/8	shot(s)	**Freshly squeezed lemon juice**
Top up with		**Prosecco sparkling wine**

Origin: Created in 2005 by yours truly.
Comment: This red drink is drier and more adult than it looks.

●●●●◐

POMEGRANATE MARGARITA [NEW]

Glass: Coupette
Garnish: Lime wedge on rim
Method: Cut pomegranate in half and juice using a citrus juicer. **SHAKE** all ingredients with ice and fine strain into chilled glass.

2	shot(s)	**Sauza Hornitos tequila**
1	shot(s)	**Freshly squeezed pomegranate juice**
1/2	shot(s)	**Freshly squeezed lime juice**
1/4	shot(s)	**Sonoma pomegranate (grenadine) syrup**

Origin: Recipe by yours truly in 2006.
Comment: Pomegranate and tequila combine harmoniously in this Margarita.

●●●●◐

POMEGRANATE MARTINI [NEW]

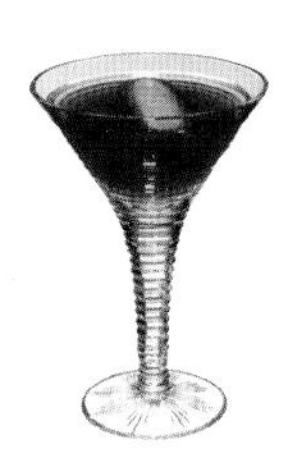

Glass: Martini
Garnish: Orange zest twist
Method: Cut pomegranate in half and juice using a citrus juicer. **SHAKE** all ingredients with ice and fine strain into chilled glass.

2	shot(s)	**Ketel One vodka**
1 1/2	shot(s)	**Freshly squeezed pomegranate juice**
1/2	shot(s)	**Sonoma pomegranate (grenadine) syrup**

Origin: Adapted from a drink discovered in 2005 at Lotus Bar, Sydney, Australia.
Comment: This drink was originally based on gin but I find that juniper and pomegranate clash.

●●●●○

POMPANSKI MARTINI

Glass: Martini
Garnish: Orange zest twist
Method: **SHAKE** all ingredients with ice and fine strain into chilled glass.

1 3/4	shot(s)	**Ketel One vodka**
1/2	shot(s)	**Cointreau / triple sec**
1 1/2	shot(s)	**Freshly squeezed grapefruit juice**
1/4	shot(s)	**Sugar (gomme) syrup**
1	spoon	**Dry vermouth**

Comment: Dry and zesty with the sharp freshness of grapefruit and a hint of orange.

●●●◐○

PONCHE DE ALGARROBINA [NEW]

Glass: Goblet
Garnish: Dust with cinnamon
Method: **BLEND** all ingredients with 12oz scoop crushed ice. Serve with straws.

2	shot(s)	**Pisco**
1	fresh	**Egg yolk**
1	shot(s)	**Condensed milk**
1	spoon	**Algarrobo extract (or malt extract from healthfood shops)**

Tip: It pays to add the condensed milk and Algarrobo (or malt extract) after starting the blender.
Origin: A traditional Peruvian drink I discovered at Tito's Restaurant, London, England. Algarrobo is extracted from the fruits of the tree of the same name. It is a sticky honey-like liquid which I find tastes a little like malt extract.
Comment: A creamy frozen drink with real character.

●●●●○

PONCE DE LEON [NEW]

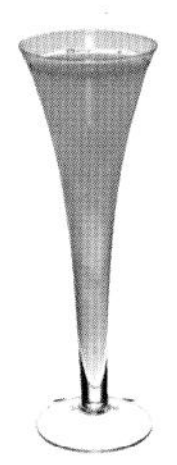

Glass: Flute
Method: **SHAKE** first four ingredients with ice and fine strain into chilled glass. **TOP** with champagne.

1/2	shot(s)	**Mount Gay golden rum**
1/2	shot(s)	**Rémy Martin cognac**
1/2	shot(s)	**Cointreau /triple sec**
1/2	shot(s)	**Freshly squeezed pink grapefruit juice**
Top up with		**Piper-Heidsieck brut champagne**

Origin: A long lost classic.
Comment: A well-balanced classic champagne cocktail.

●●●●○

PONCHA

Glass: Collins
Garnish: Orange wedge
Method: **STIR** honey with aguardiente in base of shaker to dissolve honey. Add other ingredients, **SHAKE** with ice and strain into ice filled glass.

2	spoons	**Runny honey**
2 1/2	shot(s)	**Aguardiente (Torres Aqua d'Or)**
1	shot(s)	**Freshly squeezed lemon juice**
1/4	shot(s)	**Sugar (gomme) syrup**
1 1/2	shot(s)	**Freshly squeezed orange juice**
1 1/2	shot(s)	**Freshly squeezed grapefruit juice**

Origin: My adaptation of a tradtitional drink from the island of Madeira.
Comment: This citrus refresher is reputedly an excellent cold remedy.

DRINKS ARE GRADED AS FOLLOWS:

● DISGUSTING ●◐ PRETTY AWFUL ●● BEST AVOIDED
●●◐ DISAPPOINTING ●●● ACCEPTABLE ●●●◐ GOOD
●●●● RECOMMENDED ●●●●◐ HIGHLY RECOMMENDED
●●●●● OUTSTANDING / EXCEPTIONAL

PONTBERRY MARTINI

Glass: Martini
Garnish: Blackberries
Method: **SHAKE** all ingredients with ice and fine strain into chilled glass.

1½	shot(s)	Ketel One vodka
½	shot(s)	Bols blackberry (crème de mûre) liqueur
2	shot(s)	Cranberry juice

Origin: Created by Dick Bradsell in the late 90s for the opening of Agent Provocateur in Pont Street, London, England.
Comment: A light, fruity, easy drinking cocktail.

POOH'TINI

Glass: Martini
Garnish: Lemon zest twist
Method: **STIR** honey with vodka in base of shaker to dissolve honey. Add other ingredients, **SHAKE** with ice and fine strain into chilled glass.

2	spoon(s)	Runny honey
2	shot(s)	Zubrówka bison grass vodka
½	shot(s)	Krupnik honey liqueur
1½	shot(s)	Cold black camomile tea

Origin: Adapted from a drink discovered in 1999 at Lot 61, New York City.
Comment: Grassy honey with a spicy, slightly tannic, camomile finish.

PORT & MELON MARTINI

Glass: Martini
Garnish: Melon wedge on rim
Method: Cut melon into eight segments and deseed. Cut cubes of flesh from skin of one segment and **MUDDLE** in base of shaker. Add other ingredients, **SHAKE** with ice and fine strain into chilled glass.

⅛	fresh	Cantaloupe / Galia melon
1½	shot(s)	Ketel One vodka
1½	shot(s)	Dry white Port (e.g. Dow's Fine White)
1	pinch	Ground ginger

Origin: Created in 2004 by yours truly.
Comment: The classic seventies starter served as a Martini.

PORT & STARBOARD [NEW]

Glass: Shot
Method: Refrigerate ingredients then **LAYER** in chilled glass by carefully pouring in the following order.

½	shot(s)	Sonoma pomegranate (grenadine) syrup
½	shot(s)	Bols green crème de menthe

Origin: Named after and inspired by the red and green running lights which respectively mark the 'Port' (left-hand) and 'Starboard' (right-hand) sides of a ship. The red light is called the Port side because port wine is red. The original name for the opposite side was Larboard, but over the years it was corrupted to Starboard.
Comment: Easy to layer but hard to drink. Very sweet.

PORT LIGHT [NEW]

Glass: Martini
Garnish: Passion fruit half
Method: **STIR** honey with bourbon in base of shaker to dissolve honey. Cut passion fruit in half and scoop flesh into shaker. Add other ingredients, **SHAKE** with ice and fine strain into ice-filled glass.

2	spoons	Runny honey
2	shot(s)	Bourbon whiskey
1	fresh	Passion fruit
1	shot(s)	Freshly squeezed lemon juice
½	shot(s)	Sonoma pomegranate (grenadine) syrup
½	fresh	Egg white

Origin: Adapted from a drink created by Victor Bergeron (Trader Vic).
Comment: Strong and very fruity. Too many will put your lights out.

PORT WINE COCKTAIL

Glass: Martini
Garnish: Orange zest twist
Method: **STIR** all ingredients with ice and strain into chilled glass.

3	shot(s)	Warre's Otima Tawny Port
1	shot(s)	Rémy Martin cognac

Origin: A classic from the early 1900s.
Comment: Port and brandy served straight-up and dressed up.

POTTED PARROT [NEW]

Glass: Sling
Garnish: Parrot on stick & mint sprig
Method: **SHAKE** all ingredients with ice and strain into glass filled with crushed ice.

2	shot(s)	Light white rum
½	shot(s)	Cointreau / triple sec
2	shot(s)	Freshly squeezed orange juice
1	shot(s)	Freshly squeezed lemon juice
¼	shot(s)	Almond (orgeat) sugar syrup
¼	shot(s)	Sugar (gomme) syrup

Origin: Adapted from a recipe in the 1947-72 Trader Vic's Bartender's Guide by Victor Bergeron. Popular in Trader Vic's restaurants.
Comment: Tangy orange, not too sweet.

POUSSE-CAFÉ

Glass: Shot
Method: Refrigerate ingredients then **LAYER** in chilled glass by carefully pouring in the following order.

¼	shot(s)	Sonoma pomegranate (grenadine) syrup
¼	shot(s)	Kahlúa coffee liqueur
¼	shot(s)	Green crème de menthe
¼	shot(s)	Cointreau / triple sec
¼	shot(s)	Bourbon whiskey
¼	shot(s)	Wray & Nephew white overproof rum

Origin: A pousse-café is a term for any multi-layered cocktail. (See 'Layer' in 'Bartending Basics'.)
Comment: More a test of patience and a steady hand than a drink.

A B C D E F G H I J K L M N O P Q R S T U V W X Y Z

PRAIRIE OYSTER

Glass: Coupette
Method: Taking care not to break the egg yolk, **PLACE** it in the centre hollow of the glass. **SHAKE** the rest of the ingredients with ice and strain over egg. Instruct drinker to down in one.

1	raw	**Egg yolk**
1	shot(s)	**Rémy Martin cognac**
1/4	shot(s)	**Worcestershire sauce**
1/4	shot(s)	**Tomato juice**
5	drops	**Tabasco**
2	pinches	**Pepper**
2	pinches	**Salt**
1/2	spoon	**Malt vinegar**

Origin: Thought to have been created in Germany in the 1870s. Jeeves makes something similar for Bertie Wooster in a P.G. Wodehouse tale.
Comment: Like many supposed hangover cures, this works on the kill or... basis. It tastes better than it looks.

PRESIDENT [NEW]

Glass: Martini
Garnish: Orange zest twist
Method: **SHAKE** all ingredients with ice and fine strain into chilled glass.

2	shot(s)	**Light white rum**
1	shot(s)	**Freshly squeezed orange juice**
1/4	shot(s)	**Freshly squeezed lemon juice**
1/4	shot(s)	**Sonoma pomegranate (grenadine) syrup**
1/2	shot(s)	**Chilled mineral water (omit if wet ice)**

Origin: Adapted from a recipe in Harry Craddock's 1930 Savoy Cocktail Book.
Comment: A delicately fruity orange Daiquiri.

PRESIDENTE

Glass: Martini
Garnish: Orange zest twist
Method: **SHAKE** all ingredients with ice and fine strain into chilled glass.

1 1/2	shot(s)	**Light white rum**
3/4	shot(s)	**Cointreau / triple sec**
3/4	shot(s)	**Dry vermouth**
1/8	shot(s)	**Sonoma pomegranate (grenadine) syrup**
1/2	shot(s)	**Chilled mineral water (omit if wet ice)**

Origin: This classic was created during the 1920s in Vista Alegre, Cuba. The name refers to Mario Garcia Menocal, who was president of Cuba from 1912 to 1920.
Comment: A lightly flavoured classic cocktail.

DRINKS ARE GRADED AS FOLLOWS:

● DISGUSTING ●◐ PRETTY AWFUL ●● BEST AVOIDED
●●◐ DISAPPOINTING ●●● ACCEPTABLE ●●●◐ GOOD
●●●● RECOMMENDED ●●●●◐ HIGHLY RECOMMENDED
●●●●● OUTSTANDING / EXCEPTIONAL

PRICKLY PEAR MULE

Glass: Collins
Garnish: Pear slice on rim
Method: **SHAKE** first five ingredients with ice and strain into ice-filled glass. **TOP** with ginger beer.

1 1/4	shot(s)	**Pear & cognac liqueur**
1 1/4	shot(s)	**Poire William eau de vie**
3	shot(s)	**Freshly extracted pear juice**
1/4	shot(s)	**Freshly squeezed lemon juice**
2	dashes	**Angostura aromatic bitters**
Top up with		**Jamaican ginger beer**

Origin: Created in 2002 by yours truly.
Tip: Fill the glass with ice and go easy on the ginger beer which can predominate and overpower the pear.
Comment: Subtle pear with ginger spice.

PRINCE CHARLIE

Glass: Martini
Garnish: Lemon zest twist
Method: **SHAKE** all ingredients with ice and fine strain into chilled glass.

1	shot(s)	**Rémy Martin cognac**
1	shot(s)	**Drambuie liqueur**
1	shot(s)	**Freshly squeezed lemon juice**
3/4	shot(s)	**Chilled mineral water (omit if wet ice)**

Origin: A long lost classic.
Comment: Cognac and honey with sweet and sourness in harmony.

PRINCE OF WALES [NEW]

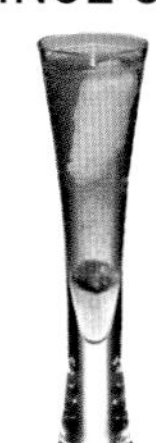

Glass: Flute
Garnish: Lemon peel twist
Method: Rub sugar cube with lemon peel, coat with bitters and drop into glass. **POUR** cognac and liqueur over soaked cube and **TOP** with champagne.

1	cube	**Brown sugar**
2	dashes	**Angostura aromatic bitters**
1/2	shot(s)	**Rémy Martin cognac**
1/2	shot(s)	**Grand Marnier liqueur**
Top up with		**Piper-Heidsieck brut champagne**

Comment: More interesting than a classic Champagne Cocktail.

PRINCESS MARINA [NEW]

Glass: Martini
Garnish: Orange zest twist
Method: **SHAKE** all ingredients with ice and fine strain into chilled glass.

1	shot(s)	**Plymouth gin**
1/2	shot(s)	**Calvados or applejack brandy**
1/2	shot(s)	**Dubonnet Red**
1/2	shot(s)	**Cointreau / triple sec**
1/2	shot(s)	**Carlshamns Swedish Torr Flaggpunsch**
3/4	shot(s)	**Chilled mineral water (omit if wet ice)**

Origin: Created in the late 1920s/early 1930s and named after Princess Marina, the late mother of The Duke of Kent, Prince Michael of Kent and Princess Alexandra.
Comment: Delicate yet loaded with alcohol and flavour.

PRINCESS MARY [NEW]

Glass: Martini
Garnish: Dust with cocoa powder
Method: **SHAKE** all ingredients with ice and fine strain into chilled glass.

1 1/2	shot(s)	**Plymouth gin**
1	shot(s)	**Bols white crème de cacao**
3/4	shot(s)	**Double (heavy) cream**
3/4	shot(s)	**Milk**

Origin: Created in 1922 by Harry MacElhone to celebrate H.R.H. Princess Mary's marriage. The original recipe featured equal parts of all four ingredients.
Comment: Slightly sweet, very creamy - drink after dinner.

PRINCESS MARY'S PRIDE [NEW]

Glass: Martini
Garnish: Orange zest twist
Method: **SHAKE** all ingredients with ice and fine strain into chilled glass.

2	shot(s)	**Calvados / applejack brandy**
1	shot(s)	**Dubonnet Red**
1	shot(s)	**Dry vermouth**

Origin: Created by Harry Craddock on 28th February 1922 to mark the wedding celebrations of H.R.H. Princess Mary. Recipe from 1930's Savoy Cocktail Book.
Comment: Apple brandy to the fore, followed by aromatised wine.

PRINCESS PRIDE [NEW]

Glass: Martini
Garnish: Orange zest twist
Method: **SHAKE** all ingredients with ice and fine strain into chilled glass.

2	shot(s)	**Calvados or applejack brandy**
1	shot(s)	**Dubonnet Red**
1	shot(s)	**Sweet (rosso) vermouth**

Origin: Adapted from a recipe in the 1947-72 Trader Vic's Bartender's Guide by Victor Bergeron.
Comment: Vic's improves version of the drink above.

PRINCETON [UPDATED]

Glass: Martini
Garnish: Lemon zest twist
Method: **STIR** all ingredients with ice and strain into chilled glass.

2	shot(s)	**Plymouth gin**
1	shot(s)	**Warre's Otima Tawny Port**
1/4	shot(s)	**Sugar (gomme) syrup**
2	dashes	**Fee Brothers orange bitters**

Origin: An old classic originally made with sweet 'Old Tom' gin and without the sugar syrup.
Comment: Overproof wine with a herbal orange garnish.

PRINCETON MARTINI [NEW]

Glass: Martini
Garnish: Lime zest twist
Method: **SHAKE** all ingredients with ice and fine strain into chilled glass.

2	shot(s)	**Plymouth gin**
1/2	shot(s)	**Dry vermouth**
1/4	shot(s)	**Rose's lime cordial**
1/2	shot(s)	**Chilled mineral water (omit if wet ice)**

Comment: The Dry Martini meets the Gimlet. They should meet more often.

PRUNE FACE

Glass: Old-fashioned
Garnish: Orange zest twist
Method: **POUR** bourbon into glass with four ice cubes and **STIR** until ice has at least half melted. Add other ingredients and additional ice and stir some more.

2	shot(s)	**Bourbon whiskey**
3/4	shot(s)	**Vieille de prune eau de vie**
1/4	shot(s)	**Mandarine Napoléon liqueur**
1/4	shot(s)	**Sugar (gomme) syrup**

Origin: Created in 2002 by Daniel Warner at Zander, London, England and named after my friend's nickname for his stepmother.
Comment: Why muddle cherries into your Old Fashioned when you can add a hint of prune?

PRUNEAUX [NEW]

Glass: Martini
Garnish: Prunes on stick
Method: **SHAKE** all ingredients with ice and fine strain into chilled glass.

1 1/2	shot(s)	**Plymouth gin**
1	shot(s)	**Amontillado sherry**
1/2	shot(s)	**Pedro Ximenez sherry**
3/4	shot(s)	**Freshly squeezed orange juice**
3/4	shot(s)	**Syrup from tinned prunes**

Origin: Adapted from a recipe in Harry Craddock's 1930 Savoy Cocktail Book.
Comment: Sherried prunes further fortified by gin.

P.S. I LOVE YOU

Glass: Martini
Garnish: Crumbled Cadbury's Flake bar
Method: **SHAKE** all ingredients with ice and fine strain into chilled glass.

1 1/4	shot(s)	**Baileys Irish Cream liqueur**
1 1/4	shot(s)	**Luxardo Amaretto di Saschira liqueur**
3/4	shot(s)	**Mount Gay Eclipse golden rum**
3/4	shot(s)	**Kahlúa coffee liqueur**
1	shot(s)	**Double (heavy) cream**

Comment: P.S. You'll love this creamy flavoursome drink.

PUCCINI

●●●◐○

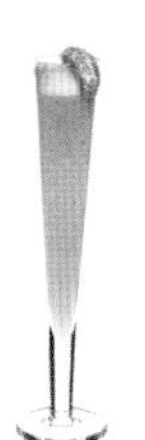

Glass: Flute
Garnish: Mandarin (tangerine) segment
Method: **MUDDLE** segments in base of shaker. Add liqueur, **SHAKE** with ice and fine strain into chilled glass. **TOP** with champagne and lightly stir.

8	segments	**Fresh mandarin (tangerine/clementine/satsuma)**
3/4	shot(s)	**Mandarine Napoléon liqueur**
Top up with		**Prosecco sparkling wine**

Origin: Named after the composer of Madame Butterfly, this cocktail is popular in Venice and other areas of northern Italy. It is often made without mandarin liqueur.
Comment: The use of mandarin (tangerine) instead of orange makes the Puccini slightly sharper than the similar Mimosa.

PULP FICTION

●●●●○

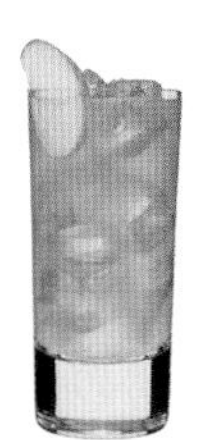

Glass: Collins
Method: **SHAKE** all ingredients with ice and strain into ice filled glass. **TOP** with 7-Up.

2	shot(s)	**Pressed apple juice**
2	shot(s)	**Rémy Martin cognac**
1	shot(s)	**Apple schnapps liqueur**
Top up with		**7-Up**

Origin: Discovered in 2001 at Teatro, London, England.
Comment: Originally made with apple pulp, this drink has a zingy apple taste.

PURPLE COSMO

●●●●◐

Glass: Martini
Garnish: Orange zest twist
Method: **STIR** all ingredients with ice and strain into chilled glass.

2	shot(s)	**Ketel One Citroen vodka**
3/4	shot(s)	**Parfait Amour liqueur**
1 1/2	shot(s)	**White cranberry & grape juice**
1/4	shot(s)	**Freshly squeezed lime juice**

Variant: Blue Cosmo
Comment: If shaken this becomes more of a grey Cosmo. The flavour and colour make for an interesting twist.

PURPLE FLIRT #1

●●●●○

Glass: Martini
Garnish: Orange zest twist
Method: **SHAKE** all ingredients with ice and fine strain into chilled glass.

1 1/2	shot(s)	**Ketel One vodka**
3/4	shot(s)	**Opal Nera black sambuca**
2	shot(s)	**Cranberry juice**

Comment: This purple drink is surprisingly balanced with subtle hints of liquorice.

PURPLE FLIRT #2

●●●○○

Glass: Old-fashioned
Garnish: Orange slice & cherry (sail)
Method: **SHAKE** all ingredients with ice and strain into ice-filled glass.

1	shot(s)	**Goslings Black Seal rum**
1/4	shot(s)	**Bols blue curaçao liqueur**
1	shot(s)	**Pressed pineapple juice**
1/2	shot(s)	**Freshly squeezed lemon juice**
1/4	shot(s)	**Sonoma pomegranate (grenadine) syrup**
1/2	fresh	**Egg white**

Comment: This popular drink is more brown than purple. It tastes OK, anyway.

PURPLE HAZE

●●●◐○

Glass: Shot
Method: **SHAKE** first three ingredients with ice and strain into glass. **POUR** liqueur down the inside of the glass. This will fall to the bottom and form the purple haze.

1 1/2	shot(s)	**Ketel One vodka**
1/2	shot(s)	**Freshly squeezed lime juice**
1/4	shot(s)	**Sugar (gomme) syrup**
1/8	shot(s)	**Chambord black raspberry liqueur**

Comment: A sweet and sour shot with a sweet, berry base.

PURPLE HOOTER

●●●◐○

Glass: Collins
Garnish: Lime wedge
Method: **SHAKE** first three ingredients with ice and strain into ice-filled glass. **TOP** with soda.

2	shot(s)	**Ketel One vodka**
1	shot(s)	**Chambord black raspberry liqueur**
1	shot(s)	**Freshly squeezed lime juice**
Top up with		**Soda water (club soda)**

Comment: Tangy, fruity, long and refreshing.

PURPLE PEAR MARTINI

●●●●○

Glass: Martini
Garnish: Pear slice on rim
Method: **SHAKE** all ingredients with ice and fine strain into chilled glass.

2	shot(s)	**Poire William eau de vie**
2	shot(s)	**Benoit Serres liqueur de violette**
1/2	shot(s)	**Sugar (gomme) syrup**

Origin: Created in 2002 by yours truly.
Comment: This floral drink suits its name.

DRINKS ARE GRADED AS FOLLOWS:

● DISGUSTING ●◐ PRETTY AWFUL ●● BEST AVOIDED
●●◐ DISAPPOINTING ●●● ACCEPTABLE ●●●◐ GOOD
●●●● RECOMMENDED ●●●●◐ HIGHLY RECOMMENDED
●●●●● OUTSTANDING / EXCEPTIONAL

PURPLE TURTLE

Glass: Shot
Method: **SHAKE** all ingredients with ice and fine strain into chilled glass.

1/2	shot(s)	Sauza Hornitos tequila
1/2	shot(s)	Bols blue curaçao
1/2	shot(s)	Plymouth sloe gin

Comment: This aquamarine shooter goes down a treat.

PUSSYFOOT (MOCKTAIL) [UPDATED]

Glass: Collins
Garnish: Orange slice
Method: **MUDDLE** mint in base of shaker. Add other ingredients, **SHAKE** with ice and fine strain into ice-filled glass.

7	fresh	Mint leaves
4	shot(s)	Freshly squeezed orange juice
1/2	shot(s)	Freshly squeezed lemon juice
1/2	shot(s)	Freshly squeezed lime juice
1/2	shot(s)	Sonoma pomegranate (grenadine) syrup
1	fresh	Egg yolk

Origin: Created in 1920 by Robert Vermeire at the Embassy Club, London, England. This non-alcoholic cocktail is named after 'Pussyfoot' (William E.) Johnson who was an ardent supporter of Prohibition.
Comment: Probably the best non-alcoholic cocktail ever.

QUARTER DECK [NEW]

Glass: Martini
Garnish: Orange zest twist
Method: **SHAKE** all ingredients with ice and fine strain into chilled glass.

2	shot(s)	Light white rum
1	shot(s)	Pedro Ximenez sherry
1/4	shot(s)	Freshly squeezed lemon juice
3/4	shot(s)	Chilled mineral water (omit if wet ice)

Origin: Long lost classic.
Comment: Hints of prune, toffee and maple syrup. Very complex.

QUARTERBACK

Glass: Martini
Garnish: Orange zest twist
Method: **SHAKE** all ingredients with ice and fine strain into chilled glass.

1	shot(s)	Yellow Chartreuse
1	shot(s)	Cointreau / triple sec
1	shot(s)	Double (heavy) cream
1	shot(s)	Milk

Comment: This white, creamy drink has a flavoursome bite.

QUEBEC [NEW]

Glass: Martini
Garnish: Orange zest twist
Method: **STIR** all ingredients with ice and strain into chilled glass.

2	shot(s)	Canadian whisky (or bourbon whiskey)
2	shot(s)	Dubonnet Red
2	dashes	Fee Brothers orange bitters

Origin: Created in 2004 at Victoria Bar, Berlin, Germany.
Comment: Canadian whisky with French accents of aromatised wine – très Quebecois.

QUEEN MARTINI [NEW]

Glass: Martini
Garnish: Maraschino cherry
Method: **SHAKE** all ingredients with ice and fine strain into chilled glass.

1 1/2	shot(s)	Plymouth gin
1/2	shot(s)	Dry vermouth
1/2	shot(s)	Red (rosso) vermouth
1/2	shot(s)	Freshly squeezed orange juice
1/2	shot(s)	Pressed pineapple juice

Comment: A 'perfectly' fruity Martini that's fit for a...

QUELLE VIE [NEW]

Glass: Martini
Garnish: Orange zest twist
Method: **STIR** all ingredients with ice and fine strain into chilled glass.

2	shot(s)	Rémy Martin cognac
1/2	shot(s)	Kummel
3/4	shot(s)	Chilled mineral water (omit if wet ice)

Origin: Adapted from a recipe in the 1930 Savoy Cocktail Book by Harry Craddock.
Comment: In Craddock's words, "Brandy gives you courage and Kummel makes you cautious, thus giving you a perfect mixture of bravery and caution, with the bravery predominating."

QUINCE SOUR [NEW]

Glass: Old-fashioned
Garnish: Lemon slice & cherry (sail)
Method: **STIR** quince jam with vodka in base of shaker to dissolve jam. Add other ingredients, **SHAKE** with ice and fine strain into ice-filled glass.

3	spoons	Quince jam /membrillo Spanish quince paste
2	shot(s)	Ketel One vodka
1	shot(s)	Freshly squeezed lemon juice
1/2	fresh	Egg white

Comment: The sweet quince both flavours and balances this sour.

INGREDIENTS APPENDIX

ABSINTHE

There are two basic styles of absinthe commonly available – French and Czech. French styles, which are mostly still banned in their country of origin, have a full-bodied aniseed flavour and a deep green colour. When water is added the colour should change and the drink should eventually go cloudy. This process of precipitation is known as the louche. Czech absinth (spelt without the 'e') usually has a bluer tinge to its green colour. The aniseed flavour is more subtle than in its French counterpart and it is not usual for it to turn cloudy with the addition of water.

Linstead ●●●●○
London Cocktail ●●●◐○
Martini Special ●●●●○
Maurice Martini ●●●◐○
Merry Widow #1 ●●●◐○
Monkey Gland #1 ●●●●○
Moonshine Martini ●●●●◐
Morning Glory ●●●●○
Morning Glory Fizz ●●●●○
New Year's Absolution ●●●◐○
Peggy Martini ●●●○○
Piccadilly Martini ●●●●◐
Pisco Punch #4 (Prosser's) ●●●●●

ADVOCAAT LIQUEUR

See 'Bols Advocaat Liqueur'

AMARETTO LIQUEUR

See 'Luxardo Amaretto di Saschira Liqueur'

AMONTILLADO

See 'Sherry – Amontillado'

ANGOSTURA AROMATIC BITTERS

44.7% alc./vol. (89.4°proof)

www.angostura.com

Producer: Angostura Ltd, Laventille, Port of Spain, Trinidad, West Indies.

US agent: Angostura International Ltd..

Tel: 414 529 1839

These famous bitters were first made in 1824 by the German Surgeon-General of a military hospital in the town of Angostura, Venezuela, to help treat stomach disorders and indigestion. In 1875, due to unrest in Venezuela, production was moved to Trinidad. It was here that the laid-back Caribbean attitude affected Angostura's packaging. One day a new batch of labels was ordered and a simple mistake led to them being too big for the bottles. The error was spotted in time but everyone thought somebody else would deal with the problem. No one did, so they simply stuck the labels on the bottles, intending to fix the next batch. No one quite got round to it and the oversized label became a trademark of the brand.

One of the smallest bottles on any bar, Angostura is packed with flavour: Turkish coffee, jasmine, dried mint, fruit poached with cloves and cinnamon, cherry, orange and lemon zest. A dash adds that indefinable something which brings cocktails to life.

Lemon Lime & Bitters ●●●◐○
Limey ●●●◐○
Liquorice Whisky Sour ●●●●◐
Lolita Margarita ●●●●◐
Luxury Cocktail ●●●◐○
Luxury Mojito ●●●●○
Mai Tai #2 (Beaumont-Gantt's Formula) ●●●●○
Manhattan Dry ●●●●◐
Manhattan Perfect ●●●●●
Manhattan Sweet ●●●●●
Manhattan Island ●●●●○
Maple Old-Fashioned ●●●●○
Marama Rum Punch ●●●●○
Martini Special ●●●●◐
Medicinal Solution ●●●◐○
Merry Widow #1 ●●●◐○
Mexican 55 ●●●●○
Mexican Manhattan ●●●●○
Mint Julep ●●●●●
Mona Lisa ●●●●○
Montego Bay ●●●◐○
Morning Glory ●●●●○
Moscow Mule ●●●●○
Navy Grog ●●●●○
Noon ●●●●○
Oddball Manhattan Dry ●●●●○
Old Fashioned #1 (Classic Version) ●●●●●
Old Fashioned #2 (US Version) ●●●●◐
Old Fashioned Caddy ●●●●○
Parma Negroni ●●●●○
Passion Punch ●●●◐○
Pegu Club ●●●●○
Pilgrim Cocktail ●●●●○
Pink Daiquiri ●●●●○
Pink Gin #1 (Traditional) ●●●●○
Pink Gin #2 (Modern) ●●●●○
Pink Gin & Tonic ●●●●○
Piscola ●●●◐○
Plantation Punch ●●●◐○
Planter's Punch ●●●●○
Playmate Martini ●●●●◐
Prickly Pear Mule ●●●●○
Prince Of Wales ●●●◐○

ANIS

See 'Pernod Anis'

APPLEJACK BRANDY

See 'Calvados'

APPLE JUICE

Apples are a good source of dietary fibre, vitamin C and vitamin B5, plus minerals such as copper, iron and potassium. Choose a flavoursome variety like Bramley over more bland types like Washington Red or Golden Delicious.

The best way to use apples in cocktails is as a juice. You can make your own in a standard electric juice extractor. There is no need to peel or core apples, as the skin and core contain over half the fruit's nutrients. Simply remove the stalks and chop the fruit into small enough chunks to fit through the feeder.

Unchecked, the juice will quickly oxidise and discolour but a splash of lime juice helps prevent this without too much effect on the flavour. You'll find that crisper apples yield clearer juice.
Most supermarkets carry at least one quality pressed apple juice and the best of these cloudy juices make DIY juicing unnecessary. Avoid the packaged 'pure', clear apple juices as these tend to be overly sweet and artificial tasting.

Lemon Butter Cookie ●●●●○
Lighter Breeze ●●●◐○
Long Flight of Stairs ●●●●◐
Love Junk ●●●◐○
Madroska ●●●○○
Mandarintini ●●●○○
Mango Rum Cooler ●●●◐○
Maple Pomme ●●●●○
The Mayflower Martini ●●●●○
Mint Limeade (Mocktail) ●●●●◐
Mitch Martini ●●●●○
Monza ●●●◐○
Moscow Lassi ●●●○○
Motox ●●●●○
Myrtle Martini ●●●◐○
New Year's Absolution ●●●◐○
Northern Lights ●●●●○
November Seabreeze (Mocktail) ●●●◐○
Orchard Breeze ●●●●◐
Palookaville ●●●●○
Palm Springs ●●●◐○
Pappy Honeysuckle ●●●●◐
Pear Shaped #1 (Deluxe Version) ●●●●◐
Pear Shaped #2 (Popular) ●●●●◐
Planter's Punchless (Mocktail) ●●●○○
Polish Martini ●●●●●
Pulp Fiction ●●●●○

APPLE SCHNAPPS LIQUEUR

The term schnapps traditionally suggests a clear, strong spirit. However, in recent years the term has come to refer to sweet liqueurs of only 20-24% alc./vol., bearing no resemblance to the strong, dry schnapps from which they take their name. I call such drinks 'schnapps liqueurs' to avoid confusion.

Northern Lights ●●●●○
Palookaville ●●●●○
Pulp Fiction ●●●●○

APRICOT BRANDY LIQUEUR

See 'Bols Apricot Brandy Liqueur'

BASIL LEAVES

This aromatic herb has a strong lemon and jasmine flavour.

Milly Martini ●●●●○

BEER

Although beer is one of the most widely consumed alcoholic beverages, sadly it does not greatly feature in the world of cocktails. At least, not yet! Suggestions to simon@diffordsguide.com, please.

Michelada ●●●○○

BÉNÉDICTINE D.O.M. LIQUEUR

Maxim's Coffee (Hot) ●●●●○
Merry Widow #1 ●●●◐○
Monkey Gland #2 ●●●●○
Mule's Hind Leg ●●●●◐
O'Henry ●●●◐○
Poet's Dream ●●●●◐

BLACKBERRIES

See 'Raspberries & Blackberries'

BLACKBERRY (CRÈME DE MÛRE) LIQUEUR

See 'Bols Blackberry Liqueur'

BLUEBERRIES

Blueberry pie is as much an American icon as the Stars and Stripes. This bushy shrub, which is related to the bilberry, is native to the States and many different types grow there – not all of them blue. The lowbush blueberry, which is called the 'bleuet' in Quebec, tends to be smaller and sweeter than other varieties and is often marketed as 'wild blueberry'. The larger, highbush blueberry is the variety most cultivated in the US.

These soft berries are best muddled in the base of your shaker or glass. Recipes in this guide specify the number required for each drink. Alternatively, you can make a puree. Just stick them in the blender and add a touch of sugar syrup. Fresh blueberries should not be stored in the refrigerator.

No. 10 Lemonade ●●●●◐

BLUE CURAÇAO LIQUEUR

See 'Bols Blue Curaçao Liqueur'

BOLS ADVOCAAT LIQUEUR

15.0% alc./vol. (30°proof)

www.grantUSA.com

Producer: Bols Royal Distilleries, Zoetermeer, The Netherlands.

US agent: William Grant & Sons.

Tel: 732 225 9000

This Dutch liqueur is derived from an alcoholic drink that colonists in South Africa made from the yellowish pulp of the abacate fruit. In Holland, egg yolks took the place of abacate and the name, already evolved into 'avocado' by Portuguese colonists, became 'advocaat' in Dutch.

Bols Advocaat is an entirely natural product. It is made exclusively from brandy, egg yolks, sugar and vanilla, without any preservatives or artificial thickeners.

Bols Advocaat has a thick, indulgent, luscious custardy consistency. The palate features subtle, creamy vanilla, cocoa powder and a hint of cooked egg yolk.

New Port Codebreaker ●●●◐○
Nutty Summer ●●●●◐
Orange Custard Martini ●●●◐○

BOLS APRICOT BRANDY LIQUEUR

24% alc./vol. (48°proof)

www.grantUSA.com

Producer: Bols Royal Distilleries, Zoetermeer, The Netherlands.

US distributor: William Grant & Sons.

Tel: 732 225 9000

Apricot Brandy is sometimes also known as 'apry'. It is a liqueur produced by infusing apricots in selected cognacs and flavouring the infusion with various herbs to bring out the finest apricot taste and aroma. Enriched with a hint of almond, this amber coloured liqueur is one of Bols' most popular liqueurs.

With a mild aroma of juicy apricots, this distinctively flavoured liqueur is suited to use in a variety of different cocktails. The light, clean taste features apricot with a hint of cognac and almond.

Leave It To Me Martini ●●●◐○
Lutkins Special Martini ●●●◐○
Mambo ●●●◐○
Mayfair Cocktail ●●●●○
The Mayflower Martini ●●●●○
Millionaire's Daiquiri ●●●◐○
Moon River ●●●◐○
Mule's Hind Leg ●●●●◐
Nacional Daiquiri #1 ●●●●◐
Nacional Daiquiri #2 ●●●●◐
Pancho Villa ●●●●○
Paradise #1 ●●●◐○
Paradise #2 ●●●●◐
Paradise #3 ●●●◐○
Park Lane ●●●●◐
Pendennis Cocktail ●●●●○
Periodista Daiquiri ●●●●○
Playmate Martini ●●●●◐

BOLS BLACKBERRY LIQUEUR

www.grantUSA.com

Producer: Bols Royal Distilleries, Zoetermeer, The Netherlands.

US distributor: William Grant & Sons.

Tel: 732 225 9000

The Latin words 'Semper Idem' inscribed on the coat of arms of the Bols family literally translate as 'always the same'. For the distillers at Bols this motto represents their goal to produce liqueurs of a consistently high quality. It is to that end that they apply their years of experience and knowledge.

Some cocktail recipe books state 'crème de mûre' instead of 'blackberry liqueur'. This comes from 'mûre', the French for blackberry, and 'crème' as in the French phrase 'crème de la crème', meaning 'best of the best'. In such cases you can use Bols Blackberry liqueur which is made from the finest fresh blackberries.

The intense blackberry flavour of this rich liqueur adds a concentrated fruit flavour to cocktails and can be used to boost the flavour when using fresh fruit in a drink.

BOLS BLUE CURAÇAO LIQUEUR

21% alc./vol. (42°proof)

www.grantUSA.com

Producer: Bols Royal Distilleries, Zoetermeer, The Netherlands.

US distributor: William Grant & Sons.

Tel: 732 225 9000

This vivid blue curaçao liqueur is probably the best known of the Bols range. Part of Remy Cointreau, Bols Royal Distilleries originated from a firm started in 1575 by a Dutchman called Lucas Bols. Prevented from distilling within the city walls due to the fire risk, Lucas distilled from a wooden shed outside Amsterdam. Today Bols is one of the largest liqueur producers in the world.

Bols Blue is distilled from a blend of predominantly natural products from around the world – herbs, sweet red oranges, the characteristically flavourful bitter Curaçao oranges and the rare Kinnow oranges. This gives Bols Blue its fresh, yet complex orange scent and taste.

Bols Blue is frequently used by bartenders due to its distinctive, deep blue colour and refreshing taste, which features orange zest with a hint of spice.

Liminal Shot ●●●○○
Liquorice All Sort ●●●◐○
Lotus Martini ●●●●○
Purple Flirt #2 ●●●○○
Purple Turtle ●●●◐○

BOLS BUTTERSCOTCH LIQUEUR

www.grantUSA.com

Producer: Bols Royal Distilleries, Zoetermeer, The Netherlands.

US distributor: William Grant & Sons.

Tel: 732 225 9000

Butterscotch is one of those indulgent flavours that take us back to our youth, a world of cookies, ice-cream toppings and candies. Sweet and creamy, it also has a wonderfully tangy bite.

The name has nothing to do with Scotch whisky, or anything Scottish at all. It comes from the term 'scotch', meaning to cut or score a surface, and 'butter' for the butter in the candy. When butterscotch candy is poured out to cool, it is scotched to make it easier to break into pieces later.

Bols Butterscotch liqueur captures the heart of butterscotch so mixologists can easily add that wonderful burnt, buttery, sugary flavour to everything from shooters to Martinis.

Met Manhattan ●●●●○
Monk's Candy Bar ●●●○○

BOLS CHERRY (BRANDY) LIQUEUR

24% alc./vol. (48°proof)

www.grantUSA.com

Producer: Bols Royal Distilleries, Zoetermeer, The Netherlands.

US distributor: William Grant & Sons.

Tel: 732 225 9000

This richly flavoured liqueur is made from the juice of ripe, dark red cherries. Crushing the kernels while pressing the cherries enhances almond notes in the cherry juice and is very evident in the finished liqueur.

Extracts of various carefully selected herbs and spices such as cinnamon and cloves produce a well-balanced liqueur. With its luscious cherry flavour and hints of almond and spice, this traditional liqueur is a versatile mixer.

Nightmare Martini ●●●○○
Nutty Berry'tini ●●●◐○
Old Fashioned Caddy ●●●●○
Pancho Villa ●●●●○
Passbour Cooler ●●●○○

BOLS CRÈME DE BANANES LIQUEUR

17% alc./vol. (34°proof)

www.grantUSA.com

Producer: Bols Royal Distilleries, Zoetermeer, The Netherlands.

US distributor: William Grant & Sons.

Tel: 732 225 9000

The French term 'crème de' (literally 'cream of') indicates that one particular flavour predominates in a liqueur - it does not imply that the liqueur contains cream. Many fruit liqueurs are described as 'crème de' followed by the name of a fruit. This refers to the liqueur's quality, as in the phrase 'crème de la crème'. Therefore crème de bananes is a banana flavoured liqueur made by infusion and maceration of the fruit in neutral spirit.

Bols Crème de Bananes is a clear yellow liqueur with the flavour of sun-ripened bananas, enhanced with a touch of soft vanilla and a hint of almond. Extracts of various carefully selected herbs and spices give this well-balanced liqueur its special taste. Like many of the liqueurs in the Bols range, Crème de Bananes is extremely mixable. A plethora of cocktails rely on its exotic ripe banana flavour.

Landslide ●●●○○
Liquorice All Sort ●●●◐○
Luxury Cocktail ●●●◐○
Mellow Martini ●●●◐○

BOLS CRÈME DE CACAO BROWN

24% alc./vol. (48°proof)

www.grantUSA.com

Producer: Bols Royal Distilleries, Zoetermeer, The Netherlands.

US distributor: William Grant & Sons.

Tel: 732 225 9000

The finest roasted cacao beans are used to prepare Bols Brown crème de cacao. The cacao seeds are first broken open and then percolated. Various herbs are added to give the liqueur its own distinctive flavour. Please note that 'brown crème de cacao' liqueurs are sometimes alternatively named 'dark crème de cacao'.

Bols crème de cacao is perfect for adding a rich chocolate flavour to any cocktail. Choose between the lighter, more delicately flavoured white or this rich, dark version.

Mocha Martini ●●●●◐
Mulata Daiquiri ●●●●◐

BOLS CRÈME DE CACAO WHITE

24% alc./vol. (48°proof)

www.grantUSA.com

Producer: Bols Royal Distilleries, Zoetermeer, The Netherlands.

US distributor: William Grant & Sons.

Tel: 732 225 9000

A number of recipes require the chocolate flavour of crème de cacao but without the dark brown colour. In order to preserve the taste but eliminate the colour, Bols extract the flavour of the finest roasted cacao beans by means of distillation instead of percolation. This process also gives Bols White crème de cacao a lighter flavour than Bols Brown crème de cacao.

Bols crème de cacao is perfect for adding a rich chocolate flavour to any cocktail. Choose between this lighter, more delicately flavoured white or the rich, dark version.

Lemon Chiffon Pie ●●●●○
Lola ●●●◐○
Melon Collie Martini ●●●●○
Nutcracker Sweet ●●●◐○
Pago Pago ●●●◐○
Pall Mall Martini ●●●●○
Pini ●●●●◐
Pink Cloud ●●●○○
Pink Sin Martini ●●●○○
Princess Mary ●●●○○

BOLS PEACH SCHNAPPS LIQUEUR

www.grantUSA.com

Producer: Bols Royal Distilleries, Zoetermeer, The Netherlands.

US distributor: William Grant & Sons.

Tel: 732 225 9000

The luscious peach originated in China, where the tree has been cultivated since the 5th century BC. It reached Europe by way of Alexander the Great and the Greeks and its sweet, succulent flavour has made it a favourite liqueur ingredient since time immemorial.

During the 80s, peach schnapps appeared on the scene, and rapidly ousted the more syrupy, heavier peach liqueurs of old. Bols Peach Schnapps is a supremely contemporary blend of fine spirits with the mild, juicy aroma and flavour of sun-ripened peaches. Its refreshing flavour and clear colour make it a versatile addition to the cocktail bartender's palette.

Love Junk ●●●◐○
Missionary's Downfall ●●●●●
Mississippi Schnapper ●●●◐○
Moonraker ●●●●○
Mystique ●●●◐○
Oatmeal Cookie ●●●◐○
Pale Rider ●●●○○
Palma Violet Martini ●●●◐○
Peach Daiquiri ●●●●○
Peach Melba Martini ●●●◐○
Pink Tutu ●●●◐○

BOLS STRAWBERRY LIQUEUR

17% alc./vol. (34°proof)

www.grantUSA.com

Producer: Bols Royal Distilleries, Zoetermeer, The Netherlands.

US distributor: William Grant & Sons.

Tel: 732 225 9000

Bols are one of the largest and oldest producers of fine spirits and liqueurs in the world. Some of their products date back as far as 1575. However, this strawberry liqueur is a relatively new addition to the Bols range. It is a distillate of refreshing citrus fruit and real strawberry juice.

The French word for strawberry is 'fraise' and cocktail recipes often call for the use of 'crème de fraise', or strawberry liqueur. Bols Strawberry liqueur is ideal for use in any recipe which calls for crème de fraise.

Bols Strawberry has a rich ripe strawberry flavour with light hints of citrus fruit. It is great served chilled, in a cocktail, over strawberries or in a fruit salad.

Liquorice All Sort ●●●◐○

BOLS WHITE CRÈME DE MENTHE

www.grantUSA.com

Producer: Bols Royal Distilleries, Zoetermeer, The Netherlands.

US distributor: William Grant & Sons.

Tel: 732 225 9000

Bols White Crème de Menthe is an aromatic liqueur, great sipped straight as a digestif or blended in a range of cocktails. Bols' master distillers derive oil from mint leaves originating in England, America and Morocco, then redistill them to produce a clear liqueur with a clean, well-defined bouquet and a definite mint finish.

Bols White Crème de Menthe was especially developed for use in the many cocktails which require a fresh, minty flavour to be added without a change of colour.

Miami Daiquiri ●●●●○
Mint Cocktail ●●●●◐
Mint Fizz ●●●◐○
Monte Carlo Imperial ●●●○○

BOURBON

See 'Whiskey - Bourbon'

BUTTERSCOTCH SCHNAPPS LIQUEUR

See 'Bols Butterscotch Liqueur'

CACAO DARK (CRÈME DE) LIQUEUR

See 'Bols Crème de Cacao Brown'

CACAO WHITE (CRÈME DE) LIQUEUR

See 'Bols Crème de Cacao White'

CACHAÇA

Pronounced 'Ka-Shah-Sa', cachaça is the spirit of Brazil. As it is based on sugar cane, it is very similar to a rum. However, maize meal is traditionally used to start the fermentation, so many brands of cachaça are not strictly rums. Further, most rums are produced from molasses, a byproduct of sugar refining, but the best cachaça is distilled from fermented sugar cane juice. (Many bigger brands, however, use molasses, which ferments more quickly as the sugars break down faster after they have been burnt. And a lot of smaller distillers use sugar cane syrup.)

Cachaça is distilled to a maximum of 75% alcoholic strength, unlike most light rums which are usually distilled to 96% strength. This lower distillation strength means cachaça retains more of the aroma and flavour of the sugar cane and is less refined than most rums.

Lemon Beat ●●●●○
Mango Batida ●●●●○
Maracuja Batida ●●●●○
Milho Verde Batida ●●●◐○
Passion Fruit Caipirinha ●●●●○

CALVADOS

Calvados is a French brandy made from apples, although some styles also contain pears. The name is an appellation contrôlée, meaning that Calvados can only be produced in defined areas of north-west France.

Like Cognac and Armagnac, the Calvados-making district is divided into smaller areas. Two of these sub-regions have their own appellations contrôlées: Pays d'Auge and Domfront.

Pays d'Auge, the area around the villages of Orne and Eure, is generally considered to produce the best Calvados and by law all AOC Pays d'Auge Calvados must be double-distilled in pot stills.

Domfront Calvados, which acquired its AOC at the end of 1997, must contain at least 30% perry pears.

Long Flight of Stairs ●●●●◐
Mule's Hind Leg ●●●●◐
Parisian Spring Punch ●●●●○
Princess Marina ●●●●○
Princess Mary's Pride ●●◐○○
Princess Pride ●●●◐○

CHAMBORD

16.5% alc./vol. (33°proof)

www.chambord online.com

Producer: Chambord et Cie, Chambord, France.

US agent: Charles Jacquin et Cie, 2633, Trenton Ave, Philadelphia, PA 19125.

Tel: 800 523 3811

Chambord Liqueur Royale de France, to use its full name, is believed to have been created in the time of Louis XIV, when hunting parties visited Chambord, the largest chateau in the French Loire Valley. It is a rich Framboise-style liqueur made from small black raspberries and herbs combined with honey and high quality neutral alcohol.

Chambord is popularly mixed as a Kir-like drink with champagne – the Cham Cham. Its distinctive orb shaped bottle is easily recognised and a 'must stock' in most cocktail bars. Although there are other raspberry liqueurs, it is Chambord that graces our shelves and those of some of the world's most noted cocktail bars.

Chambord's rich flavour is ideally suited to a variety of cocktail recipes and has a taste that includes raspberry fool, blackcurrant jam, cherry jam, honeyed vanilla, sloe and damson, plus a hint of raisins and stewed prunes.

Loved Up ●●●◐○
Lush ●●●◐○
Marquee ●●●●○
Miss Martini ●●●◐○
Mystique Martini ●●●●○
New Orleans Punch ●●●◐○
Nuts & Berries ●●●●○
Pavlova Shot ●●●◐○
Peach Melba Martini ●●●◐○
Peanut Butter & Jelly Shot ●●●◐○
Purple Haze ●●●◐○
Purple Hooter ●●●◐○

CAMPARI

Mambo ●●●◐○
Mandarintini ●●●○○
Milano ●●●●◐
Monza ●●●◐○
Negroni ●●●●◐
Night & Day ●●●◐○
Old Pal ●●●◐○
Parma Negroni ●●●●○
Pink Tutu ●●●◐○

CHAMPAGNE

The vineyards of the Champagne region are the most northerly in France, lying north-east of Paris, on either side of the River Marne. Most of the champagne houses are based in one of two towns: Epernay and Reims.

Champagne, surprisingly, is made predominantly from black grapes. The three grape varieties used are Pinot Noir (the red grape of Burgundy), Pinot Meunier (a fruitier relative of Pinot Noir) and Chardonnay. Pinot Meunier is the most commonly used of these three varieties with Chardonnay, the only white grape, accounting for less than 30% of vines in the Champagne region. Pinot Meunier buds late and ripens early so can be relied upon to ripen throughout the Champagne region, which probably explains its domination.

Limeosa ●●●◐○
Lush ●●●◐○
Luxury Mojito ●●●●○
Martini Royale ●●●◐○
Mexican 55 ●●●●○
Mimosa ●●●◐○
Monte Carlo Imperial ●●●○○
Night & Day ●●●◐○
Nine-20-Seven ●●●●○
Parisian Spring Punch ●●●●○
Perry-tini ●●●●○
Pimm's Cocktail ●●●●◐
Pimm's Royal ●●◐○○
Pisco Punch #1 (Difford's Formula) ●●●●◐
Poinsettia ●●●◐○
Ponce de Leon ●●●●○
Prince Of Wales ●●●◐○

CHARTREUSE GREEN

The Last Word ●●●●◐
Martini Thyme ●●●●○
Mary Queen of Scots ●●●●◐
Mary Rose ●●●●○
Medicinal Solution ●●●◐○
Mona Lisa ●●●●○
Mujer Verde ●●●●○
Pago Pago ●●●◐○

CHARTREUSE YELLOW

Lemony ●●●●○
Mujer Verde ●●●●○
Nome ●●●●○
Oddball Manhattan Dry ●●●●○
Quarterback ●●●●○

CHERRY (BRANDY) LIQUEUR

See 'Bols Cherry (Brandy) Liqueur'

CINNAMON SCHNAPPS LIQUEUR

Cinnamon is obtained from the bark of several tropical trees. Sri Lanka and China are the largest producers. Cinnamon liqueurs have a warm, sweet, spicy flavour.

Oatmeal Cookie ●●●◐○
Pink Sin Martini ●●●○○
Pirate Daiquiri ●●●●○
Plum Pudding Martini ●●●◐○

COCONUT RUM LIQUEUR

Coconut rums are mostly made in the Caribbean but are also common in France and Spain. They are made by blending rectified white rum with coconut extracts and tend to be presented in opaque white bottles.

Melon Collie Martini ●●●●○
Meloncholy Martini ●●●●○
Mister Stu ●●●◐○
Monkey Shine ●●●●○
Mucky Bottom ●●●◐○
Nutty Summer ●●●●◐

COFFEE (ESPRESSO)

Coffee beans are the dried and roasted seed of a cherry which grows on a bush in the tropics. There are two main species of coffee plant: Coffea Arabica and Coffea Canephora. These are commonly known as Arabica and Robusta. Arabica is relatively low in caffeine, more delicate and requires more intensive cultivation. Robusta is higher in caffeine, more tolerant of climate and parasites, and can be grown fairly cheaply. Robusta beans tend to be woody and bitter while Arabica beans have well-rounded, subtle flavours.

Most of the recipes in this guide which use coffee call for espresso and, as with other ingredients, the quality of this will greatly affect the finished drink. I strongly recommend using an Arabica coffee brewed in an espresso machine or a moka pot.

Lazarus ●●●●◐
Lotus Espresso ●●●●◐
Mocha Martini ●●●●◐
Opal Café ●●●●○
Pharmaceutical Stimulant ●●●●○

COFFEE LIQUEUR

Coffee flavoured liqueurs are made by infusing coffee beans in alcohol or by infusing beans in hot water and then blending with alcohol. Look for brands made using Arabica coffee beans.

Lazarus ●●●●◐
Lonely Bull ●●●◐○
Long Beach Iced Tea ●●●◐○
Lotus Expresso ●●●●◐
Mad Monk Milkshake ●●●◐○
Mayan ●●●○○
Mayan Whore ●●●●○
Monk's Candy Bar ●●●○○
Muddy Water ●●●◐○
Mudslide ●●●●○
Mucky Bottom ●●●◐○
New Orleans Mule ●●●◐○
Nutty Russian ●●●◐○
Pharmaceutical Stimulant ●●●●○
Pousse-café ●●◐○○
P.S. I Love You ●●●●○

COGNAC

Cognac is a fine French brandy from the region around the little town of Cognac in south-west France, recognised with its own appellation contrôlée. With its rolling countryside, groves of trees and the Charente River, the area is picturesque. It is divided into six sub-regions, reflecting variations in climate and soil. As a general rule, the best soil is the chalkiest: the most regarded (and most central) sub-region, Grande Champagne, has only a very thin layer of top soil over solid chalk. The biggest houses only use grapes from the best four sub-regions to produce their cognacs.

Lazarus ●●●●◐
Loud Speaker Martini ●●●◐○
Mandarine Sidecar ●●●●○
Manhattan Island ●●●●○
Maxim's Coffee (Hot) ●●●●○
Milk Punch ●●●●○
Mississippi Punch ●●●●○
Moonraker ●●●●○
Morning Glory ●●●●○
Nice Pear-tini ●●●●◐
Nicky Finn ●●●●○
Ole ●●●◐○
Olympic ●●●●◐
Orange Brûlée ●●●●●
Passion Punch ●●●◐○
Pear & Cardamom Sidecar ●●●●◐
Pierre Collins ●●●●○
Pini ●●●●◐
Playmate Martini ●●●●◐
Ponce de Leon ●●●●○
Port Wine Cocktail ●●●◐○
Prairie Oyster ●●●◐○
Prince Charlie ●●●●○
Prince Of Wales ●●●◐○
Pulp Fiction ●●●●○
Quelle Vie ●●●◐○

COINTREAU LIQUEUR

L.A. Iced Tea ●●●◐○
Lago Cosmo ●●●◐○
Lemon Drop Martini ●●●◐○
Lemongrass Cosmo ●●●●◐
Leninade ●●●●○
Limelite ●●●○○
Limey Cosmo ●●●●○
Long Island Iced Tea ●●●◐○
Long Island Spiced Tea ●●●◐○
Loved Up ●●●◐○
Lynchburg Lemonade ●●●●○
Mai Tai #2 (Beaumont-Gantt's Formula) ●●●●○
Mai Tai #3 (Difford's Formula) ●●●●●
Maiden's Blush ●●●●◐
Maiden's Prayer ●●●◐○
Mainbrace ●●●●○
Major Bailey #2 ●●●●◐
Magic Bus ●●●◐○
Malcolm Lowry ●●●●○
Mambo ●●●◐○
Mango Margarita #1 ●●●●○
Mango Margarita #2 (Frozen) ●●●●○
Marama Rum Punch ●●●●○
Margarita #1 (Straight-up) ●●●●◐
Margarita #2 (On the Rocks) ●●●●◐
Margarita #3 (Frozen) ●●●●○
Margarita #4 (Salt Foam Float) ●●●◐○
Marmarita ●●●●○
Martinez ●●●●●
Mat The Rat ●●●◐○
Matador ●●●●○
Meloncholy Martini ●●●●○
Menehune Juice ●●●●○
Metropolitan ●●●●○
Millionaire ●●●●○
Mississippi Schnapper ●●●◐○
Monk's Habit ●●●○○
Montego Bay ●●●◐○
Moon River ●●●◐○
Mountain Sipper ●●●◐○
Napoleon Martini ●●●●◐
Nicky Finn ●●●●○
Oh Gosh! ●●●●●
Opal ●●●●◐
Orang-A-Tang ●●●●○
Orange Bloom Martini ●●●●◐
Orange Blossom ●●●◐○
Osmo ●●●●○
Passion Fruit Margarita ●●●●○
Passion Fruit Martini #3 ●●●●○
Pear & Cardamom Sidecar ●●●●◐
Pegu Club ●●●●○
Perfect John ●●●●○
Pineapple Margarita ●●●●○
Pino Pepe ●●●●○
Playa Del Mar ●●●●○
Poinsettia ●●●◐○
Pompanski Martini ●●●●○
Ponce de Leon ●●●●○
Potted Parrot ●●●◐○
Pousse-café ●●◐○○
Presidente ●●●●○
Princess Marina ●●●●○
Quarterback ●●●●○

CRANBERRY JUICE - RED

Cranberries are native to America and are grown in large, flooded fields, known as cranberry bogs. Experts say you can tell when a cranberry is ready to eat because it bounces. Cranberries are high in vitamin C and pectin, and a popular natural remedy for cystitis.

Cranberry is the exception which proves the 'fresh is best' rule. Don't even contemplate muddling fresh berries: pure cranberry juice is extremely sour and is normally sweetened and blended to make it more palatable.

Pick up a carton of cranberry juice from the refrigerated display of your local supermarket. As with other juices, avoid the non-refrigerated products and read the small print carefully – some products end up with barely any cranberry and taste far too sweet. Look for products containing at least 20% cranberry juice.

Lemongrass Cosmo ●●●●◐
Light Breeze ●●●◐○
Lighter Breeze ●●●◐○
Lime Breeze ●●●◐○
Limey Cosmo ●●●●○
Long Beach Iced Tea ●●●◐○
Madras ●●●◐○
Madroska ●●●○○
Mae West Martini ●●●●○
Magic Bus ●●●◐○
Man-Bour-Tini ●●●●○
Maria Theresa Margarita ●●●●○
Marquee ●●●●○
Metropolitan ●●●●○
Mexican Tea (Hot) ●●●●◐
Mountain Slipper ●●●◐○
Nantucket ●●●◐○
Nautilus ●●●●◐
Not So Cosmo (Mocktail) ●●●◐○
November Seabreeze (Mocktail) ●●●◐○
Nutty Berry'tini ●●●◐○
Osmo ●●●●○
Pale Rider ●●●○○
Palm Springs ●●●◐○
Parlay Punch ●●●○○
Pass-on-that ●●●○○
Passbour Cooler ●●●○○
Pink Flamingo ●●●○○
Pink Sin Martini ●●●○○
Playa Del Mar ●●●●○
Poinsettia ●●●◐○
Pontberry Martini ●●●●○
Purple Flirt #1 ●●●●○

CRANBERRY (WHITE) & GRAPE DRINK

White cranberry juice drinks are made with white cranberries, harvested before they develop their familiar red colour. They tend to be less tart than red cranberry drinks.

Purple Cosmo ●●●●◐

CUCUMBER

The fruit of a climbing plant originating from the foothills of the Himalayas, cucumbers should be used as fresh as possible, so look for firm, unwrinkled fruit. The skin can be quite bitter so cucumber is best peeled before use in cocktails. Either muddle in the base of your shaker or juice using an extractor.

Moscow Lassi ●●●○○
Pimm's Cup (or Classic) ●●●◐○

DOUBLE (HEAVY) CREAM

I've specified 'double' or 'heavy cream' in preference to lighter creams. In many recipes this is diluted with an equal measure of milk to make half & half.

Lemon Meringue Pie'tini
Lola
Lonely Bull
Mad Monk Milkshake
Melon Collie Martini
Meloncholy Martini
Mexican Coffee (Hot)
Mexicano (Hot)
Milk & Honey Martini
Milk Punch
Miss Martini
Mocha Martini
Monk's Candy Bar
North Pole Martini
Nutty Summer
Opal Café
Orange Brûlée
Peach Melba Martini
Piña Colada
Piña Colada Virgin (Mocktail)
Platinum Blonde
Princess Mary
P.S. I Love You
Quarterback

CREAM OF COCONUT

This is a non-alcoholic, sticky blend of coconut juice, sugar, emulsifier, cellulose, thickeners, citric acid and salt. Fortunately it tastes better than it sounds and is an essential ingredient of a good Piña Colada. One 15oz/425ml can will make approximately 25 drinks. Once opened the contents should be transferred to a suitable container and stored in a refrigerator. This may thicken the product, so gentle warming may be required prior to use. Coconut milk is very different and cannot be substituted.

New Port Codebreaker
Painkiller
Piña Colada
Piña Colada Virgin (Mocktail)

CRÈME DE BANANES LIQUEUR

See 'Bols Crème de Bananes Liqueur'

CRÈME DE CACAO LIQUEUR

See 'Bols Crème de Cacao Brown' and 'Bols Crème de Cacao White'

CRÈME DE CASSIS LIQUEUR

As with other liqueurs, the term 'crème de' does not mean the liqueur contains any cream. Crème de cassis is a blackcurrant liqueur which originated in France and can be made by infusion and/or maceration. The original recipe for a crème de cassis is thought to have been formulated by Denis Lagoute in 1841 in the French Dijon region. Many of the best examples are still produced in this region.

EEC law states that crème de cassis must have a minimum of 400g of sugar per litre and a minimum alcoholic strength of 15%. Unfortunately no minimum is set for the fruit content although the best brands will contain as much as 600g of blackcurrants per litre. Brands with a high fruit content will have a more fruity taste and a deeper colour than low-fruit brands.

Liquorice Shot
Lychee & Blackcurrant Martini
Macka
Martini Royale
Mexican Martini
Parisian Martini

CRÈME DE FRAISE LIQUEUR

See 'Bols Strawberry Liqueur'

CRÈME DE FRAMBOISE LIQUEUR

See 'Raspberry (Crème de Framboise) Liqueur'

CRÈME DE MENTHE GREEN LIQUEUR

A mint-flavoured liqueur with a striking green colour.

Miami Daiquiri
Mint Cocktail
Mint Fizz
Monte Carlo Imperial

CRÈME DE MENTHE WHITE LIQUEUR

See 'Bols White Crème de Menthe'

CRÈME DE MÛRE LIQUEUR

See 'Bols Blackberry Liqueur'

DRAMBUIE LIQUEUR

Mary Queen of Scots
Mystique
Prince Charlie

DUBONNET RED

Merry Widow #2
Moonraker
Napoleon Martini
Nightmare Martini
Opera
Paris Sour
Peggy Martini
Princess Marina
Princess Mary's Pride
Princess Pride
Quebec

EGGS

The hazards of raw eggs are well known so you may decide it is safer to use commercially produced pasteurised egg white, particularly if you are infirm or pregnant (but then you probably shouldn't be drinking cocktails anyway).

Many cocktails only taste their best when made with fresh eggs. I'm sure I've suffered more upset stomachs from drinking too much alcohol than I have as a result of bad eggs. That said, it's worth taking steps to reduce the risk of Salmonella poisoning and therefore I recommend you store small, free range eggs in a refrigerator and use them well before the sell-by date. Don't consume eggs if:

1. You are uncertain about their freshness.
2. There is a crack or flaw in the shell.
3. They don't wobble when rolled across a flat surface.
4. The egg white is watery instead of gel-like.
5. The egg yolk is not convex and firm.
6. The egg yolk bursts easily.
7. They smell foul.

Lemon Sorbet
Lime Sour
Liquorice Whiskey Sour
Mandarine Sour
Margarita #4 (Salt Foam Float)
Milano Sour
The Million Dollar Cocktail
Millionaire
Morning Glory Fizz
Mountain
Noon
North Pole Martini
Paris Sour
Park Lane
Passion Fruit Martini #3
Pink Lady
Pisco Sour (Traditional Recipe)
Pisco Sour (Difford's Version)
Playmate Martini
Plum Sour
Ponche de Algarrobina
Port Light
Prairie Oyster
Purple Flirt #2
Pussyfoot (Mocktail)
Quince Sour

ELDERFLOWER CORDIAL

Elderflower cordial is a traditional Victorian British thirst quencher which found its way from the farmhouse kitchen to the supermarket shelf in the late 80s. It is made from the tiny white flowers which cover the elder bush, a common sight in the British hedgerow during early summer.

To make homemade elderflower cordial you'll need about 30 heads of elderflower, rinsed clean of dirt and bugs. Do not use the leaves or branches as they are poisonous and, if using wild flowers, be sure you have identified them correctly: a mistake could have serious consequences.

Pour 6 pints (3 litres) of boiling water over 900g (2lb) of sugar in a bowl, and stir until the sugar has dissolved. Leave to cool. Wash and slice 2 unwaxed oranges and 3 unwaxed lemons and add these along with 2 teaspoons of citric acid (available from chemists) and 30 elderflower heads. Leave in a cool place for 24 hours, stirring occasionally. Finally, strain through muslin and bottle. You can store this in a refrigerator for up to two weeks.

Lemongrad ●●●●◐
Lighter Breeze ●●●◐○
The Mayflower Martini ●●●●○
M.C. Martini ●●●●●
Monarch Martini ●●●●○
Orchard Breeze ●●●●◐
Palookaville ●●●●○
Pear & Elderflower Martini ●●●●○

FINO

See under 'Sherry – Fino'

GALLIANO LIQUEUR

Maxim's Coffee (Hot) ●●●●○
Milano Sour ●●●●○
Moon River ●●●◐○
Mrs Robinson #2 ●●●◐○
Perfect John ●●●●○
Picca ●●●●○

GIN

See 'Plymouth Gin'

GINGER ALE

A non-alcoholic drink made by adding ginger essence, colouring and sweeteners to aerated water. Not as powerful in flavour as ginger beer.

Limey Mule ●●●●○
Loch Almond ●●●●○
Maple Pomme ●●●●○
New Year's Absolution ●●●◐○
Niagara Falls ●●●◐○
O'Henry ●●●◐○

GINGER BEER

A fizzy drink flavoured with ginger - either non-alcoholic or only mildly so. Buy a quality brand or brew your own as follows:

Combine 2oz/56 grams of peeled and crushed root ginger, two lemons sliced into thick rings, one teaspoon of cream of tartar, 1lb/450 grams sugar and 1 gallon/ 4 litres water in a large stainless steel saucepan and bring to the boil. Stir and leave to cool to blood temperature. Stir in 1 oz/ 28 grams of yeast and leave to ferment for 24 hours. Skim off the yeast from the surface and fine strain the liquid into four sterilised 1 litre plastic bottles with screw caps. (Leave at least 2 inches/5cm of air at the top of each bottle and ensure all utensils are scrupulously clean.) Place bottles upright and release excess pressure after 12 hours. Check again after another 12 hours. Once the bottles feel firm and under pressure, place them in the refrigerator and consume their contents within three days.

Mandarine Songbird ●●●○○
Mexican Mule ●●●●◐
Moscow Mule ●●●●○
New Orleans Mule ●●●◐○
Prickly Pear Mule ●●●●○

GRAND MARNIER

40% alc./vol. (80° proof)

www.grand-marnier.com

Producer: Marnier-Lapostolle (Société des Produits), Paris, France.

US distributor: Marnier-Lapostolle. **Tel:** 212 207 4350

Grand Marnier is one of the best known and most widely sold premium liqueurs in the world. With a cognac base, its unique flavour and aroma come from the maceration and distillation of natural, tropical orange peels.

Founded in 1827 by Jean Baptiste Lapostolle, Grand Marnier is still a family-run business and continues to use traditional production methods and the original Grand Marnier recipe. But despite its heritage, Grand Marnier is an essential cocktail ingredient in today's leading style bars.

Grand Marnier is silky rich with a zesty, juicy flavour. It has a good underlying bite of bitter orange and hints of marmalade and cognac richness at the edges, making it the perfect cocktail partner.

Grand Marnier also produce two special cuvées or blends, 'Grand Marnier Cuvée du Centenaire', created in 1927 by Louis-Alexandre Marnier-Lapostolle to celebrate the 100th anniversary of the company's foundation; and 'Grand Marnier Cuvée du Cent Cinquantenaire', an exceptional Grand Marnier created in 1977 by the chairman of the company, Jacques Marnier-Lapostolle, to celebrate its 150th anniversary.

A number of the cocktails in this guide which call for Grand Marnier benefit from the extra complexity provided by these exceptional cuvées. I've marked these drinks with an '*' in the list below and in the recipe after Grand Marnier.

Leap Year Martini ●●●○○
Mandarinitini ●●●○○
Marny Cocktail* ●●●●◐
Met Manhattan ●●●●○
Mexican Tea (Hot) ●●●●◐
Mexicano (Hot) ●●●●◐
Million Dollar Margarita* ●●●●◐
Mimosa ●●●◐○
Morning Glory ●●●●○
Mulled Wine ●●●●○
Naranja Daiquiri ●●●●○
Niagara Falls ●●●◐○
Night & Day ●●●◐○
Olympic ●●●●◐
Orange Brûlée ●●●●●
Orange Custard Martini ●●●◐○
Park Avenue ●●●●○
Periodista Daiquiri ●●●●○
Pilgrim Cocktail ●●●●○
Pink Palace ●●●●◐
Pisco Naranja ●●●◐○
Platinum Blonde ●●●◐○
Playmate Martini* ●●●●◐
Polly's Special ●●●●○
Prince Of Wales* ●●●◐○

GRAPEFRUIT JUICE

This citrus fruit originated in Jamaica and may take its unusual name from the way the unripe fruit hangs in green clusters from the tree like bunches of grapes. Or then again, maybe some early botanist just got confused. Grapefruit is a recognised antioxidant and pink grapefruit contains lycopene, which is thought to boost the body's immune system. Consuming large quantities of concentrated grapefruit juice can, however, produce reactions with certain prescription-only medicines.

As a rule of thumb – the darker the flesh, the sweeter the juice and the more beta-carotene and vitamins. But even the sweetest of grapefruits are wonderfully sharp and tart.

I must confess that I tend to use packaged 'freshly squeezed' grapefruit juice from the supermarket. However, this is a relatively easy fruit to juice yourself using a citrus press or an electric spinning juicer. Simply cut in half and juice away, taking care to avoid the pith, which can make the juice bitter. As with other citrus fruits, avoid storing in the refrigerator immediately prior to use as cold fruit yield less juice.

LCB Martini ●●●●○
Light Breeze ●●●◐○
Lima Sour ●●●◐○
Lime Breeze ●●●◐○
Lisa B's Daiquiri ●●●●●
M.G.F. ●●●●○
Mai Tai #2 (Beaumont-Gantt's Formula) ●●●●○
Mainbrace ●●●●○
Mesa Fresca ●●●●○
Monkey Wrench ●●●◐○
Moonlight Martini ●●●●○
Mountain Sipper ●●●◐○
Mucky Bottom ●●●◐○
Nantucket ●●●◐○
Navigator ●●●●○
Nevada Daiquiri ●●●●○
Nicky's Fizz ●●●◐○
Oriental Tart ●●●●○
Paloma ●●●●◐
Palm Beach ●●●◐○
Parma Negroni ●●●●○
Passover ●●●○○
Pink Grapefruit Margarita ●●●●○
Pink Hound ●●●●○
Pink Tutu ●●●◐○
Pogo Stick ●●●●○
Polly's Special ●●●●○
Pompanski Martini ●●●●○
Ponce de Leon ●●●●○
Poncha ●●●●○

GRAPES

Oddly, many of the grapes which are classically used for winemaking are not particularly good to eat. Only a few, like Gamay, Tokay, Zinfandel and Muscat, are used for both purposes.

The main commercially available table grapes are Concord, which gives a purple juice which is used for concentrates and jellies, Emperor, which is red and thick-skinned, and Thompson Seedless, which is green and sweet. Seedless grapes are easiest to use in cocktails. Fresh grape juice has a delicate, subtle flavour which is very different from the syrupy stuff in cartons.

The best way to extract juice is to muddle the required number of grapes in the base of your shaker. Recipes in this guide call for 'seedless red grapes' or 'seedless white grapes'. Obviously, if you've opted for a grape that has seeds you'll need to remove them yourself before you muddle the grapes. Crushing seeds releases bitter flavours which can spoil a drink.

Double Grape Martini ●●●●◐
Enchanted ●●●◐○ (white grapes)
Grape Delight ●●●◐○ (red grapes)
Grape Effect ●●●●○ (white grapes)
Oriental Grape Martini ●●●●◐
Pisco Punch #4 (Prosser's Formula) ●●●●●

GRENADINE

See 'Pomegranate (Grenadine) Syrup'

HALF & HALF

This blend of 50% milk and 50% cream is relatively unknown in the UK. I've listed milk and cream as separate ingredients in both the American and the British versions of this guide.

HAZELNUT LIQUEUR

French hazelnut liqueurs are known as crème de noisette. Edmond Briottet is one of the better producers.

Mad Monk Milkshake ●●●◐○
Monk's Candy Bar ●●●○○
Monk's Habit ●●●○○
Nuts & Berries ●●●●○
Nutty Berry'tini ●●●◐○
Nutty Nashville ●●●●○
Nutty Russian ●●●◐○
Peanut Butter & Jelly Shot ●●●◐○

HONEY

Many bartenders dilute honey with equal parts of warm water to make it easier to mix. I prefer to use good quality runny honey (preferably orange blossom) and dissolve it by stirring it into the cocktail's base spirit prior to adding the other ingredients. This may be a tad time consuming but it avoids unnecessary dilution. Decant your honey into a squeezy plastic bottle with a fine nozzle for easy dispensing.

Lemon Beat ●●●●○
Lolita Margarita ●●●●◐
Lucky Lily Margarita ●●●●◐
Lucky Lindy ●●●◐○
Maria Theresa Margarita ●●●●○
Milk & Honey Martini ●●●●◐
Navy Grog ●●●●○
New Year's Absolution ●●●◐○
Nutty Nashville ●●●●○
Pappy Honeysuckle ●●●●◐
Pineapple Smoothie (Mocktail) ●●●◐○
Poncha ●●●●○
Pooh'tini ●●●●◐
Port Light ●●●◐○

HONEY LIQUEUR

There are many varieties of honey liqueur but the Polish brands claim the oldest heritage. Traditional Polish vodka-based honey liqueurs are thought to have originated in the 16th century. Besides the cocktails below, these liqueurs are worth enjoying neat and slightly warmed in a balloon glass – at London's Baltic they warm the bottle in a baby's bottle warmer.

Lemon Butter Cookie ●●●●○
Limited Liability ●●●●◐
Limousine ●●●●○
Milk & Honey Martini ●●●●◐
Nutty Nashville ●●●●○
Perfect Alibi ●●●●○
Polish Martini ●●●●●
Pooh'tini ●●●●◐

ICE CREAM (VANILLA)

Vanilla ice cream may not be exciting, but it is safe and almost universally liked. There are few people who can honestly say they hate the stuff, making it the obvious choice for a bar's freezer. Splash out on a decent brand. You'll taste the difference.

Lemon Chiffon Pie ●●●●○
Mudslide ●●●●○

INFUSIONS

Some recipes call for an infused spirit, such as vanilla-infused rum. You make this by putting three split vanilla pods in a bottle of rum and leaving it to stand for a fortnight. Warming and turning the bottle frequently can speed the infusion. Other herbs, spices and even fruits can be infused in a similar manner in vodka, gin, rum, whiskey and tequila. Whatever spirit you decide to use, pick a brand that is at least 40% alcohol by volume.

Be aware that when the level of spirit in a bottle drops below the flavouring, the alcohol loses its preservative effect and the flavouring can start to rot. Also be careful not to load the spirit with too much flavour or leave it to infuse for too long. Sample the infusion every couple of days to ensure the taste is not becoming overpowering.

IRISH CREAM LIQUEUR

In November 1974 R&A Bailey perfected the technique of combining Irish whiskey, cocoa and fresh cream without souring the cream. Sales grew quickly and Baileys is now the world's best selling liqueur. There are, however, many equally good alternatives.

Landslide ●●●○○
Lemon Meringue Martini ●●●●○
Mad Monk Milkshake ●●●◐○
Mocha Martini ●●●●◐
Muddy Water ●●●◐○
Mudslide ●●●●○
Oatmeal Cookie ●●●◐○
Oil Slick ●●◐○○
Peanut Butter & Jelly Shot ●●●◐○
P.S. I Love You ●●●●○

JENEVER

Jenever (or genever) is a juniper-flavoured spirit from Holland and Belgium. The juniper means jenever is technically a gin and in fact it was the forerunner of the London dry gins popular today. There are three basic styles of jenever - 'oude' (literally, 'old'), 'jonge' ('young') and 'korenwijn' ('corn wine'). They differ according to the percentage of malt-wine (a kind of unaged whiskey) and botanicals contained.

Jonge jenever is so named because it is a modern, contemporary style. It was first developed in the 1950s in response to consumer demand for a lighter, more mixable jenever.

Medicinal Solution ●●●◐○

KETEL ONE VODKA

40% alc./vol. (80°proof)

www.KetelOne.com

Producer: Nolet Distillery, Schiedam, The Netherlands.

US distributor: Nolet Spirits U.S.A., 30 Journey, Aliso Viejo, CA 92656.

Tel: 949 448 5700 / 800 243 3618

Ketel One vodka is the creation of one of Holland's oldest distilling families, the Nolet family of Schiedam, who have been distilling since 1691 when Joannes Nolet started his distillation business.

The Dutch refer to their pot stills as 'ketels', and this vodka is named after the Nolets' original coal-fired pot still - number one. This is still used today in the production of Ketel One. After distillation, the small batch spirit is slowly filtered through charcoal to ensure its purity.

Ten generations after Joannes, Carolus Nolet runs the company with the help of his two sons, Carl and Bob. They introduced Ketel One to the US in 1991 where it has since enjoyed phenomenal growth. This looks as if it's being repeated in the UK where the brand was launched in 1999.

Ketel One's balanced and clean palate with its classic wheat character makes beautifully smooth Martinis while still showing the character of the grain from which it is made.

L.A. Iced Tea ●●●◐○
Lavender & Black Pepper Martini ●●●●○
Lazarus ●●●●◐
LCB Martini ●●●●○
The Legend ●●●●○
Lemon Butter Cookie ●●●●○
Lemon Drop Martini ●●●◐○
Lemon Martini ●●●●◐
Life (Love In the Future Ecstasy) ●●●◐○
Limoncello Martini ●●●◐○
Liquorice Shot ●●●◐○
Long Beach Iced Tea ●●●◐○
Long Island Iced Tea ●●●◐○
Long Island Spiced Tea ●●●◐○
Lotus Expresso ●●●●◐
Love Junk ●●●◐○
Lush ●●●◐○
Lychee Martini ●●●●○
Madras ●●●◐○
Madroska ●●●○○
Mae West Martini ●●●●○
Mambo ●●●◐○
Mandarito ●●●●○
Martini Royale ●●●◐○
Melon Ball ●●●○○
Melon Martini #1 ●●●○○
Melon Martini #2 (Fresh Fruit) ●●●●○
Meloncholy Martini ●●●●○
Mellow Martini ●●●◐○
Merry Widow #2 ●●●◐○
Milano ●●●●◐
Mint Martini ●●●●◐
Miss Martini ●●●◐○
Momo Special ●●●●○
Monza ●●●◐○
Moscow Lassi ●●●○○
Moscow Mule ●●●●○
Mrs Robinson #2 ●●●◐○
Muddy Water ●●●◐○
Mudslide ●●●●○
Myrtle Martini ●●●◐○
Niagara Falls ●●●◐○
Noble Europe ●●●●◐
Nutcracker Sweet ●●●◐○
Nutty Russian ●●●◐○
Orang-A-Tang ●●●●○
Orchard Breeze ●●●●◐
Oriental Grape Martini ●●●●◐

Ouzi ●●●◐○
Palma Violet Martini ●●●◐○
Pass-on-that ●●●○○
Passion Fruit Martini #1 ●●●●○
Passion Fruit Martini #2 ●●●●○
Passover ●●●○○
Pavlova Shot ●●●◐○
Pear & Elderflower Martini ●●●●○
Perfect John ●●●●○
Pernod & Black Martini ●●●●○
Pharmaceutical Stimulant ●●●●○
Piña Martini ●●●●○
Pineapple & Cardamom Martini ●●●●●
Pineapple & Ginger Martini ●●●●○
Pink Sin Martini ●●●○○
Pink Tutu ●●●◐○
Pino Pepe ●●●●○
Plum Martini ●●●●○
Plum Sour ●●●●○
Polish Martini ●●●●●
Pomegranate Martini ●●●●◐
Pompanski Martini ●●●●○
Pontberry Martini ●●●●○
Port & Melon Martini ●●●●◐
Purple Flirt #1 ●●●●○
Purple Haze ●●●◐○
Purple Hooter ●●●◐○
Quince Sour ●●●●○

KETEL ONE CITROEN VODKA

40% alc./vol.
(80°proof)

www.KetelOne.com

Producer: Nolet Distillery, Schiedam, The Netherlands.

US distributor: Nolet Spirits U.S.A., 30 Journey, Aliso Viejo, CA 92656.

Tel: 949 448 5700 / 800 243 3618

Having already created what they and many top bartenders consider the perfect vodka for Martinis, the Nolet family wanted to create a flavoured vodka of equal excellence for making the ultimate Cosmopolitan. The family spent more than two years researching and evaluating different blending and infusion methods, before arriving at the costly but effective process of hand-crafting in small batches and infusing with natural citrus flavour until the perfect balance is reached.

Ketel One Citroen combines the smooth qualities of the original Ketel One vodka with refreshing natural essence of citrus fruit. To ensure continuity in the quality of Ketel One Citroen, a member of the Nolet family personally samples each batch prior to release.

There are few other citrus-flavoured vodkas with the rich, natural lemon peel oil flavours found in Ketel One Citroen. These combine with a clean grain character to make this vodka an ideal base for Cosmopolitans and other contemporary cocktails.

Lemon Curd Martini ●●●●○
Lemon Meringue Martini ●●●●○
Lemongrad ●●●●◐
Lemongrass Cosmo ●●●●◐
Leninade ●●●●○
M.G.F. ●●●●○
Mango Martini ●●●●○
Motox ●●●●○
Pear Drop ●●●◐○
Purple Cosmo ●●●●◐

LEMONCELLO

See 'Luxardo Limoncello Liqueur'

LEMONS & LIMES

Originally from India or Malaysia, lemons are available throughout the year and in many different varieties, distinguishable by their shape, size and thickness of skin. The smaller and more fragrant lime is closely related to the lemon. It is cultivated in tropical countries and is widely used in Caribbean and Brazilian cuisine.

Both these citrus fruits are bartender staples and their juice is used to balance sweetness and add depth to a bewildering range of cocktails. Lemon and lime juice will curdle cream and cream liqueurs but will happily mix with most other spirits and liqueurs. Limes generally pair well with rum while lemons are preferable in drinks based on whiskey or brandy.

Limes and lemons last longer if stored in the refrigerator. But you'll get more juice out of them if you let them warm up to room temperature and roll the fruit on a surface under the palm of your hand before you cut them. Save hard fruits for garnishing: soft fruits have more juice and flavour.

To juice, simply cut in half widthways and juice using a press, squeezer or spinning juicer, taking care not to grind the pith. Ideally you should juice your lemons and limes immediately prior to use as the juice will oxidise after a couple of hours.

I'd guess that, along with sugar syrup, these fruits are the most frequently used ingredients in this guide. Hence I've not even tried to index them.

LIME CORDIAL

Lauchlan Rose started importing lime juice from the West Indies to England in the 1860s, when ships were compelled to carry lime or lemon juice to prevent scurvy. In 1867 he devised a method for preserving juice without alcohol and created lime cordial, the world's first concentrated fruit drink. (What a spoilsport.) Thankfully all of the drinks in this guide that call for lime cordial are alcoholic.

Lime Blush ●●●○○ (Mocktail)
Limey ●●●◐○
Limey Cosmo ●●●●○
Limnology ●●●◐○
Luxury Cocktail ●●●◐○
Lychee & Blackcurrant Martini ●●●●○
Metropolitan ●●●●○
Mexican Surfer ●●●●○
Princeton Martini ●●●●○

LIMONCELLO LIQUEUR

See 'Luxardo Limoncello Liqueur'

LITCHI LIQUEUR

See 'Soho Lychee Liqueur'

LUXARDO AMARETTO DI SASCHIRA LIQUEUR

28% alc./vol.
(56°proof)

Producer: Girolamo Luxardo SpA., Torreglia, Padova, Italy.

US agent: Preiss Imports Ramona, CA.

Tel: 760 789 6010,

Email: info@preissimports.com

This delicate liqueur is an Italian classic, packed with the unique flavour of sweet almond, once sacred to the Greek goddess Cybele. The Luxardo family have been distilling fine liqueurs in the Veneto region of Italy for six generations now. They make their amaretto with the pure paste of the finest almonds, from Avola in southern Sicily, and age it for eight months in larch vats to impart its distinctive, well-rounded taste.

Their very contemporary amaretto is a vital tool in any mixologist's flavour armoury, with its palate of almond and marzipan.

Landslide ●●●○○
Loch Almond ●●●●○
Mae West Martini ●●●●○
Mister Stu ●●●◐○
Nutcracker Sweet ●●●◐○
Nutty Summer ●●●●◐
Orange Brûlée ●●●●●
Pink Cloud ●●●○○
Plum Pudding Martini ●●●◐○
P.S. I Love You ●●●●○

LUXARDO LIMONCELLO LIQUEUR

27% alc./vol.
(54°proof)

Producer: Girolamo Luxardo SpA., Torreglia, Padova, Italy.

US agent: Preiss Imports Ramona, CA.

Tel: 760 789 6010,

Email: info@preissimports.com

Despite its vibrant, yellow-green hue, this is an extremely traditional Italian liqueur – and, since the 90s, one of Italy's most popular. For generations, families have macerated lemon zest in spirit and sugar, encapsulating the mixologist's favourite combination of sour citrus, sweet and spirit: the formula at the heart of the Daiquiri, the Caipirinha and many more.

Luxardo Limoncello delivers a rich sweet lemon flavour in a blast of sour citrus, lemon zest and candied citrus, which somehow remain pure and balanced. It is increasingly popular among bartenders seeking new ways of delivering that vital citrus tang.

Lemon Meringue Pie'tini ●●●●○
Lemon Sorbet ●●●●○
Lemony ●●●●○
Limoncello Martini ●●●◐○
Motox ●●●●○
Navigator ●●●●○
Pear Drop Martini ●●●●○

LUXARDO MARASCHINO ORIGINALE LIQUEUR

32% alc./vol. (64°proof)

www.luxardo.it

Producer: Girolamo Luxardo SpA., Torreglia, Padova, Italy.

US agent: Preiss Imports, Ramona, CA.
Tel: 760 789 6010,

Email: info@preissimports.com

Until well into the 20th century, the bitter Marasca cherry grew only on the Dalmatian coast. Now part of Croatia, Zara, Dalmatia, was Italian territory when Girolamo Luxardo's wife began producing a liqueur from the local cherries. So popular did her maraschino become that in 1821 Girolamo founded a distillery to mass-produce it. The business prospered until the disruption of the Second World War, after which the family moved production to Italy. Today the Luxardos base their liqueur on cherries from their own 200 acre orchard and age it for two years in white Finnish ashwood vats. The silky palate features hints of dark chocolate, vanilla and marmalade alongside subtle cherry notes, with an elegant white chocolate and cherry finish, making it essential to a range of classic and modern cocktails.

The Last Word ●●●●◐
Lima Sour ●●●◐○
Lux Daiquiri ●●●●○
Manhattan Island ●●●●○
Mary Pickford ●●●●●
Monte Carlo ●●●◐○
Moonshine Martini ●●●●◐
Mystique ●●●◐○
North Pole Martini ●●●●○
Nutty Berry'tini ●●●◐○
Opera ●●●●○
Petto Martini ●●●●◐
Pink Daiquiri ●●●●○

LUXARDO SAMBUCA DEI CESARI

38% alc./vol. (76°proof)

www.luxardo.it

Producer: Girolamo Luxardo SpA., Torreglia, Padova, Italy.

US agent: Preiss Imports, Ramona, CA.
Tel: 760 789 6010,

Email: info@preissimports.com

The elder bush, with its distinctive bunches of black berries, grows wild all over Europe. Along with anise, it is the vital ingredient in Luxardo Sambuca, which takes its name from the Latin term for the plant.

This clear liqueur is crafted from green Sicilian aniseed and elderberries grown in the Euganean hills. Uniquely, it is matured in Finnish ash wood vats.

The clean, rich aniseed palate is lighter and less syrupy than some other brands, with subtle hints of lemon zest. A star performer in a number of contemporary cocktails, it is also great served 'con mosca' – flamed in a glass with three floating coffee beans signifying health, wealth and happiness, to bestow good luck.

Liquorice Shot ●●●◐○

LYCHEE LIQUEUR

See 'Soho Lychee Liqueur'

MANDARINE NAPOLÉON LIQUEUR

38% alc./vol. (76°proof)

www.mandarine napoleon.com

Producer: Fourcroy S.A., Rue Steyls 119, B1020 Brussels, Belgium.

US agent: Preiss Imports, Ramona, CA.
Tel: 760 789 6010,

Email: info@preissimports.com

Emperor Napoléon Bonaparte's physician, Antoine-Francois de Fourcroy, created a special liqueur for the Emperor based on aged cognacs and exotic mandarin oranges ('mandarines' in French). Mandarins, often known as tangerines, had been introduced into Europe from China in the 18th century and grew particularly well in Corsica, Bonaparte's birthplace.

Mandarine Napoléon was first commercially distilled in 1892, using the finest aged French cognacs and mandarin peels from the Mediterranean area blended with an infusion of herbs and spices. The distillate is aged for at least three years, until it acquires the rich mellow flavour which makes Mandarine Napoléon one of the great classic liqueurs of the world.

Mandarine Napoléon is brilliantly suited to cocktail mixing and distinctly different from other orange liqueurs on bartenders' shelves. Its luscious zesty tangerine flavour with a herbal backnote gives a sophisticated twist to a Cosmopolitan but is also superb on its own, long over ice with a splash of tonic.

Lola ●●●◐○
Man-Bour-Tini ●●●●○
Mandarine Collins ●●●○○
Mandarine Sidecar ●●●●○
Mandarine Songbird ●●●○○
Mandarine Sour ●●●◐○
Mandarito ●●●●○
Orange Mojito ●●●●○
Prune Face ●●●●○
Puccini ●●●◐○

MAPLE SYRUP

The boiled-down sap of the North American sugar maple, authentic maple syrup has a complex sweetness appreciated all over the world. Please be wary of synthetic imitations, which are nowhere near as good as the real thing.

Maple syrups are graded A or B – grade B, which is dark and very strongly flavoured, is sometimes known as 'cooking syrup'. The A grade syrups are all of equal quality and divided into categories according to their hue and level of flavour, most generally 'light amber', 'medium amber' and 'dark amber'. Confusingly, some Canadian and US states have their own names for these categories. I favour a medium amber or light syrup.

Maple syrup should be stored in the refrigerator and consumed within 28 days of opening. To use in a cocktail, simply pour into a thimble measure and follow the recipe.

Lotus Espresso ●●●●◐
Louisiana Trade ●●●◐○
Maple Old-Fashioned ●●●●○
Maple Leaf ●●●●○
Maple Pomme ●●●●○
Mule's Hind Leg ●●●●◐

MARASCHINO LIQUEUR

'See Luxardo Maraschino Originale Liqueur'

MARASCHINO SYRUP

The sweet liquid from a jar of maraschino cherries.

Lux Daiquiri ●●●●○
Manhattan Sweet ●●●●●
Old Fashioned #2 (US Version) ●●●●◐

MIDORI MELON LIQUEUR

20% alc./vol. (40°proof)

www.midori-world.com

Producer: Suntory Limited, Japan.
US agent: Suntory International Corp, New York City, NY.

Tel: 212 836 3999,

Email: si@midori-world.com

Midori is flavoured with extracts of honeydew melons and can rightly claim to be the original melon liqueur. Midori's vibrant green colour, light melon taste and great versatility has ensured its demand in bars worldwide. Launched in

1978 at New York's famed Studio 54 nightclub, Midori was shaken within sight of the cast of Saturday Night Fever. That same year, Midori won first prize in the U.S. Bartenders' Guild Annual Championship.

The name 'Midori' is Japanese for green and it is owned by Suntory, Japan's leading producer and distributor of alcoholic beverages. Midori is one of the most noted modern day cocktail ingredients due to its vibrant colour and flavour, being: fruity, luscious, lightly syrupy while retaining freshness, with honeyed melon and a hint of green apple. It is also great simply served long with sparkling apple juice or cranberry juice.

L.A. Iced Tea ●●●◐○
Love Junk ●●●◐○
Mae West Martini ●●●●○
Melon Ball ●●●○○
Melon Collie Martini ●●●●○
Melon Daiquiri #1 (Served 'Up') ●●●●○
Melon Daiquiri #2 (Served Frozen) ●●●◐○
Melon Margarita #1 (Served 'Up') ●●●●○
Melon Margarita #2 (Served Frozen) ●●●◐○
Melon Martini #1 ●●●○○
Meloncholy Martini ●●●●○
Passion Killer ●●●○○

MINT LEAVES

This perennial herb grows in most temperate parts of the world. The varieties which non-botanists call 'mint' belong to the genus mentha. Mentha species include apple mint, curly mint, pennyroyal, peppermint, pineapple mint, spearmint and water or bog mint.

Spearmint, or garden mint, is the most common kind and you may well find it growing in your garden. It has a fruity aroma and flavour and, like peppermint, has bright green leaves and purple flowers. Spearmint is generally used for cooking savouries, such as mint sauce.

Peppermint is the second most common kind. Its leaves produce a pungent oil which is used to flavour confectionery, desserts and liqueurs such as crème de menthe. The main visible difference between peppermint and spearmint is in the leaves.

Spearmint leaves have a crinkly surface and seem to grow straight out of the plant's main stem, while peppermint leaves have smoother surfaces and individual stems. Peppermint can also tend towards purple. Which type of mint you choose to use in drinks is largely a matter of personal taste: some recommend mentha nemorosa for Mojitos.

Growing your own mint, be it spearmint, peppermint or otherwise is easy – but be sure to keep it in a container or it will overrun your garden. Either buy a plant or place a sprig in a glass of water. When it roots, pot it in a large, shallow tub with drainage holes. Place bricks under the tub to prevent the roots from growing through the holes.

Life (Love In the Future Ecstasy) ●●●◐○
Lotus Martini ●●●●○
Luxury Mojito ●●●●○
Mai Tai #2 (Beaumont-Gantt's Formula) ●●●●○
Major Bailey #1 ●●●●◐
Mandarito ●●●●○
Marama Rum Punch ●●●●○
Milky Mojito ●●●◐○
Mint Cocktail ●●●●◐
Mint Collins ●●●●○
Mint Daiquiri ●●●●●
Mint Fizz ●●●◐○
Mint Julep ●●●●●
Mint Limeade (Mocktail) ●●●●◐
Mint Martini ●●●●◐
Missionary's Downfall ●●●●●
Mojito ●●●●●
Mojito de Casa ●●●●○
Momo Special ●●●●○
Monarch Martini ●●●●○
Orange Mojito ●●●●○
Palm Springs ●●●◐○
Pineapple Mojito ●●●●◐
Pussyfoot (Mocktail) ●●●●◐

OPAL NERA BLACK SAMBUCA

40% alc./vol. (80°proof)

www.opalnera.com

Producer: Fratelli Francoli S.p.A., Ghemme, Corso Romagnano, Italy.

US agent: Wine Wave, Jericho, NY.

Tel: 516 433 112,

Email: info@winewave.com

In 1989 Alessandro Francoli was on honeymoon in America and took time out to present his company's traditional Italian grappas and sambucas to a potential buyer. He noticed the interest the buyer showed in a coffee sambuca, and this dark liqueur set Alessandro thinking. He experimented with different flavours and created Opal Nera, a black coloured sambuca with a hint of lemon. Opal Nera's seductive and unmistakable colour comes from elderberries, a key ingredient in all sambucas: Francoli macerate their purple-black skins.

Opal Nera Black Sambuca is a favourite with many bartenders due to its colour and flavour, which includes aniseed, soft black liquorice, light elderberry spice and lemon zest.

Liquorice All Sort ●●●◐○
Liquorice Martini ●●●◐○
Molotov Cocktail ●●●◐○
Opal Café ●●●●○
Purple Flirt #1 ●●●●○

ORANGE BITTERS

Sadly, this key cocktail ingredient is hard to find in modern liquor stores. There are a number of brands that profess to be 'orange bitters' but many hardly taste of orange and are more like sweet liqueurs than bitters. Search the internet for suitable brands or make your own. See www.drinkboy.com/LiquorCabinet/Flavorings/OrangeBitters.htm

The Legend ●●●●○
Lemon Sorbet ●●●●○
Leninade ●●●●○
London Calling ●●●◐○
London Cocktail ●●●○○
Mac Orange ●●●◐○
Marguerite Martini ●●●●○
Marny Cocktail ●●●●◐
Martinez ●●●●●
Merry Widow #2 ●●●◐○
Met Manhattan ●●●●○
Milly Martini ●●●●○
Modernista ●●●◐○
Mystique ●●●◐○
Oil Slick ●●◐○○
Onion Ring Martini ●●●○○
Opera ●●●●○
Orange Martini ●●●●○
Pall Mall Martini ●●●●○
Palma Violet Martini ●●●◐○
Paradise #2 ●●●●◐
Pegu Club ●●●●○
Perfect Martini ●●●◐○
Princeton ●●●●○
Quebec ●●●●○

ORANGE JUICE

The orange is now so commonly available in our shops and markets that it's hard to believe it was once an exotic and expensive luxury. Although native to China, its name originates from 'naranga' in the old Indian language of Sanskrit.

There are many different types of orange but the best ones for bartending purposes are Washington Navels, which are in season from the end of October. These have a firm, rough skin perfect for cutting twists from and are juicy and slightly sour.

Simply cut in half and juice with a hand press. If using an electric spinning citrus juicer take care not to grind the pith.

Oranges are so widely available and easy to juice that as I write this I'm wondering why I so often buy packaged juice from the supermarket. My only defence is that I always buy freshly squeezed, refrigerated juice.

Lago Cosmo ●●●◐○
Limeosa ●●●◐○
Lola ●●●◐○
Loved Up ●●●◐○
Lutkins Special Martini ●●●◐○
Mac Orange ●●●◐○
Madras ●●●◐○
Madroska ●●●○○
Maiden's Prayer ●●●◐○
Magic Bus ●●●◐○
Mambo ●●●◐○
Mandarine Songbird ●●●○○
Maurice Martini ●●●◐○
Mat The Rat ●●●◐○
Mayfair Cocktail ●●●●○
Melon Ball ●●●○○
Mexican Melon Ball ●●●◐○
Mimosa ●●●◐○
Mister Stu ●●●◐○
Mona Lisa ●●●●○
Monkey Gland #1 ●●●●○
Monkey Gland #2 ●●●●○
Mrs Robinson #2 ●●●◐○
Naranja Daiquiri ●●●●○
New Port Codebreaker ●●●◐○
Nightmare Martini ●●●○○
Noble Europe ●●●●◐
Noon ●●●●○
Not So Cosmo (Mocktail) ●●●◐○
Ole ●●●◐○
Olympic ●●●●◐
Opal ●●●●◐
Orang-A-Tang ●●●●○
Orange Blossom ●●●◐○
Orange Daiquiri #1 ●●●●◐
Orange Martini ●●●●○
Oranjiniha ●●●●○
Painkiller ●●●●○
Paradise #1 ●●●◐○
Paradise #2 ●●●●◐
Paradise #3 ●●●◐○
Park Lane ●●●●◐
Parlay Punch ●●●○○
Perfect John ●●●●○
Peter Pan Martini ●●●●○
Petto Martini ●●●●◐
Pilgrim Cocktail ●●●●○
Pinky Pincher ●●●●○
Pisco Punch #1 (Difford's Formula) ●●●●◐
Pisco Naranja ●●●◐○
Planteur ●●●●○
Playmate Martini ●●●●◐
Poncha ●●●●○
Potted Parrot ●●●◐○
President ●●●●○
Pruneaux ●●●●○
Pussyfoot (Mocktail) ●●●●◐
Queen Martini ●●●●○

PARFAIT AMOUR LIQUEUR

A French, lilac coloured curaçao liqueur flavoured with rose petals, vanilla pods and almonds. The name means 'perfect love'.

Lavender Martini ●●●●○
Molotov Cocktail ●●●◐○
Purple Cosmo ●●●●◐

PASSION FRUIT LIQUEUR

Palm Springs ●●●◐○
Pass-on-that ●●●○○
Passbour Cooler ●●●○○
Passion Killer ●●●○○
Passover ●●●○○

PASTIS

See 'Ricard Pastis'

PEACH SCHNAPPS & PEACH LIQUEUR

See 'Bols Peach Schnapps Liqueur'

PEACHES

There are a number of different varieties of peach, a fruit which originated in China but is cultivated all over the world. White peaches are preferable for use in cocktails. They have finer flesh and flavour, and produce more juice than yellow peaches, which generally mature later. When peeling peaches for muddling or pureeing, try plunging them into boiling water for thirty seconds first.

PEAR & COGNAC LIQUEURS

These are liqueurs based on cognac and flavoured with natural pear essence. They are rich in flavour with hints of perfumed pear (almost pear marmalade) and spice, particularly cinnamon, fortified with cognac.

Long Flight of Stairs ●●●●◐
Nice Pear-tini ●●●●◐
Pear & Cardamom Sidecar ●●●●◐
Pear & Vanilla Rickey ●●●◐○
Pear Drop ●●●◐○
Pear Drop Martini ●●●●○
Pear Shaped #1 (Deluxe Version) ●●●●◐
Pear Shaped #2 (Popular) ●●●●◐
Perry-tini ●●●●○
Prickly Pear Mule ●●●●○

PEAR JUICE

Western varieties of pear soften when ripe and tend to have quite a grainy texture; Asian types, such as the nashi pear, are crisp when ripe. Unless otherwise stated, pear in this guide means the Western varieties. Conference is widely available and works well in cocktails.

Pears will ripen after they are picked, but spoil quickly, so care is needed in storage.

The best way to extract the flavour of a pear is to use an electric juice extractor. Surprisingly, you'll find that beautifully ripe fruits yield little and much of that is in the form of slush. Instead, look for pears which are on their way to ripeness but still have a good crunch.

Remove the stalk but don't worry about peeling or removing the core. Cut the fruit into chunks small enough to push into the juicer. If you hate cleaning an electric juice extractor then use a blender or food processor.

Nice Pear-tini ●●●●◐
Pear & Elderflower Martini ●●●●○
Pear Drop Martini ●●●●○
Pear Shaped #1 (Deluxe Version) ●●●●◐
Perry-tini ●●●●○
Prickly Pear Mule ●●●●○

PERNOD ANIS

40% alc./vol. (80°proof)

www.pernod.net
Producer: Pernod Enterprise, France.

US agent: Pernod Ricard USA.

Tel: 866 220 8713,

Email: pernod@qualitycustomercare.com

Pernod's story starts in 1789 when Dr Pierre Ordinaire first prescribed his pain relieving and reviving 'absinthe elixir' in Switzerland. Ten years later, Major Dubied bought the formula and set up an absinthe factory in Couvet, Switzerland, with his son-in-law, Henri-Louis Pernod. In 1805, Henri-Louis Pernod established Pernod Fils in Pontarlier, France. The authentic absinthe, the original Pernod was created from a recipe that included 'artemisia absinthium': wormwood, the absinthe plant.

Pernod quickly gained fame as THE absinthe of Parisian café society. But a prohibitionist propaganda movement sprang up and a massive press campaign blamed absinthe abuse as the cause of socially unacceptable behaviour, insanity, tuberculosis and even murder. On 7th January 1915, absinthe was banned and Pernod Fils was forced to close. But by 1920, anise liquors were legalised again, albeit in a more sober form, and in its new guise Pernod remained as popular as ever. The Pernod we enjoy today is an historic blend of 14 herbs including star anise, fennel, mint and coriander.

Pernod is best served long with cranberry juice, apple juice or bitter lemon, diluted five to one.

Light Breeze ●●●◐○
Lighter Breeze ●●●◐○
London Fog ●●●○○
Milky Mojito ●●●◐○
Modernista ●●●◐○
Monte Carlo ●●●◐○
Moonraker ●●●●○
Mucky Bottom ●●●◐○
Nicky Finn ●●●●○
Northern Lights ●●●●○
Pernod & Black Martini ●●●●○

PEYCHAUD'S AROMATIC BITTERS

Lychee & Rose Petal Martini ●●●●○
Pendennis Cocktail ●●●●○

PIMM'S NO. 1 CUP

Luxury Cocktail ●●●◐○
Pimm's Cocktail ●●●●○
Pimm's Cup (or Classic) ●●●◐○
Pimm's Royal ●●◐○○

PINEAPPLE JUICE

Pineapples are widely grown in the West Indies, Africa and Asia. There are many varieties which vary significantly in both size and flavour. When pineapples are ripe the skin changes colour from yellow-green to brown; over-ripe pineapples are yellow-brown.

Pineapples are tropical and tend to deteriorate at temperatures below 7°C (45°F) so are best left out of the refrigerator.

Pineapple is one of the most satisfying fruits to juice due to the quantity of liquid it yields. Chop the crown and bottom off, then slice the skin off, without worrying too much about the little brown dimples that remain. Finally slice the fruit along its length around the hard central core, and chop it into pieces small enough to fit into your juice extractor. The base is the sweetest part of a pineapple, so if you are only juicing half be sure to divide the fruit lengthways.

For convenience I still often end up buying cartons of 'pressed pineapple juice' from the supermarket chill cabinet. As with all such juices, look for those labelled 'not from concentrate'. When buying supermarket own brand pineapple juice, read the label carefully to avoid stuff made from concentrate.

Linstead ●●●●◐
Lucky Lily Margarita ●●●●◐
Major Bailey #2 ●●●●◐
Mary Pickford ●●●●●
Matador ●●●●○
Mayan ●●●○○
Mayan Whore ●●●●○
Meloncholy Martini ●●●●○
Mellow Martini ●●●◐○
Mexican ●●●●○
Mexican Martini ●●●◐○
Mexican Surfer ●●●●○

Miami Beach ●●●●○
The Million Dollar Cocktail ●●●●◐
Milly Martini ●●●●○
Missionary's Downfall ●●●●●
Mister Stu ●●●◐○
Monkey Shine ●●●●○
Monk's Habit ●●●○○
Motox ●●●●○
Nacional Daiquiri #2 ●●●●◐
New Orleans Mule ●●●◐○
New Year's Absolution ●●●◐○
Nutty Summer ●●●●◐
Painkiller ●●●●○
Palermo ●●●●◐
Pancho Villa ●●●●○
Park Avenue ●●●●○
Parlay Punch ●●●○○
Piña Martini ●●●●○
Piña Colada ●●●●◐
Piña Colada Virgin (Mocktail) ●●●○○
Pineapple & Cardamom Daiquiri ●●●●◐
Pineapple & Cardamom Martini ●●●●●
Pineapple & Ginger Martini ●●●●○
Pineapple & Sage Margarita ●●●●◐
Pineapple Blossom ●●●●○
Pineapple Daiquiri #1 (On-the-Rocks) ●●●●◐
Pineapple Daiquiri #2 (Frozen) ●●●●◐
Pineapple Fizz ●●●●●
Pineapple Margarita ●●●●○
Pineapple Mojito ●●●●◐
Pineapple Smoothie (Mocktail) ●●●◐○
Pino Pepe ●●●●○
Pisco Punch #1 (Difford's Formula) ●●●●◐
Pisco Punch #3 (Lanes' Formula) ●●●●○
Pisco Punch #4 (Prosser's Formula) ●●●●●
Playa Del Mar ●●●●○
Pogo Stick ●●●●○
Purple Flirt #2 ●●●○○
Queen Martini ●●●●○

PISCO

A type of brandy and the national drink of both Chile and Peru, pisco probably takes its name from the port of Pisco in Peru.

The best pisco is made from the fermented juice of the Muscat grape, which grows in the Ica region of southwestern Peru and in Chile's Elqui Valley. There are many varieties of Muscat. The Quebranta grape is favoured in Peru where it is usually blended with one or two other varietals such as Italia, Moscatel, Albilla, Negra, Mollar and Torontel. In Chile Common Black, Mollar, Pink Muscat, Torontel, Pedro Jimenez and Muscat of Alexandria are all used.

Lima Sour ●●●◐○
Pichuncho Martini ●●●●◐
Pini ●●●●◐
Pisco Collins ●●●●○
Pisco Punch #1 (Difford's Formula) ●●●●◐
Pisco Punch #2 (Alfredo Micheli's Formula) ●●●●●
Pisco Punch #3 (Lanes' Formula) ●●●●○
Pisco Punch #4 (Prosser's Formula) ●●●●●
Pisco Naranja ●●●◐○
Pisco Sour (Traditional Recipe) ●●●●◐
Pisco Sour (Difford's Version) ●●●●●
Piscola ●●●◐○
Ponche de Algarrobina ●●●◐○

PLYMOUTH GIN

41.2% alc./vol. (82.4°proof)

www.plymouthgin.com

Producer: V&S Plymouth Ltd, Black Friars Distillery, Plymouth, England

US distributor: The Absolut Spirits Company Inc..

Tel: 212 641 8700,

Email: enquiries@plymouthgin.com

Since 1793, Plymouth gin has been hand-crafted in England's oldest working distillery - Black Friars in Plymouth. It is still bottled at the unique strength of 41.2% alc./vol., and is based on a recipe that is over 200 years old. Plymouth gin, which can only be produced in Plymouth, differs from London gins due to the use of only sweet botanicals combined with soft Dartmoor water. The result is a wonderfully aromatic and smooth gin.

Plymouth has been used in cocktails since 1896, when it was first mixed in the original Dry Martini, and is favoured by many top bartenders due to its fresh juniper, lemony bite with deeper earthy notes.

L.A. Iced Tea ●●●◐○
The Last Word ●●●●◐
Leap Year Martini ●●●○○
Leave It To Me Martini ●●●◐○
Lemony ●●●●○
Liquorice Martini ●●●◐○
Livingstone ●●●●○
London Calling ●●●◐○
London Cocktail ●●●○○
London Fog ●●●○○
Long Beach Iced Tea ●●●◐○
Long Island Iced Tea ●●●◐○
Long Island Spiced Tea ●●●◐○
Lotus Martini ●●●●○
Loud Speaker Martini ●●●◐○
Lutkins Special Martini ●●●◐○
Luxury Cocktail ●●●◐○
Lychee & Blackcurrant Martini ●●●●○
Lychee & Rose Petal Martini ●●●●○
Lychee & Sake Martini ●●●●○
Lychee Rickey ●●●◐○
Macka ●●●◐○
Maiden's Blush ●●●●◐
Maiden's Prayer ●●●◐○
Mainbrace ●●●●○
Major Bailey #1 ●●●●◐
Mandarine Collins ●●●○○
Mango Collins ●●●●○
Marguerite Martini ●●●●○
Marmalade Martini ●●●●◐
Marny Cocktail ●●●●◐
Martinez ●●●●●
Martini Special ●●●●◐
Martini Thyme ●●●●○
Mary Rose ●●●●○
Maurice Martini ●●●◐○
Mayfair Cocktail ●●●●○
The Mayflower Martini ●●●●○
M.C. Martini ●●●●●
Medium Martini ●●●●◐
Merry Widow #1 ●●●◐○
Merry-Go-Round Martini ●●●●○
Miami Beach ●●●●○
Milano Sour ●●●●○
The Million Dollar Cocktail ●●●●◐
Milly Martini ●●●●○
Mint Cocktail ●●●●◐
Mint Collins ●●●●○
Mint Fizz ●●●◐○
Modernista ●●●◐○
Monarch Martini ●●●●○
Monkey Gland #1 ●●●●○
Monkey Gland #2 ●●●●○
Monte Carlo Imperial ●●●○○
Moon River ●●●◐○
Moonlight Martini ●●●●○
Moonshine Martini ●●●●◐
Mujer Verde ●●●●○
Mule's Hind Leg ●●●●◐
Napoleon Martini ●●●●◐
Navigator ●●●●○
Negroni ●●●●◐
Nicky's Fizz ●●●◐○
Nightmare Martini ●●●○○
Nome ●●●●○
Noon ●●●●○
North Pole Martini ●●●●○
Onion Ring Martini ●●●○○
Opal ●●●●◐
Opera ●●●●○
Orange Bloom Martini ●●●●◐
Orange Blossom ●●●◐○
Orange Martini ●●●●○
Oriental Tart ●●●●○
Paisley Martini ●●●●○
Pall Mall Martini ●●●●○
Palm Beach ●●●◐○
Pancho Villa ●●●●○
Paradise #1 ●●●◐○
Paradise #2 ●●●●◐
Paradise #3 ●●●◐○
Parisian Martini ●●●●○
Park Avenue ●●●●○
Park Lane ●●●●◐
Parma Negroni ●●●●○
Passion Fruit Collins ●●●●○
Passion Fruit Martini #3 ●●●●○
Passion Punch ●●●◐○
Peggy Martini ●●●○○
Pegu Club ●●●●○
Pendennis Cocktail ●●●●○
Perfect Martini ●●●◐○
Peter Pan Martini ●●●●○
Petto Martini ●●●●◐
Piccadilly Martini ●●●●◐
Pimm's Cocktail ●●●●◐
Pink Gin #1 (Traditional) ●●●●○
Pink Gin #2 (Modern0 ●●●●○
Pink Gin & Tonic ●●●●○
Pink Hound ●●●●○
Pink Lady ●●●●◐
Pink Palace ●●●●◐
Poet's Dream ●●●●◐
Pogo Stick ●●●●○
Princess Marina ●●●●○
Princess Mary ●●●○○
Princeton ●●●●○
Princeton Martini ●●●●○
Pruneaux ●●●●○
Queen Martini ●●●●○

PLYMOUTH SLOE GIN LIQUEUR

26% alc./vol. (52°proof)

www.plymouthgin.com

Producer: Coates & Co Ltd, Plymouth, England.

US distributor: The Absolut Spirits Company Inc..

Tel: 212 641 8700,

Email:enquiries@plymouthgin.com

The making of fruit liqueurs is a long tradition in the British country-side and Plymouth sloe gin stays true to a unique 1883 recipe. The sloe berries are slowly and gently steeped in high strength Plymouth gin, soft Dartmoor water and a further secret ingredient. It is an unhurried process and the drink is bottled only when the Head Distiller decides the perfect flavour has been reached. The result is an entirely natural product with no added flavouring or colourings.

This richly flavoured liqueur is initially dry but opens with smooth, sweet, lightly jammy, juicy cherry and raspberry notes alongside a complimentary mixture of figs, cloves, set honey and stewed fruits. The finish has strong almond notes.

London Calling ●●●◐○
Millionaire's Daiquiri ●●●◐○
Purple Turtle ●●●◐○

POMEGRANATE (GRENADINE) SYRUP

Originally grenadine was a syrup flavoured with pomegranate. Sadly most of today's commercially available grenadine syrups are flavoured with red berries and cherry juice. They may be blood red but they don't taste of pomegranate. Hunt out one of the few genuine commercially made pomegranate syrups or make your own.

Separate the seed cells of four pomegranates from the outer membranes and skin, then pulp them in a food processor. Simmer and stir the pulp in a saucepan with a quarter cup of honey for several minutes. Strain through a cheesecloth-layered sieve and store in a refrigerator.

Leave It To Me Martini ●●●◐○
Lime Blush ●●●○○ (Mocktail)
Lotus Martini ●●●●○
Maiden's Blush ●●●●◐
Mary Pickford ●●●●●
Mexican ●●●●○
The Million Dollar Cocktail ●●●●◐
Millionaire ●●●●○
Millionaire's Daiquiri ●●●◐○
Monkey Gland #1 ●●●●○
Monkey Gland #2 ●●●●○
Monk's Habit ●●●○○
Opening Shot ●●●◐○
Orang-A-Tang ●●●●○
Orange Blossom ●●●◐○
Park Lane ●●●●◐
Piccadilly Martini ●●●●◐
Pink Cloud ●●●○○
Pink Daiquiri ●●●●○
Pink Lady ●●●●◐
Pink Lemonade (Mocktail) ●●●○○
Pink Palace ●●●●◐
Pirate Daiquiri ●●●●○
Planter's Punchless (Mocktail) ●●●○○
Planteur ●●●●○
Pomegranate Margarita ●●●●◐
Pomegranate Martini ●●●●◐
Port & Starboard ●●◐○○
Port Light ●●●◐○
Pousse-café ●●◐○○
President ●●●●○
Presidente ●●●●○
Purple Flirt #2 ●●●○○
Pussyfoot (Mocktail) ●●●●◐

PORT (PORTO)

Port, or to give it its full name 'vinho do porto', is a Portuguese wine from the area known as the Upper Douro which starts 45 miles from the coast at the town of Oporto and stretches east to the Spanish border. Wine is fortified with grape brandy, which stops fermentation before it is complete by raising the alcoholic strength beyond that at which the fermenting yeasts can survive. This produces wines with residual sugars, giving port its inherently sweet style.

Mulled Wine ●●●●○
Negus (Hot) ●●●●○
Port & Melon Martini ●●●●◐
Port Wine Cocktail ●●●◐○
Princeton ●●●●○

PUREES

Fruit purees are made from fresh fruit which has been chopped up and liquidised. When making your own puree add roughly five to ten percent sugar syrup to your pureed fruit depending on the fruit's ripeness. Commercially available purees contain differing amounts of added sugar and, if using such a product, you may have to adjust the balance of your drink to allow for the extra sweetness.

PUSSER'S NAVY RUM

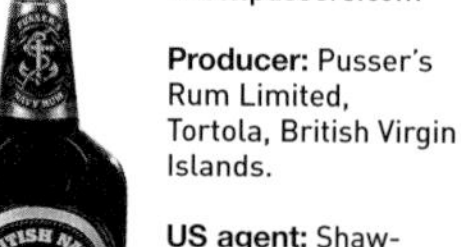

47.75% alc./vol. (95.5°proof)

www.pussers.com

Producer: Pusser's Rum Limited, Tortola, British Virgin Islands.

US agent: Shaw-Ross International Importers.

Tel: 954 430 5020,

Email: info@shaw-ross.com

The name 'Pusser' is slang in the Royal Navy for purser, the officer with responsibility for the issue of rum on board ship. For more than 300 years the British Navy issued a daily 'tot' of Pusser's rum, with a double issue before battle. This tradition, which started in Jamaica in 1665, was finally broken on 31st July 1970, a day now known as 'Black Tot Day'. In 1979 the Admiralty approved the re-blending of Pusser's rum to the original specifications by Charles Tobias in the British Virgin Islands. A significant donation from the sale of each bottle accrues to the benefit of The Royal Navy Sailor's Fund, a naval charity established to compensate sailors for their lost tot.

In our opinion, this is the best Navy rum, delivering a rich medley of flavours: molasses, treacle, vanilla, cinnamon, nutmeg, sticky toffee pudding, espresso and creamy tiramisu with subtle hints of oak.

Navy Grog ●●●●○
Nevada Daiquiri ●●●●○
New Port Codebreaker ●●●◐○
Painkiller ●●●●○
Pirate Daiquiri ●●●●○

PROSECCO SPARKLING WINE

Prosecco is a wine produced around the towns of Conegliano and Valdobbiadene in the Italian province of Treviso. It can be still, semi-sparkling or sparkling, dry, off-dry or sweet. The style called for in this guide, and the preferred style for export, is dry and sparkling. 'Frizzante' means 'semi-sparkling' and 'spumante' means 'sparkling'.

The better wines from hill-side vineyards are labelled 'Prosecco di Conegliano-Valdobbiadene'. The best are 'Prosecco Superiore di Cartizze' from the great hill of Cartizze in the Valdobbiadene sub-region.

Pomegranate Bellini ●●●◐○
Puccini ●●●◐○

RASPBERRY (CRÈME DE FRAMBOISE) LIQUEUR

Cocktail books often refer to raspberry liqueur as 'crème de framboise', its name in French. Its intense, rich flavour lends itself to use in cocktails.

Mrs Robinson #1 ●●●●○

RASPBERRIES & BLACKBERRIES

Both these berries grow on brambly bushes and are related to the rose. Both can be cultivated in a wide range of colours, from white or yellow to orange, pink or purple, as well as the more common red and black.

The juice of both raspberries and blackberries is intense and a little goes a long way. Which is just as well because there's precious little juice in each berry and you'll find putting them through an electric juicer a complete waste of time. Instead, either blend them into a puree or (as I do) muddle the fruits in the base of your shaker or in the glass. Recipes in this guide state how many fruits you should muddle for each drink.

Miss Martini ●●●◐○
Mrs Robinson #1 ●●●●○
Pernod & Black Martini ●●●●○

RICARD PASTIS

45% alc./vol. (90°proof)

Producer: Pernod (Group Pernod Ricard), Créteil, France.

US agent: Pernod Ricard USA, White Plains, NY.

Tel: 866 220 8713,

Email: info@qualitycustomercare.com

A French classic, this liquorice based spirit is Europe's number one selling spirit brand and the third biggest brand worldwide. Created by Paul Ricard in Marseille in 1932, it is now produced in Bessan, Southern France. The unique flavour of this pastis derives from liquorice root, green anise, fennel and seven different aromatic herbs from Provence. It is anethole, made from fennel and green anise, which produces Ricard's most distinctive effect: it turns milky on contact with water or ice.

Traditionally served over ice diluted with five parts of water, Ricard adds a rich aniseed flavour and distinctive cloudy appearance to a number of classic and modern cocktails. Besides the predominant aniseed, its dry palate features fennel, soft liquorice and a delicious minty lemon freshness.

Liquorice Whisky Sour ●●●●◐
Mauresque ●●●●○
La Momie ●●●○○
Momisette ●●●●○
Perroquet ●●●○○

RUM

Rum is a spirit made from sugar cane or its byproducts. The recipes in this guide call for a number of styles of rum, as explained below.

RUM - AGED (AÑEJO)

Like other distillates, rum is clear when it condenses after distillation. The fact that ageing in oak barrels improved the raw rum was discovered when ships carried rum on the long passage to Europe: it arrived darker in colour and with an enhanced flavour.

Today, rum is aged in barrels from France or the United States which have previously been used to age cognac, bourbon or whiskey. They may be charred or scraped clean to remove any previous charring before receiving the rum: the treatment of the barrels is reflected in the character they impart to the finished rum.

Orange Daiquiri #1 ●●●●◐
Platinum Blonde ●●●◐○

RUM - BERMUDAN DARK

A few recipes in this guide require the use of Bermudan rum, a distinctive dark style.

Milk Punch ●●●●○
Modernista ●●●◐○
Purple Flirt #2 ●●●○○

RUM - GOLDEN

An amber coloured rum aged in wood and often coloured with caramel.

Lola ●●●◐○
Monkey Shine ●●●●○
Monkey Wrench ●●●◐○
Pago Pago ●●●◐○
Palm Springs ●●●◐○
Pilgrim Cocktail ●●●●○
Piña Colada ●●●●◐
Pineapple Fizz ●●●●●
Ponce de Leon ●●●●○
P.S. I Love You ●●●●○

RUM - JAMAICAN OVERPROOF

Gunpowder was originally used to determine the strength of a spirit. The tester would mix the spirit with gunpowder and attempt to light it. If the spirit did not ignite, it was underproof; if it burned steadily, it was proof; if it exploded, it was overproof.

Proof is measured differently in the UK and the US, but in the States 100°proof is double alcohol by volume (measured by the Gay-Lussac scale). Hence an overproof rum is over 100°proof or 50% alc./vol. in strength.

Vic's Original 1944 Mai Tai ●●●●●
Mango Punch ●●●●○
Marama Rum Punch ●●●●○
Passionate Rum Punch ●●●●○
Pirate Daiquiri ●●●●○

RUM - LIGHT/WHITE

Rum is termed 'light' or 'heavy', depending on the purity to which it was distilled. Essentially, the flavour of any spirit comes from 'congeners' – products of fermentation which are not ethyl alcohol. When alcohol is concentrated during distillation, the levels of congeners are reduced. The fewer congeners, the lighter the rum. The more congeners, the heavier.
The fermentation process also affects whether a rum is light or heavy. A longer, slower fermentation will result in a heavier rum.

The odour, texture and taste of light rums are more subtle and refined than those of heavy rums, which have a heavy, syrupy flavour to match their dark colour.
Light rums tend to originate from countries originally colonised by the Spanish, such as Cuba, the Dominican Republic, Puerto Rico and Venezuela.

L.A. Iced Tea ●●●◐○
Lemon Chiffon Pie ●●●●○
Long Beach Iced Tea ●●●◐○
Long Island Iced Tea ●●●◐○
Lux Daiquiri ●●●●○
Mai Tai #2 (Beaumont-Gantt's Formula) ●●●●○
Major Bailey #2 ●●●●◐
Mango Daiquiri ●●●●○
Mango Rum Cooler ●●●◐○
Mary Pickford ●●●●●
Melon Collie Martini ●●●●○
Melon Daiquiri #1 (Served 'Up') ●●●●○
Melon Daiquiri #2 (Served Frozen) ●●●◐○
Menehune Juice ●●●●○
Miami Daiquiri ●●●●○
Millionaire's Daiquiri ●●●◐○
Mint Daiquiri ●●●●●
Missionary's Downfall ●●●●●
Mojito ●●●●●
Monk's Habit ●●●○○
Nacional Daiquiri #1 ●●●●◐
Nacional Daiquiri #2 ●●●●◐
Nantucket ●●●◐○
Naranja Daiquiri ●●●●○
Natural Daiquiri ●●●●●
No. 10 Lemonade ●●●●◐
Oh Gosh! ●●●●●
Orange Mojito ●●●●○
Pancho Villa ●●●●○
Passion Fruit Daiquiri ●●●●○
Peach Daiquiri ●●●●○
Pedro Collins ●●●●○
Periodista Daiquiri ●●●●○
Pineapple & Cardamom Daiquiri ●●●●◐
Pineapple Daiquiri #1 (On-the-Rocks) ●●●●◐
Pineapple Daiquiri #2 (Frozen) ●●●●◐
Pineapple Mojito ●●●●◐
Pink Daiquiri ●●●●○
Pino Pepe ●●●●○
Plantation Punch ●●●◐○
Plum Daiquiri ●●●●○
Potted Parrot ●●●◐○
President ●●●●○
Presidente ●●●●○
Quarter Deck ●●●●○

RUM - NAVY

See 'Pusser's Navy Rum'

RUM - SPICED

Spiced rums are continuously distilled light rums flavoured with spices including ginger, cinnamon, clove and vanilla.

Long Island Spiced Tea ●●●◐○
Mat The Rat ●●●◐○

RUM - VANILLA INFUSED

The pods of a tropical plant which belongs to the orchid family, vanilla has long been a prized flavouring. It is cultivated in many different tropical regions. Bourbon vanilla is generally considered the finest kind, and Mexico and the Indian Ocean islands are popularly known as the best producers. Once the pods are harvested from the parent vine, they undergo months of curing to develop and refine their distinctive flavour.

In this guide, recipes utilise the flavour of vanilla by infusing it in a spirit, most often rum or vodka. Simply take two quality vanilla pods (roughly 6in/15cm long) and split them lengthwise with a sharp knife. Place them in the bottle of spirit you want to flavour and leave it to infuse for a fortnight, turning occasionally.

Lisa B's Daiquiri ●●●●●
Palermo ●●●●◐

SAKE

Sometimes described as a rice wine, sometimes as a rice beer, sake shares qualities of both. It is fermented from specially developed rice and water by brewmasters ('toji'). But, although sake is brewed like a beer, it is served like a wine and, like a wine, can either be dry or sweet, heavy or light. But it is slightly more alcoholic than wine - 14-18% alc./vol..

Sake (pronounced Sar-Keh – heavy on the K!) is native to Japan (and parts of China). The basic outline of production has changed little since the 11th century, but complex and fragrant sake has only been generally available since the 1970s.

Lychee & Sake Martini ●●●●○
Onion Ring Martini ●●●○○
Oriental Grape Martini ●●●●◐
Osmo ●●●●○

SAMBUCA BLACK

See 'Opal Nera Black Sambuca'

SAMBUCA WHITE

See 'Luxardo Sambuca dei Cesari'

SCOTCH

See 'Whisky – Scotch'

SHERRY

A fortified wine produced around the region of Jerez, Spain. See below for styles of sherry used in this guide.

SHERRY – AMONTILLADO

An Amontillado sherry begins as a Fino, a pale, dry sherry produced under a layer of a kind of yeast known as 'flor'. Once the flor dies, increasing the oxidisation and changing the flavour of the wine, the sherry becomes an Amontillado. There are two distinct Amontillado styles. One is naturally dry, while the other is sweetened. Recipes in this guide which call for Amontillado sherry require the better quality, dry style.

Pruneaux ●●●●○

SHERRY – FINO

Pronounced 'Fee-No', this pale, dry style of sherry is best drunk young. It is produced under a layer of a kind of yeast known as 'flor' which protects the wine from oxidation.

Nome ●●●●○

SHERRY - PEDRO XIMÉNEZ

A superbly rich dessert sherry made from sun-dried Pedro Ximénez (pronounced Hee-May-Neth) grapes.

Pruneaux ●●●●○
Quarter Deck ●●●●○

SLOE GIN LIQUEUR

See 'Plymouth Sloe Gin Liqueur'

SOHO LYCHEE LIQUEUR

24% alc./vol. (48°proof)

Producer: Pernod (Group Pernod Ricard), Créteil, France.

US distributor: Pernod Ricard USA, White Plains, NY.

Tel: 866 220 8713,

Email: soho@qualitycustomercare.com

Native to South China, the lychee's distinctive floral, fragrant flavour has a luscious delicacy which is distinctly Asian. Revered for over two thousand years as a symbol of love and romance, in part for its flavour and in part for its similarity to the heart, lychee is making waves in fusion food and cocktails around the world.

Pernod Ricard distil this clear liqueur in France, from Asian lychees. It has a distinct smoothness and a light, fresh taste of rich lychee and raspberry, alongside a touch of citrus and raspberry jam.

Lychee & Blackcurrant Martini ●●●●○
Lychee & Sake Martini ●●●●○
Lychee Mac ●●●◐○
Lychee Martini ●●●●○
Lychee Rickey ●●●◐○
Mellow Martini ●●●◐○
Oriental Tart ●●●●○
Pear Drop ●●●◐○

SOUR APPLE SCHNAPPS LIQUEUR

In the following recipes, a standard apple schnapps liqueur will not work: a sour version is required.

Pink Flamingo ●●●○○

SOUR MIX

Sour mix is a term for a blend of lemon or lime juice mixed with sugar syrup. Commercial pre-mixed sour mix is available in a dried crystal or powdered form, often with the addition of pasteurised egg white. Margarita mix is a similar pre-mix, but with the addition of orange flavours. I strongly advocate the use of freshly squeezed juice and sugar syrup and in this guide they appear as separate ingredients.

SOUTHERN COMFORT

A whiskey-based spirit.

Louisiana Trade ●●●◐○
Parlay Punch ●●●○○
Plantation Punch ●●●◐○

STRAWBERRY (CRÈME DE FRAISE) LIQUEUR

See 'Bols Strawberry Liqueur'

SUGAR SYRUP

Many cocktails benefit from sweetening but granulated sugar does not dissolve easily in cold drinks. Hence pre-dissolved sugar syrup (also known as 'simple syrup') is used. Commercially made 'gomme sirop' (gum syrup) is sugar syrup with the addition of gum arabic, the crystallised sap of the acacia tree. Many bartenders don't like using gomme syrup but prefer to use simple or sugar syrup. Others prefer gomme as it adds mouth-feel and smoothness to some drinks.

Make your own sugar syrup by gradually pouring two cups of granulated sugar into a saucepan containing one cup of hot water and stirring and simmering until the sugar is dissolved. Do not let the water even come close to boiling and only simmer for as long as it takes to dissolve the sugar. Allow the syrup to cool and pour it into an empty bottle. Ideally, you should finely strain your syrup into the bottle to remove any undissolved crystals which could otherwise encourage crystallisation. If kept in a refrigerator this mixture will last for a couple of months.

A wide range of flavoured sugar syrups are commercially available. Orgeat (almond), passion fruit and vanilla are among the most popular. See also 'Pomegranate (Grenadine) Syrup'.

TEQUILA

Tequila is named after the town of the same name located about forty miles west of Guadalajara in the state of Jalisco, Mexico. Despite its lethal reputation, tequila is no stronger than other spirits and is usually bottled at 38% alc./vol. (76°proof). Another common misconception is that tequila sometimes has a worm in the bottle. This is not true. It is tequila's relation, mezcal, which comes with the 'worm' - which is in any case a moth larva. Mezcal is a very different spirit.

Tequila has a strong, herbal flavour with a slightly oily consistency. The best wood aged tequilas also have complex subtle flavours such as vanilla, a result of the ageing process.

Lavender Margarita ●●●●●
Lolita Margarita ●●●●◐
Lonely Bull ●●●◐○
Long Beach Iced Tea ●●●◐○
Long Island Iced Tea ●●●◐○
Long Island Spiced Tea ●●●◐○
Loved Up ●●●◐○
Lucky Lily Margarita ●●●●◐
Magic Bus ●●●◐○
Malcolm Lowry ●●●●○
Mango Margarita #1 (Served 'Up') ●●●●○
Mango Margarita #2 (Frozen) ●●●●○
Margarita #1 (Straight-up) ●●●●◐
Margarita #2 (On the Rocks) ●●●●◐
Margarita #3 (Frozen) ●●●●○
Margarita #4 (Salt Foam Float) ●●●◐○
Maria Theresa Margarita ●●●●○
Marmarita ●●●●○
Matador ●●●●○
Mayan ●●●○○
Mayan Whore ●●●●○
Melon Margarita #1 ('Up') ●●●●○
Melon Margarita #2 (Frozen) ●●●◐○
Mesa Fresca ●●●●○
Mexican ●●●●○
Mexican 55 ●●●●○
Mexican Coffee (Hot) ●●●◐○
Mexican Manhattan ●●●●○
Mexican Martini ●●●◐○
Mexican Melon Ball ●●●◐○
Mexican Mule ●●●●◐
Mexican Surfer ●●●●○
Mexican Tea (Hot) ●●●●◐
Mexican City ●●●●◐
Mexicano (Hot) ●●●●◐
Million Dollar Margarita ●●●●◐
Mister Stu ●●●◐○
Mojito de Casa ●●●●○
Nautilus ●●●●◐
New Port Codebreaker ●●●◐○
Paloma ●●●●◐
Passion Fruit Margarita ●●●●○
Passion Killer ●●●○○
Pineapple & Sage Margarita ●●●●◐
Pineapple Margarita ●●●●○
Pink Grapefruit Margarita ●●●●○
Playa Del Mar ●●●●○
Pomegranate Margarita ●●●●◐
Purple Turtle ●●●◐○

TOMATO JUICE

Originally from Peru, the tomato was imported into Spain in the 16th century. Buy a quality, chilled, freshly pressed juice or make your own. Avoid sweet packaged juices made from concentrate.

Peppered Mary ●●●●○
Prairie Oyster ●●●◐○

TRIPLE SEC

An orange-flavoured liqueur often used in cocktails. Cointreau makes a good substitute.

TUACA LIQUEUR

Mystique Martini ●●●●○
Orange Custard Martini ●●●◐○
Pepper & Vanilla'tini ●●●●◐

VERMOUTH DRY

Vermouth as we know it today was invented during the 18th century in the ancient Kingdom of Savoy, which is now divided between north-west Italy and parts of southern and eastern France. At that time the region had an abundance of grapes and produced only very ordinary wines. As a result, enterprising types fortified wine, added herbs and spices, and created vermouth.

Lavender Martini ●●●●○
Lemon Martini ●●●●◐
Livingstone ●●●●○
Lutkins Special Martini ●●●◐○
Lychee Martini ●●●●○
Macka ●●●◐○
Manhattan Dry ●●●●◐
Manhattan Perfect ●●●●●
Marguerite Martini ●●●●○
Maurice Martini ●●●◐○
Medium Martini ●●●●◐
Merry Widow #1 ●●●◐○
Merry Widow #2 ●●●◐○
Merry-Go-Round Martini ●●●●○
Mint Martini ●●●●◐
Moonshine Martini ●●●●◐
Mountain ●●●◐○
Noon ●●●●○
Oddball Manhattan Dry ●●●●○
Old Pal ●●●◐○
Paisley Martini ●●●●○
Pall Mall Martini ●●●●○
Parisian Martini ●●●●○
Parisian Spring Punch ●●●●○
Peggy Martini ●●●○○
Perfect Martini ●●●◐○
Peter Pan Martini ●●●●○
Petto Martini ●●●●◐
Piccadilly Martini ●●●●◐
Plum Cocktail ●●●◐○
Plum Martini ●●●●○
Poet's Dream ●●●●◐
Pompanski Martini ●●●●○
Presidente ●●●●○
Princess Mary's Pride ●●●○○
Princeton Martini ●●●●○
Queen Martini ●●●●○

SWEET (ROSSO) VERMOUTH

Popular belief has it that Italian vermouth was originally sweet and produced from red wine, while French vermouth was typically dry and white. Hence, many old cocktail books refer to 'French' for dry vermouth and 'Italian' where sweet vermouth is called for. The truth is that the division between the styles of the two countries was never that defined and producers in both countries now make both sweet (rosso) and dry styles. Although red vermouth was initially based on red wine, now virtually all is made from white wine with caramel blended in to give an amber colour.

Leap Year Martini ●●●○○
Leave It To Me Martini ●●●◐○
Little Italy ●●●◐○
London Calling ●●●◐○
Loud Speaker Martini ●●●◐○
Luxury Cocktail ●●●◐○
Macka ●●●◐○
Manhattan Perfect ●●●●●
Manhattan Sweet ●●●●●
Manhattan Island ●●●●○
Martinez ●●●●●
Martini Special ●●●●◐
Maurice Martini ●●●◐○
Medium Martini ●●●●◐
Merry-Go-Round Martini ●●●●○
Mexican Manhattan ●●●●○
Milano ●●●●◐
The Million Dollar Cocktail ●●●●◐
Moravian Cocktail ●●●○○
Mountain ●●●◐○
Negroni ●●●●◐
Noon ●●●●○
Old Fashioned Caddy ●●●●○
Opening Shot ●●●◐○
Orange Bloom Martini ●●●●◐
Orange Martini ●●●●○
Pall Mall Martini ●●●●○
Palm Beach ●●●◐○
Park Avenue ●●●●○
Perfect Martini ●●●◐○
Petto Martini ●●●●◐
Picca ●●●●○
Pichuncho Martini ●●●●◐
Princess Pride ●●●◐○
Queen Martini ●●●●○

VIOLET LIQUEUR

A liqueur flavoured with the purple flowers from a small perennial plant. Usually from France, particularly Toulouse.

Palma Violet Martini ●●●◐○
Purple Pear Martini ●●●●○

VODKA - UNFLAVOURED GRAIN

See 'Ketel One Vodka'

VODKA – BISON GRASS FLAVOURED

See 'Zubrówka Bison Vodka'

VODKA – CITRUS FLAVOURED

See 'Ketel One Citroen'

VODKA – CRANBERRY FLAVOURED

Finitaly ●●●●○
Finn Rouge ●●●◐○
Finnberry Martini ●●●●○
The Juxtaposition ●●●●○

VODKA – CURRANT FLAVOURED

Metropolitan ●●●●○
Nuts & Berries ●●●●○
Pale Rider ●●●○○
Plum Pudding Martini ●●●◐○

VODKA – LIME FLAVOURED

Lime Breeze ●●●◐○
Lime Sour ●●●●○
Limelite ●●●○○
Limeosa ●●●◐○
Limerick ●●●●○
Limey ●●●◐○
Limey Cosmo ●●●●○
Limey Mule ●●●●○
Liminal Shot ●●●○○
Limited Liability ●●●●◐
Limnology ●●●◐○
Limousine ●●●●○
Molotov Cocktail ●●●◐○

VODKA – ORANGE FLAVOURED

M.G.F. ●●●●○
Mandarintini ●●●○○
Orange Mojito ●●●●○
Oranjiniha ●●●●○
Pink Flamingo ●●●○○

VODKA - VANILLA FLAVOURED

Nine-20-Seven ●●●●○
Peach Melba Martini ●●●◐○
Pear & Vanilla Rickey ●●●◐○
Pepper & Vanilla'tini ●●●●◐
Plum Pudding Martini ●●●◐○

WATER

The dilution of a cocktail is key to achieving the right balance. This varies according to how hard you shake, how cold your ice is and how much ice you use. Even if a recipe doesn't call for a splash of water, don't be scared to add some if you feel it needs it. Use spring or filtered water and keep a bottle in your refrigerator next to the bottle of sugar syrup.

WHISKEY - BOURBON

Bourbon can be made anywhere in the USA, but it is native to the South, and only Kentucky bourbon can advertise the state where it is made. Thus, there is no bourbon with Tennessee on the label.

Bourbons are produced in a specific way. A bourbon must contain at least 51% corn (but not more than 80%), be distilled to a strength of not more than 80% alc./vol., be stored in charred new white oak barrels at a strength no higher than 62.5% alc./vol. and aged for at least two years, and be reduced at the time of bottling to no lower than 40% alc./vol..

Straight bourbon whiskey must be aged for a minimum of two years in new, charred oak casks. Any whiskey which has been aged for less than four years must state its age on the label. Generally, two to four year old whiskies are best avoided. No colouring or flavouring may be added to straight whiskey.

Little Italy ●●●◐○
Lucky Lindy ●●●◐○
Man-Bour-Tini ●●●●○
Manhattan Dry ●●●●◐
Manhattan Perfect ●●●●●
Manhattan Sweet ●●●●●
Maple Old-Fashioned ●●●●○

Maple Leaf ●●●●○
Marquee ●●●●○
Met Manhattan ●●●●○
Millionaire ●●●●○
Mint Julep ●●●●●
Mississippi Punch ●●●●○
Mocha Martini ●●●●◐
Mountain ●●●◐○
Mrs Robinson #1 ●●●●○
New Orleans Mule ●●●◐○
New Orleans Punch ●●●◐○
New Yorker ●●●●○
Nutty Nashville ●●●●○
Oddball Manhattan Dry ●●●●○
O'Henry ●●●◐○
Old Fashioned #1 (Classic Version) ●●●●●
Old Fashioned #2 (US Version) ●●●●◐
Old Pal ●●●◐○
Opening Shot ●●●◐○
Paris Sour ●●●●○
Parlay Punch ●●●○○
Passbour Cooler ●●●○○
Pinky Pincher ●●●●○
Port Light ●●●◐○
Pousse-café ●●◐○○
Prune Face ●●●●○
Quebec ●●●●○

WHISKEY - IRISH

Due to the domination of Irish Distillers, the producers' group now owned by Pernod-Ricard, as a rule Irish whiskey is triple-distilled and not peated and hence light and smooth. (The independent Cooley Distillery produces some notable exceptions to these rules.)

Pappy Honeysuckle ●●●●◐

WHISKEY – TENNESSEE

The main difference between bourbon and Tennessee whiskey lies in the Lincoln County Process, a form of charcoal filtration. In the 1820s someone (possibly Alfred Eaton) started filtering whiskey through maple charcoal.

Tennessee whiskeys are now filtered through 10-12 feet of maple charcoal before they are bottled, removing impurities and giving a 'sooty' sweetness to the finished spirit.

A Tennessee whiskey must be made from at least 51% of one particular grain. This could be rye or wheat, but most often, as with bourbon, corn is the favoured base.

Lynchburg Lemonade ●●●●○
Mississippi Schnapper ●●●◐○
Mountain Sipper ●●●◐○

WHISKY – CANADIAN

John Molson, though better known for brewing, is credited with first introducing whisky to Canada in 1799. His lead was followed by Scottish emigrants who found their new home had plentiful and cheap grain. Whisky production started at Kingston, on Lake Ontario, and spread as farming developed. However, barley was not common, so they reduced the amount of barley from that used in Scotland and added corn, wheat and rye instead.

In 1875, government regulation specified that Canadian whisky must be made from cereal grains in Canada, using continuous distillation. The rules also state that Canadian whisky must be aged a minimum of 3 years and a maximum of 18 years in charred oak barrels.

Quebec ●●●●○

WHISKY - SCOTCH

For whisky to be called 'Scotch whisky' it must be a) made in Scotland and b) aged in oak casks for a minimum of three years. Malt whisky – based on malted barley - was the original Scottish whisky and is at the core of all decent Scotch. But, although it has recently become extremely popular, the majority of pot still malt whisky is sold in blends (which include non-malt whiskies), not as single malt whiskies (which do not). Blended Scotch whisky, or 'Scotch' for short, is the world's most popular whisky and accounts for well over 85% of all Scottish whisky.

A standard blended whisky will probably contain 15-40% malt and have no age statement (though every whisky in it will have been aged at least three years). Some blends describe themselves as 'deluxe' - this is a reference to the percentage of malt whisky in the blend and the average age of the whisky. A deluxe brand will usually contain more than 45% pot still malt and will show an age statement of 12 years or more.

Linstead ●●●●◐
Liquorice Whisky Sour ●●●●◐
Loch Almond ●●●●○
Lychee Mac ●●●◐○
Mac Orange ●●●◐○
Maple Pomme ●●●●○
Mary Queen of Scots ●●●●◐
Milk & Honey Martini ●●●●◐
Morning Glory Fizz ●●●●○
Mystique ●●●◐○
Mystique Martini ●●●●○
Old Fashioned Caddy ●●●●○
Paisley Martini ●●●●○
Pear Shaped #1 (Deluxe Version) ●●●●◐
Pear Shaped #2 (Popular Version) 4.5
Picca ●●●●○
Pineapple Blossom ●●●●○
Polly's Special ●●●●○

WINE - RED

The acidity in table wine can balance a cocktail in a similar way to citrus juice. Avoid heavily oaked wines.

Mulled Wine ●●●●○
New Yorker ●●●●○

WINE - WHITE

The acidity in table wine can balance a cocktail in a similar way to citrus juice. The grassy notes in Sauvignon Blanc make this grape varietal particularly suitable for cocktail use.

LCB Martini ●●●●○
M.C. Martini ●●●●●
Mint Cocktail ●●●●◐
Mint Martini ●●●●◐
Moonlight Martini ●●●●○
Orchard Breeze ●●●●◐
Palermo ●●●●◐
Pappy Honeysuckle ●●●●◐

ZUBRÓWKA BISON VODKA

A Polish vodka flavoured with bison grass.

Lemon Butter Cookie ●●●●○
Mitch Martini ●●●●○
Northern Lights ●●●●○
Palookaville ●●●●○
Polish Martini ●●●●●
Pooh'tini ●●●●◐

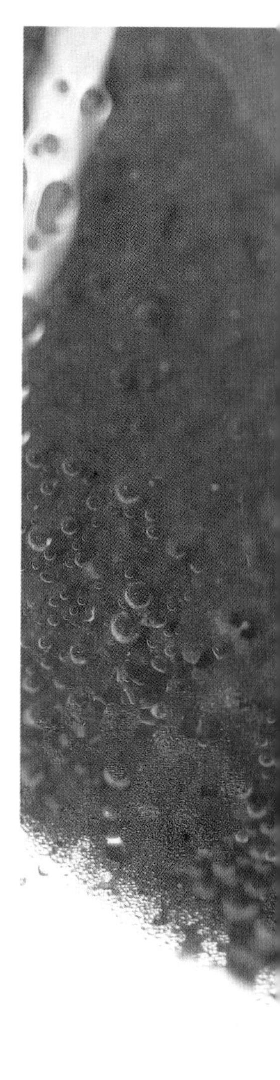

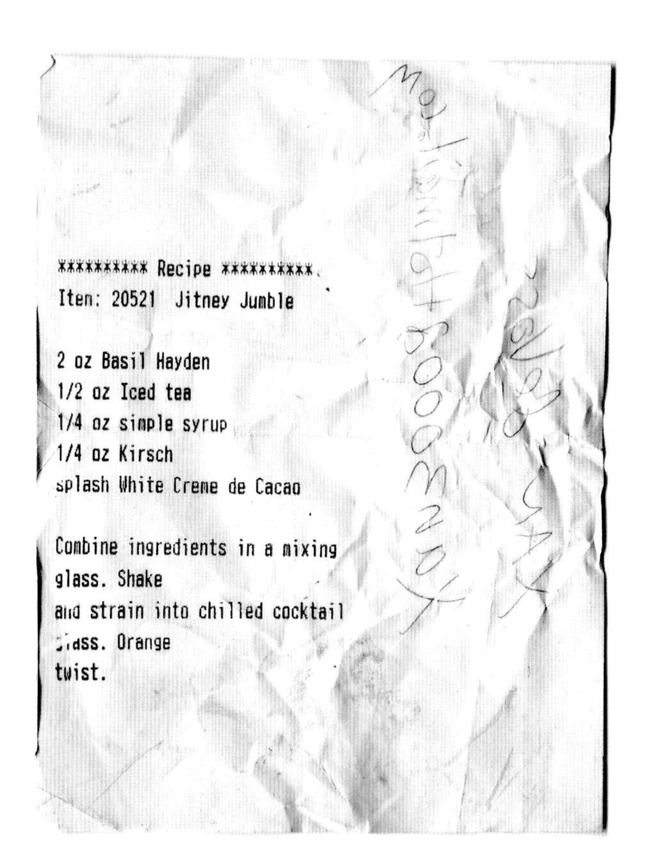

********** Recipe **********

Item: 20521 Jitney Jumble

2 oz Basil Hayden
1/2 oz Iced tea
1/4 oz simple syrup
1/4 oz Kirsch
splash White Creme de Cacao

Combine ingredients in a mixing glass. Shake and strain into chilled cocktail glass. Orange twist.

READERS' RECIPES

I pick up new cocktail recipes on a daily basis, in bars and by email. I usually adapt recipes to fit our house style, both in the liquor brands specified and the way they're made. However, the recipes over the following pages are exactly as I received them. The best will find their way into the front pages of future guides and as always I'll credit creators, so please keep sending them in.

Once again I'd like to thank the many bartenders who have contributed to our guides.

Simon Difford
simon@diffordsguide.com

Hi Simon,
Great spending time with you in Las Vegas during the Nightclub & Bar Show. Here are the recipes we conjured up for our on-trade event for our newest project, Heavy Water Vodka, which we held at the Skylofts at the MGM Grand Hotel. We'll be launching in the UK come Spring 2006.

HEAVY MULE

A light yet zesty variation on the classic Moscow Mule: the cocktail that triggered the vodka revolution during the 1940s.

60 ml Heavy Water Vodka
90 ml ginger ale
30 ml fresh lime juice
Grated fresh ginger

Build ingredients in an ice-filled highball glass. Grate a little fresh ginger into the glass. Garnish with a lime wedge.

GINZA COLLINS

Japan's number two soft drink Calpico offers a surprisingly fresh take on the classic collins recipe.

45 ml Heavy Water Vodka
30 ml Calpico
Splash of fresh lemon juice
Soda water

Build ingredients in an ice-filled highball glass. Stir. Garnish with a lemon slice.

ANASTASIA

Inspired by Professor Jerry Thomas's Egg Sours and use of tea syrups in cocktails, as well as the aroma of Russian tea, this cocktail offers a number of tastes and textures to delight the palate.

60 ml Heavy Water Vodka
60 ml fresh-squeezed pink grapefruit juice
10 ml spiced tea syrup*
10 ml fresh egg white
2 dashes Regan's Orange Bitters

Fill a shaker with ice. Add all ingredients. Shake until icy cold, about 30 seconds. Pour into a rocks glass filled with ice, or strain into a chilled cocktail glass.

*Spiced Tea Syrup: Combine 1 cup water and 18 whole cloves in a small pot. Bring to a boil and remove from heat. Add 1 darjeeling tea bag and steep for about 5 minutes. Return to heat and add 1 cup sugar and 1/4 tsp ground cinnamon. Heat and stir until sugar is dissolved. Remove from heat and add 1/4 tsp pure vanilla extract or scrape the seed from half a vanilla bean. Strain through a coffee filter, cool and store in a sealed glass jar until ready to use.

Cheers,
Anistatia Miller, New York
Heavy Water International AS

Hi Simon,
My name is Pasquale I really like what you are doing with cocktails....I love mixology and mixed drinks. At the moment I'm working at Anam bar north London. I will be really pleased if any of my recipes appear in one of your books.

CUBAN PINK

Glass: Inverness
Garnish: Pink grapefruit zest & coriander spring
Method: Muddle pink grapefruit and coriander in the base of a glass. Add syrup, rum and Licor 43. Half fill glass with crushed ice and churn with bar spoon. Fill glass with more crushed ice and serve with straws.

1/4 of pink grapefruit
handful of coriander
1/2 shot vanilla syrup
1 1/2 shot Havana Club Añejo Especial
1/2 shot Licor 43

AFTER ALL

Glass: Martini
Garnish: Basil leaf
Method: Shake first 5 ingredients with ice and strain into chilled glass. Top up with beer.

3 basil leaves
1/2 vanilla syrup
1 shot cranberry juice
1 1/2 Belvedere Citrus
1 Grand Marnier
top up with beer

Thanks.
Pasquale Corda

Hi Simon,
Just wanted to send you a few new cocktails I came up with.

PARISIAN DREAM

Glass: Rocks
Method: Shake all ingredients and strain over crushed ice.
Garnish: Flamed orange zest

25ml Hennessy
12.5ml Crème de Cassis
12.5ml Cointreau
25ml Peach Puree
12.5ml Lemon Juice
12.5ml Gomme

PICKLED CUCUMBER GIN MARTINI

Glass: Martini
Method: Muddle fresh pickled cucumber, add gin and stir with ice. Fine strain.
Garnish: 1/2 Slice of Pickled cucumber

50ml Bombay Sapphire gin
2 large slices of Pickled cucumber

Cheers,
Peter J. McAlister
Malmaison, Belfast

Hi Simon
Some of my new cocktail creations to try...

Thyme Bandit

30 ml Thyme infused Vodka
10 ml Mandarin Napoleon
10 ml Cartron Manderine
20 ml Lemon Juice
10 ml Eggwhite
3 drops Peychaud bitters
Shake vigorously, served on Rocks / Orange Spiral

DILLEMA

50ML BELVEDERA VODKA
25ML LIME JUICE
25ML BAY LEAF GOMME
FRESH DILL

MUDDLE / SHAKE

CAPERTINI
Glass: Martini

75ml Penka Vodka
1/4 Brine from cocktail caperberries
1/4 Noilly Pratt

Garnish: Caperberrie on stick
Variation: Gin or Vodka

SICILIAN ROMANCE
Glass: Martini

50ml Hendricks gin
25ml Lemon Juice
12.5ml Sugar sirop
1 bar spoon of Luxardo Sambuca

Method: Shake over ice
Garnish: Star aniz

GASPARE'S REVELATION
Glass: Long Drink

50ml Campari
12ml Grand marnier
12ml Rosemary sirop
25ml Blood orange juice
25ml Pink grapefruit

Method: Shake over ice
Garnish: Spring of rosemary

ISLAND CONNECTION
Glass: Martini

50ml Havana 7
25ml Bual Madeira wine
25ml Pineapple juice
12.5ml Vanilla sirop

Method: shake over ice
Garnish: slice of pineapple

My best regards,
Humberto Marques
Oloroso Restaurant, Edinburgh
www.oloroso.co.uk

Hey Simon, Hope all is well. Just wanted to send you in a couple of cocktails...

One is mine....
Sean Kennedy
"Kupe"
Aarhus, Denmark (yeah moved to dk from london).

M.B.P (MY BERRY PASSION)
1.5 Vanilla Vodka
1 Chambord
.25 Framboise
1 Half and Half
.25 Gome
3 fresh Blackberries
3 fresh Raspberries.
1 Fresh Vanilla Pod

Large Martini Glass
Garnished with three berries on stick on rim.
Muddle vanilla, Raspberries, Blackberries, Gome... add rest, shake and strain into chilled martini glass.
The other cocktail is a friend's, she a great bartender and I convinced her to let me send this in to you.

Mette Parkegaard
"Kupe"
Aarhus, Denmark.

SUMMER FLIRT
1.5 Citrus Vodka
.75 Blue Curacao
.25 Chambord
.5 Fresh lime
2 Passion Fruit Puree
2 Fresh Apple Juice

Sling
Garnish with lime
Blue curaçao bottom. Shake passion, apple, lime and vodka together... layer over blue curaçao... float Chambord.

Regards
Sean

Hi Simon

Pictures and recipes of the famous cocktails from AlMercante in Copenhagen. All drinks were created by Lars Vestbirk & Meik Pizzitui from the AlMercante bar lounge & restaurant in Copenhagen and bartending school barkursus.dk.

TIGERKISS

3cl Absolut Vanilla Vodka
2cl Grand Marnier
6cl Mandarin puree
1cl Vanilla syrup
Use a 1/2 teaspoon of chili powder (sweet)
Crushed ice in glass.

Method: Shake & strain over full glas with crushed ice.
Glass: Hurricane
Garnish: Tiger scratches on the side. Mix honey and chilli powder and paint on glass
Garnish: Chili and kumquatz with a dust of chilli powder
Created by Mr Lars Vestbirk
Award winning drink 2006 at the national championships (1st Place long drink).

PINK PONG!

3Cl Cruzan Rum 2 years
2.5Cl Likør43
1.5 Cl Passionfruit Syrup
9Cl Cranberry Juice
Foam of pineapple

Method: Shake pineapple juice with ice and take only
Foam to float on top of the drink.
Glass: Hurricane
Method: Shake & strain over glass filled up with ice cubes
Top with fresh pineapple foam.
Garnish: Kumquatz palmtree (Kumquatz, physalis top, cranberry and baby pineapple leaves).
Created by Mr Meik Pizziuti
Award winning drink 2006 at the national championships (3rd place long drink).

RAZZMO

4cl Absolut Rasberry vodka
1,5cl Pineapple syrup (ananas)
7cl Apple juice
Dash of angostura bitters
Glass: Cocktail glass
Garnish in the glass Muddle 2 raspberries in base and cover with crushed ice.
Method: Shake & strain over crushed ice
Garnish: Fine slice of apple on the side.
Copenhagen answer to the New York 'Cosmopolitan' cocktail.
Created by Mr Meik Pizziuti
Runner up for the Absolut Rasberry Vodka Competition 2006

A TOUCH OF RAZZBERRY

4cl Absolut Rasberry
1.5cl Chambord
4cl Elderflower cordinal
1/2 of fresh lime
Dash of chambord to the bottom

Method: Shake & strain
Glass: Martini Cocktail
Garnish: Thai Orchid and 3 raspberries on stick
Created by Mr. Meik Pizziuti from the AlMercante bar lounge & restaurant in Copenhagen and bartending school barkursus.dk
Award winning drink 2006 at the Absolut Vodka Competition (1st Place raspberry drink).

ABSOLUT RAZZMATAZZ

2cl Absolut Rasberry
3cl Chambord
2cl Plymouth Gin
1cl Gomme sirop
Limejuice
Dash Tabasco

Method: Shake & strain over glas filled with crushed ice
Glass: Highball whisky glass
Garnish: 3 raspberries on top of crushed ice
Created by Mr. Meik Pizziuti
Award winning drink 2006 at the Absolut Vodka Competition (3rd Place raspberry drink)

We hope you will post these wonderful tasty drinks in your next issues of magazines.

Best regards.
Med venlig hilsen & Meik Pizziuti
AlMercante, Copenhagen
www.almercante.dk

Hi Simon-

First of all, let me say a huge thank-you for the wonderful Difford's Guide to Cocktails. This has given my household many a happy evening- and a lot of new favourites for many of my friends. We've also experimented (in a very minor way) and come up with a twist on one of your cocktails, which we think gives it a lovely new edge. I make a standard Raspberry Collins, but add half a teaspoon of rose water to it. This gives it a lovely Turkish Delight kind of flavour. Being a pretentious science-fiction fan, I call this a 'Leisure Hive' but our more sensible friends call it a 'Turkish Collins'. Whichever name it goes under, it tastes lovely!

Keep up the good work,

Simon Exton,
Belfast
Northern Ireland

THE SPICED APPLE TINI

25ml Krupnik
12.5ml Sauza Hornitos
12.5ml Cointreau
12.5ml Elderflower Cordial
50ml Cloudy Apple juice
A shake of Black Pepper

Method: shake and double strain into a chilled martini glass
Garnish with an apple wedge or Cinnamon Stick

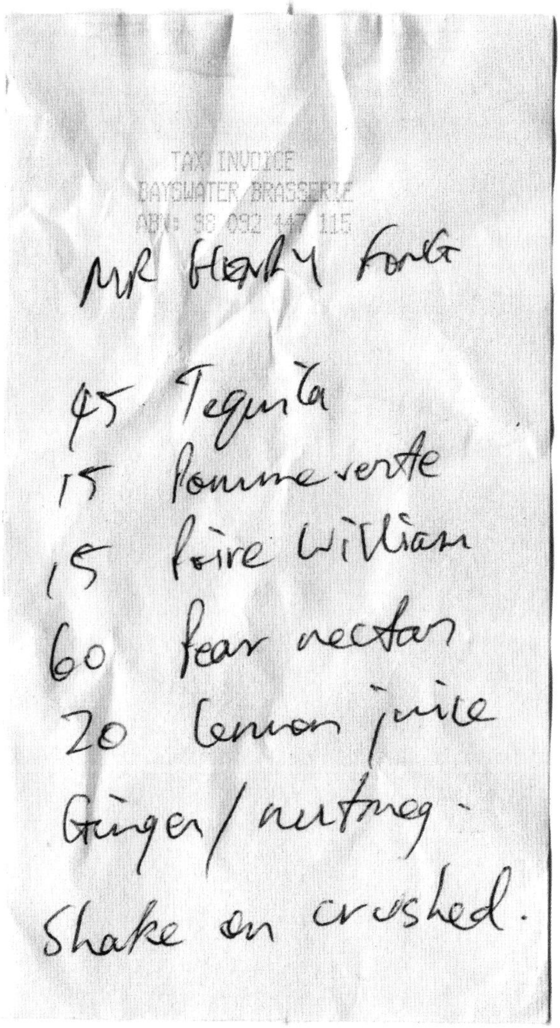

TAX INVOICE
BAYSWATER BRASSERIE
ABN: 98 092 447 115

MR HENRY FONG

45 Tequila
15 Pomme verte
15 Poire William
60 Pear nectar
20 Lemon juice
Ginger/nutmeg.
Shake on crushed.

The pepper kick at the end of this drink is something to be experienced it is selling well as our cocktail of the week.

Yours
Chris Setchell, The Orange Tree Leicester

Hello
My name is Henrik and I'm a bartender from Sweden. I used to work with Phillip Jeffrey at the GE Club in Liverpool street (you used to come in to the bar and drink only the best that we had to offer). Anyway, your guides are great.
Nordic Light Hotel is the place in Stockholm where you get great cocktails! Custom made cocktails for each guest. However they like it.
I have a lot of great recipes that would look real good in your guide to cocktails. One of them is "Snow White". It was my contribution to the Swedish championships 2004. It has now gone to a big sale all over Stockholm.

SNOW WHITE

Fresh lemongrass
35 ml Smirnoff apple vodka
15 ml Quarenta y tres (Licor 43) liqueur
50 ml Guanabana juice
10ml Fresh lemon
10 ml sugar

Shaken in martini glass.
Bash a peace of fresh lemongrass.
Then add all the ingredients.
Garnish: In Sweden we have a candy company called Malaco. They make long sweet-liquorice strings (about 1 meter long and thin). Fold it over the middle and then over the middle again. Then tie a knot in the middle and you get 4 ends. Lay the knot in the middle of the martini glass and let all ends hang out over the glass. Looks like a black spider.

Henrik Gillberg, White Room, Stockholm. www.nordiclighthotel.com

Hi Simon

THAI GIN FIZZ

Glass: Collins/Highball
Garnish: Several cross section slices of red chilli dropped on drink

50mls Plymouth Gin or Tanqueray Ten
25mls Lime Juice
20ml Homemade Thai Syrup
Soda Water

Shake the gin, lime juice and syrup and strain into the glass filled with crushed ice.
Top up with Soda water and garnish with lime.

To make the Thai syrup make a simple sugar syrup with 2-3 stalks of lemon grass, 5 lime leaves and 6-8 large slices of root ginger. When the syrup has cooled transfer to a bottle and leave the ingredients to infuse further with the syrup.
Finally add a Red chili pepper to infuse for 2-3 days.

Hope you like this.

Regards
Tomo, Black Rabbit Bartenders

Dear Simon
Hi my name is Gareth Crouth and I work in a bar called Blue Coyote in Newcastle-Upon-Tyne.

VANILLA RAINE

Glass: Martini
Garnish: Slice watermelon on rim
Method: Muddle watermelon in Boston glass. Add ingredients and shake vigorously. Fine strain into chilled glass

50ml Absolut vanilla
25ml Apple schnapps
6 chunks fresh watermelon
12.5ml fresh lime juice
12.5ml vanilla sugar syrup

Yours sincerely
Gareth Brent Crouth

Hello Simon
I'm the manager of the Luxe bar in Perth Western Australia, not sure on what merits you select drinks for your guide, but here's a twist on the Whisk(e)y Mac, which we've found to be an amazingly popular drink & it has been plagiarised (always a good sign) by several bars around Australia already.

MAPLE MAC

Glass: Rock
Ingredients:

45ml Jamesons 12 year old
15ml Stones Ginger wine
2 barpsoons of maple syrup

Method: Pour booze over ice in glass add maple syrup & stir very well with a bonzer bar spoon
Garnish: nah this is a guys drink
Notes: (gaz) – another twisted classic

Gary Beadle
Luxe Bar, Perth
www.luxebar.com

Dear Sir

My name is Michael Cloke. I am a 21 year old business graduate and I am a very keen cocktail barman. For the last year I have managed a busy cocktail bar in Leeds in which time I became an accomplished flair bartender and have been down to London

on many occasions to both sample London's delights and watch my boss in top mixology competitions.

This cocktail that did me proud in a V/X comp.

IT'S SNOW MARTINI

25ml Raisin Infused Appleton Estate V/X
12.5ml Appleton Extra
12.5ml White Cacao
2X Milky Bar (melted)
25ml half n half

add one and a half shots of Raisin V/X to a boston and slowly add melted choc stirring rapidly, add other ingredients and shake with whole ice. Strain into a prepped martini glass that has solidified white choc around the rim. Not Bad.

Hi Simon,

I've attached a few cocktails from our list here at Peachykeen which you may find of interest for the next issue of the guide. If you're ever passing by Camden/Kentish Town pop by and I'll shout you a drink.

OPAL FRUITS

1 shot Absolut Citron
1 shot Chambord
1 shot Lemoncello
1 shot Fresh Lemon Juice
1/2 shot Sugar Syrup
Splash of soda

Shake ingredients (except soda) with ice and strain into a Collins glass, top with soda. Garnish with a lemon wedge. Should taste like the sweets!

PINK & FLUFFY

1 Fresh passion fruit
1/6 Fresh Mango
1 1/2 shots Finlandia Mango
1 shot Passao
1 shot Passion Fruit Juice
Splash of soda

Muddle the fruit, add the other ingredients (except soda), shake with ice and strain into a Collins glass, top with soda. Garnish with 1/2 Passion Fruit.

LOU LOU

2 shots Jack Daniels
1 shot Chambord
6 Fresh raspberries
1 shot Lemon Juice
1/2 shot Sugar syrup

Muddle raspberries in a Boston glass, add other ingredients and shake with ice. Strain into an old fashion glass and garnish with two raspberries on a stick.

APPLE AND RASPBERRY MARTINI

6 Fresh Raspberries
1 1/2 shots Absolut Raspberri
1/4 shot Chambord
1/4 shot Apple Sourz
1 shot Cranberry Juice
1 shot Apple juice (Bramley)

Muddle raspberries in a Boston glass, add other ingredients and shake with ice. Strain into a chilled Martini glass. Garnish with an apple and raspberry stick

PRESSED TO REFRESH

1 inch Cucumber (skinned)
8 Mint leaves
1 shot Elderflower Cordial
2 shots Hendricks gin
2 shots Cranberry Juice
2 shots Apple Juice (Bramley)

Muddle cucumber, mint & elderflower in a Boston glass, add other ingredients and shake with ice. Strain into a Collins glass and garish with a cucumber wheel and mint sprig.

OUR SON PAT

1 shot Absolut Vanilla
1 shot Frangelico
1 shot Chambord
1 Large bar spoon of Crunchy Peanut Butter
2 shots Single Cream

Shake all ingredients with ice and strain into a chilled Martini Glass. Garnish with a Monkey Nut.
Cheers, Elliot
www.peachy-keen.com

Hi, My name is Drew Gladwell and I have two party cocktails that you might be able to put into your next edition of the guide.

JUBILLEE ICED TEA

Glass: Sling
Garnish: Split lemon wheel
Method: Shake first 7 ingredients with ice and strain into ice filled glass, then top up with tonic and stir.
3/4 shot gin
1/2 shot light rum
1/2 shot vodka
1/2 shot pimms no 1
1/4 shot tequila
1 shot fresh lemon juice
1/2 shot sugar syrup
top with tonic

Created by Drew Gladwell 2003 Bar Three Bar Manager

WEST COUNTRY ICED TEA

Glass: Sling
Garnish: split lime wheel
Method: Shake first 7 ingredients with ice and strain into ice filled glass, then top up with cider and stir.
1/2 shot gin
1/2 shot light rum
1/2 shot vodka
1/2 shot triple sec
1/4 shot tequila
1 shot fresh lime juice
1/2 shot sugar syrup

top with a good west country, sparkling cider. Created by Jack Midgley 2005 Bar Three Head Bartender

Cheers
Drew Gladwell
Bar Three, Bristol

Andy

Fitzmaurice

35ml Krupnik
15ml Poire William
25ml Lime Juice
20ml Honey syrup
20ml Ginger cordial
25ml Fresh apple
Juice

Shaken, crushed
ice, rocks glass
grated lime zest
drizzle honey